# Victorian Psychology and British Culture
# 1850–1880

# Victorian Psychology and British Culture
## 1850–1880

RICK RYLANCE

OXFORD
UNIVERSITY PRESS

# OXFORD
## UNIVERSITY PRESS

Great Clarendon Street, Oxford OX2 6DP

Oxford University Press is a department of the University of Oxford.
It furthers the University's objective of excellence in research, scholarship,
and education by publishing worldwide in

Oxford  New York

Athens Auckland Bangkok Bogotá Buenos Aires Calcutta
Cape Town Chennai Dar es Salaam Delhi Florence Hong Kong Istanbul
Karachi Kuala Lumpur Madrid Melbourne Mexico City Mumbai
Nairobi Paris São Paulo Singapore Taipei Tokyo Toronto Warsaw

and associated companies in Berlin Ibadan

Oxford is a registered trade mark of Oxford University Press
in the UK and certain other countries

Published in the United States
by Oxford University Press Inc., New York

British Library Cataloguing in Publication Data

Data available

Library of Congress Cataloging in Publication Data

Rylance, Rick.
Victorian psychology and British culture, 1850–1880 / Rick Rylance.
p.  cm.
Includes bibliographical references and index.
1. Psychology—Great Britain—History—19th century.  2. Great
Britain—Civilization—19th century.  3. Bain, Alexander, 1810–1877.  4. Spencer, Herbert,
1820–1903.  5. Lewes, George Henry, 1817–1878.  6. Psychology in literature.  I. Title.
BF108.G7 R95 2000  150'.941'09034—dc21  00-036748
ISBN 0–19–812283–7

1 3 5 7 9 10 8 6 4 2

Typeset by Graphicraft Ltd., Hong Kong
Printed in Great Britain
on acid-free paper by
Biddles Ltd., Guildford and King's Lynn

*Judith's book,*
*at last*

# Acknowledgements

I have many people to thank for their contribution to this book over the years. Friends offered advice on countless topics general and specific, Victorian and Modern, literary, historical, and psychological. Some—Rick Allen, Phil Davies, Maud Ellmann, Heather Glen, Rebecca Stott, and Nigel Wheale—generously read substantial parts in draft and always offered most observant, constructive, and helpful suggestions. I would also like to thank Simon Dentith, Kelvin Everest, Eamonn Hughes, Sharon Ouditt, Judy Simons, and Martin Stannard for advice and discussion of all kinds. I enjoyed conversations with Stefan Collini on interdisciplinary matters, Sally Shuttleworth on psychological matters, and Bill Myers —originally a most stimulating doctoral supervisor—on virtually everything. APU has provided various forms of research support, and John Blanchfield willingly helped with several computing tasks. I am deeply grateful to Ian Gordon, who has supported the work in innumerable ways. Annie—aged 6—remains amused by this as a plausible job of work, and wants to know why there is only one picture. Sophie Goldsworthy, Andrew Lockett, Hilary Walford, and Frances Whistler at OUP have been efficient, supportive, helpful, and good-humoured beyond patience. Errors and all, what remains is mine.

# Contents

# Prelude

What might you expect to find in this book? It has a number of aims, the first of which is to offer a systematic overview of the development of mid-Victorian psychological theory in a way that pays attention to its diverse traditions. It stresses the multiform and conflicting nature of these traditions, and the emergence of a recognizably modern form of the discipline during the last two decades of the nineteenth century. It attempts to illuminate the generalist nature of Victorian intellectual culture, examining in detail the continuing intellectual conversation between specialists and generalists, scientists and literary writers, theologians, doctors, and philosophers, that constituted the analysis of the human mind for Victorian people. It analyses these developments in a broad context, understanding psychological ideas as evolving, provisional, and frequently disputatious. It attends to particular situations of authorship, including, from time to time, the alarmed public reaction to controversial ideas. The book will hopefully enable readers of nineteenth-century texts of many kinds to grasp the nuances of individual psychological positions and their importance to the lives and beliefs of individuals. As intellectual history, the book assumes that ideas are cultivated public utterances designed to defend positions, refute alternatives, and persuade other readers, and that written style is one indication of the way relationships are negotiated with other ideas and groups (especially those that are thought to constitute orthodoxy).

In Dickens's novel *Great Expectations*, the blacksmith's child Pip is suddenly presented to the alarmingly mad, massively ragged, awesomely rich Miss Havisham and commanded to 'Play!', which, understandably, he cannot do. Pip cannot play because all the context for his natural play has been removed. A Victorian psychologist commanded abruptly to 'Psychologize!' before a late-twentieth-century Professor Havisham would, without the natural context of his discipline to hand, be similarly hard put. 'I felt myself so unequal to the performance', Pip confesses, 'that I gave it up, and stood looking at Miss Havisham in what I supposed she took for a dogged manner.'[1] Two issues are important here: the first is the need to be conscious of the nature of the intellectual and contextual gaps that separate modern from Victorian thinking. To address a distant subject, one must try to imagine a dialogue with something other than oneself, and this implies taking some measure of one's own situation. Secondly, Pip appears to Miss Havisham as dogged and sullen, and so she

---

[1] Charles Dickens, *Great Expectations* (1860–1), ed. Angus Calder (Harmondsworth, 1965), 88.

thinks him stupid. In dealing with psychological ideas more than a century old, it is necessary not to think anyone stupid, and to guard—as has not always been the case—against the condescensions of modernity. For some, the philosophical framework of Victorian psychology can, indeed, appear 'doggedly' unresponsive to modern inquisition. But the effort to contextualize brings alive the struggle for ideas, amid all the pressures surrounding them, in a way that constitutes an intellectual life across time. So, at intervals, I introduce for comparative purposes material from central psychological debates of our period. The aim is not so much to point up a difference (though that is unavoidable); rather, it is a way of emphasizing *continuity*. These comparisons have the dual function of highlighting the edges of our knowledge, and of establishing a dialogue between historical formulations that have negotiated their own responses to unsettling and unsettled issues. It is obvious, therefore, that my opinion is that certain deep conceptual problems in psychology—such as the problem of consciousness, the theory of mind–body relations, and the role social, symbolic, and cultural systems play in the psychological development—are, if not 'timeless' (because their forms are historically produced and specific), tenaciously persistent. That such issues are not amenable to solution is, I think, stimulating rather than depressing, and it is a point where a dialogue with the past can be realized. In a real way, for all their difference, we are still in active conversation with Victorian ideas.

I am, by choice, pleasure, and training, a literary critic. This gives me a particular interest in the way ideas are framed and conveyed, as well as the way in which they circulate for the use of others (few literary artists make their work directly from a specialism). It gives me expertise in certain methods of textual analysis and a sympathetic bias towards understanding utterances as contextually formed. I began this work with an interest in George Eliot's intellectual context; from her work I moved to that of her partner, G. H. Lewes; from Lewes I moved to everyone else. Eliot herself—impressively inward with psychological arguments—encouraged the expansion: she justified her novel *The Mill on the Floss* to her publisher by reference to the need for a 'widening psychology' newly responsive to the contemporary world.[2] This study was intended to follow the path of that 'widening psychology', but in writing it I have, in effect, reversed the customary priorities for contextual work in the study of literature. Commentary on literary works (especially those of George Eliot) appears regularly in this book, and extracts are considered in some detail. But they surface in relation to arguments largely constituted, centred, and continuing elsewhere. The object of study, therefore, is not literary culture in any direct sense (any more than it is, with exclusive focus, the philosophical, or theological, or biomedical

---

[2]  George Eliot to John Blackwood, 9 July 1860, *The George Eliot Letters*, ed. Gordon S. Haight, 9 vols. (London, 1954–6, 1978), iii. 317–18.

culture). The commentary on literature demonstrates the contribution made by intelligent, accomplished writers to issues of shared concern in an unfolding public network of debate over psychological problems. This was conducted in specialist psychological texts, reviews, essays in the great periodicals, novels, poems, philosophical tracts, and political polemics. What drew literary, psychological, and other writers together were the relaxed protocols of psychological investigation that made psychology, by modern standards, a less robust, but in some ways a more open discourse. The porous boundaries of the discipline accepted and enabled the movement of ideas.

I mention the literary issue because it is part of a proper and appropriate methodological self-consciousness to be aware of one's origins. But George Eliot has been influential in ways greater than giving me a start and furnishing apposite passages for commentary. I became aware, only towards the end of the writing, that the method I was using imitated her own in some major respects. This was not deliberate or considered, but it did follow from my respect for her way of dramatizing multiple perspectives (there are ample demonstrations of this in relation to her work in the chapters that follow). Often, for her, this takes the form of an invitation to the reader to converse across cultures and history, across different forms of knowledge, across assumptions, prejudice, and ideology. I think that the authentic ethical action in her work is contained in such moments (and not in sporadic moments of hectoring, doctrinal enthusiasm). I also think that, if there is an 'interdisciplinary' moment in this work, it lies in the effort to reconstruct the intellectual and cultural conditions of a now vanished formation and develop the spring of surprise and enlargement that comes with new ways of seeing and thinking. This is, I believe, what the new form of the Victorian realist novel enabled, and, as this book occasionally argues, Victorian psychology and Victorian fiction possess it in common.

What draws psychology and fiction, as well as other parties, together is, in part, a shared interest in language. As early as 1839, the eminent physician Sir Henry Holland (whose work is examined in detail in Chapter 4 and who was, as it happens, George Eliot's doctor) astutely recognized that what is sometimes perceived as progress in knowledge (in this case knowledge of the relations of mind to body) can simply be the effect of a performance in language: 'If we sometimes seem to obtain a show of further discovery . . . this arises generally from the deception of language, which gives the appearance of advancing, when in truth we are but treading on our former steps.'[3] Later, in essays written months before his death in 1873, Holland mused that over the eighty-year span of his life, in which he witnessed most of the developments we survey: 'in natural

---

[3] Henry Holland, 'On the Brain as a Double Organ', *Medical Notes and Reflections* (London, 1839), 152.

science at least, so much has been done to rescue the mind from the tyranny of words, the coinage of older times.'[4] But he still thought that 'psychology, under its various titles, is that part of science in which the dominion of words is largest and most uncontrolled'.[5]

The role of language in the formulation and impact of psychological ideas is crucial to this book, and it is so for specific historical reasons like these. Contrary to (now yielding) images of Victorian solidity and brusque empiricism, psychology emerged as confidence in abstract, general 'truth' fell away. Looking back, in an article for the psychological journal *Mind* in 1904, William James reflected on the shape of intellectual developments in the century just closed:

Up to about 1850 almost everyone believed that sciences expressed truths that were exact copies of a definite code of non-human realities. But the enormously rapid multiplication of theories in these latter days has well-nigh upset the notion of any one of them being a more literally objective kind of thing than another. There are so many geometries, so many logics, so many physical and chemical hypotheses, so many classifications, each one of them good for so much and yet not good for everything, that the notion that even the truest formula may be a human device and not a literal transcript has dawned upon us.[6]

We may argue about precise dates and turning points, but these propositions, put in general terms by James, are especially pertinent for psychology. This book respects the origins of Victorian psychological theory in earlier periods, and pays a good deal of attention to them, but it concurs with James in seeing the period following 1850 as one of a rapid growth in psychological ideas partly as a result of this kind of questioning. Psychology was, for Victorian culture, a way of reflecting upon the formation of its *own* mind as it loosened itself from the traditions of the past; it was a staging of a debate about its own identity. James therefore gives one reason why this study opens in 1850. For the reasons why it closes three decades or so later you need to turn to the Introduction.

---

[4] Sir Henry Holland, 'Progress of Human Knowledge', in *Fragmentary Papers on Science and Other Subjects* (London, 1875), 5.

[5] Holland, 'Influence of Words and Names', in *Fragmentary Papers*, 245.

[6] William James, 'Humanism and Truth' (1904), in *Selected Writings*, ed. G. H. Bird (London, 1995), 57.

# Introduction: Looking round Corners

A history has to find its object. But Victorian psychology hides round corners and three particularly chunky obstacles obstruct our view. There is, first, the change in the modern conception of the discipline of psychology brought about by its rapid professionalization at the end of the nineteenth century. This process had many strands (including the growth of therapeutic sub-specialization), but the main agent was the fundamental reorientation of psychology's methods and outlook created by the new Experimentalism of the 1890s and beyond. Secondly, there has been the ascendancy of psychoanalysis as the branch of psychology thought most appropriate to cultural analysis in the humanities, which has obscured other lines of development and other kinds of work. Finally, there has been the authority of certain versions of cultural and literary Modernism that have intervened between the Victorians and ourselves, in effect withdrawing significant lines of connection between the psychological ideas of both epochs.

The first experimental psychological laboratories were opened in British universities in 1897 at Cambridge and University College London; the British Psychological Association was founded in 1901; and the *British Journal of Psychology* was launched in 1904. In these years psychology was constituted as an academic and scientific discipline in a way quite different from that of the period covered by this book. The historiographical effects of this were specific, deliberate, and, in the event, long-lasting, for the understanding of Victorian psychology was profoundly altered by the aggressively limited interests of the new generation. Edwin G. Boring's hugely influential *History of Experimental Psychology* of 1929, many times reprinted, was explicit. The present, Boring wrote, 'changes the past; and, as the focus and range of psychology shifts in the present, new parts of the past enter into its history and other parts drop out.' This process of selection, Boring continues, 'is itself a matter of history, which is quite independent of the will of the historian'.[1]

It is tempting to connect Boring's denial of his own agency to the passivity of human subjects in laboratory investigations in his period, but the crucial point is the reduced historical sense this view promotes. For Boring, psychology—defined as 'the psychology of the generalised, human, normal, adult mind as revealed in the psychological laboratory'[2]—has a history of just over half a century, and

[1] Edwin G. Boring, *A History of Experimental Psychology* (London, 1929), p. vii.
[2] Ibid., p. viii.

his patience with pre-experimental work is limited. G. H. Lewes, for instance (who will figure prominently in this book), is dismissed: 'his influence . . . has not been so great as that of Herbert Spencer, and we can afford to pass him by.'[3] These principles of selection are congruent with Boring's positivism, but also with the crude evolutionism on which his model of intellectual transmisson is based. Lewes's work was not fit enough to survive, even as influence.

The Experimentalist revision began early and developed rapidly, and Boring was rationalizing an existing development. Edward Wheeler Scripture's *The New Psychology* of 1897 was offered as a conspectus of new developments for Havelock Ellis's influential 'Contemporary Science Series'. Scripture severs psychology from its origins in the philosophy of mind, and pictures 'the new psychology' as instead a product of sciences such as astronomy and physics (valued for their development of accurate forms of measurement) alongside German physiology, French cerebral anatomy, and the analysis of clinical data gathered across Europe. Though Scripture credits philosophers such as Hobbes, Locke, and Hume with encouraging 'observational' science, he is scathing about the 'old psychology . . . before the introduction of experiment and measurement'.[4] Disciplinary professionalism, new experimental techniques, dedicated laboratory facilities, and above all a consolidated 'scientific' outlook, based upon detailed measurement, have, according to Scripture, released psychology's potential from its 'disappointing' history. With zesty confidence, he argues that 'modern work' has in fact realized ancient hopes, bringing scientific principles to flawed techniques and mistaken outlooks. 'There is no difference in its material,' he insists, 'no change in its point-of-view, and no degeneration of its aims.'[5] But in fact all three were altered root and branch by the new outlook. The intellectual culture of the previous generation was abandoned.

Experimentalism proposed a fundamental reorientation of psychology's methods, a steep reduction in its aims, and a radically altered sense of its public role and intellectual resources. Scripture's book is dedicated to three men: the German Wilhelm Wundt, 'founder of the first psychological laboratory' (a photograph of Wundt also features as the frontispiece to Boring's *History*), G. Stanley Hall, 'founder of the first American psychological laboratory', and George Trumbull, founder of the Yale Laboratory where Scripture worked. Both Scripture and Boring were American, and the association between these Americans and the continental work they celebrate indicates the formation of fresh intellectual alliances. The move towards the laboratory coincides with a redrawing

---

[3] Edwin G. Boring, *A History of Experimental Psychology* (London, 1929), 234.
[4] E. W. Scripture, *The New Psychology* (London, 1897), 452.       [5] Ibid. 453.

of the discipline's national and international profile.[6] The specificity of national traditions is abandoned, and experimental psychology as it were joins the dots to link up the burgeoning international laboratory circuit. Though its internationalism is welcome, one loss is a sense of psychology's address to particular cultural and social situations. It also begins a move towards greater specialization, both in the definition of the field of activity and in the language in which it is to be articulated. After Experimentalism, psychological discourse circulates between professional peers rather than in the more openly public domains favoured by the earlier generation, and the shift towards the laboratory marks a shift in the public presence of the subject. Psychology now tends to address more localized areas of knowledge, in more expert language, and as part of an international traffic of communication between companion centres. It is specialist, 'measured', 'objective', and 'scientific'—a word coming into wide currency in its modern usage only around 1900.[7] It is secular and modernizing in its outlook and postures, and is a clear beneficiary of the increased professionalization of intellectual life in Britain, which historians have detected from around 1880.[8]

By contrast, the high-Victorian psychology of the years 1850–80 was a more open discourse, more spaciously framed in its address to common issues, and with an audience crossing wide disciplinary interests. Economists, imaginative writers, philosophers, clerics, literary critics, policy-makers, as well as biomedical scientists contributed to its formation. It was an unshapely, accommodating, contested, emergent, energetic discipline, filled with dispute and without settled lines of theory or protocols for investigation. The role played by the great generalist periodicals of the Victorian period is crucial in this, and the broad audience for psychology perceived the issues it raised as matters of common, not specialized, intellectual and cultural concern.[9] This, hard-eyed Experimentalists dismissed

---

[6] By contrast, British commentators were often more parochial in outlook and fond of taxonomies based on national cultures. The philosopher Shadworth Hodgson, for instance, remarks in 1876 that psychology is 'the peculiar glory of Englishmen' ('Philosophy of Mind: II—As Regards Psychology', *Mind*, 1 (1876), 223). Many also discriminated between the English and Scottish schools, as Hodgson does here. The early numbers of *Mind* have several large articles on the different national traditions in psychology, and these were also a regular feature in the discussion of 'Current Philosophy' in the *Atheneum*.

[7] Richard Yeo, *Defining Science: William Whewell, Natural Knowledge, and Public Debate in Early Victorian Britain* (Cambridge, 1993), 5.

[8] Sheldon Rothblatt, *Tradition and Change in English Liberal Education: An Essay on History and Culture* (London, 1976); Harold Perkin, *The Rise of Professional Society: England since 1880* (London, 1989); Stefan Collini, *Public Moralists: Political Thought and Intellectual Life in Britain 1850–1930* (Oxford, 1991).

[9] This claim will, I trust, be sustained by the detail of what follows. Robert M. Young ('Natural Theology Victorian Periodicals, and the Fragmentation of a Common Context', in *Darwin's Metaphor: Nature's Place in Victorian Culture* (Cambridge, 1985)) outlines the general development clearly and persuasively. See also Yeo, *Defining Science*, and T. W. Heyck, *The Transformation of Intellectual Life in Victorian England* (London, 1982).

as 'philosophy', but it was much more. What is at stake is the presence and disposition of knowledge within a culture, and it is unfortunate that subsequent historians have mainly followed the Experimentalists' lead. In synoptic histories of psychology, the long 'philosophical' past tends to be reduced to short first chapters.

Other factors, additional to the dominion of the experimental paradigm, combine to block our view of Victorian psychological thought. For many cultural historians and literary critics, psychoanalysis has long been considered the branch of psychology most appropriate for humanistic enquiry. In part, this is a reaction to the ascendancy of Experimentalism, because psychoanalysis has been seen to have a more 'personalist' orientation next to the steely science. But psychoanalysis has contributed its share to the popular myth that there was 'no psychology before Freud'. Psychoanalysis, with its clinical and personalized emphases, its discursively closed explications, and its roots in continental thought, has, over time, helped obscure that distinctively British psychology of the nineteenth century that was conceived in very different traditions and with different aims and materials. The ahistorical consequences of the application of Freudian interpretative protocols to historically distant topics and personalities have been, in their more thoughtless applications, notorious (as in the case of some speculative psycho-biography). But the psychoanalytic conception of culture has also frequently been short of localized detail and historical specificity in a way consistent with the kind of speculation encouraged in Freud's late work. *Civilization and its Discontents*, for example, theoretically equalizes and makes identical the pressures to cultural conformity across all of human history from the tribe to the skyscraper. Though there are substantial exceptions to this (especially in the work of Peter Gay), the problem is one of historical insensitivity as well as interpretative narrowness, both of which are driven by the mythicizing drives embedded in its psychological system. But the problem represented by psychoanalysis attaches itself to larger issues that lie adjacent to it.

In an essay on 'The Growth of Culture and the Evolution of Mind', the anthropologist Clifford Geertz reviews the discourse about mind in the second half of the twentieth century. He examines four principal contributors: neuroscience, humanists, evolutionary biologists, and psychoanalysts. Twentieth-century neuro- and psychological scientists are, he thinks, inhibited in even using the word 'mind'. For Experimentalists and classical neurologists, 'mind' represents a totality of functions and abilities not amenable to a kind of analysis that instinctively breaks larger categories into functionally smaller units. Scientists therefore feel uncomfortable with such an unwieldy, unrestricted term. On the opposite side, humanists and philosophers have traditionally defended the idea, finding in it ways of escaping an aggressive functionalism. As a result, in their work, the idea of mind has become over-identified with private feelings.[10] Geertz regrets the loss of a conversation between the two perspectives, but even more strongly he regrets the neglect by both traditions of a social approach to mind. Both wings of opinion, he argues, avoid discussing the mind as a social product determined by its immersion in cultural systems. It is, he affirms, through interactions within culture that personal sensibilities are formed. At the same time, the 'hardware' of the nervous system 'relies, inescapably, on the accessibility of public symbolic structures to build up its own autonomous, ongoing pattern of activity'.[11] Geertz finds similar assumptions replicated in modern evolutionary thought and in psychoanalysis. The former pays attention almost exclusively to biological mechanisms; the latter emphasizes so-called primary, largely unconscious processes (such as 'substitution, reversal, [and] condensation') rather than 'those [Freud] called "secondary"—directed, logically ordered reasoning, and so on'.[12] The combined effect has been further to divide the 'two cultures' of the humanities and the sciences, underestimate the role of culture in human development, devalue the contribution of conscious individual agency to culture, and separate the experience of the lived self from the language of science.[13]

Raymond Williams, in *Keywords*, pursued a similar line of argument. He recounted how the word 'psychological' came, in general use in the twentieth century, to be identified with inwardness and personal feeling, a privileged area of inner and usually private experience detached from social and cultural contexts. Williams argues that this was in part an understandable reaction against the depersonalization of much medical or Experimentalist discourse in psychology, and the grossly reductive generalizations made by 'group-behaviour' specialists, and 'social' and 'industrial' psychologists. Like Geertz, Williams sees this as a regrettable narrowing of intellectual interests, and a loss of balanced attention to the role of society in individual development, both of which reflect a culture whose specializations constitute an increasing inability to enquire into and understand general or interlocking processes. In *Keywords* and elsewhere, Williams argues that, in a companion development, the bifurcation of the novel into increasingly separate 'social' and 'psychological' domains reflects the same circumstance. This separation, Williams argues, has disabled the common understanding of the relationship between personal and social developments, which was the great

---

[10] Clifford Geertz, 'The Growth of Culture and the Evolution of Mind', in *The Interpretation of Cultures: Selected Essays* (London, 1993), 56.

[11] Ibid. 83.    [12] Ibid. 61–2.

[13] For companionable arguments to these, see also John Searle, *Minds, Brains and Science: The 1984 Reith Lectures* (Harmondsworth, 1984), and Steven Rose, *Lifelines: Biology, Freedom, Determinism* (London, 1997). Geertz's essay is historically close to at least one side of the Leavis–Snow 'two cultures' controversy of 1959, though both British contributors lacked the detail and sophisticated range of Geertz's analysis. See C. P. Snow, *The Two Cultures*, ed. Stefan Collini (Cambridge, 1993). Collini's introduction helpfully sets the context of the debate, including its nineteenth-century sources and antecedents.

achievement of nineteenth-century realism, and this is one unfortunate consequence of cultural and literary Modernism.[14]

There are limits to this argument. It would, for instance, be foolish to ignore the very real social, historical, and cultural engagements of Modernist writers. But there does appear to be a case to be made here. Many of the innovative narrative techniques of literary Modernism associated with writers such as Joyce, Richardson, Woolf, or Henry James—techniques such as 'stream of consciousness', intense focus on 'moments of being' or epiphany, or the emphasis on the divisibility and multiplicity of subjective perception as captured in pluralistic narratives—can be seen to privilege inwardness in such a way that it is a only a short step to identify modernity itself with psychological processes that are introspective, often socially alienated, and fundamentally private. The emphasis placed by many Modernists on the fresh and challenging representation of fluid interiority (and the corresponding polemical rejection of stiff 'Victorian' repression and conventionality) too often obscures both Modernism's relations with its own past and, in its imagined leap beyond it, the real achievements of that past itself, as other recent commentators have remarked.[15] The complicated lines of this connection can be neatly illustrated.

'Stream of consciousness' as a literary technique is usually connected with William James's *The Principles of Psychology* of 1890.[16] The metaphor James deploys is well designed to capture the analytically fugitive quality of mental events. Its flowing movements are characteristic of inwardly perceived mental experience whose entangled character baffles more invasively dissecting description. James writes:

Consciousness, then, does not appear to itself chopped up in bits. Such words as 'chain' or 'train' do not describe it fitly as it presents itself in the first instance. It is nothing jointed; it flows. A 'river' or 'stream' are the metaphors by which it is most naturally described. *In talking of it hereafter, let us call it the stream of thought, of consciousness, or of subjective life.*[17]

---

[14] Raymond Williams, *Keywords: A Vocabulary of Culture and Society*, rev. edn. (London, 1983), 246–8; see also 'Realism and the Contemporary Novel', in *The Long Revolution* (London, 1961), and *The English Novel from Dickens to Lawrence* (London, 1970).

[15] See e.g. Isobel Armstrong, *Victorian Politics: Poetry, Poetics and Politics* (London, 1993), 'Introduction', and Gillian Beer, 'The Victorians in Virginia Woolf: 1832–1941', in *Arguing with the Past: Essays in Narrative from Woolf to Sidney* (London, 1989), and, especially, 'Wave Theory and the Rise of Literary Modernism', in *Open Fields: Science in Cultural Encounter* (Oxford, 1996).

[16] Judith Ryan provides a recent example. Ryan writes that James was 'the creator of the term "stream of consciousness"' and she cites several authorities for this view (*The Vanishing Subject: Early Psychology and Literary Modernism* (London, 1991), 1, 14). Though Ryan is concerned to 'rediscover a lost element in Modernism' (p. 5), it is that of a European tradition of psychological thought developing through Ernst Mach, Franz Brentano, and various French writers, and she sets British sources aside.

[17] William James, *The Principles of Psychology* (1890), 2 vols. (New York, 1950), i. 239. James's account of the 'stream of consciousness' was first published in an article in the British journal *Mind* in 1884: 'On Some Omissions of Introspective Psychology', *Mind*, 9 (1884), 1–26.

The passage situates itself against some elements in nineteenth-century psychology ('chain' and 'train', as we shall see in Chapter 2, are semi-technical terms from associationist theory used to indicate the serial determinations by which ideas are mentally linked). But the main point for our purposes is that the metaphor did not in fact originate with James. It was actually a coinage introduced some decades earlier by G. H. Lewes that afterwards became a part of general usage in psychological circles, often adapted in various forms such as the 'stream of feeling' or the 'stream of thought'. By the turn of the century the metaphor appears almost a commonplace. It is used, for instance, in a short, popular exposition from 1902 *The Story of Thought and Feeling* by Frederick Ryland in the successful series 'The Library of Useful Stories'. Ryland begins with a chapter on 'The Stream of Consciousness' before moving to accounts of Mental Images, Perception, Feeling, Thought, and so on.[18] 'The Stream of Consciousness' is, therefore, his opening move in what is largely a psychology of perception.

However, Lewes's original use of the metaphor suggests something both richer and more complicated than later redactions, even that of James's splendidly lucid and much-quoted definition. (To be fair to James, it should be said that this passage, which is so regularly isolated from his book, is part of a much more complicated and satisfying argument.) In 1859 in *The Physiology of Common Life* Lewes wrote not only of 'the general stream of Consciousness' that characterizes the action of our minds as we fall between voluntary and involuntary, conscious and unconscious states, but also of 'the general stream of Sensation which constitutes his [the reader's] feeling of existence—the consciousness of himself as a sensitive being'.[19] This latter state, it is important to note, is largely a physical, bodily state, and it is for Lewes distinct from (though it contributes to) the mental 'stream of consciousness' emphasized by James. Taken together, the two suggest not just a sense of mental freewheeling (which is the loose, colloquial understanding of 'stream of consciousness'), but a rich, physical, ontological grounding to that activity that, to my mind, actually captures much more successfully the effect of, say, Molly Bloom's soliloquy in *Ulysses* than the usual understanding of the pure liquidity of James's 'mentalist' image. And, as it happened, Lewes's idea of the 'stream of Sensation' was itself developed in the 1890s though with as little credit given to its innovator. The description of the unconscious sensory flow that establishes and maintains our bodily and psychological presence and identity, and with it our ontological grounding, was named 'proprioception' by C. S. Sherrington in the 1890s and was developed by him into a compelling theory that has become a crucial part of general and clinical neurology, though —perversely—it has not entered very far into literary commentary or the

[18] Frederick Ryland, *The Story of Thought and Feeling* (London, 1902).
[19] George Henry Lewes, *The Physiology of Common Life*, 2 vols. (London, 1859–60), ii. 63, 66.

history of psychology.[20] Despite Edwin Boring's assertion, Lewes's contribution was not, in fact, without influence.

What does this fishing in the eddying history of the 'stream of consciousness' suggest? It obviously suggests that the Jamesian stream of consciousness, commonly understood in its 'mentalist' form, is only a partial story. Following Williams and Geertz, it appears to leave aside the social and cultural influences that shape consciousness. Following Lewes or Sherrington, it appears to grant an unwarranted autonomy to events of consciousness as distinct from physical sensation and bodily processes. But also, delaying the date of its coinage and ascribing it to James have presented cultural and literary historians with a more convenient point at which to 'break' to Modernist techniques and outlooks, and to construct a corresponding epochal narrative that is, to a degree, illusory. This process has gone alongside the recruitment of William James himself as a distinctively Modernist voice, a process that has cut him adrift from his nineteenth-century roots and antecedents and often turned him crudely against them.[21] The Victorian sources for the Modernist emphasis on 'stream of consciousness' and cognate processes and techniques have been eliminated (though not, it should once more be said, by James himself, who is always careful to stage his discussion in relation to nineteenth-century debates). The conceptual awareness of the experience of these complex mental states is evident much earlier than the received versions of the history of ideas or psychology or literature imply, and these earlier conceptions are, in some respects, richer and more suggestive. One final point is worth emphasizing. As G. H. Lewes coined the term, his partner George Eliot

[20]   Oliver Sacks, *The Man who Mistook his Wife for a Hat* (London, 1986), 42, 49–52, 68. Sacks connects Sherrington's 'proprioception' with the nineteenth-century theory of the 'muscle sense' developed by Alexander Bain, W. B. Carpenter, and others. At least one major Victorian commentator made the same connection (though, of course, without Sherrington's nomenclature), explicitly identifying Lewes as the key source: see W. K. Clifford, '*Problems of Life and Mind* by George Henry Lewes. First Series. The Foundations of a Creed. Vol. 1', *Academy*, 5 (1874), 149. For Sherrington's account of 'proprioception', see Charles S. Sherrington, *The Integrated Action of the Nervous System* (London, 1906), 308–53.

[21]   David A. Hollinger writes: 'However diverse our opinions of William James today, we generally agree that the great pragmatist was right about one thing: the pretensions of the Victorian "positivists". James exposed the epistemological naïveté of these cultural imperialists. He celebrated openness of mind over the arrogant, dogmatic closures we associate with the nineteenth-century scientific intelligentsia. We honour [James] for being one of the first to take up the cause, for being among the great prophets of epistemic humility, a founder of truly "modernist" or even "postmodernist" thought' ('James, Clifford, and the Scientific Conscience', in *The Cambridge Companion to William James*, ed. Ruth Anna Putnam (Cambridge, 1997), 69). Though, in fact, Hollinger goes on to defend Clifford, the framing assumptions are revealing. My argument, of course, does not insist that 'the' Victorians were identical with 'the' Modernists, any more than I would argue that they were absolutely different, or that the various generations composed themselves uniformly into either camp. The Victorians had their essential difference from the Moderns, as the Moderns do from ourselves. It is the mixture of resemblance and difference that allows them to be perceived at all.

was at work on *The Mill on the Floss* in another room of the house they shared at Holly Lodge, Wimbledon. Just as the line between modern and Victorian cannot be so easily drawn, the histories of psychology and literature can sometimes be as close as a hallway apart.

How, then, can the story of Victorian psychology best be told? Perhaps not as a narrative. Plain narratives (especially in post-structural times) can suggest pure linearity and closed destinations, or Whiggish or positivist history. It might imitate the severe elimination from the plot of unwanted material, and the kind of exclusive teleology and self-emphasis that was proposed by cocky Experimentalists in the 1890s. This the Freudians—not always free from it themselves —might describe as 'narcissism', or Jacques Lacan as 'the mirror stage' of historiography, whereas what actually characterize the ensemble of discourses that make up high-Victorian psychology are its many-sided interactions, its jostle of incompatible material, its multiple, fraught arenas for debate. In this book, the methodological tactic in Part One is to devise a taxonomy rather than a narrative, partly because the material yields no clear sequence, chronological or otherwise. However, the taxonomy is largely heuristic in intention, and is not meant to imply categorical distinctions or restrictions. The material contained in each chapter must flow across the boundaries set for it: the faculty psychology straddles Chapters 1 and 2, the description of the body and its passions continues across Chapters 3 and 4. The typology is, therefore, to a degree, self-cancelling.

Victorian psychology opens out everywhere, fertile in its sources, dense and turbulent in its growth. The very word was only just coming into common usage, and its vigour of development is amply specified in the *OED*. The word was coined in the mid-seventeenth century, by William Harvey in *Anatomical Exercises* (1653), to designate a branch of 'anthropology' or the study of man.[22] It was sporadically used in these ways for 150 years or so with variant spellings (included 'psichology' and 'psychologie' as late as 1800) and forms (for example 'Psychonomy: or the science of the moral powers' in 1803, or 'Psychics', Bentham's version of modern psychology in the 1830s). Different words were also used, like 'pneumatology'—the theory or doctrine of spirits or spiritual beings—a form preferred by Scottish writers. But psychology settled into recognizably modern usage in the first half of the nineteenth century. Even then, there was plenty of elasticity, as in Sir William Hamilton's eclectically jumbled definition in 1836: the study of 'States of the mind, or Conscious Subject, or Soul, or Spirit or Self or Ego'. More careful refinements followed, as, for instance, by James Pritchard, a leading and influential 'mad doctor' whose *Natural History of Man* went through four editions between 1842 and 1855. According to Pritchard, psychology is 'with

---

[22] The actual origins of the term remain disputed: see François H. Lapointe, 'Who Originated the Term "Psychology"?', *Journal of the History of the Behavioural Sciences*, 8 (1972), 328–35.

respect to the human mind, the history of the mental faculties', but his opening clause shows an awareness of variant understandings. By 1880 the word had
been established with some stability, but, the *OED* makes clear, it had by then
begun to splice itself into specialisms: experimental psychology (as we have seen),
child psychology, social psychology, developmental psychology, and so on. But
its boisterous lexical aggregation and embellishment indicate the energetic drive
of psychology's development. Words came tumbling into usage: 'psychologise'
(1830), 'psychophysiology' (1837), 'psychiatry' (1846), 'psychosis', 'psychopathology',
and 'psychopathic' (1847—though 'psychopath' not until 1885), 'psychophysical'
(1847), 'psychography' (1850), 'psychotherapy' (1853), 'psychometry' (1854), 'psychosomatic' (by the novelist Charles Reade in *Hard Cash*, 1863), 'psychopomp'
(1863), 'psychoneurology' (1865), 'psychodynamic' and 'psychogenesis' (both by
G. H. Lewes, 1874), 'psycho-motor' (1878), 'psychoneurosis' (1883), 'psychicist'
(1885), 'psychophysicist' (1886), 'psychoblast' (1889)—so many compounds, so
many coinages, such looseness in agreed usage and semantic structure. A history of high-Victorian psychology needs to begin with a sense of this variety
and fertility.

The new discipline of psychology attracted comment from virtually all major
Victorian intellectuals. Their fascination, factionalized controversy, contempt, aston-
ishment, and thirst for discussion of it rivalled the railways as a topic. But the
multivocal nature of its development, as I see it, has more in common with those
bountiful Victorian inventions that emphasize organized multiplicity than with
the smooth linear sequences expounded in the traditional disciplinary historiography. I have in mind instruments such as the kaleidoscope, invented, though
not patented, in 1816 by Sir David Brewster (whose psychological views we
will encounter shortly); or Brewster's 'stereoscope', first displayed at the Great
Exhibition of 1851; or the Great Exhibition itself, that enormous apogee of all
'the great Victorian collections' in their many shapes and forms, about which
Charlotte Brontë wrote that 'its grandeur does not consist in *one* thing, but in
the unique assemblage of *all* things';[23] or the multipart spectroscopes built in
the 1860s from a matrix of prisms to unveil spectra with such precision that
they could detect '1/100,000,000*th part of a grain* of sodium';[24] or the multi-
branching diagram in Chapter 4 of Darwin's *The Origin of Species*, designed to
represent, in a controlled way, the flux of possibilities for evolutionary life that
threaten to reduce any literal representation to heuristic chaos.[25] This diagram

---

[23] Quoted by Asa Briggs, *Victorian Things* (Harmondsworth, 1988), 52.
[24] Robert Routledge, *Discoveries and Inventions of the Nineteenth Century*, 14th edn. (London,
1903), 424.
[25] Charles Darwin, *The Origin of Species by Means of Natural Selection, or The Preservation of
Favoured Races in the Struggle for Life*, ed. J. W. Burrow (Harmondsworth, 1968), 159–60. See also
Gillian Beer's brilliant account of this in *Darwin's Plots: Evolutionary Narrative in Darwin, George
Eliot and Nineteeth-Century Fiction* (London, 1983), esp. 'Introduction' and 37–8.

opens like a stack of fans, or a multi-branching tree, evolving in many directions with myriad possibilities. It is a lavish image, ample in its abundance, and yet the mathematician W. K. Clifford later remarked that even representational analogies such as this were inadequate, because 'Space has not dimensions enough to represent the true state of the case.'[26] In literature and applied art something of this cascading multiplicity is also to be found in the illustrations that front the monthly parts of novels like *David Copperfield* (1849–50), in which a whirl of images circulates around the exuberantly embellished, Micawberish title: *The Personal History, Adventures, Experience, & Observation of David Copperfield The Younger of Blunderstone Rookery (Which He never meant to be Published on any Account)*.

The history of Victorian psychology between 1850 and 1880 may not revolve so endlessly as a kaleidoscope, or focus so fruitfully as the stereoscope, or be so publically prominent as the Great Exhibition, or determine so precisely as a spectroscope, or be so boundlessly indicative in its possibilities as Darwin's illustration of the evolution of life, or balance its design so well as Hablôt K. Browne (Dickens's illustrator in *David Copperfield*). But images such as these are necessary to register the sheer bustle of its discursive world, and help challenge those obstructive images of pinched, ungenerous anxiety and morbid repressiveness attached to classic conceptions of 'Victorianism'. In its fertile, multiplex interactions, Victorian psychology is a discourse flowing (like Lewes's twin streams of Consciousness and Sensation) as a compound with manifold sources and consequences. Lewes himself relished what he styled its 'disturbing anarchy of Investigation'.[27] He meant, primarily, its continuing challenge to orthodoxy and convention, but the phrase happily captures something of the rumbustious aspirations of the emergent discipline.

Victorian psychologists created endless, prolix, classificatory distinctions in their efforts to get to grips with this discursive turbulence and cognitive and semantic revolution. Often they sorted by schools (the Empirical school, the Rational school, the Inductive school, the Compromise school). Sometimes, they ordered by national culture (Scottish Common Sense, English Empiricism, French Materialism, German

---

[26] W. K. Clifford, *Lectures and Essays*, 2 vols., ed. Leslie Stephen and Frederick Pollock (London, 1879), ii. 90.

[27] George Henry Lewes, *Problems of Life and Mind*, 5 vols. (London, 1874–9), ii. 131. The organization of *Problems of Life and Mind* is complex. Lewes divided it into three 'series', of which the first and third appeared as two separate volumes. *First Series*: [i] *The Foundations of a Creed* (London, 1874); [ii] *The Foundations of a Creed* (London, 1875); *Second Series*: [iii] *The Physical Basis of Mind* (London, 1877); *Third Series*: [iv] *The Study of Psychology: Its Object, Scope and Method* (London, 1879); [v] untitled (London, 1879). This division is, however, cumbersome for finding one's way around its bulk. I therefore henceforth give citations by volume number followed by page number; the reader should, however, be aware that Lewes himself did not use the volume numbers. See further Chapter 7, esp. n. 16.

Speculation). They distinguished between empirical and deductive psychologies, observation and introspection, clinical evidence and (in the Enlightenment tradition) the normative knowledge of human nature assumed by all men of good will. They classified according to psychology's supposed objectivity or subjectivity, its science or its philosophy. They disputed the importance and relevance of the various different sciences whose impact was felt upon the knowledge of the mind. They squabbled about the claims of religious authority as against those of science, and of ethics against natural philosophy. They quarrelled over the distinctions to be made between the soul and the mind, the mind and the brain, the mind and the degrading forces of the body, between man and animal, male and female, civilized and primitive. They argued over the relationship between simple sentience and the multifarious sensorium, between sensation and cognition, the reflex arc and the cerebrum, the motor functions and thought, mechanisms and experience. They debated the claims of the psychological faculties against the physiological functions, the status of the higher faculties against the lower, and the proper meanings of an endless army of terms and distinctions paraded through psychological books like familiar turns in an often-visited carnival: thought, feeling, will, habit, instinct, memory, consciousness, double consciousness, and unconsciousness.

The strain and effort to classify and discriminate, to gain purchase on the co-mingling phenomena of the mind, and correlate these with functions of the organism (or to deny such correlations), is immediately apparent from a glance at the contents of almost any book of psychological theory in the nineteenth century. These books thrive on the distinctions they create. Sometimes, indeed, Victorian psychology can appear a gigantic taxonomic exchange, an extravaganza of categorization, like the feverish work of palaeontologists and naturalists opening endless crates of specimens shipped from overseas in the newly founded museums in Kensington or Paris or Dublin, and trying gamely (and for the most part successfully) to make an orderly pattern from the pile.

In this context, the subtitle of *Mind*, the first exclusively 'psychological' journal in Britain founded in the 1870s, is worth noticing: *A Quarterly Review of Psychology and Philosophy*. The conjunction expresses both an identity and a difference, a necessary relationship and a desired independence, as the science and the philosophy pulled in contrary directions, as they did in various ways throughout the period. Though the journal's first editorial offered to 'procure a decision on this question as to the scientific standing of psychology', in the event it was only by the Experimentalists' abrupt curtailment of the discussion that an answer was delivered.[28] But the pre-history of the Experimentalist assertion is not the childhood of a maturing discipline. Looking round the corners of

---

[28] George Croom Robertson, 'Prefatory Words', *Mind*, 1 (1875), 3.

such a crude obstruction, we see an epistemological passion and appetite for knowledge in the mid-nineteenth-century debate that takes us beyond the discipline to the heart of major issues in Victorian culture. But to follow this it is time to turn the corner and consider a typology of this unglimpsed, often-derided theory.

PART ONE

# Generalities: A Discrimination of Types of Psychological Theory

# CHAPTER 1

# *The Discourse of the Soul*

We can identify four strands of psychological argument in the period 1850–80 that display the different discursive fields in which Victorian psychologists operated. All historical commentary creates retrospective categories, but this taxonomy follows, as closely as possible, the various areas within which Victorian theory operated.[1] The four strands are: the discourse of the soul, the discourse of philosophy, the discourse of physiology in general biology, and the discourse of medicine. However, these are not so much four different theories (or even coherent bodies of theory) as *four different ways of looking at* the phenomena of the human mind. As one would expect, they contain factions in dispute with one another, although they operate within the same discursive orbit and with some shared assumptions. So this typology presents, as it were, four different *languages* for psychology, each entailing a different conceptual architecture and set of assumptions whose identification and analysis are major concerns of this book. Nineteenth-century psychology seems to me a mosaic always in process of completion, in which each of its many makers had a different vision of the pattern and rarely cooperated. Though the more scientific orientation of the last two items in the typology (those relating to physiology and medicine) became increasingly conspicuous and influential as time passed, this list is not intended, by any means, to suggest a progressive sequence in the Positivist manner. All of these discourses were available throughout the period covered by this book, and all were used. But they had variable effects in speaking to different constituencies with different interests in a debate that was essentially disorderly. These discourses were often at loggerheads internally and with each other. But local concord

---

[1] There have been other attempts to provide a taxonomy of Victorian psychology recently. Jenny Bourne Taylor and Sally Shuttleworth's excellent *Embodied Selves: An Anthology of Psychological Texts 1830–1890* (Oxford, 1998) collects an impressive array of material across a large span of interests distributed into five sections—'Reading the Mind', 'The Unconscious Mind and the Workings of Memory', 'The Sexual Body', 'Insanity and Nervous Disorders', and 'Heredity, Degeneration, and Modern Life'—each of which is further subdivided in different ways. The arrangement helpfully allows the reader to negotiate the sheer bulk of material, and the texts are exceptionally well chosen and edited. The volume also illustrates the links between areas by allowing writers to appear in more than one section. The broad categories, however, tend (though by no means exclusively) to reflect modern interests. The more general typology proposed here allows arguments to circulate as far as possible as they grew and developed in their nineteenth-century forms, often in corkscrew fashion, within the broad categories of Victorian psychological debate.

could be as important as conflict, and compromise agreements, reached for brief periods, often for expedient reasons, on fast-developing, frequently uncertain scientific terrain, are vital. The development of psychology is thus ungainly as well as disputatious. In this respect, it is, of course, much like any other intellectual environment. Let us begin with the discourse of the soul.

The word psychology is derived from the Greek for 'soul discourse'. For many at the beginning of the nineteenth century, psychology, functionally as well as etymologically, meant simply 'the study of the soul', and powerful popular and theological discourses sustained this meaning throughout. An early synonym was 'pneumatology', the study of 'the nature and functions of the human soul or mind' (*OED*), which derived from the seventeenth-century doctrine of the spirits or spiritual beings, and this word was preferred instead of psychology in, for example, Sir David Brewster's influential *Edinburgh Encyclopaedia* in 1830.[2] Thus, across the century, one strand of psychological discourse was always attached to a cluster of interests connected to metaphysics or the supernatural, whether these derived from orthodox theology or elsewhere. In 1803 the Scottish philosopher Dugald Stewart was not displeased to discover 'the metaphysical origins of all the words which express the intellectual phenomena, from the subtle and fugitive nature of the objects of our reasoning . . . to the subjects of our consciousness'.[3] Learned theory shared page space with popular enthusiasms such as spiritualism, mesmerism, and psychography (or 'spirit writing') in both up- as well as downmarket publications.[4] The two shared an undiscriminated language. Until late in the century, the word 'psychic' was used to mean both 'psychological' (as in the common phrase 'psychic faculties') and the more modern sense pertaining to spiritualism. Indeed, as psychology took a more materialist turn, its opponents found it polemically helpful to conflate the two in order to puncture the new theory's scientific credentials in reviews that mixed together books of both kinds. This was particularly the case with the popular discourse of cranioscopy, the phrenological theory of reading character from the bumps on one's head that we will examine in Chapter 3. Readers of the *Quarterly* or the *Edinburgh* could regularly find accounts of serious psychological texts smeared

---

[2] Anon., 'Metaphysics', in *The Edinburgh Encyclopaedia*, conducted by David Brewster with the assistance of Gentlemen eminent in Science and Literature (Edinburgh, 1830).

[3] Dugald Stewart, 'An Account of the Life and Writings of Thomas Reid' (1803), in *The Works of Thomas Reid, D.D., with Notes and Supplementary Dissertations by Sir William Hamilton, Bart.*, 2 vols., 8th edn. (Edinburgh, 1895), i. 13.

[4] Catherine Crowe's *The Night-Side of Nature: or, Ghosts and Ghost Seers*, 3rd edn. (London, 1853) is representative. It is a compendium of strange and creepy tales with analyses, and went through three editions in five years. It stirs together gothic nonsense and folklore with a hotch-potch of other material in the generally inchoate orbit of psychology in the early to mid-century including, not only mesmerism and spiritualism, but phrenology, German philosophical idealism, and physiological psychology. It protests long and hard against the Establishment abuse of marginal knowledge.

by association with controversial phrenology, or enthusiastic spiritualist nonsense, for the first half of the century at least.

Early encyclopaedias were committed to the discourse of the soul. Psychology 'consists in the knowledge of the soul in general, and of the soul of man in particular', according to the *Encyclopaedia Perthensis* of 1816.[5] The entry in Abraham Rees's best-selling *Cyclopaedia*, in the editions of both 1788 and 1819 (which was enlarged from two to thirty-nine volumes), has 'PSYCHOLOGY, the doctrine of the Soul. See Soul.' In the 1819 entry, psychology is paired with anatomy under the general heading 'Anthropology'. The former branch studies the soul, while the latter studies the body. This suggests parallel strands of spiritual and physical knowledge, but, the entry makes clear, these are not convergent.[6] In 1845 Coleridge's *Encyclopaedia Metropolitana* (completed a decade after his death) defined psychology simply as the 'Discourse of the Soul'.[7] The abruptness of such a definition implies a powerful set of assumptions that are identified in the more forthcoming *British Cyclopaedia* of 1838: 'PSYCHOLOGY, the science of the soul, or the spiritual principle in man . . . may be defined to be the scientifically conducted observation of the operations and changes of the human soul . . . It takes for granted the distinction of the spiritual substance from the body, as a matter of consciousness, and does not therefore attempt to explain it.'[8] This definition folds the mind into the categories of soul and spirit, for its qualities are entirely determined by these. It toys with a modish scientism (before, of course, the word science had hardened into its modern form), but it finesses the latent contradiction between scientific investigation and intangible spirituality. It ends by declaring two major *a priori* assumptions: that body and spirit are ontologically distinct, and that their relationship, even their natures, are beyond enquiry. These assumptions are a cornerstone of psychology as the discourse of the soul, and were recommended as matters of both principle and expediency. Readers of the *Perthensis*, for instance, were told that exploration of these questions was pointless as well as wrong: 'the most profound, the most subtile [*sic*] and abstract researches have been made, that human reason is capable of producing; and concerning the substance of which, in spite of all the efforts, it is yet extremely difficult to assert anything that is rational, and still less anything that is positive and well-supported.'[9]

[5] Anon., 'Metaphysics', in *Encyclopaedia Perthensis; or Universal Dictionary of the Arts, Sciences, Literature, &c.* (Edinburgh, 1816), xiv. 527.

[6] Anon., 'Psychology', in *Cyclopaedia: or, an Universal Dictionary of Arts and Sciences* (London, 1788); Anon., 'Psychology', in *Cyclopaedia: or, an Universal Dictionary of Arts and Sciences*, by Abraham Rees (London, 1819).

[7] Anon., 'Psychology', in *Encyclopaedia Metropolitana: or, Universal Dictionary of Knowledge* (London, 1845).

[8] Anon., 'Psychology', in *The British Cyclopaedia* (London, 1838), iii. 367.

[9] Anon., 'Metaphysics', in *Encyclopaedias Perthensis*, xiv. 527.

Encyclopaedias can, of course, promote reforming knowledge, but often, as here, they preserve and transmit orthodoxies, and the discourse of the soul was essentially conservative in relation to the developing discipline. It was also very often conservative in the political sense. As we shall see in detail later, the block on enquiry, particularly into the direct linkage of mind to body, was one of the many intellectual embargoes on new ideas felt in Britain after the French Revolution, when materialism was obsessively associated with political radicalism. Even when the encyclopaedias developed fuller accounts of psychological doctrine as the century advanced, they favoured the traditional, mentalist, or, more pointedly, spiritualist case. The *Encyclopaedia Britannica*, for instance, has no entry for psychology at all until the eighth edition of 1853–60, when the reader is referred to a long entry on 'Metaphysics' by the Christian Tory H. L. Mansel, while the ninth edition of 1886 included a long, celebrated disquisition by the idealist philosopher James Ward, which is discussed in Chapter 7 below. At the more populist end of the market, *Chambers's Encyclopaedia: A Dictionary of Universal Knowledge for the People* in 1865 also took a strongly mentalist line. Under 'Psychology' readers were referred to the entry on 'Mind', which asserted the ontological autonomy of mental events. Mind cannot be resolved into simpler elements, the entry claimed, as there is 'nothing more fundamental than itself'. Lacking qualities of extension in space and other properties of matter, it must be considered insubstantial and not amenable to material analysis.[10]

The terminological shift from 'soul' to 'mind' in this mid-century definition represents a significant adjustment in attention. But in other respects the intellectual architecture remains the same. Mind (soul continues to hover suggestively) is remote from the determinations of the body and also from other creatures. Whatever headway was made by the new physiologically oriented psychology during the nineteenth century was made against a Christian conception of humanity that stressed exclusive spiritual determinations, and the special status of humans judged in relation to animals. This was a most powerful opponent. David Newsome, in his recent *The Victorian World Picture*, finds no reason to dissent from George Kitson Clark's verdict from 1962 that 'probably in no other century . . . did the claims of religion occupy so large a part in the nation's life, or did men speaking in the name of religion continue to exercise so much power'.[11] This was the case in psychological theory as elsewhere. As we shall see in the next section, the religious perspective on psychology was supported by compelling arguments in the philosophy of mind, but it had powerful sources in theology, especially that stemming from Natural Theology.

[10] Anon., 'Mind', *Chambers's Encyclopaedia: A Dictionary of Universal Knowledge for the People* (Edinburgh, 1865), vi. 465.
[11] George Kitson Clark in *The Making of Victorian England* (1962), quoted by David Newsome, *The Victorian World Picture: Perceptions and Introspections in an Age of Change* (London, 1998), 197.

For our purposes, nineteenth-century Natural Theology argues two things: that we can know that God exists because nature is so clearly and successfully designed that it must have had a Creator, and that, knowing this, we should celebrate nature as revelation. The human constitution (both mind and body), with its marvellous abilities, is in this respect part of nature, and so should inspire the same admiration. These abilities, however, were so distinctive that they established humanity's special status according to William Paley, whose *Natural Theology; or, the Evidences of the Existence and Attributes of the Deity, Collected from the Appearances of Nature* (1802) was the key text in this line of argument for the century. The theory promotes the study of nature, including human nature, as evidence of God's ordinance, but it could also inhibit explanations that might conflict with its founding assumptions. As the history of evolutionary enquiry indicates, Darwin's work first grew within, and then beyond, and finally in opposition to Natural Theology.[12] This was also true for psychology. Paley and his followers revered man's psychological capacities, but they resisted forms of explanation for them that derive from non-orthodox sources. The stakes are obvious, for, if rival, more materialistic explanations are successful, then the edifice of faith trembles. Arguments from Natural Theology are compelling in so far as they are reassuringly purposive (everything is well in a designed world), and enlist as supportive testimony nature's spectacular beauty and efficiency. But, potentially, these are also high-risk arguments, because the metaphysical case is so firmly attached to the physical one, and evidence produced in the latter area might compromise the former. As a result, natural theologians often resisted too close an enquiry into man's psychological capacities. Paley offered a lead in his remarks on the human eye and powers of vision. What distinguishes a living being from a machine, he argued, is the fact that machines are thoroughly knowable. A living being, by contrast, is inscrutable, a joyous, benign, mysterious gift, and to trace the sequence of events between light striking the retina and human perception is best not attempted.[13]

Guarding against materialistic trespass was a major feature of the invigilation of psychological theory by the discourse of the soul. The views of natural theologians were not the only Christian views of nature available (the Anglo-Catholic J. H. Newman, for instance, attacked Natural Theology's complacent, establishment Protestantism and its ignoring of the flawed, fallen, evil-beset condition of the natural world[14]); none the less, it was the orthodoxy. It embedded mystery into

---

[12] Dov Ospovat, *The Development of Darwin's Theory: Natural History, Natural Theology and Natural Selection, 1839–1859* (Cambridge, 1981); Robert M. Young, *Darwin's Metaphor*; Adrian Desmond and James Moore, *Darwin* (London, 1991).

[13] William Paley, *Natural Theology; or, the Evidences of the Existence and Attributes of the Deity, Collected from the Appearances of Nature* (London, 1802), ch. 3.

[14] John Henry Newman, *The Idea of a University Defined* (1873), ed. I. T. Ker (London, 1976).

the study of nature and the human mind, and where there was mystery there could also be faith. As the century progressed, Natural Theology proved a resilient argument, partly because, in deft hands, it could retreat gracefully under pressure. Faced with scientific evidence that suggested that natural forms were not made directly by God at all but, like landscapes and living beings, were evolved, there was a natural line of defence. If He did not actually make these things Himself, He did at least create the processes that made the things.[15] This argument was deployed by many, perhaps most successfully and coherently by Frederick Temple, ex-Headmaster of Rugby and future Archbishop of Canterbury, in his Bampton Lectures of 1884 on *The Relations between Religion and Science*. Temple attempted to make peace between Darwinism and Christianity by conceding the broad story of evolutionary development. But he insisted that the 'gaps' (his word) in the proposed evolutionary sequence from animal to human, and the scientifically incomplete nature of Darwinian theory itself, left a substantial place for human spirituality. As humans undoubtedly possess a distinctive capacity for spiritual feeling, and a historically demonstrable appetite for religious behaviour, he argued, it is reasonable to assume that this stems from a distinctively human disposition towards universal norms of spiritual and ethical conduct. In which case, psychological investigation (for instance) remains unaffected by the new findings. 'His [man's] dignity consists in his possession of the spiritual faculty, and not in the method by which he became possessed of it.'[16] Once this is assumed, some believed that science and the discourse of the soul could continue to run happily in reassuring parallel, just as they had for the encyclopaedists half a century earlier.

The discourse of the soul as it relates to psychology made two major assumptions: first, that human beings occupy a special place at the pinnacle of Creation, and, secondly, that, by virtue of this, humans, for the most part, are exempt

---

[15] There is a recent revival of interest in natural theological argument, and, to some extent, the modern debate replicates Victorian arguments. The strongest general objection to natural theology is that nature lacks foresight: there can be no design because there is no predictable future to design for, let alone an agent to do the predicting or designing. Nature is thus a blind force. This case is powerfully put, for example, by Richard Dawkins in *The Blind Watchmaker* (Harlow, 1986) and Daniel Dennett in *Darwin's Dangerous Idea: Evolution and the Meaning of Life* (Harmondsworth, 1995). Modern natural theology implicitly concedes this, but instead grounds itself in *unpredictability*, for example, in the strangeness and indeterminacy of the world revealed by quantum physics. This argument is continuous with some nineteenth-century versions because it promotes mystery as the end of nature's empire, and some have pushed this towards a new spiritualized 'scientific' psychology (e.g. Danah Zohar, *The Quantum Self* (London, 1990)). The other source for modern natural theology lies in environmentalism. Here, nature offers us no proof of anything, but it does offer wisdom and insight. For an overview of both strands of argument, see W. Mark Richardson and Wesley J. Wildman (eds.), *Religion and Science: History, Method, Dialogue* (London, 1997).

[16] Frederick Temple, *The Relations between Religion and Science* (1884), in Tess Cosslett (ed.), *Science and Religion in the Nineteenth Century* (Cambridge, 1984), 203.

from the messy determinations of nature. Humans are not only higher in the scheme of things; they are different. The discourse of the soul disconnected mind from the tyranny of its unpredictable earthly origins and structured its ontology, as it were, from above. It discriminated higher minds from lower (for instance, men from women and 'civilized' minds from 'primitive') and saw itself as defending the special dignity of human nature. In extreme forms of the argument, it expresses a violent fear of contamination. Man's special dignity may be compromised even by an acknowledgement of adjacency to other life forms, let alone kinship with them.

As a result, psychologically, human beings were thought to possess relatively autonomous, distinctively human, mental *faculties*. This is a key idea in the development of nineteenth-century psychology. The faculties are arranged hierarchically with the so-called 'higher faculties', such as reason, faith, love, spiritual apprehension, a sense of the numinous, exercise of the will, and so on, at the top, and the 'lower faculties', such as sensation, feeling, appetite, desire, and so on, at the bottom. Clearly, this implies a mind–body separation. At the apex was the unlocated soul, which, exempt from material determinations, focused human hopes and expressed our status in Creation. Ideally, the relationship between the higher and lower faculties would be orderly and integral, but for most it was imagined to be either one of conflict, as the spiritual part strives to subdue the animal, or a matter of mere arbitrariness. In the latter case, the biological or motor functions are acknowledged as necessary to sustain life, but are thought to have little constitutive relationship to the higher or more splendid of human capacities.

Faculty psychology was inherited from the eighteenth century, when much energy was spent settling its taxonomy, in particular which faculty belonged where in the hierarchy. By the nineteenth century it had become so central a feature in the conceptual scenery that it sometimes appears easier to note its absence than mark its presence. Faculty psychology is the orthodoxy, the 'common sense', the 'default position', the 'doxa' (as Roland Barthes called it) of the psychology of the age. It is the background that shapes and establishes the foreground when other theories are under consideration. Its supporters were easily offended, and its normative and hierarchical ideas were deeply persistent. Gary Hatfield notes that its influence has been such that even twentieth-century textbooks follow 'the traditional division of the faculties' it established.[17] Often, in the nineteenth century, it springs to notice only in the attacks it makes on new ideas. Here is

---

[17] Gary Hatfield, 'Remaking the Science of Mind: Psychology as Natural Science', in Christopher Fox, Roy Porter, and Robert Wokler (eds.), *Inventing Human Science: Eighteenth-Century Domains* (London, 1995), 227 n. 74. See also Carroll C. Pratt, 'Faculty Psychology', *Psychological Review*, 36 (1929), 142–71.

an undistinguished but typical example from a review of work by the anthropologist E. B. Tylor in 1872. The review attacked the 'contemporary fetichism [*sic*] of modern science' and claimed that

the attempt, indeed, to bridge over the gulf that separates animal from human intelligence, by any analysis of the conscious elements that constitute the latter, or the necessary products of those elements, appears to us the result of psychological confusion and mistake. It rests on the assumption . . . that there is no difference in kind between animal and human intelligence; that will may be resolved into appetite, and reason into sense; and that, as the lowest forms of life have rudimentary appetites and senses, the mind of an oyster is identical in kind with the mind of a Newton or a Shakespeare.[18]

Several points are worth making about this passage.

The first is the obvious point that, in the nineteenth century, psychological issues percolate through the modern boundaries between disciplines to address questions of broad public concern. This is a generalist culture. Here, psychological issues are discussed with reference to anthropological research by a reviewer, T. S. Baynes, who was a Shakespeare scholar, and, from 1873, editor of the *Encyclopaedia Britannica*. At the time he occupied the chair of Logic, Metaphysics, and English Literature at St Andrews. The debate about psychological issues, in other words, was common, not specialist, intellectual property and this contributes its share to the aggressively sarcastic tone. This style of polemical rhetoric, especially the heavy use of bathos, is found everywhere on the traditionalist side and makes its appeal to conventional understanding.[19] But beneath this derision lies anxiety. This review is worried by the mingling of lower and higher, and makes its appeal to the common sense of the acknowledged demarcations between animal and human, as well as between the lower faculties (appetite and sense) and the higher (will and reason). Also, this is a review of Tylor's two-volume *Primitive Cultures* of 1871, and anthropological work like Tylor's provoked a worry that racial distinctions between 'primitive' and 'civilized' would not hold. The passage, therefore, illustrates a world view under pressure. This can be felt in the unwitting acceptance of the idea of 'animal intelligence'. Animal intelligence, the reviewer insists, is absolutely different in kind from human intelligence. But the acknowledgement that animals may have any kind of intelligence at all admits a leakage from the new conceptual world. Intelligence, of course, is a higher faculty and the use of the same vocabulary to discuss both human and animal worlds is a concession. George Eliot, a supporter of the new

---

[18] [T. S. Baynes], 'Tylor on Primitive Culture', *Edinburgh Review*, 135 (1872), 113.

[19] As Gillian Beer notes, there was widespread irritation produced by speculative leaps across the yawning gaps between species, and this became a feature of anti-evolutionary polemic (Beer, *Darwin's Plots*, 105–6, 129). G. H. Lewes was one of the many pro-scientific psychologists who became exasperated with tired, polemical talk of 'an intelligent gas or a sentient molecule' (*Problems*, v. 31).

psychology, made the same post-evolutionary point with quiet insistence in her systematic deployment of animal imagery to describe the mental habits of the human communities in *The Mill on the Floss* (1860), *Middlemarch* (1871–2), and—in its most barbed form—the English country house in *Daniel Deronda* (1876).

The polemically combative, but conceptually defensive stance of Tylor's *Edinburgh* reviewer is one of the ways in which faculty psychology maintained a noisy presence in the mainstream of nineteenth-century psychological debate. The case against it will be illustrated throughout this book, but W. K. Clifford put it with typical acuity. Clifford—who, as a mathematician, was much concerned with conceptual modelling—was troubled by the strange world produced by an obsession with phenomena graded relentlessly into lower and higher. In a lecture to the Royal Institution in 1868, 'On Some of the Conditions of Mental Development', he found no such boundaries in nature and concluded that, in terms of function, 'what we mean by higher and lower . . . [amount to] much the same thing'.[20] To think, for instance, in terms of a orderly, ascending chain of living forms was, he felt, to be captured by metaphor: there was no smooth growth, no harmonic scales of species, or neat sets of characteristics that he could see. Instead all was process: 'Men acquire faculties by practice . . . Everybody knows how the mental faculties open out and become visible as a child grows up.'[21] For the republican Clifford, this adaptive, developmental world makes talk of higher and lower, or superior and inferior, all but meaningless in these contexts. There is only the slow 'process of simultaneous differentiation and integration which goes on in the paths of consciousness, between the mind and external things, between the mind and other minds'.[22] Mind is not the expression of already existing faculties, it is an active agent in its own development.[23] For him, this is a better definition of human-ness than the mere passive reception of God's arrangements. After all, he slyly argued later, were one to be rigorous about the traditional faculties as agents in psychological development, one would also have to include, with grave theological consequences, not just propensities towards human betterment, but the capacity for inflicting harm, for feeling terror, and, indeed, for 'resisting evidence'.[24]

If the discourse of the soul had been faculty psychology's only sustenance it would have perished much earlier as scientific naturalism started to take the ground from beneath it. But it had a more intellectually robust constitution and diverse feeding habits, which kept it going. Indeed, it has been argued that, just as in the long run Natural Theology contrarily encouraged the studies that led to evolutionary theory, so eighteenth-century faculty psychology assisted the secular

[20] Clifford, 'On Some of the Conditions of Mental Development' (1868), in *Lectures and Essays*, i. 83.

[21] Ibid. 94.    [22] Ibid. 100–1.    [23] Ibid. 104.

[24] Clifford, 'Body and Mind' (1874), in *Lectures and Essays*, ii. 68.

investigation of the human mind by setting it safely at a distance from direct theological invigilation. By centring itself on normative and familiar experiences, and by using categories recommended by both their obviousness and their theological innocence, it avoided metaphysical suspicion, whilst, at the same time, it encouraged the systematic, empirical observation of mental processes and behaviour.[25] That it later became entangled with nineteenth-century theological and scientific disputes might be a return of the repressed, but this should not confuse our sense of its other functions. Eighteenth-century faculty psychology promoted distinctively humanistic, Enlightenment values which fed into nineteenth-century debates alongside those of Natural Theology. These values advocated rational, individual self-improvement as a means to general social benefit through the wise and careful scrutiny of one's own mental habits. It is a confident, wide-ranging vision, whose secular orientation sat at ease with conventional Christian faith, and survived well into the nineteenth century, especially in Scotland.[26] The work of Sir David Brewster is a case in point.

Born in Jedburgh and Edinburgh educated, Brewster was a powerful advocate for Enlightenment humanism well into the heart of Victoria's reign, recommending and supporting its values through a distinguished and influential career as both a man of letters and an internationally known scientist in the fields of optics and the theory of light. He created, and for twenty-two years edited, the *Edinburgh Encyclopaedia* whilst sustaining a role as an unusually busy public man even by Victorian standards. He was a leading activist in the Royal Society and, later, the British Association for the Advancement of Science, became Principal of both St Andrews and Edinburgh universities, and played a prominent role in the establishment of the Free Church of Scotland in the 1830s and 1840s.

---

[25] C. C. Gillespie, *The Edge of Objectivity: An Essay in the History of Scientific Ideas* (Princeton, 1960); Hatfield, 'Remaking the Science of Mind'; Richard Olsen, *Scottish Philosophy and British Physics: A Study of the Foundations of the Victorian Scientific Style* (Princeton, 1975); G. S. Rousseau, 'Nerves, Spirits, and Fibres: Towards Defining the Origins of Sensibility', in R. F. Brissington and J. C. Eade (eds.), *Studies in the Eighteenth Century III* (Toronto, 1976), 137–57; Robert M. Young, 'The Impact of Darwin on Conventional Thought' and 'Natural Theology, Victorian Periodicals and the Fragmentation of a Common Context', in *Darwin's Metaphor*.

[26] There is a considerable secondary literature on these ideas. The following have been especially useful: Gladys Bryson, *Man and Society: The Scottish Inquiry of the Eighteenth Century* (Princeton, 1945); R. H. Campbell and Andrew S. Skinner (eds.), *The Origins and Nature of the Scottish Enlightenment* (Edinburgh, 1982); Nicholas Phillipson, 'The Scottish Enlightenment', in Roy Porter and Mikulas Teich (eds.), *The Enlightenment in National Context* (Cambridge, 1981); J. Charles Robertson, 'A Bacon-Facing Generation: Scottish Philosophy in the Early Nineteenth Century', *Journal of the History of Philosophy*, 14 (1976), 37–49; G. S. Rousseau and Roy Porter (eds.), *The Ferment of Knowledge: Studies in the Historiography of Eighteenth-Century Science* (Cambridge, 1980); Donald Winch, 'The System of the North: Dugald Stewart and his Pupils', in Stefan Collini, Donald Winch, and John Burrow (eds.), *That Noble Science of Politics: A Study in Nineteenth-Century Intellectual History* (Cambridge, 1983).

There is an anonymous, seventy-page entry on 'Pneumatology' in the *Edinburgh Encyclopaedia* in 1830 under the general heading of 'Logic'. Whether this was by Brewster himself is unknown, but there appears to be little in it with which he might have disagreed, and the entry symptomatically reveals the transition from Enlightenment confidence to Victorian anxiety. It illustrates how and why the somewhat lordly discourse of the soul was dragged into the messy, uncongenial details of Victorian psychological dispute.

'Pneumatology' argues that psychological argument is important because of the present, pressing need to counter the subjectivism and chaotic relativism that modern versions of the discipline encourage. If 'our feelings are so mixed up with all our moral reasonings, that they too frequently give a distortion to the truth, and render it repulsive to those whose minds are influenced by different associations and prejudices', the author writes, then it is 'absolutely necessary for the knowledge and right management of human nature, and for our own improvement as moral and social beings' that psychological theory itself should put things straight.[27] This strongly normative, benignly corrective position is applied to cultures as well as individuals. Though truth may be 'worshipped . . . under different forms, and sometimes even with opposite rites, she has, nevertheless, generally speaking, the same attributes assigned to her, and her identity may be recognized, though disfigured under fantastic or absurd appearances'.[28] Psychology's duty, therefore, is diagnostic and restitutive. From the 'accurate examination of notions and feelings, we can ascertain how far they are consistent with known general principles, and how far they are sanctioned by the order and course of nature'.[29] This disposition towards invigilation and psychological management makes clear the social function envisaged for psychology through much of the nineteenth century. The Enlightenment project, whereby rational self-improvement releases civic benefit, connects with darker Utilitarian imaginings of closed, supervised, institutional environments—school, workhouse, workplace, prison—in which they hoped to train those they deemed the 'deserving' as well as the 'undeserving' population. The corrective supervision of the boundaries between natural and artificial, normative and eccentric, is closely related to the medicalized policing of psychological illness that passed for therapy in much Victorian psychiatry (see Chapter 4 below).

The managerial component in post-Enlightenment psychology extends to the regulation of psychological discourse itself. The *Edinburgh Encyclopaedia* is severe on new modes, on 'the jarring and perpetually changing opinions of physiologists and chemists', for instance, who attempt to link body and mind.[30] The psychological faculties are at the centre of pneumatological theory, but, typically,

---

[27] Anon., 'Logic', in *Edinburgh Encyclopaedia*, xiii. 149.
[28] Ibid.    [29] Ibid. 117.    [30] Ibid. 118.

their substance remains elusive, and can remain so because it is a matter of confident, common assumption. This, the author explains, is so because there is nothing new to be said: 'no new views can be given of our faculties' because 'nobody ever dreams of being put in possession of a new sense, or of a faculty, different from those already felt and recognized by the generality of mankind'.[31] This carefully oiled, traditional world, with its bland assumption of universal knowledge, is representative of what was to be traumatically disrupted by evolutionary theory and cognate developments. But, in the meantime, the serene fittingness of the psychological faculties to nature and supernature, and the personal and social benefits that were thought to follow from their alignment, secured its standing in significant parts of the intellectual as well as the social establishment. The theory is at best complacent, but that does not mean it is without intellectual prestige, staying power, or influence. 'Pneumatology' peeps uncomfortably into a new vision of a multipartite world, but the changes envisaged in this new world were to come far from rapidly, and many intermediate steps needed to be taken. Robert Chambers's enormously influential *Vestiges of the Natural History of Creation*, written a decade or so later and published in 1844, illustrates clearly the theoretical and cultural negotiations that the new psychological ideas needed to accomplish.

There is little doubt that *Vestiges* was among the most influential books of the mid-century and played a crucial role in mediating the feel, if not the detail, of new scientific ideas to an expanding public interested in such material. Emanating from the same Edinburgh-based intellectual hotbed as Brewster's *Encyclopaedia* (though Brewster detested it for what he perceived to be its intellectual vulgarity and moral implications), the book covers topics across the scientific spectrum from cosmology to the formation of the human mind. Its racy success—it ran through eleven editions in sixteen years and spawned a shoal of replies whose sales sometimes exceeded even those of the original—did much to popularize interest in the new intellectual paradigms for understanding the natural world. Though senior figures like Huxley disparaged its scientific credentials, few doubted, as Darwin himself realized, that the book's importance lay in preparing the ground for better ideas than its own.[32] Yet in reading *Vestiges* one is conscious of a powerful, Janus-faced aspect to it. If it looks to the future, it does so in moments of release from gazing steadily towards the past. This is because Chambers manages the argument in such a way as to make it appear congruent with existing conceptions. The book's support for a materialistic theory

[31] Anon., 'Logic', in *Edinburgh Encyclopaedia*, xiii. 117.
[32] James Secord's excellent introduction to his modern edition of *Vestiges* provides a good account of the circumstances of the book's publication and reception: Robert Chambers, *Vestiges of the Natural History of Creation and Other Evolutionary Writings*, ed. James A. Secord (London, 1994), pp. ix–xlv. I am grateful to Rebecca Stott for impressing on me the importance of Chambers's work to the psychological debates of the 1840s and beyond.

of the mind, and its reforming politics, are carefully integrated with more traditional conceptions. Reading Chambers is like watching an elegant performance
of a gracefully managed transition from the world of Natural Theology to that
of the new naturalism. If the *Edinburgh Encyclopaedia* entry on 'Pneumatology'
responds to the same change in accents of regret, Chambers's book is calculated
to win the forward-looking enthusiasm of a different audience—that of an emergent, newly prosperous group with awakened interests in rational accounts of
moderate change. This version of Victorian evolutionary theory was by no
means 'red in tooth and claw'; *Vestiges* was, as James Secord puts it, a reassuring 'scientific romance for the middle classes'.[33] Opposing both the increasingly
stiff-necked clerics of an earlier world, and the noisy street radicals of popular
materialism, the new world view was ushered by Chambers directly into the
Victorian parlour.

The seventeenth of *Vestiges'* unnumbered chapters is abruptly entitled 'Mental
Constitution of Animals' and its topic is psychology, though it uses the word
only adjectivally. The title might give us pause, oriented as it is towards the
animal world to which it ascribes mental characteristics of an unspecified kind.
The chapter begins reassuringly with a tribute to Paley and the safe world of
Natural Theology. In his comfortable way, Chambers ruminates on the pleasures of tracing 'the wonderfully exact adaptations of animals to the physical
circumstances amidst which they are destined to live'.[34] 'Destined' here is well
chosen: it appears there will be no surprises in this world, and Chambers delivers
a familiar lesson. The harmonious adaptation of the animals to their environment proves 'clearly that *design* presided in the creation of the whole—design
again implying a designer, another word for a CREATOR', and Paley is then
recommended.[35] But, Chambers muses on the next page, if the physical constitution of animals is of 'the nicest congruity', what of the mental? Here a
problem halts his cheery analysis, because the traditional theological and metaphysical embargo on considering the attachment of body to mind prevents, he
sorrowfully thinks, the emergence of some of the best evidence for the nicety
of that congruity: 'There is a general disinclination to regard mind in connexion
with organization, from a fear that this must needs interfere with the cherished
religious doctrine of the spirit of man, and lower him to the level of brutes.'[36]

I enjoy observing the skill with which this argument is deployed and developed, and find it easy to deduce, from its deft attention to tone and argumentative structure, what Chambers must have perceived to be his audience's
mind-set, an audience, it should be added, that he undoubtedly succeeded in
winning. Reassurance comes first, followed by a thoughtful pause, before a profoundly heterodox argument for the materialization of mind is recommended

---

[33] Ibid., p. xxv.    [34] Ibid. 324.    [35] Ibid.    [36] Ibid. 325.

as supplying an absence in the prevailing theory, not as a challenge to it. The tone is equable, reasonable, helpful. Problems are acknowledged: the suspicion of materialism is real enough, he admits, and human minds can be fickle things, too 'irregular and wayward', 'unstable and 'various', perhaps, to be put alongside that always-reliable, omnipresent 'immortal spirit'.[37] None the less, Chambers believes that statistics can demonstrate that, overall, encouraging, normative conclusions about populations can be sustained: man is 'an enigma only as an individual; in the mass he is a mathematical problem'.[38] What might be wayward in you and me, averages out in the long run.

This may well be the first use of statistical evidence in psychological analysis, and it is one of a number of strikingly modern uses of data now common in psychology (others, in the same chapter, include the observation of animal behaviour and clinical evidence from the dissected brains of lunatics). But the conclusion towards which Chambers is heading is cleverly managed. Not only is the materialization of mind unlikely to pollute a secure sense of the Design of Nature; the evidence it yields will confirm it. The embargo on such ideas is actually, Chambers maintains, an obstruction to *Christian* argument. The fitness for purpose of both mind and brain (which includes the ability to reverence beauty and intuit God's existence) is every bit as revealing of Natural Design as the dexterity of the hand, which was, after Paley, the conventional, emblematic evidence of Design in early nineteenth-century Natural Theology. So Chambers writes that the 'old metaphysical character vanishes in a moment, and the distinction usually taken between physical and moral is annulled, as only an error in terms. This view teaches, that mental phenomena flow directly from the brain.'[39] So 'wondrous' is this brain, it enables 'communion to the councils of God himself [*sic*] . . . in its living constitution, designed, formed, and sustained by Almighty Wisdom, how admirable its character! How reflective of the unutterable depths of that Power by which it was formed, and is so sustained!'[40]

Though corny, this is very accomplished, and it indicates that, in this arena of debate, the management of rhetoric can be as important as persuasion by evidence in winning a case. The rhapsodic register at this moment carries its own positive, stylistic assertions and supplies sufficient 'uplift' to ennoble a suspect, materialistic opinion. As we shall see in Chapter 5, influential objections were made to the new psychology by an important wing of the Christian literary community who protested against the spiritually demoralizing effect of materialism and its elimination of the poetry of nature. Chambers seems, intuitively, to have responded to these fears.

[37] James Secord's excellent introduction to his modern edition of *Vestiges* provides a good account of the circumstances of the book's publication and reception: Robert Chambers, *Vestiges of the Natural History of Creation and Other Evolutionary Writings*, ed. James A. Secord (London, 1994), 326–7.
[38] Ibid. 331.    [39] Ibid. 331–2.    [40] Ibid. 332.

His discussion of psychological issues in *Vestiges* centres on a number of crucial issues. The first, as we have seen, is the removal of 'metaphysical' obstacles to a materialistically inclined discussion of the mind. This is done through manipulation of the arguments of Natural Theology and by bringing an outlaw discourse within its terms of reference. The symbolic values of the physiological apparatus Chambers describes are, throughout, immediately emphasized, for in the supercharged world of Natural Theology everything manifests a figurative as well as a literal significance. Thus, the lesson of the nervous system is its 'great principle of unity';[41] that of the brain, its role in devoting the mind to encouraging characteristics such as love, reverence, and faith; while the energy in the system, too, is theologically benign. The mind–body circuit runs on electricity, Chambers declares (somewhat hopefully), but 'electricity is almost as metaphysical as ever mind was supposed to be', and so 'mental action may be imponderable, intangible, and yet a real existence, and ruled by the Eternal through his laws'.[42] He concludes his chapter thus: 'the sum of all we have seen of the psychical constitution of man is, that its Almighty Author has destined it, like everything else, to be developed from inherent qualities, and to have a mode of action depending solely on its own organization.'[43] This, characteristically, has it both ways at once: 'the psychical constitution' depends 'solely on its own organization', but always under the benign, reassuring—if somewhat distant—invigilation of its Author. The paradigm of Natural Theology is being adjusted very carefully.

The real kernel of the psychological argument, however, concerns the nature of the psychological faculties. In a way typical of his generation, this is the key concept in Chambers's psychological vocabulary. Characteristically, he derives it from contradictory sources. There is, first, the orthodox psychological language of the period embedded in the discourse of the soul as we have been describing it. Then there is the newcomer, materialist phrenology, whose provocative assertions he soothes by bathing them in the sort of calming theological waters in which he specialized. Phrenology (which is described in detail in Chapter 3 below) scandalized orthodox opinion by asserting that the mental faculties were derived from localizable parts of the brain. Chambers accepted this for reasons given openly in *Vestiges* (he thought it the only contemporary philosophy actually 'founded on nature'[44]). So, again, we find Chambers facing two ways intellectually and carrying off the equivocation with aplomb.

The faculties were for him, as they were for many in his period, the building blocks of psychological life, and *Vestiges* simply confirms this. But the key issue that interests him concerns the vexed question of the extent to which humans are different from animals. If humans possess faculties to enable them to go about their duty, what is it that animals possess when they display social behaviour,

---

[41] Ibid. 333.     [42] Ibid. 334–5.     [43] Ibid. 359.     [44] Ibid. 341.

for instance, or the ability to communicate, or are able to learn new feeding repertoires?[45] Orthodoxy, as we have seen, would insist on an absolute distinction between man and brute, but Chambers is uncomfortable with a segregated conception of the organic kingdom, and the real innovation in his work is to line up the animal and human worlds in a continuous conceptual framework. He accomplishes this with only moderate offence by a verbal sleight of hand: what we find in animals (as well as infants, primitives, and simpletons) are 'instincts'; what are found in humans at a more advanced stage are 'faculties'. He clearly insists that the difference between them is merely quantitative, not qualitative ('a difference in degree only'[46]), but the rhetorical advantage of dual terminology (one 'lower' and bodily, the other 'higher' and mental) allows a slippage in the conceptual distinction that he is not slow to utilize. Even here he can never help but be reassuring: 'Bound up as we thus are by an identity in the character of our mental organization with the lower animals, we are yet, it will be observed, strikingly distinguished from them by this great advance in development.'[47] Again, we observe his rhetorical shrewdness. This sentence—with its easy tone—places the bad news first, but ends by calming the imagined alarm of the reader by the scale of the differences still revealed. Chambers has both his homology and his hierarchy at once. Instincts in animals are 'limited', he claims, the human faculties 'unlimited', thus installing the requisite degree of freedom for humans to act, create, and be distinguished.[48] At no stage does the thoughtful Chambers trouble his reader with the question of whether an instinct might become a faculty, or a 'limited' faculty become 'unlimited' (as they undoubtedly do as infants grow). He lets the inference settle that these are species distinctions.

Actually, it would have been surprising if Chambers had been able to respond to these questions, and even more surprising had he been able to postulate a mechanism for such development. But the crux of the issue is skilfully defrayed, and the overall management of the argument is as cleverly emollient as one would expect. With the calm, predictable rhythms of a swinging pendulum, Chambers alternates statements about the proximity of the animals to man with statements that support the opposite view, especially concerning those

parts of mind . . . which connect us with the things that are not of this world. We have veneration, prompting us to the worship of the Deity, which the animals lack. . . . We have reason, to enable us to inquire into the character of the Great Father, and the relation of us, his humble creatures, towards him. . . . The face of God is reflected in the organization of man, as a little pool reflects the glorious sun.[49]

[45] James Secord's excellent introduction to his modern edition of *Vestiges* provides a good account of the circumstances of the book's publication and reception: Robert Chambers, *Vestiges of the Natural History of Creation and Other Evolutionary Writings*, ed. James A. Secord (London, 1994), 337.

[46] Ibid. 335–6.    [47] Ibid. 347.    [48] Ibid. 343.    [49] Ibid. 348.

The smooth swinging of this rhetorical pendulum is lubricated, when necessary, by his lyricism and the language of Providential Design. The argument may swing between competing ideas, but there is no doubting that the rhetoric manages it splendidly.

Robert Chambers's *Vestiges of Creation* illustrates two converging things about the psychology developing from the discourse of the soul in the 1840s. The first is that the paradigms for understanding the mind's relation to nature are shifting appreciably. The second is that, at least for the time being, the negotiation of that shift is conducted in relation to the discourse of orthodoxy in a placatory fashion. Later, things got substantially rougher, but *Vestiges*—like the Scarecrow in *Wizard of Oz*—is able to point simultaneously in entirely different directions. In such a situation, the ability to persuade by an accomplished mixture of lucidity, charm, and adroit argumentative reassurance represents a spectacular success. According to James Secord, Chambers's religion in the *Vestiges* was 'largely strategic', and Chambers's real opinions were both anticlerical and anti-evangelical.[50] And there is, we might note in this remarkable chapter of *Vestiges*, a very significant absence. Chambers notes, in passing, that mind is 'a received synonyme [*sic*] with soul', but nowhere else does the soul make an appearance.[51] For all the careful rhetorical manœuvring, and the stagecraft of divine rhapsody, this is an imminently secular world view in which God is, at best, comfortably and politely distant. If the *Edinburgh Encyclopaedia* entry on 'Pneumatology' indicates something of the intellectual complacency and instinct for superiority (as well as the appetite for social surveillance) buried in Enlightenment Natural Theology, *Vestiges* is perhaps itself the last vestige of the same tradition's secular, liberal encouragement to naturalistic investigation. It reinforced the conceptual dominion of the language of the faculties in psychology, but it grounded them in a new world of nature, a world that was extended to include the human brain.

As we shall see in the next chapter, the faculty psychology remains a major part of the developing discursive landscape of nineteenth-century psychological theory. Chambers's work indicates something of the gravitational pull it exerted on emergent theory through a complex series of intellectual, cultural, and social pressures. It may, to a degree, represent a vanishing intellectual world, but that world persisted in a way that only the most sanguine of progressives could call merely residual. Faculty psychology, as derived from the discourse of the soul, and elaborated—as we shall see in the next chapter—in the discourses of certain kinds of philosophy, is much more than a remnant in the evolving debate. Before leaving the discourse of the soul, therefore, it is worth pondering briefly why the language of the faculties should have such attractions for subsequent generations.

[50] Ibid., p. xxii.    [51] Ibid. 325.

The appeal of faculty psychology rests upon two features. First, its language is recognizably close to the experience of mental events in everyday terms. When we think about our own psychological processes, they usually present themselves as acts of memory, or will, or ratiocination, and so on. This is the familiar language nineteenth-century people especially were accustomed to using, and it thereby had the value of spontaneous recognition in public dispute. Whether this spontaneous recognition is a product of real conceptual power, or (as opponents claimed) mere discursive habit, is an issue. But it is certainly true that many of the newer languages for describing the mind—for example, as unconscious patterns of association, or versions of the reflex mechanism, or the workings of 'nucleated protoplasm' (a temporary fad)—lacked its authority and instant credibility. Faculty psychology, therefore, was clearly at an argumentative advantage in general discourse and its supporters were not slow to mobilize this.

From a modern perspective, however, there is a more powerful argument. Some modern psychological theory has not been compelling when it has spoken of the experience of personhood. Its inclination to discuss humans as broken machine parts is not only alienating and dehumanizing; it is, some argue, a major conceptual error. The ethical and existential case against, for example, Behaviourism or the treatment of mental illness by severe mechanical means has been familiar since the early 1960s. More recently, the clinical neurologist Oliver Sacks has argued against neuropsychology's 'mechanical' or 'animal' reduction of the human person in terms that refloat the importance of the idea of the mental faculties. 'Traditional neurology,' Sacks writes, 'by its mechanicalness, its emphasis on deficits, conceals from us the actual life that is instinct in all cerebral functions —at least higher functions such as those of imagination, memory and perception.'[52] In his view, the abandonment of the idea of the psychological faculties, especially the faculty of conscious judgement, is gravely damaging: 'Judgement and identity may be casualties [in neurological injury]—but neuropsychology never speaks of them. And yet . . . judgement is the most important faculty we have . . . the *first* faculty of higher life or mind—yet it is ignored, or misinterpreted, by classical (computational) neurology.'[53] Ironically, Sacks remarks, mechanical neuropsychology's neglect of personhood replicates some of the very same cognitive disabilities suffered by his patients.

The rights and wrongs of this argument are not our immediate concern. Sacks's crusade for a reconvened faculty psychology resumes a long set of arguments in nineteenth-century theory, as he acknowledges.[54] But, by the end of the century

---

[52] Sacks, *The Man who Mistook his Wife for a Hat*, 83.    [53] Ibid. 18–19.

[54] Sacks himself dates these developments to the dominion of experimental neurology from the late nineteenth century, when it was a ready companion of the experimental psychology discussed in the Introduction above (see *An Anthropologist on Mars: Seven Paradoxical Tales* (London, 1995), 17). In *The Man who Mistook his Wife for a Hat*, he laments the loss of, as it were, the literary

the 'doxa', the 'common sense', had swung another way. In 1891, in the new edition of *Chambers's Encyclopaedia* (the very Chambers, indeed, who wrote the *Vestiges*), W. R. Sorley, Knightbridge Professor of Moral Philosophy at Cambridge, noted in the encyclopaedia's first ever entry on 'Psychology' that 'the view that mind is a congeries of distinct faculties, and psychology a process of labelling facts and putting each into its proper compartment . . . is to mistake a name for an explanation'.[55] Slowly, nineteenth-century enquiry demanded more than verbal tags for commonly understood processes. It wanted to understand the faculties, not as static categories, but as part of multiple, interactive processes.

dimension to neuropsychological case histories, that 'tradition of richly human clinical tales [which] reached a high point in the nineteenth century, and then declined, with the advent of an impersonal neurological science' (p. x).

[55] W. R. Sorley, 'Psychology', in *Chambers's Encyclopaedia: A Dictionary of Universal Knowledge*, new edn. (London, 1891), viii. 474.

# CHAPTER 2

# The Discourse of Philosophy

If there is a dominant source for the majority of what passed for psychology in the Victorian period, it is to be found in the philosophy of mind. By this I mean that the conceptual heritage derived from philosophical discussion determined to a great extent the appearance and substance of the leading psychological issues addressed by nineteenth-century minds. It determined the vocabulary and rhetorical style selected by psychological writers, as well as the location and types of publication. It influenced the personnel who involved themselves in psychological debate (through, for example, appointments to academic posts), the mode of argumentation in which it was conducted, and the deep structure of the conceptual issues it considered.

As we shall see, and as virtually all nineteenth-century commentators agree, just two schools of thought dominated debate. The first, like the psychologists of the soul, believed that the faculties of the human mind were innate and, though these faculties might be developed in experience, they were not constituted by it. The second school (sometimes called 'the school of Locke', or 'the experience philosophy', or, simply, 'associationism') maintained the opposite view. For thinkers in this line, the mind was primarily created in experience and the role of innate ideas was negligible. Exchanges between these two positions dominated discussion and the debate fell largely within the terrain mapped out by argument around four classical philosophical problems, which are briefly described below. The formulation of positions in relation to these problems controlled the development of psychological ideas for at least the first two-thirds of the nineteenth century. What occurred on a larger scale was an adjustment in the philosophical conception of nature, including human nature, which part followed and part created the decline of Enlightenment values. What replaced these values was a much more troubled and uncertain form of knowledge reflecting a much more troubled and uncertain view of nature. But the stake also concerned the role of philosophy itself in the formulation of psychological propositions. In the next chapter we will see the issue of this development as philosophy came into direct conflict with a more confident and assertive material science. This chapter, however, traces the deployment and adjustment of philosophical argument concerning the mind in its broad, public context, bearing in mind the fact that philosophy carried a greater share of the intellectual and cultural conversation of nineteenth-century British society than it may do today, and that its language and forms of publication (particularly essays in the great periodicals) enabled and reflected this.

The four classical philosophical problems under discussion are:

1. *The mind–body problem*: to what degree are mental states derived from, or determined by, physical states understood as either states of the whole nervous system (including the sensory apparatus) or of the brain alone?

2. *The epistemological problem*: is our knowledge of the world derived from, and determined by, experience, or is it somehow intuited by way of innate cognitive faculties? (The latter of course was the position taken by the faculty psychology.)

3. *The psychological growth problem, or the nature/nurture argument*: is what we become, psychologically, the result of innate—possibly God-given— qualities, or does the environment, conceived as broadly as one could wish (biological, social, cultural, familial, educational, and so on), determine our being?

4. Finally, there is what is sometimes called *the 'first-person/third-person' problem*, which is, first, an issue concerning reductionism, and, secondly, an issue concerning the language considered most appropriate for the description of mental processes. In reporting or analysing psychological events, should we take the primarily introspective stance of the experiencing individual using the natural language of that person's experience ('I felt . . .')? Or should we strive for a purportedly more objective ('scientific'), and certainly more distanced, account by an uninvolved observer who adopts a 'third-person' stance ('the results of thalmic microstimulation correlate closely with observed behaviour . . .')? If we take the latter stance, there is the possibility (some would say likelihood) that the 'third-person' perspective arrogates a vocabulary and address so chilly and alien to the person whose experiences are being described that he or she can barely recognize what occurred as his or her own.

Of these four problems, the first three are reasonably familiar, and are an established part of the ordinary texture of discussion in these areas. The fourth, however—which was particularly pressing in the nineteenth century, as psychology attempted to constitute itself as an independent discipline—may need more elaboration. In what follows immediately, I will concentrate on this, but the issues raised in Problems 1–3 occupied an equal share of psychological debate and will be addressed as coverage proceeds.

There is a crucial difference between observing an experience in someone else and having that experience oneself. This ordinary human difference is greatly enlarged if the observer and transcriber of the experience happens to be, say, a neuroscientist deploying the rhetoric, postures, techniques, and conceptual equipment of his or her science in a way that might take the experience some distance from the experiencing individual's personal sense of what occurred. The 'third-person' perspective and the 'first-person' perspective may, in fact, express themselves incommensurably, articulating different interests, value systems, priorities, and estimates of consequences.

Scientists have come to recognize this. One of today's leading clinical neurologists, V. S. Ramachandran, writes that the 'need to reconcile the first-person and the third-person accounts of the universe (the "I" view versus the "he" or "it" view) is the single most important unsolved problem in science'.[1] This, however, is by no means an exclusively modern issue, though it is one exacerbated by the development of specialized, technical expertise. Nineteenth-century writers were alert to the question of 'first-person/third-person' perspectives, and the adequacy of the language and conceptual structures adopted by the psychology of the day. The poet Wordsworth, for example, had this much in mind in his great autobiographical poem *The Prelude*, first written in the late 1790s but published after his death, with refreshed pertinence, in 1850. Wordsworth's standing as the senior poet of his generation, and as Poet Laureate, guaranteed public attention.

> But who shall parcel out
> His intellect by geometric rules,
> Split like a province into round and square?
> Who knows the individual hour in which
> His habits were first sown, even as a seed?
> Who that shall point as with a wand and say
> 'This portion of the river of my mind
> Came from yon fountain?' Thou, my Friend! art one
> More deeply read in thy own thoughts; to thee
> Science appears but what in truth she is,
> Not as our glory and our absolute boast,
> But as a succedaneum, and a prop
> To our infirmity. No officious slave
> Art thou of that false secondary power
> By which we multiply distinctions, then
> Deem that our puny boundaries are things
> That we perceive, and not that we have made.
> To thee, unblinded by these formal arts,
> The unity of all hath been revealed,
> And thou wilt doubt with me, less aptly skilled

[1] V. S. Ramachandran and Sandra Blakeslee, *Phantoms in the Brain: Human Nature and the Architecture of the Mind* (London, 1998), 229. For further discussion, see Rose, *Lifelines*, esp. ch. 2.

Than many are to range the faculties
In scale and order, class the cabinet
Of their sensations, and in voluble phrase
Run through the history and the birth of each
As of a single independent thing.
Hard task, vain hope, to analyse the mind . . .[2]

The sciences invoked by 'geometric rules' and the natural historian's (or maybe druggist's) cabinet are not those we would now identify as especially problematic. Nor would we now opt so sternly and readily for a rival language so obviously derived from psychology as a discourse of the soul (the 'Friend' mentioned here is, of course, Coleridge, a great public champion of this discourse, whom we will encounter much in this chapter). But the issue Wordsworth addresses is clearly recognizable, and the impact of his discussion is aided by the potency of the personal testimony. The autobiographical poem encapsulates the reflective self-confidence of the 'first-person' perspective utterly.

The most pressing form of the 'first-person/third-person' problem occurred to many Victorians in the same way as it oppressed Wordsworth, and the language of psychological polemic is soaked in indignation at the purported science's obtrusive meddling and desecration. In recoil, many fell back on the familiar phrases and concepts of the faculty psychology. Educated people asked themselves what purchase the language of psycho-physiology could have on interior mental events. What rights did it have when many felt it a distorting invasion, and what obligations did it have to protect the sanctity of individual feelings and beliefs? For those who felt this response, it could be considered impertinence at best; at worst, it was a gross falsification, and the outraged, somewhat blimpish tone of some of the responses encountered in subsequent chapters should be read in this light. One must remember that even liberal opinion was confronting the scientific way of looking at the mind pretty much for the first time, and it came with the same shock (and excitement, for some) as fast, alarming technologies such as the railways or telegraphy, from which, in fact, it often borrowed its metaphors (see Chapter 5 below). Even on the progressive, pro-science, 'physicalist' side there were anxieties. John Tyndall expressed the issue well in his infamous Presidential Address to the British Association for the Advancement of Science in Belfast in 1874: 'We can trace the development of a nervous system, and correlate with it the parallel phenomena of sensation and thought. We see with undoubting certainty that they go hand in hand. But we try to soar in a vacuum the moment we seek to comprehend the connection between them.'[3]

[2] William Wordsworth, *The Prelude* (1850), book II, ll. 203–28, in *The Prelude: 1799, 1805, 1850*, ed. Jonathan Wordsworth, M. H. Abrams, and Stephen Gill (London, 1979).
[3] John Tyndall, *Address Delivered before the British Association Assembled at Belfast, with Additions* (London, 1874), 59.

Tyndall's address became notorious as a statement of the extreme 'physicalist' position, yet it concedes limitation. He is partly concerned with the limitations to modern knowledge as a technical matter, but his point also concerns deeper conceptual perspectives and suggests a stalling of the conceptual imagination before huge issues.

This, as much as the technical problems, preoccupied psychological theorists across the century and, as we shall see, was a leading feature of writing by prominent contributors such as Huxley and Lewes. But a version of it is also to be found in the work of a novelist like George Eliot, who, thoroughly acquainted with philosophical debate in this area, is preoccupied, almost, it sometimes seems, above all else, by issues relating to how we see, what we see, and the points of view that allow or disallow that always-limited vision. This intelligent perspectivism resisted the traditional conception of the psychological faculties on the grounds of their essentialism.

During the nineteenth century, faculty psychology was sustained and elaborated by three currents in philosophical discourse: the Scottish Enlightenment tradition, the influential work of Coleridge, and appropriations of the philosophy of Immanuel Kant. What these have in common is an account of the mind as a unitary, self-activating, self-sustaining, and ontologically independent structure that possesses distinctive human and spiritual attributes that distinguish humankind from the rest of Creation. In the practice of argument in the nineteenth century, these sources overlap to the point where, like Wordsworth's river of the mind, one cannot discriminate the origins of particular ideas, though many felt that Kant, particularly, was both appropriated and distorted.

The so-called Common Sense school of Scottish Enlightenment philosophy developed from the work of Thomas Reid and others.[4] It had little truck with fancy analytical elaborations, and, insisting on the self-presentation, innate resilience, and universal predictability of the faculties of the human mind, Reid and his followers tried to settle the ghosts of both Humean scepticism and the challenge posed by associationist theory, which, they believed with good reason, was likely to lead to materialism. The nineteenth century received this work through a number of channels: new, heavyweight editions, essays in the great Scottish periodicals, popularized versions in encyclopaedias like the *Edinburgh*, and through direct teaching. Born in Aberdeen, Alexander Bain recounts in his *Autobiography* that Reid was regarded as 'the acknowledged chief' of philosophy and standard fare in the Mechanics' Institutes where he studied as a young man.[5]

---

[4] See G. S. Brett, *Brett's History of Psychology*, ed. and abridged by R. S. Peters, rev. edn. (London, 1962); S. A. Grave, *The Scottish Philosophy of Common Sense* (Oxford, 1960); G. S. Rousseau, 'Psychology', in Rousseau and Porter (eds.), *The Ferment of Knowledge*, 143–210; also the items on eighteenth-century theory mentioned in the previous chapter.

[5] Alexander Bain, *Autobiography* (London, 1904), 17, 73.

The Scottish faculty psychology, therefore, was a central part of the intellectual inheritance the nineteenth century took from the eighteenth. Of later thinkers directly attached to it, probably the most important for our purposes was Sir William Hamilton, Reid's nineteenth-century editor and commentator, whose influence reached deep and wide. (Amongst his many protégés was T. S. Baynes, the future editor of the *Britannica* whose review of Tylor's *Primitive Cultures* we noticed in the previous chapter.) Hamilton took Reid towards Idealism, a direction Reid would have disliked (as Hamilton recognized), but which did not surprise many contemporaries.[6]

Hamilton began with a political perception of the purpose of philosophical psychology. He attacked what he called the selfish and materialist 'dirt philosophy' of the French Revolutionary period and proposed Reid as an antidote.[7] Like the writers for the encyclopaedias, he feared the corrosive consequences of psychological 'Sensualism', by which term was insinuated not just the supposed debauchery of the revolutionaries, but a psychological theory that took for granted the physical basis of mind. This became the established term of abuse.[8] For Hamilton its consequences were clear:

From the mechanical relations of sense with its object, it was attempted to solve the mysteries of will and intelligence; the philosophy of mind was soon viewed as correlative to the physiology of organization. The moral nature of man was at last formally abolished, in its identification with the physical: the mind became a reflex of matter; thought a secretion of the brain.[9]

This 'melancholy' doctrine, Hamilton argued, levelled the higher and lower faculties by abolishing them altogether in non-moral matter. A fundamental reorientation was therefore required, he thought, to restore a philosophical psychology that 'does not revolt against the authority of our natural beliefs'.[10]

This sort of argument was repeated endlessly by those alarmed by agitation at home and the succession of revolutionary episodes in Europe across the nineteenth century. Reid's supposedly exemplary private life, indeed, became a sort of fetish to be waved in moments of crisis to judge from the solemn frequency with which it is offered as a model of probity and steadiness each

---

[6] See e.g. Hamilton's own comment on Reid's 'superstitious horror of the ideal theory' in *Discussions of Philosophy and Literature, Education and University Reform, Chiefly from the Edinburgh Review; Corrected, Vindicated, Enlarged, in Notes and Appendices*, 2nd edn. (London, 1853), 53. G. H. Lewes represented the views of many in thinking that Reid's differences with idealism were 'merely nominal' (*The History of Philosophy from Thales to Comte*, 2 vols., 4th edn. (London, 1871), ii. 406).

[7] Hamilton, *Discussions*, 39.

[8] John Stuart Mill, 'Coleridge', in *Mill on Bentham and Coleridge*, ed. F. R. Leavis (London, 1950), 111.

[9] Hamilton, *Discussions*, 3.      [10] Ibid. 63.

time the French got into difficulties.[11] In the mid-century, Reid and Hamilton found an influential advocate in A. Campbell Fraser, Professor of Philosophy at Edinburgh and editor of the *North British Review* until 1857, when he was forced to resign following protests from more liberal-minded contributors.[12] In 1848, the year of European-wide revolutions, Fraser saluted the pair's 'speculative purity' and 'motives of religion and duty' in a review of Hamilton's edition of Reid.[13] In 1853 he repeated the tribute in the light of the spiritual, intellectual, and moral anarchy he saw across the Continent. Thus, over the first half of the century, Enlightenment optimism turned to its opposite for Scottish faculty psychologists as events disturbed their faith in the scale of being. In reaction, the theory of the higher faculties was boosted to levels of metaphysical grandeur. Thomas Brown, in wartime Edinburgh, complained that materialism eliminates 'heroic virtue', leaving 'but a certain aggregation of particles, which . . . must rot in the grave, with the other parts of the withered and ulcerated body'.[14] For Fraser, Hamilton's virtue was that he transcended the political emergency by establishing 'the metaphysical or necessary conditions of human consciousness, and the psychological modifications which that consciousness is discovered to manifest when studied experimentally'. At this level, Hamilton could become 'positive, synthetic, and conciliatory'.[15]

Metaphysical ideas in psychology became crucially attached to the defence of the status quo. With God on their side, it was hoped, the metaphysical faculties might hold together peoples and cultures, and verify the 'common truths which everyone apprehends, but which few have the talent to develop', as Hamilton put it.[16] Amongst conservative theorists, a metaphysical alliance developed that John Stuart Mill dubbed 'the Germano-Coleridgean doctrine', though the Scottish contribution, as he acknowledged, was just as important.[17] Hamilton and Coleridge both aligned themselves with versions of Kantianism; Fraser connected Hamilton to Coleridge, and spoke of the 'epoch of Reid and Kant',

[11] e.g. Dugald Stewart, 'Life and Writings of Reid', 3; [Francis Jeffrey], 'Stewart's *Life of Reid*', *Edinburgh Review*, 3 (1804), 269–87; James McCosh, *The Scottish Philosophy: Biographical, Expository, Critical: from Hutcheson to Hamilton* (New York, 1875), 206–7, 425; John Veitch, 'Philosophy in the Scottish Universities II', *Mind*, 2 (1877), 221. Veitch, a poet and critic as well as philosopher, wrote a similarly hagiographic life of his old mentor, whose work he also edited: *Memoir of Sir William Hamilton, Bart.* (Edinburgh, 1869).

[12] *The Wellesley Index to Victorian Periodicals 1824–1900*, ed. Walter E. Houghton *et al.*, 5 vols. (London, 1966–89), i. 663–4.

[13] [A. Campbell Fraser], 'Sir William Hamilton and Dr. Reid', *North British Review*, 10 (1848), 146, 149.

[14] [Thomas Brown], 'Belsham's *Philosophy of the Mind*', *Edinburgh Review*, 1 (1803), 479–80.

[15] [A. Campbell Fraser], 'Scottish Philosophy', *North British Review*, 18 (1853), 367–8.

[16] Quoted by [Fraser], 'Hamilton and Reid', 170.

[17] John Stuart Mill, *Bentham and Coleridge*, 108, 115. G. H. Lewes spotted the same thing, but called it 'the *a priori* school' (*History of Philosophy*, ii. 480).

claiming Hamilton as the progeny of the 'fusion' of these two giants.[18] Countless subsequent commentators rationalized the federation.[19] This ensemble had a major impact upon psychological, physiological, and medical debate in the first half of the nineteenth century, despite its provenance in sources not apparently immediately cognate with their main concerns. The influence of the poet, critic, all-round theorist, and conservative commentator and ideologian Samuel Taylor Coleridge was conspicuous. As Adrian Desmond shows, Coleridge's ideas profoundly influenced not only psychology but the development of comparative anatomy and training in the medical schools. The powerfully conservative Royal College of Surgeons came to see itself as one part of a Coleridgean clerisy leading the opposition to materialism.[20]

So, what was Victorian metaphysical faculty psychology, and in what ways can it be distinguished from its more humanistic Enlightenment forerunner? We have already noted that, for the first half of the nineteenth century, because of its discursive pre-eminence, faculty psychology worked mainly by allusion to its founding principles rather than by a detailed reformulation of its case. This was especially so when it could draw upon the alarmed political ambience of the post-Revolutionary years to refresh its audience's attention. This tactic tells us something about its social role and intellectual constitution. Faculty psychologists obstructed new enquiries as often as possible (especially in psycho-physiology), and promoted the view that the development of any kind of substantive psychological theory on empirical lines was misplaced effort. But arguments based only on stubborn resistance have limited life. The recruitment of Kantian critical thinking to the ensemble added another dimension. Faculty psychology now proclaimed, on up-to-date intellectual as well as political grounds, that the attempt to create a materially grounded psychology was doomed.

---

[18] Hamilton, *Discussions*, 5–6; S. T. Coleridge, *Biographia Literaria, or Biographical Sketches of my Literary Life and Opinions*, ed. George Watson (London, 1975), 84–5; [Fraser], 'Scottish Philosophy', 353; 'Hamilton and Reid', 157.

[19] See e.g.: Edward Lytton Bulwer, *England and the English* (1833), ed. Standish Meacham (London, 1970), 321; H. L. Mansel, *A Lecture on the Philosophy of Kant* (Oxford, 1856); [J. C. Shairp], 'Samuel Taylor Coleridge', *North British Review*, OS 43, NS 4 (1865), 251–322; McCosh, *Scottish Philosophy*; Andrew Seth, *Scottish Philosophy: A Comparison of the Scottish and German Answers to Hume* (1885; repr. New York, 1971). Several of these reflect on differences as well as similarities between the three. For discussion, see: Rosemary Ashton, *The German Idea: Four English Writers and the Reception of German Thought 1800–1860* (Cambridge, 1980); Giuseppe Micheli, 'The Early Reception of Kant's Thought in England, 1785–1805', and Manfred Kuehn, 'Hamilton's Reading of Kant: A Chapter in the Early Scottish Reception of Kant's Thought', both in George MacDonald Ross and Tony McWalter (eds.), *Kant and his Influence* (Bristol, 1990), 202–314, 315–47; Bernard Lightman, *The Origins of Agnosticism: Victorian Unbelief and the Limits of Knowledge* (London, 1987), esp. ch. 2; René Wellek, *Immanuel Kant in England 1793–1838* (Princeton, 1931).

[20] Adrian Desmond, *The Politics of Evolution: Morphology, Medicine, and Reform in Radical London* (London, 1989), esp. chs. 6–7. See also Heyck, *Transformation of Intellectual Life*, 50–67; Yeo, *Defining Science*, 'Introduction'.

In the *Critique of Judgement* of 1790 (the 'Third Critique'), Kant asserts that psychology can provide only a 'negative conception of our thinking being. It tells us that not one of the operations of the mind or manifestations of the internal sense can be explained on material lines.'[21] At first sight this appears a standard warning against materialism congruent with other such warnings by, for example, Thomas Reid, who, in *An Inquiry Into the Human Mind* (1764), warned, in an image that remained popular for a century, of the 'deep and dark gulf' separating mind and body 'which our understanding cannot pass'.[22] But Kant had more than this in mind. Psychology's 'negative conception of our thinking being' implies for the discipline a critical or solvent role in intellectual life rather than one of simple, obstructive embargo. Psychology's strength, according to Kant, is that it can dismantle 'speculative' propositions; its limitation is that it cannot provide substantive knowledge, 'neither enlightenment nor determinant judgement', as Kant puts it.[23] In a radical sense, then, any substantive psychology of whatever discursive stamp that makes positive propositions about mind and behaviour is lost—even that of pneumatology, or the discourse of the soul: 'rational *psychology* can never become *pneumatology*, as a science that extends our knowledge. . . . On the contrary we see that it is really a sort of mere anthropology of the internal sense, a knowledge, that is to say, of our thinking self *as alive*, and that, in the form of theoretical cognition, it also remains merely empirical.'[24] At best, Kant states, substantive or empirical psychology consists of routine introspective observation, a 'mere anthropology of the internal sense'. Its authentic task is self-reflection upon the processes of intellection themselves, in particular the fundamental category structures inherent in thought: 'the universal laws apart from which nature in general (as an object of sense) cannot be thought'.[25] These are the '*a priori* laws' that 'understanding prescribes . . . for nature'.[26] Examples would be our sense of Time, Space, and Extension, or Unity, Difference, and Limitation, a sense of which, Kant believed, was innately embedded in human minds.

Nineteenth-century commentators received this analysis in somewhat different ways, depending upon preferences and perspectives. In fact it has two distinct careers, the first of which favours the faculty psychology. Faculty psychologists, building upon the discourse of the soul, take from Kant two supportive affirmations: first, that the mind possesses innate ideas (time, space, and so on); and, secondly, that as an intellectual discipline the scope open to psychology is very

---

[21] Kant, *The Critique of Judgement*, trans. James Creed Meredith (Oxford, 1952), 'Part II: Critique of Teleological Judgement', 131–2. (Parts I and II are separately paginated in this edition.)

[22] Reid, *The Works of Thomas Reid*, 2 vols. ed. Sir William Hamilton, 8th edn. (Edinburgh, 1895), i. 187.

[23] Kant, *Critique*, 'Part II', 132.    [24] Ibid.

[25] Kant, *Critique*, 'Part I: Critique of Aesthetic Judgement', 22.    [26] Ibid. 36.

limited, and its methods remain restricted to the increasingly old-fashioned-looking ones of introspection. Indeed, in this truncated version of Kantianism, psychology cannot get much beyond the repetition of these fundamental principles and suggest their ramifications for epistemology, ethics, and spiritual faith. It certainly cannot enquire into their origin (especially their physiological origin), nor analyse very deeply their mode of operation. Inscrutability thus became a structural requirement of the faculty psychology, and this is a powerful reason why faculty-based arguments were usually critical rather than substantive. Despite his high-falutin manner, early commentators brought Kant four-square with Reid, who posited 'certain principles . . . which the constitution of our nature leads us to believe, and which we are under a necessity to take for granted in the common concerns of life'.[27] Thomas Brown, for instance, complained of Kant's obscurity, but he honoured his 'deductions from the opinions of others', especially 'the *common sense* of the later Scotch philosophers' and the 'three great faculties' (cognition, volition, and judgement) whose study they encouraged.[28] Some modern commentators support this interpretation of Kant, and argue that he was indeed at heart a faculty psychologist.[29] But his ideas had another nineteenth-century destination.

Despite Kant's leaning towards innate ideas, a significant strand of advanced opinion relished another aspect of his work, the corrosive power of his critical intelligence. T. H. Huxley, 'Darwin's bulldog', the 'devil's disciple', and arch-exponent of psycho-physiology, was particularly prominent in this respect, for he, not inaccurately, found in Kant a confirmation of his own agnosticism. Cheekily, he praised Kant, not for his alliance with Reid, but for his development from Hume of 'that more modern way of thinking which has been called "agnosticism"'. For him, the 'critical philosophy' was 'essentially the same' as scepticism.[30] The bones of this argument are easy to grasp. If Kant's self-described 'negative conception of our thinking being' makes it difficult to sustain substantive beliefs about the mind, it becomes just as difficult to believe in God, received truths, immaterial principles, or entities like the soul. Huxley summarizes:

In short, nothing can be proved or disproved, respecting either the distinct existence, the substance, or the durability of the soul. So far, Kant is at one with Hume. But Kant adds, as you cannot disprove the immortality of the soul, and as the belief herein is very

---

[27] Reid, *Works*, i. 108.

[28] [Thomas Brown], 'Villers' *Philosophie de Kant*', *Edinburgh Review*, 1 (1803), 264, 266.

[29] Wayne Waxman, *Kant's Model of the Mind: A New Interpretation of Transcendental Idealism* (Oxford, 1991). See also Patricia Kitcher, *Kant's Transcendental Psychology* (Oxford, 1990). Others acknowledge the 'faculty' perspective but highlight the overall ambiguities in Kant's position—for instance, Karl Ameriks, *Kant's Theory of Mind: An Analysis of the Paralogisms of Pure Reason* (Oxford, 1982).

[30] T. H. Huxley, *Hume* (London, 1879), 60. For helpful commentary, see Lightman, *Origins of Agnosticism*.

useful for moral purposes, you may assume it. To which, had Hume lived half a century later, he would probably have replied, that, if morality has no better foundation than an assumption, it is not likely to bear much strain; and, if it have a better foundation, the assumption rather weakens than strengthens it.[31]

It may be morally convenient to believe in God, as the psychology hung from innate ideas claimed, but the argument cannot bear much weight, and Huxley adroitly exploited against the faculty psychology its own 'negative' powers. Kant is now understood to support, not the reassuring commonplaces of faculty psychology, but 'nothing less than a scientific basis for Scepticism', as Lewes put it (though personally Lewes, unlike Huxley, took his distance from it).[32] Epistemological sceptics such as Huxley, Clifford, and Tyndall received gleefully what they took to be Kant's assertion that one may not know anything with certainty. This corresponded to their view that scientific propositions were permanently open to revision.

In his own work, Kant conceals the epistemological abyss his critical reasoning might open by insisting that innate categories of thought happily agree with the order of nature. The normal mind does not freewheel towards mysticism or madness because the fundamental categories are coincident with sensory intuition. The correspondence of 'two entirely heterogeneous factors, understanding for conceptions [i.e. the fundamental categories] and sensuous intuition for the corresponding Objects' enables us to distinguish the fancied from the actual, he claims.[33] But the Janus-faced aspect presented by Kant's work stirred the psychological waters a good deal. Faculty psychologists took reassurance, while sceptics like Huxley delighted to tease them with their own mentor. Meanwhile, other non-faculty psychologists went along with the underpinning provided by 'sensory intuition' and more or less ignored the rest. In the end, some lost patience. Lewes thought the overall argument had become pointless as well as arcane, while others more enthusiastic about Kant, like the Irish lawyer and freelance speculator in ideas T. E. Webb, wished to jettison the drag-anchor attachment to 'Common Sense' to liberate Kantian principles. Webb tried for a sort of physiological Kantianism and speculated that innate ideas might be located in the organs that received sensory information, a position that at least illustrates the heavy limitations of compromise.[34] None the less, the prominence of Kantian ideas in the mainstream of argument does indicate a decisive shift in psychological theory.

[31] Huxley, *Hume*, 181.

[32] G. H. Lewes, *A Biographical History of Philosophy from its Origin in Greece down to the Present Day*, 2nd edn. (London, 1857), 547.

[33] Kant, *Critique*, 'Part II', 56. See also Mansel, *Lecture on Kant*, 20.

[34] Lewes, *History of Philosophy*, ii. 460–5; T. E. Webb, 'The Metaphysician: A Retrospect', *Fraser's Magazine*, 61 (1860), 503–17.

The older faculty psychology of the Enlightenment placed mind in 'the great chain of being'.[35] Though in most of its forms this line of argument resisted physiological explanations, it did allow mind simultaneously to have a worldly as well as a celestial ontology and underwrote it with Natural Theology.[36] In the conservative tradition, the mind's faculties provided evidence of God's blessed Design, and this was exploited by reforming newcomers like Robert Chambers. However, as several commentators have noted, nineteenth-century developments in this tradition are oriented much more profoundly towards the severance of mind —especially consciousness itself—from nature.[37] Despite sniffy complaints about continental 'obscurity' (Kant himself had called aspects of his ideas 'unfathomable, though still thinkable'[38]), many British commentators promoted a conception of mind that emphasized its mystic and transcendental potentials and were happy to kick away the ladders (or chains) traditionally linking such minds to earth. In 1868 T. Collyns Simon, a representative contributor to the *Contemporary Review*, rejected Reidian common sense as 'superficial', remarked on Britain's 'silence' during the great period of German Idealism, and promoted a new vision of the 'spiritualist interest' in attacking the 'materialistic' psychologies of Spencer and Lewes.[39] He styled this new vision 'Phenomenalism', a school that, he claimed, had its roots in Berkeley and grew to Hamilton. Like his mentor Hamilton, therefore, Simon gave a decisive Idealist tilt to what was once Common Sense.

Simon's emphasis on Hamilton's transcendental conception of consciousness is as symptomatically revealing as his rejection of the Scottish Enlightenment. According to Hamilton, consciousness is the 'generic condition' of all the faculties and underpins all their operations. Though knowing and knowing-that-we-know can be logically distinguished, they are in fact ontologically identical as properties of consciousness, he argues. In all its manifold but unified operations, consciousness now becomes the defining attribute of mind and the defining attribute of humanity, 'not as a particular faculty, but as the universal condition

[35] The classic exposition of this remains Arthur O. Lovejoy, *The Great Chain of Being: A Study in the History of an Idea* (1930; repr. New York, 1960).

[36] David Hartley's uneasy, but influential marriage of physiological speculation, associationism in psychology, and Enlightenment Natural Theology in *Observations on Man, his Frame, his Duty, and his Expectations* (1749) is the most vivid illustration of this. See Benjamin Read, 'The Early Development of Hartley's Doctrine of Association', *Psychological Review*, 30 (1923), 306–20, and, especially, Robert Marsh, 'The Second Part of Hartley's System', *Journal of the History of Ideas*, 20 (1959), 264–73.

[37] G. S. Rousseau, 'Science and the Discovery of Imagination in Enlightened England', *Eighteenth-Century Studies*, 3 (1969), 108–35; Lightman, *Origins of Agnosticism*, 56–8.

[38] Kant, *Critique*, 'Part II', 23.

[39] T. Collyns Simon, 'The Present State of Metaphysics in Great Britain', *Contemporary Review*, 8 (1868), 246–61. See also John Tulloch, 'Professor Ferrier's *Philosophical Remains*', *Edinburgh Review*, 126 (1867), 71–94, and Alfred Barry, 'The Battle of the Philosophies—Physical and Metaphysical', *Contemporary Review*, 12 (1869), 232–44, for similar sentiments.

of intelligence'.[40] Psychology, Hamilton adds, 'is only a developed consciousness, that is, a scientific evolution of the facts of which consciousness is the guarantee and revelation'.[41] It is difficult to make exact sense of this, but the restricted role of psychology as a mode of enquiry is clear, as is its inverse relation to the aggrandisement of consciousness, which now takes the place of the conglomerate of separate faculties in importance.

At times, Hamilton has an energetic vision in the Romantic manner, and can sound a bit like the radical poet and artist William Blake turned parsonical: 'We *exist* only as we energise; pleasure is the reflex of unimpeded energy; energy is the *means* by which our faculties are developed; and a higher energy the *end* which their development proposes.'[42] Several of these metaphysical psychologists were not shy of daunting mystical obscurity as they exhorted the transcendent self into vital being, and much of their project attempted the kind of fundamentally conservative Romantic allure satirized by Byron in *Don Juan*. In the writing of these psychologists, a patina of obscurity appears to add to its transcendental credibility. J. H. Green, for instance, was Coleridge's friend, disciple, and literary executor, who, after inheriting substantial private means, dedicated the second half of his life to the elaboration of the thought of his master. What was particularly significant about Green was that he joined his philosophical pursuits to a career as a distinguished Professor of Anatomy who twice served as President of the Royal College of Surgeons.[43] His transcendental vision for psychology is given below, but it was not a piece of quirky or marginal Idealism. It is central to his work as a doctor and teacher at the heart of the scientific establishment. In a passage in his prestigious Hunterian Oration to the Royal College in 1840, some years before he gave up the day job entirely, he records that:

My position is this:—Man finds in examining the facts of his consciousness, and the essential character of his rationality, the capability of apprehending truths universal, necessary, and absolute; the grounds of which being underived from, must be antecedent, and presupposed in order, to experience:—man finds in himself the capability of inferring the reality of that which transcends his sensuous experience, and of contemplating causality, efficiency, permanent being, law, order, finality, unity:—man finds in himself the capability of apprehending, in a world of relations, the supra-relative; in a world of dependencies, the unconditional; in a world of imperfections, the perfect.[44]

---

[40] Hamilton, *Discussions*, 47.     [41] Ibid. 87.     [42] Ibid. 40.

[43] See Desmond, *Politics of Evolution*, 260–75.

[44] Joseph Henry Green, *Vital Dynamics: The Hunterian Oration before the Royal College of Surgeons in London 14th February 1840* (London, 1840), 19–20. This passage was reprinted with special emphasis by the editor of Green's posthumous *Spiritual Philosophy: Founded on the Teaching of the Late Samuel Taylor Coleridge*, ed. John Simon, 2 vols. (London, 1865), pp. xxvi–xxvii. The emphatic obscurity of Green's pulpit manner could be disconcertingly dependent on inspiration for a man with a scalpel: 'And it is in meditating on the conditions of and causes of this capability, that man becomes conscious of an operance in and on his own mind, of the downshine of a light from above, which is the power of Living Truth, and which, in irradiating and actuating the human mind, becomes for it (reveals itself as) Reason;—yea!' (*Spiritual Philosophy*, 161–2).

This, again, is not as clear as it might be (Green seems to have invented the bullet point without grasping its purpose), and in reading such passages one cannot help regretting the loss of Enlightenment lucidity. Yet the hope of 'permanent being, law, order, finality, unity . . . the supra-relative . . . the unconditional . . . the perfect' is a recognizable, if more yearning, expression of familiar values.

So the destination of this vision in Victorian culture was, after all, quite un-Blakean. Among the most important of Kant's nineteenth-century interpreters was the Tory, High-Church apologist H. L. Mansel, one-time Waynflete Professor of Moral and Metaphysical Philosophy at Oxford and eventually Dean of St Paul's. Mansel's famous Bampton Lectures of 1858 on *The Limits of Religious Thought*, in a further twist to the story, took the sceptical component of Kant's philosophy and created from it a defence of revealed religion, and an account of the psychology of religious experience, which set the Natural Theology tradition, already under pressure, decisively aside. Mansel's defence of Christian faith acknowledged the limitations of human cognition and severed knowledge of God decisively from any that might relate to the mundane world. But it argued forcefully that this existential vacuum actually *increased* the potency, as well as the piquancy, of our intuited sense of His existence.[45] Mansel's lectures were widely influential, though their arguments, like Kant's, were somewhat uncontrollalbe, as they could as easily recommend disbelief as its opposite. *The Limits of Religious Thought* reputedly spurred Huxley to conceptualize his agnosticism, for instance, and Spencer developed similar lines of thought to very different, non-Christian ends.[46] But from the point of view of the history of psychology, Mansel's importance lies in his representative, mid-century reconceptualization of the psychological problem. This was for him no longer an issue about the functioning of mind in the world of here and now. It was an argument about the transcendence of this world and the orientation of the mind towards these ambitions. The Bampton Lectures had a wider brief, but it is important to recognize that their intellectual origin lay in Mansel's earlier work on psychological issues specifically, especially *Psychology the Test of Moral and Metaphysical Philosophy*, his inaugural lecture as Reader in Moral and Metaphysical Philosophy at Magdelene College in 1855. Drawing again on Kant, Mansel argued that psychology was the systematic reflection on the intuitive sense of truth and morality that arises from the 'facts and laws of the consciousness', which are, in fact, 'the facts and laws of the soul'.[47] Such an enquiry asks: 'What are the presentative faculties of the human mind?

[45] The excellent account of Mansel in Lightman's *Origins of Agnosticism* is instructive for present purposes.

[46] Adrian Desmond, *Huxley: The Devil's Disciple* (London, 1994), 285; Lightman, *Origins of Agnosticism*, ch. 3.

[47] H. L. Mansel, *Psychology the Test of Moral and Metaphysical Philosophy: An Inaugural Lecture Delivered at Magdalen College, Oct. 23 1855* (Oxford, 1855), 17–18.

. . . [for] without such a faculty, positive thought can have no place.'[48] We can clearly see here the emergence of a transcendentally 'positive' psychology from Kant's 'negative' characterization of it. As such it represents a confluence (which is also an appropriation) of the discourses of the soul, the faculties, and the transcendental critique.

Mid-nineteenth-century philosophers maintained the eighteenth-century emphasis on the innate, normative, and uniform faculties of mind, and retained powerful convictions about mind's place in the teleological architecture of 'the great chain of being'. But what now connected the individual to the universal mind were not Creation's gradual, ascending steps, but leaps of the intuitive imagination. For Hamilton, intuition establishes spiritual belonging and epistemological certainty; for Mansel, intuition reveals God, guarantees truth, and sanctions morality (which is 'a peculiar faculty of the intuitive consciousness'); for Coleridge, according to Ian Wylie's excellent study of his relation to natural philosophy, the Imagination (in Coleridge's special sense) becomes the bridge between the human and divine worlds and replaces what were traditionally envisaged as more tangible links in being's great chain.[49]

Under the influence of Kant, Coleridge, and the philosophy derived from the 'Scotch School', metaphysical psychologists brought the faculties together under a conception of a unitary, transcendent consciousness identified with the soul. This created a powerful argumentative ensemble that, in the mid-century, was a ready and persuasive opponent for the new psycho-physiology. The new investigations threatened to disaggregate mental life into its material and cognitive components. In response, the transfigured faculty psychology envisioned ever grander and more unified meanings and purposes. It satisfied evangelical appetites and reassured traditionalists by a vision that was at once spiritually consoling and metaphysically ambitious, yet it also held to a cautious conception of the psychological faculties recognizable in the obviousness of common experience. By these means it sustained a major presence in the minds of many Victorian people. This is one reason why (as we shall see in Chapter 7) the psychology of the higher faculties remained readily available to return as a component in the revival of philosophical Idealism at the end of the century, whence it was transmitted to some of the more influential architects of literary Modernism like T. S. Eliot.[50] To opponents, however, its methods and assumptions remained

[48] H. L. Mansel, *Psychology the Test of Moral and Metaphysical Philosophy: An Inaugural Lecture Delivered at Magdalene College, Oct. 23 1855* (Oxford, 1855), 18.

[49] Hamilton, *Discussions*, 55–63; Mansel, *Psychology*, 12; Ian Wylie, *Young Coleridge and the Philosophers of Nature* (Oxford, 1989), 135–6. Stefan Collini comments helpfully on the instinctive 'moral Kantianism' of most Victorian ethical theory and thus how widely these ideas were disseminated: *Public Moralists*, 63, 98.

[50] For further comment, see Rick Rylance, 'Twisting: Memory from Eliot to Eliot', in Matthew Campbell, Jacqueline Labbe, and Sally Shuttleworth (eds.), *Memory and Memorials 1789–1914* (Routledge, 2000).

chronically flawed. To use the traditional taxonomy of the mental faculties as tools for psychological enquiry seemed rather like analysing nutrition using categories such as 'breakfast' or 'pudding', let alone the transcendental category of pie in the sky. So we need now to look at faculty psychology's Victorian rival within the philosophy of mind.

The great competitor was the theory of associationism, a body of thought probably now best known by negative images. It was the target for famous assaults by Coleridge in *Biographia Literaria*, by Wordsworth in *The Prelude*, and, in connection with Utilitarian social and educational programmes, by Dickens in *Hard Times*, all of whom emphasized what they took to be its heartless, soulless, joyless, mechanical reductions of human behaviour. Yet, despite these debilities, associationism retained an impressive hold on the psychological imagination throughout the nineteenth century. Indeed, of the two, associationism is probably better remembered than faculty theory. This is partly due, ironically, to the genius of those who attacked it, but it is also because it presents as a more consolidated body of doctrine with circumscribed historical parameters and clear labels. Historical memory loves doctrinal lucidity, and it loves finality, and associationism has both. The faculty psychology, by contrast, was too hazy in its outlines, too pervasive, and too inconsistent (or flexible) a doctrine to remain visible and distinctive, despite the taxonomic grid it bequeathed to the discipline. Faculty psychology lingered; associationism crashed. It fed the emergent psycho-physiology, but in doing so was comfortably swallowed.

None the less, during the period covered by this book, faculty psychology and associationism are as inseparable as quarrelling siblings. This metaphor recognizes their antagonism, but it also acknowledges a considerable degree of interdependent development. Associationists, for instance, used the same generic terms (memory, will, reason, and so on) as their antagonistic brothers (though faculty psychologists used them with more exhortatory gravitas). Faculty psychologists, meanwhile, recognized the usefulness of some features of associationist theory and circumspectly pilfered its vocabulary. Thomas Reid, though asserting the superior and anterior role of the faculties, declared himself easy in the modest usage of associationist concepts, for the association of ideas can 'tie together' the stray strands of complex experience and thus help the faculties in their binding operations.[51] Other Scottish colleagues, such as Thomas Brown and Dugald Stewart, adopted similar principles. Dickens, too, though violently caricaturing methods of child rearing and teaching based on associationist beliefs in *Hard*

---

[51] Reid, *Works*, i. 112, 117. See also Dugald Stewart, *Elements of the Philosophy of the Human Mind* (1814), ed. G. N. Wright (London, 1843), 157, 206–7. For general comment, see Martin Kallich, *The Association of Ideas and Critical Theory in Eighteenth-Century England: A History of a Psychological Method in English Criticism* (The Hague, 1970). Despite its specialist orientation, this is a most detailed account of associationist ideas in the texture of intellectual life in the period.

*Times* (1854), widely used associationist language to describe his hero's mental development in *David Copperfield* (1849–50). The following is a typical example: 'I don't know why one slight set of impressions should be more particularly associated with a place than another, though I believe this obtains with most people, in reference especially to the associations of their childhood.'[52] In its elaborated doctrine, which struck many as dogma, and, in the social and political conclusions sometimes drawn from it, associationism troubled general opinion. But on neutral ground, such as David Copperfield's childhood in Yarmouth, and at a level of common experience ('I believe this obtains with most people,' says David), there is a clear degree of cooperation between the rival theories, and associationism gained credence and, virtually unconsciously, a place in the psychological vocabulary of the era (hence the frequency with which it appears in the language of fiction). It was as if faculty psychology named the parts of speech while associationism parsed the petty clauses. However, the real quarrel lay below, in fundamentally opposed accounts of the deep structures of mind. As is the nature of such structures, these might remain hidden or ignored for a time, but the driving energies of the dispute are always there none the less.

As nineteenth-century supporters frequently remarked, associationism has a long, swanky, philosophical pedigree stretching back to Aristotle, but for our purposes its significant elaboration is by John Locke in the 1690s. For most nineteenth-century historians of philosophy 'the school of Locke' or 'Locke's descendants' are the common phrases used to indicate the whole line of thought. What made it controversial was its strong claim that the mind's structure, organization, and development are derived entirely from interactions with the environment. Thus, in relation to the list of general philosophical issues with which we began this chapter, associationism had very decided answers to Problems 2 and 3. On the epistemological question (Problem 2) they answered that knowledge depends on experience (indeed, 'the experience philosophy' was an alternative label to 'the school of Locke' or 'associationism'). Intuition, the innate faculties, or other sources of knowledge not derived from experience are, they believed,

---

[52] Charles Dickens, *The Personal History of David Copperfield* (1849–50), ed. Trevor Blount (Harmondsworth, 1966), 91. *David Copperfield* sustains its interest in associationist principles and is actually quite thorough in its coverage. It satirizes, for instance, the fashionable, sentimental associationism of the post-Romantic generation in the girlish posturings of Dora Spenlow and Miss Mills, as well as David (see ch. 38 especially). Like many novelists, Dickens also uses associationist principles to articulate scenes of grief, trauma, or passion when high feeling is communicated by description of associated circumstantial detail, a technique Ruskin shortly afterwards called 'the pathetic fallacy'. (For an example see the description of David's mother's death and funeral.) He also exploits the comic potential of the maverick compulsions induced by unfortunately associated ideas—for example, Aunt Betsy's obsession with donkeys, which 'turned the current of her ideas in a moment' (p. 251). In this respect, the most relevantly associated text is, of course, Sterne's *Tristram Shandy*.

false assumptions resulting from intellectual or religious prejudice or, more char-
itably, from the fact that most associative pathways are facilitated automatically,
independently of consciousness. What might appear an independent source of
knowledge, therefore, is simply one whose origins are forgotten. On the nature/
nurture question (Problem 3), they were similarly decisive: 'human nature' is
not a given, but a product of circumstances. We are what our environment has
made us, and the association of ideas is the psychological mechanism through
which this occurs. Of the two remaining problems, associationist theory favoured
the psycho-physiological approach to the mind–body issue (Problem 1), though,
especially in its early forms, this was not an obligatory part of the doctrine.
However, its response to the 'first-person/third-person' question (Problem 4) was
much less certain, as we shall see.

Associationism assumes that mental life is derived from sensory and perceptual stimulation. In childhood, these stimuli establish the fundamental structures
of mind, which is empty without them. In later life, these structures regulate
the flow of sensory data and prevent the mind becoming an inferno of chaotic
and random stimuli. For associationists, the mind is thus self-organizing around
the initiatory clusters. It does not need the direct intervention of a Creator, and
nor is there any need to consider the soul as a psychological entity. Christian
faith is perfectly compatible with this doctrine (indeed it appealed to many
dissenters, especially Unitarians like the scientist Joseph Priestley). But so is
agnosticism and atheism, as no one was slow to realize.

So how do the mind's contents organize themselves in associationist theory?
The simplest explanation was that the structures of the mind replicate the structures of the experienced environment. For example, ideas occur in the sequence
they do because those are the actual sequences in phenomena, and important
ideas are given their importance by the frequency of their recurrence. The mind's
dominant ideas are therefore a self-electing reflection of the way the world is.
Complex ideas are accrued from simple ones, and abstract concepts are established by the averages of repetition. In later life, the relationship between stimulus and categorization becomes more dialectically complicated, but the root
principles are clear. Much associationist writing therefore stopped at the level
of abstract description and rested on the exchange of nature/nurture statements
of principle: a good deal of associationist debate is merely a game of being 'more
nurturist than thou'. Whatever the emphasis, however, all agreed that the data
flow coheres in patterns of associated ideas that accurately reflect the environment from which they derive. Associationists, therefore, felt some epistemological confidence, theoretically.

Clearly, though, the argument begs several questions, and there appears to be
something radically missing from its account of the process by which any but
the most primitive of mental ideas are formed. This is not simply because of

the lack of a clearly articulated mechanism to specify the ways in which sensory information is conveyed to consciousness (faculty psychology lacked this too). It is a question of how a vision of mental life that is serial in composition and passive in disposition can function synthetically and actively in real life. How does the mind initiate as well as receive processes? How can the imagination operate? How can the mind possibly entertain multiple versions of reality? How can sane people disagree? This is the first of associationism's difficulties with the 'first-person/third-person' question. How mind is experienced (as a synthesizing, self-acting agent) is at odds with a description of it as a relatively passive response to environmental circumstances.

Two central components of associationist theory in the nineteenth century are fundamental to this question.[53] The first of these is the specification of the means by which ideas are linked in the mind. In most accounts, the links between ideas occur in one of two ways: either by contiguity (that is, by direct adjacency in time or space) or by the perception of resemblance. James Mill, for instance, under the heading '*The Ultimate Analysis of the Laws of Association*', writes that 'it is easy to reduce all the laws ever assigned, as governing the reproduction of our ideas, to three, Contiguity, Similarity, and Contrast', and of these Similarity and Contrast are, he asserts, different modes of the same thing.[54] However, the perception of resemblance—the association of similar ideas—is a tricky issue. It is sometimes ascribed to the frequency with which ideas are associated in the environment, in which case, for strict theorists, the perception of resemblance is only a special case of heavily repeated contiguity. But, if ideas are associated by means other than contiguous occurrence, then the theory is in difficulties, because this line of thought suggests that the mind might be able to recognize resemblance by a faculty that is not itself a product of association. This is a classic difficulty in Locke's development of associationist doctrine in *An Essay Concerning Human Understanding*, and it dogged the theory for nearly 200 years thereafter.[55] If a relatively independent faculty to adjudicate comparisons and

---

[53] For the most detailed overview, see Howard C. Warren, *A History of the Associationist Psychology* (New York, 1921).

[54] James Mill, *Analysis of the Phenomena of the Human Mind* (1829), 2 vols., ed. J. S. Mill (1869; repr. New York, 1967), i. 120.

[55] 'The mind, receiving the *ideas* mentioned in the foregoing chapters from without, when it turns its view inward upon itself and observes its own actions about those *ideas* it has, takes from thence other *ideas*, which are as capable to be the objects of its contemplation as any of those it received from foreign things' (John Locke, 'Of Simple Ideas of Reflection', in *An Essay Concerning Human Understanding*, 4th edn. (1700), ed. John Yolton (London, 1961), i. 98. For helpful discussion of Locke's sometimes bumpy account of this classic associationist dilemma, see: Morris Mandelson, 'Locke's Realism', in *Philosophy, Science and Perception* (Baltimore, 1964); John Yolton (ed.), *John Locke: Problems and Perspectives* (Cambridge, 1969); Richard L. Gregory, *Mind in Science: A History of Explanations in Psychology and Physics* (London, 1981); John Dunn, *Locke* (Oxford, 1984), E. J. Lowe, *Locke on Human Understanding* (London, 1995). Even the purest of subsequent

detect similarities is conceded—Locke's general name for it is 'reflection'—the purist rigour of associationism falls, and important ground is given up to jeering faculty psychologists. If it is not conceded, however, a serious gap appears in the theory. What is at stake is the acquisition and use of conceptual categories by a self-reflexive, attentive consciousness whose development is not satisfactorily explained by massive doses of multiply repeated contiguous associations. What so irritated faculty psychologists about this debate was not just the weakness presented by this theoretical aporia, but the refusal to recognize innate ideas as a solution. Locke was unequivocal on this point (chapter two of the *Essay* is entitled 'No Innate Principles in the Mind') and his followers were equally unyielding. The mind was to be understood as an entity constituted within its own history and not under any terms of reference outside this process.[56] To exasperated Victorian opponents, associationism appeared a theory not only shockingly worldly and inhumanly determinist in its machine-like rigour, but one dogmatically pig-headed in the face of a simple, traditional solution that folk of good sense recognized from their own experience.

The second important strand of associationist doctrine central to these concerns is the theory known as 'sensationalism'. Like 'the experience philosophy', the term was often used as a label for the whole body of associationist doctrine, especially by opponents pronouncing 'sensationalism' with the sneer usually reserved for 'sensualism'. As a theory, sensationalism proposes that ideas (the 'thought' components of mental life) derive simply and directly from sense experience. James Mill put the matter straightforwardly: 'we have two classes of feelings; one, that which exists when the object of sense is present; another, that which exists after the object of sense has ceased to be present. The one class of feelings I call SENSATIONS; the other class of feelings I call IDEAS . . .'.[57] Sensations and

---

theorists, like James Mill, retain at least the rhetorical compulsion to aggrandize the faculty of perceiving resemblance among the mind's proudest achievements. They thus create for it an aura at odds with strict principles. Mill describes the perception of resemblance as 'that mighty operation on which, as its basis, the whole of our intellectual structure is reared'. His discussion of the 'mighty operation' does little to clarify the difficulty; indeed he finesses the issue by an argumentatively shrewd, but unsatisfying attack on Platonic theory. See James Mill, *Analysis*, i. 270 ff.

[56] C. C. Gillespie quotes Voltaire: 'Just as a skilled anatomist explains the workings of the human body, so does Locke's *Essay Concerning Human Understanding* give the natural history of consciousness. . . . So many philosophers having written the romance of the soul, a sage has arrived who has modestly written its history' (*Edge of Objectivity*, 159). Voltaire's anatomical simile, the apparent interchangeability of mind and soul (to the ontological advantage of the former), and the developmental model of the mind's formation through time are all worthy of note. See also G. H. Lewes: '[Locke] is the founder of modern Psychology. By him the questions of Philosophy are so boldly and scientifically reduced to the primary questions of the limits of human understanding. By him is begun the *history* of the development and combination of our thoughts. Others had contented themselves with the thoughts as they found them: Locke sedulously inquired into the *origin* of all our thoughts' (*Biographical History of Philosophy*, 458–9).

[57] James Mill, *Analysis*, i. 52.

ideas are different, but not in kind. Despite his rather watery manner, Mill is playing for high stakes here, for sensationalist theory declines the expected onto-logical distinction between mind and body, and a good deal follows from this. For example, the customary hierarchy of the faculties must go because absolute distinctions between, for instance, rudimentary sensations, and activities such as prayer or philosophical thought, cannot be maintained.

Everyone realized that this opened the way to a physiologically based study of mind by placing cognition, perception, sensation, the functioning of the organs of sense, and general physiology all in one line of development. Mill himself had neither the physiological knowledge, nor the interest, to pursue the enquiry, but he was conscious of it as a line of development. The *Analysis* speaks of homo-logous nervous tissue criss-crossing the body and conveying sensations to the whole sensorium.[58] Though he concludes that it is a 'mystery' why one network produces visual sensations, while another produces hearing, and so on, what is interesting is, again, what is *not* said, which is the conventional wisdom that the brain is master of the nervous system as the higher faculties are masters of the lower, as man is master of creation, as God is Lord of man; in short, the ladder of Creation or Great Chain of Being. Mill's model is instinctively dis-persed, systemic, non-pyramidal, and implies a key drift in the metaphoric and conceptual structure of psychology to which we shall regularly return. This is a movement from systems based on ascending hierarchy to ones based upon flat networks. Again, it is easy to see how conservatively tempered faculty psy-chologists would be offended, as they were by Mill's Benthamite support for pleasure–pain conditioning as the sole developmental motor for psychological growth. Mill himself may have been uninterested in physiology (as his son regret-ted in his edition of the *Analysis*), but his readers were not. James McCosh, an opponent, exaggerates, but the point behind his antagonism is worth hearing: 'It is clear that Mill's analysis has been the main book, or the only book on mental science, carefully studied by a certain class of London physiologists—such as Carpenter, Huxley, and Maudsley—who seldom rise above the contemplation of sensations and sensation reproduced.'[59]

We will come back to some of the problems that the associationist model produces, but it is worth pausing for a moment to take note of its strengths. Associationism has an ordered, sequential, and coherent (if narrow) theoretical programme. It develops complex entities from simple ones in an orderly way, and has a promising (if speculative) rigour, parsimony, and consistency of

---

[58] James Mill, *Analysis*, i. 10. Hartley's speculations on the physiological engineering of the sensation –perception model of associationism lies behind Mill's remark: see the next chapter for a description.

[59] McCosh, *Scottish Philosophy*, 380. For limited confirmation of McCosh's point, see Carpenter's essay 'The Brain and its Physiology' (1846), repr. in William B. Carpenter, *Nature and Man: Essays Scientific and Philosophical* (London, 1888), 159–63.

explanation, as John Stuart Mill noted in praising his father's work forty years later.[60] It rejects metaphysical, or quasi-metaphysical, entities and explanations that tend towards mind–body dualism. It thus encourages new work on psychophysical interaction and lays a notional foundation for such work in its psychological 'sensationalism'. It orients knowledge of the mind towards the natural and social environments, thus opening psychology to methods and findings in natural science and to developmental perspectives (hence its utilization in educational theory). Finally, because of its strong 'nurturist' stance against normative conceptions of human nature and innate ideas, it has the potential to develop a social critique of ideological conditioning and to launch social hopes based upon a reform of human nature. Dickens may have thought that the utilitarian appropriation of associationism was on the way to creating Frankenstein monsters in unfortunate northern industrial centres in *Hard Times*,[61] but many others derived more benign and hopeful programmes from associationist principles, including radicals of William Godwin's generation, Owenite socialists, and post-Wollstonecraft feminists, such as John Stuart and Harriet Taylor Mill.[62]

The potential for reformist hope and social critique glowed at the heart of associationism's appeal because the theory asserted that human nature might be improved by revisions to circumstances. As the faculty psychology sustained the status quo, associationism carried radical hopes, despite the paradox that an environmentally determinist psychology can have little logical expectation of amending the environment by which it is determined. Even after the defeat of the most optimistic of these hopes in the aftermath of the French Revolution, associationism appealed to reformers of the post-Napoleonic generation, particularly among the Philosophical Radicals and their ideological descendants, who built psychological considerations into revisionary programmes in politics, economics, and social policy.[63] Harriet Martineau, who shared these ideological ambitions,

---

[60] John Stuart Mill, 'Preface', to James Mill, *Analysis*, i, p. v.

[61] See Chris Baldick, *In Frankenstein's Shadow: Myth, Monstrosity, and Nineteenth-Century Writing* (Oxford, 1987), ch. 5.

[62] William Godwin, *Enquiry Concerning Political Justice and its Influence on Modern Morals and Happiness*, 3rd edn. (1789), ed. Isaac Kramnick (Harmondsworth, 1976); Robert Owen, 'Essays on the Formation of Human Character' (1813–14), in *A New View of Society and Other Writings*, ed. John Butt (London, 1972); John Stuart Mill and Harriet Taylor Mill, *Essays on Sex Equality*, ed. Alice S. Rossi (London, 1970). For commentary, see J. F. C. Harrison, *Robert Owen and the Owenites in Britain and America: The Quest for a New Moral World* (London, 1969), Barbara Taylor, *Eve and the New Jerusalem: Socialism and Feminism in the Nineteenth Century* (London, 1983).

[63] C. H. Driver, 'The Development of a Psychological Approach to Politics in English Speculation before 1869', in F. J. C. Hearnshaw (ed.), *The Social and Political Ideas of Some Representative Thinkers of the Victorian Age* (London, 1933), 251–71; Paul McReynolds, 'The Motivational Psychology of Jeremy Bentham', *Journal of the History of the Behavioural Sciences*, 4 (1968), 230–44; William Thomas, *The Philosophical Radicals: Nine Studies in Theory and Practice 1817–1841* (Oxford, 1979); Collini, *Public Moralists*, ch. 3; Margaret Schabas, 'Victorian Economics and the Science of Mind', in Bernard Lightman (ed.), *Victorian Science in Context* (London, 1997), 72–93.

records in her *Autobiography* how she debated with herself as a young woman in the 1820s between the principles of 'the Locke and Hartley school', on the one hand, and the 'seductions' of 'the Scotch proposition of Common Sense', on the other, as she tried (in that most revealing of Victorian phrases, which mixes physical force and mental craving) to 'grasp a conviction'.[64] Lacking formal education, and 'yearning for a teacher', she pictures herself 'floating and floundering among metaphysical imaginations' until the plain, liberating razor of associationism's simplicity cut through her difficulties and Hartley's account of the association of ideas became 'perhaps the most important book in the world to me, except the bible'.[65] She later recanted somewhat (partly repelled by the adoption of associationism by Owenite Socialists), but her story is a summary of the experiences of those of her generation—she was born in 1802—who craved secular doctrine to anchor belief. Her personal need indicates something of why associationism's appeal should extend beyond the theoretical fascinations of devotees.

The political orientation of the two schools was a leading determinant of the role each branch of the philosophy of mind played in the development of psychological theory in the nineteenth century. Clearly, the two occupied different camps. But it would be a mistake to assume that attachment to one doctrine or the other followed to an inevitable political conclusion. From time to time in this book, faculty psychology is characterized as 'conservative', but this intellectual or disciplinary conservatism was not the same thing as political Toryism (though it often included that). A study of the early British reception of Kant, for instance, reveals bewildering confusion in the estimate of the political consequences of his ideas.[66] In the same period, the intellectual adventurousness of the Scottish psychologist Thomas Brown, an instinctive ally of 'Common Sense', none the less attracted the enmity of the 'church and king' party, as Leslie Stephen emphasized in his *DNB* entry on Brown in the 1880s. During the Napoleonic Wars, fresh thinking in psychological theory was risky, the pressure towards orthodoxy was especially strong, and suspect affiliations (as Brown discovered) could jeopardize a career. Dugald Stewart likewise regretted (but more speedily retracted) an early interest in the French sensationalist Condorcet. But key later figures were still sometimes cantankerously wedded to orthodoxy. Sir William Hamilton, for example, was known as a liberal and educational reformer, politically some distance from the Tory sympathies of, for example, H. L. Mansel. Hamilton's famous confrontation with John Stuart Mill in the 1860s was a fight between a traditional Whig and a progressive Liberal, rather than one between notional

---

[64] Harriet Martineau, *Autobiography* (1877; 2 vols. London, 1983), i. 106.
[65] Ibid. 107, 104.
[66] Micheli, 'The Early Reception of Kant's Thought in England'.

representatives of the 'right' and 'left' wings of political opinion, even though Mill leagued Hamilton with the Tory interest.[67] But, despite these grey areas, the distances often remained significant. The heartland of associationist support lay among the emergent community of middle-class, freethinking, urban liberalism, and its distance from the Whig traditionalism of Scottish Common Sense is conveniently illustrated by this methodological metaphor from Dugald Stewart, which suggests the very different social landscape envisaged by the faculty psychologist:

the grand and fundamental *desideratum* [for a psychological theory] is a bold and comprehensive outline; somewhat for the same reason that, in the cultivation of an extensive country, forests must be cleared and wildernesses reclaimed, before the limits of private property are fixed with accuracy; and long before the period when the divisions and subdivisions of separate possessions give rise to the details of a curious and refined husbandry.[68]

Certainly rural, perhaps a plantation fantasy, suggestive of a landscape garden, the metaphor speaks to a world innocent of factories and radicalism. Associationism rarely found itself in this world.

There is, however, no denying the politics of probably the most trenchant of associationism's critics. The astringency of Coleridge's masterful demolition of associationism in his compellingly quirky *Biographia Literaria* (1817) was invigorated by the changed convictions of an intelligent turncoat. An enthusiast for radical associationism in his youth, Coleridge, like many of his generation, later found solace in God, country, and German philosophy.[69] But, even if his motives were peccant, his case against associationist psychology has authority. In less than twenty pages Coleridge puts virtually all of the arguments that were to goad associationism across the reminder of the century. These are the main charges.

Coleridge argues that associationism renders the human mind both passive and mechanical. There is a loss of human agency amid the 'despotism of outward impressions and that of senseless and passive memory' that makes the mind 'a slave of chances' and the mechanical actions of habit.[70] Like many of

[67] Alan Ryan, 'Introduction', to John Stuart Mill, *An Examination of the Sir William Hamilton's Philosophy and of the Principal Philosophical Questions Discussed in his Writings* in *Collected Works of John Stuart Mill*, ix (London, 1979). Ryan also points out that among Mill's targets were a number of true Tories, including Mansel. See also Leslie Stephen's entry on Hamilton in the *DNB*.

[68] Stewart, 'Life of Reid', 16.

[69] Marilyn Butler, *Romantics, Rebels, and Reactionaries: English Literature and its Background 1760–1830* (Oxford, 1981), ch. 3. For relevant studies of Coleridge's developing thought, see Richard Haven, 'Coleridge, Hartley and the Mystics', *Journal of the History of Ideas*, 20 (1959), 477–94; Thomas McFarland, *Coleridge and the Pantheist Tradition* (Oxford, 1969); Trevor H. Levere, *Poetry Realized in Nature: Samuel Taylor Coleridge and Early Nineteenth-Century Science* (Cambridge, 1981); Wylie, *Young Coleridge*.

[70] Coleridge, *Biographia Literaria*, 64, 68.

his contemporaries, Coleridge believed that psychological authority rested with the higher faculties and, eventually therefore, with God. But he significantly changes the orientation of the psychological problem. Now it is one not so much of regulation, but of the elimination of creative independence of thought and action. There is in associationism, Coleridge argues, a basic poverty in the psychological landscape: it cannot generate 'such faculties as those of the will and the scientific reason'.[71] Nor can it account for the faculty of the Imagination, which, for Coleridge, mediates between the active and passive powers of the mind and helps us thereby to negotiate life by considering possibilities prior to action. Later in the *Biographia*, Coleridge makes much greater claims for the Imagination as the ground for human ontological and existential identity. For him, it links the individual to the higher mind, as in his famous (but obscure) statement that Imagination is 'a repetition in the finite mind of the eternal act of creation in the infinite I AM'.[72] But this daunting argument is grounded in a more intelligent, practical conception of the role of the imagination in everyday life than sometimes appears from commentaries. The imagination's active role in problem solving, in exploratory and creative behaviour, in playfulness, and in human personal and cultural interaction is one the associationists—especially the utilitarian associationists—not only ignored, but also could not imagine.[73]

For Coleridge, associationism cannot originate any form of mental activity not tied to sequence and contiguity. It cannot, therefore, generate mental classes or sets other than those adventitiously put in front of it.[74] This damages its account of human intelligence to be sure, but it is, for him, part of a general disaggregation, not only of the individual psyche, but of individuals from each other, and of the present from the past. For Coleridge, human experience aims to be unitary, psychologically, socially, spiritually, and morally, and he is typically rhapsodic about the 'probability' that 'all thoughts are in themselves imperishable; and that if the intelligent faculty should be rendered more comprehensive, it would require *only* a different and apportioned organization, the body celestial instead of the body terrestrial, to bring before every human soul the collective experience of its whole past existence'.[75] Rarely can so much have hung from the single, frail hook of an 'only', but Coleridge's point should not be lost in his enthusiasm. Associationists maintained that their theory permitted access to the real record of human history rather than its transcendence (James Mill wrote

---

[71] Coleridge, *Biographia Literaria*, 70.    [72] Ibid. 167.

[73] James Mill's narrow conception of the imagination, as the mere retracing of existing trains of associated ideas, is typical (*Analysis*, i. 239 ff.). His characterization of poetical imagining as pleasurable, nostalgic whimsy has always irritated literary critics, but his rejection of the idea (ascribed to Dugald Stewart) that the imagination is the constructive formation of *new* combinations is especially damaging for his psychological as well as his literary theory.

[74] Coleridge, *Biographia Literaria*, 56.    [75] Ibid. 66, emphasis added.

a six-volume *History of British India*, for instance), and pointed to Coleridge's prejudice against sudden historical change. (His critique of associationism takes due note of its popularity in 'an unfortunate neighbour-nation', and concludes sternly that 'such men need discipline, not argument'.[76]) But, associationism's disaggregating tendency, and, through Utilitarian theory, its impact upon perceptions of human community as well as the human mind, were charges that attracted not only Dickens among subsequent critics.

Finally, Coleridge censures associationism's covert materialism. He cannot see, for instance, 'how any affection from without can metamorphose itself into perception or will'. The issue is not just a matter of the physiologist's inability to explain a mechanism; it is mainly, for Coleridge, a fundamental confusion of categories. 'Matter has no Inward', he remarks on the same page. He means by this two things: first, that matter has no properties in itself to convert a physical into a mental event (a sensation into a perception, for instance); and, secondly, that what we perceive in the material world has purposes and significances that have little to do with the mere material forms and properties of objects. His example is a bell whose nature cannot be explained by its 'iron tongue' alone.[77] The music of its 'bell-ness' is something added to its iron, just as the perception of its sound is something more than the reception of a sensation of clanging in the ear. This was essentially Wordsworth's point also about the human response to nature. Nature's significance exceeds any of its individual features or modes, and this forms the basis of his critique of associationism in *The Prelude*, which followed from Coleridge's ideas.

Two important issues in the development of psychological theory follow from this. The first asks how psychologists might theorize the relationship between physical and mental states. Sensationalists insisted upon homology, but crucial issues remain, including the question of origins. As G. H. Lewes later pithily put it: 'Sensations develop our mental faculties, they do not create them. Condillac might as well say that exercise creates the faculty men have of running.'[78] We shall return to this debate in the next section, but, as Coleridge notes, the failure to leap across that gap in the theory generally issues in dualism: 'the most consistent proceeding of the dogmatic materialist is to fall back into the common rank of *soul-and-bodyists*,' he claims.[79]

The second important issue concerns complexity. *Biographia Literaria*, like many protests against associationism, presents itself as a voice for the complexity of individual cognition and human culture, and as a voice respectful of human achievement. It is an honourable protest against what we would now call crude stimulus-response models of human behaviour, and faculty psychology thus claimed

---

[76] Ibid. 71.      [77] Ibid. 75–6.      [78] Lewes, *Biographical History of Philosophy*, 523.
[79] Coleridge, *Biographia Literaria*, 76.

the advantage of care for human integrity and values. But it is worth repeating that faculty psychology itself possessed no more compelling account of these issues, and it is easy to be respectful and rather pious when it is your adversary who is in the dock suffering under the burden of having to prove his innocence. Such was the pattern throughout much of the century.

None the less, associationism does present an intensely streamlined model of human behaviour. What arrives as sensation becomes an idea, but these appear to have identical status. Nothing is added or lost in the conversion; nor is anything added or lost by the accumulation of ideas. Associationism has certain mechanisms for retaining efficiency (such as classification by resemblance), but it has none for added value. Two sensations lead to two ideas, three to three, and so on. There are no synergistic energies in the ideal, trimly run, smoothly associated mind: input equals output like balls rolled through a tube. Associationism is also an intensely *rationalist* model that has considerable difficulty with experiences it cannot explain, name, or account for. It is not good with shadowy ideas or emotional states. Its primary mechanisms are the binary switches of true/not true or pleasurable/not pleasurable. John Stuart Mill's account of his breakdown in his *Autobiography* deliberately emphasized the limitations of his associationist upbringing, and he highlighted the role the theory played in his crisis, citing Coleridge's poem 'Dejection' to describe his state of mind. Disturbed by the thinness of the utilitarian–associationist way of categorizing the world, exhausted by self-scrutiny, and disorientated by the withdrawal of emotion once invested in abstract ends, Mill doubted the psychological efficacy of 'pains and pleasures thus forcibly associated with things'.[80] Mill is disturbed by exactly that blockage and turbulence in the system—the withdrawal of emotion from once-cherished objects, the psychological entropy of too long-sustained goals and the habit of self-analysis, the realization that eyes fixed on the distance have ignored the here and now—that (most galling of all) associationism is simply unable to recognize. His depression is compounded by the collapse of the theoretical frame of reference that should allow him to understand his own mind.

The issue, however, is not just a matter of ignoring emotion in a crude, Gradgrindian way. Mill's point is that, even in acts of human cognition, there is a complex interaction of feeling and thought, and associationism is unable to respond to this. Associationist theory was, in fact, often heavily invested with emotion of a certain type, usually sentimentality or moral loftiness or both, as though to compensate for its own tart rationalism. The 'associationist romance' (as we might call it) in Victorian culture whereby individuals become powerfully attached to the scenes and people of childhood, provoking emotions that last a lifetime (and regularly issue in a marriage), is a fixture in Victorian fiction

---

[80] John Stuart Mill, *Autobiography*, ed. Jack Stillinger (1873; Oxford, 1971), 83.

and other discourse, often (as in *David Copperfield*) conveyed through the language of associated ideas. Lucy Snowe, Charlotte Brontë's mordant narrator in *Villette* (1853), coldly but succinctly describes the process with respect to the marriage of Dr Bretton and Paulina: 'out of association grows adhesion, and out of adhesion, amalgamation.'[81] Intentional or not (and the language is coloured by the narrator's envy), it is difficult to imagine a better parody of the textbook Utilitarian voice confronting the sentimental world. Even the intellectually hard-boiled George Eliot had, in *Middlemarch*, her Fred Vincys and Mary Garths, and explored in *The Mill on the Floss* the tangled attachments and trains of association of Tom and Maggie Tulliver. But sometimes these attachments are cruelly insufficient, as Tom and Maggie both tragically discover in their different ways. This is one lesson of Mill's experience also, and it is a case impressively sustained in another of the great mid-century voices against psychological regulation, Wordsworth's *The Prelude*.

As we saw at the beginning of the chapter, Wordsworth criticized the associationist 'cabinet of sensations', but he did not revert automatically to unconsidered faith in the abstract faculties. It is one virtue of literature, in relation to psychological debates, that it can explore the ground from diverse perspectives, sometimes *relatively* untroubled by doctrinal affiliation in the war of the psychological schools. The account of the growing mind in Wordsworth's poem not only refrains from too particular a conceptualization of psychological processes, it makes a positive epistemological and literary virtue from its restraint. Like George Eliot's work, it is committed to a degree of radical perspectivism, and dramatizes both the mind of the boy as he thinks and feels, and the mind of the man trying to understand what the boy was and became. Book Four of *The Prelude* has a splendidly appropriate metaphor for this. The poet hangs over the side of a boat and looks down. He cannot separate, in the shimmering images, what is reflection and what really lies below the water. The experience suggests itself as a metaphor for thinking about one's past, but also for any kind of introspective reflection.[82] So, in terms of theory, the poem is unpredictable in the explanatory conceits and arguments it offers for the psychological development it describes, and this generates both its acuity and its intellectual energy. Psychologically, the poem seems full of vagrant entities bubbling out of lakes, streaming over mountains, hanging from cliffs, just as Wordsworth's actual landscape contains many itinerant and wandering inhabitants. The paragraph-by-paragraph rhythm of the poem, whereby an event is described and then followed by reflection upon it, sustains the feel of problems under revisionary enquiry, and this is matched in phrasing and detail as ideas glide by following their 'quaint associations',

---

[81] Charlotte Brontë, *Villette* (1853), ed. Mark Lilley (London, 1979), 372.
[82] Wordsworth, *The Prelude* (1850), bk. 4, ll. 256 ff.

'unconscious intercourse', 'dim similitudes', and 'invisible links | allied to the affections', while fugitive spirits, genii or presences flicker or impose themselves on the mind in a flowing trail of 'invisible links'.[83] This processes of creative apprehension became, in *The Prelude*, a mode of concept formation in itself as Wordsworth sets aside the rigor of the schools, just as perception itself is described in his poem 'Tintern Abbey' as a matter of what eye and ear both 'half-create, | and what perceive . . .'.[84]

Both Wordsworth and Coleridge thought associationism horribly restrictive and dogmatic; Dugald Stewart thought that a psychology built upon the levelling principles of associationism threatened an expansive 'culture of the heart'; and Edward Lytton Bulwer thought it 'cabined and confined in the unennobling materialism of Locke'. Both Stewart and Bulwer considered Scottish thought grand and spacious by comparison.[85] So, despite its sporadic hopes for universal amelioration, associationism remained a doctrine for small spaces: the untidy, scratchy intimacies of primitive sensation, the petty linking of tiny ideas, cramped streets and dwellings, urban alleys, the dwarfing regimes of the Utilitarian prison and teaching factory, the intensely localized patrician communities of the Owenites, the unaffiliated intellectual's parlour or kitchen table on which such things might be explained in theorems, with dreams of correction attached. There was also the question of emotion, and thereby arises one of the most trenchant of the humanistic critiques of the theory: that arising from the self-imprisoning, emotional deformity of emergent, subaltern professionals, brought up through associationist programmes, like Dickens's schoolmaster Bradley Headstone in *Our Mutual Friend* (1864–5).

Dickens describes Bradley Headstone's mind as like 'a mental warehouse', an image also used of Gradgrind on the first page of *Hard Times*. Both characters have the emotional resources of a penny receipt. Dickens describes Headstone's mind as like a stock ledger in which ideas are in transit, like temporary goods associated by clip and docket. These the schoolmaster checks anxiously to satisfy himself that nothing is missing:

From his early childhood up, his mind had been a place of mechanical stowage. The arrangement of his wholesale warehouse, so that it might be always ready to meet the demands of retail traders . . . imparted to his countenance a look of care. . . . He always seemed to be uneasy lest anything should be missing from his mental warehouse, and taking stock to assure himself.[86]

---

[83] 'Quaint associations' is the phrase used by Wordsworth in the 1799 version of *The Prelude* (bk. I, l. 421); it was changed to 'quaint accidents' in 1805.

[84] William Wordsworth and Samuel Coleridge, *Wordsworth and Coleridge: Lyrical Ballads*, ed. R. L. Brett and A. R. Jones (London, 1968), 116.

[85] Stewart, 'Life of Reid', 17; Bulwer, *England and the English*, 208.

[86] Charles Dickens, *Our Mutual Friend* (1864–5), ed. Stephen Gill (Harmondsworth, 1971), 267–8.

Dickens has larger targets than psychological theory in view here, but his account of Headstone's mind follows coherently from that of his other Utilitarian, associationist casualties such as Bitzer and Louisa Gradgrind in *Hard Times*. Headstone's is a mind without proportion, self-understanding, and anything more than habituated egotism. As a result, Dickens argues, his human desires remain childishly vindictive. He lives in a toytown world as grotesquely messy and selfishly infantile as his self-proclaimed (and entirely unreciprocated) 'love' for Lizzie Hexam:

The schools were newly built, and there were so many of them all over the country, that one might have thought the whole were but one restless edifice with the loco-motive gift of Aladdin's palace. They were in a neighbourhood which looked like a toy neighbourhood taken in blocks out of a box by a child of particularly incoherent mind, and set up anyhow; here, one side of a new street; there, a large solitary public-house facing nowhere; here, another finished street already in ruins; there, a church; here, an immense new warehouse; there, a dilapidated old country villa; then a medley of black ditch, sparkling cucumber-frame, rank field, richly cultivated kitchen garden, brick viaduct, arch-spanned canal, and disorder of frowziness and fog. As if the child had given the table a kick, and gone to sleep.[87]

This is partly a passage about unplanned urban development, but it is also about the mind of a child whose careless petulance provides its comic focus. The two are connected by the theme of incoherent, unbalanced growth in both cities and minds.

*Hard Times* made the complaint that associationist-led education made monsters by regimentation. *Our Mutual Friend* is concerned with monstrosity by neglect. If this passage is read (only a little against its will) as an image not just of Headstone's ruin, but of his emotionally stunted mind, it also reveals the discredit into which associative Utilitarianism had fallen in psychological circles by the 1860s. It appears a theory in which the higher faculties have no more coherent and telling role than that of an ignorant, dozy child. Dickens's account of Bradley Headstone is divided in its attitudes: is this tragedy or villainy? Either way, his nasty, incoherent, helpless fate illustrates some of the central problematics of psychological theory in the mid-century: how might it best be integrated with the body and its desires, and how might the mind be maturely regulated? With this in view, let us leave the philosophy of mind and move to the two final discourses that constitute psychology's development in the nineteenth century: the discourse of physiology and then that of psychiatric medicine.

---

[87] Ibid. 267–8.

CHAPTER 3

# The Discourse of Physiology in General Biology

Modern historians concur with Victorian commentators that the decade of the 1870s was crucial in the development of British physiology and psycho-physiology, and that it represented an important turning point in the move to scientific definitions of psychological theory. Most agree that it was only from the end of the 1860s that psycho-physiology was able to make a sustained, well-supported challenge to the prevailing philosophical and theological paradigms.[1] William James, for instance, in *Principles of Psychology* (1890) thought that a significantly detailed, modern knowledge of cerebral anatomy, and the physiology of the brain, began its development around 1870, and he considered it among the 'achievements of the present generation'.[2] Several factors contributed to this British resurgence. Path-breaking European work was gradually readmitted to the mainstream of domestic enquiry from the 1840s after a period of post-Revolutionary suspicion. By the 1870s, though the extension of physiological knowledge to psychology continued to be vigorously attacked, physiology itself was more securely anchored to undismissable scientific findings, and better techniques and instrumentation had been developed to enable further work. David Ferrier at King's College, London, for example, provided conclusive evidence of the cerebral localization of the major brain functions in the early part of the decade. In experiments on dogs and other animals, Ferrier for the first time demonstrated predictable responses in motor functions to ablations and galvanic

---

[1] For discussion of the developments described in this paragraph, see Lorraine J. Daston, 'British Responses to Psycho-Physiology, 1860–1900', *Isis*, 69 (1978), 192–208; Richard D. French, 'Some Problems and Sources in the Foundations of Modern Physiology in Great Britain', *History of Science*, 10 (1971), 28–55; Gerald L. Geison, 'Social and Institutional Factors in the Stagnancy of English Physiology, 1840–1870', *Bulletin of the History of Medicine*, 26 (1972), 30–58; Marc Jeannerod, *The Brain Machine: The Development of Neurophysiological Thought*, trans. David Urion (London, 1985), 56; Karl E. Rothschuh, *History of Physiology*, ed. and trans. Guenter B. Risse (New York, 1973), 305–18; J. Schiller, 'Physiology's Struggle for Independence in the First Half of the Nineteenth Century', *History of Science*, 7 (1968), 64–89; Roger Smith, 'The Background to Physiological Psychology in Natural Philosophy', *History of Science*, 11 (1973), 83; Robert Young, *Mind, Brain and Adaptation in the Nineteenth Century: Cerebral Localization and its Biological Context from Gall to Ferrier* (Oxford, 1970), 234.

[2] James, *Principles of Psychology*, i. 14.

stimulations of the cortex. His results were announced in lectures at the Royal Society in 1874–5, and his internationally influential book, *The Functions of the Brain*, was published a year later. Though tentative, these developments checked the ideological accusation that physiological psychology was simply a materialist fantasy. In addition, in line with general trends in Victorian intellectual and scientific life at this time, physiology as a discipline became more thoroughly professionalized in a way that secured a more substantial presence in the culture. The first specialist physiological laboratories were opened towards the end of the 1860s; the Physiological Society was founded in 1876; the *Journal of Physiology* began publication in 1878; and physiological scholarships were established at major universities, including, in 1879, the George Henry Lewes Studentship at Cambridge.

It is not difficult to see why a figure such as Lewes might play a significant role in the emergent discipline. His interests remained primarily at the psychological end of physiology, but, as a freelance, he was untroubled by institutional pressures that might discourage initiative. He had an established, general audience through the great periodicals, as well as the specialist ear of the strengthening scientific community in London. As a Germanist of some reputation (who also had fluent French and Italian), he had important contacts on the Continent and ready access to the new work being produced there. As an intellectual generalist of a distinctively Victorian kind, with an established reputation in the history of philosophy, he was already well placed to try a synthesis between the new science and the earlier psychological traditions.

It is with writers such as Lewes, rather than specialists such as Ferrier, that this book is primarily concerned. However, in the Victorian period, one should not overestimate the division between specialist and generalist, as the careers of representative figures such as Huxley or Darwin illustrate. Our contemporary awareness of this division, and a corresponding suspicion of the inexpert or non-specialist, perhaps reveals more about our intellectual culture and needs than it does about that of the Victorians. Scientists in that period moved with authority between domains, and the role and impact of the generalist intellectual was considerable, even in specialist areas like physiology. They performed important work of synthesis as well as developing informed speculation; they mediated and disseminated new knowledge; and they nurtured the discipline's emerging reputation in the public domain. It is unlikely to have occurred to the Victorians that they might need specialist professors in the public understanding of science.

We might think about 1876, the year in which the Physiological Society was founded, and about G. H. Lewes's activities in that year, for a revealing snapshot. In December of 1875 Lewes had given evidence to the Royal Commission on Vivisection on behalf of the physiological community, and in the early months of the new year he was still actively concerned with the issue amid fears that the growing anti-vivisection lobby would push through legislation disabling new work. Unregulated vivisection was an emotional and deeply conflicted issue that contributed—not always helpfully—to physiology's prominent place in public attention.[3] Lewes, as a man who thought himself a scientist (among other things), defended the practice, though he argued for more rigorously controlled conditions. In March 1876, with others, he established the Physiological Society, partly to defend the interests of scientists in the vivisection debates as legislation became imminent (the Cruelty to Animals Act was passed later that year). He was promptly elected to the Society's Council and, in May, became its Chairman. In the previous year he had been among those consulted on the foundation of the first specialist psychological journal, *Mind*, which was launched in January 1876, spotlighting psychology's scientific credentials as these debates rumbled on. The first number carried a lengthy critical notice by Lewes of a new Italian book on the central nervous system, and he contributed the lead essay to the second asking 'What is Sensation?'. Meanwhile, his best-selling *History of Philosophy* (previously *The Biographical History of Philosophy*) was into its fourth edition; the third edition of his *Life of Goethe* had just appeared; and the second edition of *On Actors and the Art of Acting* had recently been delivered to the shops. As he counted his royalties from these sources, he sorted through the proofs of his specialist *The Physical Basis of Mind*. This was volume three of his magnum opus *Problems of Life and Mind*, which eventually ran to five large volumes by the time of his death in December of 1878. *The Physical Basis of Mind*, published in July 1877, was a 500-page assessment of new scientific work in physiology, especially that coming from Europe. Articles based on the research appeared during 1876 in both *Mind* and the pro-science *Fortnightly Review* (of which Lewes had, in the mid-1860s, been the first editor). Meanwhile, George Eliot's *Daniel Deronda* came out in eight parts between February and September. The novel famously begins with reflections on the construction of scientific units of measurement: 'Men can do nothing without the make-believe of a beginning. Even Science, the strict measurer, is obliged to start with a make-believe unit . . . and pretend that time is at Nought.'[4] One should be careful, therefore, not to indulge too freely in the make-believe that physiological psychology begins only with the twitchings in the cortical anatomy observed under laboratory stimulation.

Physiology's advance made psychological traditionalists and cultural conservatives doubly anxious, and the effect of progress in psycho-physiological work was widely felt. Many thought it a particularly threatening part of the general, bulldozing 'march of science'. In 1874 Henry Sidgwick declared, in Arnoldian accents, that the scientific method

[3] Geison, 'Social and Institutional Factors', 35–6, 41; Nicolaas Rupke (ed.), *Vivisection in Historical Perspective* (London, 1987); Rosemary Ashton, *G. H. Lewes: A Life* (Oxford, 1991), 267–8.

[4] George Eliot, *Daniel Deronda* (1876), ed. Barbara Hardy (Harmondsworth, 1967), 35.

has steadily grown both intensively and extensively, both in clearness and certainty of conviction, and in the universality of explication, as the human mind has developed and human experience has been systematized and enlarged. Step by step, in successive departments of fact, conflicting modes of thought have receded and faded, until at length they have vanished everywhere, except for the mysterious citadel of the will.[5]

Sidgwick's selection of the will as the central faculty holding out against the march of science was typical of the period. For many Victorians, the exercise of the will, particularly the ethical will, was the behavioural feature that most clearly distinguished humans from other species. So the stakes were high in these discussions, and Sidgwick's remark illustrates the plight of the beleaguered humanist: the will, once a proud, independent faculty, is now a defensive redoubt, and the citadel of the higher faculties is surrounded by the brutish hordes of the physiological functions.

Sidgwick's is a skirmish in what one commentator, Alfred Barry, called, in the *Contemporary Review* in 1869, 'The Battle of the Philosophies—Physical and Metaphysical'. Barry's sympathies lay with the metaphysicians, and his essay dismisses physiological psychology. But what is once again revealing is his defensiveness, including an alarmed sense that he might be on the losing side. The aim of the essay, he writes, 'is to enter a protest on behalf of Metaphysical against Physical Philosophy, chiefly on a ground which appeals to the interest of all—a desire to vindicate the weak and the oppressed'.[6] The fortunes of metaphysical philosophy (briefly in the ascendant in the psychological debates of the late 1850s and early 1860s) now appear in decline, and Barry worries that science might 'finally absorb and obliterate . . . the philosophy of mind, and its objects'. He lists the probable casualties: Christian belief, the integrity of the moral life, and 'the great distinction between right and necessity'.[7] So, for Barry as well as for Sidgwick, the splendid autonomy of the ethical life is among those treasures likely to be pillaged by invading scientific brutishness. It is in this climate of discussion that one should understand one element in the contribution of George Eliot's fiction. Her work, which can now appear to some modern readers (as it did to a few contemporaries like Nietzsche[8]) as a rather stuffy defence

[5] Henry Sidgwick, *The Methods of Ethics* (1874), quoted by Daston, 'British Responses to Psycho-Physiology', 194.

[6] Barry, 'Battle of the Philosophies', 235–6. Alarm bells sounded even earlier: an anonymous writer in 1864 urged psychologists to wake up lest physiology steal 'the best part of their science' (Anon., 'Mind and Brain', *British Quarterly Review*, 40 (1864), 440).

[7] Barry, 'Battle of the Philosophies', 240, 236.

[8] 'G. Eliot.—They have got rid of the Christian God, and now feel obliged to cling all the more firmly to Christian morality: that is the *English* consistency, let us not blame it on little blue-stockings *à la* Eliot' (Friedrich Nietzsche, *Twilight of the Idols* (1889), in *Twilight of the Idols and The Anti-Christ*, trans. R. J. Hollingdale (Harmondsworth, 1968), 69). For commentary, see William Myers, *The Teaching of George Eliot* (Leicester, 1984), ch. 7.

of old-fashioned duty, is in fact a contextually highly pertinent attempt to discriminate the basis for an authentic moral life as an alternative to the 'unreflecting moral Kantianism' (to use again Stefan Collini's happy phrase) of mainstream Victorian ethical theory.[9] With its careful specification of the exacting, contextual pressures placed on individual moral choices, it participates in a debate between those who understood the laws of ethical behaviour as stern, self-validating injunctions announced at some distance from history, and those who understood morality as a matter of intense, experiential negotiation. Like her psycho-physiological friends, George Eliot could not accept that ethics were a simple enactment of ideal principles standing outside the determining context of choice. Her work is an enquiry into how a life of moral integrity might be lived in the exacting, complexly determined circumstances of post-Utilitarian Britain.[10]

Psychological debate in the 1870s often made use of the language of warfare and/or disputed intellectual territory. This partly reflects, in a general way, a darkening sense of the implications of evolutionary strife, as well as the brewing nationalist conflicts in Europe (both can be detected, for instance, in Eliot's *Daniel Deronda* (1876), but also in her sibylline reflections in *Impressions of Theophrastus Such* of 1879).[11] Henry Calderwood was another who used this language. Professor of Moral Philosophy at Edinburgh, he was an elder in the Presbyterian Church and followed the physiological debates with great care, eventually publishing his summative reflections in *The Relations of Mind and Brain* (1879). He opened the debate with an essay in 1871: 'the new sciences encroach on the territory of the old, and by the strong hand of conquest take from them some part of their ancient possessions, or even enter into occupancy of the whole region.'[12] Fundamental changes in intellectual life, or upheavals within a discipline, can often be characterized as warfare.[13] But two particular issues for

---

[9] See above, ch. 2 n. 49.

[10] Pertinent discussion of these issues can be found in the work of Alasdair MacIntyre, especially *A Short History of Ethics* (London, 1967) and *After Virtue: A Study of Moral Theory* (London, 1981).

[11] Frank Turner notes that 'after approximately 1875 the spokesmen for British science shifted their rhetoric and the emphasis of their policy from the values of peace, cosmopolitanism, self-improvement, material comfort, social mobility, and intellectual progress towards the values of collectivism, nationalism, military preparedness, patriotism, political elitism, and social imperialism' ('Public Science in Britain: 1880–1919', in *Contesting Cultural Authority: Essays in Victorian Intellectual Life* (Cambridge, 1993), 205).

[12] Henry Calderwood, 'The Present Relations of Physical Science to Mental Philosophy', *Contemporary Review*, 16 (1871), 225.

[13] Twenty years later, in *The Principles of Psychology*, William James used the same language to characterize the 'invasion' of the Experimentalists: 'The simple and open method of attack having done what it can, the method of patience, starving out, and harassing to death is tried; the Mind must submit to a regular *siege*, in which minute advantages gained night and day by the forces that hem her in must sum themselves up at last into her overthrow.' What distinguishes James's use of the metaphor is the spirited intellectual confidence displayed in his irony. German Experimentalism, he writes, 'could hardly have arisen in a country whose natives could be *bored*' (*Principles of Psychology*, i. 192–3). His is a psychology still in the ascendant—but only just.

consideration might be teased from this particular battle. The first concerns the role of philosophy in relation to the new physiological psychology. The second concerns the relationship between psychology and the physiological body, what we might call the somatization of the new theory. Let us take these in order.

Two arguments were made in defence of the traditional importance of philosophy in psychological enquiry. In the first, opponents of the new physiological psychology tried to stop the headlong advance of psycho-physiology and preserve specific territory as philosophy's own. Henry Calderwood argued that, however extensive the reach of physiology might be presumed to be, aspects of mind would always remain beyond it, especially Consciousness, which was fast acquiring a permanent capital letter and rivalling the Will as the last redoubt of the older psychology. 'What is within Consciousness,' Calderwood writes, 'physiology cannot account for; what belongs to physiology, Consciousness cannot account for.'[14] The drastic, dualistic implications of this argument were not lost on anyone, and Calderwood formally declared an end to the long 'struggle towards unity in a theory of all life' in post-Enlightenment philosophy.[15]

However, pro-science writers refused to let go of philosophical problems, even as the emerging Experimentalist movement spurred the science towards narrower goals. Lewes, a great auto-didact with his own laboratory facilities in the basement of his home, was not, as future generations would be, acculturated into the hermetic world of laboratory science, and in this he was not alone. T. H. Huxley, in a lecture 'On Sensation and the Unity of Structure of the Sensiferous Organs' at the Royal Institution in 1879, was, as always, as direct as could be: 'The man who seeks sanctuary from philosophical questions within the walls of the observatory or of the laboratory', he declared, will find 'the germs, if not the full-grown shapes, of lively metaphysical postulates rampant amidst his most positive and matter-of-fact notions.'[16] The metaphor of metaphysics growing unnoticed in laboratory preparations is particularly neat, not least because it comes from a man whose life was, in major respects, dedicated to establishing such facilities. But the triumphalism and restricted horizons of the coming Experimentalist generation were not, by and large, features of the intellectual life of their seniors. If younger researchers saw the future in ever-more precise laboratory measurement, and in methodologically unselfconscious fieldwork, their vision

---

[14] Calderwood, 'Present Relations', 229.

[15] Ibid. 230. Cf. John Duns, editor of the *North British Review* from 1857, commenting on Richard Owen's conservative anatomy: 'In science then, as in grace, the distinct recognition of the personality of God, as the primal source of being, is thrust upon us at that point at which mind cannot penetrate further, even while it feels that there is much to be known beyond; a point, then, at which those of noblest faculties are constrained to acknowledge their littleness, weakness, and ignorance' ([John Duns], 'Professor Owen's Works', *North British Review*, 28 (1858), 329).

[16] T. H. Huxley, 'On Sensation and the Unity of Structure of the Sensiferous Organs', in *Science and Culture and Other Essays* (London, 1892), 247.

was not widely shared in the 1870s. Huxley's lecture (which was promptly published in *The Nineteenth Century*) admonished the 'cocksureness' and primitivism of underdeveloped ideas, and warned that the modern understanding of even rudimentary terms like 'sensation', as used by the Experimentalists, had hardly got beyond that of the eighteenth century.

So the battle between science and philosophy for discursive mastery in psychological theory of the second half of the century was fought in several ways. It was fought as a territorial dispute by conservative philosophers who, like once-dominant groups everywhere faced with declining influence, threatened unilateral declarations of independence. But it was also fought by pro-science writers maturely aware of the philosophical issues their work opened. If the tactic of conservatives was to try to drag iron barriers between professional domains, that of the most forthright, and often aggressive, of the scientific lobby, like Huxley, Clifford, or Tyndall, was to return a challenge in the form of the philosophical issues they believed their scientific work opened. As a result, traditionalists conceded ground, and the open, public 'battle of the philosophies' was now being fought largely on terms dictated by the scientific interest. The key issue concerned the limits of human knowledge. Some of the more exuberantly thoughtless articulated a raw, expansionist view of scientific knowledge, but most were conscious of limitations. These could be of a technical kind, but the debate also focused on the conceptual structure of science itself. Could science really offer the prospect of total knowledge? What areas might always lie, by definition, beyond discovery? Clearly, the candidacy of psychology, the knowledge of the human mind, was proposed as a key instance or test case. Among scientists, the informed position was agnostic, the word itself suddenly capturing an unnamed mood after Huxley's inspired coinage of it in 1869 at a meeting of the Metaphysical Society.[17] But scientific agnosticism was not just a matter of reserving judgement about the existence of God. In these debates, agnosticism was more of an epistemological issue than a religious one (though the latter grabbed the headlines), and to some degree it expressed an anxiety on the part of scientists that their territorial adventure might be overextended. It implied a declaration of limitation about the real extent of human knowledge, and an attitude of open-minded provisionality in relation to it. Some things, agnostics declared, we will know; many things we will not. Epistemological agnosticism accepts that error and limitation are structural features of human knowing.

These were strong, attractive arguments to liberal minds in the climate of post-Darwinian debate over the legitimacy of inferences about general purposes in nature. But we should not necessarily take them at face value, or underestimate the shaping context of their formulation. The apparent flaunting of scientific limitation was often, in fact, an aggressive, carefully stage-managed confession

---

[17] Desmond, *Huxley: The Devil's Disciple*, 373–4.

devised for disputatious purposes and aimed not so much at perceived short-comings in the scientific community as at the general debate in which, it was thought, unprovable metaphysical propositions needed to be shouldered aside. Questions about cosmic order were always being opened and they prowled in the background of all discussion. But the corrosive effect of the emphasis on agnostic provisionality changed the parameters of psychological debate. In advanced circles, conventional discussion of the qualities of consciousness, or taxonomical disputes about the proper ranking of the faculties, was no longer interesting. What was interesting, in this at times impetuous adventure in human enquiry, was the limits and possibilities of psychological knowledge. Could naturalistic knowledge of *all* human behaviour be achieved? Would this embrace all behaviour uniformly, from the reflex mechanism to the exercise of the ethical will? Could complex psychological entities—like Consciousness or the Will—be generated from what was known of the biological conditions of the organism alone? The posing of the questions profoundly readjusted the orientation of the debate.

Some, on the scientific side, remorselessly claimed that top-level questions concerning, for example, modes and qualities of consciousness, were merely fancy distractions. But the plangency of 'first-person' responses to such functional 'third-person' programmes could not so easily be gainsaid. Writers like Huxley were acutely aware of these issues, but they could be cleverly blunt in their postures of ignorance in order to finesse awkward questions: 'We class sensations along with *emotions*, and *volitions*, and *thoughts*, under the common head of *states of consciousness*. But what consciousness is, we know not; and how it is that anything so remarkable as a state of consciousness comes about as the result of irritating nervous tissue, is just as unaccountable as any other ultimate fact of nature.'[18] It is not so much the declaration of ignorance that is the key issue here. It is the refusal to read significance into natural processes. One result of this is (as we shall see in detail in Part Two of this book) that epistemology takes over from ontology as the main philosophical terrain of the dominant intellectual conversation in psychological circles in the latter part of the century. That this conversation quickly turned into an argument, and just as quickly became a furious row, was a sign of the times. The two armies circled each other, trying to begin a dialogue with assumptions and language both might acknowledge.[19]

---

[18] T. H. Huxley, *Lessons in Elementary Physiology*, rev. edn. (London, 1886), 202.

[19] Several contributors to James Paradis and Thomas Postlewait's collection *Victorian Science and Victorian Values: Literary Perspectives* (New York, 1981) make clear not only the inaccuracy of some literary characterizations of Victorian science, but also the way in which some scientific writers tried eagerly to explore common ground to mediate between increasingly splintered sections of the intellectual community. This was part of the original intention of the journal *Nature*—which featured a quotation from Wordsworth on its masthead—when it was founded in 1869. See David A. Roos, 'The "Aims and Intentions" of *Nature*' (pp. 159–80), and Donald R. Benson, 'Facts and Constructs: Victorian Humanists and Scientific Theorists on Scientific Knowledge' (pp. 299–318).

But the field was mined with polemic, and each side deployed itself in ornate manœuvres armed with the latest, penetrating rhetorical ammunition.

Once again, it is Huxley who provides the best example. In his book on the philosopher David Hume, published, like his essay 'On Sensation', in 1879, Huxley defined psychology in a way that would have horrified the encyclopaedists of the discourse of the soul:

Psychology is a part of the science of life or biology, which differs from the other branches of that science, merely in so far as it deals with the psychical, instead of the physical, phenomena of life.

As there is an anatomy of the body, so there is an anatomy of the mind; the psychologist dissects mental phenomena into elementary states of consciousness, as the anatomist resolves limbs, into tissues, and tissues into cells.[20]

This seems an assured and succinct declaration of psychology's new procedure, but we need to read it contextually and, in so doing, distinguish between a methodological statement and a programme of actual research, and between both of these and a provocative metaphor. The image of the psychologist as anatomist is one we shall encounter many times in this book. It was used regularly throughout the century (as the impish Huxley well knew) by physiological psychology's opponents to characterize what they wanted their readers to understand as the new science's offensive, morbid invasiveness into the human mind. So here Huxley is playing a game he delighted in: baiting traditionalists with their own language. His statement *looks* programmatic, but we need, therefore, to take even more note of its context, because it expresses a hope more than a reality.

It comes from a book in the popular 'English Men of Letters' series, written to the moment for a handsome advance and a general readership. It is a book of philosophy (not science), and treats a philosopher still understood as controversial. Writing at top speed, Huxley was encouraged to be topical by John Morley, Lewes's radically minded successor as editor of the *Fortnightly* and the general editor of the series.[21] Though statements such as the one quoted above appear confidently programmatic, because of Huxley's characteristically assertive manner, they in fact cover a degree of uncertainty, which, in part, follows from his awareness of difficulties in both research definition and data collection. The statement appears to assume, for instance, that there is an agreed, stable corpus of psychological data of a kind similar to the anatomical fact that the normal human body contains 206 bones. Huxley's statement implies that these data are not a matter of active enquiry but are already available to be worked over in theory. However, there is plenty of evidence that Huxley did not think this at all. As we have seen, in the *Lessons in Elementary Physiology*, he considered the

[20] Huxley, *Hume*, 50.
[21] Adrian Desmond, *Huxley: Evolution's High Priest* (London, 1997), 115–18.

problem of consciousness 'unaccountable', and it was Huxley who promoted the virtues of rigorous epistemological agnosticism. The buoyant, no-nonsense, 'moralizing materialism' of his book on Hume (in Adrian Desmond's phrase[22]) successfully caught the mood of the times, as revealed in its substantial sales. But it illustrates the trickiness involved in separating fact from polemic in the still interdependent relationship between philosophy and physiological psychology. If physiological psychology was a new growth in this period (and it was), it occurred somewhat in the way new crops do in an already existing field structure. Physiological psychology needed to solve its scientific problems. But it also needed to change the general terms of debate about psychological issues, a task that Huxley, Lewes, and others took as their own.

A knot of broad conceptual issues dominated. These were succinctly summarized by Leslie Stephen in his *History of English Thought in the Eighteenth Century* (1876), in which Stephen amplified arguments he found in 'the school of Locke' for the post-Darwinian, physiological generation:

the tendency of the materialists was to get rid of reason. Not only innate ideas, but innate faculties, seemed to disappear. The reasoning process itself became nothing but a particular case of the mechanical action and reaction of material particles; and so far from the order of the universe being deducible from some primitive and necessary truths, the ultimate basis even of order must be chance, in the sense of essentially unknowable processes.[23]

Stephen's synopsis gathers the crucial topics. There is the question of how the 'higher' faculties (like reason) can be generated from 'lower' processes; there is the perception of an abrupt draining of significance as vital, human processes are reduced to mechanical actions; and there is the loss of teleological or other forms of ultimate meaning in processes whose significance appears either inscrutable or haphazard. This sense of bewildered loss was aggravated, for sensitive minds, by the apparently irrefutable nature of the new scientific findings.

This agenda dominated the physiological development of psychology across the nineteenth century. However, we need to be clear about the historical nature of the issues it proposed for itself. Though the forms taken by these problems present a characteristically 'Victorian' cluster of anxieties, the issues themselves are not, in essence, peculiar to that period. These are issues that transcended their time. One indication of this might be the appeal of modern treatments of them in popular, late-twentieth-century fiction about Victorian life by modern novelists such as John Fowles or A. S. Byatt.[24] Such fiction establishes a dialogue

---

[22] Ibid. 117.
[23] Leslie Stephen, *History of English Thought in the Eighteenth Century* (1876), 2 vols. (London, 1962), i. 55.
[24] I have in mind, especially, John Fowles's *The French Lieutenant's Woman* (1969) and A. S. Byatt's two novellas *Morpho Eugenia* and *The Conjugal Angel* (1992).

between the two ages on the basis of divergent responses to shared questions. But this does not mean that Victorian problems quietly awaited modern solutions. A good deal of recent popular scientific writing displays a fascination with concerns that are recognizably convergent with those of the Victorians (a number of these are examined in this book). Indeed, some of this writing (for example, that of Richard Dawkins) shows the same polemical drives and crusading need to persuade that are familiar from the immediately post-Darwinian climate of debate. Often this writing deals with identical topics, such as the issue of teleological purposes, or the elimination of wonder by what is perceived as 'scientific meddling', or—very popular presently—the understanding of consciousness. In the twenty-first century, we are more comfortable with the idea of chance development and worldly or provisional causality, and there is less emotional investment in a governing teleology from which we might be torn in pain and regret. We are less troubled, too, by the idea that meaning and significance are produced by human acts not metaphysical sanctions, and that a sense of purpose might be a creative act rather than a stoical necessity. We also have a better informed (though still far from complete) account of how physiological processes emerge as acts of mind. But, at the same time, recent writers struggle to agree on even the broad outlines of a theory of the evolutionary function of consciousness, and still seem at sea in 'first-person/third-person' issues, especially the piquant detail and intractable quiddity of 'me-ness'. Now as then, evolutionary neurophysiology is more comfortable with processes described at the level of populations rather than that of individuals. So, to a large extent, this book examines historically specific formulations of historically persistent issues. It looks at the forms envisaged for repeated problems, and at the particular answers imagined for them. In the period 1850–80, the main source of anxiety concerns psychology's imagining of the mind's comprehensive embodiment for the first time in history. It is a development that excites attention to issues in general biology, as well as at the specific level of the individual mind. So how might we characterize the Victorian vision of psychology's somatization as psycho-physiology?

The first thing to say is that the physiological body of nineteenth-century theory is curiously abstract. Most writers in the physiological tradition empty their language of the experience of bodily process, which is at first sight curious for a discipline centred on developmental growth. Lewes, for instance, described physiology as 'Anatomy in Action'.[25] But the 'first-person' perspective is rarely present in the nineteenth-century physiological literature except as rather barren anecdotage or in occasional, brief clinical references. The former is often as fleeting as it is uninteresting and lacks the sustained density of an engaging account of personhood. The latter, especially under nineteenth-century conventions, has

---

[25] G. H. Lewes, 'What is Sensation?', *Mind*, 1 (1876), 161.

the problem posed by the peculiarity of the atypical. As we shall see in the next chapter, Victorian clinical histories are rarely connected to average experience. So, in the mainstream of the discourse of physiology, it appears as though the ordinary body's most significant quality is its anonymity. There is a detached, curiously impersonal, even faintly *dis*embodied quality about it, even in the best writers. In a literal as well as a metaphorical sense, it is bloodless.

At first, this might appear a characteristic 'Victorian' evasion. But, as a good deal of recent work on both Victorian medicine and Victorian sexuality has shown, other discourses were not so reticent (though they could be negative). Sally Shuttleworth's work on Charlotte Brontë, the anthology she co-edited with Jenny Bourne Taylor, histories by Michel Foucault, Peter Gay, and Michael Mason among others, all show that, however one may assess their value, the discourses that described the Victorian body in these areas were not shy of sheer material viscosity.[26] But the body in *physiological* discourse is something else. The anonymous body described in the physiological literature, which appears to function as discretely as an efficient butler, of course owes a good deal to the calculatedly cool conventions of scientific description where purposes are heuristic, and representations diagrammatic. But issues arise from the universal adoption of this convention in physiological writing. Medical discourse also carries these heuristic requirements, yet the language of nineteenth-century medicine is often lurid with metaphor, and cantankerous with transplanted hopes and fears, as the scholars mentioned above have shown. This is partly explained by the stresses of human illness, no doubt, and the anxieties of the attempted cure, but why not in physiology also?

A clue to the sober, anonymous qualities considered desirable in physiological discourse is, in fact, given in the passage from Huxley's book on *Hume* quoted above. Huxley's model and point of reference is the *anatomist*. Anatomy, of course, is the technical rendition of body structures. Its skill lies in careful dissection and accurate rendition and, for obvious reasons, it works (mainly) on the dead. It has its own distinct representational conventions, and Huxley, a skilled draughtsman, often prepared his own drawings, like the one reproduced in Fig. 1 from his frequently reprinted textbook *Lessons in Elementary Physiology*. The disposition of this figure carries with it the hush and passivity of the dissecting room. It is, it appears, a death mask. As such, it falls, half-willingly, into the hands of

---

[26] Michel Foucault, *A History of Sexuality*, i. *An Introduction*, trans. Robert Hurley (Harmondsworth, 1979); Catherine Gallagher and Thomas Laqueur (eds.), *The Making of the Modern Body: Sexuality and Society in the Nineteenth Century* (London, 1987); Peter Gay, *The Bourgeois Experience: Victoria to Freud*, i. *The Education of the Senses* (Oxford, 1984) and *The Bourgeois Experience: Victoria to Freud*, ii. *The Tender Passion* (Oxford, 1986); Michael Mason, *The Making of Victorian Sexuality* (Oxford, 1994) and *The Making of Victorian Sexual Attitudes* (Oxford, 1995); Sally Shuttleworth, *Charlotte Brontë and Victorian Psychology* (Cambridge, 1996); Taylor and Shuttleworth (eds.), *Embodied Selves*.

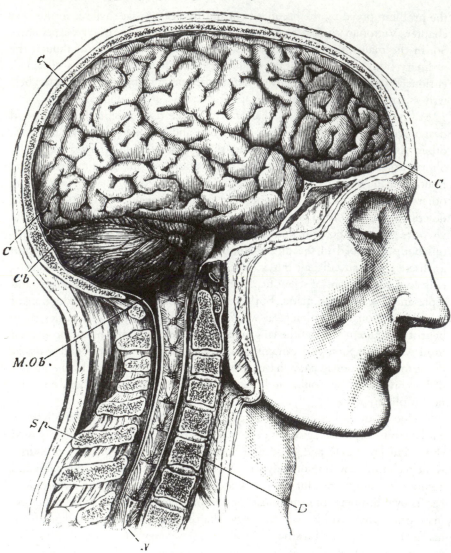

FIG. 1. From T. H. Huxley, *Lessons in Elementary Physiology* (London, 1886), 293

the opponents of physiological psychology, who accused it of morbidity, of
Frankensteinian meddling, of pathological reductionism. The flawless skin, peeled
away to reveal the innards, is a grotesquely fascinating image. The contrast between
the eerie, slack repose of the musculature, and the flenching violence imagined
in the process of laying it bare, plays a part in this. The flanged face also has
something in common, I think, with modern representations in science fiction

of the interface between the human and the machine, the RoboCop, the Terminator, the Six-Million-Dollar Man, in which skin surfaces are peeled away to reveal the clean lines of electrodes and microchips. This filmic iconography is, of course, itself borrowed from anatomical drawing.[27]

The comparison is not idle. In his autobiographical essay, Huxley described his early scientific interests:

my great desire was to be a mechanical engineer, but the Fates were against this; and, while very young, I commenced the study of Medicine under a medical brother-in-law. But, though the Institute of Mechanical Engineers would certainly not own me, I am not sure that I have not, all along, been a sort of mechanical engineer *in partibus infidelium*. . . . The only part of my professional course which really and deeply interested me was Physiology, which is the mechanical engineering of living machines . . .[28]

So the 'mechanical' side of Huxley's physiology is not accidental. Physiology understood as 'the mechanical engineering of living machines' crank-starts the style of Huxley's illustrations. It also motors the smooth-running lucidity of his verbal descriptions of physiological processes—as here, for example: 'Thus a living, active man, constantly exerts *mechanical force*, gives off *heat*, evolves *carbonic acid* and *water*, and undergoes a *loss of substance*.'[29] The pedagogical function of this is clear, and it is well executed (which was why *The Lessons* were so popular). However, this, from the essay 'On Sensation', has a less obviously compelling rationale:

Sensation is a product of the sensiferous apparatus caused by certain modes of motion which are set up in it by impulses from without. The sensiferous apparatuses are, as it were, factories, all of which at the one end receive raw materials of a similar kind— namely, modes of motion—while, at the other, each turns out a special product, the feeling which constitutes the kind of sensation characteristic of it.[30]

Dickens compared Bradley Headstone's mind to a warehouse in *Our Mutual Friend* to indicate his human deficits. Though a factory, unlike a warehouse, makes things of its own, and though Huxley intends his metaphor to be normative rather than aberrant, his comparison somehow appears even more chilling.[31]

[27] Jonathan Sawday makes a similar point, and dates the beginning of these conventions of anatomical drawing to the late sixteenth century when, under the influence of Descartes and others, the body came to be regarded as a machine (*The Body Emblazoned: Dissection and the Human Body in Renaissance Culture* (London, 1995), 133–4, 293).

[28] T. H. Huxley, 'Autobiography', in *Charles Darwin and T. H. Huxley: Autobiographies*, ed. Gavin de Beer (Oxford, 1983), 103.

[29] Huxley, *Lessons in Elementary Physiology*, 3.

[30] Huxley, 'On Sensation', in *Science and Culture*, 269.

[31] Again, Huxley's metaphor is not aberrant. Political economists of the period repeatedly used the same comparison. Alfred Marshall, who drew heavily on associationist theory, wrote in an early essay that, in industrial economies, 'the most important machine is man, and the most important thing produced is thought' (quoted by Schabas, 'Victorian Economics and the Science of Mind', 84). Dickens's satire on factory Utilitarianism in *Hard Times* makes much of this, of course.

It would be wrong to see this as a merely personal issue. Georges Canguilhem points out that nineteenth-century conceptions of the physiology of the nervous system 'were based in part upon analogies with operations or objects which were familiar by dint of construction and/or use of machines'. This helped secure acceptance of ideas that could be visibly correlated with startling advances in the technological world. The revelation of the body's mechanisms could command by association the prestige of astonishing technology (as we ourselves have seen in modern psychological models based upon computers). 'Progress in this branch of physiology,' Canguilhem writes, 'whose discoveries were incorporated into psychology, earned it widespread recognition.'[32] Historians have also pointed out that physiology in this period was generally dominated by a static anatomical model rather than one that emphasized energy systems or transformative processes.[33] The reasons for this lay in the nature of medical education as well as intellectual and scientific history, but all developments were based upon the centuries-old tradition of understanding the body as a form of machine. Known as 'iatro-mechanism', this view dominated a good deal of eighteenth-century physiolo-gical thought and was encouraged by, among other things, a post-Cartesian dualism that divided humans into body and soul, machine and spirit, with the implica-tion that the body could be conceptualized as a passive, reified non-participant in mental life.[34] It is a view that is very pronounced, for example, in David Hartley's influential marriage of the association of ideas, sensationalist theory, Natural Theology, and iatromechanical physiology in *Observations on Man* (1749), which was such an influence in the nineteenth century. Writers such as Huxley, Lewes, and Mill championed Hartley as a pioneer of the physiological psychology of the 1860s and 1870s.[35]

---

[32] Georges Canguilhem, *A Vital Rationalist: Selected Writings*, ed. François Delaporte, trans. Arthur Goldhammer (New York, 1994), 122–3.

[33] William F. Bynum, 'The Anatomical Method, Natural Theology, and the Functions of the Brain', *Isis*, 64 (1973), 445–68; Desmond, *Politics of Evolution*; Geison, 'Social and Institutional Factors'; Schiller, 'Physiology's Struggle for Independence'.

[34] Theodore M. Brown, 'From Mechanism to Vitalism in Eighteenth-Century English Physiology', *Journal of the History of Biology*, 7 (1974), 179–216; William Coleman, 'Mechanical Philosophy and Hypothetical Physiology', in Robert Patter (ed.), *The Anus Mirabilis of Sir Isaac Newton 1666–1966*, (Cambridge, Mass., 1970), 322–32; P. M. Heimann and J. E. McGuire, 'Newtonian Forces and Lockean Powers: Concepts of Matter in Eighteenth-Century Thought', *Historical Studies in the Physical Sciences*, 3 (1971), 233–306; R. E. Schofield, *Mechanism and Materialism: British Natural Philosophy in an Age of Reason* (Princeton, 1970); John W. Yolton, *Thinking Matter: Materialism in Eighteenth-Century Britain* (Minneapolis, 1983).

[35] Huxley, 'On Sensation', in *Science and Culture*, 250–1; Lewes, *History of Philosophy*, ii. 368, 372; John Stuart Mill, 'Bain's Psychology', in *Essays on Philosophy and the Classics: Collected Works of John Stuart Mill*, xi, ed. J. M. Robson (London, 1978), 341; George Croom Robertson, 'Psychology and Philosophy', *Mind*, 8 (1883), 5; Ribot, *English Psychology*, 37. For comment, see *Brett's History of Psychology*, 437; R. C. Oldfield and K. Oldfield, 'Hartley's *Observations on Man*', *Annals of Science*, 7 (1951), 371–81; Robert M. Young, *Mind, Brain and Adaptation*, 97.

The physiology of Hartley's speculations is unswervingly, if adventurously, iatromechanical. He imagined the nervous system as a network of 'solid capillamenta'—cords or fibres—that transmit vibrations along their surface to the white medullary substance of the brain, which somehow translates them into sensations and ideas. In the reverse direction, the same network enables the execution of motor tasks through a system of 'diminutive vibrations' called by Hartley 'vibratiuncles'. These are copied from the primary system, which is derived, in the tradition of post-Lockean philosophy and the association of ideas, from environmental stimulation.[36] Overall, the two systems resemble, or are a sort of forerunner of, the sensory-motor arc, whose neurology was established at the beginning of the nineteenth century.

Hartley's system implies strict homogeneity of structure and function across not just the physical system but the mental also, and it proposes a vanishingly small role for consciousness. Medullary vibrations, to all intents and purposes, are identical to sensations and ideas in their aetiology and psychological status, and the system functions by virtue of this regularity just as a machine can only function by consistency of input and process. Metaphors derived from machines and other human contrivance dominate Hartley's language: the action of pendulums, particles in sounding bodies, the transmission of heat and light, the operation of ground lenses and musical strings, mechanical friction, the action of magnets in mechanical parts, and the discharge of guns all feature in the first fifty pages. The 'higher' faculties are derived on a similar pattern. The will, for example, is 'that desire or aversion, which is strongest for the present time', and, since 'all love and hatred, all desire and aversion, are factitious, and generated by association, *i.e.* mechanically, it follows that the will is mechanical also'.[37]

Hartley's neurological conceits had strong influence. Huxley's essay 'On Sensation', in which the nervous system is imagined as a factory, places itself explicitly in this tradition. 'In truth,' Huxley writes, 'the theory of sensation . . . is, at the present moment, very much where Hartley . . . left it a hundred and twenty years since . . . [and] Hartley's propositions embody the most probable conclusions which are to be drawn from the latest investigations of physiologists.'[38] Hartley also made a bequest of metaphor. His networked body, criss-crossed by fibrous capillamenta, drew on a common eighteenth-century image pool used by writers seeking to express complex, intermingled states of feeling and thinking.[39] Feelings and ideas zoomed up and down this networked body, and as they did so the metaphorical register of the mechanical wires evolved

[36] Hartley, *Observations*, 5, 37.    [37] Ibid. 233.
[38] Huxley, 'On Sensation', in *Science and Culture*, 250–1.
[39] Rousseau, 'Nerves, Spirits, and Fibres'.

into organic filaments and tissues.[40] There is an observable development from the neurophysiology of 'first causes' (i.e. divine ordinance) to one focused on observable phenomena, and from a neurology of effluvia (the movement through tubular nerves of spiritous substance) to that of energetic impulses like Hartley's vibrations.[41]

These images were taken up and adapted by Victorian writers. George Eliot's often-noted deployment of images of tissues, threads, and vibrations is a direct descendant, but usage was general. Here is George Borrow in 1851. He is describing his feelings as a child on receiving his first present of a book. This opens a new world for him:

All at once a strange sensation came over me, such as I had never experienced before— a similar blending of curiosity, awe and pleasure, the remembrance of which, even at this distance of time, produces a remarkable effect upon my nervous system. What strange things are the nerves—I mean those more secret and mysterious ones in which I have some notion that the mind and soul, call it what you will, has its habitation; how they constantly tingle and vibrate before any coming event closely connected with the future weal and woe of the human being. Such a feeling was now within me, certainly independent of what the eye had seen or the ear had heard.[42]

Physiological and literary discourses interpenetrate here in an account of the physicality of memory and premonition embodied in nerves that 'tingle and vibrate'. The register is obviously Hartleyan, and the passage is clearly composed in the sensationalist tradition (though whether the author was as conscious of this as Huxley is less certain). Borrow equivocates somewhat in his distinction between ordinary nerves and 'those more secret and mysterious ones', but 'the soul or mind, call it what you will' (the terminological prevarication was itself not without significance in 1851), definitely has a physical location as well as physical properties. The significant points in this passage are not only its claim that intuition has organic sources, and its unforced willingness to give this an explicitly physiological basis, but also its participation in an established metaphorical tradition with a clear, if imprecise, physical basis and register of effects.

---

[40] George Dyson's fascinating recent book *Darwin among the Machines* (London, 1998) demonstrates the longevity of this idea. Dyson hypothesizes that the conditions for genuine machine intelligence are created, not so much by the capacities of individual machines, but by the interlinked power of machines connected over the web. This interlinking, he argues, replicates some of the conditions for the production of animal intelligence.

[41] W. P. D. Wightman, 'Wars of Ideas in Neurological Science—from Willis to Bichat and from Locke to Condillac', in F. N. L. Poynter (ed.), *The Brain and its Functions* (Oxford, 1958), 144.

[42] George Borrow, *Lavengro: The Scholar—The Gypsy—The Priest* (1851; London, 1961), 21. For a representative medical endorsement of similar metaphors, see J. G. Millingen, 'Memory and the Mental Faculties', in his *Curiosities of Medical Experience*, 2nd edn. (London, 1839), 408.

One direct response to iatromechanism in physiology was biological vitalism, and, by the beginning of the nineteenth century, this was an equally dominant presence in public debate, almost as though it were the companion half of the Cartesian dualism of soul and body. Vitalism provided the physiological spirit for the body's machine.[43] With roots in German *Naturphilosophie*, vitalistic theories emphasized, for the Romantic generation, a superadded principle of life that animated inert matter and created the special character of all life forms, but of human life especially. Radical materialists might picture people as anonymous, self-activating machines, but vitalistic theories distinguished human life by its special, superadded, vital spark. Such reasoning was clearly congruent with Christian arguments concerning the soul, and was pressed by such influential post-Romantic proselytizers as Carlyle—for example, in 'Signs of the Times' (1829). It was also congruent with arguments in Natural Theology concerning nature's favouritism towards human beings. Indeed, such was the strength and influence of this tradition that Christian and conservative theorists in the first third of the nineteenth century considered nervous anatomy and physiology their own particular preserve, and it dominated the Royal College of Surgeons and other powerful institutions. According to L. S. Jacyna, 'the nervous system was a favoured object of inquiry for British investigators precisely because it offered an especially promising field for the display of divine providence and of man's unique place in the natural order'.[44] Among those attracted to it were Coleridge and his followers. Coleridge's vision of the ideological role of vitalistic theory, as well as his own biological speculations and conception of the human mind's special powers, attracted influential Tory patrons like J. H. Green.[45] However, Anglican orthodoxy and Tory politics were not essential for belief in biological vitalism. The theological implications of vitalistic doctrines also appealed to young professional scientists like the Unitarian William Carpenter, who exclaimed in 1838

[43] E. Benton, 'Vitalism in Nineteenth-Century Physiological Thought: A Typology and Reassessment', *Studies in the History and Philosophy of Science*, 5 (1974), 25–9; Brown, 'From Mechanism to Vitalism'; Hilde Hein, 'The Endurance of the Mechanism–Vitalism Controversy', *Journal of the History of Biology*, 5 (1972), 159–88; L. S. Jacyna, 'Immanence or Transcendence: Theories of Life and Organization in Britain, 1790–1835', *Isis*, 74 (1983), 311–29; Jacyna, 'The Romantic Programme and the Reception of Cell Theory in Britain', *Journal of the History of Biology*, 17 (1984), 13–48; Jacyna, 'Principles of General Physiology: The Comparative Dimension of British Neuroscience in the 1830s and 1840s', in William Coleman and Camille Limoges (eds.), *Studies in the History of Biology 7* (London, 1984), 47–92; Everett Mendelsohn, 'Physical Models and Physiological Concepts: Explanation in Nineteenth-Century Biology', *British Journal for the History of Science*, 2 (1965), 201–19.

[44] Jacyna, 'Principles of General Physiology', 48. See also Desmond, *Politics of Evolution*.

[45] Timothy J. Corrigan, '*Biographia Literaria* and the Language of Science', *Journal of the History of Ideas*, 41 (1980), 399–419; J. H. Haeger, 'Coleridge's "Bye Blow": The Composition and Date of *Theory of Life*', *Modern Philology*, 74 (1976), 20–41; Levere, *Poetry Realized in Nature*, 206 ff.; Wylie, *Young Coleridge*, 122 ff. For Green, see the previous chapter.

over the 'beauty and harmony [revealed by physiology] in which the contemplative mind delights to recognize the wisdom and beneficence of the Divine Author of the universe'.[46]

Though vitalistic theory was widely challenged in scientific circles in the mid-century, its arguments could still be mobilized effectivley in the 1870s, when their pertinence appeared refreshed by post-Darwinian controversies. A typical review of Darwin's *The Descent of Man* (1871) in the *Edinburgh* neatly collects the standard arguments directed towards psychology. The reviewer objected to evolutionary theory and noted that:

still less can the theory explain the phenomena of mind. We owe indeed to Mr Darwin some gratitude for his attempt to explain the origin of the intellectual faculties by the purely materialistic argument, since his failure is that of one of the greatest natural philosophers who has ever attempted to approach this most difficult problem. It might indeed occur to some that this method of dealing with the subject would be about as likely to result in the discovery of truth as that of a chemist who should approach the deepest and most abstruse phenomena presented to physiology by means of analysis, without taking into account the vital processes which transcend his skill. Mr Darwin, before he can fairly argue from matter to mind, must prove that they are both the same thing, which is manifestly impossible.[47]

These arguments assume a categorical difference not only between species but also between mind and matter. The purchase of physiological analysis on man's higher faculties is denied, partly by a rhetorical sleight of hand that reduces physiology to chemistry. Throughout this period, vitalistic arguments are attached to psychological propositions to inflate humanity's special status. T. S. Baynes, also in the *Edinburgh* the following year, claimed that there is

in human life and human history a new power, manifesting itself by new and distinctive products, of which no traces are found in any form of merely animal life. This power is conscious intelligence, which determines a vital difference in kind in all the activities of the human mind, from the highest to the lowest. . . . Even the operations of sense, in a being endowed with self-consciousness, are conditioned by the higher attribute.[48]

This argument reverses all the priorities of physiological psychology. Here, the attributes of human consciousness, specifically intelligence, create biological and physiological conditions, not the other way round.

---

[46] William B. Carpenter, 'The Method and Aim of the Study of Physiology' (1838), in *Nature and Man*, 157. Originally entitled 'Physiology an Inductive Science', this essay was first published in the specialist *British and Foreign Medical Review*. For helpful comment on Carpenter in relation to these debates, see Jacyna, 'Principles of General Physiology', and Roger Smith, 'The Human Significance of Biology: Carpenter, Darwin and the *vera causa*', in U. C. Knoepflmacher and G. B. Tennyson (eds.), *Nature and the Victorian Imagination*, (London, 1977), 216–30.
[47] [W. Boyd Dawkins], 'Darwin on the Descent of Man', *Edinburgh Review*, 134 (1871), 207.
[48] [Baynes], 'Tylor on Primitive Culture', 118.

The collision between mechanistic and vitalistic theories troubled psychological debate through most of the century. For example, June Goodfield-Toulmin has shown how the ideological pressures of the post-Revolutionary period forced William Lawrence to abandon his tentative work on nervous organization under pressure of public attacks that associated it with 'French Materialism'. As she makes clear, the scientific groundwork was in this instance too slender to maintain explanations that were thought to challenge the prevailing vitalism, and Lawrence quickly withdrew his book—*Lectures on Physiology, Zoology and the Natural History of Man* (1819)—and retreated to his (thereafter, highly successful) medical practice.[49] No doubt the political pressures of this period were particularly severe, but the implications of the 'Lawrence affair' rumbled on through the century and became a reference point for quarrels between the new science and old philosophy, innovatory knowledge and reactionary inhibition. Lawrence's book was pirated by the radical press, and Coleridge was still sneering at it in *On the Constitution of Church and State* a decade later as a byword for immature, freethinking speculation.[50] By the mid-century, materialistic physiologists had a more secure standing ground, but one need only mention the evolution debates to recognize a fraught public context for an area of investigation seen to interfere with prevailing conceptions of man. Goodfield-Toulmin notes that, in his preface to *Man's Place in Nature* of 1863, T. H. Huxley (who was a friend of Lawrence) explicitly invoked parallels between his own predicament as a champion of evolution and the hostility visited on Lawrence in 1819.

G. H. Lewes, too, was alert to the ideological force that could be mobilized behind charges of 'materialism', and to the complex mediations between science, philosophy, and politics that the period demanded. In 'The Present Condition of Philosophy', the conclusion to his enlarged *History of Philosophy* in 1867, Lewes lambasts a culture ideologically geared to reject unpalatable scientific findings. Science 'should be refuted as false, not denounced as dangerous. Research is arduous enough without obstructing the path with bugbears.'[51] Like Huxley, he made a parallel with the period after the French Revolution to indicate the difficulties experienced by contemporaries. It is a passage worth quoting at length, because it reveals a physiological psychologist's own sense of the means by which historical pressures deform ideas. Of the post-Revolution period Lewes writes:

The reaction against the Philosophy of the Eighteenth Century was less a reaction against a doctrine that had proved to be incompetent than against a doctrine believed to be the source of frightful immorality . . . Associated in men's mind with the Saturnalia of the

[49] June Goodfield-Toulmin, 'Some Aspects of English Physiology, 1780–1840', *Journal of the History of Biology*, 2 (1969), 283–320. See also Jacyna, 'Immanence or Transcendence'.

[50] S. T. Coleridge, *On the Constitution of Church and State According to the Idea of Each* (1830), ed. John Barrell (London, 1972), 7–8.

[51] Lewes, *History of Philosophy*, ii. 745.

Terror, the philosophical opinions of Condillac, Diderot and Cabanis were held responsible for the crimes of the Convention; and what might be true in those opinions was
flung aside with what was false, without discrimination, without analysis, in fierce impetuous disgust. Every opinion which had what was called 'a taint of materialism', or seemed
to point in that direction, was denounced as an opinion necessarily leading to the destruction of all Religion, Morality, and Government. Every opinion which seemed to point
in the direction of spiritualism was eagerly welcomed, promulgated, and lauded; not because
it was demonstrably true, but because it was supposed capable of preserving social order.
And indeed when, looking back on those times, we contemplate the misery and anarchy
which disgraced what was an inevitable movement, and dimmed what was really noble
in that movement, we can understand how many generous hearts and minds, fluctuating in perplexity, did instinctively revolt not only against the Revolution, but against
all the principles which were ever invoked by the revolutionists. Looking at the matter
from this distance we can see clearly enough that 'Materialism' had really no more to
do with the Revolution than Christianity had to do with the hideous scenes in which
the Anabaptists were actors; but we can understand how indelible was the association
of Revolution with materialism in the minds of that generation.

Towards the end of the paragraph, the reader is pushed towards a comfortable
historical retrospect. However, in his next—in a manner not unlike many
moments in George Eliot's fiction—Lewes surprises the reader with a return to
the pressing problems of the present:

So profoundly influential has this association been, that a celebrated surgeon of our own
day periled his position by advocating the opinion, now almost universally accepted,
but then generally shuddered at, that the brain is the 'organ' of the mind. He had to
retract that opinion, which the pious Hartley and many others had advanced without
offence. He had to retract it, not because it was scientifically untenable, but because it
was declared to be morally dangerous.[52]

Lewes presumably had William Lawrence in mind here, but the broad point is
central to his thinking and typical of the period.

John Morley, Lewes's successor as editor of the *Fortnightly Review* from the
mid-1860s, recollected that advanced physiological research inevitably mixed in
political company, at least for the readers of his review:

people justly perceived that there seemed to be a certain undefinable concurrence among
writers coming from different schools and handling very different subjects. Perhaps the
instinct was right which fancied it discerned some common drift, a certain pervading
atmosphere. People scented a subtle connection between speculations on the Physical
Basis of Life and the Unseen Universe, and articles on Trades Unions and National
Education; and Professor Tyndall's eloquence in impugning the authority of miracles
was supposed to work in the same direction as Mr Frederic Harrison's eloquence in

---

[52] Lewes, *History of Philosophy*, ii. 743–4.

demolishing Prince Bismarck and vindicating the Commune as the newest proof of the political genius of France.[53]

The political as well as scientific contention between vitalism and materialism thus persisted. Because vitalistic theories were seen to introduce occult entities into biomedical science, many found them unsatisfactory. But others were often unable to dispense with them entirely, not least because the rival theory was distastefully inhuman. Mary Shelley's *Frankenstein* (1817) provides a neat, if literary, illustration of a continuing theoretical dilemma. Her novel was directly influenced by William Lawrence, and Frankenstein's Creature is mechanistically contrived and animated by galvanic electricity.[54] He appears a 'material' creature through and through. But the theoretical status of the galvanic spark that gives him life is equivocal. Is it a purely mechanical ingredient, or a superadded, vitalizing force? Mechanistic theories in psychology presented similar difficulties. If 'the mechanical engineering of living machines' (in Huxley's words) was like a factory, where did the particularities of human consciousness and culture find their resources? The Frankenstein story in this respect haunts a century of debate, with commentators on both sides abusing opponents for Frankensteinian proclivities.[55] The scientific problem, writes G. J. Goodfield, 'was to find the relation between the two realms—physico-chemical and vital—to find terms that would both allow for the plasticity of organic processes, and at the same time relate them to the familiar regularities of the inorganic world'.[56] But the broader issues appeared even more intractable.

One important aspect of this debate concerned the prospect of human automatism. This controversy was familiar from the 1840s, but it came to a head in the 1870s when post-Darwinian debate amplified anxieties over the direction of psychological theory.[57] The controversy turned on the mechanistic implications immanent in physiological psychology when extended not only to the higher

[53] John Morley, 'Valedictory' (1882), in *Nineteenth-Century Essays*, selected and introduced by Peter Stansky (London, 1970), 290–1.

[54] Marilyn Butler, 'The First *Frankenstein* and Radical Science', *Times Literary Supplement*, 9 Apr. 1993, 12–14. Robert Chambers, a quarter of a century after *Frankenstein*, had not got much further. He insisted that electricity was the force that powered both mind and body, but, he asserted positively, 'electricity is almost as metaphysical as ever mind is supposed to be' (*Vestiges*, 334).

[55] For example, H. L. Mansel describes the monstrosity of materialist 'speculation' in these terms (*Lecture on Kant*, 31–9). More cheekily, W. K. Clifford reversed the argument picturing the vitalistic, Kantian human being as a 'Frankensteinian monster' made by God without free will ('Body and Mind' (1874), in *Lectures and Essays*, ii. 58.) This allegorical possibility is, of course, suggested by Mary Shelley's tale itself. For extended discussion, see Baldick, *In Frankenstein's Shadow*.

[56] G. J. Goodfield, *The Growth of Scientific Physiology* (London, 1960), 101. See also Mendelsohn, 'Physical Models and Physiological Concepts'.

[57] Roger Smith, 'The Human Significance of Biology', 222. For general discussion, see L. S. Jacyna, 'The Physiology of Mind, the Unity of Nature, and the Moral Order in Victorian Thought', *British Journal for the History of Science*, 14 (1981), 109–32.

faculties, but to the concept of the whole person. Psycho-physiological humanity increasingly appeared to resemble machines in the writing of energetic and
aggressive polemicists such as Huxley, Tyndall, and Clifford. Their pronouncements actively encouraged speculation in this direction, and, if the physiological
body could appear mechanistic, so too might the mind. They denied holding
such views, and usually stopped short of a full assertion of this position (their
agnosticism, avoiding universalist statements on principle, would not allow such
generalization, nor would their political tact). But they often left little braking
distance between the momentum of their arguments and this conclusion.

John Tyndall's position, in a celebrated address to the British Association for
the Advancement of Science at Norwich in 1868, was representative. Tyndall restated
the view that, for the scientist, natural processes were 'a purely mechanical
problem'. The materialist, he declared, argues that 'the growth of the body is
mechanical, and that thought, as exercised by us, has its correlative in the physics
of the brain', though it is not legitimate to infer that 'molecular groupings, and
motions, explain everything'.[58] Most heard the first part of this statement, found
the implication, and set aside the rest. Tyndall's caution was a proper scientific
hesitation, as well as prudent intellectual and ideological abstention, but it only
checked, and did not halt, the direction of the argument.

Tyndall's views were much cited and discussed by parties on both sides.[59] But
the issue was alive in other hands. Huxley, in his consideration of the subject
in 1874, scorned the doctrines of dualists, vitalists, and Idealists and proposed
a more specific correlation of physiology and consciousness:

It is quite true that, to the best of my judgement, the argumentation which applies to
brutes holds equally good of men; and therefore, that all states of consciousness in us,
as in them, are immediately caused by molecular changes of the brain substance. It seems
to me that in men, as in brutes, there is no proof that any state of consciousness is the
cause of change in the motion of the matter of the organism . . . it follows that our
mental conditions are simply the symbols in consciousness of the changes which take
place automatically in the organism; and that, to take an extreme illustration, the feeling that we call volition is not the cause of a voluntary act, but the symbol of that state
of the brain which is the immediate cause of the act. We are conscious automata, endowed
with free will in the only intelligible sense of that much abused term—in as much as
in many respects we are able to do as we like—but none the less we are parts of the
great series of causes and effects which, in unbroken continuity, composes that which
is, and has been, and shall be—the sum of existence.[60]

---

[58] John Tyndall, *Fragments of a Science: A Series of Detached Essays, Addresses, and Reviews*,
2 vols., 9th edn. (London, 1902), ii. 85–7.
[59] See e.g. Calderwood, 'Present Relations', 231, and James, *Principles of Psychology*, i. 147.
[60] T. H. Huxley, 'On the Hypothesis that Animals are Automata, and its History' (1874), in
*Science and Culture and Other Essays*, 239–40.

Huxley denied fatalism, materialism, and atheism, and hid his swashbuckling message in liturgical rhythms. Ducking and diving with characteristic agility, and looking for convenient allies, he claimed that 'predestinarian' theologians and philosophers authorized his case. Augustine, Calvin, Leibnitz, Hartley, and others, he asserted, all recommended Christian faith on identical premises. But the spectre of automatism was not exorcised. The abstraction of the physiological body, neither fully disappearing nor yet becoming fully corporeal, and haunting the liminal area between machine and animal, troubled scientific speculation and conservative nightmare alike. Its function remained primarily heuristic and schematic, but this quality nourished the fears and, as a result, the physiological automaton clanks into humanistic and traditionalist dreams as one part of a monstrous Siamese twin whose other head is that of a Darwinian beast. This composite monster, half meccano, half brute, plods out of the nineteenth century as a dual-purpose fantasy of the scientific future. For scientific optimists, the physiological body represents a dream goal of rational (and remedial) enquiry, but for others it represents an invasive creature created by the intellectual perversity of the secular mind. Both conclusions are available in the studied neutrality of Huxley's vision: 'as surely as every future grows out of the past and present, so will the physiology of the future gradually extend the realm of matter and law until it is co-extensive with knowledge, with feeling and with action.'[61]

There were, of course, pro-scientific voices who opposed automaticist doctrines. Carpenter, as a Unitarian, criticized Huxley for abolishing the higher faculties, especially the will, in an obsession with mechanism.[62] G. H. Lewes was conscious of extremist arguments on both sides, and his discussion of 'Mechanism and Experience' in *The Study of Psychology* (1879), the fourth volume of *Problems of Life and Mind*, was one of the few genuinely judicious attempts to stand apart from the main lines of battle. This was partly because he situated the debate in the context of comparable European work, and avoided overinflating the tentative and provisional claims of physiological investigation. But it is also because he takes the sensible step—strangely rarely pursued—of insisting that mental development is not just a question of physiological processes. For Lewes, as we shall see in detail in Chapter 7, it was just as much a question of social development.[63] Others, meanwhile, were troubled by the ersatz metaphysics implied in the more extreme of automaticist pronouncements. Huxley may have intended to pre-empt Christian objections by linking his physiological psychology to predestination (though his extreme rationalist determinism led him in that direction anyway), but it also alienated secular-minded supporters. William James,

---

[61] T. H. Huxley, 'On the Physical Basis of Life', *Fortnightly Review*, NS 5 (1869), 143.
[62] William B. Carpenter, 'On the Doctrine of Human Automatism', *Contemporary Review*, 25 (1875), 397–416.                    [63] Lewes, *Problems*, iv. 29–38.

reviewing the debate in 1890, dismissed 'the automaton theory' as 'an *unwarrantable impertinence*' because it mirrored the assertions of its opponents when urged 'on *a priori* and *quasi*-metaphysical grounds'.[64]

Part of the problem lay in the inherent limitations of nineteenth-century psycho-physiological projects, and their sporadic, but massive, theoretical over-extension. Relevant physiological research was primarily found in two areas of investigation: that of the sensory-motor arc (which linked brain and mind to the environment through the nervous system), and that of the localization of the cerebral functions in the anatomy of the brain. A linkage between these two, it was thought, would specify physiologically the circuitry of human behaviour. In retrospect, it is easy to see how rudimentary a basis this was for understanding the capacities of human beings. But it is also easy to underestimate the excitement of original discovery. The sensory-motor arc (established in the first decades of the century by Sir Charles Bell in Britain and François Magandie in France, and developed by Marshall Hall in Britain and Johannes Müller in Germany thereafter), and the more elusive hope of localizing the cerebral functions, provided research foundations for general models of considerable (if rather wide and provisional) explanatory power over a long period. What Clifford Geertz, in 1962, described as physiological psychology's 'long enthralment with the wonders of the reflex arc' persisted well into the twentieth century.[65]

It bears repeating at this point that we are not by and large dealing in this book with scientific work that satisfied the theoretical hopes it inspired. Nor with discoveries that, passing all tests of verification, turned the direction of all subsequent work. We are dealing, instead, with a range of arguments, assumptions, opinions, and knowledge which both prepares, and inhibits, the fortunes of disputed theory as it rises and falls. With hindsight, the overinflation of the explanatory power of physiological models based upon the sensory-motor arc and cerebral localization can appear as absurd to us as it appeared alarming to contemporaries. To explain the whole of human activity in terms of the sensory-motor arc is like explaining how a computer works in terms of the flow of power from the electrical grid. Explaining the same thing by cerebral localization is—to follow the metaphor (and without wishing to imply that minds are computers, because they are not)—like pinning one's explanatory hopes on the simple spatial positioning of microchips. Both are crucial, but hardly sufficient. On the other hand, nor is a computer explained by the witnessing of the operations it performs (which might be an analogy for the arguments of the faculty psychologists). Physiological psychology in the nineteenth century was at work somewhere between the extremes of mechanical determinism and

[64] James, *Principles of Psychology*, i. 138.
[65] Geertz, 'The Growth of Culture and the Evolution of Mind', in *The Interpretation of Cultures*, 70.

airy denial, and it is well to remind ourselves that such denials could go to extra-ordinary lengths.

John Gordon, an influential anatomist in Edinburgh in the early decades of the century, was an extremist. He denied not only iatromechanical theories but vitalistic ones also. For him, even the notion of a vital spark smacked too much of the materialization of the soul.[66] Gordon reviewed the psycho-physiological debate in an essay on 'Functions of the Nervous System' in the *Edinburgh Review* in 1815. He begins on a note of ill-founded optimism: 'Speculations respecting the nature of Mind seem now universally abandoned as endless and unprofitable. Metaphysicians rest satisfied with the truth that the mental phenomena are ultimately dependent on something essentially distinct from mere Matter; and content themselves with the patient study of the laws, by which these phenomena are regulated.'[67] This is a classic, programmatic statement of the traditional faculty psychology. What is more interesting, however, is the extraordinary and lengthy vehemence of Gordon's denial, based upon purported clinical evidence, not just that the higher faculties might be located in the cerebrum, but that the brain has any role *at all* in the workings of the mind. The bulk of the article is a cata-logue of autopsy results from the examinations of brain-damaged individuals, many of them soldiers returning from the war, whose lives had either been little affected by spectacularly gross injury, or who lived a surprisingly long time after it. As well as stories of sword stabs and musket shots, there is a boy of 14 with a three-inch cavity in the left hemisphere full of pus, a man 'whose sensibility remained unaffected till within a few hours of his death; and yet there was found in his brain, an abscess occupying nearly one third of the substance of the right hemisphere, communicating by a large ulcerated opening with the anterior extremity of the right ventricle, and penetrating, by a small orifice, to the inferior surface of the anterior lobe',[68] a man with the whole right hemisphere destroyed by suppuration, a man 'who had not been insensible in any part of the body' whose *corpus striatum* was 'converted into matter like the dregs of wine', a woman whose cerebellum was 'converted into a bag of purulent matter', and a man whose cerebellum was 'without the last vestige of natural structure'.[69] There are abscesses found in the brain weighing half a pound, discharges of brain matter the size of hen's eggs, pigeon's eggs, and nutmegs, accompanied by quarts of liquid; brains have shrunk to two inches diameter, there is a 'brown vascular mass' instead of a brain,[70] and children live without any brain at all, including one whose vital functions were unimpaired for eighteen months. On his sudden, unexpected death, the cranium was opened and 'more than five quarts

---

[66] [John Gordon], 'Abernathy on Vital Principles', *Edinburgh Review*, 23 (1814), 384–98.
[67] [John Gordon], 'Functions of the Nervous System', *Edinburgh Review*, 24 (1815), 439.
[68] Ibid. 441.    [69] Ibid. 443–4.    [70] Ibid. 447.

of very limpid water were found within it; but there was not the smallest trace of membrane, or of brain, except opposite the orbits and *meatus auditorius*, where something like *medulla* still remained'.[71] 'Although we have no doubt', Gordon preposterously concludes, 'that the total destruction of the brain alone . . . will in general be followed by partial or total insensibility, yet we think it has already been shown, that this is not always the consequence.'[72]

Aspirations are as important in scientific as in any other kind of enquiry, and hopes can influence theories. The increasingly confident acceptance that mind was dependent on the architecture of the brain and the nervous system, the inherent, if incautious, fascination aroused by the new neurological discoveries, the enticing possibility of consistent, naturalistic explanations crossing the barriers between mental and physical events, the yearning urgency of linking mind and body like two separated members of an unfortunate family, all of these played a part in the imaginative expectations of physiological psychology in the nineteenth century.[73] Put like this, investigations in physiological psychology present themselves as epic enticements. But hopes are not facts, nor causes necessarily uniform and simple; correlations are not always exact, nor desirable explanations full and thorough. The discovery by Pierre Paul Broca in the 1860s, through the dissection of the brains of recently deceased motor aphasiacs, that a specific part of the left hemisphere of the brain is necessarily implicated in the use of language, validated the hypothesis that the advanced cerebral functions are anatomically localizable.[74] However, the significance of this and other findings is difficult to measure. It is clearly a major physiological breakthrough. But the identification of 'Broca's convolution' in the lowest frontal gyrus of the brain does not explain what conditions and processes govern the acquisition of language in general human development. Nor does it tell us much about its use in individual circumstances. Nor does it explain very much about its role in human cultures. Nor, for that matter, does it specify very thoroughly the role of these localized centres in the whole neurobiological system. The same point

---

[71] [John Gordon], 'Functions of the Nervous System', *Edinburgh Review*, 24 (1814), 446–7.

[72] Ibid. 451.

[73] For acknowledgement of this, see G. H. Lewes's own account of the long gestation of *Problems of Life and Mind* in his preface to the first volume dated September 1873. He had first planned 'a treatise on the philosophy of Mind in which the doctrines of Reid, Stewart, and Brown were to be physiologically interpreted' in lectures delivered at Fox's Chapel, Finsbury, in 1837. With its origins in dissenting radicalism, autodidacticism, breathtaking, transdisciplinary ambition, and eventual progress to an unfinished five volumes and 2,000 pages, *Problems of Life and Mind* might stand as a sort of simulacrum of much of the mid-Victorian psycho-physiological project. The physiological interpretation of Common Sense philosophy, incidentally, was abandoned because of lack of progress in physiology and 'growing dissatisfaction with the doctrines of the Scotch school'. That, too, is typical (Lewes, *Problems*, i, p. v).

[74] For discussion, see Robert M. Young, *Mind, Brain, and Adaptation*, ch. 4; Jeannerod, *Brain Machine*, 71 ff.

can be made about David Ferrier's even more complicated localization of sight. In this case, after Ferrier's results were announced, German work quickly distinguished between 'sensorial blindness' (total insensibility to light) and 'psychic blindness', the 'inability to recognize the *meaning* of optical impressions'. The psychological, let alone the physiological differences between these two conditions —whose discrimination was based on clinical evidence rather than pathological data and animal vivisection, as Ferrier's were—was not resolved even by the time William James came to comment on the matter in 1890.[75]

The conceptual and explanatory gap between the hypothesis of a mechanism and an account of sophisticated behaviour can be illustrated by the frequently discussed example of phrenology. Phrenology was, for many in the nineteenth century as well as later, a nonsense science, but it is a useful example for these purposes for three reasons. First, it had an extraordinary popularity and a powerful public presence. It has been claimed, for instance, that George Coombe's *The Constitution of Man* (1828), the leading phrenological text of the period written in English, was perhaps the fourth most popular book in Britain between 1825 and 1850 after the Bible, *Pilgrim's Progress*, and *Robinson Crusoe*.[76] Secondly, phrenology had an influence on genuine research into the localized faculties, not least by providing a theoretical model that invited a programme of investigation.[77] Thirdly, this model provided a specified account of how actual behaviour might be correlated with anatomical and physiological features. In other words, it offered to bridge the gap, not just between mind and body, but also between the different discursive levels of 'first- and third-person' description.

Phrenological theory claimed to correlate specific brain portions directly with behaviour. Thus, in the familiar phrenological headmaps (which reminded John Gordon, the anatomist of brainless people, of the redrawn maps of Revolutionary France[78]), the skull is divided into small, unevenly sized areas that correspond to both the traditional faculties used by faculty psychologists (volition, ratiocination, etc.), and to others invented by phrenology ('Alimentiveness', 'Concentrativeness', 'Destructiveness', and so on). The correlations are manifested in the contours of the skull, and reading these 'head bumps' constituted the much ridiculed art of cranioscopy. Phrenology, therefore, argued for a determining relation between anatomy and character (and therefore destiny), and phrenology was seen as a 'gross materialism' by many, including the Christian commentator

[75] James, *Principles of Psychology*, i. 41 ff.

[76] Newsome, *Victorian World Picture*, 211. The gigantic success of Coombe's book was not lost on contemporaries. In 1852 an opponent, reviewing yet another new edition, reckoned it had already sold over 90,000 copies: [G. D. Campbell], 'Phrenology: Its Place and Relations', *North British Review*, 17 (1852), 41.

[77] Robert M. Young, *Mind, Brain and Adaptation*, ch. 1; R. J. Cooter, 'Phrenology: The Provocation of Progress', *History of Science*, 14 (1976), 211–34.

[78] [John Gordon], 'The Doctrines of Gall and Spurzheim', *Edinburgh Review*, 25 (1815), 251.

G. D. Campbell (the 8th Duke of Argyll) in an intelligently argued piece in 1852.[79] The 'Man of Bumps' (as Campbell wittily put it) was of the same kind as the machine man of anatomy-dominated physiology. Indeed, historians have since argued that the nineteenth-century fascination with cerebral localization is only a particularized version of the dominion of anatomical models in physiology.[80]

Phrenology had a number of points of appeal. The simplicity of the relationships it posited, and the possibility it offered of do-it-yourself, drawing-room application, brought a slang science to the multitudes. Phrenologists may use a portentous, pseudo-technical term like 'philoprogenitiveness', but everyone could recognize 'love of children' (its meaning) as an attribute at a 'first-person' level while enjoying the rhetorical thrill of 'third-person' jargon. So a patina of intellectual seriousness was harnessed to a personalized, future-predicting, and character-divining appeal similar to that of astrology. At the same time, the intellectually serious side of phrenology (that engaged with cerebral localization) was reinforced by its outlaw reputation in the medical establishment and among the stuffy pundits of respectable knowledge who lambasted it routinely in the great periodicals. It was also boosted by its adoption by weighty figures on the intellectual fringe, especially in a provincial culture like that of early nineteenth-century Coventry, where it briefly appealed to the awakened, secularized interests of the young George Eliot.[81] Phrenology could be captivating, and discipleship was common.

It also had its place in the mesh of ideas and allegiances of cosmopolitan science, and psychology in particular. Phrenology was embraced by Auguste Comte's Positivism, and, through Comte's influence on Lewes, Mill, Frederick Harrison, and others who were well placed among London intellectuals, it reached mainstream psychological debate. In *Comte's Philosophy of the Sciences*, his book-length exposition of 1853, Lewes devoted a chapter to 'Psychology: a New Cerebral Theory'. This, in fact, carved out a space for psychology from Comte's theories that the master himself did not allow. Comte had denied that psychology could have independence because, traditionally, it had an inadequate scientific methodology

---

[79] [Campbell], 'Phrenology', 50.
[80] Schiller, 'Physiology's Struggle for Independence', 74.
[81] For helpful discussion of this milieu, see the opening chapters of Rosemary Ashton, *George Eliot: A Life* (London, 1997). For an insider's view from the East Midlands, which makes clear phrenology's connection with 'mainstream', materialist psychology, see J. Millott Severn, *The Life Story and Experiences of a Phrenologist* (Brighton, 1929). For general discussion, see Steven Shapin, 'Homo Phrenologicus: Anthropological Perspectives on an Historical Problem', in Barry Barnes and Steven Shapin (eds.), *Natural Order: Historical Studies of Scientific Culture* (London, 1979), 41–71, and Roger Cooter, *The Cultural Meaning of Popular Science: Phrenology and the Organization of Consent in Nineteenth-Century Britain* (Cambridge, 1984). Cooter argues that Coombe's phrenology had the additional attraction of a psychological theory of self-improvement. For an informative study of phrenology's influence on another writer, see Shuttleworth, *Charlotte Brontë and Victorian Psychology*, esp. ch. 4.

based only on introspection. One portion of psychology was, therefore, to be given over to biology (where phrenology provided the basis for a theory), while the other was to be given to sociology, which would study the exercise of the intellectual powers in societies.[82] Comte also rejected philosophical psychology's intellectualist emphasis and stressed instead the importance of the affective and physical life (hence the importance of phrenological faculties like 'Amativeness'). He argued for the 'relational study of the mind and the ways of animals' and, above all, a more rigorous attention to the physiological and anatomical foundation of the human faculties, especially their cerebral localization.[83] Though Comte took issue with the conventional division of the phrenological faculties, he none the less believed that, once a true classification had been settled, a 'phrenological psychology' could be based upon the redescription of the faculties as instincts. The concept of instinct could theoretically connect the intellectual and affective parts of human nature and the human and the animal worlds.[84] In effect, the theory ran in parallel to that of Robert Chambers in *Vestiges of the Natural History of Creation*, discussed in Chapter 1 above.

The problems in phrenological theory were not lost on contemporaries. A Positivist fellow-traveller like John Stuart Mill, in *Auguste Comte and Positivism* (1865), could see the pitfalls, and a fierce opponent like T. H. Huxley showed no mercy in blistering polemics from the same period.[85] Lewes too had doubts, even in 1853, when his enthusiasm for Comte was at its height. However, Comte's analysis had strengths. For example, the stress on the affective life as a central component of any psychology was undoubtedly necessary, and was one of Comte's attractions for both Lewes and George Eliot.[86] Equally attractive was his emphasis on a conflictive model of psychological life. Human nature, Comte wrote, is inclined 'in various directions by distinct and independent powers, among which equilibrium is established with extreme difficulty'.[87] Finally, his critique of philosophical dualism, and the psychology of transcendental Consciousness derived from German Idealist metaphysics, became commonplace positions among scientific psychologists, as we have seen.

But there are serious difficulties in Comte's reliance on phrenology. Mill's critique was incisive and widely supported. He pointed out that the idea of

---

[82] Auguste Comte, *Auguste Comte and Positivism: The Essential Writings*, ed. Gertrude Lenzer (New York, 1975), 79–80.

[83] Ibid. 192.

[84] Ibid. 186–91; G. H. Lewes, *Comte's Philosophy of the Sciences* (London, 1853), 218–32.

[85] See esp. T. H. Huxley, 'The Scientific Aspects of Positivism', *Fortnightly Review*, NS 5 (1869), 653–70. For commentary, see Sidney Eiser, 'Huxley and the Positivists', *Victorian Studies*, 7 (1964), 337–58.

[86] Lewes, *Comte's Philosophy*, 5–6. Lewes did not change this view: see *Problems of Life and Mind: First Series*, i, ch. 16, 'The Place of Sentiment in Philosophy'.

[87] Comte, *Essential Writings*, 186.

generalized faculties could not develop a psychology of specific individual contents and differences. These, Mill believed, were accessible only through careful, introspective self-observation. (Throughout his life, Mill remained wedded to the introspective methodologies of philosophical associationism.) Further, Comte's classification of the faculties on the basis of supposedly objective categories of personality type involved a grave methodological flaw:

To establish a relation between mental functions and cerebral conformations, requires not only a parallel system of observations applied to each, but (as M. Comte himself, with some inconsistency, acknowledges) an analysis of the mental faculties, 'des diverses facultes elementaires' [*sic*], conducted without any reference to the physical conditions since the proof of the theory would lie in the correspondence between the division of the brain into organs and that of the mind into faculties, each shown by separate evidences.[88]

In other words, the supposedly relational analysis was nothing of the kind. There were no scientifically specified correlations between the two discrete sets of phenomena. Furthermore, the choice of the faculties appeared arbitrary, and, Mill argued, Comte's belief that such faculties were instinctual seriously underestimated the influence of environment in determining mental character. Comte's views implied a severe reductionism, a kind of anatomical determinism, in which apparently scientific categories were in fact tendentious inventions whose effect was to regularize the diversity of human character and therefore, by implication, constrain personal liberty.

Mill's are strong arguments and are all the more so for being launched from a broadly sympathetic position. Similar points were made by other sponsors like Lewes, as well as opponents like G. D. Campbell.[89] Drawing on earlier remarks by Mill, Lewes felt that positive philosophy must modify the hierarchy of the sciences to provide a space for psychology, so that the study of human nature should not be consumed by Biology and Sociology. An independent discipline must be formulated with its own procedures and object, Lewes argued, just as Biology should not itself be reduced to organic chemistry.[90]

The theoretical function of phrenology's claims, and its at first sight unlikely influence, have to be understood in the context of the dominant dualism of nineteenth-century psychological thought. In an uncertain theoretical domain in the nineteenth century, few psychologists made a specific, thoroughly imagined

---

[88] John Stuart Mill, *Auguste Comte and Positivism*, 2nd edn. (London, 1866), 65–6.

[89] [Campbell], 'Phrenology', 45–56.

[90] Lewes, *Comte's Philosophy*, 210–11. Lewes's later position on phrenology is, as usual, admirably lucid and provides a judicious epitaph: 'We think its Psychology excessively imperfect. We think its Physiology crude and inaccurate . . . We think its pretence of reading character a mischievous and misleading error. Yet . . . we are by no means hostile to any moderate claims Phrenology may set up' ([G. H. Lewes], 'Phrenology in France', *Blackwood's Edinburgh Magazine*, 82 (1857), 673).

attempt to see the functional identity of physical and mental states. As a result, comprehensive efforts to do so could be inspiring. But phrenology also illustrates the theoretical difficulties which beset psycho-physiology. These included an over-insistent, determining correlation between anatomy and behaviour, which rendered human agency somewhat passive or even irrelevant, and an inflated trust in oversimplified models, which included the closed circuitry of the sensory-motor arc and the cruder cerebral localizations. In a effort to understand all mental phenomena in a uniform, naturalistic way, physiological psychologists ignored the problems set by the major differences between the 'higher' and the 'lower' attributes of mind. They tended to think in terms of point-for-point anatomical correlations, or predictable, closed circuits of energy flow, rather than in the spirit of more complex, system-based models like those now favoured by modern writers. What can be said of phrenology in this respect can also be said of automaton theory, which left the prevailing dualism in place by providing inadvertent support for biological vitalism by its uncompromising iatromechanical stance.

One major writer who understood this clearly was William James. Though his work falls a little outside the period covered by this book, his overview of physiological psychology in *The Principles of Psychology* (1890) provides an excellent conspectus of developments, as well as presenting a formidable counterweight to the increasingly rigid Experimentalism emerging from the new psychological laboratories by the 1890s. James was well disposed to, and thoroughly acquainted with, physiological work. In *The Principles* he described psychology generally as the study of 'the empirical correlation of the various sorts of thought and feeling with definite conditions of the brain'.[91] None the less, he criticized 'automaton-theory' and other passive or mechanical models in psychology for their assumption of 'a circle of pure receptivity' rather than active agency.[92] His desire to reincorporate consciousness (of the non-transcendental variety) into the psychological equation, and to understand the relationship between the lower and higher functions on a discriminatory and correlative, rather than homeostatic basis, led to a far-reaching revision of the psycho-physiological model.

In his discussion of 'automaton-theory' in chapter five of *The Principles*, James noted that it proposed no significant role for consciousness. Yet clearly, for evolutionists, something as complex and highly developed as consciousness must offer an advantage to human beings, otherwise there is little evolutionary point in it. James, therefore, proposed that, at a functional level, consciousness has a regulative purpose. It checks 'hair-trigger' reflexes and thus adjusts an unavoidable instability in the psycho-motor system, an instability that is necessary for

---

[91] James, *Principles of Psychology*, i, p. vi. Note also his opening critique of the 'facultative' psychology in these terms (i. 1–3).     [92] Ibid. 402.

some purposes (such as a response to danger), but not for others. This perspective provides him with his basic definition of a psychological entity: '*the mark and criterion of the presence of mentality* in a phenomenon', he asserts, is the organism's ability to select means in pursuit of future ends.[93] For him, consciousness is a '*fighter for ends*', a functional, and not transcendental, component of a psychological system within which the brain is 'an instrument of possibilities, but of no certainties'.[94] This marriage of adaptive functionality with a system that allows for self-regulation and a degree of self-determination is the hallmark of James's psychological system and he rejects as 'anti-psychological' any 'conception of consciousness as a purely cognitive form of being, which is the pet way of regarding it in many idealistic-modern as well as ancient schools'.[95]

James's Darwinian conception of consciousness specifically opposed the Idealist revival at the close of the century (see Chapter 7 below).[96] But it also answered hard-line physiological psychology, which ignored or undervalued consciousness or favoured automaticist models. This included writers such as Huxley in physiology, the associationists in psychology, and the clinician Thomas Laycock, who was influenced by phrenology, in the treatment of mental health.[97] James castigated alike religious transcendentalists (who consider 'the Kosmos as a whole' to be 'an expression of intelligence'), and 'atheist materialists' (who understand 'the present only as so much mere mechanical sprouting from the past').[98] For reasons quite other than those of conservative writers, James questioned whether 'machine-like' acts were a proper subject for psychology, and discriminated between 'mechanical' and 'intelligent' behaviour.[99] Drawing on Lewes, and a number of German writers, he made the simple point that adaptive behaviour is beyond machines, and that this is the conclusive difference between them and living creatures. In an anti-Huxleyan image (of which Huxley himself would have been proud) he comments that a broken electrical sewing machine never 'gets restless because it can only emit sparks, and not hem pillowcases'.[100]

James's conception of humans as adaptive, active, purposive, creative, and conscious creatures within an evolutionary framework breaks the dualistic log-jam decisively. It is a strikingly modern view to which recent thought has again started to attend. It characterizes what is distinctively human as an ability to respond to uncertain and unpredictable internal and external environments freed (unlike machines) from programmed routines and responses.[101] It does not, however

---

[93] James, *Principles of Psychology*, i. 8.     [94] Ibid.     [95] Ibid. 141.

[96] James debates whether an evolutionary conception of consciousness should be Darwinian or Lamarckian and comes down on the Darwinian side (ibid. i. 79; ii. 683–4). This important choice will be revisited in Part Two of this book.

[97] For discussion of Laycock, see Jacyna, 'Physiology of Mind', 116.

[98] James, *Principles of Psychology*, i. 6, 8.

[99] Ibid.     [100] Ibid. 9.     [101] Ibid. 17–18.

—and this should be emphasized—believe in a free-floating, independent consciousness as some of James's 'Modernist' admirers propose. (That, actually, is a view more characteristic of Idealist thinkers like F. H. Bradley, who influenced the distinctive tradition of Modernist conservatism associated with T. S. Eliot.[102]) James's view, that consciousness evolved from the organism's response to difficulty, gives it a strong biological and environmental specification. At the same time, his critique of phrenology, like his critique of automaton theory, rests on the fundamental point that such theories either do not recognize the importance of conscious human activity (or do so only minimally), or, by too deterministically linking behaviour to anatomy, they, in effect, eliminate the object they are trying to explain. Anyway, even setting aside its anatomical and methodological mistakes, phrenology, according to James, 'hardly does more than restate' the taxonomies of the faculty psychology.[103] Perceiving the psycho-physiological argument to lie between the work of the 'cerebralist' and that of the 'nerve physiologist', James favours the approach of the latter because it offers opportunities for a more extended, systemic model.[104] The localization issue, he argues, has mired the debate in schematic falsehoods determined largely by heuristic aims, however worthy: 'too much anatomy has been found to order for theoretic purposes, even by the anatomists.'[105]

Chapters two and three of *The Principles of Psychology*, 'The Functions of the Brain' and 'On Some General Considerations of Brain Activity', are generally little remarked by recent commentators, perhaps because they appear either arcane or out of date. James, in line with most Victorian physiological psychologists, divides the neurological system into the lower and higher functions, though he stresses the dynamism of their interrelation in an evolutionary perspective: 'like all other organs, however, they [the nervous centres] *evolve* from ancestor to descendant, and their evolution takes two directions, the lower centres passing downwards into more unhesitating automatism, and the higher ones upwards into larger intellectuality.'[106] Therefore James's developmental story (like that of Lewes, as we shall see in Chapter 7) unfolds in multiple, complex dimensions. Indeed James, like his novelist brother Henry, distrusts (as William put it) the 'smoothness of the tale' beneath which he detects oversimplified descriptions characteristic of stimulus-response or automaticist models.[107] So what did he suggest by way of replacement?

James's alternative model is suggested (and suggestive) rather than fully developed, and he relies on a good deal of metaphor. He proposes a 'loop-line' conception of the relationship between lower and higher centres in which it is a characteristic of the latter that they can revisit sequences just as water can be

<hr/>

[102] See Rylance, 'Twisting: Memory from Eliot to Eliot'.
[103] James, *Principles of Psychology*, i. 28.      [104] Ibid. 4–5.
[105] Ibid. 81.      [106] Ibid. 79.      [107] Ibid. 402.

drawn again and again from the same reservoir. He writes: 'In the "loop-line" along which the memories and ideas of the distant past are supposed to lie, the action, in so far as it is a physical process, must be interpreted after the type of the action in the lower centres.'[108] There is, therefore, identity of structure and, to a degree, process, but increased differentiation of function. James now images this as a reversible electrical circuit (the dangerously mixed 'reservoir' image had occurred two pages earlier) and such images abound throughout the book. Though he disliked the mechanistic implications of the language of fibres, James took from the associationists their webs and networks.[109] He is interested in the flow of organic energy that passes through these systems, speaking, for instance, of consciousness as a 'pulse'.[110] The traffic up and down these pathways is the most common metaphorical formulation (for example, 'the brain is essentially a place of currents, which is run in organized pathways'[111]), and, like several of his contemporaries (Charlotte Brontë's casual use of an alternative phrase 'the stream of electricity' reveals the buried metaphor[112]), he makes happy, if potentially explosive, use of the dual associations of 'current' in the flows of both water and electricity. Outlandishly, at one point, he imagines the sensory-perceptual system as a kind of hybrid of electric cables running from 'motor zones', and a subterranean network of caverns in which the 'stream' of excitation pours down the specialized 'funnels' at the head of channels leading to the different sensory systems.[113] It is like—I have no idea whether it actually is—an extraordinary vision of the underground railways tunnels, or sewerage channels, then being excavated beneath large cities.

The organization and interlinking of pathways are at the heart of these systems. Thinking about the difference between blindness as an organic deficit and so-called psychic blindness (the inability to interpret signals once received by the optic nerve), it is once again the interwoven circuitry that claims his main interest. James concludes that 'psychic blindness' must be related to the 'interruption of the paths between optic centres and the centres for other ideas', and it is not a problem that can be defined by crude principles of cerebral localization.[114] James's requirement is that the system be understood dynamically, and *not* in a closed, point-for-point, passive, or static way, and he writes of 'such a dynamic connection amongst all the brain-parts that the activity of any one of them will be likely to awaken the activity of all the rest'.[115] Consciousness, therefore, is a dispersed function of the whole system. But it is also a requirement of it that thrives on the synergy ('summation' is James's word) of interlinked processes whose ramifying input, networked across interacting pathways, is dauntingly greater than the sum of its parts.[116]

---

[108] James, *Principles of Psychology*, i. 23.    [109] Ibid. 81.    [110] Ibid. 405.
[111] Ibid. 70.    [112] Brontë, *Villette*, 445.    [113] James, *Principles of Psychology*, i. 65.
[114] Ibid. 48.    [115] Ibid. 55.    [116] Ibid. 82–5.

Despite the self-acknowledged provisionality of its formulations, the clarity, thoroughness, and sophistication of the overall conception of James's ideas were unusual in this period and are a major part of the book's genius.[117] But they draw upon important seed elements in earlier work. G. H. Lewes, for instance, features frequently, and James is noticeably interested in Lewes's terminology (we have already seen that James's most celebrated coinage—'the stream of consciousness'—was in fact Lewes's). Lewes's work was cognate with that of James in a number of important respects, as James acknowledged. Lewes, for example, is credited as an influence on James's discussion of consciousness as systemic potential rather than an act of a particular organ or centre; and Lewes's idea of 'pre-perception', or 'anticipatory imagination', is saluted by James as an important development in the theory of psychological attention.[118] Though Lewes possessed neither the clarity of James's conceptual architecture, nor his commanding historical perspective, nor his organizational gifts on this kind of material, none the less there is evidence that Lewes was heading this way. His critique of mechanistic physiology in *The Study of Psychology* (posthumously published in 1879) focuses upon the substitution of 'a single incidental force' (that is, the reflex mechanism) by 'the whole complex of conditions' and 'whole group of forces' that constitute the interaction of physiological mechanisms and states of consciousness and sentience.[119] As we shall see in Chapter 7, Lewes, like James, developed increasingly complicated conceptual models for his psycho-physiological system, and registered these in similar image strands. Even in three early papers delivered at the conference of the British Association for the Advancement of Science at Aberdeen in 1859, and based upon his own laboratory research, Lewes argued that the composition of nerve tissue is homogenous throughout the system, there being no separate histological structure for the sensory as distinct from the motor systems (as prevailing speculation had it). The property and function of a nerve thus depend on its location in relation to the somatic periphery, and thus, Lewes suggested, to environmental use. In the light of this, Lewes indicated the inadequate taxonomy of nerve physiology as it is related to these variable functions, and claimed to demonstrate a special class of sensations localized in the muscles rather than the skin.[120] This last is notable, for, as Roger Smith has shown, the importance of muscle sense, and hence of the volitional control of sensation, was central to nineteenth-century physiologists' attempts

[117] For a typically self-aware moment, see James's comment on his idea of the sensory 'funnels': 'some broad and vague formulation like this is as much as we can safely venture on in the present state of science' (ibid. 65), or his remarks on the way inorganic metaphors distort understanding of problems of consciousness (ibid. 454).

[118] Ibid. 78, 439–44.    [119] Lewes, *Problems*, iv. 31.

[120] *Report of the Twenty-Ninth Meeting of the British Association for the Advancement of Science held at Aberdeen, Sept. 1859* (London, 1860), 166–70.

to theorize the human organism as capable of active learning and interaction with the environment.[121]

Lewes's was by no means the only effort in this direction in British physiological psychology on which James could build. W. B. Carpenter, another opponent of automaton theory, had developed more responsive and creative, rather than merely reactive, models for psycho-physiological processes. His deliberations, revealed in successive editions of his influential textbooks *Principles of Human Physiology* and *Principles of Mental Physiology*, revised his ideas progressively in a Jamesian direction. Carpenter's thinking about what happens when people *see* provides a case in point. In the mid-1850s he equivocated between two different viewpoints that in themselves recapitulate the disagreement between the older, more mechanistic psycho-physiology and the newer, more dynamic outlook. The following passage displays both in a long, single sentence:

The sense of Vision depends, in the first place, on the excitement of our sensational consciousness by the ocular picture impressed upon the retina, which represents the outlines, lights and shades, colours, and relative positions, of the objects before us; and the ideas respecting the real forms, distances, &c., of bodies, which we found upon these data, are derived through the perceptions, either instinctively or experientially suggested by sensations.[122]

There are two rival models in play here: that associated with the inert reception of visual images, which, in the old, Lockean metaphor for psychological ideas, are 'impressed upon the retina', and that associated towards the end of the passage with the experientially derived *interpretation* (not mere reception) of visual data. In the first, older model the mind is passive; in the second, it is busy receiving and deciphering stimuli. Carpenter admits he cannot specify a mechanism, but none the less insists that 'visual perception is not a mere *transfer* of the sensorial impression, but is *a mental state excited by it*'. We don't '*look at* the retinal picture with the "mind's eye", just as we look at the picture formed by a camera with the bodily eye'.[123] Carpenter cites as evidence cases of 'recovered sight'—that is, of patients who, born blind, later acquire sight through surgery. What such patients report is not a sudden 'turning on of the light', but a sudden, distressing, baffling chaos of visual signals that they have slowly, and painfully, to learn to interpret.[124]

By the mid-1870s, Carpenter was even more confident. Continuing his interest in 'recovered sight', taking note of the results of laboratory experiments with

[121] Smith, 'The Background to Physiological Psychology'.
[122] William B. Carpenter, *The Principles of Human Physiology: With their Chief Applications to Psychology, Pathology, Therapeutics, Hygiene, and Forensic Medicine*, 5th edn. (London, 1855), 710.
[123] Ibid. 711.
[124] For a modern discussion of this issue, see Oliver Sacks's account of his patient 'Virgil' in 'To See and Not to See', in *An Anthropologist on Mars*, 102–44.

hooded chicks, and experimenting a good deal himself with human subjects using new laboratory gadgets like the stereoscope, he was intrigued by the processes of *acquisition* of sight and the processes of interpretation that must be involved in, for instance, binocular vision. He concluded generally that 'the Nervous Mechanism *grows to* particular modes of activity' and that perceptions are acquired. They do not simply 'belong to our original constitution' and their apparently automatic character is merely the result of habit.[125] In Carpenter's work, physiological processes were turning into intelligent systems, and it is this development that, in the end, is able to bypass the old, fraught, automaticist dualisms of mind and body.

There is, then, beside the battle of the old binary stalemates, a strong, developmental impetus in physiological psychology in the nineteenth century. The models and assumptions that writers like Carpenter, Lewes, and James used were, as yet, immature in both detail and overall conception, but they point forward directly to important twentieth-century work. Indeed, some modern commentators regret lost opportunities. Nicholas Humphrey, for example, whose *A History of the Mind* (1992) develops adjacent arguments and models to those examined above, begins by remarking that, 'in many respects, this is a book that could have been written a hundred years ago. Only it wasn't.'[126] Humphrey retraces theoretical steps to begin again with the same 'sentient self' examined by nineteenth-century psychologists. Oliver Sacks, too, as we have seen, has attempted to recover some of the guiding principles of nineteenth-century clinical work, and he links V. S. Ramachandran to the same enterprise.[127] Ramachandran, in turn, sees himself participating in a tradition of serious popular-science writing on psycho-physiological issues running from great Victorians such as Darwin and Huxley, through to twentieth-century writers such as Sacks, Francis Crick, Stephen Jay Gould, and Richard Dawkins.[128] Ramachandran, it might be noted, admires the contribution of William James, as do others in this circle.[129] In this work, the results of sustained investigation can be conveyed to a significantly larger audience, but there is also an opportunity to reflect on wider implications, to open, as the Victorians did, speculative questions, and to assess fundamental values.

Like James, modern thinking works on the assumption of neurological 'feedback loops' as a way of conceiving of the operations of the neuro-physiological system in such a way that it is capable of the kind of advanced behaviours

[125] William B. Carpenter, *The Principles of Mental Physiology with their Applications to the Training and Disciplining of the Mind and the Study of its Morbid Conditions* (London, 1874), 181–2.
[126] Nicholas Humphrey, *A History of the Mind* (London, 1992), p. xv.
[127] Oliver Sacks, 'Foreword', to Ramachandran and Blakeslee, *Phantoms*, p. ix.
[128] Ramachandran and Blakeslee, 'Preface', in Ramachandran and Blakeslee, *Phantoms*, pp. xi–xii.
[129] Ibid. 276.

characteristic of intelligent beings. Nicholas Humphrey, for example, reconsiders the role of sensation. The 'self-characterizing' quality of sensation, he argues, supplies our sense of the 'density' of experience as well as acting as an epistemological guarantee. But to maintain this guarantee, the mind needs to 'echo back to the source' in a dispersed system that is able to authenticate itself by interactive self-checking among its parts.[130] The cognitive and existential density of experience can, in this way, be sustained. Because most real-life stimuli are very brief, 'what constitutes the conscious present is largely the immediate sensory *afterglow* of stimuli that have just passed by—the dying-away activity in reverberating sensory loops'.[131] It is these 'reverberating sensory loops' that secure a personal natural history and sense of identity.[132] As though replying to ghostly Victorian predecessors, Humphrey maintains that 'consciousness is uniquely the "having of sensations"' rather than 'embracing the whole range of higher mental functions'.[133]

For Humphrey, as for James, neurological loops are an evolutionary development, and his 'contention is that consciousness did in fact emerge in evolution as and when these recurrent feedback loops came into being'.[134] This idea seems generally accepted. It is endorsed by Ramachandran, who puts a radical case, on clinical evidence, for the Huxleyan view that all human knowledge (including even that of our own bodies) is, as it were, a functional illusion. These 'massive feed forward and feedback projections', Ramachandran writes, 'are in the business of conducting successive iterations that enable us to home in on the closest approximation to the truth. To overstate the argument deliberately, perhaps we are hallucinating all the time and what we call perception is arrived at simply by determining which hallucination best conforms to the best sensory input.'[135] On this basis, Ramachandran objects to the kind of sensationalist realism espoused by Humphrey, but especially to the doctrines of innate ideas that, like many Victorian forebears, he associates with Kantianism.[136] Others draw less sceptical or formalist epistemologies from these premisses, but the degrees of difference between realism and constructivism in these debates is often difficult to measure. G. H. Lewes, for instance, a committed and sophisticated realist, as we shall see in Chapter 7, also objected to Kantian innate ideas on the grounds that they neglected the dependency of cognitive categories on 'organic conditions',[137] and this view is also taken by the Nobel Prize-winning neuroscientist Gerald Edelman, whose '*qualified* realism' holds that our belief systems are dependent upon their 'evolutionary morphology'.[138] Both realist and

---

[130] Humphrey, *History of the Mind*, 73–87.    [131] Ibid. 176.    [132] Ibid. 197.
[133] Ibid. 180.    [134] Ibid. 179.    [135] Ramachandran and Blakeslee, *Phantoms*, 109.
[136] Ibid. 115.    [137] Lewes, *History of Philosophy*, ii. 485.
[138] Gerald Edelman, *Bright Air, Brilliant Fire: On the Matter of the Mind* (Harmondsworth, 1994), 157–64, 228–37.

constructivist turns to the argument, in both their nineteenth- and twentieth-century forms, rest upon the claim that knowledge is provisionally formulated in systems dependent on change and revisability as the very condition of conscious human intelligence.

Edelman, in fact, provides the most comprehensive, sophisticated, and compelling account of the neurological system as both a looping network and a stochastic evolutionary construction. In so doing, he abandons entirely the mechanical and anatomical framework for conceiving these matters in the Huxleyan tradition. Epigenetic and self-organizing, the brain and the neurological system are, for Edelman, unlike 'any other natural or man-made network'.[139] They lack stable point-for-point 'wiring', and are fluctuating and developmental. 'Indeed,' Edelman writes, in a startling but brilliant metaphor, 'the chemical and electronic dynamics of the brain resemble the sound and light patterns and the movement and growth patterns of a jungle more than they do an electric company.'[140] The comparison to a heaving, self-maintaining eco-system like a jungle represents a daring conceptual break from previous models. But the dynamics were immanent in earlier work. As James, Lewes, and others saw consciousness developing in an evolutionary environment, Edelman internalizes evolutionary principles to explain the morphology of individual brain and neurological systems. The internal environment of neuronal groups and complex interconnecting linkages are, Edelman argues, massively diverse. As in the general biological environment, it is this variety, and the ability of the system to use and select parts of its abundance competitively for different developmental tasks, that establishes the foundation of evolutionary consciousness, and sustains evolutionary advantage through the distinctively human characteristic of intelligent adaptability and performance enhancement. If the physiological system was, for Huxley, like a factory, Edelman, at the end of the line of reasoning that fed Huxley's evolutionary commitments, breaks from the predictable, restricting, unexplaining walls of that metaphor into a new vision of self-maintaining, evolutionary complexity in physiological psychology.

[139] Ibid. 25.     [140] Ibid. 29.

# CHAPTER 4

# *The Discourse of Medicine*

The discourse of medicine is the final contributory stream in the flow of psychological ideas in the nineteenth century. It is also the one that has been most closely researched recently, and modern studies have enriched the complex profile of medical and, especially, psychiatric theory.[1] Scholars have also investigated the overlapping world of Victorian sexuality, and described the frequently pathologized images of both female and male sexuality with which the period distressed itself.[2] Further work still has linked these ideas to the literary writing of the period. This research has produced analyses that are genuinely interdisciplinary in their achievement, and demonstrate beyond doubt the close relationship in the period between biomedical discourse and literature.[3]

To some extent, this chapter follows these insights, though it will not try to review this research. Nor will it attempt an overview of the exceedingly complicated development of Victorian medical theory overall, much of which, even

---

[1] Significant studies include Michel Foucault's enormously influential *Madness and Civilization: A History of Insanity in the Age of Reason*, trans. Richard Howard (London, 1967); William F. Bynum *et al.* (eds.), *The Anatomy of Madness: Essays in the History of Psychiatry*, i. *People and Ideas*; ii. *Institutions and Society*; iii. *The Asylum and its Psychiatry* (London, 1985–8); Michael Donnelly, *Managing the Mind: A Study of Medical Psychology in Early Nineteenth-Century Britain* (London, 1983); George F. Drinker, *The Birth of Neurosis: Myth, Malady and the Victorians* (New York, 1984); Anne Harrington, *Medicine, Mind and the Double Brain* (Princeton, 1987); Janet Oppenheim, 'Shattered Nerves': Doctors, Patients and Depression in Victorian England* (Oxford, 1991); Andrew Scull, *Museums of Madness: The Social Organization of Insanity in Nineteenth-Century England* (London, 1979); Scull (ed.), *Madhouses, Mad-Doctors and Madmen: The Social History of Psychology in the Victorian Era* (London, 1981); Scull, *The Most Solitary of Afflictions: Madness and Society in Britain 1700–1900* (New Haven, 1993); Elaine Showalter, *The Female Malady: Women, Madness and English Culture, 1830–1980* (London, 1987); Taylor and Shuttleworth (eds.), *Embodied Selves*.

[2] Foucault, *A History of Sexuality*; Gallagher and Laqueur (eds.), *The Making of the Modern Body*; Gay, *The Bourgeois Experience Victoria to Freud*, i, ii; L. J. Jordanova, *Sexual Visions: Images of Gender in Science and Medicine between the Eighteenth and Twentieth Centuries* (London, 1989); Mason, *The Making of Victorian Sexuality* and *The Making of Victorian Sexual Attitudes*; Jill L. Matus, *Unstable Bodies: Victorian Representations of Sexuality and Maternity* (Manchester, 1995).

[3] Evelyn Ender, *Sexing the Mind: Nineteenth-Century Fictions of Hysteria* (Ithaca, NY, 1995); Ekbert Faas, *Retreat into the Mind: Victorian Poetry and the Rise of Psychiatry* (Princeton, 1988); Peter Melville Logan, *Nerves and Narratives: A Cultural History of Hysteria in Nineteenth-Century British Prose* (Berkeley and Los Angeles, 1997); Shuttleworth, *Charlotte Brontë and Victorian Psychology*; Helen Small, *Love's Madness: Medicine, the Novel and Female Insanity, 1800–1865* (Oxford, 1996); Jenny Bourne Taylor, *In the Secret Theatre of the Home: Wilkie Collins, Sensation Narrative and Nineteenth-Century Psychology* (London, 1988).

in the field of psychiatry, lies beyond its remit. Because of the diversity and scale of medical discourse in the nineteenth century, it is less easy to sustain responsible generalizations in a single chapter. For this reason, this chapter takes a different line of approach to the survey of developments in Chapters 1, 2, and 3. It will examine the way medical opinion considered psychological questions through an analysis of the work of two individual doctors, John Gideon Millingen and Sir Henry Holland, both of whom wrote in detail on psychological issues. Though they are now both somewhat forgotten figures (especially Millingen), in their day both were well known. They were not, however, theorists in the same way as other figures included in this study—that is, they did not attempt a consciously elaborated body of theory, speculation, or sustained research. Both were practising doctors, concerned instead with clinical efficacy and thoughtful reflection on their practice. Their discourse, therefore, is somewhat different from that of the professional scientists or intellectuals examined elsewhere. It is pragmatic rather then systematic; eclectic rather than bound to a theoretical school; case-oriented rather than philosophically considered; pragmatic and assertive rather than conceptual or abstract. Millingen and Holland belonged to different sectors of the medical community, but their work illustrates typical features of medical discourse as it relates to psychology. It also illustrates something of the general difficulty and confusion of direction that typify psychological theory at the mid-century. In focusing on the work of two individuals, and in highlighting the uncertain, and to a degree contradictory, features of the claims they made about psychosomatic and mental illness in particular, this chapter will prepare the way for Part Two of this book.

But we might start by asking, in a general way, what it was that medicine added to psychology that is not to be found elsewhere. Non-medical psychological theory in the nineteenth century was, by and large, both normative and essentialist in its conception of psychological processes. Its instinct was to look at the situation of what it imagined to be the typical rather than the unusual individual. That this individual would be characteristically male, relatively affluent, healthy, Anglo-Saxon, and live in a southern (or Scottish) town or city tells its own tale of limitation, and it was a perspective encouraged (especially in the philosophical tradition) by the inherited method of introspection that, in the nature of things, tended to be the introspection of male, relatively affluent, healthy, etceteras.

At the same time, nineteenth-century theory is inclined to consider important psychological entities, such as the faculties, as both positive and self-authoring. It lacks the idea, so powerful in twentieth-century thinking, that the foundations of mental life lie in the response made to psychological *deficit*. Particularly in the faculty psychology and its derivatives, nineteenth-century theory is essentialist in the sense that it understands psychological action to be an expression of essential faculties that pre-exist experience. Experience may check the exercise of these faculties, but few theorists claimed that this was deeply constitutive. Even though the association psychology emphasized experience and opposed faculty-based theories, in fact it often contributed to this assumption. Not only did much associationist theory continue to rely upon a conceptual residuum drawn from the older faculty psychology, its lordly emphasis on *intellectual* processes (it was, after all, the psychology of the association of *ideas*) created a psychology curiously uninterested in emotion, physicality, desire, or the many frustrations of all of these. Though the new psycho-physiology was interested in the body, and the physical aetiology of psychological processes, it shared the intellectualist emphasis of its philosophical neighbours and, as we have seen, was often more interested in machines than feelings. The incomplete relationship between nineteenth-century psychology, the human body, sensibility, and emotion, therefore, dogged the steps of theory across the century. As we shall see in the next chapter, the titles of Alexander Bain's best-selling textbooks, *The Senses and the Intellect* and *The Emotions and the Will*, pointedly try to bring together the body and the mind, the 'lower' and the 'higher' faculties. But their success in this enterprise was limited.

As a practice attentive to debility and the body, medicine might offer important, missing perspectives on nineteenth-century psychological debate. There are three issues to consider: first, the role of clinical data in the development of psychological theory; secondly, the role ascribed to the body as a particular kind of animal energy system (as distinct from a machine, a house for the soul, or an irrelevant stand for a philosophical head to nod upon); lastly, there is the question of the impact that human failure and dysfunction have upon the psychological constitution. By and large, mainstream, nineteenth-century psychology was not strong in these areas and this shaped the way Victorians considered the aetiology and dynamics of psychological processes. In much theory, the mind was a stable-state system in which the essential features, once established, needed little attention. Few mainstream theorists used psychological concepts that implied a contingent, self-checking, and self-revising system dependent upon probabilities rather than absolutes. The discourse of medicine, however, emphasized the diagnosis not of ability but of debility. In this discourse, the correction or management of potential or actual dysfunction is paramount.

Twentieth-century, clinically based theories, from Freud to modern neurology, highlight the propinquity of the ordinary and the aberrant, and many, of course, have questioned the foundations of any distinction between them. For such theorists, clinical data are a route towards the understanding of general experience. But many of these theories are also committed to an image of normality that assumes that the self is constituted by its response to deficit. Such theories conceive of the mind (as nineteenth-century theorists by and large did not) as a response to incompletion, insufficiency, partial capacity, or debility. The primary mechanisms of the psychoanalytic tradition (repression, displacement, denial, 'the mirror stage', and so forth) are of this kind. Avoidance, coping, compromise, let alone neurosis or worse, are its keynotes. This 'deficit model', wherein the mind is understood as a structure whose primary function is to try to make the best of things, also features in modern clinical neurology. As we have seen at the close of the previous chapter, V. S. Ramachandran describes normal human cognition as a selection among more or less compelling illusions. This view follows not only from Freud (whose work influences Ramachandran), but also from a post-Darwinian outlook that stresses evolutionary adequacy rather than any form of essentialist positivity. The question of how we might value this retreat from fullness—whether the emphasis should fall, as in Freud, on discontent and incapacity, or, as in Oliver Sacks, on the potential for growth and the resilience of personhood—is a separate matter. The real difference between Freud and his nineteenth-century predecessors may lie not so much in his 'invention' or 'discovery' of 'the unconscious' (plenty of Victorian theories of unconscious psychological activity preceded him), nor in his attempts to 'biologize the mind' as a system of competing energy flows or 'drives' (as we shall see shortly, in the case of J. G. Millingen, some Victorians conceived of the mind in just this way, though with a great difference in outlook). The main difference may lie, instead, in his view that the mind is constituted by its negative dialectics and inevitable discontents. The slide in meaning of the terms 'neurosis' and 'psychosis' over the last quarter of the nineteenth century illustrates the point neatly. They now designate types of illness, but these terms were originally coined, by T. H. Huxley, to indicate a value-neutral 'state of mind' (psychosis) and its companion 'state of the nerves' (neurosis).[4] They have been pathologized from this basis.

Mainstream Victorian psychological (as distinct from psychiatric) theory had no full or adequate vocabulary for mental debility. Indeed, by and large it had neither conceptual nor experiential interest in the subject. A characteristic tactic of the psychologist of the soul, the philosopher of mind, and the psychophysiologist alike, was to discard the issue. When associationists occasionally considered the question of mental illness, they considered it as a case of diseased associations, possibly ascribable to a vicious education. When faculty psychologists considered the same thing, they saw it as a case of a diseased faculty. The tautological character of these diagnoses indicates more than sloppy thinking and failure of interest. It also reflects the hard divide, in much Victorian thinking and social policy, that separates the sane from the mad as ruthlessly as the quarantine separates the healthy from the suspect. The diagnosis of mental pathology in

---

[4] James, *Principles of Psychology*, i. 186; Lewes, *Problems*, iv. 26.

nineteenth-century psychological theory is largely an all-or-nothing game. Theorists liked to think that insanity was either all there, and the lunatic is therefore a pariah to the human community (as in literary representations like that of Bertha Mason in *Jane Eyre*), or not there at all. Though this position was increasingly contested as the century progressed (not least in Charlotte Brontë's later novel *Villette*), the iconographic impact of a tale like Stevenson's *The Strange Case of Dr Jekyll and Mr Hyde* (1886)—which draws upon the binary separations of sane from insane, man from beast, reason and memory from unconscious compulsion, and civil from criminal behaviour—indicates the persistence of well-worn conceptual archetypes. Psychologists of many kinds may have become increasingly conscious of the porousness of these boundaries, but the conceptual architecture remained and is very visible in influential late works, such as Galton's eugenicist tomes *Hereditary Genius, its Laws and Consequences* and *Inquiry into the Human Faculty and its Development*, which abruptly segregate 'the deviant' from the rest.[5]

None the less, this does not mean that the Victorian sense of self was secure, for the cost of a repression is generally an anxiety. Jenny Bourne Taylor notes the disorder endemic in nineteenth-century psychological visions of the self as they came under increasing pressure on different theoretical and administrative fronts. The new conception of the self was inherently more complicated and unstable. It embodies, Taylor writes, 'an implicit dialogue between different layers, currents or sections of the mind'. It was, she argues persuasively, 'in the clashes and correspondence within a fissured, multiple consciousness that the self becomes a social being' in the period, and it was this that made the self so amenable for literary exploration for an emergent generation of novelists preoccupied with questions of identity.[6] But how was this freshly energized vision of the self articulated by the discourse of medicine? Let us turn first to the work of John Gideon Millingen.

Millingen (1782–1862) was a brightly coloured, Thackerayan character. Eccentric from the point of view of modern, highly certificated professionalism, he was not, one suspects, so unusual among Victorian doctors. Born in London, he was the second son of a Dutch businessman who dealt largely in the Indian trade. His mother was the daughter of the Dutch governor of the island of Batavia. His brother, James, became an eminent antiquarian and scholar-collector, who roved the world buying for the leading European collections. The family's religious background lay in nonconformist dissent, particularly the fashionable Anabaptist sect in London's Grafton Street. Millingen himself came to detest

---

[5] Francis Galton, *Herditary Genius, its Laws and Consequences* (London, 1869), and *Inquiry into the Human Faculty and its Development* (London, 1883).

[6] Jenny Bourne Taylor, 'Obscure Recesses: Locating the Victorian Unconscious', in J. B. Bullen (ed.), *Writing and Victorianism* (Harlow, 1997), 141.

the overheated claustrophobia of this milieu, and later espoused a fierce anticlericalism. But the political culture of this milieu was strongly pro-Revolutionary, and, after the fall of the Bastille, the family moved its business to Paris. For twelve years, therefore, between 1790 and 1801, Millingen experienced the most extreme of the Revolutionary disturbances and their Napoleonic aftermath. At first, the family resided contentedly, expecting every day to hear of a companion revolt in Britain, but, as for so many, things went sour. Now unable to remove their capital from France, they witnessed the Terror at close quarters and were subject to the anti-English backlash after war was declared. Millingen's brother was imprisoned, while the rest of the family stayed at liberty only by claiming to be Dutch. None the less, Millingen gained a medical education in the advanced Parisian medical schools and graduated from the École de Médecine. Fleeing Paris in 1801 (after his involvement in a plot to kill Napoleon, he later claimed), he joined the allied forces as an army doctor, and served in Egypt, the Peninsula, and at Waterloo. In peacetime, he was sent to the West Indies, where health problems ended his military career. Thereafter, for a time, he wandered across Europe, living on half-pay, by occasional doctoring, and by his pen, until he chose to specialize in the treatment of insanity, working first for the Military Lunatic Asylum at Chatham, then as resident physician to the Middlesex Pauper Asylum, before opening a private establishment in Kensington, where he became something of a reform-minded authority, sketching progressive, model asylums in works such as *Aphorisms of the Treatment and Management of the Insane* (1840). His career as a jobbing writer—as distinct from a professional intellectual or medical professional—shows a profusion of styles and subjects typical of the London 'Grub Street' of the period in a way that mirrors in some respects the early career of the polymathic Lewes, who also began his adult life 'walking the wards' in the London hospitals. In addition to an autobiography, and books and essays on medical and related matters, Millingen wrote travel sketches, a racy novel (*Adventures of An Irish Gentleman* (1830)), essays on 'Remarkable Suicides', 'Fortune Hunters', and similar topics for *Bentley's Miscellany*, comic opera libretti and popular farces (e.g. *Who'll Lend Me A Wife?* (1825)), and a history of duelling. He had the intellectual and professional eclecticism typical of the medical community of the period and claimed, for instance, to have learned more about the treatment of lunacy from the 'productions of our poets, than all the metaphysical disquisitions of the learned'.[7] (Given the nature of these disquisitions, this is not an unworthy claim.) But most of all he learned from experience, and his

---

[7] J. D. Millingen, *Mind and Matter, Illustrated by Considerations on Hereditary Insanity and the Influence of Temperament in the Development of the Passions* (London, 1847), p. vii. This is the first edition of the book later called (because another writer had scooped the title 'Mind and Matter') *The Passions; or Mind and Matter, Illustrated by Considerations on Hereditary Insanity, etc., etc., etc.* (London, 1848).

insouciance reflects his detached relationship to the medical and intellectual establishment. His main work on medical issues, *The Passions; or Mind and Matter*
(1848), was published by John and Daniel Darling, a house that specialized in
military literature, and his *Curiosities of Medical Experience* (1839) is an extraordinary ragbag of pieces on, for example, being buried alive, ventriloquism, human
hair, coffee, love potions, the abuse of food, spectacles, spontaneous combus-
tion, flagellation, cretinism, Chaucer, and lettuce.

Millingen's career is significant as well as curious. His background in trade,
and—however thoroughly he later disowned it—religious dissent and political
radicalism, and his unconventional education in 'materialistic' Paris, set him upon
the cultural and professional margins and left him impatient with, and often
contemptuous of, authorities both intellectual and administrative. He was a noisy
opponent of closed, self-regulating institutions, and a powerful advocate of homeopathy, partly because of the rampant dishonesty and venality of the drug trade.
He wrote a defence of homeopathy in *A Popular View of the Homœopathic Doctrine*
(1837), and snarled at the corruption of the magistrates regulating the treatment
of lunatics, and the profiteering evils of 'mad-doctoring'. He was furious, by turns,
about cruelty towards the insane, vivisection, religious fundamentalism of any
kind, 'priestcraft', the depraved aristocracy, racial prejudice, women, and revolution. In his voice, even in its inconsistencies, prejudices, and maverick enthusiasms, one can recognize the tones of a highly coloured, but none the less
representative, male, liberal, bourgeois humanitarian of the period. In his political views, he desired the amelioration of class antagonism, and an end to social
and economic injustice. But he thought these things should be brought about
by a benign authoritarianism, and he loathed revolution, systematic agitation,
and any civil unrest. He supported private property and the Empire, and
favoured the professions, especially the military. Above all, he looked for institutions that encouraged industry and science and promoted the meritocratic
advancement of talent. His ideas pivot around that powerful nineteenth-century
conundrum that set the unshakeable necessity for order against the claims of
liberal culture and the need for more porous institutions. Freedom and regulation
are two equally weighted, if thereby inharmonious, watchwords in his political
opinions, his medical views, and, as we shall see, his psychological theory.

By his own account, the experience of the French Revolution was formative,
not just personally but professionally. The Revolution was traumatic, and he
makes a therapeutic virtue of this, claiming that his psychiatric credentials arise
from his Parisian experiences, in particular his first-hand acquaintance with shock
and the evil consequences of uncontrolled passion. This knowledge, he states
with contempt, was not 'gained in the shades of the academy'.[8] Millingen's

---

[8] Millingen, *Mind and Matter*, p. iv.

narrative of his experience of the Revolution, written up in *Recollections of Republican France from 1790–1801* (1848), the first of an uncompleted autobiographical series, outlines the pattern he detects in the revolutionary incidents. It is a pattern that he also finds in the internal dynamics of the psychological system. For him, both history and the psychology of the individual follow the same, pulsing rhythm, which oscillates between regulation and anarchy, control and disorder, calm and passion, sympathy and brutality, steadiness and feckless unpredictability. Needless to say, the first of these paired opposites is always positive, the second not, and Millingen's attitudes are, in this respect, comparable to those of other writers in the nineteenth-century bourgeois tradition.[9] For Millingen, the Revolution represented a mass pathology, a collective madness closely connected to the derangement of individuals: a 'maniacal excitement, with a few moments of lucid intervals', a 'vortex of confusion . . . verging on insanity', an expression of 'the instability of a people', and the 'evil passions' of a 'vacillating mind'.[10]

Millingen's work is an example of the tendency in nineteenth-century theory to transfer social feelings and categories directly into psychology and vice versa. Published in 1848, and excited by the revolutionary episodes of that year, his book portrays political events as savage expressions of mass delirium. But his storytelling also carries an ambiguity sometimes found in similar descriptions by Carlyle or Dickens. His strongly written denunciations of revolutionary excesses display a slightly discomforting excitement at the horrors described. Millingen the dramatist, for instance, is stimulated by the transgressive theatre of a world turned upside down: 'the theatre of every possible depravity' (as he calls it), the 'bloody carnival', the 'ferocious Saturnalia'.[11] These things thrill him even as he condemns the debauch, and the sound of lips smacking is interrupted only by carefully placed tut-tutting. This relish for the gruesome and the titillating shows his Grub Street instincts as well as a more personal ambivalence over a human and political emergency of enormous scale. But it also articulates his sense of a confusing psychological problem. Only weeks after another outbreak of Parisian streetfighting in the February Revolution of 1848, and while running a private asylum for the insane, Millingen cannot help but find the obvious, disturbing parallel. History turns pathological when enough people in enough significant places go mad, or are allowed to express their madness. But why should this madness arise, and why should it be so contagious? Millingen's answer to these

[9] A relevant analysis is to be found in Roland Barthes's book on Millingen's contemporary Jules Michelet. Barthes reads Michelet's history as an articulation of the thematic pulse of the author's 'network of obsessions', some of which were personal, some epochal and ideological. See Roland Barthes, *Michelet*, trans. Richard Howard (London, 1979), 3.

[10] J. D. Millingen, *Recollections of Republican France from 1790–1801* (London, 1848), 75, 126, 142.

[11] Ibid. 68, 250.

questions now sounds glibly 'Victorian' in the worst sense. It is, he says, a result of the indulgence of passion, a subject on which he wrote his most substantial treatise, *The Passions; or Mind and Matter*, also published in 1848. However, we have to judge the significance of this familiar Victorian theme in context.

For Millingen, passion did not mean mere intemperance about which one might primly moralize. Nor did it imply a silly fear or hostility towards sex as such. By passion, he meant an engulfing, violent, destabilizing loss of control, which, he thought, lies potentially at the heart of all human behaviour and brings with it ruin, illness, and destruction. What he had in mind has a much more Freudian cast than any supposed 'Victorian' prissiness, and as a theory it has a powerful, structuring ambivalence. It is the product of a medical imagination haunted by, and partly attracted towards, the abolition of psychological regulation and comprehension by the controlling faculties. Passion means not only a loss of personal control, but the loss of understanding itself, and the secret allure of this vertigo is very strong. Thus, he is intrigued by sado-masochistic passions, which transgress the borderlines between pleasure and pain.[12] His vision of nature, too, became radically Manichaean. Both human and inhuman nature are battle-fields (his metaphor) on which fight the theoretically underdeveloped fore-runners of Freud's Eros and Thanatos, the life and death instincts. There is, therefore, for Millingen, a radical disequilibrium at the heart of human beings, which is expressed in disruptive, anarchic outbursts of passion. His writing enjoys these, even as it announces its formal disapproval.

The prospect of a Manichaean biology, in which life was imaged as the con-tention of hostile energies, troubled other medical commentators in the period confronted by such bewildering behaviour. Sir Henry Holland, for instance (whose work we shall examine shortly), was concerned that post-Darwinian theory would unsettle not only the isomorphism of the natural and moral worlds, but the unitary conception of nature itself, now to be conceived as jagged and discon-tinuous. Acknowledging the force of the Darwinian conception, none the less Holland saw no need for 'any Manichaean doctrine of an antagonistic power to meet the difficulty'.[13] But Millingen, writing before Darwin, did. Outwardly, he did his best to appear a conventional Natural Theologian, and his work makes widespread use of the comfortable phraseology of this position. 'The Creation is ruled by immutable and uniform laws', for instance, is an early statement that pithily assumes the validity of all the leading propositions in Natural Theological argument (that is, that the world is created, ruled, and unchangeable).[14] But the

---

[12] See e.g. his complementary accounts of the Jacobin fanatic Théroigne de Méricour in ibid. 123–6, and *The Passions*, 451–3.

[13] Sir Henry Holland, 'Unity of the Creative Power through Creation', in *Fragmentary Papers*, 24. The essay was written in 1867.

[14] Millingen, *The Passions*, 2.

security of this position is threatened by monsters. Rather as educated people after the Second World War asked how cultivated Germans could perpetrate atrocity and so despaired of human nature, Millingen took revolutionary trauma to the heart of his vision. He hypothesized 'a war implacable, in which strength overwhelms the feeble, and might too frequently tramples upon right'.[15] The view that Millingen characterizes would have been described a quarter of a century later as 'Darwinian' (though it is more strictly Spencerian or Social-Darwinist), but Millingen runs ahead of this debate. He tries to recoup this violent, energized vision for the complacencies of Natural Theology by arguing that history is cyclical and compensatory, and that moral anarchy and brutality eventually bring forth order, just as evil ultimately brings forth good. But this is an argument of convenience, for his major interests are not emphatically directed towards the celebration of cosmic balance. Like Freud, in fact, he sees civilized living itself as an enemy of human contentment, because of the limitations it sets to egoistic, passionate desire. Indeed, madness itself, he claimed in a Rousseauist moment, is only a disease of the civilized, and 'of rare occurrence in barbarous nations'.[16] Civilization inhibits desire, and is thus an obvious source of immediate discontent, but this process is compounded because civilization also raises appetites and expectations by manufacturing both wishes and opportunity, and hence 'the advance of civilization [opens] the sluice-gates of every evil passion'.[17] Unlike Freud, he sometimes piously imagined that desire, reason, and civilized living might be reconciled, but the closing remarks of *The Passions* emphasize the impossibility of human perfectibility, and the inevitability of disharmony. It is a vision that has more in common with the cataclysmic thinkers of the *fin-de-siècle* (of whom Freud was, in a sense, one), or indeed with Marxian ideas on the psychological impact of manufactured desires in commodity-based economies. Civilization's advance, Millingen argues, produces the prospect not only of an endless train of freshly unsatisfied wishes, but the return of destructive, atavistic longings that humans ordinarily (and rightly) suppress. These he images throughout the book as natural calamities: volcanic eruptions, earthquakes, hurricanes, and deluge—exactly the same train of images that were being used by female novelists particularly to indicate the force of personal yearning in heroines such as Charlotte Brontë's Jane Eyre (1848) or George Eliot's Maggie Tulliver in *The Mill on the Floss* (1860). The primitive, 'superstitious' emotions, Millingen writes, have embedded a mental structure even in the 'civilized' community that 'to the present day . . . pervades the mind'.[18]

---

[15] Ibid.

[16] J. G. Millingen, *Aphorisms of the Treatment and Management of the Insane; with Considerations on Public and Private Lunatic Asylums, Pointing out the Errors in the Present System* (London, 1840), 12.

[17] Ibid. 266.        [18] Millingen, *The Passions*, 254.

There are two key elements in the dynamics of this apparently permanent psychological structure. One is Millingen's version of the inheritance of acquired characteristics, whereby, for instance, insanity, once established in a family, is likely to be transmitted to future generations. As there is little parallel emphasis in his work on the acquirement of beneficial acquisitions, and as Millingen returns to the subject of hereditary insanity at every opportunity, his books carry a somewhat doom-laden vision of an inexorable, Malthus-like progression of madness and related debilities trampling inevitably through the 'civilized' population.[19] 'If the power of our reason could controul [*sic*] our mental aberration,' he gloomily concludes one discussion, 'no reasonable being would be mad.'[20] But it cannot.

Millingen hypothesizes a biological mechanism for these transmissions that provides his psychological theory with its second key component. Acquired characteristics, he claims, are reproduced by the transmission of 'germinal granules'.[21] This neo-Lamarckian process is either encouraged or discouraged by the civilization of the day, and by factors such as diet. But an 'organic germ' always lies within human beings 'ready to receive the plastic impressions of the vivifying secretion' of actual existence.[22] The gendered, prejudicial nature of this imagining is obvious: nature is female and passive, while worldly experience is active, male, and secreting. But this process is the key for Millingen not just to biological transmissions, but psychological ones also. What are transmitted are fundamental physical and temperamental features determined by the significant incidents of life (drunkenness during conception is one he names) and the cultural habits of the epoch and/or social group.

Like many a biological speculator of his generation, Millingen struggled to contain imaginatively the monstrous potential for unpredictable variation and transformation that a theory such as this unleashes. He tried to control it practically by moral exhortation, arguing that people should control their passions for the sake of their children as much as themselves, and he tried to control it theoretically, as we noted above, by the rather vague prospect of an eventual cosmic balancing of historical, ethical, and psychological forces, which allowed the flat iron of Natural Theology to smooth the creases revealed in Nature's rumpled fabric. But at the biological level neither of these arguments carries much weight. Instead, Millingen tried to contain proliferating change by invoking the great shibboleth of pre-Darwinian biology, the stability and permanence of species. However, even this invited a hit at another totem of Victorian civilization, that of faith in progressive optimism:

We have reason to believe that everything in the creation, endowed with vitality and the faculties of nutrition and reproduction, arose from a fundamental prototype, most probably co-eval with the creation of the animal world. Each species procreates its like.

---

[19] See e.g. Millingen, *The Passions*, 7 ff.   [20] Ibid. 13.
[21] Ibid. 33–4.   [22] Ibid. 32.

Races of animals may have been destroyed in the various revolutions of our globe; they may have ceased to exist; but we have no reason to suppose, that any transition has taken place from species to species. Variations may have been observed—the result of climate, locality, and the experiential industry of man; but so far from its being a fact, that any of the species which people our earth, subject to the laws of mundane economy, are advancing by generation to a higher or more perfect type of being—where the fostering hand of civilization is withdrawn, every species has a tendency to revert to its original and normal state.[23]

The syntactical confusions in this passage reflect an overall argument that wants to do several contradictory things at once. It wants to claim that acquired characteristics are passed to subsequent generations and determine their natures; but it also wants to assert a natural intolerance to mutation that encourages reversal to original type. Species are, therefore, both transformable and permanent at once, and nature is both changeable and unchangeable at the same time. Natural Theology is under acute, contorting pressure in this pre-Darwinian imbroglio of ideas. The kind of juggling act that enabled Robert Chambers to balance his intellectual books and bring biology into line with theology was, a few years later, beyond Millingen.

Millingen veers from a powerful materialist determinism (for example: 'Man is incessantly decomposed and reproduced according to chemical laws, in the laboratory of nature'[24]) to a position that flatly and contradictorily denies this. Associating materialism with French revolutionary ideology, he spurned both psycho-physiology and psychological determinism.[25] In a passage that rivals for hyperbole that most conservative of anatomists, John Gordon (whose work we encountered in the previous chapter), Millingen also produces a catalogue of brain-damaged individuals whose gross injuries none the less, he claims, barely inhibited their mental functions: a man with one hemisphere of the brain entirely destroyed, another whose brain leaked out through his wound, a third with an abscess weighing half a pound. 'These cases', Millingen remarks blandly, 'show that cerebral diseases have but little influence on the manifestations of mind.'[26] Once again, my point is not that individuals do not survive deep injury in remarkable ways. It is that clinical information is being used to validate anti-materialist (and anti-scientific) conclusions—namely, that physiological structures have no relation to mental processes.

The original title of *The Passions* was *Mind and Matter*. This became the subtitle in the second edition after another author claimed priority rights to it, but the original title declared the book's psychological interests very clearly. What stance does Millingen take on this key issue in mid-century psychological

[23] Ibid. 27–8.     [24] Ibid. 105.
[25] Millingen, *Curiosities*, pp. vii–ix; *Recollections*, 261–5; *The Passions*, 122–5.
[26] Millingen, *Curiosities*, 406–7.

theory? Though he explicitly attacked materialism as an outlook, and opposed physiological 'speculation' in psychology, his theoretical views were once again deeply equivocal in ways that are easily read as symptomatic of the general mid-century debate. Biomedical discourse was under theoretical and ideological pressure to sustain the orthodox separation of mind from matter. But simultaneously it was pushed in the contrary direction by emergent ideas supported by some scientific findings. In Millingen's case, the eagerness for psychological and social order, which was one component of his temperament, was backed by his need to be seen to have a respectable reputation in the competitive markets of the 'mad trade'. However, these forces were counteracted by experiential ambivalences supported by his clinical observations. When it came to the crunch, he inevitably finessed the problem, carefully separating contradictory utterances by several closely argued pages in *The Passions*, or, in *Curiosities of Medical Experience* and *Aphorisms of the Treatment and Management of the Insane*, disintegrating his theories into miniature particles in essays which could sometimes be as tiny as one page long. He made himself an expert at issuing self-refuting, Janus-faced estimates of controversial, but important ideas such as those of phrenology.[27]

For a writer such as Nietzsche, the aphoristic style became a way of articulating complexity, but for Millingen it is a way of avoiding ideological exposure and too-explicit contradiction. When forced to consider a question directly, he habitually reverted to the orthodox, default position of the times. For instance, when considering 'The Influence of Corporeal Agency on the Mind' in Section IV of *The Passions*, Millingen alerts his reader to the obnoxious possibility of 'plunging headlong into the chaotic quagmire of materialism, by endowing matter with a mind'.[28] However, because he needs to preserve some 'corporeal' presence to sustain his neo-Lamarckian theories, for the moment he converts his version of evolutionary biology into a pious vitalism wholly compatible with orthodoxy: 'there is a principle implanted in the living form, equally distinct from all mechanical, chemical, and rational powers, which directs the agent by unerring impulse—or, in other words, impels it by a prescribed and *unerring* law.'[29] That this vitalism is a mere idea of convenience is suggested by the glaring contradiction between the emphasis on '*unerring* law' and the radical instability that engrosses his attention elsewhere. Anyway, he shrugs, concluding his discussion as if the butter was still whole in his mouth, 'whatever may be our presumptuous notion of the subject, we must admit that the whole of creation is governed by the Supreme Intelligence that has been called by philosophers the *anima mundi*'.[30] The moment is typical. Whether it is sincere, I do not know. It is certainly impeccably orthodox. However, the gap between the assertion of orthodoxy, and the specification of biological and physiological

[27] Millingen, *The Passions*, 149–50.    [28] Ibid. 125.    [29] Ibid. 126.    [30] Ibid.

mechanisms and processes, was widening for Millingen's generation and the cracks in consistency in Millingen's theoretical writing seem emblematic in this as in other respects.

So what were the crucial concepts in Millingen's psychology? In a passage proximate in spirit and position to the one just quoted, Millingen endorses the Scotch School of philosopher-psychologists and names Reid, Beattie, Campbell, and Stewart in particular.[31] Certainly, the vocabulary of the faculties and other associated, rather old-fashioned terminology, such as character, temperament, and the humours, play an important role in *The Passions*. But what does the idea of a faculty mean in Millingen's usage? Characteristically, he equivocates, and is, once again, representative. Sometimes, 'faculty' signifies no more than a capability, a potential in the human mind for, for example, reason or will power. This anodyne sense was acceptable in most camps of psychological argument. However, Millingen also gave the word a quite other inflection. In phrases such as 'the reasoning faculty', 'the faculty of the will', or 'the faculties of perception', or in the proposition that 'certain organs and faculties [are] more irritable and excitable than others',[32] it is used as though to denote an agent, a thing that performs reasoning or willing, for instance. This verbal slippage was handy for faculty psychologists, and was exploited by carefully ambivalent theorists like Millingen. The faculties are permitted a degree of rhetorical independence while also carrying, for those that want it, the implication of a systematic relationship. This can be ignored as easily as it can be exploited. What is also clear is that Millingen, whatever he might say declaratively, did not think that the faculties possessed the kind of psychological autonomy or authority that Scotch-School philosophers, for instance, assumed.

For example, he believed (as did most of his contemporaries) that children could not be mad, and that mental illness was a post-pubescent condition. But one implication of this view is that the mind and its faculties must, in one very central respect at least, be heavily developmental in nature because they must change. They must also, if the following passage is to be given any weight, be strongly dependent upon physiological and nervous conditioning:

One might say that our nervous system is educated with our minds. This is most conspicuous at the age of puberty: as that period developes [*sic*] the power of reproduction, so do our moral faculties undergo a corresponding change, when mental energies and vigour are called forth to fulfil our future destinies and support our progeniture—a wise provision of the Supreme Intelligence.[33]

This illustrates all the tensions in Millingen's position. The existence of moral faculties, the idea of destiny, the wise provisions of the Supreme Intelligence,

---

[31] Ibid. 123.      [32] Ibid. 88.      [33] Ibid. 114.

all gesture towards a calm orderliness in development. But the turbulent influx of sexual energy, and his awareness of 'morbid, imperfect or vitiated' development (as he puts it on the following page), allows little room for theoretical composure. In fact, Millingen, though proclaiming the virtues of the faculty psychology, regularly wrote with a quite different psychological template in mind, one that tries to come to terms with

strange, anomalous sensations, producing impressions that prompt not only the most extraordinary desires, but to the commission of the most heinous crimes, utterly uncontrollable by the reasoning faculties. Our senses may be in a morbid condition; so can our minds. In the one instance we indulge in the most extraordinary appetites; in the other, we entertain most extraordinary desires. We see chlorotic girls and pregnant women eating chalk, charcoal, tar, spiders—nay, the most disgusting substances.[34]

Alongside the misogynistic implications carried by the examples (which are of a piece with other features in the book and continue, on this occasion, in lurid detail over a good deal of the next page), we might recognize also a struggle within psychological doctrine.

In Millingen's work, the psychological faculties are contorted in conception. They are, for him, a product of growth not Creation, and are always potentially frail in their development. At the same time, he contradictorily claims that they are persistent and reassuring, establishing bulwarks against insanity, and providing recognizable signatures of normalcy. Just as, in his general biology, species may be twisted out of shape, but can never evolve into anything different, so, though the faculties may develop in wild directions, their essential nature endures. The 'instinctive mental faculties prevail even in the embryo', Millingen claims, and form the basis of our 'temperament'.[35] Alongside visions of spider-eating women, therefore, Millingen has an account of normative development. But it is a description of extraordinary blandness and tedious conventionality that does no more than verbally elaborate, over tiresome pages, capacities whose nature can be safely recognized as part of common, inoffensive knowledge. Thus, for instance, as we develop towards adulthood, our judgement becomes less fickle, our reason less sluggish, and our memories more reliable. Millingen's guiding interpretative principle depends upon the identification of different kinds of temperament (sanguinous, choleric, bilious, atrabilious, and so on), and this taxonomy is tabulated in the most numbing, Victorian classificatory manner.[36]

For all the authority claimed for his clinical experience, Millingen prefers his psychological concepts to operate at a level of genial generality, which permits

---

[34] Millingen, *The Passions*, 112–13.   [35] Ibid. 132.

[36] Ibid. 135–6. The tabulation of psychological 'types' is a recurrent motif in some Victorian psychology, which perniciously became a universally applied mode of discrimination in Eugenicist theory.

a helpful theoretical imprecision. But the rhetorical and ideological advantages of this are, in a sense, only collateral products of a psycho-medical discourse, which, anyway, had little vocabulary for the strange phenomena of human behaviour it struggled to acknowledge, and often equally earnestly struggled to misrecognize. Millingen often emphasizes processes of development, but his root categories are quaint and theoretically torpid. He is fond of ideas of temperament, character, and the humours, and sometimes his psychology seems to get little beyond that of a contemporary of Ben Jonson: 'notwithstanding the many revolutions that have taken place in the doctrines of physiology,' he writes primly, 'this ancient classification [of the humours] prevails, to a certain extent, to the present period.'[37] From this point the discussion is free to degenerate into topics such as hair colour: 'carroty' people, he maintains, are more likely to go mad.[38]

Psychology thus construed is, to use the old-fashioned image Millingen himself favours, a battlefield between Reason and Passion. He notionally believed in Reason, in the abstract Enlightenment sense, as a safeguard for life, morality, and property. But the more original image he chose to convey the role of Reason in *The Passions* leaves it at some distance from Enlightenment optimism. The exercise of Reason is like:

casting a pebble in a rivulet to check its course: for a moment, the current may eddy around the obstacle, but still the stream will pursue its destination, until the waters have attained by Nature's laws. In like manner will our train of thoughts continue uninterrupted until forcibly drawn away by a more powerful diversion, and in the ratio of the comparative power, will one passion succeed or supersede another . . . *Reason* may check the indulgence of our appetites and desires, but it cannot alter their essence.[39]

The change here, from Reason standing outside mental activity to Reason plunged helpless in its midst, is revealing, as is the selection of flowing water as an image for the mind. As later advocates of the 'stream of consciousness' were aware, this modern image of swirling energy disrupts the stability of the old mental classifications and the role assumed for the traditional faculties. 'The traditional psychology', wrote William James later, 'talks like one who should say a river consists of nothing but pailsful, spoonsful, quartpotsful, barrelsful, and other moulded forms of water. Even were the pails and pots all actually standing in the stream, still between them the free water would continue to flow. It is just this free water of consciousness that psychologists resolutely overlook.'[40]

It is easy to see that the selection of a turbulent energy system as an image for the mind, and the relative powerlessness of faculties like the reason and the will implied by it, is a transposition of Millingen's way of understanding the events of the French Revolution. (This proposition might be put the other way

---

[37] Ibid. 66.    [38] Ibid. 91 n.    [39] Ibid. 163.
[40] James, 'On Some Omissions of Introspective Psychology', 16.

round, of course.) For him, as a psychologist, 'impulses are instinctive, totally independent of volition . . . unaccountable, uncontrollable . . . an overwhelming power'.[41] The passions pit the mind against the body and, in cases of insanity, the mind is overwhelmed by its energies.[42] As a result, though the conceptual structure of Millingen's analysis maintains an abstract distinction between, for example, mind and body (or reason and passion), in fact this distinction is impossible to sustain in practice. Indeed he concludes that 'to ascertain and fix the limits of mind and body, of spirit and matter . . . [would be] a futile attempt'.[43] Similarly, the atrocities of the French Revolution, though deplorable, were unavoidable. Millingen's memoir of the Revolutionary events has no other notion of causality than that of a vast soup of irrational, unstoppable passions: 'Every passion that could drive to acts of desperate daring was excited, and the whole population of Paris kept in a state of feverish fermentation.'[44] The dominant interpretative motif is of a gigantic, gross, cultural morbidity, an episode of 'Romantic mania',[45] which leads to cults of suicide and erotic violence. And, at the fascinated, enrapt, disgusted centre of Millingen's account stands a lunatic. Robespierre is, for him, a figure of demonic, twitching, sado-masochistic passions: 'His whole frame shook in convulsive rigors; his teeth chattered, his articulation became difficult, and foam issued from the angles of his mouth. On such occasions, he has been known to thrust one of his hands in his bosom, and lacerate it with his nails. Such was the violence of his passions, that he sometimes appeared threatened with suffocation.'[46] After probably imaginary interviews with Robespierre held to secure his brother's release (Robespierre was executed when Millingen was 12), he unsurprisingly returned to tell his father that 'he appeared to me to be a madman'.[47]

Like much nineteenth-century psychological theory, Millingen's account of the psychology of passion lacks clarity in the roles it ascribes to the mental faculties and the bodily impulses, and, urging the authority of reason and the will, it, in fact, concedes their helplessness. Clinical data are used opportunistically and without rigour or analytic safeguards, and the emphasis on dysfunction is

---

[41] Millingen, *The Passions*, 167.    [42] Ibid. 62–3.    [43] Ibid. 62.
[44] Millingen, *Recollections*, 55–6.    [45] Ibid. 372.    [46] Ibid. 289.
[47] Ibid. 292. The late 1840s saw several topical attempts to reinterpret the significance of the French Revolution. G. H. Lewes's biography of Robespierre, published in 1849, provides an interesting point of contrast to Millingen's version. Lewes, too, tried to understand Jacobin ruthlessness from the perspective of 'the psychologist' (see p. 349), but he deliberately tried to counteract Tory images of a Revolutionary ogre. Writing for the radical publisher John Chapman, Lewes concedes Robespierre's fanaticism, but places it historically. Robespierre, he argues, represents the culmination of the 'metaphysical philosophy' in politics—that is, an attempt to legislate human action by inhuman laws. His biography thus becomes a Positivist analysis of the political dangers of the Metaphysical Stage of society, to be succeeded, Lewes hoped at the time, by his own 'scientific' generation. See G. H. Lewes, *The Life of Maximilien Robespierre with Extracts from his Unpublished Correspondence* (London, 1849).

counteracted only by a recurrent, abstractly declared optimism. Untroubled by, or unable to cope with, either intellectual or ideological contradiction, Millingen fell back on optimistic shibboleths such as Reason, the tenets of Natural Theology, and old-fashioned psychological conceptual equipment, to enable a retreat backwards to the future that covered his inconsistencies as gracefully as possible. But the picture that emerges from his work is one in which human beings are an object of some sadness. Harassed by insanity, traumatized by mass pathology, subject to passion in its strong form, deluded by civilized reason and authority, abandoned by the once-reliable faculties, his individuals (to borrow some of his own metaphors) stand bewildered on battlefields, or lonely below volcanoes holding no more than conceptual umbrellas thick with holes. At the heart of the Victorian period, in an asylum in Kensington, sits a forerunner of Freudian pessimism writing at his table in his model bucolic garden created specially, and with great care, for the incarcerated insane.

Millingen was a doctor on the unstable radical fringe of medical opinion. The second figure to be examined in this chapter, Sir Henry Holland (1788–1873), inhabited a different world. Where Millingen was passionate, Holland was urbane; where Millingen was an outsider, working in the rough trade of the management of the mad, Holland had a lucrative society practice that allowed him many months a year for foreign travel, his real passion, where, it was rumoured, he conducted clandestine 'diplomatic' missions. Where Millingen was disconnected and eccentric, Holland appears to have been one of the most worldly, likeable, and well-connected men of his age.[48] His poised, charming autobiography, *Recollections of Past Life* (1872), at first privately printed for the family, then published publicly as demanded by his 'friends', reads, compared to Millingen's Grub Street potboiler, like the silver address book or collected calling cards of the best of Victorian 'society'. He seems to have known everyone in and out of the Whig establishment. He was familiar at court, an intimate of Lords Landsdowne and Holland (though no relation), a cousin of Elizabeth Gaskell and related to the Wedgwood family (and through them to the Darwins), a friend (he recollects in his autobiography) of Byron, Abraham Lincoln, Walter Scott, Thomas Browne, Sir William Hamilton, Darwin (whom he admired), Lord Jeffrey, Lord Macaulay, Dugald Stewart, Dean Stanley, George Grote, Madame de Staël, Maria Edgeworth, Humphrey Davy, Canning, Tallyrand, Guizot, Lord Aberdeen, Lord Melbourne, and others. He was three times President of the Royal Society and a Fellow of the Royal College of Physicians. Among his patients were Queen Victoria, Prince Albert, six Prime Ministers, George Eliot, and G. H. Lewes.

[48] An indication of the friendly esteem in which he was held can be gained from David Brewster's review of 'Works on Mental Philosophy, Mesmerism, Electro-Biology, &c.', *North British Review*, 22 (1854–5), 179–224, and the anonymous review of 'Sir Henry Holland's *Recollections*' in *British Quarterly Review*, 55 (1872), 461–78.

According to L. S. Hearnshaw, Holland was one of a number of eminent medics interested in psychological theory who formed an informal grouping with W. B. Carpenter at their head.[49] Carpenter dedicated his major work *Principles of Mental Physiology* to Holland in 1874, in tribute to 'the wonderful suggestiveness' of his work.[50] But the group also included: Sir Benjamin Brodie (1783–1862), court surgeon to George IV and William IV, Professor of Comparative Anatomy and Physiology at the Royal College of Surgeons, President of the Royal College in 1844, President of the Royal Society from 1858 to 1861, and author of *Psychological Inquiries: in a Series of Essays intended to Illustrate the Mutual Relations of the Physical Organization and the Mental Faculties* (1854); Thomas Laycock (1812–1876), Professor of the Practice of Physic at Edinburgh from 1855 and author of *Mind and Brain* (1859); Robert Dunn (1799–1877), author of *An Essay on Physiological Psychology* (1858), and Daniel Noble (1810–1885), author of *The Brain and its Physiology* (1846), *Elements of Psychological Medicine: An Introduction to the Practical Study of Insanity* (1855), and *The Human Mind in its Relation with the Brain* (1858). Dunn and Noble were attached to hospitals in London and Manchester respectively, and the group as a whole formed a significant, and representative, body of liberal medical opinion that, in effect, mediated between the older body of ideas and the emergent generation of psychological radicals. G. H. Lewes's review of Brodie's *Psychological Inquiries* suggests something of the relations between this group and the ideas of the new generation. Brodie's book, Lewes says, 'fall[s] in with the current opinions of the day' but is, in fact, rather behind advanced theory in both physiology and psychology, especially in its conception of the relations between mind and body. The style was agreeable, and the book pleasant, but there 'is no headache in these pages'. Despite his criticisms, Lewes's review is not of the contemptuously dismissive kind he sometimes wrote in this period.[51]

[49] L. S. Hearnshaw, *A Short History of British Psychology 1840–1940* (London, 1964), 19–20. S. S. Schweber identifies Holland as a representative scientific intellectual of the early Victorian period: 'Scientists as Intellectuals: The Early Victorians', in James Paradis and Thomas Postlewait (eds.), *Victorian Science and Victorian Values: Literary Perspectives* (New York, 1981), 3.

[50] Carpenter, *Principles of Mental Physiology*, p. xiii.

[51] [G. H. Lewes], 'Brodie's Psychological Inquiries', *Saturday Review*, 1 (1856), 422–3. Lewes's perception that Brodie's work leaned both ways was shared by his less radical friend William Henry Smith ('Psychological Inquiries', *Blackwood's Edinburgh Magazine*, 77 (1855), 402–20), and Brodie's work appealed to Samuel Smiles, an opponent of the new psychology (see Smiles, *Self-Help; with Illustrations of Conduct and Perseverance*, 2nd edn. (London, 1866), 314). Smiles's views will be discussed more fully shortly. Either way, there is little doubt that the book was widely read. Smith's review begins: 'By this time everybody has read Sir Benjamin Brodie's interesting little book. Everybody at least should read it. There are no professional terms to embarrass, and no crabbed style to repel, the reader. It may lie with as much propriety on a lady's table as on a student's desk. It can weary no one, it will instruct most, it will suggest something to all.' The book was twice reprinted between 1854 and 1856. For discussion of Brodie's conservatism within the medical politics of the day, see Desmond, *Politics of Evolution*, esp. 269 ff.

Like his colleagues, Holland was interested in the newer medical theories and practices and was informed and serious about new biological ideas, especially, in the manner of a much more successful Tertius Lydgate, innovatory neurological and histological theory. Like Eliot's fictional doctor in *Middlemarch*, and like Carpenter, Holland was trained in Edinburgh, and Edinburgh was perceived as the British centre for new, excellent medical practice and teaching.[52] At the same time, Holland was an opponent of too-hasty speculation on the physiological basis of psychology and was a vigorous opponent of phrenology in the lively Edinburgh debates in the early part of the century.[53] This is indicative of the general range of his opinions, which were based upon an opposition to mere theoretical speculation in medical matters and a faith in the free, autonomous activity of the higher human faculties, particularly the will.

Holland was especially interested in psychosomatic phenomena, in the psychological action of alcohol and narcotics, and in the therapies that might become available from such investigation for a practising doctor. He is not interested in theoretical speculation, but his writing shows awareness of some of the latest physiological and biological literature, both British and French. What distinguishes him is his rejection of the strict demarcations between mind and body, and the healthy and the ill, current in his period. His interest in psychosomatic illness, for instance, set him aside as a thoughtfully 'advanced' physician. The preface to *Medical Notes and Reflections* (1839) announces that he has 'sought especially to associate pathology with physiology, the morbid with the natural and healthy states of the body, believing this principle of modern enquiry to be above all others fertile in sound conclusions'.[54] Likewise, the preface to *Chapters in Mental Physiology* (1852) states that the book is an investigation into the 'reciprocal actions and relations of mental and bodily phenomena, as they make up the totality of life', and he is particularly interested in the bearings of mental action upon 'morbid disease' either 'directly or indirectly—as cause or as effect'.[55]

Physiology is for Holland necessary, but not sufficient for investigating phenomena of mind. This is a repeated refrain. In discussing the physiology of automatic action, for instance, in which the most spectacular progress had been made in research, Holland is careful to say that 'it is still a knowledge of the instruments only that we have obtained'.[56] This way of putting it suggests there

[52] Charles Newman, *The Evolution of Medical Education in the Nineteenth Century* (Oxford, 1957).
[53] Sir Henry Holland, 'On Phrenology', in *Chapters in Mental Physiology* (London, 1852). G. N. Cantor, 'The Edinburgh Phrenology Debates: 1803–1828', *Annals of Science*, 32 (1975), 199.
[54] Sir Henry Holland, *Medical Notes and Reflections* (London, 1839), p. v.
[55] Holland, *Chapters*, p. v. Holland made a name here. Sir David Brewster wrote that he 'has particularly distinguished himself in the investigation of that branch of mental physiology which treats of the influence of the mind over the body' ([Brewster], 'Works on Mental Philosophy', 182).
[56] Holland, *Chapters*, 218.

is some other force wielding these instruments. Likewise, in his general assessment of the state of this research and its bearings on the study of psychology, he makes the sensible and accurate point that, 'in truth, both anatomy and physiology are still engaged in settling points of structure far below those of the ultimate organization of the brain', and he speaks of the 'undiscovered and impassable space that lies beyond it'.[57] Therefore the 'highest attainment is that which can best define the boundary of research, and labour for truth and knowledge within it'.[58] This is responsible caution in a physician (and the language of uncrossable boundaries is frequent in the book), but it also suggests a mind perhaps resistant to the conclusions that more daring thinkers such as Lewes, Huxley, or Spencer were venturing. In some respects, as in the work of John Stuart Mill and Bain, there is a backward-looking aspect to some of Holland's thought. For instance, he claims that in the investigation of the higher phenomena of consciousness only introspection will serve methodologically: 'The faculty, or principle, described under this name, can alone furnish us with those elementary facts which lie at the bottom of all mental phenomena, under whatever name propounded.'[59] The argumentative landscape of his work is furrowed and pitted with chasms, barriers, crevices, and obscurities that separate mind from body: 'Our existence may be said to lie on each side of this boundary [between mind and body]; yet with a chasm between, so profound and obscure, that though perpetually traversing it in all the functions of life, we have no eye to penetrate its depths.'[60]

Holland's work was well known to Lewes and George Eliot, not least because he was their doctor, and they respected it. Lewes made use of it in *The Physiology of Common Life*, *Problems of Life and Mind*, and several essays.[61] Eliot read the book too. It is mentioned in an informed, though passing, way in one of her notebooks for *Middlemarch*, and we can assume it formed a part of her research for Lydgate, as well as her more general thinking.[62] More widely, Holland held views whose general tenor would have been compatible in some major respects with those of both Lewes and Eliot—especially perhaps Eliot, for she was not so rigorously tied to the close exploration of disputed and demandingly technical sets of ideas, and would not have been so troubled by the conservative tendencies in Holland's physiological psychology.

It would be a large claim on slender evidence, that Holland's work exerted any considerable influence on George Eliot. But there are some striking connections

---

[57] Holland, *Chapters*, 266.    [58] Ibid. 241.    [59] Ibid. 47.
[60] Holland, *Medical Notes*, 152. Holland was pleased with this passage and repeated it in *Chapters*, 171.
[61] Lewes, 'Hereditary Influence, Animal and Human', *Westminster Review*, NS 10 (1856), 141; *Physiology of Common Life*, ii. 386; *Problems*, v. 180, 295–306.
[62] *George Eliot's 'Middlemarch' Notebooks*, ed. John Clark Pratt and Victor A. Neufeldt (London, 1979), 41.

between it and some features of *Middlemarch*. The metaphors that Holland uses to describe the operations of the mind—blending currents and merging streams, for instance, or the twining-together of thread—are shared by her, but they were not uncommon in the science and literature of the period. Nevertheless there is a recognizable similarity of thinking both in the description of certain detailed features of the mental operations, and the formulation of some general problems concerning moral behaviour.

Holland is interested in the intersections of different states of consciousness, which were often, in the prevailing taxonomic method of the time, described as discrete and separate. This was a feature of his work picked out for particular attention by Sir David Brewster.[63] Holland has in mind such everyday phenomena as the blurring that can occur between dream and fully attentive wakefulness, but also larger questions such as the discrimination between sanity and madness (I will return to this shortly). Similar ambiguous and complex states of mind are found widely and carefully described in George Eliot's fiction, and both she and Holland are interested, in a very fundamental way, in states of reverie when memory, desire, and perception become twisted together, and perception is coloured by subjectivity. Holland states that 'past images and memories rise up unbidden to perplex both sensations and acts by mingling with them, without control or direction of the rational will'.[64] He gives as an example the way we perceive those known to us in a daguerreotype. Ordinarily, we match a memory with the silhouette to produce the likeness, but this partial image can summon up other associated mental traces and our apparently secure recognition can become tangled.[65] Holland is, therefore, alert to a potential instability even in mundane mental life, and this is of a piece with his general outlook. For instance, he is concerned with the treatment of the insane, and is conscious—partly through personal experience to which he touchingly alludes[66]—that mental trouble is not peculiar to a small and segregable section of the population: 'how slight the line is, if line there be, which separates the healthy actions of mind from those of a morbid nature.'[67] He takes sensitive account of the problems of stress, depression, neurological dysfunction, illness, and circumstances. More widely, he is aware of the potential instability of all character, even in those who appear most firm, stable, and purposive.[68]

The force of this argument is best understood in context, for it is made at a time of wide-ranging popular discourses on 'character', which exploited and celebrated the ideological potential of the idea.[69] Samuel Smiles wrote probably the best known of these—*Character*—in 1871. But books of popular instruction

[63] [Brewster], 'Works on Mental Philosophy', 185–6.     [64] Holland, *Chapters*, 29.
[65] Ibid. 23.     [66] Ibid. 144.     [67] Ibid. 126.     [68] Ibid. 139–40.
[69] Stefan Collini has an excellent discussion of this in chapter 3 of *Public Moralists*.

on character, or fictional versions of them (often featuring that robust achiever Robinson Crusoe), were widely distributed, often as prizes, through church organizations like the Sunday Schools, and Utilitarian-backed organizations like the Mechanics' Institutes.[70] They formed a powerful body of ideological preconception in Victorian culture. Holland's guarded remarks on the possible complex instability of character thus have a relevant social context. Popular accounts of character conflated product and agency: what could be seen as a result of the interaction between individual potential and environmental life chances was, instead, offered as motive, role model, and moral desideratum. Smiles's account in *Self-Help* (1859) emphasizes this very clearly. The book concludes with chapters on 'Example—Models' (chapter 12) and 'Character—The True Gentleman' (chapter 13), in which it is proposed that:

Character is human nature in its best form. It is moral order embodied in the individual. Men of character are not only the conscience of society, but in every well-governed State they are its best motive power; for it is moral qualities which rule the world. Even in war, Napoleon said that the moral is to the physical as ten to one. The strength, the industry, the civilisation of nations—all depend upon individual character; and the very foundations of civil security seat upon it. Laws and institutions are but its outgrowth. In the just balance of nature, individuals, nations, and races will obtain just as much as they deserve, and no more. And as effect finds its cause, so surely does quality of character among a people produce its befitting results.[71]

The social and political context of theories of individual character are here very plain, and constitute another version of that political and ideological alarm that dogged psychology's footsteps in the mid-century. Smiles exhorts morally ('The crown and glory of life is Character'[72]) while offering both reward and threat in political and material terms. It is, therefore, significant that 'character' was a key term in the business of assessing social reputation (as Smiles's association of it with the idea of the gentleman suggests), and, probably more importantly, in the conduct of employer–employee relations through the 'character reference'. It was also common to generalize about 'national character' on the same basis. J. G. Millingen used the idea of a firm individual character as a moral barrier to insurgent passion, but he was also inclined to take a typically Podsnappish view of the giddy and feckless French: 'I have shown what the French *were*— what, in my humble opinion, they still *are*, and what most likely they *will be*, until time, and dearly-bought experience may effect a total change in their national character, and qualify them to be ruled by gentle means,—fitting them to appreciate the blessings of free institutions.'[73]

---

[70] These can be regularly found in second-hand bookshops, often with the prize labels still attached. The title of a recent find, the Anglo-American *Stories for Character Training: A Suggestive Series of Lessons in Ethics* by Ella Lyman Cabot and Edward Eyles (London, 1912), gives a clear indication of their intentions.    [71] Smiles, *Self-Help*, 383.

[72] Ibid. 382.    [73] Millingen, *Recollections*, p. x.

These ideas were regularly attacked by more radically minded psychologists and literary figures. Dickens's Bradley Headstone and Charlie Hexam, in *Our Mutual Friend*, are portraits in the psychological cost of this obsession with character, and its emphasis on denial and negativity, as is George Eliot's Tom Tulliver in *The Mill on the Floss*. Of Tom, Eliot writes: 'a character at unity with itself—that performs what it intends, subdues every counteracting impulse and has no visions beyond the distinctly possible, is strong by its very negations.'[74] But the novel makes clear the limitations of this strength, as, explicitly, does Philip Wakem when chiding Maggie: 'It is mere cowardice to seek safety in negations. No character becomes strong in that way. You will be thrown into the world some day, and then every rational satisfaction of your nature that you deny now, will assault you like a savage appetite.'[75] The psychologists made similar points. Like Eliot in *Middlemarch*, Lewes in *Problems of Life and Mind* described character as 'a process and an unfolding', not a stable entity.[76] These processes, he argues, are often unconscious and beyond the control of the will.[77] Alexander Bain, too, criticized Smiles's emphasis on will power: 'to bid a man be habitually cheerful . . . is like bidding him to triple his fortune, or add a cubit to his stature.'[78] In the same year, in a lecture to the Royal Institution, W. K. Clifford linked the work of novelists to the newly envisaged psychology of fluid processes:

Is it not regarded as the greatest stroke of the novelist that he should be able not merely to draw a character at any given time, but also sketch the growth of it through the changing circumstances of life? In fact, if you consider it a little further, you will see that it is not even true that a character remains the same for a single day: every circumstance, however trivial, that in any way affects the mind, leaves its mark, infinitely small it may be, imperceptible in itself, but yet more indelible than the stone-carved hieroglyphics of Egypt. And the sum of all these marks is precisely what we call character, which is the history of the entire previous life of the individual; which is therefore continually being added to, continually growing, continually in a state of change.[79]

Holland then, like his more radical contemporaries, was writing in the context of an ideologically loaded debate about the stability of character and the fluidity of psychological processes.

We should not, though, overestimate his radicalism. He was a man of his time, and a member of the Whig establishment, and there are limits to his

---

[74] George Eliot, *The Mill on the Floss* (1860), ed. A. S. Byatt (Harmondsworth, 1979), 407.

[75] Ibid. 428–9.

[76] George Eliot, *Middlemarch: A Study of Provincial Life* (1871–2), ed. W. J. Harvey (Harmondsworth, 1965), 178.

[77] Lewes, *Problems*, v. 140, 196–204.

[78] Alexander Bain, 'Common Errors on the Mind', *Fortnightly Review*, NS 4 (1868), 161.

[79] W. K. Clifford, 'On Some of the Conditions of Mental Development' (1868), in *Lectures and Essays*, i. 77.

psychiatric and psychological liberalism. He retains, for instance, the special category of 'moral insanity', a disease whose symptoms consist of behaviours that offend the consensual codes of moral and social behaviour and whose origin is to be found, he very typically says, largely in a depraved, vicious, and perverted prior life.[80] In other words, the cause is created by the diagnosis. As G. H. Lewes later put it, 'we say that drunkenness or sexual excess has caused insanity, when perhaps it was only a symptom of an undeclared disease'.[81] The real function of such diagnoses was, as Elaine Showalter makes clear, the regulation of what was perceived as abnormal or disruptive behaviour, especially by women.[82] But, by and large, Holland puts a good case for regarding the mental life as restless and complicated. For Holland, looking at a daguerreotype is a complex matter.

Let us turn now to a related moment in George Eliot. In chapter 28 of *Middlemarch* Dorothea's sensation of 'moral imprisonment' at Lowick on her return from her honeymoon in Rome is insistently conveyed by images of disordered perception. This continues an idea begun in the famous passage in chapter 20, which describes Dorothea's response to Rome in which the city appears 'like a disease of the retina'.[83] In her sitting room at Lowick she suffers from semi-hallucination. The world outside becomes a reflection of the decoration of her room; it is shrunken, inert, ghostly, and pale. 'Each remembered thing in the room was disenchanted, was deadened as an unlit transparency', and her eyes wander to a group of miniatures on the wall, particularly a picture of Casaubon's aunt Julia, Will Ladislaw's grandmother. She finds it companionable, for 'here was a woman who had known some difficulty about marriage'. The passage goes on:

Nay, the colours deepened, the lips and chin seemed to get larger, the hair and eyes seemed to be sending out light, the face was masculine and beamed on her with full gaze which tells her on whom it falls that she is too interesting for the slightest movement of her eyelid to pass unnoticed or uninterpreted. The vivid presentation came like a pleasant glow to Dorothea: she felt herself smiling, and turning from the miniature sat down and looked up as if she were again talking to a figure in front of her.[84]

The passage works by organizing a series of contrasts to convey meaning. It contrasts light against dimness, warmth against pallor, pleasure against unhappiness, animation against ennui, and finally—and ironically—clear-sightedness against

---

[80] Holland, *Chapters*, 137–8.　　[81] Lewes, *Problems*, v. 138.
[82] Showalter, *The Female Malady*, esp. ch. 1. For a helpful, general discussion of the issues raised by the problem of diagnostic attribution of cause in mental illness, and the social and professional consequences of it, see Scull, *Museums of Madness*, esp. ch. 4.
[83] Eliot, *Middlemarch*, 226.　　[84] Ibid. 308.

drabness. This last is ironic because it is only in hallucination that Dorothea perceives reality. Below her consciousness is hidden her desire for Will, and her subjective desires engulf perception and threaten, though do not engulf (and this is crucial), her sense of her moral duty and the life this sense of duty has offered her in the consequences of her choice of Casaubon for a husband. This is a central area of enquiry in the novel (it is reflected in the conflict between Lydgate and Rosamond), which details with superb acuity the intangible psychological tensions at work in the making of such choices where will, desire, perception, ambition, and habit are blurred. It is very typical of George Eliot's practice—and that of the intellectual circle in which she moved—that she should choose topical and relevant metaphors from the psychology and science of the day to convey these issues. The imagery of perception that dominates the account of Dorothea's dilemmas is closely related to that deployed by Sir Henry Holland to discuss the same kinds of notions in his psychological enquiries.

Similarly, Lydgate's case is conveyed by an equally apt scientific metaphor as he trembles on the edge of his proposal to Rosamond in chapter 31. Rosamond spills two tears.

That moment of naturalness was the crystalizing feathertouch: it shook flirtation into love. Remember that the ambitious man who was looking at those Forget-me-nots under the water was very warm-hearted and rash. He did not know where the chain went; an idea had thrilled through the recesses within him which had a miraculous effect in raising the power of passionate love lying buried there in no sealed sepulchre, but under the lightest, easily pierced mould. His words were quite abrupt and awkward; but the tone made them sound like an ardent, appealing avowal.[85]

Once more, and characteristically, the meanings and effects of this are gained by a virtuoso organization of contrasting metaphor and image, which carries a foreboding irony, but the passage is even more complexly organized than that from chapter 28. The implied reference to Christ, or the raising of Lazarus, brings death close to this scene of love—in book 4 entitled 'Waiting for Death'—but the offered, though unstated, prospect of redemption is undercut by what we know the fate of these lovers will be, and by the stressed materiality of the language and reference: the heavy 'sealed sepulchre' and the top dressing of leaf mould, the importance of which for the regeneration and fertility of the soil, along with the action of worms, was just becoming understood.

But the ironies reach further. Lydgate is a man ever peering into a microscope at micro-phenomena, including those of pond life and the actions of water. In the opening two sentences we have two related images: first the formation of crystal in a supersaturated saline solution at the touch of a needle (Lewes also

[85] Ibid. 335.

uses the image in *Problems of Life and Mind*[86])—a phenomenon usually observed only under the microscope; and then, secondly, there is a kind of mawkish parody of this—the blue of Rosamond's eyes are the botanical specimens (Forget-me-nots) examined under the lens of her tears. This second image is sentimental in mood and language, and reflects Lydgate's ornamental (and sexist) expectations of what is fitting in a woman and a wife. This, in turn, is undercut by the gothic language of graves and decomposition that follows, and the scientific register associated with the microscope. The scientific language carries a further irony. It is as a comprehending scientist that Lydgate wishes to think of himself, but here he 'did not know where the chain went' and eventually his ambition and prospects are broken. He cannot see what he should see, and when, fifty pages later, Farebrother visits him, he finds Lydgate's 'tableful of apparatus and specimens in confusion'.[87]

Lydgate is unable to resolve with happiness the quarrel between will and desire; Dorothea manages to do so only by the fortunate death of Casaubon. This benign event resolves a dilemma that, under the prevailing moral and literary standards of the period, could not have been settled otherwise. It is inconceivable that Eliot might have portrayed a scandalous liaison outside marriage for Dorothea and Will such as the one she and Lewes enjoyed. But her understanding of the problem and the situation, and her careful and telling deployment of images and ideas used in the scientific, psychological, and medical worlds to render moments of crisis in these dilemmas, illustrate something of the significance of the kinds of arguments about the will and the exercise of the higher mental faculties that psychologists in the mid-century were making. In formulating theories about psychological categories such as the will, these writers were coming very close to questions of conduct and ethics, and many of them were alert to the fact that a too-rigorous investigation of such matters under a medical or physiological light might well compromise values and approved behaviours in a far-reaching way.

Henry Holland, for instance, realized the implications of his belief in the close relationship between mind and body, subjectivity and perception, and is quick to close the doors when it looks as though a too-frisky ideological horse may bolt. More than once he calls off discussion by raising the spectre of dangerous metaphysics. The train of thought started by the daguerreotype analogy is scared away with the comment that the subject is 'very obscure, and blends itself with

---

[86] Lewes is writing of the way in which meaning and understanding flash into being. It is an image of extraordinary sophistication: 'The words float suspended, soulless, mere sounds. No sooner are these floating sounds grasped by the copula, than in that grasp they are grouped into significance: they start into life, as a supersaturated saline solution crystallizes on being touched by a needle-point', Lewes, *Problems*, ii. 145.          [87] Eliot, *Middlemarch*, 383.

the most abstruse points of metaphysical inquiry'.[88] Likewise, later, he says that 'the influence of the mental passions and emotions on the bodily economy' is a question far too wide to admit a helpful treatment and moves on.[89] In other words, the discussion is truncated at a point at which it might throw categories into question that elsewhere form a cornerstone of his beliefs. This tactic is rather revealingly typical of the intellectual procedure of the book as a whole. Alongside the fair-minded, informed, scientific caution, and the helpful scepticism about a too-exorbitant extension of the newer physiological findings, there runs a deep, conventional understanding of the special place of the higher human faculties in man's destiny in relation both to his own development and to God.

Holland's conception of the will is of a free-acting autonomous agency that is independent of neurology and has no material basis.[90] He is concerned to separate the will from other mental entities that might be related to it such as instinct or habit. Habit is morally fickle, for habits are as liable to be bad as good. Morality cannot be generated from habit, and thus Holland opposes the cruder kinds of Utilitarian thinking on such topics as education. This, too, is a position he shared with George Eliot and Lewes. Of habits he says: 'some minister directly to the power and integrity of intellect, or to the moral discipline of the mind. Others are faulty and injurious associations, which by repetition become almost compulsory on their nature, and usurp the place and prerogative of reason.'[91] Of education Holland concludes that forcing children too severely merely wrecks 'the condition and culture of every faculty of body and mind'.[92] Children should be allowed to develop in a way that is congenial to their temperament and abilities and not to a pattern. This seems to have been George Eliot's belief in the late 1850s also, to judge from the account of Tom and Maggie Tulliver's education in *The Mill on the Floss*.

It is noticeable that both these accounts, of habit and of education, juxtapose mental acquisition to mental endowment, and that priority is given to the latter over the former. The passage on habit suggests that habit needs to be controlled by the superior mental powers of intellect and reason, which should have a natural prerogative. Likewise, it is these abilities that educational practice should develop. This, of course, is a perfectly sensible position. Theorists of environmentally derived mental abilities—such as the stricter associationist Utilitarians—have severe and compromising difficulties when they come to explain the active exercise and functioning of these abilities. There is a problem, however, on the other side when the status and origin of these abilities come to be theorized in

---

[88] Holland, *Chapters*, 23.      [89] Ibid. 45.

[90] Roger Smith, 'Physiological Psychology and the Philosophy of Nature in Mid-Nineteenth-Century Britain' (D.Phil. diss., Cambridge, 1970), 56.

[91] Holland, *Chapters*, 223. Note again the political analogy implied in the notion of prerogative.

[92] Ibid. 157–8.

accounts, like Holland's, that favour the nature rather than the nurture pole of the argument. This is because Holland is keen to exempt these higher abilities from the conditioning of their material means—that is, the state of the nervous organism in contact with the environment. At best, Holland is prepared to grant that faculties like the intellect and the will, and the power of attention (which renders possible the first two), have the status of instincts. But these instincts, Holland suggests, are 'derived from higher power'—that is, God—and he traces in support similar arguments in Bacon, Newton, Descartes, and Locke.[93] In other words, they have no formally specified relationship to the physiological circumstances of the individual, and can in no real sense be thought of as instincts in any biological sense.

However, Holland is not really satisfied with such a view, which is at odds with the scientific cast of his profession and general outlook, and the tone of this discussion is subdued and rather half-hearted. This aspect of his work finds itself in a contradiction whose consequences can be only postponed and not resolved. In one manner Holland can speak as a pious Natural Theologian of his period, sketching out a blandly benign view of the divine harmony of nature.[94] Thus he wishes to insist that moral and physical causes are identical because both spring from God. The evidence of God's work in nature, indeed, is the exercise of those higher faculties that perceive His existence. The argument is charmingly circular:

In pursuing science along this path (the happiest exercise of man's divination), we obtain certainty of an intelligent cause from a source hardly separable from the consciousness of our own intellectual existence. And in thus making the highest efforts of the human faculty the interpreters of the principle of divine causation, we bring our conception of moral cause into closest relation with the physical, and acquire not only elevation, but distinctness and stability in all our views on the subject.[95]

Holland's argument is structured by such separations. In the absence of absolute proof of the material foundations of the higher mental activities, consideration of the material determinants of mind should be kept clear of the question, allowing the higher faculties free rein to be considered independent entities. There is thus the characteristic language of gulfs, lines, or boundaries that separate the two spheres of research on which we have already remarked. The brain, in one of Holland's most repeated phrases, is a 'double organ', an assembly of functions that nevertheless are not, and cannot be, equal to the capacity of mind as a whole. Consciousness, will, reason, intellect, all the higher faculties are more than this. A line or boundary 'separates material organization and actions from

[93] Holland, *Chapters*, 207–9.
[94] Holland, 'Natural Theology', in *Fragmentary Papers*, 195–205.
[95] Holland, *Chapters*, 173 n.

the proper attributes of mind—the instruments of voluntary power from the will itself'.[96] 'Materialistic' explanation cannot be considered, because priority must be given to the 'intellectual existence, of which consciousness and personal identity are the simplest expressions, but which spreads itself out into the endless varieties of thought and feeling'.[97]

Nevertheless, as Holland is quick to say, those who argue 'for an immaterial principle' alone do not convince, because it is useless to deny 'the close and constant action of matter upon mind'.[98] As a result, Holland was particularly impatient with Coleridge and his followers.[99] Instead, he tried to reconceive the problem. The will and the other higher faculties *may* have their origin in matter (though this is subject always to God's ordinance), but they quickly liberate themselves from this to become self-acting entities. This was the solution proposed also by Carpenter, who argued for 'a *will* which, alike in the Mind as in the Body, can utilize the Automatic agencies to work out its own purposes'.[100] Holland and his school thus have the best of both explanatory worlds and can picture drastically alternative scenarios for describing the operations of nature. On the one hand, as we have said, he posits a bland harmony in the arrangement of things to which praises are from time to time sung in the book. But, on the other hand, these higher faculties are also pictured in struggle and difficulty: people go mad, their perceptions and beliefs are uncertain, the organism on which they rely is subject to disease and dysfunction. There is 'an unceasing conflict between the will and the material conditions which surround it'.[101] The juxtaposition of these two scenarios is sometimes quite extraordinary:

The struggle, for such it may often be termed, between voluntary and involuntary acts—between the intellectual and the automatic functions—is, in truth, a dominant fact in the mental constitution of man; one upon which all the phenomena, both of mind and body, closely depend at every instant of life. In using the term struggle however let it be added that there is no provision of our nature which better illustrates the wisdom and prescience to which we owe our being. Man might have been created with larger powers than he has—but under the limitation manifestly designed by his Creator, we must ever admire that wonderful adaptation, by which faculties, different in nature, and often opposed in action, do yet concur and harmonize in general results; giving order and stability to

---

[96] Ibid. 171.
[97] Ibid. 172. See also the late essay 'Materialism As a Question of Science and Philosophy', in *Fragmentary Papers*, 206–13.                                    [98] Holland, *Chapters*, 173.
[99] 'I never took a place among the worshippers at his shrine. I recollect him only as an eloquent but intolerable talker; impatient of the speech and opinions of others, very inconsecutive, and putting forth a plethora of words, misty dogmas in theology and metaphysics, partly of German origin, which he never seemed to clear up to his own understanding or that of others. What has come out posthumously of his philosophy has not removed this imputation upon it' (Sir Henry Holland, *Recollections of Past Life* (London, 1872), 205).
[100] William B. Carpenter, 'The Physiology of the Will', *Contemporary Review*, 17 (1871), 192.
[101] Holland, *Chapters*, 65.

all the complex functions of life, and admitting of increase of power to those of the highest kind by their due and sufficient exercise. We might have been constituted, so as to regulate by will those actions which are now automatic or instinctive. Were these functions suddenly committed to us, disorder and death would speedily ensue.[102]

The contradiction in this passage between the language of struggle and the language of harmony is representative. Holland mixes the propositions of the older Natural Theology with a newer vocabulary, which toys with evolutionary language—hence the hypothesis of the evolution from willed to automatic mental functions—and the notion of intra-organic struggle. (We will discuss the former, quasi-Lamarckian idea of the inheritance of habitualized functions—it is not the only reference to it in the *Chapters*[103]—in more detail in Chapters 6 and 7.) The tenor of the passage is to posit a teeming, unwilled life going on beneath our consciousness, which, once more, unites Holland with the adventurous scientific minds of his period, and, for that matter, once again, with George Eliot and *Middlemarch*.

I have briefly called attention to the famous chapter 20 in Rome and pointed to the way Dorothea's mental confusion is related to bodily processes and even to organic dysfunction ('a disease of the retina'). There is another famous image in these marvellous paragraphs:

That element of tragedy which lies in the very fact of frequency, has not yet wrought itself into the course emotion of mankind; and perhaps our frames could hardly bear much of it. If we had a keen vision and feeling of all ordinary human life, it would be like hearing the grass grow and the squirrel's heart beat, and we should die of that roar which lies on the other side of silence. As it is the quickest of us walk about well wadded with stupidity.[104]

There are several propositions at work here that are worth serious consideration in the light of the passage from Henry Holland. There is the same quasi-Lamarckian idea that emotion can with frequency work its way into the emotional habits of the race (though George Eliot's attitude to this seems, at best, equivocal); and there is the idea of an abounding life going on beneath our ken and beyond our capacity to respond. Our conscious life is here understood to be limited by the very structure of consciousness itself and its customary modes of comprehension ('stupidity'). This is not an absolute limitation in an extremist phenomenological sense (for one can break from isolated, habitual subjectivity in moments when emotion claims our comprehending sympathy). Nor is it a Freudian proposition, which would imply that our being is structured by the shape of the repressions that form our unconscious being. It is, rather, a powerfully

---

[102] Holland, *Chapters*, 27.
[103] See also p. 224, where the apparent tendency for habit to be transmitted in domestic animals is noted.                                      [104] Eliot, *Middlemarch*, 225.

*historicized* view of active consciousness of a kind that has become, maybe, somewhat unpopular in the late twentieth century.

This argument of George Eliot's—one sustained throughout *Middlemarch*—is deeply impressive, and it is one towards which the most exciting of the mid-to-late Victorian psychologies were reaching. (It is the task to which Lewes dedicated himself in *Problems of Life and Mind*.) The argument is this. Our subjectivities are historically, culturally, and temperamentally limited. We are limited as biological beings, and by the era and location of our birth. Our culture feeds us with obstinacies, blindnesses, and prejudices of many kinds. But by emotions that excite us beyond ourselves ('sympathy'[105]), and by acts of historical comparison and comprehension, the limitations of our own understandings can be overcome sufficiently. And, because understanding can become sufficient, we can begin to understand beyond ourselves. Cultural, national, social, sexual, and historical differences (all of which feature in *Middlemarch*) do *not* necessarily mean relativism, or cognitive scepticism. They mean that, at the heart of our being, in the organism, and at the heart of our morals, politics, and cognitions, we can comprehend, make effort, and thus enable 'the growing good of the world'. The whole effort of *Middlemarch*, and of George Eliot's other work, and of the most closely related psychology of the period, was towards this kind of comprehension. *Middlemarch* (like *The Mill on the Floss* or *Adam Bede* or *Scenes of Clerical Life*) says: we need to understand those people and that culture of forty years ago, in a remote provincial town, and thus come to understand ourselves, for that past is part of our identity as well as part of our difference as we are here, in 1872—or in 2000.

Both George Eliot and Henry Holland, for all their emphasis on the will, are profoundly opposed to the simple-minded ideological appropriations of it. In *Self-Help* Smiles writes that:

Whatever theoretical conclusions logicians may have formed as to the freedom of the will, each individual feels that practically he is free to choose between good and evil—that he is not as a mere straw thrown upon the water to mark the direction of the current, but that he has within him the power of a good swimmer, and is capable of striking out for himself . . . There is no absolute constraint upon our volitions, and we feel and know that we are not bound, as by a spell, with reference to our actions. It would paralyze all desire of excellence were we to think otherwise. The entire business and conduct of life, with its domestic rules, its social arrangements, and its public institutions, proceed upon the practical conviction that the will is free. Without this where would be

[105] This idea is present in several works by psychologists in Eliot's circle—Lewes most obviously, but see Alexander Bain: 'Distinct from the gift of reading accurately what is passing in the mind of a fellow-being, is the susceptibility to take on the precise excitement that actuates a second person, and follow out, and cherish, that strain of excitement to the suppression of our own separate feelings at the time. This last is the true meaning of sympathy' (*The Emotions and the Will* (London, 1859), 109).

responsibility?—and what the advantage of teaching, advising, preaching, reproof, and correction? What were the use of laws, were it not the universal belief . . . that men obey them or not, very much as they individually determine?[106]

Smiles's exhortation is designed to encourage under-confident entrepreneurs. As a mode of comprehending a culture, and the various participants in that culture, it is, in its individualism and refusal to think of variation in time, circumstance, and temperament, wholly inadequate. But it draws its effect and confidence from a powerful, prevailing mode of psychological discourse of the period.

We have examined the work of Sir Henry Holland as a representative of the middle ground of informed psychological opinion in the mid-century. Alert to the newer findings in psycho-physiology and to the arguments launched from them, Holland nevertheless does not wish to abandon the older modes and categories of analysis handed down to him. In the absence of firm proof to the contrary, he maintains faith in the old categories of special human faculties whose activities cannot be otherwise than autonomous—even though that may contradict other elements of his beliefs. Perhaps in this situation we can detect another legacy of his Scottish education: both an advanced medical man's inductivist scepticism, and the heritage of Scottish 'Common-Sense' faculty psychology. Whatever the reasons, Holland's work tells us something of the situation that confronted the new generation of psychologists whose work began to appear in the 1850s. Holland's is a way of thinking that resists, ultimately, all the forms of exclusive psychological explanation available at the beginning of the decade. At various points he has harsh words for vitalism, for materialism, for the arguments made by analogy, and the arguments made from anatomy (phrenology). He applies only a limited and constrained associationist terminology and method, and, though informed of its findings, wishes to be circumspect in his applications of physiology. His refusal of commitment, though, leaves him with a typology of the mental functions that has some unhelpful ideological neighbours, and a bland assurance of the triumph of the will, of divine causation and purpose, and of the unity of the mental functions in the *sensorium commune* (an old concept still used by him).[107] Given the impossibility of closing the gap between mind and body because of the state of our knowledge, he concludes, it is perhaps best not to try. Such conclusions again courted dualism and were unappetizing for the writers whose work will be examined in Part Two of this book.

But Holland also gloried in diversity—in the range of cultures he encountered on his many foreign travels, in the varieties of provincial and metropolitan life in Britain, in the 'wonderful diversities' life itself produces from 'unity of origin'.[108]

---

[106] Smiles, *Self-Help*, 227.    [107] Holland, *Chapters*, 264 for example.
[108] Holland, 'Natural History of Man' (1849), in *Essays on Scientific and Other Subjects Contributed to the Edinburgh and Quarterly Reviews* (London, 1862), 465.

In his autobiography, Holland writes of 'our systems of Psychology', and the plural was crucial for him for the 'subject indeed is too vast and complex to be approached from any single point, or comprised in any one scheme'.[109] This pluralism is revealing of both the variety of psychological debate in the period, and of the discourse of medicine's uncertain response to the new issues it disclosed. For both Holland and Millingen, the pressure of their clinical experience, and their professional interest in mind–body states, brought their ideas into conflict with psychological orthodoxy and exposed some of the tensions and contradictions in mid-century theory. Holland is interested in the complex minutiae of perception and cognition, the epistemological ambiguities of ordinary states of mind, and the potentially entangled aetiology of feeling. His work is, in this aspect, compatible with the growing interest in mind as a fluid energy system in which physical processes play a significant role. He is uneasy, however, when analysis leads him to confusions at the boundaries of theoretical propriety. Millingen, too, is racked by the tension between theological and material ways of explaining human behaviour, and he has none of Holland's urbane insouciance to smooth the way. His work—like the clientele with whom he worked —has a raw, exposed quality. It is a world of violent contest, of the volcano and the guillotine rather than the daguerreotype. Though more luridly than Holland, he too is disturbed by the collision between mind and body, spirit and nature, and readily perceives the social consequences of unstable and uncertain psychological boundaries.

The discourse of medicine exposes the faultlines and makeshifts in the psychological theory of the mid-nineteenth century. The confusion over the status of the faculties, the enquiry into the unexpected complexity of their operation, the mingling of mind and body, a generally unsettled conception of nature, anxieties over the increasing somatization of psychological theory, as well as apprehension about the pressing public context of debate, are all evident. The cosmopolitan Holland and the adventurer Millingen, from their different worlds, converge in defining the most immediate of the psychological issues in the mid-century. That neither of them sits comfortably in the discursive camps thus far defined for Victorian psychology is as it should be, for theirs was a less than tidy field of activity. The plurality of psychologies Holland welcomed also seems the right note on which to close Part One of this book. For, like an improvising jazz quartet, the four discourses of Victorian psychology made tunes and discords without strong, inevitable closure.

---

[109] Holland, *Recollections*, 327.

# Particulars: Three Writers in their Times and Contexts

# CHAPTER 5

# Alexander Bain and the New Psychology of the Higher Faculties

Part Two of this book turns attention from the general discursive configurations of Victorian psychology to the work of three individuals: Alexander Bain, Herbert Spencer, and G. H. Lewes. There are several reasons for this alteration in focus. The shift from general to particular makes visible the profile of individual careers in ways not possible in more generalized description. It allows us to study the particular circumstances of these ideas under development, and to see their hesitations, lacunae, and abrupt spurts of growth. Through the study of reviews and other response to the work of these individuals, it also continues to allow us to attach individual developments to the larger picture and to see how, in the complex architecture of Victorian psychological theory, individuals made choices and pushed arguments within a heterogeneous discursive framework.

I am conscious that, to some extent, this approach conflicts with a key emphasis in important, recent work in the history of ideas, particularly that following from Michel Foucault's path-breaking studies. Work in this line has stressed, above all, the importance of general descriptions of discursive formations, and especially their regulatory powers. Sometimes (not least in Foucault's own hands) it has resulted in habits of analysis that set aside the agency of individuals in a way that carries consequences not only for the study of intellectual history, but for the political conception of the thinking human individual, whose role, to a significant extent, it depreciates. Foucault's programmatic depersonalization of authors, in his classic polemical essay of 1969 'What Is An Author?', is symptomatic: 'In short, it is a matter of depriving the subject (or its substitute) of its role as originator, and of analysing the subject as a variable and complex function of discourse.'[1] To elide agency in this way, and to characterize discourses monolithically, as Foucault's turn of mind is apt to do, belittles creative activity and neglects the situations of specific intellectual imaginations. This, for me, is a matter of intellectual and historiographical, as well as political and ethical regret. Exciting in its generalizations, indispensable in its emphasis on power and authority, discerningly intelligent in its interdisciplinary conceptions, post-

---

[1] Michel Foucault, 'What Is An Author?', in *The Foucault Reader*, ed. Paul Rabinow (Harmondsworth, 1986), 118.

Foucauldian work can diminish acts of conscious intelligence and creative will and therefore, in the end, an important potential for human freedom.

Yet, to put the opposite case, overemphasis on the work of individuals that is heedless of general discursive pressures is liable to underestimate the power of discursive regulation to shape and set limits to enquiry, and is unlikely to generate much analysis of the underlying structures of the theory it studies. All individual insight is, of course, accompanied by blindness, and very often its un-perceptiveness issues from a structure of assumptions that, unspoken, regulate its operation. Thus, Victorian psychology was clearly overwhelmingly rationalist and intellectualist in methodological demeanour. It made little of apparently irrational experience, and avoided the instinctive. It evaded experiences of physic-ality and of the body except as issues of abstract sensation considered epistemo-logically, or, in physiology, as psychological bodies imagined in the anatomical inertias of death. Sometimes, especially in the medical literature, it was given to outbursts of regulatory enthusiasm and sermonized on the passions. It was almost always captured—and, as often, captivated—by the gravitational pull of the discourse of the soul in a way that applies equally, if differently, to those who wished to avoid religious perspectives as to those who wished to celebrate them. Victorian psychology was also powerfully normative and, on the whole, sought a bland elimination of unruly subjectivity, suppressing the dense particularity of the self by tactics of relentless generalization and thematic emphases on the type rather than the person, the abstract process rather than the individual, the standard and not the aberrant. These are the elements of deep consensus where analysis that follows from Foucauldian commitments can shape its strongest story.

However, a different kind of methodological model—one free of strangula-tion by discourse on the one side, and the autarky of the individual on the other—is desirable, and might be found close to our materials in the nineteenth century. Darwin taught that development occurs by way of profuse diversity rather than closed uniformity, and this, it seems to me, is true in the intellectual as in the biological realm. Variety, contest, provisionality, discordance, opposition, revis-ability, capacities for logical or loose integration, temporary powers of rhetoric and persuasion, the suggestibility of language, and especially of metaphor, to advance speculation or ease the path of a controversial or unfinished theory—all of these are key ingredients in the development of a discipline, especially one as fluid, polyglot, prolix, and contested as Victorian psychology. It is the porousness and loose-weaving of psychological debate in the nineteenth century that allows specific creative activities to take place.

By contrast, in *The Order of Things*, Foucault describes the emergence of 'the psychological region' from sources in three nineteenth-century disciplines (or 'epistemological regions'): biology, economics, and philology. The ' "psycholo-gical region" ', he writes, 'found its locus in that place where the living being, in extension of its functions, in its neuro-motor blueprints, its physiological regulations, but also in the suspense that interrupts and limits them, opens itself to the possibility of representation'.[2] The idea that representational possibility is a key concern both of nineteenth-century psychological theory itself, and for the historian of its development, is a perspective shared by this book. But Foucault's calculated depersonalization of psychology's development, its attribution to a girdle of confining 'regions' the brief 'suspension' of whose vigilance allows growth, and his influential, geopolitical conceit of discourse as a set of competing powers allowing development only in the interstices of their activities, is—I feel—more questionable. Foucault's images (the metaphors are the same in French) appear to be derived from the imperialist geopolitics of the nineteenth-century European states, or of the Cold War, which constituted the historical 'region' of Foucault's own book (it was first published in 1966). These lend an imperiously static character to his descriptions of intellectual development. The rivalry between biology, economics, and philology, he asserts, is not a 'limited episode', but a 'matter of ineffaceable fact, which is bound up, for ever, with their particular arrangement in the particular space'.[3] Alongside the simple question 'why only these three?', we might also query the limiting force of this perception of an imprisoning discursive 'space', and the strange conception of historical time entailed in that crude 'for ever'.

On the whole, therefore, the model with which I work in this book is closer to that offered by George Eliot in *Middlemarch* when she muses in chapter 11 on the coming of her enthusiastic, young doctor Tertius Lydgate (himself a psycho-physiologist of promise) to the 'old provincial society' of the town. In a cascade of details and metaphors, Eliot indicates the complicated ways in which changes of perception and relation occur in the 'double change of self and beholder', the 'stealthy convergence of human lots', the 'slow preparation of effects from one life on another', and the 'less marked vicissitudes which are constantly shifting the boundaries . . . and begetting new consciousness of interdependence' and 'fresh threads of connection'.[4] The history of Victorian psychology sits more comfortably in the emergent properties of such a descriptive environment than in more abstract methodological models of discursive power. It is a feature of Eliot's analysis, of course, that her reflections on process emerge relatively late in the experience of reading the novel. They do not establish her world, they are sustained by their embeddedness in the detail that surrounds them. It is a technique similar to that named 'thick description' by the anthropologist Clifford Geertz, and it is one that might be considered to be at the heart of realist aesthetics.[5]

---

[2] Michel Foucault, *The Order of Things: An Archaeology of the Human Sciences*, translator and editor unnamed (New York, 1973), 355.

[3] Ibid. 356.    [4] Eliot, *Middlemarch*, 122–3.

[5] Clifford Geertz, 'Thick Description: Towards an Interpretive Theory of Culture', in *The Interpretation of Cultures*.

Accordingly, the three chapters in Part Two of this book concentrate on the careers of three individuals. But they are equally concerned to place their work in its public context, principally by giving substantial and detailed attention to the reviews each received. Usually, as was the way with the Victorian 'higher journalism', these reviews are generous in length, openly discursive, and intellectually unimpeded in their engagements whether supportive or hostile. It is a conversation in print across an intellectual culture, and a study of these responses opens the works of a particular writer to the ebb and flow of general debate. What follows may spotlight the soloist, but it is crucial to continue to hear the combination playing—including its discords—which establishes the solo's effects.

Why Bain, Spencer, and Lewes? Their selection is determined on several criteria. They were central to the debates of the period and initiated, influenced, or responded to most of the leading psychological ideas of the period. At the hub of key arguments, their work is both representative and illustrative of the spread and progress of discussion, and all three were prodigious writers, both generalist and specialist. They produced sustained, authoritative work on psychological questions and occupied significant positions in the movement of ideas. Unlike Huxley, John Mill, or Carpenter (three who commanded similar generalist respect, but who were best known for work in other areas), Bain, Spencer, and Lewes had, for their peers and subsequent historians alike, reputations as innovatory psychological specialists who influenced the conduct of the discipline in the second half of the nineteenth century. Bain transformed the associationist paradigm in the discourse of the philosophy of mind; Spencer and Lewes contributed most significantly to the development of psychology within the framework of evolutionary biology and the study of society. All three knew each other well and considered themselves engaged in a common enterprise. With George Eliot and others, they represent a distinct and important interdisciplinary formation in Victorian intellectual culture within which the individual careers of Bain and Lewes, especially, have been too little studied. One aim of this book is to bring these achievements into a better light, where the lights and shadows of Victorian interdisciplinary endeavour can be more clearly seen.

## BAIN, MILL, AND THE POLITICS OF PSYCHOLOGICAL THEORY IN THE MID-CENTURY

Alexander Bain (1818–1903) did not arrive an innocent in the turbulent psychological debates of the 1850s, for London was already disposed to receive the Scotsman with suspicion. Thus his arrival was somewhat like that of another incomer, Tertius Lydgate in *Middlemarch*, and—to use George Eliot's phrase— those who received them 'counted on swallowing . . . and assimilating [them] very comfortably'.[6] Bain, however, was crucially unlike Lydgate in important respects. Where Lydgate is significantly 'better born than other country surgeons',[7] hailing from the gentry and enjoying a cosmopolitan education in Edinburgh and Paris, Bain was a man of the working class, the son of an Aberdeen weaver, and among the objections made to his work were the sneers of the 'better born'. He was also self-educated, and a significantly more astute street-fighter in intellectual politics. More profoundly and skilfully aware than Eliot's naïve and instinctively haughty doctor, of the value and pitfalls of patronage, Bain, when he arrived in London, was well known as a confederate of John Stuart Mill, and the party of radical and liberal Utilitarianism. This guaranteed the suspicion, but it also supplied the advantage. Bain managed the success of his career as thoroughly as Lydgate spoiled his.

Victorian reviewers and modern scholars universally agree that Bain's work came at an important juncture in the history of British psychology.[8] He entered the psychological debates of the 1850s and 1860s as the voice of a modernized associationism alert to the possibilities of the new physiology, and with a determined instinct to marry the two while making the latter subordinate to the former. Whether supportive or hostile, contemporary reviewers accepted this view of the project, and many welcomed its recognizably synthetic ambitions. But for opponents, especially those reared in the faculty psychology and the conservative opposition, new physiological error merely compounded ancient offence, and Bain felt much of the angry hostility one might anticipate from the intellectual and cultural commotion described in previous chapters. He was one of the unsettling strangers described in *Middlemarch* as arriving with what was thought to be 'an alarming novelty of skill [and] an offensive advantage in cunning'.[9] His psychology, therefore, was shunned on religious and political grounds alike.

The Unitarian William MacCall is representative. His pieces on Bain in the early 1860s—'Morbid Psychology' and 'On *The Study of Character*'—use ideas and language characteristic of those embracing the 'spiritualist position' (to use MacCall's self-description). Bain's psychology, he asserts, lacks 'charm' in the face of the 'mystery of the universe'. Instead of seeking 'self-oblivion in nature', or the 'grand', 'great', or 'infinite' experiences of religion, it is morbidly introspective in its 'hideous self-anatomy', or cockily assertive in its 'Liliputian' antics. The 'microscopic intelligencies' and 'barren gaze of logicians and psychologists' are

---

[6] Eliot, *Middlemarch*, 183.    [7] Ibid. 179.

[8] *Brett's History of Psychology*, 456–64; Boring, *History of Experimental Psychology*, 236; Hearnshaw, *Short History of British Psychology*, 2; D. B. Klein, *A History of Scientific Psychology: Its Origins and Philosophical Backgrounds* (London, 1970), ch. 22; Thomas Hardy Leahey, *A History of Psychology: Main Currents in Psychological Thought* (Englewood Cliffs, NJ, 1980), 169–70; W. S. O'Neil, *The Beginnings of Modern Psychology*, 2nd edn. (Brighton, 1982), 2; Robert M. Young, *Mind, Brain and Adaptation*, 150, 182.    [9] Eliot, *Middlemarch*, 122.

'boundlessly breaking what is already too much of a fragment already'. The notions of proper boundaries in nature, and, more importantly still, the proper parameters of human enquiry, are central to such arguments. But, for MacCall, Bain adds social offence, and his descriptions of Bain's psychology chide his presumption as well as belittling his findings: it is like a tailor watching a strutting bantam cock, or an old woman unpacking rubbish from a cupboard.[10] This treatment of Bain was not singular, and Lewes's and Harriet Martineau's expositions of Comte, for instance, are, according to MacCall, 'potations of Cockney caudle and Ambleside small-beer'.[11] Such criticisms open important questions about the resources and perspectives of the dominant intellectual culture as these incomers appear on the threshold. George Eliot's contemporary defence of seventeenth-century Dutch genre painting in *Adam Bede* (1859) is absolutely to the point. She delights in the 'rare, precious truthfulness . . . which lofty-minded people despise' in 'faithful pictures of a monotonous homely existence, which has been the fate of so many more among my fellow-mortals than a life of pomp or absolute indigence'.[12] The appeal to common experience at the common end of the middle rank, to scenes of tailors, cockerels, and old women, is one shared by these painters, this novelist, the Comteans, and Alexander Bain the psychologist alike.

MacCall's reviews also indicate another important component in British culture's response to the new psychology at this period—that is, the distinctively *literary* nature of the objections made to it. The attitudes that inform his polemics continue and represent certain features in the heritage of English, literary Romanticism as interpreted by conservative mid-century Victorians for whom Wordsworth was a central figure. He had, after all, been dead for less than a decade. I have particularly in mind his hostility to science and strenuous 'intellectual' enquiry generally. The point of view represented by Wordsworth's famous lines on the 'meddling intellect' was widely shared, and the lines themselves were often quoted. The analytical and bookish intellect, Wordsworth wrote,

> Misshapes the beauteous forms of things;
> —We murder to dissect.

---

[10] William MacCall, *The Newest Materialism: Sundry Papers on the Books of Mill, Comte, Bain, Spencer, Atkinson and Feuerbach* (London, 1873). This volume reprints MacCall's essays and reviews over a decade or so. Quotations are taken from pp. 78–87. The grouping of writers discussed is interesting, particularly the inclusion of Feuerbach—the piece on whom is a review of George Eliot's translation of 1854—among the scientists and radicals. He is held unpleasantly to 'materialize' religion. MacCall also takes this opportunity to attack women intellectuals, whose 'disgusting excesses' are turning the 'homes of our countrywomen into casinos of blasphemy' (p. 120).                                                                              [11] Ibid. 70.

[12] George Eliot, *Adam Bede* (1859), ed. Stephen Gill (Harmondsworth, 1980), 223.

> Enough of science and of art;
> Close up these barren leaves;
> Come forth, and bring with you a heart
> That watches and receives.[13]

Wordsworth's comments are, of course, contradictory (they too are contained in 'leaves', and leaves cannot be fertile). Nevertheless such attitudes exerted a powerful pressure that became progressively more organized and vocal, particularly in an educational world dominated by the literary community.[14] Tennyson's mournfulness in *In Memoriam* (1850) is perhaps the best-known example of this literary reaction to science, but attitudes hardened and persisted. James Ward (an influential idealist psychologist whose work will be considered in Chapter 7) echoed Wordsworth's vocabulary, as well as his emphasis on seeing Nature as inspired revelation, as late as 1926:

No, the reality of your thoughts and emotions—so far as reality stands for meaning and worth—lies in these as they are when you think and feel them, just as the reality of Nature lies in the living form and face of Nature, not in the decompositions, whether logical or material, which aid our curiosity when we try to know not *it*, but *about it*. A chill disappointment is sure to seize us if we imagine the reality is what we have reached by our analyses and dissections, instead of being what we left behind.[15]

Other responses were more militant still, such as that of the Tory High Anglican W. H. Mallock. In Mallock's *The New Republic* (1877) the ludicrous, scientific Mr Saunders (probably a caricature of W. K. Clifford) proclaims the death of both religion and 'that most treacherous handmaiden of priestcraft, poetry',

which, professing to heighten the lights of life, did, in reality, only deepen its shadows, will delude him no longer—she will be gone—gone for ever. Science the liberator of humanity, will have cast its light upon her; and the lying vision will vanish. But why do I talk of poetry? Is not that, and every other evil—reverence, faith, mysticism, humility, and all the other unclean company—comprised in this one word, Religion?[16]

Literature and religion are indissolubly associated in the minds of both Mr Saunders and his satirist, as they were for many. Matthew Arnold became the leading

---

[13] 'The Tables Turned' (1798), in *Wordsworth and Coleridge: Lyrical Ballads*, 106.

[14] For an overview, see Chris Baldick, *The Social Mission of English Criticism, 1848–1932* (Oxford, 1983). Taking note of these developments, incidentally, helps place the distinctiveness of George Eliot's literary achievement, for in a literary climate where such attitudes were widespread her interest in, and use of, science are both brave and significant.

[15] James Ward, *Psychology Applied to Education* (1926); quoted by Daston, 'British Responses to Psycho-Physiology', 206.

[16] W. H. Mallock, *The New Republic: Culture, Faith, and Philosophy in an English Country House* (1877; Leicester, 1975), 218.

champion of anti-scientific, anti-technological 'Culture', but, despite the mood of lonely alienation in much of his poetry, he was far from a solitary voice in his intellectual community. The reception of the psychology of Alexander Bain and others in the 1850s and 1860s is representative of attitudes that went very deep.

As a matter of rhetorical habit, opponents deployed a belittling imagery and turn of phrase. We have taken note of MacCall on Lilliputian antics and rummaging in cupboards, but this kind of polemic was common. The Catholic literary critic and Shakespeare scholar Richard Simpson pictured the new psychology attempting to 'weigh worth by avoirdupois pounds, to measure humanity by the imperial quart, and to reduce all virtue to statistical tabulation and numerical values. It is, after all, only a genteel way of denying the existence of heaven and any future life.'[17] J. C. Shairp, a future Oxford Professor of Poetry, echoed Wordsworth's celebrated remarks from 'A Poet's Epitaph', which scornfully describe the natural philosopher as

> a fingering slave
> One that would peep and botanize
> Upon his mother's grave.[18]

For Shairp, the psychologist's error is to attempt to 'botanize' the human personality.[19] Similarly, a *Westminster* reviewer of James Garth Wilkinson's eccentric *The Human Body and its Connexion with Man* (1852)—which mixed Swedenborgian mysticism, vitalist physiology, and astrology, amongst other things—paid tribute to a work that measures the inadequacy of 'chemical formulae' against the 'empire of the soul'. Despite Wilkinson's absurdities, the 'deathly fetters of chemical formulae are here shaken off with scornful indignation, and we confess to some rejoicing that the aggressive powers of the "natural sciences" should meet a repulse, and that the empire of the soul should be so violently contended for'.[20] Meanwhile, the Unitarian divine James Martineau found an arrestingly effective image to encapsulate the negative relationship between anatomically based psycho-physiology and the reverent appreciation of art and religion in his essay on Bain. The reduction of human experience to the new psychologist's lawmaking is, he says, like painting a Madonna with the skin off.[21] Bain's psychological method destroys the whole texture and significance of human experience,

---

[17] [Richard Simpson], 'The Morals and Politics of Materialism', *Rambler*, NS 6 (1856), 447–8.

[18] William Wordsworth, *The Poems*, 2 vols., ed. John O. Hayden (Harmondsworth, 1977), i. 396.

[19] [J. C. Shairp], 'Moral Theories and Christian Ethics', *North British Review*, NS 8 (1867), 10.

[20] Anon., 'Notice of *The Human Body and its Connexion with Man* by James Garth Wilkinson', *Westminster Review*, NS 1 (1852), 275–9.

[21] [James Martineau], 'Cerebral Psychology: Bain', *National Review*, 10 (1860), 506.

and Martineau echoes Wordsworth once more: Bain's analysis of our ideas is 'a cruel operation,—a cold-blooded dissecting of them to death'.[22]

These attitudes were elaborated most fully in relation to Bain in an essay review by J. C. Shairp in 1867, which indicates clearly the ways in which literary and religious opposition to the new psychology meshed with broader political objectives. Shairp was then Professor of Latin at St Andrews (he became Oxford Professor of Poetry in 1877) and he reviewed Bain's work alongside Arnold's *Essays in Criticism* (1865), James Martineau's *Essays* (1866), and two works by J. S. Mill, *On Liberty* (1859) and *Utilitarianism* (1863). The review appeared in the *North British Review*, which, though officially carrying old-school Whig affiliations, was attached to the Scottish Free Church and, conservative and traditionally minded, consistently opposed the new psychology.[23] The book of Bain's under review was—rather belatedly—the first edition of *The Emotions and the Will* of 1859. The review thus groups some very disparate texts and, because of the obvious dysymmetry in the dates of publication, we can assume Shairp chose to collect them so rather than follow the schedules of his editor. The decision to link Bain and Mill was definitely no accident, for Mill had forcefully championed Bain's psychology in a long article in the prestigious *Edinburgh Review* in 1859, and the two were associated in many minds as part of the radical-liberal vanguard. (I will have more to say on this topic, and on Mill's important essay on Bain, as we go on.) Shairp's conspectus of the work of a decade thus leagues the radicals in psychology and politics (Bain and Mill) against the traditionalists (Martineau and Arnold), the pro-science party against the apostles of religion and verse.

The political context of Shairp's essay was more wide-ranging than a specific intellectual dispute, and important public issues formed the atmosphere in which Shairp's review was read. The debate over the Second Reform Bill is perhaps the most obvious of these, but other matters of public concern included the 'culture and anarchy' arguments that Arnold had launched in 'Culture and its Enemies', his valedictory lecture as Oxford Professor of Poetry in 1867 (quickly published in the *Cornhill* ), and the 'Governor Eyre' controversy of 1864–6, which had divided British intellectual opinion sharply. Eyre, as Governor of Jamaica, had suppressed an uprising with extraordinary brutality. Against him were grouped progressive and liberal intellectuals, among whom were many of the leading scientific psychologists and evolutionists of the day, including Darwin, Huxley, Wallace, Lyell, Bain, Spencer, and Lewes. These were leagued with prominent radicals, dissenters, and positivists such as Mill and the Leweses' friend Frederic Harrison. Mill (who

---

[22] Ibid. 511.
[23] [Shairp], 'Moral Theories'. The Whig party was favoured by the Free Church. See Joanne Shattock, 'Problems of Parentage: The *North British Review* and the Free Church of Scotland', in Joanne Shattock and Michael Wolff (eds.), *The Victorian Periodical Press: Samplings and Soundings* (Leicester, 1982), 145–66.

was still an MP) took a leading part, with Harrison and others, in the 'Jamaica Committee' formed to lobby for the prosecution of Eyre for murder, and the controversy ranged widely in the press. Lewes, for instance, as editor of the *Fortnightly Review*, pitched in and placed the new journal behind the anti-Eyre lobby in its first issue in 1865. Thus, in the mind of the public at large, many of the leading supporters of the new psychology were firmly identified with the liberal side in a celebrated political cause, which settled deep in the minds of its leading figures. At the height of the agitation, Mill was receiving death threats about once a week.[24] Spencer claimed that his father died dreaming of the incident.[25] James Sully, a psychologist of the next generation who was to be one of Lewes's literary executors, was then a student at Regent's Park Baptist College. Angered by the opinions of the college authorities and the student body alike, he resigned from the College Union and refused ever after to read *The Times* because of its pro-Eyre reporting.[26]

On the other side, in defence of Eyre, were grouped a number of prominent literary intellectuals including Kingsley, Carlyle, Ruskin, Tennyson, and (surprisingly perhaps) Dickens.[27] Not all literary intellectuals, of course, ranged themselves on the pro-Eyre side: Trollope did not, for instance, and nor did George Eliot. The Eyre incident, indeed, forms a significant context for her novel *Daniel Deronda* (1876), which is set in the mid-1860s. As Sally Shuttleworth notes, Grandcourt's brutal attitudes to the Jamaican Negro—'a beastly sort of baptist Caliban'—connects the attitudes of a complacently authoritarian British ruling class with the exercise of colonial power and white supremacism in racial theory.[28] In terms of the quarrels over science, Negroes were associated with monkeys— or subhumans like Caliban—and therefore the Eyre arguments touched scientific controversy in the context of the evolutionary debates. This connection was not lost on Herbert Spencer, whose anti-Eyre views were formed from an amalgam of liberal politics, lifelong opposition to imperialism, and a pro-science outlook.[29] The Eyre incident was another instance of the public parting of intellectual opinion between, very broadly, the 'literary' wing of British intellectual opinion and (just as broadly) the 'scientific' wing. The split between the two groups loomed large in the public mind in the 1860s, and incidents such as the Eyre controversy gave it a recognizable political edge. Readers of Shairp's review of Bain in the *North British Review* of 1867 would have had this much in mind.

[24] John Stuart Mill, *Autobiography*, 174–7.

[25] Herbert Spencer, *An Autobiography*, 2 vols. (London, 1904), ii. 139.

[26] James Sully, *My Life and Friends: A Psychologist's Memories* (London, 1918), 64 ff.

[27] Bernard Semmel, *The Governor Eyre Controversy* (London, 1962); E. M. Everett, *The Party of Humanity: The Fortnightly Review and its Contributors 1865–1874* (Chapel Hill, NY, 1939).

[28] Sally Shuttleworth, *George Eliot and Nineteenth-Century Science: the Make-Believe of a Beginning* (Cambridge, 1986), 182.

[29] J. D. Y. Peel, *Herbert Spencer: The Evolution of a Sociologist* (London, 1971), 11.

The review begins with an attack *tout court* on physical science, which is contrasted unfavourably with the endeavours of modern literature. Physical science, Shairp argues, has 'drained off' ethical thought and threatens to bankrupt man's spiritual being. Modern materialist philosophers are preoccupied by 'a cut-and-dried conventional psychology', which, thin and repetitious, fails to uplift or absorb like more conventional metaphysical enquiry. By contrast, modern literature is concerned with ennobling spiritual topics, and contemporary literary and religious 'giants' (his word), emphasizing their spiritual struggles, are better placed to act as guides. Shairp cites a distinctively conservative Romantic lineage running between Wordsworth, Coleridge, Carlyle, Newman, and the eclectic Broad Church divine and literary critic Frederick Robertson as evidence for his case.[30]

For Shairp, both Mill and Bain are representative of the shrivelled morality and spirituality of Utilitarianism that, he asserts, lies at the heart of contemporary science. Utilitarian theory has a reduced conception of human possibility; it posits self-interest as the sole motive for self-government; and it ignores the human instinct for generous or philanthropic action. The activities of the human will are thus reduced, and man made incapable of self-generating moral activity. Shairp attacks Mill particularly. Mill's language is without style (thus speaks the future Professor of Poetry); it is poor and muddled in expression and thought alike, and full of special pleading. Special cases are exaggerated into general cases, and the run and texture of general human experience is ignored.[31] In philosophical terms, Shairp offers himself as a follower of Plato and other *a priori* thinkers such as Kant or Bishop Butler: 'dynamic' philosophers who refuse the inert, materialist passivity of Utilitarianism. The Platonic doctrine of the 'Essential Form or Idea of the Good' gives men a glimpse of something better, and provides them with a vital moral and spiritual centre.[32] Shairp attaches this meta-ethical idea to other elements, and posits an 'irradicable craving for a Power behind all phenomena . . . a craving which no form of Comtian [*sic*] philosophy will ever exorcise'.[33] This power is expressed in several ways: in the 'dynamic or motive power in moral life'; in a compelling belief in a special or vital power (the Creator himself) operating through Nature; and in the special, imaginative apprehension of this to be found in literature of the highest quality.[34] The psychological mechanism by means of which these moral, ontological, imaginative, and spiritual certainties are gained cannot, Shairp asserts, be explained. They are grasped only by intuition, by sudden, stunning perception. No mere argument or proof can validate them, and Shairp finds support for his view in Coleridge's conception of 'instinctive perceptions'. What these yield is a glimpse of the beneficence of Nature, and of a regularity and harmony at the heart of

---

[30] [Shairp], 'Moral Theories', 1–3.     [31] Ibid. 22–3.
[32] Ibid. 13.     [33] Ibid. 29.     [34] Ibid. 11.

things that is also to be found in the works of Shakespeare and other literary geniuses.[35] The essay is consequently generous in quotation and literary allusion, and ends enlisting Arnold to the cause of philosophical and religious Idealism. Arnold's attacks on philistinism and the machine age are enthusiastically embraced. Shairp merely wishes that he would give greater prominence to religion in Culture, for Culture is the Will of God.

So the essay opposes literary culture to science's alarmingly empty view of nature. In terms of the discipline of psychology, Shairp favours the older methods of introspection and casual observation of others. The new psychology, by contrast, produces only tabulation and the stale repetitions of scientific law. Bain, he grants, has gathered some new mental facts, but only, as it were, by accident arising 'from the wider survey of human history, and the deepened human experience which our present civilization has opened up'.[36] Overall, his work remains vitiated by flawed procedure and supposition. Modern scholars have noted that Bain's books establish the organization of the modern psychological textbook by beginning with the physiological foundations.[37] But, for Shairp, it is this that most clearly represents his failure: he starts from the wrong end. Psychology should begin with 'moral psychology' and engage with 'the fundamental ideas which underlie [human experiences]; that is, [psychology] will land us in theology or religion'.[38]

By refusing to allow that big capacities have smaller origins, Shairp's psychology is Idealist through and through. It resists the tactics of analytic deconstruction favoured by the associationist tradition, and even turns its back on the traditional psychological faculties of the Scottish school. It favours instead the German-influenced transcendentalism popular in the mid-century described in Chapter 2. The crucial psychological entity for Shairp is the 'mysterious conscious "I", the fully formed personal will', which is 'the centre, the core of man's being'. Moral science deals with character, and character is defined as 'a completely fashioned will'. The only conceivable use of psychology is, therefore, to enable the achievement of this state of the will, and to bring it into harmony with spiritual needs. Psychology should emphasize the desirability of such states, and to that end trace 'the historical growth of the individual as well as the race'; that is, its progress from primitive instincts and desires to a civilized European will power created by the deliberate frustration of desire and, thereby, the acquisition of prudence. From selfishness and egoism, according to Shairp, we develop the 'spiritual order' of the 'higher consciousness'. From acknowledgement of others, and the restraint of our own desires, we come to acknowledge

---

[35] [Shairp], 'Moral Theories', 12–13.    [36] Ibid. 7.
[37] David J. Murray, *A History of Western Psychology* (Englewood Cliffs, NJ, 1983), 120–3.
[38] [Shairp], 'Moral Theories', 7.

God. In a characteristic nineteenth-century way, Shairp marks this progress in stages: from the 'emotional' to the 'prudential' to the 'moral'. At the close, there is a cultured, religious, and unified personality, which issues in an ordered, stable social system.[39]

The connection between this view and the wider, ideological context of psychological argument is clear, for Shairp's providentialist ethics are, socially, a recommendation of the status quo and social discipline (among Jamaican Negroes, for instance). Like Samuel Smiles or Carlyle, Shairp recommends the study and celebration of character for moral improvement, and, again, this was common. Protesting against subversive, materialist politics in the wake of the 1848 revolutions, Richard Simpson recommended the psychological efficacy of the study of the lives of heroic soldiers, martyrs, and priests. The current obsession with 'literary and scientific persons', Simpson argued, was mere idolatry. Culture was a power game, and science was winning, he feared, in the self-applauding philosophic coteries. In the wake of the revolutions, Simpson cried for strong measures, and spoke (in the manner of one later voice of Arnold's and a regular one of Carlyle's[40]) of the need for authority to settle the cultural decline, just as soldiers and strong government were needed to settle rebellions.[41] The appeal to a disinterested cultural élite in Arnold, to heroes and aristocracy in Carlyle, and to Shairp's culture of poetry and the will, are reflections of this same demand for social authority and obligation made in agitated political circumstances. It is against this that the emphasis on doctrines of liberty made by Mill and Bain should be understood. Their psychological programme, in its political aspect, was aimed at the release of the individual from ideological incorporation.

Mill's championship of Bain was absolute and forthright. His *Edinburgh Review* essay of 1859, 'Bain's Psychology', begins with an unequivocal salute. After years of decline, Mill writes, 'the sceptre of psychology' has at last returned to England, the home of the 'experience' or '*a posteriori*' tradition, and Bain's work (though by a Scot) 'deserves to take rank as the foremost of its class, and as

---

[39] This is a summary of the argument in ibid. 6–13.

[40] Raymond Williams called attention to the origins of *Culture and Anarchy* in Arnold's alarmed and draconian response to the Hyde Park riots of 1866: 'I remember my father ... *As for rioting, the old Roman way of dealing with that is always the right one; flog the rank and file, and fling the ringleaders from the Tarpeian Rock!* And this opinion we can never forsake, however our liberal friends may think a little rioting, and what they call popular demonstrations, useful to their own interests and to the interests of the valuable practical operations they have in hand.' Quoted from the initial 'Culture and Anarchy' lectures by Williams in 'A Hundred Years of Culture and Anarchy', in *Problems in Materialism and Culture: Selected Essays* (London, 1980), 6–7. Carlyle, of course, also fulminated against 'Swarmeries' in this period and the collapse of social and cultural discipline, as, for example, in 'Shooting Niagara: And After?' (1867), one of whose subjects was the Eyre controversy (in Thomas Carlyle, *Essays: Scottish and Other Miscellanies*, 2 vols., ed. James Russell Lowell, (London, 1915), i. 299–339.

[41] [Simpson], 'The Morals and Politics of Materialism'.

marking the most advanced point which the *a posteriori* psychology has reached'.[42]
This judgement appears less startling now, when Bain's reputation is secure, than
it would have done in 1859. But we have only to glance at the company in which
Bain is mentioned in the opening pages—Hobbes, Locke, Hartley, James Mill
(on the *a posteriori* side), Descartes, the German Idealists, Reid, Stewart, Brown,
and Hamilton (on the *a priori* side)—to begin to wonder a little. For Bain had
no substantial reputation in 1859. He had written some twenty or so essays—
though only a handful of these were published in prestigious, or widely circu-
lating, liberal journals like the *Westminster* or *Fraser's*. He had also published
his two large, though rather dry, psychology books, and three educational
instructors on popular scientific topics, though none of these was well known.
*The Senses and the Intellect* was widely reviewed, but its sales had been small—so
small, indeed, that the publisher insisted that the long-planned companion
volume, *The Emotions and the Will*, be financially underwritten (by Mill and George
Grote, in fact) before proceeding with publication. As it turned out—and partly
because of Mill's championship—the sales of *The Emotions and the Will* were
good, and Mill's guarantee against the publisher's losses proved unnecessary; the
reception of the book even stimulated sales of *The Senses and the Intellect*.[43]

Why, then, was Mill so concerned to boost Bain's career and make these heady
claims for his work? By 1859 the two had known each other for nearly twenty
years, after Bain had contacted Mill through John Robertson (an acquaintance
of Mill's and one of Bain's early mentors in Aberdeen) when beginning his
intellectual career in the early 1840s. He had taken an early interest in psychological questions, and Mill sent him a copy of his father's *Analysis* in 1841, encouraging him to write for the *Westminster*, which he did for the first time that year.[44]
In return, Bain helped Mill with his famous *System of Logic*, which appeared in
1843. Indeed, Bain was the only person Mill mentioned in the *Autobiography* as
helping with the book.[45] But the reasons for Mill's championship of his friend
were more than personal. Bain's psychological programme was what Mill needed
in the late 1850s. It offered a politically compatible psychological theory securely
within the associationist (experience/*a posteriori*) tradition, which took some
account of the new physiological psychology, but did not hand the discipline
entirely over to it.[46] Bain's work took the weight of the standard critique of
associationism (best put, for Mill, by Coleridge[47]), that associationism was
too passive in its theorization of the human personality, and attempted to
remodel it without losing touch with founding principles. In this way, the

---

[42] John Stuart Mill, 'Bain's Psychology', 342.    [43] Bain, *Autobiography*, 251.
[44] Ibid. 112.    [45] John Stuart Mill, *Autobiography*, 147 n.
[46] John Stuart Mill, 'Bain's Psychology', 348.
[47] Ibid. 354; also *Mill on Bentham and Coleridge*, esp. 115 ff.

post-Benthamite ensemble of liberal Utilitarianism would not be unduly disturbed by the new physiology, for, as we noted in Part One, Mill was personally committed to the old introspective and observational methods in psychology. What is more, he leaned some distance towards the 'literary' critique of the new science. As is well known, because of the rigours of his early upbringing, he too had come to relish the culture of the feelings and share the consolations of the natural world envisioned by Wordsworth and Coleridge. Though he realized very clearly the importance of the new scientific findings, he was reluctant to grant them the kind of priority that others of a slightly younger generation came to do over the next decade. Bain, who was to become a professor of English as well as Philosophy, was attractive because he could both rescue and advance the specifically *associationist* psychology within its traditional theoretical format.

In his essay on Bain, Mill offers a footnote to explain why he chose Bain not Spencer (a thinker of 'kindred merit') for his essay on the state of the discipline. Whereas Bain thinks within the accepted traditions, Mill says, Spencer does not. He is 'less sober', though more original; and he is therefore 'likely to obtain a much less unqualified adhesion from the best minds trained in the same general mode of thought'.[48] The comment illustrates the bias of Mill's mind towards the psychology in which he had been trained and of which Bain's work was the latest and—modern scholars agree—culminating representative. But there is in this comment also the voice of the propagandist, shrewdly alert to his cause. For Mill was quite right. In 1859 Spencer was, indeed, a maverick in psychological theory as far as the popular conception of the discipline went. His *Principles of Psychology*, as we shall see, looked a very odd book indeed compared to the work of his contemporaries, and it would have seemed both intellectually eccentric and politically compromising for Mill to pin his colours to it. So it was Bain, for personal, intellectual, and political reasons whom Mill chose, quite consciously, to promote. In his *Autobiography* he is clear about this: he wished, as 'a duty particularly incumbent upon me', to make Bain's work better known.[49] He hoped that 'my father's great Analysis of the Mind, my own Logic, and Professor Bain's great treatise' would form a trio of books to combat the mid-century orthodoxies represented most clearly for Mill by the work of Sir William Hamilton.[50] The essay on Bain was part of Mill's larger programme, which included his own *An Examination of Sir William Hamilton's Philosophy* (1865), and his edition of his father's *Analysis*, finally published in 1869 with contributions by Bain and others.

Mill is frank about the political bearing of this collective work. He says in the *Autobiography* that he wished to combat

---

[48] John Stuart Mill, 'Bain's Psychology', 342.
[49] John Stuart Mill, *Autobiography*, 155.　　[50] Ibid. 163.

a philosophy which is addicted to holding up favourite doctrines as intuitive truths, and deems intuition to be the voice of Nature and of God, speaking with an authority higher than our reason. In particular, I have long felt that the prevailing tendency to regard all the marked distinctions of human character as innate, and in the main indelible, and to ignore the irresistible proofs that by far the greater part of those differences, whether between individuals, races, or sexes, are such as not only might but naturally would be produced by differences in circumstances, is one of the chief hindrances to the rational treatment of great social questions, and one of the great stumbling blocks to human improvement. This tendency has its source in the intuitional metaphysics which character-ized the reaction of the nineteenth century against the eighteenth, and it is a tendency so agreeable to human indolence, as well as to conservative interests generally, that unless it is attacked at the very root, it is sure to be carried to even a greater length than is really justified by the more moderate forms of intuitional philosophy. That philosophy, not always in its moderate forms, had ruled the thought of Europe for the greater part of a century.[51]

There is much here worthy of comment, for this is the associationist case put at its best. We can note Mill's shrewd sense of how the idea of God—or the philosophy of Nature—is used to confiscate argument; of how, too, these argu-ments about intuition in cognition are related to those that think of human character as innate; of how, again, these theories of innate character are used to buttress the status quo and the protection of 'conservative interests generally'; of how even moderate forms of intuitionist argument need to be scrutinized carefully because they have the weight of tradition and interest behind them; and we can finally note that Mill is quite specific in his understanding of the origins of this orthodoxy—it dates from Romanticism ('the reaction of the nine-teenth century against the eighteenth') or, rather, that conservatively coloured version of Romanticism stemming from German Idealist philosophy that was actively promoted for the right in Britain by such thinkers as Coleridge and Carlyle.[52] The political bearing of these psychological arguments, then, is very plain, and the analysis is one that would have appealed to Alexander Bain for reasons that have received little comment in the existing secondary literature.

Bain was born in 1818, the son of a farmer on a small tenancy outside Aberdeen. The family lost the farm during the post-war depression and his father joined the army. Subsequently, he became a weaver at a time when weaving was one of the most politically vocal of trades in the post-war world.[53] In 1831 Bain him-self became an apprentice weaver at a moment when, he recalled, 'the Reform agitation [was] at its crisis'. This moment, as he joined the Reform demonstra-tions as a 13 year old, marked the beginnings of 'Reform sympathies, which,

[51] John Stuart Mill, *Autobiography*, 162–3.
[52] Butler, *Romantics, Rebels, and Reactionaries*, esp. chs. 3, 6.
[53] E. P. Thompson, *The Making of the English Working Class* (Harmondsworth, 1967).

in the shape of liberalism in general politics, stuck with me through life'.[54] His intellectual career began in the local Mechanics' Institute and he was a product of a working-class, largely autodidact educational community that was in fact a community for 'Mutual Instruction'. (The distorting image of Hardy's solitary Jude often obscures the collective enterprise in much nineteenth-century, working-class education.) His particular friends in this circle were the local blacksmith's sons, who introduced him to psychological theory through their heated (in all senses) discussions of Thomas Reid. It was through Bain's dislike of Reid that he was led to read Hume and the sceptics. By 1835 he was teaching classes at the Institute, and in 1836 he gave up full-time work to attend Marischal College, Aberdeen, though he continued to work as a weaver in the vacations.

Everything in Bain's early experience then, as well as the intellectual outlook he quickly and readily adopted, was conducive to a radical political position. His first published piece, in 1836 for the *Aberdeen Herald*, was 'On Civil and Religious Liberty' and was originally a political speech given in the city. Sixty years later, in 1894, he was still writing for the *Aberdeen Free Press* against the hereditary principle in the House of Lords and contemplating the 'ultimate extinction' of that body if it persisted in its present form.[55] Bain's *Autobiography* contains plenty of frank discussion of his political opinions, about which he was quite open. He followed the progress of Chartism keenly in the 1840s, and noted with disgust (and a wry sense of the ridiculous in retrospect) that, in April 1848, clerical workers at the Board of Health (where he was working for Chadwick's Metropolitan Sanitary Commission) were issued with weapons and instructed to barricade their buildings. He made many speeches on public issues and was invited, in March 1885, to stand as an MP in the Radical interest in Sheffield in the general election caused by the dissolution of Parliament over Gladstone's Home Rule measures. Bain declined, but, he says, on the grounds of age (he was then 67) and not 'from difficulties as to party allegiance'.[56] He had decided views on the Irish question and delivered a speech at a demonstration against the Irish Crimes Bill in August 1888 that was reprinted in the *Aberdeen Free Press*.[57] He did not believe that political trouble could be solved by draconian legislation or violent suppression, a position he maintained at the time of the Governor Eyre incident.

[54] Bain, *Autobiography*, 15.
[55] William L. Davidson, 'Supplementary Chapter 1890–1903', to Bain's *Autobiography*, 416. Bain wrote the bulk of his *Autobiography*—which is rather a flat, unengaging narrative—at a leisurely pace between 1890 and 1897. He ended the story in 1890. Davidson added the last chapter after Bain's death. Davidson was an ex-pupil of Bain's and succeeded him as Professor of Logic at Aberdeen. He was also one of Bain's literary executors and wrote an interesting appreciation of him in *Mind* that stressed especially the far-reaching practical effects of his work, particularly in education. For many, Bain's 'philosophy' had genuine, far-reaching consequences. See 'Professor Bain's Philosophy', *Mind*, NS 13 (1904), 79–161. Davidson remarks that Bain maintained his political opinions until his death in 1904.
[56] Bain, *Autobiography*, 377.       [57] Ibid. 434.

However, Bain remained an intellectual and an academic. He was not an activist in the manner of J. S. Mill, or even a political journalist, as Lewes was in his early years editing the *Leader*. It was in his academic career that he involved himself most closely in matters of practical policy, including issues of curricula development and teaching methods. He was a tireless expositor in his writing, and a lively seeker after new opportunities to widen the constituency for his— and therefore psychology's—ideas. He wrote for *Chambers's Papers for the People* in the 1850s, and *Chambers's Encyclopaedia* in the 1860s; he wrote English grammars and other textbooks in the 1870s; he founded and managed *Mind* partly using his own funds; and he digested his two large psychological tomes (updated and revised) into a book, *Mental and Moral Science: A Compendium of Psychology and Ethics* (1868; revised and divided again in 1872), which served as a university-level textbook for a generation. According to one commentator, Gardner Murphy, who was fairly close to Bain's legacy, 'never had a psychologist been so widely read in his own day'. Murphy compared Bain's influence in psychological theory to that of Mill in political economy: 'Associationism became through him almost "popular".'[58] However, this career was not untroubled. Throughout, he was dogged by political opposition and, from time to time, particularly in his early progress, political discrimination. He was, for one thing, militantly anti-religious.

In his diary of June 1866 (that is, just prior to Shairp's attack on the religious outlook of the school with which Bain associated himself), G. H. Lewes records Bain engaging in an 'antiChristian [*sic*] onslaught' whilst dining with Lewes and George Eliot.[59] There is no indication from Lewes's reactions, or the tone of his remarks, that this tirade was either shocking or unusual, for Bain had very early rejected the Calvinism in which he had been reared. He comments in his *Autobiography* that, while still a child (that is under the age of 13 when he went into full-time work), listening to adults talking about religious matters, and noting the contradictions, 'made me a ready listener to sceptical criticism'.[60] In the long run, he concludes, this prepared the way for his acceptance of Utilitarian theory and an interest in psychology. Just as his politics never wavered, nor did his views on religion. Bain remained opposed to it on principle. Whilst never actually declaring himself an atheist (which would have been out of the question for a man pursuing an academic career), he nevertheless clearly identified himself with non-believers, and with ideas and intellectual groups that brought him into conflict with authorities.

In the early 1840s on a visit to London, and partly through the influence of Mill and Lewes (whom he also met in 1841), Bain became interested in Comte.

[58] Gardner Murphy, *Historical Introduction to Modern Psychology*, 5th edn. (London, 1949), 107. Murphy's book was first published in 1928, not so long after Bain's death.
[59] G. H. Lewes, Diary, 1–7 June 1866, in Eliot, *Letters*, iv. 266.      [60] Bain, *Autobiography*, 12.

He recommenced study of Comte in Scotland with others, including William Walker, who subsequently wrote on Comte for Lewes's radical paper, the *Leader*, and whose work was later used by Lewes in his book on Comte in 1853. Bain recalls the atmosphere of the time in his *Autobiography*:

Such studies had, no doubt, the effect of marring the orthodoxy of all concerned, and had to be kept in great measure secret, although it was impossible to avoid giving indications that in those days were calculated to bring the individual students into trouble. Nevertheless, the society [an Aberdeen reading group to which Bain belonged] allowed itself to be mentioned by Mill to Comte as one of the centres of Positivism.[61]

This, and other incidents, did indeed 'mar his orthodoxy', for Comte was associated not only with scientific materialism, but also with atheism, political radicalism, and loose living. Scurrilous Tory journalism was thick with accusations.[62] Even in respectable quarters these connections were emphasized: in *Culture and Anarchy*, Arnold associated the English Positivists directly with Jacobinism.[63] For Bain, gaining an academic appointment was never going to be easy.

Seeking a job in 1845–6, he was told he would need to become a 'licentiate of the Church' to become eligible for any chair of moral philosophy in Scotland.[64] In 1851 he was refused appointment at Aberdeen because he was 'obnoxious to the Church party'.[65] In 1860 he failed to gain a chair at St Andrews because of his 'desolating' philosophy and lack of religious orthodoxy.[66] The Principal at St Andrews was John Tulloch, whose hostility to both Comtists and the Utilitarian liberals spread over decades. Especially hostile to Mill, Tulloch was also sharply opposed to Bain. His summative *Movements of Religious Thought in Britain during the Nineteenth Century* (1885) contains a chapter-long attack on 'John Stuart Mill and his School' (including Bain), which unfavourably contrasts Mill with Carlyle, partly because of Mill's, and especially his father's, supposed default from the Scots heritage from which, Tulloch felt, Carlyle gained such spiritual resource.[67]

---

[61] Ibid. 157.

[62] See e.g. Anon., 'M. Comte's Religion for Atheists', *British Quarterly Review*, 28 (1858), 422–46; [Marie Blaze de Bury], 'Victor Cousin', *North British Review*, NS 7 (1867), 162–71. For commentary, see Christopher Kent, *Brains and Numbers: Elitism, Comtism and Democracy in Mid-Victorian England* (Toronto, 1978).

[63] Matthew Arnold, *Culture and Anarchy*, ed. Ian Gregor (Indianapolis, 1971), 54–5.

[64] Bain, *Autobiography*, 181.    [65] Ibid. 231.    [66] Ibid. 261–6.

[67] John Tulloch, *Movements of Religious Thought in Britain during the Nineteenth Century* (1885; Leicester, 1971), 240. Tulloch's arguments against Mill's psychology are familiar: he fails to account for the free exercise of the higher faculties, he eliminates conscience, moral responsibility, and the religious instincts, and he offers a contradictory account of the growth of self-consciousness. He also attacks the 'analogy between mental force and other forms of force' in the materialist account of the will, a position that, as we shall see, Bain made distinctively his own.

In 1860 Bain was a candidate for the Aberdeen chair in logic. His principal rival was an opponent of the new psychology, James McCosh, who took a strongly conservative line, attacking 'materialistic psychology' and associationism indiscriminately.[68] McCosh had the support of both the Scottish Free Church and the Established church members of the University, and Bain was publicly described as an 'infidel'. The decision, however, went in Bain's favour—though as a political appointment in the teeth of university opinion. The then Liberal Home Secretary, Sir George Cornewall Lewis, used his influence on Bain's behalf, despite the view that it would cost the government four seats in Scotland. Bain comments that there 'was always a lurking dissatisfaction with the appointment, but it was seldom shown openly'.[69] The consequences of Bain's views on politics and religion dogged him throughout his career. He tried to postpone his resignation from his Aberdeen chair in 1880, though ill, because he knew the appointment would fall 'into the hands of the Tory government'.[70] In 1890 he was excluded from the Scottish Universities Commission, 'by political prejudice' notes William Davidson.[71] But, more generally, Bain's perception of academic prejudice against the new psychology was widely shared.[72] Even the Idealist philosopher T. H. Green thought his early career had been blighted by a youthful reputation as 'a radical, a Comtist, and a materialist unfit to instruct young men'.[73] Though probably untrue in its assessment of personal consequences, the story indicates an important element in academic attitudes.

This, then, is the context in which Bain developed his career and ideas. Of all the leading members of the circle of new psychologists at work in the mid-to-late nineteenth century, Bain was the only one to pursue an academic career. Though Huxley (who had strong views on the faults of the British higher education system, especially its neglect of science) held a lectureship at the Royal School of Mines, he considered himself an outsider, opposed to the mainstream system, and turned down the offer of the new Oxford chair in physiology, and the Mastership of University College, in 1877.[74] These facts are, I think, significant, for a newly emerging discipline needs new career structures to enable it. Bain made his way in the academic world, but James and John Mill, Huxley, Spencer, and Lewes—to name but a handful of the most eminent—remained very much outside it. It is also significant that, in their social origins, none of these men (except perhaps John Mill, in his odd way) was born to the intellectual purple or to any significant social rank. Bain, as we have seen, was the

---

[68] McCosh, *Scottish Philosophy*, iii. 154, 193–4.    [69] Bain, *Autobiography*, 264–9.
[70] Ibid. 344.    [71] Ibid. 402.    [72] Sully, *My Life and Friends*, 184 ff.
[73] Quoted in Melvin Richter, *The Politics of Conscience: T. H. Green and his Age* (London, 1964), 92.
[74] William Irvine, *Thomas Henry Huxley* (London, 1973), 25–6; Desmond, *Huxley: Evolution's High Priest*, 135–6.

son of a weaver, James Mill of a Kincardineshire shoemaker, Huxley of an impecunious Ealing schoolteacher, Spencer of a freelance teacher in Derby, while Lewes came from an eccentric lower-middle-class family in London. (His grandfather was a celebrated and somewhat scandalous harlequin and comic actor in the Regency, his father a minor literary man who maintained two families independently—Lewes was illegitimate—before absconding to Bermuda, where he became a Customs Officer.) Clearly, to be sustained, speculation about the relationship between social origin and choice of intellectual career and interests would need much more detailed specification and argument—rather in the way perhaps that Richard Altick has described the sociology of literary authorship in this period[75]—but it does seem possible to speculate that the enthusiastic development of the new psychology is related to these kinds of facts. The new psychologists chose a new discipline, relatively free from established interests, with an unformed career structure, to pursue their enquiries. This lack of both social and intellectual establishment goes some way to explain the social sneering that enters the polemics of lofty, forgotten men like William MacCall, for it is indeed likely that Alexander Bain would—though a weaver rather than a tailor—regularly have watched bantam cocks or rubbish emptied from cupboards. However, it is time to turn from the social and ideological contexts of Bain's work to its place in the intellectual development of mid-nineteenth-century psychological theory overall.

BAIN AND THE DEVELOPMENT OF PHYSIOLOGICAL ASSOCIATIONISM

Mill was not the only commentator to perceive that Bain's work offered a substantial adjustment to the paradigms set for mid-nineteenth-century psychology in its emergence from and within the philosophy of mind. From their different perspectives, David Masson, J. D. Morrel, G. H. Lewes, and James Martineau also quickly placed his work in the context of the rival English and Scottish traditions of psychological theory. Masson (another Scot who, like Bain, had been something of a protégé of Mill's) reviewed *The Senses and the Intellect* in the liberal *Fraser's Magazine* in 1856, and began by contrasting Bain with the early century Scots philosopher Thomas Brown. The basis for the contrast is political: Brown is the old Whig (like Lord John Russell), whereas the new psychology is Radical. (Masson is very alert to the political bearing of the various psychological theories, and notes the conservatism of the new 'Scoto-German' transcendentalism.[76]) Compared to Brown's incisive, rapid thinking and bright

[75] Richard D. Altick, 'The Sociology of Authorship: The Social Origins of 1,000 British Writers, 1800–1935', in *Writers, Readers, and Occasions: Selected Essays on Victorian Literature and Life* (Columbus, 1989), 95–109.

[76] D[avid] M[asson], 'Bain on The Senses and the Intellect', *Fraser's Magazine*, 53 (1856), 212–13.

extemporizing manner, the tone of Bain's work is patiently accumulative, indeed rather plodding. The book is remarkable, says Masson, for its cautious autodidacticism, polemical restraint, and careful avoidance of explicit controversy. Though it is clearly in the manner of 'thorough-going English Sensationalism', Masson does not feel that its originality depends upon 'the fundamental metaphysical doctrine with which it is associated'—that is, the strict Utilitarianism of James Mill.[77] So, Bain's work participates in, but does not slavishly follow, that of his predecessors. With hindsight, one can see in it the foundations of a style for a new, professionalised discipline, one that parallels the secular, academic career structure Bain was seeking to define in his life. His books are structured to develop from body to mind in logical, progressive order, sticking steadily to the specialist aim-in-view, and are written in a style that cultivates a tone of professional detachment. The new style aided Bain's success as a writer of academic textbooks, but it was also a way of managing the various transitions, intellectual and political, in which he was a more than willing participant. What is being conducted, under the guiding light of John Stuart Mill, is a quiet, modernizing revolution in the disposition of the associationist psychology.

Other reviewers understood this clearly. J. D. Morrel, for instance, was an ex-pupil of Sir William Hamilton and a shrewd, German-educated thinker who had written the highly regarded *Elements of Psychology* (1853). For all their differences, and despite his instinctive fear of the materialist, Morrel could, to a degree, recognize himself in Bain, for he, too, became an educational professional as inspector of schools in the nonconformist interest. Like Masson's, his review—in the specialist *British and Foreign Medico-Chirurgical Review*—is fair-minded and perceptive, and he, too, emphasizes the way Bain's work offered to modernize English empiricism.[78] The same point was made by Lewes, who reviewed the second editions of both *The Senses and the Intellect* and *The Emotions and the Will* for the *Fortnightly Review* in 1866. Lewes placed Bain in 'the inductive experimental school of Locke' and felt that Bain's was the 'most advanced inductive psychology of our day'.[79] This view was endorsed by James Martineau, though Martineau—an out-and-out enemy of the new psychology—interpreted it very differently. Bain, Martineau claimed, like James Mill, unsoundly jettisoned the 'claims of the native Scottish philosophy', caught 'the infection of our [English]

---

[77] D[avid] M[asson], 'Bain on The Senses and the Intellect', *Fraser's Magazine*, 53 (1856), 214.

[78] J. D. Morrel, 'Modern English Psychology', *British and Foreign Medico-Chirurgical Review*, 17 (1856), 347–64.

[79] [G. H. Lewes], Critical Notice of *The Senses and the Intellect* and *The Emotions and the Will* by Alexander Bain, *Fortnightly Review*, 4 (1866), 767. Lewes distinguished between 'inductive' psychology (about which he had reservations) and the kind of physiological psychology in which he himself was most interested in the 1860s. The inductive approach, coloured by associationist introspection, was not exacting enough in empirical method, nor sufficiently physiological for his taste.

scepticism', and injudiciously strayed from the tried and tested methods of common sense.[80]

Bain had, of course, rejected traditional Scottish philosophy very early. On his own account he had done so by the age of 21, following his reading in the sceptics at the Mechanics' Institute, and the attack on Reid's work developed there formed a part of his mature psychology. Reid had argued that even basic, everyday activities like feeding were innate instincts, but Bain pointed out that even very basic activities need in some part to be learnt. Motor-uncoordinated infants, for instance, need to learn certain procedures to find satisfaction, and it was ludicrous to claim that all activity was spontaneous: 'Dr Reid might just as well assert that the movements of a ballet-dancer are instinctive.'[81] As a good associationist, Bain was resolutely opposed to all *a priori* assumptions about the mind's innate faculties, positions he buttressed by reading in Hartley, James Mill, and Comte.[82] He also developed an early interest in phrenology, on which he taught classes at the Mechanics' Institute as early as 1835, when phrenology was still hotly controversial.[83] Robert Young argues convincingly that phrenology exerted a powerful, constructive pressure on Bain to move his ideas from a more conventional associationism towards a more physiologically grounded theory, but Bain was determinedly eclectic in his sources.[84] Young also makes the point that Bain derived some of his physiology on the roundabout of European ideas. Bain took inspiration from the celebrated German physiologist Johannes Müller, who in turn took ideas from Erasmus Darwin, who in turn adapted Hartley's physiological outline. As these ideas revolved, their exact provenance mattered little. What we are observing is the gradual conceptual consolidation of multiple sources. There are interesting, direct resemblances in phrasing between Hartley and Bain (for instance, Bain describes the nervous system in terms of the transmission of nervous 'force', and speaks of the 'vibrations' and 'waves' in the system[85]), but this became the standard descriptive language within the associationist tradition, especially in its physiological forms.

Bain, however, remained interested in phrenology long after many of his contemporaries had abandoned interest in it. *On the Study of Character* (1861), for instance, makes a (largely unsuccessful) effort to argue against the ideological

[80] Martineau, 'Cerebral Psychology: Bain', 500.

[81] Alexander Bain, *The Senses and the Intellect* (London, 1855), 293. All subsequent references are to this edition unless otherwise noted.

[82] For Hartley, see Bain, *Autobiography*, 46, and, for comment, J. A. Cardno, 'Bain and Physiological Psychology', *Australian Journal of Philosophy*, 7 (1955), 108–20; Theodore Mischel, ' "Emotion" and "Motivation" in the Development of English Psychology: D. Hartley, James Mill, A. Bain', *Journal of the History of the Behavioural Sciences*, 2 (1966), 123–44; Robert M. Young, *Mind, Brain and Adaptation*, 116–19.

[83] Bain, *Autobiography*, 27.    [84] Robert M. Young, *Mind, Brain, and Adaptation*, ch. 3.

[85] Bain, *The Senses and the Intellect*, 333–6.

use of the idea of character by basing an account of the formation of personal-ity on phrenological theory; that is, he argues that character is in part physio-logically derived and not merely a matter of moral effort or failure.[86] The book does not succeed as a defence of this position, because its physiology—like that of phrenology itself—is too reductive, and because Bain himself was rather limited in his understanding of the idea of character. But the principle was an important step, and became a central point of doctrine. Like Spencer, Bain was concerned, as Roger Smith argues, with the substitution of physical for moral mechanisms in his psychological programme:

Bain and Spencer provided non-mentalist theories of efficacious human activity and thereby hoped to reconcile common sense with traditional sensationalism. They took 'effort' from its purely moral context and redescribed it in physiological terms of motor discharge or in biological terms of interaction between organism and environment. They argued that their contribution was to describe humans as active centres of learning and behaviour in a manner compatible with a scientific and non-mentalist physiology.[87]

Phrenology, a modified psychological 'sensationalism' and, later, a more advanced neurology are all placed back-to-back by Bain with an early interest in John Stuart Mill's sketchy ethological programme announced in 'Of Ethology, or the Science of the Formation of Character', book IV of Mill's *System of Logic*, which Mill discussed with Bain in 1843.[88] Traces of Mill's ethological ideas survive in late editions of *The Senses and the Intellect* and *The Emotions and the Will* where Bain argues that character is formed by the interaction of 'natural impulses' and acquired habits.[89] But, again the important point concerns the psychologist's will-ingness to amend and develop the broad associationist programme to produce a strongly *relational* theory, one that sets itself to explore connections not just between the contents of consciousness but also between mind and body, and mental organism and environment.

The relational aspect of Bain's work is clear from the simple titles of his books: both *The Senses and the Intellect* and *The Emotions and the Will* relate one of the higher faculties—intellect and will—to what would at the time have been regarded as subaltern mental phenomena, sensations, and emotions. In *The Senses and the Intellect* Bain insists that sense should not be seen as inferior to the supposedly 'higher' forms of mental life because of these old classificatory habits, and he takes issue with Reid, Stewart, Brown, and James Mill on the question of appetite and instinct. These writers classed appetite and instinct among

[86] Alexander Bain, *On the Study of Character Including an Estimate of Phrenology* (London, 1861).
[87] Smith, 'The Background to Physiological Psychology', 95.
[88] Bain, *Autobiography*, 159, 164.
[89] Alexander Bain, *The Emotions and the Will* (London, 1859), 521. All subsequent references are to this edition unless otherwise noted.

the phenomena of sensation. Bain, however, separates them, on the grounds that appetite and instinct are active properties of the mind.[90] The argument may appear taxonomically arcane, but it is central. Not only is Bain beginning to disrupt settled—if somewhat threadbare—categories; he is also taking up key issues of theory. For example, where James Mill's orthodox Utilitarian associationism had portrayed the mind as fundamentally passive, Bain insists that it is capable of initiatory action in its dealings with the world. Meanwhile, at the other pole of the argument, he maintained against the orthodox faculty psychologists that mind and body form a continuum. Sensation, appetite, and instinct were no longer to be classed apart, beyond the pale of the special human capacities.

This quiet, but far-reaching disruption of the standard classificatory systems is very deliberate and sustained in Bain. In *The Emotions and the Will*, he once more quickly altered perceptions of how mental phenomena should be grouped. Emotion, he says, is 'here used to comprehend all that is understood by feelings, states of feelings, pleasures, pains, passions, sentiments, affections. Consciousness, and conscious states also for the most part denote modes of emotion, although there is such a thing as the Intellectual consciousness.'[91] As we have seen, the special quality of consciousness was a key issue for the opponents of the new psychology, and here it is seen as a less than privileged entity with a definite emotional aspect. Likewise, Bain's list of emotions is interesting because it includes both rudimentary feelings and appetites, and emotions such as the moral sentiments and the gentle affections that had such a special place in the Victorian ideology of love and the family, as can be seen from many a novel of the period. As time went on, and Bain developed his ideas, this classificatory pattern altered from edition to edition of *The Emotions and the Will*, but the principle remained the same, and the process was, if anything, made more radical. In the first edition Bain discriminated between those emotions that were based directly on sensational components (terror, say, or surprise), and those that were apparently remote from sensation like moral love or the aesthetic responses. Indeed, he discovered eleven discrete families of emotions.[92] In the second edition of 1865, however, though these family groupings were preserved, the classificatory principles were altered. They are now based either on the decomposition of the emotions into their constituent elements such as sensation, ideas, or objects, or on the categorization of the psychological mechanisms of which they make use such as transfer, coalition, aggregation, or compounding. These changes naturally have the effect of making the 'higher' emotions more clearly resemble the 'lower', as they do not accept any qualitative distinctions between these psychological states.[93] Bain was almost certainly pushed in this direction by Spencer's critique of *The*

---

[90] Bain, *The Senses and the Intellect*, 65–6.   [91] Bain, *The Emotions and the Will*, 3.
[92] Ibid., ch. 2.   [93] Bain, *The Emotions and the Will*, 2nd edn. (London, 1865), ch. 2.

*Emotions and the Will* in 1860. (Spencer objected that Bain's classification blurred the specificity of mental phenomena by insisting on a typology.[94]) But Bain was, in any case, moving that way. In the third edition of 1875, the notion of families or 'Natural Orders' of emotions is dropped altogether, and a less mechanical classification is offered based upon generic resemblances across ranges of phenomena both conventionally 'high' and conventionally 'low'. These include, for example, 'Emotions of Relativity', 'Ideal Emotions', 'Tender Emotions' (which includes feelings of sexual desire), and so on.[95]

Grasping his purpose, opponents like James Martineau accused Bain of levelling down the finer attributes of mind, but in breaking from the standard taxonomies Bain is not, of course, proclaiming an identity between 'lower' and 'higher' phenomena, as his polemically minded opponents would have it. He is very clear that mind functions as a hierarchy of structures, retaining, for example, a vocabulary of 'primitive' and 'cultivated' in *The Senses and the Intellect*. But he does affirm that the 'higher' attributes are built from, and to a degree are dependent upon, the 'lower', though they supersede them. He insists that one cannot understand the 'higher' capacities of human beings without understanding their 'lower' antecedents. This principle is basic to nineteenth-century associationism, and indeed to much twentieth-century descriptive psychology also, and Bain is particularly firm with semi-physiological compromise notions such as that of the *sensorium commune*, the idea that the brain acts as a kind of mental clearing house for sensations and ideas, or generally as an 'organ' of the mind: 'We must discard forever the notion of a *sensorium commune*, the cerebral closet, as a central seat of mind, or receptacle of sensation and imagery.'[96] His reasoning is consistent. Though the *sensorium commune* appears to be a materialization of the mental faculties, in fact, rather like the idea of biological vitalism, it merely gives a physical form or location to an immaterial principle. On the contrary, insists Bain, the relationship between body and mind must be understood as one transacted throughout and across the nervous system: 'our present insight enables us to say with great probability, no [nervous] currents, no mind', and the transmission of nervous impulses 'is the very essence of cerebral action'.[97]

---

[94] Herbert Spencer, 'Bain on The Emotions and the Will' (1860); repr. in *Essays: Scientific, Political, and Speculative*, 3 vols. (London, 1891), ii. 258–9. For Bain's acknowledgement of Spencer's point, see the third edition of *The Senses and the Intellect* (London, 1868), 668.

[95] Bain, *The Emotions and the Will*, 3rd edn. (London, 1875), ch. 2.

[96] Bain, *The Senses and the Intellect*, 61. This attack on the *sensorium commune* was particularly welcomed by Lewes. Bain, Lewes wrote, thereby placed himself 'at the true physiological point of view'. 'It is the man who thinks; not the brain only; not an entity having a shadowy residence somewhere in the brain' ([G. H. Lewes], 'Bain on The Senses and the Intellect', *Leader*, 6 (1855), 771).   [97] Bain, *The Senses and the Intellect*, 61–2.

These pages of Bain's book have an excited, combative tone somewhat unlike the calm, expository manner of much of it. In them, Bain is discovering new ways of conceiving of the mind and knows himself to be at the edge of new work: 'we may be very far from comprehending the full and exact character of nerve force, but the knowledge we have gained is sufficient to destroy what has until lately prevailed as to the material processes of perception.'[98] He hypothesized that memory, for instance, is the revived action of the whole system, and not merely that of some central, receptive, storage system, and declared it likely that a brain cut from its spinal cord and nerves would lose 'even thought, reminiscence, or the emotions of the past and absence'.[99] Thus it is only partly true to say, as Robert Young does, that Bain was unwilling to accept sensory-motor analysis of the nervous system any further up the neuraxis than the subcortical structures.[100] In its cautious, piece-by-piece way, this was the direction in which his work was tending. Though, in 1855, he made categorical distinctions between, on the one hand, the spinal cord and the medulla oblongata (where routine activities such as digestion and respiration are controlled without feeling or consciousness), and, on the other, the cerebral hemispheres (where the mind proper—he thought—could be said to belong), he was very willing to believe that the higher functions involved the operation of the whole nervous system.[101] Only as time went on, and physiological findings outstripped and challenged his own (associationist-based) modes of analysis, did he take exception to them and attempt to preserve something of the autonomy of the higher faculties. Young, harder-line psycho-physiologists provoked feelings of resistance in a professional senior, and a defence of more traditional methods.[102]

The keynote remained the emphasis on relational theory. The third edition of *The Senses and the Intellect* (1868) formulated a law called the Law of Relativity, in which Bain insisted that it is only by seeing things relationally that we can understand anything at all. This applies cognitively and epistemologically ('change of impression is an indispensable condition of our being conscious, or of being mentally alive either to feeling or to thought . . . [in] everything we are capable of knowing'). But it also applies to the relations of mind and body.[103] In both the 'Preface' to the first edition of *The Senses and the Intellect*, and in his *Autobiography*, Bain made it clear that the leading arguments of *The Senses* were prompted by his reading in contemporary physiology, a programme of which he had set himself in 1851.[104] The physiological components of the book, indeed,

---

[98] Ibid. 61.    [99] Ibid.    [100] Robert M. Young, *Mind, Brain and Adaptation*, 112–14.
[101] Bain, *The Senses and the Intellect*, 47.
[102] Alexander Bain, 'The Respective Spheres and Mutual Helps of Introspection and Psycho-Physical Experiment in Psychology', *Mind*, NS 2 (1893), 42–53.    [103] Ibid. 8–9.
[104] Bain, *The Senses and the Intellect*, p. v; *Autobiography*, 227–34. See also Cardno, 'Bain and Physiological Psychology'.

struck its first reviewers as the most evidently innovative feature of it and many welcomed its contribution and the access it gave to modern thinking. Mill praised the book's impressively full exposition of the 'necessary material substratum'.[105] Masson thought that not only did the book's originality lie in its physiology; it was also the 'best *résumé* of that topic yet offered to the psychologist'.[106] Lewes thought the same in 1855 (though by the time he came to review the second edition in 1866, he felt that the physiological element had lost its edge).[107] Nevertheless, as late as 1877, Théodule Ribot considered Bain's work to be 'the most complete repository in existence of exact and positive psychology, placed *au courant* with recent discoveries'.[108] Other sympathetic readers had reservations —most notably Spencer, as we shall see—but the book was broadly and warmly welcomed by those on the side of the new psychology. Even amongst more guarded neutrals the effort was greeted sympathetically. J. D. Morrel praised Bain's efforts, though he thought them a little too inhibited by the classificatory apparatus and regretted Bain's reluctance to open his work to grander speculations. *The Senses and the Intellect* made 'no attempt at any generalization between organic life as existing in mind or nature', he noted.[109] This charge, a product in part of Bain's careful management of the transition within associationist theory so as not to ruffle feathers in his own camp, became more common as time went on, and, as we shall see, it was Spencer, in his *Principles of Psychology*, and not Bain, who broke more decisively from the older ways of conceiving of a psychological theory, and who offered these bolder generalizations. But, once again, Bain's limitations were also a source of strength as he carried the argument forward.

In retrospect, the detailed physiology in *The Senses and the Intellect* does not appear very startling. The descriptions of the physiological processes Bain offers closely follow standard textbooks of the period—Quain, Todd and Bowman, Carpenter, Müller, and Bell—and these are freely acknowledged. Bain did not, unlike Lewes or Huxley, undertake any experimental work of his own on structure or morphology. Nor did he speculate much about the details of the working of the nervous system, though he was intensely interested in the general principles of its mode of operation. The main burden of the physiological component of his work is to support the contention that the nervous system is a dynamic and transformative one. It is an energy system, he argues, which relays 'nerve force' (the precise character of which is undetermined) from point to point in the body. This is transformed (in ways also yet to be determined) into information, feeling, and other elements in the cerebral hemispheres. This

---

[105] John Stuart Mill, 'Bain's Psychology', 352.
[106] M[asson], 'Bain on The Senses and the Intellect', 216.
[107] Lewes, 'Bain on The Senses and the Intellect'; and Critical Notice.
[108] T. Ribot, *English Psychology*, 2nd edn. (London, 1877), 248.
[109] Morrel, 'Modern English Psychology', 359.

kind of description—of the psycho-physiological system as an energy system—subsequently became very common among leading psychologists in this period, and Bain gave an eye-catching portrait of it in terms of recognizable, up-to-the-minute technology. It is like 'the course of a railway train' by the side of which run telegraph wires. The individual wires cannot be said to run the whole length of the country (or the body), but they form a network that does.[110] As telegraph wires run from station to station, so the nerves run from 'nerve centre' to 'nerve centre'. The nerves—like the wires—originate nothing, they merely conduct. Each nerve has only one function (either sensory or motor), and the endogenous (efferent) and exogenous (afferent) systems are entirely separate.[111] The 'nerve centres'—like the stations on the railway line—have the property of 'sending out motor power', especially through the spinal chord, which is regarded as one big centre.[112]

In *The Emotions and the Will* Bain uses a similar analogy to drive home the point that it is the functioning of the organism as a whole that is the important fact: 'The transformations of the food and tissue are the *sine qua non*, the consciousness is the accidental part.'[113] But whence comes the energy which is thus transformed? Bain claims this is understandable, on 'the analogy of the steam-engine, where active chemical combinations give birth to moving force, through the medium of a certain mechanism. Physiologists are pretty well agreed on this point.'[114] The argument behind Bain's analogy here comes from the law in physics of the transformation and correlation of physical force—that is, as Bain puts it, the 'interchangeability of the natural powers—Heat, Electricity, Chemical Affinity, Mechanical Force'.[115] The same idea is suggested in *The Senses and the Intellect*. There, 'nerve force' is said to be analogous to electricity or magnetism, though it is not the same as these.[116] Something like 'nerve force', I suppose, is indeed now recognized to be both electrical and chemical—though not in any way Bain could have imagined—and we can see behind Bain's analogies something of the same iatromechanical impulses that stirred Hartley and, later, Huxley (see above, Chapter 3).

[110] Bain, *The Senses and the Intellect*, 30.    [111] Ibid. 36–8.
[112] Ibid. 46. For a later use of the same analogy, see W. K. Clifford, 'Body and Mind' (1874), in *Lectures and Essays*, ii. 51–2. Interestingly, some commentators later reversed the parallel, explaining the technology of telegraphy by the principle of the association of ideas: see Robert Routledge, *Discoveries and Inventions of the Nineteenth Century*, 14th edn. (London, 1903), 547–8. The forces of magnetism and the association of ideas were commonly compared—for example, by Ribot, *English Psychology*, 207, who was saluting Bain's discoveries.
[113] Bain, *The Emotions and the Will*, 476.    [114] Ibid. 477–8.
[115] Ibid. 478. This passage was preserved in the second edition, but removed from the third and used almost *verbatim* in Bain's *Mind and Body: The Theories of their Relation* (London, 1873), which deals with this idea at greater length.
[116] Bain, *The Senses and the Intellect*, 57–8.

The doctrine on which Bain is drawing—ostensibly based on a proven physical law, and illustrated by clear instances of that law in operation in the modern world—was a powerful influence in developing both Bain's reputation and the shape of his psychological theory. It was an idea that, as it were, became current, and George Eliot's use of electrical imagery in *Middlemarch*, for instance, may owe something to it. (*Middlemarch* deploys metaphors of electric currents and galvanic batteries to describe the action of human sensibilities, particularly that of Dorothea.) But it should be said that Bain's idea is not original—as he says, 'physiologists are pretty well agreed'—and Sally Shuttleworth finds other plausible—and not only physiological—sources for her use of such ideas.[117] More widely, the idea of the mutual convertibility of physiological and psychological force was one that a number of Bain's contemporaries also espoused at the mid-century. Spencer uses it in *The Principles of Psychology* (1855), as does Lewes in *The Physiology of Common Life* (1859–60), and (as Shuttleworth shows) George Eliot also used analogies that suggest organic transformations at parallel levels of society, history, morality, and individual psychological development in *Adam Bede* (1859).[118] The convergence of these ideas, illustrating a general interest in 'flat' networks of contacts between different points (as in Bain's railway system and George Eliot's familiar image of the web as a metaphor for social inter-relation) suggest a significant turn in direction in theory away from the hier-archical models that absorbed much of the interest of earlier thinkers.

One of the important original ideas in Bain's *The Senses and the Intellect*, and one that enthusiastic reviewers such as Masson, Lewes, and Mill applauded, was directly connected with these speculations.[119] In contrast to traditional associ-ationism, and partly in response to stinging criticisms by Coleridge and others, Bain conceives of the psychological system as *active*—that is, it is a system that has spontaneous resources of energy at its disposal. It is a structure with dynamic resources that pre-exist the encroachments of culture. For Mill, Masson, and Lewes, this was the key to psychology's advance in the 1850s. As Masson put it, it was 'one of the germs of a new psychology which make the present volume so interesting'.[120] Bain posits a system subject to waves of spontaneous internal energy, though the analogy he uses fails to catch the attention as effectively as that of the railways: 'The nervous system may be compared to an organ with bellows constantly charged, and ready to be let off in any direction, according to the particular keys that are touched. The stimulus of our sensations and

---

[117] Shuttleworth, *George Eliot and Nineteenth-Century Science*, 158–9.

[118] Ibid., ch. 2. See esp. pp. 39 ff. for a discussion of physiological psychology, though she does not discuss Bain's work.

[119] M[asson], 'Bain on The Senses and the Intellect', 220–3; Lewes, 'Bain on The Senses and the Intellect', 772; Mill, 'Bain's Psychology', 354.

[120] M[asson], 'Bain on The Senses and the Intellect', 223.

feelings, instead of supplying the inward power, merely determines the manner and place of the discharge.'[121] Bain suggests that the operation of this energy discharge follows the 'Law of Diffusion'. There is 'a freely diffused current of nervous activity, tending to produce movements, gesture, expression, and all the other effects described in the course of the next few pages.' These unconscious actions provide an important clue to the functioning of the mind (a principle Freud, of course, developed and extended). They are 'a constituent part of the complex fact of consciousness in every form and variety' and 'little attention has been paid to them in the scientific consideration of the mind'.[122]

Bain's idea was not new. Arguments about the existence and nature of some kind of nerve force stretch back to Hartley, and even to Locke, and it was still a lively topic of debate in the mid-nineteenth century. There is, for instance, an interesting discussion that relates to Bain's proposal in Henry Holland's work. Regarding 'the separate existence and attributes of the nervous power', Holland, in his leisurely cautious way, argues that:

Whatever censure has been thrown, justly or unjustly, upon this term, it is certain that we cannot dispense with some phrase equivalent to it, in reasoning on the phenomena of animal life. At every step we are obliged to admit the conception of the fact thus expressed; and however inadequate our present means to determine its nature, and relations to the mental and physical parts of our being, we can no more deny reality to such a power, than we can to the effects of which it is the obvious source. Other terms— energy, agency, element, principle, and force—have, on the same grounds, been applied to denote it; all readily lending themselves to any relation with physical agents which may hereafter be ascertained; but liable in common to the preliminary objection of designating one principle or element, that which we do not know to be really such. For the inquiry brings us at once to the most essential of the questions regarding the nervous power, viz., its unity:—whether it be actually one and the same agent, producing diversity of effect from the manner of its transmission, or from the various fabric and vitality of the parts on which it acts;—or whether there are two or more powers coming under this common appellation as acting through nervous structure, but really different in nature, and thence producing different effects in the economy of life.[123]

Holland identifies the crucial point. Materialists would argue that there can be only one type of nerve force that is functionally different depending upon its place in the 'economy of life' (Lewes, for example, held this view). On the other hand, those opposed to this idea want to defend the notion of more than one

---

[121] Bain, *The Senses and the Intellect*, 291. Bain often uses musical metaphors in these contexts; for instance, in his discussion of sexuality he says that, after puberty, the 'nervous waves diffused from the cerebrum, alters the whole tone of the mind, like the addition of a new range of pipes to a wind instrument' (p. 281). He seems to have been unaware of the comic effects.

[122] Ibid. 272 n. The Law of Diffusion is further expounded in the 2nd and 3rd editions of *The Emotions and the Will*, ch. 1.    [123] Holland, *Chapters*, 241–2.

such force in order to account for the moral or spiritual life, or the exercise of the 'higher' faculties, without reducing them to 'mere' material effects. As we have seen, the notion of 'special human vitalism' (an independent power superadded to any primitive material force) was a frequent response to the materialist case.

It will be clear that Bain's theory belongs in the former camp. He takes the idea of nerve force and gives it a width of application that is both new and daring. This was not in itself original; none the less, no one had attempted to explore the idea with the same level of rigour or thoroughness. And it gave Bain much opportunity. It offered the possibility of a uniform, consistent, material explanation for the nervous system and its links to the mind. But it also gave the opportunity to reinterpret and change the direction of the association psychology, to give it not only the 'material substratum' John Mill required, but also a way of explaining, within associationist rules, human agency, and activity, something it bleakly lacked in classical Utilitarianism. Within a couple of decades, Bain's theories of the spontaneity, conservation, and retention of energy were perceived to be a helpful way of short-circuiting what were seen as fruitless metaphysical arguments about the freedom of human agency—fruitless, that is, from the point of view of a developing scientific psychology.[124] As Edwin Boring pointed out, after Bain's work, it became impossible to think of the transfer of activity without the transfer of energy.[125] Bain's notion that the mind was an energy system pulled the rug from beneath neo-Coleridgean arguments that any realistic account of mind required a belief in special, self-acting faculties because matter itself was too inert to explain human activity. Henceforth, it was necessary to find an equivalence in energy terms between cause and effect for psychological actions, and eventually this became the norm of scientific explanation. In the meantime, however, Bain's ideas did not go unchallenged.

There were two sorts of objection. One came from the scientific community, the other from the religious. Both types, though, raised a common problem, that of the transference in conceptual terms from accounts of the physical world to those of mind and consciousness. This problem beset all psychologists in the period. Though Bain kept insisting that one should regard consciousness as an effect of the material processes of the organic system and not identical with them, religious thinkers, on the one side, refused to accept this, and scientific thinkers, on the other, were concerned at the analogous nature of the argument. It was all very well to talk about steam engines and telegraph wires in a way that impressed non-scientists like David Masson (who was particularly taken with the helpfulness of the latter metaphor[126]), but, in the end, the organism was not a steam

---

[124] e.g. Ribot, *English Psychology*, 252–3; Davidson, 'Bain's Philosophy', 172.

[125] Edwin G. Boring, *Sensation and Perception in the History of Experimental Psychology* (New York, 1942), 86–7.

[126] M[asson], 'Bain on The Senses and the Intellect', 217.

engine, and the nervous system was not a line of telegraph poles. As Roger Smith notes, both Bain and Spencer 'argued with professional physicists over the nature of physical force and refused to accept force as merely a mathematical function devised by physicists to aid understanding of matter in motion'.[127] In particular, Bain's ideas were challenged directly by the mathematician, lawyer, and classical scholar—and future author of *The Doctrine of Energy* (1874)—D. D. Heath, who took issue with Bain's lectures at the Royal Institution in 1866–7 'On the Correlation of Force and its Bearing on the Mind'.[128]

Heath argued that Bain had, simply, failed to understand 'those departments of science in which the precision of the mathematician and the experimentalist is required'.[129] In the absence of detailed knowledge of the mode of operation of the nervous system, substitutes from explanations of other phenomena would not do. Bain's analogies betrayed him into scientific nonsense because analogy was treated as fact:

Professor Bain, in 'The Senses and the Intellect', has an odd notion that this 'undying endurance of an electric wire'—that is, the fact that its electric state, while chemical actions and reactions are going on, is temporary—is owing to the wire being a 'compact, resisting and sluggish mass'; which seems like saying that an elastic ball is more sluggish than a lump of putty. . . . [the doctrine of the correlation of force] teaches us that there is a certain condition of equivalence in all changes, but it does not tell us what kind of changes will take place under any given circumstances. In what direction the parts of a machine will begin to move, what the reactions will be in a mass of chemical materials, and so forth, are questions to be answered by the engineer or the chemist.[130]

Processes observed in the inorganic world, Heath argued, cannot be extrapolated to the organic, and he made much of the uncertainties in the present state of physiological and biological knowledge. Despite Bain's confidence:

physiologists are apparently not yet agreed whether there is any special 'nerve force,' or agent requiring a name; that is, any special condition of the matter of the active brain and nerves apart from its state of motion, temperature, electric and chemical energy, analogous to the electric tension of a galvanic pile or frictional electrical machine, the production of which abstracts, for the time being, a definite quantity of physical energy from other forms, to restore it again, in heat or some equivalent, when 'nervous excitement' abates. Professor Huxley, lecturing in 1857, maintained the affirmative: whereas Professor Du Bois Raymond, in another lecture, inclined to think that 'what we have termed the nervous agent is some internal motion, perhaps even some chemical change,

[127] Roger Smith, 'Physiological Psychology and the Philosophy of Nature', 217.
[128] Bain's essay of the same title, which drew on the lectures, was published in *Macmillan's Magazine*, 16 (1867), 372–83.
[129] D. D. Heath, 'Professor Bain on the Doctrine of the Correlation of Force in its Bearing on the Mind', *Contemporary Review*, 8 (1868), 58.          [130] Ibid. 69–70.

of the substance contained in the nerve-tubes,' which he conceives as the result of a special arrangement of 'minute centres of chemical action, acting upon each other electrically, and controlling their mutual deviations from their position of equilibrium'.[131]

Du Bois Raymond's theory sounds like some rocky seventeenth-century speculation of the kind entertained by the contemporaries of Locke and Hartley, and it is presumably deliberately chosen by Heath for this reason, because the essay has a consistent, though subdued, mocking tone. But Heath's point is real. Theories like Bain's have a cogency in principle, but are difficult to sustain in detail, and Heath asks some hard questions. For instance, he points out that Bain wilfully blurs proper scientific discriminations and that his 'false physics and equivocal terminology' do not distinguish between 'stimulus, moving force, and energy'.[132] Bain also simply finesses the problem of criteria for measurement, and Heath issues a hard experimentalist's challenge to prove that causal force is equivalently correlated with effect:

It is fit that the psychologist should give us some hint how he would have us proceed. What is the proportion, as matter of pure consciousness, between a sound, a colour, a touch, and an emotion of surprise or grief, that Mr. Bain should tell us[;] the truth of his theory depends on these proportions being found to be the same as those of their respective physical supports.[133]

I suppose that the answer to Heath's question would lie in the measurement of electrical 'evoked potentials' in the neurological 'wiring' of the brain, something that modern-day psycho-physiologists undertake.[134] But his question was unanswerable in these or any other experimental terms in the 1860s. The issue, once again, raises that of the value of scientific theories that are now defunct. In Positivist or Experimentalist terms they are of historical interest (in its pejorative sense) only; yet they prevailed for a time, and therefore they were 'true', on some Popperian criteria of falsifiability, for instance, for the disciplinary purposes for which they were devised. At the same time they also led to better theories and better findings, and fundamentally changed the paradigm within which psychology was being thought. In this light it is interesting, once again, to consider the publishing circumstances and wider intellectual context of Heath's essay, for they shed light on the way knowledge propositions circulated in Victorian society.

The essay was originally published in the *Contemporary Review* in 1868. The *Contemporary Review* had been founded two years earlier as an Established Church

---

[131] D. D. Heath, 'Professor Bain on the Doctrine of the Correlation of Force in its Bearing on the Mind', *Contemporary Review*, 8 (1868), 73.

[132] Ibid. 73–4.    [133] Ibid. 75.

[134] For a useful description, see John Boddy, *Brain Systems and Psychological Concepts* (Chichester, 1978), pt. 4.

response to the successful, pro-scientific, and politically liberal *Fortnightly Review* edited initially by Lewes and, later, by John Morley. Though it originated within the Church camp, and was controlled by the Dean of Canterbury, it was undogmatic in editorial policy. The Dean banished 'all sectarian and class prejudices', and published writers with diverse views.[135] Spencer, for instance, had a long association with it, and the journal welcomed contributions by Catholics also. There was no point, the editors realized, in being dogmatic; the journal needed to be able to put a respectable religious case in the context of serious-minded scientific work. However, it is tempting to connect the cultural mission of the *Contemporary* with the intentions of Heath's essay, which were to compromise the scientific credentials of the new psychology. Heath was, in fact, a broad churchman of some steel and conviction, and a friend of Tennyson within the cultural and intellectual establishment. This needs to be borne in mind, for the doctrine of the correlation of force became an issue in wider religious controversy.

The doctrine was attacked by orthodox churchmen like John Tulloch in his influential *Movements of Religious Thought* (the remarks are part of a general attack on John Mill's religious views):

once suppose that there is more in heaven and earth than we can gather from the knowledge of phenomena—that man is more than matter—that mind is more than any combination of matter, and all analogy between mental force and other forms of force disappears. Does it not disappear when the facts are looked at in themselves? All forms of material force are obviously in themselves mere transformations. They operate unconsciously; they are merely *changes*—transferences. *We* recognize force in them because we have experience of force in ourselves; but they do not themselves yield the idea of force. We could never get the idea from them; and therefore Comte . . . would have the term disused as misleading—as implying something of which we have no knowledge. The idea of force is only given in the action of the mind; it is the product of self-consciousness—of nothing else. And does this not separate conscious Will from all other facts of Nature? It is confessedly untranslatable. No process of merely natural change can generate it. Does it not, therefore, by its very character, stand apart from the category of matter, and compel us to recognize its distinction? Does not, in short, the purely scientific view of mind, as something in experience absolutely apart from all other motor forces in the world, lead us up to the theological view that mind, as self-conscious, is a singular power—an efflux from a higher Source than matter?[136]

This is an adroit, but eventually weak, argument. It is also, in the history of these debates, a remarkable one, for here—as in the work of H. L. Mansel—is

---

[135] Quoted by Walter E. Houghton, 'Periodical Literature and the Articulate Classes', in Shattock and Wolff (eds.), *The Victorian Periodical Press: Samplings and Soundings*, 13. For further details, see also *The Wellesley Index*, i. 210–13.
[136] Tulloch, *Movements of Religious Thought*, 239–40.

the arsenal of sceptical argument used to support, not attack, religious conviction. Because the grounds for belief in the materialist case for the relationship between mind and matter are dubious, then sceptical epistemology is turned against itself and doubt produces the invitation to certainty in religious conviction. The argument is poor, because it invites belief in case *A* merely because it preceded case *B*, which is shown to be unverifiable. No effort is made to adjudicate the relative worth of the two cases, because the whole is written in the interested need to validate one of them. Whatever its value, however, Tulloch's argument is historically significant in the context of the development of the realist epistemologies subsequently produced to ground materialist programmes for a scientific psychology. These kinds of epistemologies are in fact to be found in Spencer and Lewes, as we shall see in subsequent chapters, and they accept provisionality wholeheartedly as the cornerstone of scientific belief.

In the context of these opposing arguments from the overlapping scientific and religious communities, how did Bain resolve the conceptual difficulty of describing the transition from matter to mind, from force to consciousness, from organic function to the higher faculties? The answer was by what one commentator—Edwin Boring—called a 'metaphysical makeshift'.[137] This was a version of the doctrine of 'psycho-physical parallelism'. This doctrine, sometimes known as 'double-aspect theory', was, for the new psychologists, a common way of approaching the apparent ontological hiatus between physical and mental phenomena. An extreme version of the argument would hold that mental and physical events are separate orders of phenomena with their own regularities and procedures of analysis. But an equally strong version held that, though the two orders need discrete modes of analysis to reveal the full specificity of each, there is a necessary, inevitable, and determining connection between them, and that they are, in the end, subject to the same laws. Mill, for instance, held this view. Such an argument, of course, still has purchase today, but in the mid-to-late nineteenth century its application was often a matter of expediency forced on defensive psychologists by the weak state of research, its distance from the conceptual armouries of the philosophy of mind, and a hostile public context. Opponents regarded it as a dodge, while some supporters thought it tainted by the ghost of metaphysical dualism.[138] Either way, it could not satisfy the instinct for conviction, and the makeshift only allowed the battle to continue. For the new psychologists the mental and physical planes were only two aspects of one phenomenon, and—as Bain argued firmly—priority in terms of analysis and causality had to belong to the physical order. The higher faculties, even consciousness itself, were only the results of sensitive neurological processes. For others, however, they remained utterly separate entities.

---

[137] Boring, *History of Experimental Psychology*, 237.
[138] Davidson, 'Bain's Philosophy', 163.

James Martineau was one who held this view. Responding to Bain, Martineau defined 'Mental Science as self-knowledge: Natural Science, the knowledge of something other than self'.[139] This distinction, Martineau argued, runs through all of our knowledge: for example, vision is the inner, mental form of light, which is the outer, natural phenomenon, and these 'spheres are of necessity mutually exclusive . . . twins in their birth but without contact in their career'. The one cannot be subordinated to the other in a deterministic relationship. The two modes of knowledge are 'absolutely parallel and co-ordinate, and can never be transposed into subordination'. There is a 'necessary duality', and the sciences themselves form a 'dualistic grouping' not a 'monistic' one. 'Neither can question, no[r] either may borrow, the language and methods of the other.'[140]

This is an extreme version of the 'parallelism' argument, used to make all the dualistic separations Martineau needs. He claims that science and literature, for example, represent different kinds of mental event and types of enquiry. Whereas science is arcane, speculative, and uncertain, literature possesses a 'community of nature between knower and known', a kind of self-validating self-evidence. Further, the introspective apprehension of inner mental life is not a solipsistic reduction. We can match the evidences of our self-knowledge to the records of human history, politics, jurisprudence, philology, and art, where the 'whole essence lies in the internal meaning of which they are the record and the sign, in the invisible and spiritual facts of which they compel the very elements to take charge'.[141] Thus Martineau's epistemological dualism sponsors two further dualisms: a dualism of kinds of discourses, and a dualism of kinds of reading. There are in the world different kinds of writing, one of which is trustworthy, while the other (science) is speculative and unfortunate. The physiological elements in Bain's psychology are thus, by definition, 'foreign and intrusive'.[142] At the same time there are different ways of reading: a reading for spiritual 'essence', and a reading of the texts of 'Natural Science', the nature of which is not specified by Martineau but does not look promising.

This is not a strong argument, because the indivisibility of such knowledge for the psychologist is exactly the issue. We may ask, for instance, what happens to these absolute separations if the object of scientific knowledge is itself that of the inner phenomena? This, after all, is what the psychologist is after—knowledge of the properties of vision, say, in both their physiological and psychological details as patterns of light are both received and interpreted. In this case, Martineau would have to acknowledge that 'inner' certainties have become objects of knowledge like any other, and the two carefully discriminated domains inevitably become contaminated. Nevertheless, despite its weakness, this might be an effective (if not a valuable) argument. It is firmly and tellingly written,

---

[139] Martineau, 'Cerebral Psychology: Bain', 502.
[140] Ibid. 502–3.    [141] Ibid. 504.    [142] Ibid. 505.

for one thing, and could command agreement from an audience already persuaded of its principles (for example, committed readers of literature of a certain kind). As we have seen in Chapter 3, it became common for writers alarmed by the scale of science's advance to retreat into a defensive dualism of this sort.

But, even so, the argument does not clearly separate the scientists from the believers, for many could be both. As we saw in Chapter 3, William Carpenter for some time resisted the advance of the physiological analysis in which he was so eminent when it entered the psychological domain, and retained his belief in the essential independence of the higher faculties. Carpenter's position was taken up by the philanthropist, religious writer, and early feminist Frances Power Cobbe in her interesting examination of Carpenter's theory of 'unconscious cerebration' in 1870. (Carpenter had advanced the idea that the brain works efficiently though unconsciously.) Cobbe—like Carpenter a Unitarian—outlines the extreme physiological case for materialistic monism, and continues:

But if this possibility be accepted provisionally, and the possibility admitted of its future physiological demonstration, have we, with it, accepted also the Materialist's ordinary conclusion that *we* and our automatically thinking brains are one and indivisible? If the brain can work by itself, have we any reason to believe it ever works *also* under the guidance of something external to itself, which we may describe as the Conscious Self? It seems to me that . . . there are two kinds of actions of the brain, the one automatic, and the other subject to the will of the Conscious Self; just as the actions of a horse are some of them spontaneous and some done under the compulsion of his rider. The first order of actions tend to indicate that the brain 'secretes thought'; the second order (contrasting with the first) show that, beside that automatically-working brain, there is another agency in the field under whose control the brain performs a wholly different class of labours.[143]

This is a more moderate, and not uninformed, dualism compared to that of Martineau, but the argument is still built upon a rigorous separation of the various 'orders' of mental life. Cobbe's—and Carpenter's—concern in the late 1860s was partly excited by the extent to which Huxley, principally, but others too, were pushing the direction of the physiological argument at the end of the decade. It will be remembered that the terminus of the argument was felt to be the alarming prospect of human automatism, but forms of this defensive dualism were continuous from the mid-century.

For instance, the 'so-what?' version of the dualistic argument was also available, and could be put by very sensitive and intelligent people, like Tennyson towards the close of *In Memoriam* (1850):

---

[143] Frances Power Cobbe, 'Unconscious Cerebration: A Psychological Study', *Macmillan's Magazine*, 23 (1870), 36–7.

CXX

I trust I have not wasted breath:
I think we are not wholly brain,
Magnetic mockeries; not in vain,
Like Paul with beasts, I fought with Death;

Not only cunning casts in clay:
Let Science prove we are, and then
What matters Science unto men,
At least to me? I would not stay.

Let him, the wiser man who springs
Hereafter, up from childhood shape
His action like the greater ape,
But I was born to other things.[144]

It is not to belittle the emotional and poetic power of the poem, nor the pressure of grief, anxiety, and struggle recorded in it, to say that its position *vis-à-vis* physiological psychology amounts to little more than turning one's back and asserting other beliefs. In terms of the larger structure and argument of the poem, this section gathers emotional weight and argumentative point from its renewed assertion of purpose, despite the prospect of an alarming pre-history of ape-ish origins, and an apparently spiritually flattening theory of the material organization of the brain. At the same time, as a specific, detailed, and contemporary intervention, it gains its effect from the prestige of its literary form *per se*. By virtue of the fact of being poetry, one might say, it becomes invested with ideas of a fine caring for human values against the mutinous tinkerings of psychology. Frances Cobbe, like Martineau and many of the writers examined in the first section of this chapter, believed that literary works should continue to be properly literary and concern themselves with the spirit and fine feeling. Modern literature placed too much emphasis on the influence of environment, and Cobbe believed, like Henry James, that science had spoiled George Eliot's work.[145]

In truth there was little alternative to some form of dualism. The softer version of 'psycho-physical parallelism'—in which the two realms shadowed each

[144] *The Poems of Tennyson*, ed. Christopher Ricks (London, 1969), 970–1. Ricks notes that the reference in line 3 to the 'magnetic mockeries' of the brain (which are reminiscent of Bain's theories in *The Senses and the Intellect*) are thought to have been derived by Tennyson from a speculation in Robert Chambers's *Vestiges of Creation* (1844). Another possibility is that Tennyson refers to the telegraph, which, of course, works by altering magnetic fields by fluctuations in electric current in order to move the dial pointing to the letters. Such a system had been patented in 1837 and was in operation on the railways in the 1840s, but it was far from reliable (hence the 'mockeries'). Either way, a general, if not direct, pertinence to Bain's idea can be claimed. See also n. 112 above.

[145] Frances Power Cobbe, *The Scientific Spirit of the Age: And Other Pleas and Discussions* (London, 1888), 30, 18.

other without a clearly specified determining relationship—was deployed by Mill, Bain, and, at this stage, Lewes too.[146] It was a necessity of the times, as responsible arguments could not be made any stronger. As D. B. Klein argues, following Boring, Bain was an ontological monist, but perforce an epistemological dualist.[147] He tried to develop a psychological theory that was grounded in a thorough-going application of materialist explanation, but he also worked within the mentalist tradition of the association psychology. His amalgamation of associationism with theories from physiology (and Spencer's joining of it to a general biological theory) were regarded as the most advanced and successful of psychological theories of the mid-nineteenth century.[148] Yet the marriage of associationism and physiology was not so smooth.

Associationist theory is prominent in *The Senses and the Intellect* and *The Emotions and the Will* in a number of ways. As a good associationist, and one who felt himself in the vanguard of the latest scientific psychology, Bain is very clear in his opposition to any conception of innate human faculties.[149] Nevertheless he retains faith in some of the older methods and approaches, founding many of his ideas on the evidence of introspection, or appeals to common experience, or to the evidence of literature. For example, he discusses depression (or, as he calls it, nervous exhaustion or fatigue) by reference to Tennyson's poem 'Mariana' (1830) and makes an 'appeal to each person's experience for the perception of it'.[150] In *The Emotions and the Will* he defends the use of introspection, and the casual observation of others, for the understanding and classification of the emotions. But he is cautious about the extrapolation of theories from remembered feelings, and so insists that we have to follow the physical evidence, in expressive gesture and other manifestation of strong feelings in others, as a check on the suspect evidence of memory.[151] Though he understands the limitations of introspection and proposes the construction of controlled experiments to monitor the exercise of the will, much of this has the feel of makeshift.[152] His clear-minded sense that complex emotional states are rarely 'pure, detached, or isolated', and that therefore all record of them is in some sense a reconstruction, and that such reconstructions are sometimes coloured by overbearing desire ('Impassioned or Exaggerated ends') or other present emotion, does not lessen his recommendation of introspection and unstructured observation.[153]

---

[146] See e.g. [G. H. Lewes], 'Voluntary and Involuntary Actions', *Blackwood's Edinburgh Magazine*, 86 (1859), esp. 305–6, in which Lewes endorses Bain's view, though a little reluctantly. Later—in *Problems of Life and Mind*—Lewes rejected Bain's moderate line and adopted a much more forceful interactionist position.

[147] Klein, *A History of Scientific Psychology*, 804.      [148] Ribot, *English Psychology*, 207.

[149] See e.g. *The Senses and the Intellect*, 340; *The Emotions and the Will*, 290.

[150] Bain, *The Senses and the Intellect*, 124. He likewise discusses the perverted pleasures of power by reference to Dickens's Quilp from *The Old Curiosity Shop* (1841).

[151] Bain, *The Emotions and the Will*, 50–3.      [152] Ibid. 447–8.      [153] Ibid. 452, 455.

It would be wrong to suggest that Bain's deployment of associationist theory is tired, reluctant, or makeshift. He was an enthusiast for these methods, on which he had been intellectually reared, until the end, and was widely credited as the leading and most comprehensive expositor of associationist ideas in the second half of the nineteenth century.[154] Rather I am suggesting that, coming at the end of this tradition, he has a lively sense of its limitations as well as its strengths, and he sees the edges of it in ways that were, apparently, invisible to either James or John Mill, for example. His perception of the writing of history (a central concern of many, like George Eliot, who moved in the circle of the new psychologists) is markedly different from that of James Mill. The difference in part follows from Bain's reservations about the accuracy of memory, and brings into focus a more substantial difference in attitude to the mind's operations. Mill's *History of British India* doggedly tramps through a six-volume wasteland of arcana and civil-service detail (an often bizarre jumble of exotica and statistics) organized on lines that stress above all the easy comprehensibility and accessibility of this giant, complex, and alien history. (One of his preferred forms of expressing it is the list or catalogue.) It is not in the least self-conscious about its own scale or ambition, nor aware of difficulties in method or presupposition. It is, in short, an imperial (and imperious) civil-service record.[155] By the time Bain, Spencer, Lewes, and George Eliot came to consider these problems, they could not be so blithe about their assumptions. Without relinquishing their faith in the reasoned understanding of the past, the problem of history, and the writing of history, for them became a more complex, intellectually taxing business. I will have more to say about this in discussion of Spencer and Lewes, who are even more acutely aware than Bain of these emergent problems and (partly as a result) were less attached to associationist theory. But Bain was not oblivious to them. He writes in *The Senses and the Intellect*: 'Human history at large is a grand ensemble of succession, which no mind can totally comprehend, and which consequently presents itself in innumerable aspects to the intellects of men.'[156] The caveat appears in the context of a long discussion of the associationist Law of Similarity, and the connection between James Mill's lists and the pure version of the associationist 'ensemble of succession' that he maintained is easily grasped.

The processes included under the Law of Similarity come into being, Bain argues, by a reactivation of a sensory-nervous disposition previously acquired. The system, as it were, recognizes a prior state of itself. Obviously this becomes more effective through repetition, and, in cases of partial similarity, this law shares

[154] Ribot, *English Psychology*, 206–7; John Stuart Mill, *A System of Logic: Ratiocinative and Inductive*, 8th edn. (London, 1895), 557.
[155] James Mill, *The History of British India*, 3rd edn., 6 vols. (London, 1826).
[156] Bain, *The Senses and the Intellect*, 500.

its effects with that of the Law of Contiguity. Bain's idea is not far removed from one of Hartley's and is therefore classical, but Bain also posits the formation of 'such a thing as an energetic power of recognizing similarity in general'; that is, it is not simply a passive, reactive mechanism, but a power that, in its own right, impels the mind forward.[157] His wording is rather equivocal. He speaks in phrases like 'the attractive force of similarity behoves to be very energetic', which sounds portentous and magnetic but, apart from anything else, occludes the question of agency.[158] Is Bain saying that the perceiving subject is energetic in such a way? Or that his or her nervous system is energetic? Or that the sensational counterparts of objects-in-the-world eagerly seek out their fellows by means of some unacknowledged property of the nervous system? The point is an interesting one for Bain's conception of the functioning of the mind in general, for his conception of the workings of associationist law, and for questions like the epistemological one raised by the writing of history. Bain's answer, though, is actually a finesse. He stampedes the point through in thirty pages of detailed example that look like classical associationist case law, and therefore disguise a little the import of his proposal (for it could be a significant amendment to associationist theory). He talks rather unclearly and unhelpfully about the idea of history as repetition, but one cannot help feeling that the thrust of the argument has not been followed through. It is another indication, perhaps, that associationism is coming to its very edges. Bain does not declare himself a naïve or spontaneous realist (like Hartley or James Mill, for example), but this is the implication. The mind can jump to its ideas automatically.

Bain's detailed technical amendments to the various laws of association are thoroughly set out elsewhere, so I will not dwell on the details.[159] In major respects he is close to the classics. His analyses of many of the 'higher faculties'—like the intellect—follow associationist lines for the most part. (Intellect is built up by the combined operation of the various laws of association working on the exogenous stimuli.) He also widely and continuously applies the Utilitarian pleasure/pain theory as a motor for psychological development.[160] This idea is not peculiar to associationism (it is used in psychoanalysis, for instance), but Bain's ethical outlook is Utilitarian through and through, as his contemporaries realized.[161] He draws on James Mill's *Fragment on Mackintosh* and holds that conscience, for instance, is 'moulded upon external authority as a type'; it is

---

[157] Bain, *The Senses and the Intellect*, 456.    [158] Ibid. 491.

[159] The most comprehensive account is given, as ever, by Warren, *History of the Association Psychology*, 104–17.

[160] See e.g. *The Senses and the Intellect*, ch. 2, and the discussion of the types of pleasure available from each of the senses, and, especially, the account of the formation of the will, in *The Emotions and the Will*, ch. 6, esp. 441–3.

[161] Davidson, 'Bain's Philosophy', 173.

not 'a distinct attribute', as Dugald Stewart and others of the Scottish school maintained.[162] He is alert to the strong case for this view (that conscience is culturally specific and not a universal, abstract entity, and that it may be coercive) and he argues this with confidence.[163] Finally, his physiological ideas are clearly constructed on associationist lines. The development of the embryonic nervous system into a functioning individual sounds, in the description of the storage and discharge of energy, like the development of the mind by the laws of association, and this aspect of Bain's work has already received some commentary.[164] However, there are also ways in which this is *not* like associationist thought, and Bain takes significant distance from it.

John Stuart Mill highlighted the most important of these. As we have seen, Mill seized upon Bain's psychology as a solution to the problem of active agency in associationism, which had been highlighted by Coleridge and others. For Mill, Bain made two 'great additions' to associationism: the physiological parts of his theory, and 'the recognition of an active element, or spontaneity, in the mind itself'.[165] This active element follows from Bain's physiological hypothesis of reserves of energy in the system that seek discharge and use. The system—which includes both mind and body—is capable of initiating, controlling, and developing its own activity as part of its development and in its mature constitution. Learning is possible, and Bain's account of the sensitive system has sophisticated mechanisms for this, particularly the muscle sense, as George Croom Robertson, the editor of *Mind*, noted in 1877. Robertson saluted the major importance of Bain's 'discovery (for it's hardly less) of the element of muscular activity in objective perception' but suggested its analysis was still too 'analytic' and 'formal' in the manner of Hartley—that is, it was not yet dynamic enough to get beyond classical associationism.[166]

Bain's description of learning, however, is subtle. Learning is not merely a matter of intellectual or conceptual understanding. It includes learning beyond ratiocination, including that obtained through feeling.[167] Bain's account of the

---

[162] Bain, *The Emotions and the Will*, 313.     [163] Ibid. 290–7.

[164] Mischel, ' "Emotion" and "Motivation" '; Robert M. Young, *Mind, Brain and Adaptation*, 114 ff.

[165] John Stuart Mill, 'Bain's Psychology', 354.

[166] George Croom Robertson, 'How we Come by our Knowledge', *Nineteenth Century*, 1 (1877), 120. Bain's account of the importance of the muscle sense in cognition is given in *The Senses and the Intellect*, 73–111, 362–404. The former describes mechanisms and inferences, while the latter discusses more generally the epistemological questions raised by it. Roger Smith, 'Physiological Psychology and the Philosophy of Nature', covers this topic widely, including Bain's contribution.

[167] See Bain's note to John Stuart Mill's 1869 edition of James Mill's *Analysis of the Phenomena of the Human Mind*, i. 36. The note discusses the origin and growth of the 'tender affections in human beings' through initial contact with the mother. This enlarged sense of knowledge growth would have been understood and approved by George Eliot.

'natural history of the feelings' was widely approved—by Mill and Lewes, for instance.[168] It attempted to give a classification of the emotions on the model of the taxonomies used in the orthodox natural histories, and hence give them a status they lacked in the mentalist bias of associationism and in classical Utilitarianism (as, for example, in John Mill's account of his upbringing in the *Autobiography*).[169] Bain also described a psychological system that does not run in one uniform direction. The mind and the body are full of conflicting and, in the initial stages especially, unformed energies and impulses: 'Perhaps the compliancy and conflicting impulses of the human frame are the cause of all this uncertainty and mistake [in the early years], rendering it necessary for us to resort to experience and science, and a higher volition than appetite, for the guidance of our daily life.'[170] This is an argument that would appeal to evolutionists, and it is one to which Bain is attached. He repeats it in *The Emotions and the Will*, for instance: it is frustration, pain, and the 'cycle of annoyance' in the child that stimulates the acquisition of the higher faculties.[171] It is human *inability* that encourages the acquisition of ability; the human faculties are not derived passively from the world outside on a smooth learning curve, as classical Utilitarianism held.

Theodore Mischel has claimed that John Mill misinterpreted Bain on the question of spontaneous activity. He argues that Mill illegitimately converted what is clearly a *physiological* concept into a *psychological* one and ignored the question of agency. How can a rudimentary power in the system be said to wield authority in the exercise of the higher faculties in the mind?, he asks. Mischel concludes that Bain is thus not, as Mill thought, an answer to Coleridge.[172] However, though Mischel does identify a genuine conceptual problem, it is one that is settled in outline, if not in detail, by the shape and direction of Bain's theory. We have noted that he anticipates the modern psychological textbook in the arrangement of his material, which develops from an account of the simplest of phenomena to the most complex. Bain's is thus a genetic and dynamic account in both form and content. The adult mind emerges from the complicated, relational interaction of diverse forces, some physiological, some social,

---

[168] Mill, 'Bain's Psychology', 361–4; Lewes, 'Bain on The Senses and the Intellect', 771; Davidson, 'Bain's Philosophy', 170. Ribot though, following Spencer's critique, is less happy: the coverage of the emotions, he concludes, is the weakest part of Bain's psychology (*English Psychology*, 222 ff.). For details of Spencer's criticisms, see Chapter 6 below.

[169] The 'natural-history' method is described by Bain in *The Senses and the Intellect*, 83 ff., and *The Emotions and the Will*, 'Preface'. It might be interestingly compared to Nicholas Humphrey's modern account along similar lines, which also rests on the importance of the historical development of the feelings and the motivating power of neo-Utilitarian self-interest (*History of the Mind*, esp. chs. 26–7).

[170] Bain, *The Senses and the Intellect*, 255.     [171] Bain, *The Emotions and the Will*, 352.

[172] Mischel, '"Emotion" and "Motivation"', 142–3.

some (eventually) the (relatively) free-acting forces of the higher faculties, which can set goals, solve problems, and control behaviour. Mischel's point seems rather trapped in the mid-nineteenth-century dualistic opposition that Bain's theory was in part trying—if not wholly successfully—to avoid. Bain's relational psychology was a genuine step towards a resolution achieved by redescribing psychological qualities as emergent properties rather than as fully-formed mental capacities, a prematurely advanced stage in the argument that inevitably locked debate into an abstract opposition of mind to body.

Bain was not an automatist; he did not believe that human beings acted in unwitting response to the promptings of physiological or environmental forces. The weight of his attention, in both *The Senses and the Intellect* and *The Emotions and the Will*, is all the other way, towards the analysis of very obviously sophist-icated forms of adult behaviour in an advanced industrial culture. Indeed, he was accused by some of neglecting comparative psychological data from less apparently sophisticated subjects, children, and 'primitive' races and cultures.[173] Against more traditional opponents, he denied holding automatist beliefs in the first edition of *The Senses and the Intellect* and repeated and expanded this through subsequent editions of his work. In 1855 he thought the purchase of reflex analysis on mature human behaviour to be 'comparatively (not entirely) insigni-ficant'.[174] He preferred to see humans as acting through complex emotional and intellectual sequences. Thus, in responses to art, for instance, an initial feeling of organic pleasure is only the beginning of conscious, more sophisticated, though no-less emotionally grounded, reactions.[175] In the third edition of 1868—when the debates about automatism were again becoming furious—he expanded this section to make a more prominent and careful denial.[176] In fact, Bain offers an interesting and original account of the higher faculties, which never loses sight of their origins in the lower forms of organic and mental action.

To begin with he attempts to redefine consciousness. He takes issue with the standard definition of the time, that consciousness is only to be distinguished from sleep, death, or other forms of insensibility. He lists twelve variants of this definition—such as responsiveness to pleasure and pain, the capacity for acts of attention, the ability to discriminate, and so on. However, says Bain, these are simply subsidiary restatements of the initial assumption in which consciousness is 'co-extensive with mental life', and it is this he wishes to challenge.[177] Consciousness should not be defined in such a way that it is restricted to inward-looking, passive contemplation. To confine it to introspection damages the scope

---

[173] e.g. by Spencer: 'Bain on The Emotions and the Will', in *Essays*, 252–3; also Ribot, *English Psychology*, 249.     [174] Bain, *The Senses and the Intellect*, 260.

[175] Ibid. 260.     [176] Bain, *The Senses and the Intellect*, 3rd edn., esp. 257.

[177] Bain, *The Emotions and the Will*, 605.

of mental science.[178] Instead, Bain divides the phenomena of consciousness into two: emotional and intellectual. Emotional consciousness comprises feelings, overt mental excitements, and the apparently neutral state (*vis-à-vis* pleasure or pain), which is nevertheless a state of nervous arousal whose most common form is an act of attention. Intellectual consciousness includes all the standard forms of the activity of intelligence (discrimination, perception, sensitivity, and so on). However, throughout, Bain insists that these two modes of consciousness in fact overlap: there is an intellectual component in feeling (for example, in acts of attention), and an emotional component in the activity of the intellect (in the reception of sense data, for instance). Even apparently very simple mental events are in fact very complex and bring 'into play those very functions of the intellect that make its development and its glory in its highest manifestations'.[179] Above all what distinguishes consciousness from not-consciousness is the registration of change and difference. It is this—the discrimination between active and passive, inside and outside, self and other, and so on—that enables the mind to build and develop. Consciousness is not merely a state of not-being-dead; it is a state of energetic activity. This new definition of consciousness as the perception of change was crucial to the development of mid-nineteenth-century psychology, as we shall see in the following chapters. It is at the core of the new scientific and realist epistemologies, and was, as Bain's supporters realized, an important advance, because it conceived of the mind as actively developing and growing.[180]

This *relational* view of consciousness (that feeling and thought, simple and complex, even conscious and unconscious contents—that is, those things that, through habit, have ceased to be conscious—are mixed inextricably together) is a cornerstone of the new psychology. It is, incidentally (but not accidentally), mirrored in the fictional procedure of George Eliot. Her novels—uniquely perhaps in the period—deploy such a striking range of intellectual reference and information alongside such a detailed and sensitive rendering of human emotional situations that the effect on the reader is to blur any conventional or casual assumptions about psychological categories he or she may entertain in relation to, for example, the distinction between intellect and emotion, or mind and body. Thus her account of Lydgate's scientific research in chapter 16 of *Middlemarch*, which conveys so well the pleasures of this activity, is rendered almost entirely through description, vocabulary, and imagery drawn from physical and emotional activities and states. Lydgate is 'enamoured' of 'arduous invention' (an emotional vocabulary to describe an intellectual venture):

---

[178] Bain, *The Emotions and the Will*, 609.     [179] Ibid. 631.
[180] John Stuart Mill, 'Bain's Psychology', 371–2; Davidson, 'Bain's Philosophy', 166.

As he threw down his book, stretched his legs towards the embers in the grate, and clasped his hands at the back of his head, in that agreeable after-glow of excitement when thought lapses from examination of a specific object into a suffusive sense of its connections with all the rest of our existence—seems, as it were, to throw itself on its back after vigorous swimming and float with the repose of unexhausted strength—Lydgate felt a triumph-ant delight in his studies, and something like pity for those less lucky men who were not in his profession.[181]

The mixture of emotion, thought, and physical (organic) feelings of pleasure is very striking here, and Lydgate and Bain once more recall each other.

Bain stressed the intertwining of thought and feeling, and is continuously keen to alert the reader to the *organic* basis of this. We have quoted him to this effect earlier, but it should be understood how persistently he makes the point, along-side the related one that complex intellectual achievements have their origins in simpler mental facts. So, the complex pleasures of expended effort—as here in the description of Lydgate's research, or in Bain's example of energetic thinking during vigorous walking (note the pairing of a physical and a mental activity) —mingle the pleasurable expenditure of energy with the exercise of abilities (motor or mental), and the cognitive development to be derived from *effort*, especially muscular effort. The organic factor underlies all this: 'Thus we derive another illustration of the accidental, temporary, and intermitted presence of the mental property, and the indispensable and perennial character of the corporeity in giving origin to moving power.'[182] It is 'organic energy' that is the 'general and fundamental fact', he says. Consciousness is just an adjunct of it, an 'occasional and accessory fact attached to it'.[183]

Bain, here, has not tried to develop a theory of the *unconscious*—save the account of what might be performed without attention through habit—and cannot, there-fore, be thought to be very much in the line that reaches towards the 'Freudian Revolution'. His ideas are not in this respect as far-reaching or daring as some contemporaries such as Carpenter (with his notion of unconscious cerebration), or Spencer (with his quasi-Lamarckian ideas about group—or race—memory), or Lewes (with his sophisticated sense of the 'stream of consciousness'). But Bain's examination of the question of consciousness does, in its theoretical trajectory, look towards this. Its best elements are concerned with a more complex exam-ination of the components of the higher faculties, and a consistent and coherent attempt to theorize them in significantly new relations between simple and complex, body and mind, and feeling and thought. It is here that Bain's main achievement lies, in developing a great advance through the characteristic dualisms that inhibited the development of nineteenth-century psychological theory. He

---

[181] Eliot, *Middlemarch*, 194.
[182] Bain, *The Emotions and the Will*, 479.     [183] Ibid. 475.

does not always develop these new relationships fully, nor specify (for example, physiologically) their modes of operation. But the effort is made to reconceptualize important psychological elements that connected directly with important areas of general public discussion and ideological argument. Of these none was more crucial than the theory of the will, because the will, in Victorian Britain, was perceived to be the cornerstone of the psychological architecture of so many different ideological buildings at once: the factory and counting house; the churches and other ethical centres; the schools, prisons, reformatories, poor houses, and wherever it was that learning flourished in mid-nineteenth-century Britain (not always the universities). In all these places—in the recommended regimes of moral behaviour and religious duty, in the formation of appropriate character, and in the destinies of individual economic advancement—the triumphant dominion of will power was held to be paramount. This chapter will therefore conclude discussion of Bain's psychology with a discussion of his theory of the will, thus again joining the psychological to the social context.

### BAIN'S THEORY OF THE WILL

As we have already seen, the will was central to Victorian notions of economic performance and success in the Smilesian ideologies of the self-made man and postponed gratification. It was important to religious experience, because of the stress placed on the effort to salvation through individual striving and worth, and because contemporary theological argument held that the will was an indication of the special distinction between man and brute. It was important in ethical argument, because it justified ethical prescriptions and rewards. It was important in ontological arguments, because it declared man to be more than the sum of his determining causes. It was important in epistemological arguments, because it was deeply connected with theories of belief. It was important in arguments over social policy and education for a variety of these reasons, and finally it was important in psychological argument, because psychology was at the junction of all these things, and because it appeared at the very top in most hierarchical taxonomies of the human faculties. If a new beginning could be made towards its explanation, then psychology could start to think itself on the road to an integrated scientific programme and a new way of conceiving of the human mind. How, then, did Alexander Bain theorize the human will?

In his *Autobiography* Bain records that the section on the will in *The Senses and the Intellect* gave him the most trouble. He had to draft and redraft, and still remained dissatisfied.[184] Nevertheless, Lewes, in his review in the *Leader* in 1855, recognized the importance of Bain's idea and urged him to expand it, which

---

[184] Bain, *Autobiography*, 234.

Bain did in *The Emotions and the Will*.[185] Lewes praised Bain for his analysis of the formation of the will from reflex action, as did Spencer.[186] Following the publication of *The Emotions and the Will* in 1859, Lewes commented that Bain had 'furnished more suggestive and instructive contributions than any psychologist we are acquainted with, to the difficult and still unresolved problems of the Will'.[187] His contribution was therefore distinctive for his fellow workers in the new psychology. A glimpse of the standard account of the role of the will— that against which Bain and Lewes were reacting—is given by J. A. Froude, friend and biographer of Carlyle, friend of Arnold, and strict churchman, in an essay on Spinoza in 1855. Spinoza, it is important to note, was regarded in the mid-1850s by Lewes (and others—George Eliot translated him) as inaugurating the 'First Crisis in Modern Philosophy', by shifting the burden of argument from ontological to psychological grounds.[188] He was, therefore, a crucial figure. Froude's article discusses the free-will ('necessitarian') question, and Spinoza is held, in effect, to argue against man's possession of free will. Froude concludes that, if Spinoza's argument about the will were to be accepted, then man will not be

what he has been hitherto supposed to be—an exception in the order of nature, with a power not differing in degree but differing in kind from those of other creatures. Moral life, like all life, is a mystery, and as to dissect the body will not reveal the secret of animation, so with the actions of the moral man. The spiritual life, which alone gives them meaning and being, glides away before the logical dissecting knife, and leaves it but a corpse to work with.[189]

This is a style of argument with which we are acquainted: rhetorically belittling (and again making ample use of the language of dissection), anti-rationalist, and arguing for the end of argument. Its substance, too, is familiar: there are categorical differences between man and the rest of nature, between humans and animals, and between the moral and spiritual life and the rest of existence. The will is the special arena of action for the first terms in all of these pairings.

---

[185] Lewes, 'Bain on The Senses and the Intellect', 772. Lewes felt that Bain did not persevere far enough with the 'organic' perspective. He repeated this criticism even after the publication of *The Emotions and the Will* four years later in 'Voluntary and Involuntary Actions', 304. These criticisms tell us something about the direction his own work was taking. He is impatient with Bain's mentalist (associationist) emphasis, despite his enthusiasm for his work as a whole. This was a view echoed by Spencer. It is noticeable that all three of Lewes's pieces on Bain written in the 1850s are markedly more enthusiastic about those aspects of his work that have a more prominent physiological perspective, though the call for expansion of the section on the will in 1855 must have been in part an attempt to publicize future work for Bain when sales were low. Lewes, who had known him for fifteen years, would have been well aware of his plans for a second volume.

[186] Spencer, 'Bain on The Emotions and the Will', in *Essays*, 244.

[187] Lewes, 'Voluntary and Involuntary Actions', 299.

[188] Lewes, *Biographical History of Philosophy*, 415–16.

[189] [J. A. Froude], 'Spinoza', *Westminster Review*, NS 8 (1855), 37.

This view was shared by James Martineau in his critique of Bain. Martineau believed that Bain's theory (that the will emerges from the organism and not the mind alone) is delusive, because it 'comes out of nothing' psychologically speaking. It is 'numb and foreign to us'. If Bain had placed the functions of the will 'within the limits of consciousness', then his problems over the higher functions would be over. Martineau denies that the muscle sense can play any part in the cognition of space and extension, because mere sensation cannot render an awareness of qualitative difference. Our perception of, say, length is an act of 'personal causation', and such cognitions are inseparable from the agencies of self and personal identity.[190] Bain's theories do 'nothing else than, in the very act of patronizing experience, destroy its fundamental postulates, and open the way to every idealistic dream'.[191] Bain, of course, would deny all the principles on which Froude and Martineau base their arguments, but his supporters realized the need to tackle the problem. J. S. Mill thought it necessary to place Bain's work in the context of 'the Free-Will controversy', and, argued that Bain, rather than adopting a Necessitarian position, 'adheres, in a unqualified manner, to the universality of Cause and Effect, or the uniformity of sequence in natural phenomena, to which he does not think the determinations of the will are in any manner an exception'. Mill and Bain both believe that 'the free-will question is emphatically one of law'.[192] Thus the bare bones of the controversy are laid out: is the will a function or a special faculty?

A more interesting, moderate defence of the religious conception of the will, and one that takes account of the 'uniformity of sequence in natural phenomena', was offered by the nonconformist J. D. Morrel in his composite review of psychology books in 1856. Morrel summarizes the state of play in psychological debate in the 1850s very lucidly. After the advance in knowledge of the nervous system, the reflex mechanism 'has begun to claim for itself the origination of many phenomena which were before attributed to the direct effort of the mind, or the will'. So, 'many actions are performed by us, and performed *consciously*, which are not in any way the result of purpose, forethought, desire, or adaptation, and which therefore cannot be cited as any illustrations [*sic*] of our voluntary activity'. Further, the 'physical economy of our being' operates 'independently of anything connected with our own personal will or intelligence'. It harmonizes 'a pre-arranged system of impulses' to perform certain functions, but the will can operate only through the nervous system. It has no extra-material being, and willed actions can even be unconscious, which establishes that the nervous

---

[190] [Martineau], 'Cerebral Psychology: Bain', 507–10.

[191] Ibid. 511. Martineau calls Bain's theory 'idealistic' because it relinquishes any outside authority for cognition: 'all externality disappears in the *Ego*' (p. 512). Martineau's argument is a travesty of the epistemology of the new psychology.

[192] John Stuart Mill, 'Bain's Psychology', 365–6.

system is 'really automatic'. There is a 'great automatic centre' (presumably located in the spinal column and lower brain), which is capable of executive action independent of consciously willed activity and which can respond to exogenous stimuli, as exemplified by hypnotic states.[193]

Morrel's interpretation of these findings is benign. The human organism, with its integrated functions and abilities, enacts the 'most beautiful and harmonious co-ordination' between thought, the organism, and 'the order of universal nature in the midst of which we are placed'. This harmony is reflected in 'a constant tendency throughout all being to advance from the more material form of existence to the more immaterial; from the more instinctive regions of intelligence to the more rational; from the passive to the active; from the dependent to the independent; from complete identification with nature to the higher life of a self-determining individual'.[194] Morrel sees that 'the regions of physical law and moral order' must remain adjacent. If they are forced apart, disaster threatens. The 'old watch-cries of *materialism* and *pantheism*' must be abandoned by traditionalists, and cooperation with science must be sought by religious minds seriously interested in defending their faith. It is *religion* that must adjust to a new scientific age.[195] This is an interesting mix of ideas. It is laudable in the sophistication of its information, and the independence of its outlook. It is also—from Bain's point of view—incoherent.

It is incoherent, because its conclusions do not follow from its premises. Morrel was critical of Bain's *The Senses and the Intellect*, because it failed to offer a significant 'generalization' of 'organic life'.[196] But Bain's theory did posit a relational model for the mind, and he does offer a graduated account of the ascension from the simple to the sophisticated in the formation of the adult consciousness. Both of these things are theoretically reconcilable with Morrel's teleologically smooth account of the mind's progress. But Bain also posits a *conflictual* model that is not so easily assimilated. Bain's underlying conception is that intelligence, will, and the other higher faculties are born from, and find their principle of growth and change in, turbulent difficulty. They grow by materially dialectical, and not by ideally teleological, activity. Bain is plain about this in his books, both in statement, and in rhetoric. He frequently uses images, metaphors, and illustrations drawn from combat and battle, the invasions of destroying Vandals, the training of violent animals, the struggles of the entrepreneur, or the deeds of the fanatic or Irish terrorist (his example is Daniel O'Connell). These things, and the underlying conception that provokes them, cannot be smoothed into generalization in the way Morrel would wish. Morrel argues that our faculties are organic in origin and process. But, by the time he has come to his conclusion,

---

[193] Morrel, 'Modern English Psychology', 351–6.
[194] Ibid. 356.   [195] Ibid. 358–9.   [196] Ibid. 359.

these things might as well never have been; for instead there is as agreeable a prospect as any crusty churchman would wish. From such a vantage point, science and religion could indeed gambol together freely.

Though a fierce opponent like James Martineau could hold that Bain's theory of the will was as mechanical and shrivelled as that of the classical Utilitarian theorists, in fact Bain took his distance from this position.[197] He attacked the notion that personality and human agency are only reward stimulated.[198] Instead, he offered an account of the origins and initial growth of the will that attempted to be wholly organic, spontaneous, and developmental. In *The Senses and the Intellect* he posits an innate *stimulus* to volitional action, but this is not an innate mental faculty in the Scottish manner. Rather, Bain finds his inspiration in the physiologist Müller, and it is a proposition about energy rather than entity.[199]

In *The Emotions and the Will* this idea is developed further. There it is argued that there is a spontaneous discharge of nervous energy (though Bain notes that, at present, it is impossible to specify the actual anatomical mechanism or physiological nature of this discharge). Gradually, through repetition and other factors (like environmental conditions), certain of these paths of discharge become facilitated and regularized, most particularly those related to certain organs or muscles. The will originates in the complex development of these neurological processes.[200] Bain relates this to a number of observable features in the normal human constitution and regular human behaviour. For example, one of the will's sources of origin lies in the action of the muscles, the 'organic condition' of which stimulates their exercise and the exploration of their powers.[201] (George Eliot touches on this in her account of Lydgate's research.) Bain finds a related instance in the growth of appetites, which he defines as 'a combination of instinct and education'—that is, renewed 'primitive cravings' demand regular satisfaction by action undertaken by the will.[202] Likewise, Bain notes the provocation of a restraining will by counterproductive displays of emotion.[203] And so on: the will is built up from complex sequences of such half-organic, half-mental developments.

The will is not, therefore, born fully formed. Nor does it exist in that way even in maturity. The rules that govern its development are derived from associationist thought, and the prime mechanism that governs their operation is the pleasure/pain matrix. It is thus that feeling and action become linked: 'The power of cohesion or association operates to join together the two facts thus brought into accidental embrace, and after a time, the pain can stimulate the precise action,

---

[197] [Martineau], 'Cerebral Psychology: Bain', 507.
[198] Bain, *The Senses and the Intellect*, 80.        [199] Ibid. 257, 289.
[200] Bain, *The Emotions and the Will*, 331–3. For the latter point, see also p. 348.
[201] Bain, *The Senses and the Intellect*, 83 ff.        [202] Ibid. 249–50.
[203] Bain, *The Emotions and the Will*, 34.

without any spontaneous coincidence of the two.'[204] The linking-together, by originally accidental association, of feeling and necessary action drives forward the development of a willing power to encourage or prevent certain events. Pleasure/pain is paramount: 'Without some antecedent of pleasurable, or painful feeling, primary or derivative, the will cannot be stimulated. Throughout all the disguises that wrap up what we call motives, something or other of these two grand conditions can be detected.'[205] Though other auxiliary forces will come into play at a later date, such as imitation of approved or desired behaviours from the outside world, these acquired abilities only encourage the development of a psychological force already in place and that has already been developed directly from the conditions of the organic system.[206]

Bain is very clear that the whole process is conflictual and difficult. There is nothing either inevitable or teleological in it: 'The first steps in our volitional education are a jumble of spluttering, stumbling, and all but despairing hope-lessness. Instead of a clear and distinct curriculum, we have to wait upon accidents, and improve them when they come.'[207] The will, in a striking phrase, is 'a machinery of detail' in a process that emphasizes development, change, and growth.[208] That the growth is opportunistic, even random, is its essence. It is dialectical and evolutionary—allowing for all of that word's mid-Victorian weight —and not inevitably progressive. Bain was conscious of the consequences of this. In an essay from 1871 on 'Darwinism and Religion', written as a contribution to the heated discussion of Darwin's *Descent of Man*, Bain argues for a conciliat-ory position between science and religion. In the end, evolutionary theory

neither shuts out God, degrades our conscience, checks our belief in the power of com-munion with the Divine mind as far as our faculties will permit, nor diminishes our hope of immortality, may we not then even while allowing the theory as probable, give rein to glorious conceptions and inspirations which flash upon us in happy moments of thought, and feel that all things are possible to us—that we have a never-ending future, and a hope of drawing nearer and nearer to the Almighty Being from whom we derive all and hope for all.[209]

Given the vehemence of his own anti-religious convictions, this is a very elastic usage of 'our', but we can see what Bain is up to at a fraught moment. He is willing to trade off public professions of orthodoxy against a potentially very damaging charge, public opinion being what it was. It may be thought that he makes compromises with conscience in doing so, but actually the weight of his attention and commitments in the essay as a whole are all towards the evolu-tionary side, and his argument asserts a basis for morality in an evolutionary

[204] Ibid. 343.    [205] Ibid. 394.    [206] Ibid. 381.
[207] Ibid. 343.    [208] Ibid. 381.
[209] A. B[ain], 'Darwinism and Religion', *Macmillan's Magazine*, 24 (1871), 51.

age unmuddled by ideological distractions. Our descent may be from sources, and by a mechanism (natural selection), insulting to species pride, but the miracle is we have our reason and intellect, and our will, and our morals, still. Nothing need change, and morality, he implies, need only become more human and secular: 'Thus the good of the community becomes at last the end and aim of our moral nature.'[210] This is the end and aim of Bain's psychological work and his theory of the will also.

Bain was a man reacting to close historical events and tendencies, as we all are. His conception of the will is not immune from some of the prevailing beliefs, which may interestingly reflect his own social origins and his difficult—though successful—career as an academic. After all, Bain thought of himself as a Utilit-arian in ethical theory, though on the 'soft' side. The shape, details, and effects of his theory of the will do powerfully challenge traditional and accepted ideas, but the metaphors he chooses to illustrate its action are interesting. They are predominantly concerned with endurance, career advancement, and accountancy. Sometimes, indeed, the psychological economy sounds like the running of a bank, or the general circulation of money, as in this discussion of mental concentra-tion: 'The fixing of a single feature has by diffusion a tendency to fix all the rest, and although these effects imply a certain draft upon the central brain, they are less costly than rapid alternations from one attitude to another.'[211] There are several descriptions of the circulation of energy in the economy of the will in similar terms.[212] Related to this are the quasi-Smilesian images of success offered in both books, like the making of fortunes, or the gaining of knowledge and learning when one's social background is unpromising for such achievement.[213] The latter, at least, has a clear personal application.

Both *The Senses and the Intellect* and *The Emotions and the Will* have plenti-ful quantities of advice for their readers of a moral or 'self-help' kind, and it is useful to remember that Bain was also, like many of his period, a writer of books and essays to help the tyro intellectual or student, or the 'coming' and ambi-tious young man. The account referred to above, for instance, which sets out the psychological economy of attaining success—resolution, fortitude, prudence, endurance, and so on—is of a piece with the *Practical Essays* of 1884.[214] So, 'Intemperance, indolence, prodigality, neglect of opportunities, giving offence to those that would assist us, and all sorts or reckless behaviour, are sins against

---

[210] A. B[ain], 'Darwinism and Religion', *Macmillan's Magazine*, 24 (1871), 51.

[211] Bain, *The Emotions and the Will*, 193–4.

[212] For example: 'The expenditure of power in the case has to be entered in the column of the accounts which is headed "Will"' (ibid. 415 n.) or the comparison of pleasure and pain to credit and debt (ibid. 441).    [213] Ibid. 489–90.

[214] Alexander Bain, *Practical Essays* (London, 1884). For example, compare the essay on 'The Art of Study', which deals with methods of self-education, with the example of autodidacticism from *The Emotions and the Will*. *On the Study of Character* sometimes strikes this note too.

prudence'. As failures of the will, they are examples of 'moral weakness'.[215] The too close identification of morality with the exercise of the will is a problem in the argument here. At points like this it seems that the will is being stiffly offered almost, indeed, as an end in itself.

As ever, though, Bain pictures the acquisition of 'The Moral Habits' as a struggle. They are here pictured as embattled:

It is necessary, above all things, in such a situation, if possible never to lose a battle. Every gain on the wrong side undoes the effect of several conquests on the right. It is therefore an essential precaution so to regulate the two opposing powers, that the one may have an uninterrupted success, until repetition has fortified it to such a degree as to cope with the opposition under any circumstances. This is the theoretically best career of moral progress, not often realized in practice.[216]

In its picture of the 'still small voice of daily duty' in combat with 'fleshly indulgences', this sounds like 'Victorian' moralizing at its most dour.[217] But it is also a voice that is sometimes not very far away in some of George Eliot's writing. Like her, Bain was a person of the time.

As a 'soft' Utilitarian, Bain held some attitudes to human feeling and desire that, in the 1850s, were sharply attacked by intellectuals and writers such as Ruskin, Carlyle, and Dickens (principally, of course, in *Hard Times*), and some features of Bain's psychology are open to the same kinds of objections as the ideas of Mr Gradgrind. For instance, he has an alarmingly shrivelled sense of human desire. Bain characterizes desire as an 'irritating, uneasy, distracted state, fretting the temper, and unfitting the mind for operations demanding a cool and concentrated attention'. It is an entirely negative state of mind, a mere wanting of something that is probably not worth the having, a 'peculiar mode of pain'.[218] The will can restrain desire, however, and, though this produces a new pain, when that ceases pleasure is the result: a net gain in the psychological accounts, which encourages the regulation of desire for industrious pursuits.[219] 'Too rampant appetites' and 'too roving desires' should be discouraged by the formation of new regulatory 'associating links'.[220] One enjoys thinking what William Blake or D. H. Lawrence (to name two writers from a similar social background to Bain's) would make of this.[221]

---

[215] Bain, *The Emotions and the Will*, 523–4.      [216] Ibid. 500–1.      [217] Ibid. 503.

[218] Ibid. 481.      [219] Ibid. 481–2.      [220] Ibid. 486–7 n., 492.

[221] In fact, in his 'Study of Thomas Hardy' (1914–15), Lawrence attacks the 'utterly bloodless', desexualized line of thought 'in the great scientists or thinkers of the last generation, even Darwin and Spencer and Huxley' (*Study of Thomas Hardy and Other Essays*, ed. Bruce Steele (Cambridge, 1985), 98). It is nevertheless interesting to find Herbert Marcuse, who shared Lawrence's view, using intact the conceptual vocabulary deployed by Bain and his contemporaries 100 years earlier. Marcuse protests against 'the perpetual internal conquest of the "lower" faculties of the individual: his sensuous and appetitive faculties' (*Eros and Civilization: A Philosophical Inquiry into Freud* (1955; London, 1969), 96).

Bain's psychology is an innovative, impressive development of the association psychology towards a more complex and sophisticated theorization of the psychological system in relation to the physiological functioning of the organism. As we have said, he looks both forward (to the new biological and evolutionary perspectives in psychology) and backward (to the methods and traditions of psychology within philosophy). He continued to defend the validity of these older methods to the last, and by the end of his long career had begun to sound distinctly old-fashioned in method. In a piece for *Mind* in 1893 he assesses the state of the field, and one cannot help feeling that it is written as he faces the redundancy of his own methods and approaches as the bifocal elements in psychology's constitution begin violently to pull apart at the end of the century towards explicit Idealism in philosophy, and laboratory Experimentalism in psychology proper. Bain's essay concerns 'The Respective Spheres and Mutual Helps of Introspection and Psycho-Physical Experiment in Psychology', and he defends introspection as the 'alpha and omega of psychological inquiry; it is alone supreme, everything else subsidiary'.[222] 'Psycho-physics' has no purchase on 'grand Metaphysical issue [*sic*]—Thought and Reality, Knowing and Being'.[223] Introspection is needed for the analysis of the higher faculties 'almost exclusively'. Though he says that experiments have purchase on the analysis of sense and instinct, he does not consider experimental work able to correlate physiological findings with mental phenomena. What is odd about Bain's last arguments is the contradiction between them and some of those of the earlier work. He insists on the need to reconstruct the origins and development of individuals. (It is perhaps not idle to recall he was writing his autobiography at the time.) In this process the accounts of memory and the findings of introspection are crucial, yet in the earlier work he had been more cautious about such criteria.

'Respective Spheres and Mutual Helps' is indeed the work of a man who is being bypassed by the development of psychological work. But this moment in the 1890s has its own context too, and there is a more positive way of putting things. As work in scientific psychology went on, the response, for very complex reasons, of Idealist philosophy was very strong. This line of thought took issue with the philosophic grounds of the psychology of writers such as Spencer and Lewes. Bain's essay, therefore, can be understood as an assertion of the realist premises of the 'new' (now old) psychology. To the end he remained combatively committed to the ideas of the school he so profoundly helped develop. It is now time to consider the other facet of this school—the evolutionary psychology developed by Spencer and Lewes from the premises of general biology.

---

[222] Bain, 'Respective Spheres and Mutual Helps', 42.     [223] Ibid. 43.

CHAPTER 6

# Herbert Spencer and the Beginnings of Evolutionary Psychology

CHANGES IN MODELS OF THE MIND IN THE SECOND
HALF OF THE NINETEENTH CENTURY

Of all the shifts in psychological opinion in the period covered by this book, probably the most far-reaching was the remodelling of it in the light of evolutionary (or 'developmental') theories. The reasons for this are not difficult to grasp. The evolutionary paradigm placed the mind in the general analysis of nature and the biological functions. The increasingly sound findings, perceived relevance, and intellectual prestige of physiology secured a hearing for views that only twenty years earlier would have seemed violently offensive. Meanwhile, a general loss of conviction in many opposing arguments partly resulted from, and partly encouraged, this process. Traditional religious or metaphysical arguments began to seem a little tired in a rapidly changing intellectual culture. Evolution changed not just the nature of psychological argument; it changed the culture in which it occurred.

Thus, for many leading writers psychology became a discipline that was biological (rather than 'mentalist' or 'intellectualist') in orientation, and 'scientific' (rather than 'philosophical') in method, notwithstanding the continuing debate over this issue in *Mind* and elsewhere. It should, however, be understood that 'scientific' here does not mean that the leading psychologists of the day were experimentalists. Only Lewes and Huxley conducted any laboratory research among the writers considered here, and the paradigm shift that moved psychology into the laboratory was yet some decades away. 'Scientific', therefore, means only that the dominant mode of explanation and analysis was conducted with reference to the principal general theories of scientific explanation of the period. Of these, evolutionary theory emerged as the most important, but it was by no means the only one. As we have seen, general physical theories concerning energy ('Force'), for instance, were also immediately relevant and there was a continuing substratum of psychological literature in the medical community.

However, despite these advances, the new psychology had as yet neither secure intellectual nor institutional standing in the culture at large, and continued to be opposed by many intellectuals in the traditional institutions and with more

traditional outlooks. This opposition, however, should not immediately be identified with a reactionary conservatism, even if criticism of this kind persisted.
The new psychology was bitterly challenged by James Martineau and T. H. Green,
but neither could be described as hailing from the conservative orthodoxy.
Martineau we have already discussed in the previous chapter, and will do so again
in this; while Green had a major impact on the reform of Oxford philosophy,
and on the ideological outlook and public policy of the Liberal Party in one of
its reforming hey-days between 1880 and 1914.[1] Once again, we are largely dealing
with arguments *within* liberal intellectual culture, and not arguments between
it and some reactionary and ill-informed traditionalism. The fact that some of
these liberal opponents *sound* to modern ears like reactionary and ill-informed
traditionalists is a difficulty for our retrospective cultural taxonomies.

This chapter and the next will examine the development of 'materialist', evolutionary psychological theory in the work of two of its leading writers, Herbert
Spencer and George Lewes, in detail and in context. Attention will be given to
the rearmed 'Idealist' reaction to it in the later part of the century, principally
in the work of its most successful thinker, T. H. Green, whose epistemologically based critiques of both Spencer and Lewes were the most formidable either
received. The critiques of Green and his allies brought into focus several major
areas for debate that provide continuity with earlier responses: the conditions
for human knowledge and the sufficiency of 'scientific' explanations of the 'higher'
faculties, the status and definition of the self and consciousness, especially in
relation to the determinations of history, society, and biology, and, finally, the
question of the cultural role of these new fields of enquiry. In 1870, when the
development of a properly 'scientific' method for psychology seemed assured,
Lewes looked, in a review in the first number of *Nature* (itself a new attempt
to bring science closer to the 'intelligent public'), not just to the success of the
discipline, but to a general alteration in cultural outlook:

The daily increasing recognition of the importance of Physiology as an element of liberal culture, no less than as a distinct branch of science, may be said to be intimately
connected with the gradual displacement of the old vitalistic conception. The old conception of Life as something essentially mysterious and removed from out [*sic*] the circle
of natural causes, has been set aside in favour of the conception of Life as something
more complex, indeed, but not otherwise more mysterious than other natural phenomena,
and dependent upon the physical and chemical agencies recognized in operation in other
provinces of research. The consequence of this changed view has been to disclose the
need of an incessant application to Physiology of those instruments and methods which
have enlarged and given precision to our views of Nature; and a further consequence
has been that the problems are found to be capable of popular exposition, that is to say,

---

[1] Richter, *The Politics of Conscience*; I. M. Greengarten, *T. H. Green and the Development of
Liberal Democratic Thought* (London, 1981).

the great results of research can now be shown to an intelligent public, and thus made to form an element in general culture.[2]

This comprehensive cultural project formed a leading feature of much of this work. It is to be found in Spencer's massive 'synthetic philosophy', George Eliot's fiction, and Lewes's and Bain's career-long efforts to see literature and philosophy, science and politics, original work and popular exposition, as complementary and not contradictory intellectual practices. The fact that this was articulated at just the same moment as rival visions of the totality of the national culture, such as Matthew Arnold's in *Culture and Anarchy* (1869), is significant. It seems to have been a moment when British intellectual and cultural life struggled self-consciously with its own image and direction, partly because it became freshly aware, in different ways, of the significant cultural presence of a new, general readership.

This book examines not just the theoretical cogency of individual arguments, but the cultural opportunities and difficulties that shaped them. The immediate audience of any writing exerts pressures on meaning (including questions about logical efficacy) in any period. What appeared coherent to, say, a theologically inclined thinker in 1850, appeared gratuitous and incoherent to an agnostic or 'practical atheist' in 1875, because the central term holding together the description of the operations of the physical world—that is, God Himself—was no longer taken for granted by the latter. Modes of argument (to follow one of the insights of post-structuralist thinkers) were reconfigured around new patterns of presence and absence, and the chains of sometimes unspoken emphasis and assumption that linked them. The existence, or not, of God is the most spectacular example, but others proliferate. For instance, the work of the new psychologists illustrates an intellectual shift from static, entity-based accounts of the mind (the mental faculties, the phrenological brain), to dynamic, process-based conceptions embracing the entire neurological system and the link between organism and environment. The negotiation from the one position to the other was continuous, and involved both massive shifts and piecemeal adjustments in accepted criteria of logicality, relevance, and accuracy in a battle that was also controlled in the wider domain by what was considered either scandalous or 'mentionable'. The analysis of shifts in opinion on this scale and of this complexity, when standards of 'truth' and validity were so volatile, needs therefore to include an account of tone, language (including organizing metaphors and rhetorical structures), manner of address, and perceptions of a likely audience. Is this a popular or specialist work? In what kind of edition or periodical did it appear? Was its mode of publication by subscription, appeal to the general market, or through the backing or subsidy of other—usually religious—bodies?

---

[2] George Henry Lewes, 'Popular Lectures on Physiology', *Nature*, 1 (1870), 353.

What this new intellectual world of the last third of the nineteenth century looked like for those interested in psychological theory (though not particularly involved with its creation) I will illustrate by two examples. The first is an article on 'The New Psychology' from the *Fortnightly Review* in 1879 by William Courtney. The second, once again, concerns George Eliot's *Middlemarch*. I will begin with Courtney's review.

William Leonard Courtney (1850–1928) was, like Bain, Spencer, Lewes, and Eliot, a man of diverse interests. He wrote on politics and literature (especially drama), as well as having a professional interest in philosophy. Formerly a fellow and tutor in philosophy at Oxford, he became a staffer on the *Daily Telegraph*, was editor of the *Fortnightly Review* between 1894 and 1924, and a contributing editor of the *Dictionary of National Biography*. He was thus on the liberal wing of intellectual opinion (the *Telegraph* was not then a Tory newspaper). He was not, though, an activist or ideologue in the same way that Spencer, James Martineau, or Green, for example, were perceived to be by many. He was known as a safe, compromise choice as editor of the *Fortnightly* in the political battles between liberals and conservatives over its editorship in the 1890s.[3] As a philosopher, he favoured the empirical tradition best represented by John Stuart Mill. He was sympathetic towards evolutionary psychology, but was not a partisan. His article is a kind of obituary tribute to Lewes, who had died the previous year, and whose two posthumous volumes of *Problems of Life and Mind* were published in 1879. (It is probable, given the range of arguments to which he refers, that Courtney has only the fourth, and less specialist volume, *The Study of Psychology*, in mind.) It should be said that Courtney's essay is neither particularly distinguished nor original. But its moderation of tone and argument, as well as its careful identification of leading issues, makes it usefully representative in an area so governed by polemic, assertion, and rebuke.

Courtney begins by identifying a 'new order' in psychological theory, and characterizes this as the difference between Lewes's newly published volume and the sixth book of John Stuart Mill's *Logic* ('On the Logic of the Moral Sciences' —a moderately libertarian adaptation of Utilitarian associationism tuned to Mill's interest in 'Ethology', the study of the social and cultural construction of character). The difference between Mill and Lewes, says Courtney, is as great as that between Hume and Kant—that is, the former stimulates the eventually very different thought of the latter. The difference between Lewes's intellectual generation (which includes Bain and Spencer also) and that of Mill 'can be summed up in one word—the study of biology'. Lewes is 'much more the disciple of Fechner, Lotze and Wundt, than he is of John Stuart Mill'.[4] The lack of biology

---

[3] *Wellesley Index*, ii. 181–2.
[4] William L. Courtney, 'The New Psychology', *Fortnightly Review*, NS 26 (1879), 318–19.

in Mill's work means not just an absence of important findings and conceptions, but a reduced sense of the relevant philosophical theories also. Courtney argues—like Everett Mendelsohn much more recently[5]—that the critiques of naturalistic explanation offered by the German Idealist tradition provided a powerful stimulus for biologists and psycho-physiologists in Germany. By contrast, Kant was 'a closed book' to Mill and he was thus unable to think through the deficiencies in classical sensationalist associationism. (In fact, Mill had realized these problems quite early—in the essay on Coleridge, for instance—but was unable to carry the point much further than an opposition of Coleridge to Bentham.) For Courtney, just as Kant could provide a way of thinking beyond passive, exclusively experience-based associationism, so biological thinking could significantly address a related problem in the older theory, which had neglected questions of heredity and the 'organic antecedents' that determine an individual's lot. Courtney speculated that a joining of theories of hereditary transmission with Kantian ideas of 'forms of thought' would be the way forward. Cannot 'forms of thought' (basic perceptions of time, space, and so on) be transmitted, just as 'his inherited aptitudes, his temper, and his moral disposition' can be passed from father to son? How otherwise can one explain the differences between Goethe and 'a Carib'? In this way Idealist philosophy can join with biology to destroy crude sensationalist psychology and refurbish the claims of faculty psychology for a new generation.[6]

Several features of Courtney's account are significant. First, there is an emphatic interest in biological theories of inheritance and transmission based on the Lamarckian model. These were probably derived from Spencer, who made these notions his own. Secondly, there is increasing interest in race and racial categories as a way of biologizing social and historical differences, as here in the loose example of the difference between Goethe and 'a Carib'. This implies that racial origin can be a disqualification from literate cultural achievement.[7] Thirdly, there is an increasingly lively recognition of the limitations of the associationist model for psychology and a renewed interest in Kantian and neo-Kantian philosophy. Courtney correctly identified the 'forms-of-thought' issue as central to these arguments and saw clearly that 'the battle of the psychologies rages fiercest round the so-called Forms of Mind'.[8] We shall follow this in detail in the objections made by Idealists to the work of Spencer and Lewes.

---

[5] Mendelsohn, 'Physical Models and Physiological Concepts', 201–19.

[6] Courtney, 'The New Psychology', 320.

[7] Courtney's reductive argument is easily embarrassed: if race, or hereditary transmission generally, is so important, then why were Goethe's father, son, or neighbour not also great writers? (We might also wonder what happens to mothers and daughters.)

[8] Courtney, 'The New Psychology', 325.

These themes were repeated through much of the psychological literature of the 1870s and 1880s. Courtney recognized the innovative efforts of the new psychology, and acknowledged that the ground rules of psychological argument had changed. But the essay is also marked by a note of regret, and a wish to recuperate psychological argument for a more traditional form of philosophical enquiry. He notes the damaging absence of biology in Mill's psychology, but his own essay pays only lip service to the science, and the bulk of the argument is directed towards the integration of German Idealist philosophy into the mainstream of psychology. He pictures Lewes reading carefully in Kant and trying to steer a course between reductive materialism and 'vague nebulous spiritualism'.[9] But this already places the argument on *philosophical* rather than scientific ground, and Spencer and Lewes had rather different ways of conceiving of these problems. Courtney saluted the 'new order' in psychology, but his essay ends wistfully. Lewes has set the agenda for 'the future speculation of English Psychology', and 'Science and Experience' will prevail over the religious arguments that once dominated debate. However, asks Courtney, striking an early note of modernist anxiety, does this mean that truth can be understood only as culture, ethics only as psychology?[10] His widely shared apprehension that certainties were vanishing lubricates the return of philosophical Idealism to British psychological theory.

But elsewhere the significant change was from static, faculty oriented conceptions of the mind to ones oriented towards process. The decisive step was the effective abandonment of associationist theory in its 'pure', mentalist form. In its place was substituted a range of new emphases. First, theoretical models were oriented towards enlarged time scales and an increased perception of the relevance of organic processes within an evolutionary framework; secondly, individual psychology was seen as part of 'group' (or sometimes racial) psychology; and, thirdly, an effort was made to account for man's *active* powers and potential, and not merely the constitutive processes that left him passively formed in experience. (This last, of course, had been a persistent difficulty for associationism.) Though associationist theory remained alive, and in many ways strong, in the work of Bain, and in the vocabulary and sometimes technical analyses used by Spencer, Lewes, and others to describe the mind's contents, none the less it lost its place alongside the faculty psychology as the dominant model for understanding the formation of the mind. New questions were asked instead. With what does the individual organism begin as a result of the biological history of its species? What power does it have to change or effect its inheritance? Is the means of transmission of this inheritance organic or cultural? To what extent is the mind only a phenomenon of consciousness and habit? What relative weight is to be

[9] Courtney, 'The New Psychology', 324.    [10] Ibid. 327–8.

given to the various descriptive languages and conceptual frameworks available to the informed psycho-physiologist? Is he to write in the registers of science or philosophy, of specialization, or of the wider culture? All of these problems mark the texts examined in this book, but they also enable their uniquely rich intellectual possibility.

To turn now to the second example, there is a well-known passage in chapter 11 of George Eliot's *Middlemarch* (1871–2) that illustrates neatly the changes in theoretical outlook I am describing:

Old provincial society had its share of this subtle movement: had not only its striking downfalls, its brilliant young professional dandies who ended by living up an entry with a drab and six children for their establishment, but also those less marked vicissitudes which are constantly shifting the boundaries of social intercourse, and begetting new consciousness of interdependence. Some slipped a little downward, some got higher footing: people denied aspirates, gained wealth, and fastidious gentleman stood for boroughs; some were caught in political currents, some in ecclesiastical, and perhaps found themselves surprisingly grouped in consequence; while a few personages of families that stood with rock firmness amid all this fluctuation, were slowly presenting new aspects in spite of solidity, and altering with double change of self and beholder. Municipal town and rural parish gradually made fresh threads of connection—gradually, as the old stocking gave way to the savings bank, and the worship of the solar guinea became extinct, while squires and baronets, and even lords who had once lived blamelessly afar from the civic mind, gathered the faultiness of closer acquaintanceship. Settlers, too, came from distant countries, some with an alarming novelty of skill, others with an offensive advantage in cunning. In fact, much the same sort of movement and mixture went on in old England as we find in older Herodotus, who also, in telling what had been, thought it well to take a woman's lot for his starting point; though Io, as a maiden apparently beguiled by attractive merchandise, was the reverse of Miss Brooke, and in this respect perhaps bore more resemblance to Rosamond Vincy . . .[11]

The language of this passage registers a world in process and motion. The syntax extends sentences to encompass the processes of decades, and the metaphors express a bewildering array of turbulent motion and different media. People slip and climb and topple down, get caught by currents of water and culture, gather and mix together, trek from afar; connections are made and broken. Lives, personalities, careers, and viewpoints throng the passage, and there is a radical, and deliberate, instability of focus, as various narratives, perspectives, glimpses of histories, stories, and ranges of reference briefly surface. The sense of the pace of life and action alters from abrupt downfalls to the patient weaving of threads. Above all, the time scales are shifted as the narrative stresses the need for a nimble historical understanding; perspectives are mobile, and engage the limits of the

[11] Eliot, *Middlemarch*, 122–3.

reader's comprehension. All this information is piled up, but, with a deceiving irony, its apprehension seems light and easy. 'Old' England is wryly made to seem so much further away than the 'real' forty years between 1871, the year of its writing, and 1831, the year in which it is set. This history seems a finished thing, as distant from our modernity as the provinces from our sophistication. It is somewhere else, just like the vanished worlds of Herodotus, whose myths are, in another twist, somehow relevant to the Misses Brooke and Vincy. The reader is pushed towards a comfortable, but misleading, certainty, so that what is at stake is the reader's cognitive activity in trying to comprehend the different and remote. This is a common practice in *Middlemarch*, which frequently dramatizes the reader's too ready and confident (mis)understanding. It is the kind of failure of comprehension that, for instance, might turn a struggling tenant farm into picturesque landscape, or might motivate the self-flattering, semi-feudal fantasy of the landlord Mr Brooke on his visit to Dagley's farm at Freeman's End in search of votes.

This episode, from chapter 39, has been interpreted as an unselfconscious, naïvely realist endorsement of the way things are.[12] But, in fact, it is full of caution about the way we understand the different, and interpret it as the familiar, particularly the artistically familiar: 'It is true that an observer, under that softening influence of the fine arts which makes other people's hardships picturesque, might have been delighted with this homestead called Freeman's End . . .'.[13] This is how the episode is introduced, and as it continues it is worked through in the same searching, critical way, highlighting the epistemological (and moral) problems involved in trying to understand and represent, as a glance down the opening paragraph clearly reveals. The cognitive action of *Middlemarch*, that is to say, is not so naïve, nor is the epistemology of Eliot's realism.

The passage describing Middlemarch's 'old provincial society' sets out the epistemological organization of the novel. It is caught in a drama of understanding that emphasizes change, difference, and process: 'the double change of self and beholder' that stems from historical processes forever moving the field of vision. Both subject and object are in relative motion, and the novel seeks to understand the extent to which we can comprehend the world so conceived. It is a world that can look now like a comforting home, now like an alien and threatening trap, like the web that is home to the spider, but death to the fly. This epistemological problem is exactly that described and understood by the new psychologists who were writing as contemporaries. For these writers the world, and man's place in it, looked (in any ultimate sense) purposeless but lawful, contingent but meaningful. It seemed to be now full of the riches of human

---

[12] e.g. by Colin MacCabe, *James Joyce and the Revolution of the Word* (London, 1978), ch. 2.
[13] Eliot, *Middlemarch*, 429.

achievement and potential, now as empty as dust and atoms, now explicable as acts of human agency and will, now only the result of the volitionless processes of evolutionary biology. *What* you understood depended on *where* you stood. But this perspectivism did not disqualify knowledge, or throw the sciences of man into relativism and scepticism, or indeed a generalizing ignorance of, as Eliot has it, 'this particular lot'. The description of this world—which seeks to integrate the near and far, the particular and the general—and the justification for thinking about it in these ways, is one more of the tasks confronting psychologists in the mid-to-late nineteenth century. *Middlemarch* is, profoundly, a novel written from the new evolutionary conception of the world, and this aspect of the novel has been seminally discussed by Gillian Beer. She describes a mode of representation that foregrounds sequences of connectives at a verbal level, and multiplies analogies at the level of plot: in short, it is a Darwinian narrative.[14] Beer's account of *Middlemarch* emphasizes the diversity of the stories these new perceptions made available, and how this created a way of seeing the world that stresses the necessary multiplicity of narrative action. The Darwinian world contains the need for both change and persistence, mutability and continuity, fecundity and extinction, conformity and variety, all of which are registered in action, theme, character, and language.

Similarly, Sally Shuttleworth has pointed out that the conception and organization of *Middlemarch* is very different from Eliot's earlier work. There she had written with the model of the natural historian in mind. In *Middlemarch*, 'the role of natural historian, passively transcribing a given order, will no longer suffice. George Eliot turns instead to the more dynamic methodology of experimental biology, a stance which receives paradigmatic expression in the novel in the research of Lydgate.'[15] Shuttleworth draws out the ways in which the novel is structured as a series of interlocking portraits of 'conditions' and results, rather as a scientist of the day would construct hypotheses. These various ways of seeing the world's change and development are not, though, self-cancelling. They are mutually enabling and ramifying portraits of different aspects of the same phenomena, exactly in the way that the various features in the life of an organism might be described in biology—or indeed other phenomena that intellectuals in her circle considered analogous, like society itself, or the human mind.

Shuttleworth's description of the transition in Eliot's work from natural historian to evolutionary biologist mirrors the shift I have been seeking to identify in psychological theory. It is, as it were, the shift from the work of Alexander Bain, associationist natural historian of the feelings, to Herbert Spencer, evolutionary psychologist. However, in making such demarcations in

[14] Beer, *Darwin's Plots*, 165. For further comment, see George Levine, *The Realistic Imagination: English Fiction from Frankenstein to Lady Chatterley* (London, 1981).
[15] Shuttleworth, *George Eliot and Nineteenth-Century Science*, 143.

the history of a discourse, one should not lose sight of the complexities of that history on the ground. Eliot's shift in analytical model from, say, *Adam Bede* to *Middlemarch* does not crudely mirror an advance in theory from Bain to Spencer. Bain's and Spencer's psychological work was exactly contemporary; both were available to Eliot in the 1850s and 1860s, and the influence of both is visible in *Scenes of Clerical Life* (1858) and *Adam Bede* (1859).[16] To describe *Middlemarch* as 'Spencerian', then, can be misleading, if that implies that the novel is written under the influence of Spencer's theories. The real situation is more complicated and interesting. Eliot, Spencer, Bain, and Lewes all participated in an intellectual culture that produced diverse, but overlapping work. Each had different emphases and aims, and drew upon different sources. Putting things in this way reduces the risk of working only with 'text' and (relatively distant) 'background'. It should also reduce the possibility of seeing one of this heterogeneous group as 'greater', or more 'correct', than the others. All shared a common intellectual heritage, all developed common methods and theories, all relished detail and sought the exhaustive anatomy of human consciousness. In considering the intellectual culture of psychological theory in the mid-nineteenth century we are dealing with a network, and not a hierarchy, just as the psychologists themselves were seeking to understand the mind as 'threads of connection', and not as the exercise of selective, presiding faculties.

### SPENCER'S PSYCHOLOGY: FROM ASSOCIATIONISM TO EVOLUTIONARY THEORY

The careers of Spencer and Bain developed at much the same pace. Yet their peers, and more recent commentators, note that they belong to different intellectual generations. Spencer's new psychology, launched in 1855, was portrayed by both radicals (such as Lewes or the secularist George Jacob Holyoake) and conservatives as marking a fresh and strikingly original turn in the development of psychological theory. Lewes, described by George Eliot in 1855 as 'nailed to the book',[17] hailed its appearance in a three-part review in the *Leader*. It marked a new era in psychological thought, it struck a decisive blow against the faculty psychology, and, with Bain's *The Senses and the Intellect*, it staked out the ground for future investigation into the intersection between physiological and psychological studies.[18] Eliot herself also praised the book as forming a new epoch in psychological thought. A year before publication, she imagined a 'Biographical

---

[16] Shuttleworth, *George Eliot and Nineteenth-Century Science*, ch. 2, and Myers, *The Teaching of George Eliot*, esp. ch. 2.

[17] George Eliot to Sara Hennell, 24 Aug. 1855, *Letters*, ii. 213.

[18] [G. H. Lewes], 'Herbert Spencer's Psychology', *Leader*, 6 (1855), 1012–13; 'History of Psychological Method', *Leader*, 6 (1855), 1036–7; 'Life and Mind', *Leader*, 6 (1855), 1062–3.

Dictionary for 1954' in which twentieth-century psychologists looked back to Spencer with gratitude for his 'great work *XXX* which gave a new impulse to psychology and has mainly contributed to the present advanced position of that science'.[19] Holyoake's response, in the radical weekly the *Reasoner*, was more immediately political: 'The greatest book of the year on the side of Freethought—the ablest and most important issued from the press for a long time, is unquestionably, Mr. Herbert Spencer's "Principles of Psychology".' Holyoake (who had not himself read the book at this stage) quoted with glee a juicily antagonistic review from the *Spectator*: *The Principles of Psychology* was 'audaciously speculative, subversive of ordinary morality, and anti-Christian'.[20]

These encomiums came in private or in openly radical publications. The overall situation was more complex. With a different audience in prospect, Lewes, for one, could be more circumspect, as he tried to recommend Spencer's work to what he perceived to be a less spontaneously enthusiastic readership. He reviewed Spencer's book a second time in the *Saturday Review*. Though he is no less alert to the originality and far-reaching theoretical implications of *The Principles of Psychology*, his tone is more guarded. He stresses the continuity of the book with earlier theory (it is not capricious), and pleads that readers make allowances for the manner (by which he really means the conclusions) on the grounds of the book's path-breaking ambitions. He admits that Spencer 'cannot hope for much acceptance from the English public', but his review is adroitly calculated to intrigue cautious, but liberal-minded opinion:

Whatever pain may be felt [in reading] so remarkable an intellect on the side of opinions which most readers must regard as opposed to their most cherished convictions, there will be a counterbalancing pleasure and a high moral influence in the contact with a mind so thoroughly earnest and sincere in the search after truth as every page of this work shows Mr. Spencer's to be.[21]

This is a good illustration of Lewes's alert and versatile sense of the audience to be won.

Lewes was right about the atmosphere in which *The Principles of Psychology* was received. Spencer's secretary, James Collier, recalled in 1874 that its

---

[19] George Eliot to Sara Hennell, 10 July 1854, *Letters*, ii. 165.

[20] [G. J. Holyoake], 'Current Literature', *Reasoner*, 2 (2 Mar. 1856), 66. For an account of the context of Holyoake's championship of Spencer's book within the radical politics of the day, see William Baker, '"A Problematical Thinker" to a "Sagacious Philosopher": Some Unpublished George Henry Lewes—Herbert Spencer Correspondence', *English Studies*, 56 (1975), 217–21. Holyoake was very active in the political arguments that surrounded Lamarckian theory, and had already been imprisoned in the early 1840s for blasphemous attacks on natural theology (see Desmond, *Politics of Evolution*, 74, 111). The *Reasoner* carried a fuller, but equally laudatory, review at the end of the month: [F. B. Barton], 'Spencer's "Principles of Psychology"', *Reasoner*, 13 (30 Mar. 1856), 99.

[21] [G. H. Lewes], 'Herbert Spencer's Principles of Psychology', *Saturday Review*, 1 (1856), 352–3.

publication in 1855 did not make a sensation. The persistent efforts of Mill had not yet succeeded in stemming the muddy tide of the prevailing scholasticism. The bastard Kantism of Hamilton did duty for metaphysics, and the Common Sense philosophy of Reid, with the common sense left out, usurped the place of Experimental Psychology. Experimental Psychology was, as usual, busy with analysis, and had no eye for a synthetical effort. Mr. Spencer's work had accordingly a chill reception. Greeted by the aristocratic metaphysicians with a few words of courtly compliment, but treated practically with supercilious disregard, it was received by psychologists of the Association school with hardly more favour than the snarling approval with which a Constitutional Whig views the entry into the Cabinet of a Birmingham Radical. Mr. Spencer was ahead of his generation, and paid the penalty of his prescience in twenty years of neglect. But now the wheel is coming round. The bovine British public . . . is at last awakening to the fact that the peer of Bacon and Newton is here.[22]

As the closing remarks indicate, this is a partisan account written by a disciple, but the parallel drawn between psychological debate and political infighting is neither wayward nor irresponsible. It does indicate something of the mood of the period, both in the lack of attention the book was initially given (Bain, a more traditional psychologist, was much more widely reviewed), and in some of the hostility it attracted, for it was accused of the usual sins: materialism, atheism, and nihilism.[23]

   Nevertheless, Collier does exaggerate, and Spencer did receive more considered responses. Morrel's careful, level-headed account in the specialist journal the *Medico-Chirurgical Review* praised the book's relentless search for first principles. Spencer had made 'one of the most vigorous attempts which has yet been made in our country to place mental philosophy upon a broad and positive basis'. This had been achieved in a situation where 'we cannot but see how the old landmarks of mental philosophy are breaking down and disappearing under the steady advance of physiological science; and yet how imperfectly we can complete . . . that vast psychological structure, the foundations of which we see already laid out'.[24] Spencer's achievement was to find a new direction for

   [22] [James Collier], 'The Development of Psychology', *Westminster Review*, NS 45 (1874), 400. This essay is unsigned, and unattributed in *The Wellesley Index*. Lewes, however, refers to it as by 'Mr. Collier' in *Problems* (iv. 39), and, in view of the fact that the essay closes with an exaggerated paean to Spencer, 'the greatest of psychologists', attribution of it to Collier, his Secretary and disciple, seems probable.
   [23] By e.g. [H. B. Wilson?], 'Theology and Philosophy', *Westminster Review*, NS 9 (1856), 221–42, and [R. H. Hutton], 'Atheism', *National Review*, 2 (1856), 97–123. Hutton's piece also attacked Holyoake, and the *Reasoner* in particular. Both the Unitarian Hutton (a pupil of James Martineau) and Wilson (a divine and Anglo-Saxon scholar) focused on the free-will problem, the sacrifice of moral agency, and the obliteration of distinctions between humans and other forms of life. Hutton's piece was the first in a series of hostile responses to Spencer written over nearly twenty years to which we will return.
   [24] Morrel, 'Modern English Psychology', 361, 363.

psychology and his originality was readily appreciated, even if his conclusions were not always endorsed. Writers in the 1860s and 1870s, though they often had substantial reservations, credited his innovations.[25]

Spencer, not a man to undervalue himself, recognized his originality early, and knew where it lay. The central 'Objective' (that is, the physiological and biological) portions of *The Principles of Psychology* were 'so little akin to those of preceding psychologists, that no extensive study of their writings was necessary', he states in his autobiography with characteristic loftiness.[26] His originality lay in the ability to conceive of a coherent theoretical framework, and (as Lewes and Collier saw) to take as a starting point not the 'Scholastic' questions of the philosophy of mind, nor the 'analytic' procedures of associationism, but the framework of general biology. In his review of Bain in the *Medico-Chirurgical Review* in 1860, Spencer lamented the current lack of theorizing in an age given over to mere observation. It was now necessary to try to reshape conceptions of the mind's activity. Bain's work was 'characteristic of this transition' and of the 'inchoate state of psychology'. His book was a 'classified collection of materials' wanting an organizing conception. Instead of the old methods of proceeding by correlating the 'objective' findings of observation and (where available) physiology, with the 'subjective' findings of introspection, Spencer saw the need to resolve mental components back to their simple, biological elements. In this way psychology could comprehend not just analysis, but *development*, and this would form (picking up Bain's phrase) a more thorough 'natural history method'.[27]

Spencer is alert to the practical and theoretical difficulties, but insists that it is now necessary to see the human mind in a developmental perspective, in terms of the growth not only of the individual (which associationist psychology *was* capable of doing), but also of the species and the race. This could be done only by a comparative psychology that studied 'the evolution of the emotions up through the various grades of the animal kingdom' taking cognisance of the differences

---

[25] See e.g. anon., 'Mr. Herbert Spencer's First Principles', *British Quarterly Review*, 37 (1863), 84–121. For twentieth-century comment on the reception of Spencer's work and its originality in the 1850s, see *Brett's History of Psychology*; J. W. Burrow, *Evolution and Society: A Study of Victorian Social Theory* (Cambridge, 1966); George Bion Denton, 'Early Psychological Theories of Herbert Spencer', *American Journal of Psychology*, 32 (1921), 5–15; Hearnshaw, *Short History of British Psychology*; Leahey, *A History of Psychology*; Murphy, *Historical Introduction to Modern Psychology*; Murray, *A History of Western Psychology*; Peel, *Herbert Spencer*; Robert J. Richards, *Darwin and the Emergence of Evolutionary Theories of Mind and Behaviour* (London, 1987); C. U. M. Smith, 'Evolution and the Problem of Mind: Part I. Herbert Spencer', *Journal of the History of Biology*, 15 (1982), 55–88; Warren, *History of the Association Psychology*; Robert M. Young, *Mind, Brain and Adaptation*. However, with the exception of Young and Richards, none of these attempts to recover the context of contemporary psychological debate in much detail.

[26] Spencer, *An Autobiography*, ii. 171.

[27] Spencer, 'Bain on The Emotions and the Will', in *Essays*, 241–61.

between the 'lower and higher human races'.[28] Thus, beginning with the study of rudimentary biological action, psychology could carry analysis forward to a specification of culture and society. Because emotional habits became ingrained, and were hereditarily transmissible, a biologized psychology could be used to 'generalize . . . the phenomena of habit, of national characteristics, of civilization in its moral aspects'.[29] What was necessary was a redrawing of the taxonomies of psychological theory so that one did not begin with the apparently stable (though in fact very complex) phenomena posited by the older traditions. Simply put, analytic, descriptive psychology began its account of the genesis of the human mental faculties historically too late. With a good eye for the contentious example, Spencer chose the will, which, as we have seen, was of particular concern in the debate, because it immediately engaged questions of human moral and spiritual agency.[30]

Spencer's contention is that the will should be classified as a developed reflex. Volition is 'a simple homogenous mental state, forming the link between feeling and action'.[31] The special category of what rival Victorian theorists often capitalized as 'The Will' should be dropped; it required no special explanation, and should have no special taxonomic or theoretical status. This was also true of all the other traditional higher faculties such as reasoning, remembering, or responding to beauty, which were usually used to distinguish men from animals. In the 600-plus pages of *The Principles of Psychology*, Spencer gave just nine to the problem of the will. The will becomes active, he says, when automatic action ceases and a selection needs to be made among competing, though nascent, motor changes—that is, the psychical state is 'imperfectly coherent' and needs to be organized. The higher forms of voluntary action develop from these states because of increasing complexity; the principle, however, remains the same.

Spencer recognized his radicalism and wrote: 'Long before reaching this point, readers will have perceived that the doctrines developed . . . are quite at variance with the current tenets respecting the freedom of the Will.' The 'current illusion' proposes that 'the *ego* is something more than the composite state of consciousness which then exists', and that there is a separate faculty presiding over the self and its activities. The hypothesis of an independent will is an understandable error, says Spencer, but an error none the less.[32] Spencer's

---

[28] Spencer, 'Bain on The Emotions and the Will', in *Essays*, 250.     [29] Ibid. 255.

[30] There is no doubt that Spencer would have been aware of his contentious choice. The problem of the will had already been singled out in reviews of *The Principles of Psychology*, and not just by opponents. Morrel and Lewes (in his piece for the *Saturday Review*) had both identified Spencer's conception of the will as a controversial difficulty in the theory.

[31] Spencer, 'Bain on The Emotions and the Will', in *Essays*, 260.

[32] Herbert Spencer, *The Principles of Psychology* (London, 1855), 617. Subsequent reference will be to this edition unless otherwise stated.

supporters picked up the idea. Douglas Spalding, in a review of the second edition of *The Principles of Psychology* in *Nature* in 1873, argued that Spencer's new ideas rendered the old conceptions null, and that they were being kept alive only by disputatious 'veterans' anxious to preserve their achievements and laurels. Spencer's evolutionary conception of the will makes Bain's, for instance, seem 'only a highly ingenious account of what does not happen'. Spencer's psychology means 'giving up much of what has hitherto passed for mental science'.[33]

Spencer's evolutionary theories, as articulated in *The Principles of Psychology*, have a number of aspects. For him evolution was progressive and purposive. Though Spencer impatiently dismissed the teleologies of, for example, Erasmus Darwin or Robert Chambers, nevertheless his own conception of the process contained a directional element that he needed as a moral mainstay in a world without traditional religious or teleological goals.[34] According to Spencer, the process of evolution was governed by the working-out of laws embedded in the constitution of nature. These included two general, but very gradual, processes, and a number of enabling mechanisms. The two general processes are: the tendency for organisms to develop from homogeneity to heterogeneity, and the tendency of organisms to seek 'co-ordination of actions' among their heterogeneous parts in order to develop increasingly sophisticated and exact 'correspondences' between themselves and their environment. (The terms indicated by quotation marks are Spencer's own, and I have also tried to retain the voluntaristic cast of his account.) 'Co-ordination of actions' was, indeed, Spencer's definition of Life itself, just as the various parts of the human body are integrated to produce its vital activity.[35] Thus, the guiding law of nature was division, but the goal was the establishment of 'consensus'. Among the biological mechanisms that came into play in these processes were: first, the transmission of those acquired characteristics that enabled organisms to flourish (or, indeed, as a stick to that carrot, were encouraging them to become dysfunctional); and, secondly, the biological division of labour whereby the organism could maintain its responsiveness to the heterogeneity of stimuli, *and* the specialization necessary to find finer and finer correspondence with the environment. These processes were the same at all levels of analysis, from the development of multi-cellular organisms, through the generation of consciousness, to the formulation of scientific theories, like Spencer's own, which recapitulated the integrational dynamics of nature itself. Scientific hypotheses, for Spencer, tend 'constantly towards larger and larger generalizations'.[36] The whole of 'Synthetic Philosophy', encompassing increasingly diverse information, has an 'organic' unity offering multiplicity within

---

[33] Douglas A. Spalding, 'Herbert Spencer's Psychology, Part 1', *Nature*, 7 (1873), 298–300.
[34] Peel, *Herbert Spencer*, 135–6.  [35] Spencer, *Principles of Psychology*, 354.
[36] Ibid. 345.

an integrated whole. Intelligence itself, as the highest of the vital phenomena, must display the most 'constant maintenance', so that 'the internal order shall be continually adjusted to the external order', life being impossible without this 'adaptation'.[37] This is the ground of Spencer's realist epistemology, to which we will return.

*The Principles of Psychology* challenges the classificatory categories of associationist and faculty psychology alike, and Spencer does not tire of making this explicit. The 'divisions we make between the various mental processes have merely a superficial truth' he says, developing the point that the mind must be seen as a relational and developing process, and psychology as a comparative activity.[38] Thus,

the classifications current in our philosophies of the mind, can be but superficially true. Instinct, Reason, Perception, Conception, Memory, Imagination, Feeling, Will, &c., &c., can be nothing more than either conventional groupings of the correspondences; or subordinate divisions among the various operations which are instrumental in effecting the correspondences. . . . these various forms of intelligence cannot be anything else than either particular modes in which the adjustment of inner to outer relations is achieved; or particular parts of the process of adjustment.[39]

The organization of *The Principles of Psychology* as a text reflects these concerns. It begins with large epistemological questions and sketches of evolutionary processes. It is only at the very end that Spencer settles to a more conventionally arranged account of, as it were, the micro-psychology of the individual, and then, as we have seen in the case of the will, Spencer gives this comparatively perfunctory attention.

So, though Spencer praised Bain's *The Emotions and the Will* as 'indispensable' for the establishment of a scientific psychology, his own work jettisoned the detailed analysis of mental contents that had been the task of associationists from Locke to Bain. In response, Bain continued to defend associationist methods against the takeover of psychology by evolutionary biology. As late as 1881, in a review of the third edition of Spencer's *Principles*, he was pointing, rather sniffily, to the fact that evolution was not yet a validated theory. Though Bain agrees with Spencer's 'cardinal doctrines', Spencer was neglectful of the complexities of the mind's workings. His psychology, and in particular his residual associationism, was therefore too crude.[40] This anxiety about the reductiveness of Spencer's programme was also expressed in the 1850s by sympathetic readers such as Morrel

---

[37] Spencer, *Principles of Psychology*, 506.    [38] Ibid. 188.    [39] Ibid. 486.
[40] Alexander Bain, 'Mr. Spencer's Psychological "Congruities"', *Mind*, 6 (1881), 266–70, 394–406. In his autobiography, Spencer records that, though his criticisms of Bain 'touched fundamentally on his method and his general conceptions', Bain took them in good part, 'philosophically', and their relationship developed to friendship (*Autobiography*, ii. 46).

and Lewes, and by later commentators such as Howard Warren. In an effort to cut through existing practice and reformulate general principles, Spencer put sensitivity to individual differences, and the variety and complexity of psychological process, at risk. As we shall see, this feature of his psychology, and with it his epistemology, became a substantial difficulty for him later.

Yet despite Spencer's opposition to a psychology based on a traditional analysis of mental contents, his theory did make some use of associationism. This has been analysed by Warren and, especially, Robert Young in *Mind, Brain, and Adaptation*. There was, after all, no other language available or appropriate for describing the details of the mind's workings. Though Spencer, like many others, flirted with phrenology early in his career, he rejected it for cogent reasons in *The Principles of Psychology*.[41] Phrenology's fixed faculties could not be assimilated to Spencer's psychology of process and development. In reality, he argued, there was no '*precise* demarcation of the faculties', only an 'insensible shading-off' of the brain portion dedicated to particular functions.[42] Associationism, though, did not suffer from this problem. Its language, analysis, and underlying assumptions were able to describe the genesis of mental functions and their development. Though Spencer objected to associationism's restriction of psychological analysis to that of ideas, at the expense of emotions and feelings,[43] associationist language could offer an appropriate means for describing the processes Spencer was after.

In the second and third editions of *The Principles of Psychology* Spencer makes the point explicit: 'The congruity between the established laws of association and the several implications of the physical principle here laid down [on the coordination of the different structures of the brain], is conspicuous.'[44] Indeed, Howard Warren has claimed that in essence *The Principles of Psychology* is an associationist text, and that 'the transformation of the analysis brought about by the evolutionary view effects the details, the distribution of emphasis, and the terminology, without modifying any of the essential factors or laws of association. The principle of association remains an effective working hypothesis; its physiological meaning is practically unaltered.'[45] But this overstates a case. Spencer did make use of associationism, and he would probably have called

---

[41] Young's chapter is the best account of this. Interestingly, George Eliot regretted the lack of attention to phrenology when the *Principles* appeared in 1855. See letter to Sara Hennell, 16 Oct. 1855, *Letters*, ii. 219.

[42] Spencer, *Principles of Psychology*, 609.

[43] 'The Feelings are not, scientifically considered, divisible from other phenomena of consciousness' (ibid. 584).

[44] Spencer, *The Principles of Psychology*, 3rd edn., 2 vols. (London, 1881), i. 577. The second (1870–2) and third editions are identical except for the addition of an independently numbered fifty-page part 8 in the third edition.

[45] Warren, *History of the Association Psychology*, 135.

himself an associationist, given the options available. But the broad direction and achievement of *The Principles of Psychology* lies elsewhere, and Spencer shifted the premises of psychology decisively, as was recognized by many of his contemporaries. He was an associationist, it seems to me, rather in the way that George Eliot was an associationist. She, too, used associationist language from time to time, because it was able to articulate processes and developments with sufficient complexity for her purposes. But this does not mean that she was an associationist psychologist committed, like Bain or John Mill, for example, to that programme of analysis.

Spencer's adaptation of associationism to evolutionary biology did, however, offer to solve some vexing associationist problems. By adapting associationism to a biological paradigm, Spencer shifted the nature of the proposed model. Instead of being static and passive, he made it dynamic and energetic. The mind was pictured as having *powers* at its disposal. The self could explore the limits of its own being through the experience of resistance and effort, especially through the quickly developed muscle sense. Indeed, according to Spencer, the experience of resistance was the 'primordial, the universal, the ever-present constituent of consciousness'.[46] In addition, the theory of the hereditary transmission of acquired characteristics could overcome the kind of problem identified by Coleridge, Hamilton, and others; that is, that the mind, in the associationist model, started with too little and ended with too much. There was, they argued, a kind of developmental hiatus between the rudimentary and contingent development of associations, from the *tabula rasa* at one end of the process, and the spectacular generation of highly advanced human faculties at the other. The problem of how a few individual repetitions of experiences can repeatedly build such sophisticated systems in the course of a single lifetime was a standard and powerful objection, as Spencer recognized:

Doubtless, the individual experiences furnish the concrete materials for all thought; doubtless, the organized and semi-organized arrangements existing among the cerebral nerves, can give no knowledge until there has been a presentation of the external relations to which they correspond; and doubtless, the child's daily observations and reasonings have the effect of facilitating and strengthening those involved nervous connections that are in the process of spontaneous evolution: just as its daily gambols aid the growth of its limbs. But this is a quite different thing from saying that its intelligence is wholly *produced* by its experiences. That is an utterly inadmissible doctrine—a doctrine which makes the presence of a brain meaningless—a doctrine which makes [?it] unaccountable [*sic*].[47]

As Young and Warren, and contemporaries like William Courtney, note, Spencer's emphasis on hereditary transmission offered to solve this problem by shifting the emphasis from the individual to the race. Spencer could thus account for

---

[46] Spencer, *Principles of Psychology*, 265.    [47] Ibid. 582.

individual growth, and posit the progressive acquisition of better abilities, because our ancestors had done most of our preliminary development for us. The basic postulates of the sensational and associationist psychologies could be maintained, but so too could ideas of continuity, evolution, and progress. The idea of innate mental endowments was brought as a solution to a persistent associationist problem, but without conceding ground to the conservative argument for special, spiritualized faculties.[48]

Spencer's psychology, then, changed the old sensationalist–associationist model by shifting its leading principles into a different register of understanding, that of evolutionary biology, and by adding a new mechanism, that of the inheritance of acquired characteristics. These principles were developed by Spencer from the early 1850s, especially in the essay 'The Development Hypothesis' (first published in Lewes's the *Leader* in 1852) and the first edition of *The Principles of Psychology*. They remained the leading ideas of his psychological and biological thought, and a keystone of his social and political ideas as well, which, partly as a consequence, were tainted by a not wholly untypical Victorian racism.[49]

Like Bain, Lewes, Eliot, and, in his rather different way, John Mill, Spencer was an autodidact. What formal training he had was in engineering, and he came to the subjects of his principal intellectual work independently, by working through some of the diverse intellectual currents of the period, as Peel and Burrow have described. His origins were in provincial dissenting radicalism, and he, like Bain and Lewes, was, in his early career, a political radical—a supporter of Chartism, for instance, and an enthusiast for Shelley.[50] Later though, unlike Bain and Lewes, he became a spokesman for the ultras of 'free-market' liberalism. He was early, and continually, influenced by mainstream mid-century political economy, and this is visible in his biological and social theories, most evidently in the concept of the survival of the fittest and the dark fears of racial degeneration (because of the swelling ranks of the poor), which haunt some of his later work. As Burrow has argued, evolution was for Spencer the justification for *laissez-faire* economics and social theory, but, at the same time, his conception of the evolutionary process was influenced by the same social theories that were then supposed to be legitimized by it. Biology thus served as both justification and model, and

[48] See Robert M. Young, *Mind, Brain, and Adaptation*, 178–82; Warren, *History of the Association Psychology*, 171–2. Also Hearnshaw, *Short History of British Psychology*, 43–5.

[49] See Michael D. Biddiss (ed.), *Images of Race* (Leicester, 1979), and Nancy Stepan, *The Idea of Race in Science: Great Britain 1800–1960* (London, 1982). Biddiss, as others have done (e.g. Peel, Burrow, and Young), notes a contradiction in Spencer's thought here (pp. 187–8). On the one hand, he offers environmentalist explanations—human characteristics are derived through experience and then hereditarily transmitted—but at others times (as for instance in the review of Bain) he speaks in terms of inevitably superior and inferior races, presumably irrespective of environmental considerations.

[50] Spencer, *An Autobiography*, i. 217–21, 260–1; Peel, *Herbert Spencer*, chs. 2–3.

Spencer's position involved more than one contradiction, for Spencer remained as resolutely individualist in his social beliefs as he was collectivist (or racial) in his biological theory.[51]

A version of this contradiction (which also lies at the heart of his racial views) compromises his social theory. A resolutely environmental determinist, who would not countenance the idea of a free-acting will in psychology, Spencer none the less insisted, as a political economist, a pacifist, an anti-colonialist, and a believer in altruism and the effects of human sympathy, that people were able to exert moral agency to make a difference to things.[52] These contradictions in social and political opinion are directly relevant to arguments in psychological theory, for the point concerns the degree of independence granted to individuals, and the emphasis to be given to the various determining factors acting on them.

In Spencer's psychology the man-made environment of society and culture functions, to all intents and purposes, as an ersatz biological medium—that is, it operates in the same way as the raw biological world of nature, providing more or less favourable conditions for the individual, who is more or less equipped to take advantage of them. Society does not significantly function by cooperation, and the transmission of skills and culture does not enable the individual to survive or significantly enrich the quality of existence. In *The Principles of Psychology* he attends to society only incidentally, and only then as an entity that offers the individual increased protection.[53] Spencer's views in this respect are unlike those of Lewes or George Eliot. As we shall see, Lewes is keen to distinguish categorically between biology and society. Spencer, in the end, is not— though, as Peter Medawar and others have pointed out, the analogizing of biological evolution and psycho-social evolution is not sustainable for a variety of hard scientific reasons, including infringement of the second law of thermodynamics.[54] Nevertheless, Spencer's *Autobiography*, for example, is written in accordance with just these theoretical premisses.

He remarks for instance, apropos education, that 'inherited constitution must ever be the chief factor in determining character'.[55] Thus he begins his 'natural history of myself' (the phrase used in the Preface and which, we recall

[51] Burrow, *Evolution and Society*, ch. 6. See also Robert M. Young, 'Malthus and the Evolutionists: The Common Context of Biological and Social Theory', in *Darwin's Metaphor*, 23–55; Barry G. Gale, 'Darwin and the Concept of a Struggle for Existence: A Study in the Extra-Scientific Origins of Scientific Ideas', *Isis*, 63 (1972), 321–44; and John C. Greene, 'Biology and Social Theory in the Nineteenth Century: Auguste Comte and Herbert Spencer', in *Science, Ideology and World-View: Essays in the History of Evolutionary Ideas* (London, 1981), 60–94. Peel remarks that Spencer covers his tracks by assuming that society can be considered as a totality, though this assumption is never argued (*Herbert Spencer*, 155).

[52] Peel, *Herbert Spencer*, 158–65.    [53] e.g. *Principles of Psychology*, 465.

[54] P. B. Medawar, 'Herbert Spencer and the Law of General Evolution', in *The Art of the Soluble* (London, 1967), 39–58.    [55] Spencer, *An Autobiography*, ii. 18.

from his review of Bain, Spencer interpreted in evolutionary terms) with an account of the 'ancestral traits' he has inherited. What many would regard as the obvious result of growing up in a nonconformist culture, Spencer attributes to biologically transmitted characteristics. These include resistance to established authorities, prudence, self-restraint, late marriage, and the 'relinquishment of present satisfactions with the view to obtaining future satisfactions'. This is Samuel Smiles paddling in the gene pool. Members of his family are similarly portrayed. Of his mother he writes, 'habits of thought and feeling continued for many years, had made organic in her the two dominant ideas of fulfilling domestic obligations and the ordinances of her creed'.[56] The key phrase is 'made organic'. Similarly, his own early life is described as a network of associations, habits, and routines expressive of his hereditary inheritance, and of achievements that predict later successes as the seed does the plant. Volume two begins in the same pattern, with comments on his father's intellectual legacy, which includes the tendency to enquire directly into 'natural necessities and probabilities', an innate ability that explains Spencer's lack of citation of others' work, he says.[57] In other parts of his work, Spencer could be more comprehensive in his account of the complexities of the educational process, but the central drive of his *psychological* theory is to eliminate the social aspects of human mental development.[58]

This type of evolutionary thinking was, however, neither self-evident nor self-validating to Spencer's contemporaries, and is not scientifically reputable today. In fact it had ceased to be so by the middle of the 1880s and it is a feature of his work that has spoilt his reputation, for Spencer held to a 'Lamarckian' view of evolution as distinct from a 'Darwinian'. The difference is simple and devastating. Lamarckian theorists believed that traits acquired in a lifetime could become 'organic' (to use Spencer's word) and therefore were transmissible from generation to generation, each incrementally increasing the former's moral capital or debts (as it were). Thus the evolutionary process is directional, and is capable of some control by the individual whose moral or practical gains—or losses—need not end at death. Furthermore, this more 'humanized' biological process did not necessarily entail the moral bankruptcy that was claimed for evolutionary theory by anxious commentators. Putting the Lamarckian argument in terms of monetary metaphors does reveal the theoretical homology between it and some distinctive nineteenth-century theories of banking and money circulation, and Smilesian ideas of social and economic advancement. Indeed, Lamarckian theory had been consistently understood in Britain in political terms. As Adrian Desmond notes, 'among the artisan atheists . . . Lamarckism was . . .

---

[56] Ibid. i. 3–12, 58.    [57] Ibid. ii. 6.

[58] See e.g. the essays collected in *Essays on Education and Kindred Subjects* (London, 1911), especially 'Moral Education' and 'On Manners and Fashion'.

used to legitimate a priest-free democratic republic' in the 1820s.[59] It was consistently used by radicals thereafter, and by middle-class *laissez-faire* liberals like Spencer. Lamarck's ideas could be used in this way because they disturbed prevailing conceptions of an inevitable, hierarchical order. Those with ability could now be seen to 'develop' and prosper. It was the biological equivalent of a free, mobile society. By contrast, opponents of evolutionary theory—and the new psychology—tended towards rigidly hierarchical politics.[60]

The Darwinian account of the evolutionary process is quite different, and it is not readily available for the kind of theoretical and ideological appropriation indicated here. For Darwin, the evolutionary process is not driven by the hereditary transmission of acquired characteristics, but, first, by 'natural selection' and, second, by 'sexual selection'. 'Natural selection' is the term given to indicate the success of species, and variations within species, in accommodating themselves to a given environment in order to survive and breed. 'Sexual selection' indicates the competition within a species for the attainment of sexual goals. By definition, the more successful—and those therefore best fitted, at this (biological) level of judgement, to continue the species—are those who do breed. Biologically speaking, however, each generation inherits nothing from its parents that has been acquired during the parent's lifetime. Evolution occurs at the sexual level through competition, and at the environmental level because of the chance success of variant forms. That is, it may turn out that a random mutation is better equipped for survival than 'normal' siblings. This strain will then prosper, perhaps at the expense of the 'normal' strain. But its success will not come from any 'progressive' or purposive feature in the process, nor from acquired biological structure, nor from any particular moral accomplishments—other, of course, than those that mitigate the effects of environmental damage for any given generation. The ability to build shelters (say) is culturally, and not biologically, transmitted. It is no wonder, then, that opponents were alarmed. Evolutionary theory in this form can easily be seen to threaten conceptions of the end and aims of man in a spiritual light, the special and particular distinctiveness of human beings as a species, the customary moral guarantees that continuity and perpetuation offer, and the gains in morale that even the illusion of perpetuity encourages.[61]

---

[59] Desmond, *Politics of Evolution*, 60. It should also be said that it would be wrong to conflate Lamarck's actual theories with these nineteenth-century appropriations. Indeed it has been convincingly argued that what we now think of as distinctively 'Lamarckian'—the theory sketched here—was in fact not original to him, and that its importance to his biology has been overestimated. This is argued, for instance, by L. J. Jordanova, *Lamarck* (Oxford, 1984).

[60] Jacyna, 'Physiology of Mind', 122–3.

[61] For a relevant nineteenth-century discussion of the question of the 'moralizing' of the evolutionary process, see T. H. Huxley, *Evolution and Ethics and Other Essays* (London, 1894). Huxley and Spencer fell out over this issue. For comment, see Peel, *Herbert Spencer*, 141–53; Irvine, *Thomas Henry Huxley*, 32–4; Desmond, *Huxley: Evolution's High Priest*, 191–6.

In scientific terms Spencer was wrong, and Darwin right.[62] However, this twentieth-century verdict should not blind us to the historical situation in the mid-to-late nineteenth century, for these two versions of 'the development hypothesis' existed side by side for at least a quarter of a century and their differences were frequently blurred even by informed commentators. It has been convincingly argued that George Eliot, for instance, did not fully appreciate the difference between the two theories when she read Darwin in 1859.[63] G. H. Lewes, who was as informed as anybody, also had difficulty in sorting out the issues, as we shall see. Part of the reason for this was that the difference was not in fact immediately clear from the primary texts. As Robert Young and others have argued, Darwin's theory was complete except for the specification of a *mechanism*. Darwinian theorists could not call upon the science of genetics. (Indeed, the account of Darwin's theory given above is essentially neo-Darwinian; that is, an extrapolation made from the synthesis of Darwin and Mendel made in the 1930s.) As a result, the language of *The Origin of Species* contains ambiguity at crucial points, and even falls back towards that of the natural theology Darwin had learned at Cambridge.[64] Derek Freeman, in an excellent account of the differences between Spencer and Darwin, notes that, in some respects, Darwin became painted with Spencer's political brush, and 'Social Darwinism' became the usual term for the biologization of nineteenth-century political economy.[65] As Freeman makes clear, the differences between the two theories, and the errors contained in Spencer's, were not established even in scientific circles until the mid-1880s following the path-breaking work of German cytologists.[66] Subsequently, Spencer conceded that he had been wrong to insist that 'the sole cause of organic evolution is the inheritance of functionally-produced modifications'.[67] But he continued to search for a means of reconciling his neo-Lamarckian ideas with those of Darwin. After

[62] For discussion of the differences in their conclusions and scientific careers, see Derek Freeman, 'The Evolutionary Theories of Charles Darwin and Herbert Spencer', *Current Anthropology*, 15 (1974), 211–37.

[63] Beer, *Darwin's Plots*, 157.

[64] See Robert M. Young, 'Darwin's Metaphor: Does Nature Select?' in *Darwin's Metaphor*, 79–125. The other essays in this collection are all worth attention in relation to this problem. For detailed discussion of the language of *The Origin*, see Beer, *Darwin's Plots*, pt. 1. The result of this 'language' problem was a confusion that has survived in certain forms until very recently. For a succinct account, see Antony Flew, *Darwinian Evolution* (London, 1984).

[65] Freeman, 'Evolutionary Theories of Darwin and Spencer'. See also Raymond Williams, 'Social Darwinism', in *Problems in Materialism and Culture*, 86–102. There is regular comment on the origins of evolutionary theory in political economy and Malthus's population theories. See, in addition to these, Robert M. Young, *Darwin's Metaphor*, Burrow, *Evolution and Society*, and Peel, *Herbert Spencer*.

[66] See also Everett Mendelsohn, 'Cell Theory and the Development of General Physiology', *Archives Internationales d'Histoire des Sciences*, 16 (1963), 419–29.

[67] Spencer, *An Autobiography*, ii. 50.

all, the stakes were high. As Huxley realized, the overthrow of Lamarckianism meant the overthrow of much more. 'Spencer is bound to it *a priori*,' he wrote in a letter in 1890, 'his psychology goes to pieces without it'.[68]

Spencer, though, was not alone in defending neo-Lamarckian ideas, which maintained a considerable presence in both scientific and extra-scientific circles until well into the twentieth century.[69] They were certainly regarded with great seriousness and respect in the period we are dealing with here, as is evident from the periodical literature. An article on Lamarck in the *Westminster Review* in 1874, for instance, is not at all defensive. Recognizing the similarities between Spencer and Lamarck (Spencer as usual had not cited his sources), the writer commented on the 'somewhat peculiar' reception of Lamarckian ideas in Britain. Attacked in the 1810s and 1820s by religious and metaphysical philosophers as materialistic, they had been attacked again by Darwinists and anti-Darwinists alike in the writer's own day. The writer thought that such attacks from both sides probably exonerated the middle and, like many others, noticed that a Lamarckian doctrine would solve the difficulty over the question of innate ideas. For surely 'innate ideas . . . would almost seem a necessary consequence of his [Lamarck's] theories'. A neurological mechanism was even sketched: mental impressions are conveyed by the 'nervous fluid which traverses the hyper-cephalon, and engraves traces of its course on that organ'. This mental 'sculpture' is then transmitted from generation to generation and Man begins his spiritual ascent.[70]

The metaphors, as well as the speculation, here remind one more of Hartley or Locke than the era of Darwinian biology, but such examples are not isolated. Lamarckian considerations recommended themselves to J. D. Morrel in his review of Spencer and Bain in 1856 because they appealed to his convictions about progress.[71] Gilbert Child, a practising doctor, also endorsed Lamarckian conceptions in the *Westminster* in 1868. Child took the occasion of a review of Henry Maudsley's *The Physiology and Pathology of the Mind* to examine the state of the whole field of 'Physiological Psychology'. It is a cautious, judicious, informed, and empirically minded account of research by a man who, by temperament and profession, is sensitive to the hazards of speculation. None the less, he concludes that the state of an infant's nervous system 'is the result of the combination of the two original constitutions of its parents, plus the effects of their life-experience upon them; life experience meaning the modifications effected in the original constitution by the whole circumstances of the whole existence

---

[68] Quoted by Freeman, 'Evolutionary Theories of Darwin and Spencer', 217.
[69] Jordanova, *Lamarck*, ch. 10.
[70] Anon., 'Lamarck', *Westminster Review*, NS 46 (1874), 197.
[71] Morrel, 'Modern English Psychology', 356.

of the individual'. His point has additional weight: he is summarizing Maudsley, whose conclusions, on this question, 'can hardly be denied'.[72]

Two things, then, are apparent. Spencer had an ultimately mistaken conception of evolutionary processes, but this error was none the less historically comprehensible, and, within its period, significant for the development of psychology. As Young remarks, the Lamarckian mistake was, for Spencer and other theorists, heuristically effective. It encouraged thought within the evolutionary paradigm, and did so partly because it could build a bridge between the new 'biologized' psychology and the old associationism in such a way as to solve some of the persistent theoretical difficulties of the latter.[73] It also had a wider integrative function. As Burrow demonstrates, despite its scandalous reputation, evolutionary theory did meet the needs of many Victorian intellectuals who, unable to accept traditional accounts of man's place in the scheme of things, none the less hankered after some overarching justification for life. Spencer's Lamarckian doctrines, as part of the overall 'Synthetic Philosophy', were, like Comte's positivism, well suited to serve such quasi-religious needs, because they offered themselves as coherent, monolithic explanations built on an appetizing, morally regular, progressive optimism. As Burrow argues, the collapse of previous integrative social theories (like Burkean conservative organicism or the Utilitarianism of the Philosophical Radicals) created the opportunity for a new corporatist explanation that could accommodate a more diverse range of social facts and that stressed gradual evolution and not turbulent revolution.[74] The smooth transmission of psychological characteristics from parent to child could offer a comfortingly ordered conception of a changing society based on traditional and hard-won values, while providing the opportunity for 'vertical' advancement and integration. Meanwhile, there was no 'Darwinian' alternative in evolutionary psychological theory to challenge this conception outright. Darwin noted in *The Origin* that, among the 'far more important researches' that the theory made possible, 'Psychology will be based on a new foundation'.[75] But he did not attempt such an account, despite the chapter in *The Descent of Man* on the 'Comparison of the Mental Powers of Man and of the Lower Animals'

---

[72] [G. W. Child], 'Physiological Psychology', *Westminster Review*, NS 33 (1868), 63. Child was a follower of William Carpenter, as was Spencer, as is attested in his autobiography. Spencer reviewed the third edition of Carpenter's *Principles of Physiology*, again in the *Westminster*, in 1852. (He had begun his own *Principles of Psychology* in 1851.) He took it as the 'state-of-the-art' text, which would save investigators 'many journeys to libraries, much searching through catalogues, and a great deal of reading' (Spencer, notice of *Principles of Physiology, General and Comparative* by W. B. Carpenter, *Westminster Review*, NS 1 (1852), 274–5).

[73] Robert M. Young, *Mind, Brain and Adaptation*, 186–9.

[74] Burrow, *Evolution and Society*, 263–71.     [75] Darwin, *The Origin of Species*, 458.

that provoked much of the furore *The Descent* caused in 1871. The impact of Darwinian theory proper on psychology was thus delayed for some time.[76]

SPENCER AND THE RELIGIOUS MIND: THE CHANGING<br>RESPONSE TO PSYCHOLOGICAL THEORY

The integrative potential of Spencer's work, however, should not conceal its disturbing consequences for many Victorians for whom the certainties Spencer might offer were no more attractive than the moral and religious chaos being articulated (they thought) by Darwin, and noisily defended by Huxley. Spencer, of course, received his share of abuse and denigration in the years of his principal publications, and, as ever, the leading issues were religious. The difficulties began before publication. He recalls in the *Autobiography* that he had difficulty finding a publisher at all, in part because of 'religious difficulties'.[77] Subsequently Spencer, like all the leading psychologists of the period, was attacked by Anglicans, nonconformists, and Catholics alike. We are, by now, familiar with these polemics and their frequent political edge. But the period also revealed a telling, though gradual, shift towards the liberalization of religious responses.

Criticism of Spencer's psychology among Anglicans took an expected course. Thomas Birks, Professor of Moral Philosophy at Cambridge, was representative. In *Modern Physical Fatalism and the Doctrine of Evolution, including an examination of Mr. H. Spencer's First Principles* (1876) Birks thought it his academic, intellectual, religious, and moral duty (he tells us in the preface) to expose Spencer's 'radically unsound' thinking, and restate faith, morality, and truth. Evolutionary theory destroys moral value, our sense of Providence, and the importance of the will. It is fatalistic and nihilistic. It eliminates choice, and abolishes mystery and 'the Unknowable'. Birks's book is full of this kind of routine objection to the new psychology, though Birks had troubled to read his opponents carefully and sometimes uses them astutely. (For instance he turns Mill's strictures against *a priori* propositions against Spencer, Comte, and Tyndall.[78]) His position, however, remains that of a theological traditionalist of the old school for

[76] See D. R. Oldroyd, *Darwinian Impacts: An Introduction to the Darwinian Revolution* (Milton Keynes, 1980); Robert M. Young, 'The Role of Psychology in the Nineteenth-Century Evolutionary Debate', in *Darwin's Metaphor*, 56–78; *Brett's History of Psychology*, 670–2; Hearnshaw *Short British Psychology*, ch. 3.

[77] Spencer, *An Autobiography*, i. 462. Spencer remarks that, after John Chapman's retirement in 1858 (Chapman was Spencer's first publisher, though he did not publish *The Principles of Psychology* because of the probable losses), London lost its foremost radical publisher. In the 1850s, 'Chapman was the only respectable publisher through whom could be issued books which were tacitly or avowedly rationalistic' (*An Autobiography*, ii. 33).

[78] Thomas Rawson Birks, *Modern Physical Fatalism and the Doctrine of Evolution, Including an Examination of Mr. H. Spencer's First Principles* (London, 1876), 15 ff., 218 ff.

whom, without religion, 'the whole universe would contain nothing more than dense, whirling balls of lifeless matter, or scattered and floating patches of nebulous vapour and confusion, and remain a dreary and barren wilderness, a waste and desolation for ever more'.[79]

Among nonconformists (Spencer's own background) the Unitarians were, perhaps surprisingly, particularly stern. *The Wellesley Index* records that the Unitarian periodical the *National Review*, though occupying the middle ground politically (a proposed early name was 'The Liberal'), was strongly led editorially. Two of its leading editors—R. H. Hutton and James Martineau—were fiercely opposed to the new psychology and, more generally, the 'loose' and 'atheistic' circle gathered around John Chapman and the *Westminster Review*. Spencer, like others, had a rough ride.[80] Martineau rejected a piece by J. D. Morrel, for example, because, after Morrel's early favourable review of *The Principles of Psychology*, he was 'so obviously taken captive by Spencer, and so ill able to resist the positivist doctrine'.[81] William MacCall was similarly dismissive. Spencer's *First Principles* (1862) was the 'Hard and Dry Philosophy', the old Utilitarianism hitched to French materialism. *First Principles* is 'really a bundle of psychological crotchets dragged by the old rope of French materialism along a desert of scientific aridities'. Philosophy 'in the diviner sense is dead in England'.[82]

Spencer was one of Hutton's guilty men in his piece on 'Atheism' for the *National Review* in 1856. Holyoake and others received critical attention, but Hutton reserved the bulk of his article for *The Principles of Psychology*. Because Spencer dismisses faith in God, he, like all modern atheists, 'props up the higher faculties of man completely and solely on the lower organization, and denies them any independent spring'.[83] The result is devastating for morals and the community. It means the collapse of 'all moral ties and the dissolution of every sacred social organization'.[84] Once again this is a transposed political anxiety, and Hutton seems to fear some kind of class treachery. The new psychology is a 'levelling' theory in which the reduction of the moral faculties to physical nature produces the same kind of '*soreness*' that there is 'between essentially different ranks, where the higher is induced by some theoretic conviction to disavow its special birthright'. Hutton's language pictures urban riot and insurrection eight years after 1848: 'How can any true Baconian induction dissolve the moral will of man into a contest between a mob of "motor changes" in the brain?', he asks.[85] The 'Order' of nature and the faculties, and the 'Force' of the human will, are the necessary conditions for satisfying human life. Spencer, though the most able of the new generation of psychologists, can see differences only of degree, and not of kind.

[79] Ibid. 260.    [80] Ashton, *George Eliot: A Life*, 110, 124–5.
[81] Quoted in *The Wellesley Index*, iii. 140.    [82] MacCall, *The Newest Materialism*, 94, 89.
[83] [Hutton], 'Atheism', 103.    [84] Ibid. 97.    [85] Ibid. 104, 122.

As a result (and this, once again, is the central arm of the attack), Spencer cannot understand the action, nature, and special status of the human will, for it is the will that generates the 'creative force' of the moral life. Alongside it, 'all the so-called "material forces" are but the mapped-out courses of an invisible power'.[86]

Hutton's arsenal of arguments is familiar and eloquent. But his acuity is greater than these vivid commonplaces may suggest. Hutton was a shrewd and sensitive moral thinker (as his stimulating criticism of George Eliot's fiction suggests[87]), and his uncompromising commitment to the defence of religion independent of the findings or theories of science led him to a trenchant objection to Spencer's Lamarckianism. In 'A Questionable Parentage for Morals' (1869) Hutton resumed his attack on Spencer. Specifically, he attacked the theory of acquired characteristics as a basis for the moral life as lived by individual moral agents. Hutton notes the similarity between Spencer's evolutionary scheme and that of the conventional Utilitarian argument for the acquisition of moral values. Though the time scale may be radically different, both theories hold that morals are acquired from without, from the social pressures and conventions obtaining at birth— that is, says Hutton, from 'a dry habit or tendency, which it is *uncomfortable* to resist'.[88] Not only does this substitute mere 'inertia' (the avoidance of disturbance from settled routines) for moral choice and activity; it also cannot account for the particularity of any moral life. How might value be discriminated from habit? In what possible form can moral conceptions be passed from parent to child biologically?

These are intelligent and interesting questions, and they put in doubt Spencer's proposed solution to the old associationist difficulties, for Spencer's theory needs to convert particular associations, and the resultant moral concepts they generate, into general instincts and intuitions. But he cannot specify a means, or even a mode of existence, for such a process, let alone a formal description of an infant's moral inheritance. In reply, Spencer maintained that morals were generated from 'moral sentiments', a non-specific inheritance that comes in the shape of the emotional life, and whose motor is the experience of pleasure.[89] However, though this answers one problem (morals are generated from the active desire for pleasure, and not the passive avoidance of pain), the argument is still where Hutton wants it to be. Spencer's 'new' psychology is a refurbished old Utilitarianism. In his concluding contribution to the exchange, Hutton in fact, though of course unwittingly, indicates the point from which a more developed evolutionary

---

[86] [Hutton], 'Atheism', 119.

[87] See the pieces, both entitled 'George Eliot', in the *National Review*, 11 (1860), 191–219, and the *Contemporary Review*, 47 (1885), 372–91.

[88] R. H. Hutton, 'A Questionable Parentage for Morals', *Macmillan's Magazine*, 20 (1869), 269.

[89] Herbert Spencer, 'Morals and Moral Sentiments', *Fortnightly Review*, NS 9 (1871), 419–32.

ethics might begin. From the point of view of biology, the generation of moral concepts is (in Hutton's strongly pejorative sense) variable and arbitrary, even irrelevant.[90] But, as Huxley and others were to argue, this does not, of itself, make ethics irrelevant to human life or, indeed, evolutionary survival. On the contrary, our ability to intervene ethically not only defines our humanity; it gives an evolutionary advantage because ethical behaviour emphasizes cooperation rather than predation.[91]

Hutton had been a pupil of James Martineau, and, though he formally broke from Unitarianism in 1862, his attitude towards the new psychology remained that of his early mentor. His identification of the personal life as the weak spot in Spencer's theory, and his rejection of Spencer's Lamarckian theories as an unsatisfactory ground for the moral life, were powerful arguments. They indicate a central feature of religious responses to Spencer, and also real weaknesses in his psychological theories. More than most, Spencer's books suffer from an absence of detail. Their theoretical rigour and innovation seems almost in inverse ratio to their human engagements. Thus the concentration on the personal life by critics indicates something about their tone and organization, as well as something about a change in religious argument in the period. The defence of religion was gradually abandoning any claim that the world was, in its material being, organized and directed by God. The weight of evidence, even in the human sciences, was too formidable. Instead theological argument took two directions.

First, religious writers defended the idea of human particularity. Either (in the strongest version of this argument) human beings were categorically different from other orders of creation; or (in its more flexible form) humans were simply too complex for the kinds of analysis offered by the likes of Spencer. Evolutionary theories of the moral life (the most common point of argument) were, if not wrong (though most held them to be so), then dangerously reductive. Therefore, in the absence of a satisfactory theory from psychologists, the arguments of theologians and religious writers were better able to provide the necessary concepts and language for fuller, more sensitive analysis.

If this is an essentially aggressive argument aimed at psychology's weak points, then the second argument was more defensive. Many saw that, because old-school theological accounts of the world had lost credence, it was necessary to build some *rapprochement* with the new sciences. But to do this two conditions were necessary from the religious point of view. First, some effort had to be made to say that psychology had changed over recent years, and was now

---

[90] R. H. Hutton, 'Mr. Herbert Spencer on Moral Intuitions and Moral Sentiments', *Contemporary Review*, 17 (1871), 463–72. For a full discussion of the idea of a 'Darwinian' ethics, see Michael Ruse, *Taking Darwin Seriously: A Naturalistic Approach to Philosophy* (Oxford, 1986).

[91] T. H. Huxley, 'Prolegomena' and 'Evolution and Ethics', in *Evolution and Ethics and Other Essays*, 1–116.

closer to religious ideas than formerly. The crucial issue concerned innate ideas, and, as we have seen, Spencer's theory was equipped to deliver a possible compromise. The second condition (a version of the first) was that psychology should leave sufficient space for religious language in the description of mental activity. Indeed, it is possible to see the quarrels in liberal intellectual circles over the new psychology in the late nineteenth century as quarrels about the purchase rival languages might have on, in particular, the description of the inner life and moral choice. It is possible, for instance, to understand George Eliot's fiction in this way. Her novels are formed from a complex, multi-vocal discourse in which the competing languages of the period vie for descriptive adequacy. Hence the complex range of her conceptual vocabulary, the proliferation of ways of seeing that a narrative such as *Middlemarch* develops, and the fascinatingly diverse range of moral predicaments, or ways of seeing similar moral predicaments, that her best work engages.

These two strands of late-nineteenth-century theological argument can be seen in James Martineau's critique of Spencer. Martineau attacked Spencer in much the same terms, and with much the same expressive flair, as he had attacked Bain in 1860. He argued that the new psychological theories came at the (temporary) end of a long line of explanations—from mythological deities, through notions of divine architecture, to conceptions of the biological processes—which man had concocted through the ages to express his sense of place in the world. Martineau therefore begins with a strong sense of historical change, but this generous historical sense is provisional and illusory, for 'Time counts for nothing with the Eternal'.[92] Martineau's argument is that man perversely tries to construct elaborate accounts of the machinery of the universe when the underlying processes—those that God Himself has established—remain the same. His opening gambit aligns new psychology with ancient error, diminishes the role of non-religious heuristic activity, replaces evolution with teleology, and insists on the autonomy of Mind, which, capitalized, is identified with God and Spirit. Thus, scientists and others may seek elaborate and more or less fanciful 'interpreting conceptions', but patient religion insists only 'that Mind is the first, and rules for ever; and whatever the process be, is its process, moving towards congenial ends. Let this be granted and it matters not by what path or method the Divine Thought advances, or [*sic*] how long it stays on the road.'[93] Some of man's 'interpreting conceptions' can be beneficial to faith, but evolutionary theory is a harmful error. It 'infuses distrust in our self-knowledge, [and] weakens our subjective religion or native faith in the intuitions of thought and conscience'.[94]

[92] James Martineau, 'The Place of Mind and Intuition in Man', *Contemporary Review*, 19 (1872), 607.
[93] Ibid. 607.    [94] Ibid. 608.

Martineau, then, is concerned (as befits a nonconformist analysis) with the under-standing of the inner world of man communicating directly with God. The spiritual advice of Martineau's critique of Spencer is to trust the sanctity of one's inner light, and not theoretical error.

Meanwhile, Martineau set about these errors in familiar terms. Evolutionary psychology, as the latest version of the 'Experience Philosophy', is strained by oversimplification and crude reduction. Complex phenomena are generated from simple premises and from these are supposed to be woven 'the patterned story of imagination, the delicate web of the affections, or the seamless robe of moral purity'. All moral and spiritual achievements are thus merely 'transformed sensations . . . spun out of the coarse fibre of self-love'.[95] The textile metaphors here are typical of the period, and they are—with the exception of the senti-mental robe of purity—shared by Bain, Spencer, Lewes, George Eliot, and others—though Martineau, of course, gives them a very different inflexion. This sharing of metaphors, and the resulting difficulties over how their usage should be read in any given case, is an example of the kind of struggle over language outlined above. George Eliot uses them to express the complexity of the inner life amid a web of determinations; Martineau uses them to validate a case for the autonomy of that life based on connotations of rich, quasi-biblical personal garments. The preoccupation of both writers with egoism is another illustration of the proximity of their concerns, and the variety of ways of understanding them.

A similar example is provided by Martineau's pejorative conception of habit. The mechanism for psychological development in Spencer, and other psycho-logists writing in the associationist tradition, is merely, Martineau claims, the routine of ingrained habit. A comparison with George Eliot is again useful. Eliot has a richer sense of the claims and limitations of habit. In novels such as *Middlemarch* or *The Mill on the Floss*, habit—with its associated ideas of mem-ory and attachment to the past—can be seen as stifling and ensnaring. It restricts intellectual, emotional, and cultural possibility. But it is also seen as an import-ant force in the formation of moral attachments and the making of moral choices. Martineau accuses Spencer of a passive conception of moral activity, a slavish 'deification of public opinion', whose motor is habit.[96] But both Eliot and Spencer had a more robust and incisive sense of the claims of habit on the moral life, and a stronger conviction of its power in the formation of inner and outer creeds, as the career of Maggie Tulliver in *The Mill on the Floss*, for one, illustrates.

Martineau's theory, like many of the same stamp, is essentially an ethical intuitionism. He believes that the moral faculties are innate, and self-acting, and that their origins and functions do not need to be explained or described. Even

[95] Ibid. 609.     [96] Ibid. 610–11.

if the moral faculties did originate in 'animal sensation', he says, psychology 'is not on that account entitled *to measure all that comes after it*' on the same terms.[97] In other words, Martineau rejects evolutionary psychology as an adequate language for attending to the inner life and 'the sacredness of Personal Communication' with God.[98] If, he continues, the analysis of human beings is merely the analysis of power, struggle, and competition (Martineau notes that Spencer's theories are a clear reflection of orthodox political economy), then what is the point and function of human reason and the moral faculty?[99] Spencer, who rarely missed an opportunity for a public defence, replied on both ontological and epistemological grounds. He and Martineau disagreed about the composition of reality, and, he argued, Martineau travestied the version of it given by scientists. For Martineau, matter, reality, was composed of discrete, simple entities held together by an unknown force. Spencer, however, thought of reality, matter itself, as compound. Its diverse forms were built from shared properties and elements, the compounding of which created the world's variety. Conversely, these compounds could be analytically reduced to their component parts, and this was the practice of science. The fact that we did not fully understand this complexity was not, however, a reason to posit an underlying, mysterious entity that controlled, though did not participate in, the functioning of matter or physical forces.[100]

Again, this is a familiar argument. It is essentially the same argument that physiological psychologists had been making about the relation of mind to brain (or body) for some years. As an argument about the composition of matter, it replays quarrels at least as far back as the eighteenth century over the status of physical forces. Were they moved by God, or their own natures? Eighteenth-century Unitarians tended to believe the latter. James Martineau believed the former, and his general argument affected the specific. Because Martineau could not understand this process-based view of matter, claimed Spencer, he could not understand how the new psychology could theoretically generate the complexity of advanced mental phenomena from rudimentary beginnings. Martineau's view of the world, therefore, was based on massive ontological *differences* ('the chasm between the living and the not living', for instance[101]), whereas Spencer's own view was modelled on their 'community'. Nevertheless, Spencer denied charges of materialism, and quoted from *The Principles of Psychology* to the effect that matter and spirit could not be separated. It was not Spencer, therefore, who was dividing spiritual concerns from the world, but Martineau. Such a division was ingrained in his conception of matter. Spencer's are strong, confident arguments,

---

[97] James Martineau, 'The Place of Mind and Intuition in Man', *Contemporary Review*, 19 (1872), 611.

[98] Ibid. 623.      [99] Ibid. 612–19.

[100] Herbert Spencer, 'Mr Martineau on Evolution', *Contemporary Review*, 20 (1872), 141–54.

[101] Ibid. 143.

long-made but only recently accepted, and Martineau's perception of the world is on the defensive. As Spencer noted at the time in a letter to his American friend and patron E. W. Youmans, 'the concessions [in Martineau's article] are large; and its criticisms feeble. It illustrates what continually happens with all parties who stand by the old. If they do nothing, things go against them still more.'[102]

Perhaps as a result, the effort to counteract the perceived anti-religious tendency in Spencer's thought sometimes took on desperate, epic proportions. A case in point is the campaign of St George Mivart (1827–1900), a Catholic convert, ex-barrister, biologist, zoologist, Fellow of the Royal Society, and lead-ing campaigner against evolutionary theory in the 1870s and beyond.[103] Mivart had been on good terms with several leading evolutionists in the 1860s, includ-ing Huxley, who respected his work on anatomy and was influential in Mivart's election as an FRS in 1869. In 1871, though, Mivart played a substantial role in the anti-Darwinian furore over *The Descent of Man* and continued to attack Darwin thereafter for biological anthropomorphism in attributing human qualities to 'brutes'.[104] He maintained his conviction of the essential disparity between organic and inorganic, human and animal, and the higher and lower faculties of mind throughout his career. His truculent, disputatious disposition, and heady mixture of science and faith, dogma and free speech, made him an unusual personality, but a man whose conflicts and quarrels are nevertheless—or even thereby—representative. In a last, pitiful, tragically ironic act, in 1900, the year of his death, he was excommunicated by the Catholic Church for defying their authority by writing, in defence of Catholicism, for the liberal periodicals the *Fortnightly Review* and the *Nineteenth Century*.

His campaign against Spencer began in 1873 in an article for the Tory peri-odical the *Quarterly Review*, which reviewed the second edition of *The Principles of Psychology*, the *Essays*, and the second edition of *First Principles*. The article placed Spencer in the context of the age-old dispute between empiricists, scep-tics, and materialists, on the one hand, and the school of Kant and Reid, on the other. The point at issue was the question of whether the mind possesses innate, *a priori* principles or faculties. Mivart holds that it does. He recognizes Spencer's novel, Lamarckian solution to the problem (what is *a priori* to the individual is *a posteriori* to the race); nevertheless in Spencer, Huxley, Lewes, Bain, and Mill 'Hume lives again'. Added to this is the 'grossest sensationalism' of Comte, and now the evolutionary theories of Spencer and Darwin, who derive

---

[102] Spencer to Youmans, 8 Apr. 1872 (*An Autobiography*, ii. 245).

[103] For details of Mivart's life and career, see the entry in the *DNB Supplement*, ed. Sidney Lee (London, 1901), and J. W. Gruber, *A Conscience in Conflict: The Life of St George Jackson Mivart* (New York, 1961).

[104] William Irvine, *Apes, Angels and Victorians: A Joint Biography of Darwin and Huxley* (London, 1955), 154–5; Beer, *Darwin's Plots*, 68; Desmond, *Huxley: Evolution's High Priest*, 25–8.

the multiplicity of Creation from singularity by 'development'. Thus Shakespeare, Plato, Raphaele (*sic*), and Newton are seen as 'the ultimate outcome of an unconscious primal mist' and men are identified with brutes.[105] Spencer's thought denies 'truth', and threatens moral conviction by denying the efficacy of duty, the capacity to choose freely, and the autonomy and capacity of the will. In addition, human capacities are brought into contagious proximity to the passions of brutes. In an age when 'calamitous social and political dangers are urged upon us with the reckless but pertinacious zeal of democratic passion', these kinds of ideas will rot the marrow of the nation whose bones are formed by 'philosophic ideas'. The 'social consequences' of Spencer's ideas are 'manifestly evil in the highest degree', for a 'passionate hatred of religion . . . lies at the bottom of much of the popular metaphysical teaching now in vogue'.[106]

Mivart's article oscillates between this kind of apocalyptic Tory hysteria and more informed and telling comment on Spencer's work (his comments on Spencer's epistemology are very shrewd). However, Mivart was by no means content to leave matters there. In 1874 he commenced an extraordinary, nine-part, 240-page, six-year-long account of Spencer's psychology for the Catholic *Dublin Review*. 'An Examination of Herbert Spencer's Psychology' is, I think, the most extraordinary thing I have read in the course of research for this book. Polemical, repetitive, furiously accusatory, and deeply out of date, Mivart's series of articles is an indication not just of the heat such debates produced in this period, but also of a generational crisis among Christians involved in scientific dispute. For, on the one hand, such men and women wanted to maintain their faith and convictions, but, on the other, the weight of argument and evidence was forcing them to concede ground rapidly.

The arguments Mivart offers in the 'Examination' are little different from those of his *Quarterly Review* piece, and little different too from many others in the period. But it is their extraordinary length and passion that are fascinating, for what they present is a personality at the edge of its tolerance for rational enquiry, yet pulled back towards such enquiry as if by compulsion. Mivart is facing, on every page, questions of the deepest implication and emotional conviction. 'All the highest questions of philosophy, those concerning God, the human soul, its nature and destiny, have now come to depend on questions of psychology' is the proposition with which he begins the series.[107] Thereafter he is struggling with angels and demons. It is the spectacle of a man wrestling not merely with his enemies, but with the two sides of his own convictions. By the close, after rejecting the major founding principles on which Spencer's psychology rests

---

[105] [St George Mivart], 'Herbert Spencer', *Quarterly Review*, 135 (1873), 512.
[106] Ibid. 532, 537.
[107] 'M.' [St George Mivart], 'An Examination of Mr. Herbert Spencer's Psychology: Part I', *Dublin Review*, NS 23 (1874), 476.

—the priority of the biological, the evolutionary continuity between lower and higher (in mental capacity as a well as living species), the Protestant origins of Spencer's intellectual world—Mivart seeks a reconciliation between his own religious faith and an outlook that, one strongly suspects, he knows must carry the future with it. Part nine seeks to enquire how Spencer's philosophy can be reconciled with, even recouped for, Catholicism, and he finds the material for this in the stress on the unknown in Spencer's epistemology, his refusal of Cartesian dualisms, and his acknowledgement that, in the matter of human understanding and belief, mere rationalism will not suffice. Men's convictions are formed in the 'perceptions of the senses' and the hunches of the intellect. At the heart of Spencerian rationality, Mivart claims, is the core of an incipient theology.[108]

The 'Examination' did not end Mivart's struggle to reconcile the basic arguments of the new psychology with religious faith. Some of the pieces that caused his break with Catholic authority were published in the *Nineteenth Century* between 1878 and 1899. In 'Modern Catholics and Scientific Freedom' (1885) he saw no contradiction between his twin vocations as a Catholic and a scientist, and protested against the increasing hostility to science in the church hierarchy. His argument is an off-the-peg one (science looks after its province, and theology takes care of the rest, just as physiology and biology examine the 'merely animal nature of man' leaving other disciplines to nurture and describe other needs), but he ends wishing 'good speed' to the new psychology, and there is no doubting the spiritual bravery of his decisions.[109] In 'The New Psychology' (1899) he appeals to scientific men not to shut themselves off from theological, moral, and spiritual questions, and thus to follow the path of Cartesian dualism. Instead, he argues for a 'unified' view of man and nature, for seeing all living creatures as 'the result of the coalescence of two factors into one absolute unity'. As oxygen and hydrogen are combined in water, so the body and 'immaterial energy' are combined in human beings.[110] Mivart thus goes some way towards meeting the objections Spencer made against Martineau without losing sight of the standard religious arguments of the period. He asks that psychologists, while they continue their study of biological processes, should not neglect the individual and the personal life. It is in the study of the individual that the 'psychical' and spiritual aspects are uppermost. It 'is the immaterial energy, or soul, which thus shows itself, revealing . . . the essential nature of the individual man or woman whose personality may so powerfully yet so mysteriously affect us.'[111]

[108] 'M.' [St George Mivart], 'An Examination of Herbert Spencer's Psychology: Part IX', *Dublin Review*, NS 34 (1880), 26–73.

[109] St George Mivart, 'Modern Catholics and Scientific Freedom', *Nineteenth Century*, 18 (1885), 30–47.

[110] St George Mivart, 'The New Psychology', *Nineteenth Century*, 45 (1899), 264–6.

[111] Ibid. 267.

Mivart's talk of 'immaterial energy' was, of course, unpalatable nonsense for scientifically inclined thinkers, and illustrates that his reconciling intentions were not infinitely tolerant or capable. In an 1878 essay, 'Force, Energy and Will', Mivart rejected absolutely the fashionable notions of the 'transformation of Force' we have encountered in connection with Bain's work and that Spencer also, though rather ambiguously, endorsed.[112] The idea that there was one force running through all things was too much of a 'transformational' idea for Mivart, because it would imply the collapse of hierarchical distinctions, in particular those between species. (The conviction that man was biologically distinct from other animals never left him.) He was, however, prepared to accept the notion as symbolic, as a kind of scientific jargon for the First Cause or God.[113] Elsewhere, responses to the idea varied, though others too found it unpalatable. Thomas Birks could not see why, if such an idea were to be posited, one could not go the whole hog and call it God. 'Positivists' were inconsistent, he claimed: 'Instead of excluding the idea of Force as metaphysical they seem ready to invest it with Divine attributes and place it on the throne of the universe. It is Something uncreated, invariable, indestructible, almighty, and eternal.'[114] On these grounds he also attacked the use of evolutionary theory by liberal theologians. Likewise, though from a different perspective, J. F. Moulton objected to the extended use of the idea of Force beyond its proper scientific meanings by Spencer and others. Spencer turned experimental law into *a priori* positions, thus ruining their scientific status and usefulness.[115] The ambiguity in the idea was teasing. T. H. Green correctly perceived, in his critique of Spencer, that it was unclear whether the knowledge of force was the outcome of simple sensation (therefore epistemologically immediately valid) or an 'intellectual synthesis', in which case its epistemological status was more complicated and dubious.[116]

None the less, the direction of Mivart's intellectual career is representative of a significant turn in the reception Spencer received in religious quarters. Spencer himself detected a change in mood. He recalled in his *Autobiography* that the exchanges with Martineau in 1872 (of which he decisively had the better) seemed

[112] Spencer equivocated on the idea of 'Force', because in the end it does appear a rather metaphysical idea. For discussion, see H. I. Sharlin, 'Herbert Spencer and Scientism', *Annals of Science*, 33 (1976), 457–80, and Oldroyd, *Darwinian Impacts*, 210. Spencer claimed he had drafted a 'one-force' argument in writing *The Principles of Psychology* in the early 1850s (which would have made him an innovator here also) but suppressed it because of his uncertainty about its validity (*An Autobiography*, ii. 13–16).

[113] St George Mivart, 'Force, Energy and Will', *Nineteenth Century*, 3 (1878), 933–48.

[114] Birks, *Modern Physical Fatalism*, 218.

[115] [J. F. Moulton], 'Herbert Spencer', *British Quarterly Review*, 58 (1873), 472–504.

[116] T. H. Green, 'Mr. Spencer and Mr. G. H. Lewes: Their Application of the Doctrine of Evolution to Thought. Part Two: Mr. Spencer on the Independence of Matter', in *Works*, ed. R. L. Nettleship, 2 vols. (London, 1906), i. 434.

to mark a liberalization of theological opinion that continued.[117] Certainly several Christian writers welcomed—more or less enthusiastically—the possible reconciliation between science and religion that Spencer's theories, and their overarching 'system', appeared to offer. A reviewer of *First Principles* in 1863 for the *British Quarterly Review*, a nonconformist evangelical periodical committed to free discussion, seized on the 'force' idea with more enthusiasm than Mivart, or, for that matter, Spencer. He vividly pictured it at work in the crashing of cannonballs, in the clumping steps of dinosaurs through primeval forests, and the whizzing molecules of the rings of Saturn. It was the 'actuality underlying phenomena . . . beyond the reach of human intellect . . . Ever near us, the one Divine and Omnipotent mystery of the world, it remains unchanged and insoluble for all the petty strivings of our reason', surpassing 'immeasurably the most transcendental analysis that man has ever been able to invent'.[118] But this is intellectual gold-plating. The reviewer was sceptical of most of Spencer's theories. He ends attacking him for 'practical Atheism', and advising him to surrender his intellectual pride for the beauty of the idea his theories contain, but scarcely acknowledge.

Similarly, another *British Quarterly* writer in 1874 attacked the 'rubbish heaps' and 'dwarfs' of Positivism, but found in Spencer's work the possibility of a reconciliation of science and religion made possible by the loosening of the 'materialistic dogmatism' he had detected in scientific circles of late. Spencer acknowledged the mystery of existence beneath rationalistic enquiry. As a result, 'science cannot scorn religion as dealing any more itself with the "*unknowable*"; and religion must not frown down science as a traitor to the highest interests of humanity'. Spencer is to be welcomed because of his 'tone of brotherhood towards religion'.[119] What is also interesting about this piece is that the writer is clearly a Germanist (it offers itself as a review of a recent lecture by Carpenter and *Gott und die Natur* by Dr Von Hermann Ulrici, which dates from 1866), and he sees a connection between Spencer and the Romantic *Naturphilosophie* that influenced Coleridge.[120]

For his own part, Spencer, perhaps cannily, continued to keep his options open. In a postscript added to part 1 of the sixth edition of *First Principles* dated March 1899, he wrote:

But an account of the Transformation of Things, given in the pages which follow, is simply an orderly presentation of facts; and the interpretation of facts is nothing more than a statement of the ultimate uniformities they present—the laws to which they

[117] Spencer, *An Autobiography*, ii. 247.   [118] Anon., 'Spencer's First Principles', 9.
[119] Anon., 'Science, Philosophy, and Religion', *British Quarterly Review*, 60 (1874), 107–8.
[120] There is some evidence for such a connection, though Spencer never really read very far in anything. See the discussion of Spencer in Robert M. Young, *Mind, Brain and Adaptation*.

conform. Is the reader an atheist? The exposition of these facts and these laws will neither yield support to his belief nor destroy it. Is he a pantheist? The phenomena and the inferences as now set forth will not force on him any incongruous implication. Does he think that God is immanent throughout all things, from concentrating nebulae to the thoughts of poets? Then the theory to be put before him contains no disproof of that view. Does he believe in a Deity who has given unchanging laws to the Universe? Then he will find nothing at variance with his belief in an exposition of those laws and an account of the results.[121]

The distinction between fact and interpretation that Spencer uses here is a familiar one from many hermeneutic theories. It also repeats an argument that, by the time Spencer wrote this, had been in use for half a century to make friends between science and religion. As we saw in Part One of this book, it had been offered by H. L. Mansel in his Bampton lectures in 1858, in which he had argued that religion was beyond science, because the latter deals only with objects that can be conceived rationally in finite terms. Religion, therefore, had no need to feel threatened by science, and vice versa. As Peel argues, this argument was opportunely similar to the kind of arguments Spencer himself wanted to make in the 1850s, and, as we have seen, continued to make until his death.[122] A discussion of how this argument related to the epistemology Spencer offered in *The Principles of Psychology*, and an assessment of the strengths and limitations of that epistemology, will close this chapter.

### EPISTEMOLOGY, EVOLUTIONARY PSYCHOLOGY, AND THE IDEALIST CRITIQUE

The *British Quarterly* writer on 'Science, Philosophy, and Religion', who, as we have seen, was well disposed towards Spencer, none the less attacked Bain for basing his epistemology on the direct apprehension of phenomena alone, irrespective of the activities of the mind perceiving these phenomena. As a result, he says, Bain's classically associationist theories rest on an infinite regress like 'the Hindoo sense of the elephant upon the tortoise'.[123] What, then, was so different about Spencer's account, and why did it appeal to writers such as this?

The first edition of *The Principles of Psychology*, unlike subsequent editions, begins with a consideration of epistemological questions. By the second edition (begun in 1867) Spencer had altered the arrangement to bring the book into line with the increasingly standard practice, pioneered in influential textbooks by Bain and Wundt, to begin with physiology and work up to psychology. Thus the form of these books mimicked the genetic account of the formation of mind

---

121 Herbert Spencer, *First Principles*, 6th edn. (London, 1904), 95–6.
122 Peel, *Herbert Spencer*, 127.
123 Anon., 'Science, Philosophy, and Religion', 109–10.

the theory proposed. In the second and third editions of *The Principles of Psychology*, Spencer began with his evolutionary theories. Part 1 of the first edition, which tackles epistemological questions, now forms part 7, and the entire first volume is concerned with biological and physiological topics. In the preface, he speaks of the 'philosophical' topics being 'relegated' in importance.[124] Yet Spencer had chosen the organization of the first edition quite deliberately. In the *Autobiography* he says that the four parts of the original were written in the order three, one, two, four[125]—that is, Spencer had conceived of the biological part first. He then chose to organize the book differently. We may wonder why.

Part of the answer is, no doubt, that, in spite of his innovative introduction of biology, he was writing in the early 1850s in a discipline that was predominantly still thought to belong to philosophy rather than the natural sciences. Anyone opening a book called *The Principles of Psychology* would have expected attention to epistemological or other philosophically oriented topics. But I think there was a deeper reason also concerned with the book's originality. An enthusiastic review of the second edition by Douglas Spalding for *Nature* in 1873 gives a clue. Spencer, says Spalding, is the first serious defender of a realist epistemology since the time of Hume and Berkeley—thinkers who rendered a defence inconceivable for the best part of a century.[126] Spalding exaggerates, but associationism *was* beset by epistemological difficulties, because it could not, except by assertion, negotiate the transition from physiological to mental events—that is, it tended to finesse its epistemological difficulties by assuming that the brain and nervous system stored or copied replicas of external events. The idea of representation was, therefore, in classical associationism, not problematic enough. Bain, for instance, as late as the 1880s, could see the fierce realism versus Idealism quarrels of those years only as an unnecessary and distracting difficulty provoked by the Idealist's refusal to think with common sense, as people did spontaneously if left to themselves.[127] His reluctance to engage may well signal that he had no answers.

Meanwhile the essentially Idealist tradition of faculty psychology was as intuitionist in its epistemology as in its ethics. Expert Idealist thinkers such as T. H. Green splendidly diagnosed Spencer's failings, but did not move the argument much beyond the old stand-off between the 'experience' and the 'intuitionist' schools. The stakes were high. The revival of interest in German Idealist thought, to which Green's critiques of Spencer and Lewes were a contribution, reopened these quarrels, partly because the refurbished realism promulgated by Spencer and others, flowing with the general scientific tide, was bidding powerfully for

---

124 Spencer, *Principles of Psychology*, 3rd edn., p. vii.
125 Spencer, *An Autobiography*, i. 460–1.
126 Douglas A. Spalding, 'Herbert Spencer's Psychology: Part 2', *Nature*, 7 (1873), 357–9.
127 Bain, 'Mr. Spencer's Psychological "Congruities"', 394–406.

the current of mainstream opinion, including that of liberally minded religious thinkers. Meanwhile, Spencer, attempting to launch an innovative psychological theory based on scientific rather than philosophical grounds, needed to deliver an epistemology that would reach that main current, but which would also satisfy the expectations of the discipline within which he was working. He needed to establish a philosophical defence for switching that discipline from philosophy to biology, and try to negotiate the religious and political debate that surrounded psychology in the mid-century. The language to hand for such an enterprise was that of the classical problems of philosophy addressed in Chapter 2 of this book. This is why epistemological questions are at the very front of our attention when we read the first edition of *The Principles of Psychology*. As C. U. M. Smith notes, making a strong case for the success of Spencer's modernizing ambitions, his epistemology has sometimes been seen as only tangentially related to the biological part of his psychology (perhaps, one might think, because he himself 'relegated' it). In fact, though, the two elements are closely and necessarily entwined.[128]

*The Principles of Psychology* of 1855 begins with some fundamental questions. What is the test that validates any knowledge? On what terms do we think we know the properties of matter, or other minds? On what grounds can we construct knowledge propositions about ourselves, when the subject that proposes that knowledge is also its object? Spencer rejects introspection, or 'unaided internal perception', as he calls it. We do not know things spontaneously, he argues, otherwise how could error ever have existed? The faculties do not simply leap into being. (This, by the way, was also Spencer's answer to those in the realist camp who wondered why he bothered making an epistemological case at all.[129]) What special mode of cognition is it that rescues psychology, and other forms of knowledge, from 'a mere aggregation of opinions'? Spencer's answer is to seek to 'make a particular mode of perception the guarantee of all other modes'.[130] In other words, he will not accept that there is a mode of cognition, categorically different from perception (such as divine revelation, for instance), that stands as a guarantee of truth. Thus, the validity of a knowledge proposition must be gauged *in relation to* other perceptual operations, and Spencer's epistemology is, like his psychology generally, a strongly relational theory. As the French writer Ribot—whose *English Psychology* Spencer praised in the preface to the second edition of *The Principles*—put it, Spencer gives to perception the 'supremacy which metaphysicians ascribe to reason', for perception is the 'organic classification of relations' obtaining in the world outside the perceiving self. Realism is,

---

[128] C. U. M. Smith, 'Evolution and the Problem of Mind: Part 1: Herbert Spencer', 82–4.

[129] This question was asked, for instance, by the freethinker F. B. Barton in his review in the *Reasoner* in 1856 and, as we have seen, later by Bain.

[130] Spencer, *Principles of Psychology*, 4.

therefore, justified, because it is simpler, and does not require psychological machinery other than the standard forms of cognitive activity. It does not, that is, sever subject from object.[131]

Spencer rejects Idealism (Fichte and Schelling) and scepticism (Hume). He also rejects Reid's—or, for that matter, Bain's—common-sense realism ('right as Reid may have been in his convictions, he cannot be said to have demonstrated he was so'). He rejects, too, Hamilton's neo-Kantian intuitionist identification of subject and object as simultaneously present in consciousness in acts of cognition. Spencer believes that such moments of apparent intuition can be decomposed into simpler, more rudimentary elements.[132] As Ribot explained, Spencer held that there were two series of events, the internal and the external, which have their own regularities, but which do correspond, though the connecting (Spencer would say 'causal') chains were sometimes complex and indirect. Epistemological questions, for Spencer, were questions of belief in the connections proposed. Any account of the epistemology of science, as of ordinary behaviour, was an effort to establish '*not any substantive proposition believed, but some canon of belief itself*'.[133] As Burrow, Peel, and others point out, Spencer thus substitutes psychological categories for logical ones within his epistemology, and has a causal, rather than logical, approach to meaning.[134]

Spencer called his epistemological theory 'the universal postulate' and, later, 'transfigured realism'. By the universal postulate he meant to indicate an idea in some ways similar to Karl Popper's criterion of falsifiability—that is, one cannot know the truth about the world absolutely. Instead one devises more or less adequate theories about it, which, it is likely, will be falsified as time goes on. None the less, while they prevail, these function with more or less adequacy, as though they were true. Spencer's idea is similar. (Though it should be said that

[131] Ribot, *English Psychology*, 180–4. Subsequent editions of *The Principles of Psychology* incorporated Ribot's point directly. Spencer warned against the 'usurpation' of cognition by reason. The cultivation of the reason often led to it becoming itself 'the final object of superstition', and the 'worship' of abstract metaphysics, 'an amputated limb in empty space'. 'Perception' (i.e. empiricism) was much better (*Principles of Psychology*, 3rd edn., ii. 314–35). The point was virtual anyway in the first edition, which very early rejected such devices in logic as the analysis of the syllogism as a means for psychological investigation. Intelligence, for Spencer, was more than reasoning.

[132] Spencer, *Principles of Psychology*, 5–10. The attack on Idealism is much expanded in subsequent editions. See e.g. ii, pt. VIII.                    [133] Ibid. 12.

[134] The general mid-nineteenth-century context of these arguments, particularly that of the Mill/Whewell disputes about scientific procedure, is well set out by Peel, who also points to Spencer's influence on American 'pragmatists' like Dewey and James in the early twentieth century. He further notes that the kind of theory Spencer is outlining has been widely influential in science under the name 'operationalism' (Peel, *Herbert Spencer*, 117–20). See also Burrow, *Evolution and Society*, 209–13. Maurice Mandelbaum points out that Spencer's epistemology, and his emphasis on belief rather than 'truth' (and therefore a fundamental 'unknowingness' in an absolute sense), is typical of a general turn in nineteenth-century thought. See Mandelbaum, *History, Man, and Reason: A Study in Nineteenth-Century Thought* (London, 1971), ch. 14.

the design of his theories is not at all Popperian, because they are designed to assert truth claims and not to encourage falsification. We shall return to this contradiction.) Spencer holds that we believe when the alternative is inconceivable. The burden of validation is thus shifted away from the notional, inherent *properties* of mind, such as the faculties, towards the *activities* of the mind in experience. The mind does act as though its beliefs and convictions are held *a priori*, but, in reality, the mind discovers them, and maybe revises them, as it matures. Spencer's 'universal postulate' is that a belief prevails in the absence of a better belief, or because rival beliefs are not so irreplaceable, necessary, or easy to adapt. But a principle of economy holds good in Spencer's theory, for beliefs are less easily sustainable the more complicated they are, and it is axiomatic that beliefs can, like all mental contents, be themselves decomposed into simpler elements. The essential beliefs, therefore, are those that have fewest components.[135] This, however, is a 'transfigured' and not a 'naïve' realism. It does not assert that mental contents correspond in an unmediated way to the world outside the mind's operations.

There is a clear homology between Spencer's epistemological and biological theories. Both claim to be based on experience rather than *a priori* principles, and both develop ideas of competition among their elements rather than relying on pre-established hierarchies. Indeed, it seems that an idea prevails in much the same way as a creature: by being able to concentrate on essential features, meet the needs and challenges of the environment, and form part of a structure of adjacent, similar, or supporting ideas. Thus, the reason why Spencer's psychology prevailed (for example) might be because its structure is clear and coherent, because it responded to the demands of the intellectual environment to look at relevant new facts and resist antagonistic conceptions, and because it was able to integrate with relevant existing paradigms (which included the associationist tradition in psychology, evolutionary thought in the natural sciences, Utilitarian social theory, political economy, and, with more limited success, the liberal element in religious thought).

Spencer's epistemology is dynamic in intention and substance, and it is theoretically coherent in relation to the rest of his psychology. Its realism is posited on the fact that viewpoints are multiple, but changeable, and that, though human cognition works by the construction of its world, these constructions are readily open to embarrassment by the world outside them. This, as Smith, Peel, and others have pointed out, is a very modern style of thinking, and, just as George Eliot's novels are not, as has been claimed, written in a mode of naïve, expressive realism, so Spencer's epistemology is not dumbly transcriptive either. Indeed, it is tempting to push the parallel further and recall once again the incident at Dagley's farm in chapter 39 of *Middlemarch*. That incident is constructed by

---

[135] Spencer, *Principles of Psychology*, 14–35.

Eliot (and it is very typical of her practice) in terms of the differences in perception of no fewer than *seven* subjectivities: the sentimental, artistically inclined, upper-class 'observer' who finds the scene picturesque and with whom the episode starts, Mr Brooke, Mr Dagley, Mrs Dagley, the tartly observed habitué of intellectual London with whom the episode ends, the narrator, and the reader, who may be imagined to share some of the traits and blindnesses of the visiting observer and the London intellectual. (In fact one might even want to say there are two readers—and therefore eight subjectivities in play—if a distinction is made between the reader of the 1870s and that of today.) The episode gains its epistemological (and ethical) effect by juxtaposing these subjectivities in the knowledge that each is partial, and none shares precisely the others' preconceptions or interests. Each (some more evidently than others) is constructing a way of understanding, and the overall account of particular, contingent, and sometimes disrupted and changing pictures of the world is strikingly similar to the epistemological and cognitive world envisaged by Spencer, and, as we shall see, G. H. Lewes in psychological theory. The episode is also representative of the world of the novel, for *Middlemarch* is a work concerned with limitation, with characters who do not *know enough*—about their own worlds, about the other worlds with which they come into contact, or about themselves.

This is the radical, realist epistemology at the heart of the fictional technique of George Eliot and the new psychology of Spencer and Lewes. But, as regards Spencer, this is not the whole story, for Spencer's theory can also appear a dogmatic positivism of an intimidating, creed-building, assertive, 'typically nineteenth-century' kind, which has been scorned by twentieth-century thinkers from Wittgenstein and Popper to contemporary literary theorists. The manner of the multiple tomes of the 'synthetic philosophy', and its ambition to be a complete 'system', appears to contradict at every turn the exacting, critical epistemology it announces. To many contemporaries—younger readers especially—Spencer's psychology appeared every bit as 'metaphysical' as those it claimed to scorn. T. H. Green (1836–82) accused Spencer of this (though in order to reinstate metaphysics), and J. F. Moulton (1844–1921), a young London barrister and MP, whose heavy criticisms of Spencer's conception of 'Force' we have already encountered, was more forthright still. Spencer's theories do have an elegant appeal, he says, but they are metaphysical through and through. Though appearing to proselytize for science, Spencer in fact 'bullies the poor physicist as other metaphysicians do', and the resulting pseudo-metaphysics is a '*mélange* of absurdities and contradictions'. As a result, Spencer is not even 'to be trusted in the inductive portion of the work, since he is strangely incapable of distinguishing between superficial and deep-seated resemblances'.[136]

---

[136] [Moulton], 'Herbert Spencer', 474, 479, 501.

The contradiction in Spencer's work is not merely a matter of 'metaphysical appearance' contradicting 'scientific substance'. There are genuine difficulties at the heart of the epistemological part of Spencer's psychology that compromise it. But it is again important to stress that these also enabled it, in the late nineteenth century, to appear attractive to Christians and others who would ordinarily be scandalized by its evolutionism, its materialism, and its, if not atheism, then blank absence of any substantial attention to God, however adroitly coy Spencer may have been in public pronouncement on the issue. In the chapters on perception in part 2, Spencer argues that every perception involves recognition and classification, and vice versa. Perception thus involves placing things in classes on the basis of likeness: 'the perception of any object, therefore, is impossible save under the form either of Recognition or Classification.' Further, 'All psychologists concur in the doctrine that most of the elements which go to make up the cognition of an observed object, are not known immediately through the senses, but are mediately known by an instantaneous and unconscious ratiocination.' For instance, perceptions of solidity, weight, dimension, and so on, are inferential, and not direct sensations. All cognitions are *acquired*, even 'those apparently simple though really very complex cognitions, by which we guide ourselves through the street'. These, too, involve classification and recognition. Spencer's conclusion is, therefore, that 'the divisions we make between the various mental processes have merely a superficial truth'. For example, the distinction between reasoning (which seems indirect) and perception (which seems direct) will not hold, for the mental operations we think of as distinctive to each of these operations are actually a part of the other also. All perception is mediate, 'the directness and indirectness is wholly a matter of degree'.[137]

Spencer's analytical method is to decompose the complex into the simple. But what is the simple here? Analytical decomposition would seem more like an endless regress, because perceptual acts always seem to depend on prior acquisitions, 'before-known attributes, before-known relations, and before-known conditions'.[138] The argument is circular when one considers it genetically. How did the first classifications arise? How is the transition from sensation to perception affected? The condition of existence of the latter is the classification of the already known: 'the *process* of perception consists in the unconscious classing of these impressions, relations, and conditions, with the like before known ones.'[139] Spencer's epistemology can appear as though it cannot distinguish its chickens from its eggs. The difficulty is threefold. First, Spencer has handed over the genetic problem (how classificatory sets get started) to evolutionary theory (we are born with the acquisitions of our ancestors). He can thus finesse the difficulty by pointing down the mists of time, without having to worry too much about the

[137] Spencer, *Principles of Psychology*, 185–9.    [138] Ibid. 207.    [139] Ibid. 229.

cognitive adequacy of the categories in place (they have been tried and tested through generations of experience).

Secondly, because previous psychological theories have built false distinctions between the various perceptual or cognitive operations, Spencer can gain a rhetorical victory by insisting that the differences we imagine between, say, reasoning and perceiving are not absolute. However, this still leaves the distinctions he does use (for example, those between sensation, perception, and cognition) unexplained and undefined. Further, he derives these from just those earlier psychologists whose taxonomies he so strongly rejects. The problem is genetic and developmental: how does an individual (or indeed a race) get from a sensation to a perception? But it is also a relatively simple conceptual problem concerning the definition of terms that, in Spencer's hands, seem to slide about rather too easily in ways that baffle or compromise his meaning from time to time. For example, when he distinguishes between sensation and perception, he is forced to backtrack alarmingly. Sensation *is* a rudimentary kind of perception (because there are no absolute distinctions between mental processes), but it is distinguished *from* perception proper because the latter is 'the cognition of an external object'.[140] There are two problems with this. First, what is the difference between a perception and a cognition, and, if there is none, why are two different terms used? Secondly, from where do we get the essential distinction between inner and outer that organizes the whole cognitive field at this level, and that seems to imply that there *is* a categorical difference between sensation and perception? As Spencer had earlier admitted, the whole of his account of perception is dependent on a sense of 'outness', of 'something separate from consciousness—something belonging, not to the mind, but to an object out of the mind'.[141] His argument that the distinction between inner and outer is then partly one of degree ('intensity' or 'vividness'), and partly one of experience stretching back into evolutionary time, is theoretically consistent, but does not answer the substantial epistemological difficulty, as T. H. Green realized with glee. Green accuses Spencer (quite rightly it seems to me) of confusing 'Fact and logical thing, real essence and nominal essence, events in the way of sensation and events in our mental history' by insisting on only *quantitative* distinctions.[142]

Given the obstructive hierarchies and distinctions made among mental activities in Spencer's day, one can understand why he wished to reject the very idea of distinction in a psychology that is process based. And one can understand too that, at basic levels of activity like the neurological, Spencer's insistence on seeing all processes as similar (sometimes to the point of identity) has an arguable truth also, especially in the context of the neurological knowledge of his period.

---

[140] Ibid. 279.     [141] Ibid. 220.
[142] T. H. Green, 'Spencer on the Independence of Matter', in *Works*, i. 421.

It adds weight to his adjustment from hierarchical to 'flat' or 'networked' systems across his whole psychology. However, his failure to make necessary distinctions at other levels is very damaging, and was a hostage to fortune to acute critics like Green. An influential modern writer on psycho-biology, Steven Rose, conceptualizes the problem in a way that exposes Spencer's difficulty. Rose argues that the psycho-biological account of mental activity must be organized in a hierarchy of explanatory levels. These might, typically, stretch from (this is taken from Rose's own diagram) the physical, through to the chemical, anatomical–biological, physiological, psychological (mentalistic), and the social.[143] The boundaries between these levels are not absolute, but operational. They are ways of organizing data and explanation such that the relevant phenomena are respected and given due account. In this way the statement 'He is in love' can be described in terms of 'the movement of electrons, the turnover of molecules or the firing of cells' but not *only* in that way.[144] The flexibility of Rose's operational hierarchy does much to clarify the problems endemic to nineteenth-century arguments, which, understandably, were often of the 'all-or-nothing' kind, and, in ignorance and polemic, made too few distinctions when more and different were needed from both sides.

The third problem in Spencer's epistemology is more philosophically oriented, but none the less follows pretty directly from these considerations. It too concerns distinctions and differences. As we have seen, for Spencer, the perceptual process is organized by recognition and classification. That is, it is organized by the apprehension of similarity. To place things into classes is to organize them on the basis of perceived likenesses among the members of that class. Yet, once again, it is difficult to perceive how the organization of this system of resemblances originates. In Spencer's explanation of the origin of this process (which, in his book, appears somewhat later than his original account of perception), he stresses the importance of *unlikeness*, not similarity. The cognition of likeness is 'two relations of likeness which neutralize each other', but 'the relation of unlikeness is the primordial one—is the relation involved in every other relation'.[145] The strength of this theory is its stress on the *relations* between phenomena, and on the apprehension of difference as the foundation of perception. One weakness is its commitment to the old mode of analysis, whereby sensations, perceptions, and other mental events are parsed out like sentences on the principle of uniform origin and development. Another weakness is the difficulty of seeing how, from a system of differences, any structure of resemblances begins to occur.

---

[143] Steven Rose, *The Conscious Brain*, rev. edn. (Harmondsworth, 1976), 28–33.
[144] Ibid. 340.    [145] Spencer, *Principles of Psychology*, 316.

Spencer regularly insists that the perception of relationships, as of phenomena themselves, is founded in experience. (The following is a typical example: 'the reader should be reminded that this analysis of the relation of co-existence, resulting as it does from the conclusion that it is a relation disclosed by experience, supplies the ultimate disproof of the hypothesis that Space is a form of thought.'[146]) But it is still difficult to envisage how the mind's construction of sets or classes develops. Spencer, as in this example, is keen to deny that the mind possesses *a priori*, Kantian 'forms of thought' like Space or Time, yet it does seem that resemblance is one such form of thought, because it is generated from nothing in the formal description of the system and its mechanisms. These difficulties seem to have struck a reviewer for the *Westminster* in 1856. The writer—probably H. B. Wilson, a liberal theologian—comments that the realist epistemology is endangered by the lack of a 'permanent fulcrum' that can make sense of the 'consciousness of change'.[147] That is, Spencer's epistemology lacks a steadying mechanism that can hold the ensemble of differences together. The strong sense of the differences between phenomena, which is stressed in parts of *The Principles of Psychology*, threatens to produce an atomistic mental world that cannot generate the classes of phenomena and relations on which the rest of the epistemology depends. If similarities cancel ('neutralize') each other, one is left with a very long string of different things. The problem is part of a paradox rather like that exploited much more recently by Jacques Derrida. If one is going to talk about structured phenomena, what is it that structures the structure?[148] Is it a property of the things that make up the structure, or is it composed from without?

The problem is a persistent one in all set theory, of course, but it is one that was ruthlessly exposed by T. H. Green, who claimed, with some justice, that it was typical of all epistemologies written in the Lockean 'experience' tradition. The error lies in the confusion of sensations with perceptions of relations. For Green they are categorically different things, and he charges Spencer, like Locke, with confusing feelings of touch with judgements of solidity. The one is a passive reception of stimuli, the other an active construction by the mind. As a result, he says, Spencer blurs subject and object, fails to define what he understands by consciousness (which seems to be a 'limbo of fleeting states' for the most part, says Green), and fails to answer Hume's sceptical challenge, for Hume had driven a wedge into realism on the basis of such distinctions. Thus, most of Spencer's supposedly 'realist' epistemology might legitimately be claimed as their own by Hume or Berkeley. Spencer covers the case with a fog

---

[146] Ibid. 309.     [147] [Wilson?], 'Theology and Philosophy', 42.
[148] Jacques Derrida, 'Structure, Sign and Play in the Discourse of the Human Sciences', in *Writing and Difference*, trans. Alan Bass (London, 1978).

of 'mechanical or physiological metaphors', but the figurative language of streams, threads, and so on is merely an attempt to fashion 'a shelter for the ambiguity'.[149] In the preface to the third edition of *The Principles of Psychology* (1880), Spencer, responding in part to Green's criticism, pictures himself as a victim of 'political or theological' warfare between realism and Idealism, science and religion. Attacked from both sides, he can see 'an element of truth in each' and argues that a compromise is to be found in his 'Transfigured Realism'.[150] It is a weak argument.

Such, then, were the difficulties and achievements of Spencer's theory. He played a principal part in shifting the paradigm of British psychology towards biology, and in doing so offered to update its model of analysis by refurbishing classical associationism and defending and defining a realist epistemology. These achievements were not without the problems we have outlined. As ever, however, the construction of psychological discourse was not the work of one individual. Others of the same generation working in the same areas had other proposals, and tackled these problems with other theories. We therefore turn now to the related, but different, efforts of G. H. Lewes towards ends recognizably cognate, but approached quite differently.

[149] T. H. Green, 'Spencer on Subject and Object' and 'Spencer on the Independence of Matter', in *Works*, i, *passim*.　　　　[150] Spencer, *Principles of Psychology*, 3rd edn., p. vi.

CHAPTER 7

# G. H. Lewes: History, Mind, and Language

## PROBLEMS OF TEXT AND CONTEXT

A consideration of the work of G. H. Lewes is an appropriate place to close this book, for Lewes is representative of the kind of intellectual whose work has formed its substance. Living and working outside the mainstream institutional life of his times, profiting by the career available to Victorian freelance writers through the periodical press, and drawing upon intellectual resources that were unorthodox and challenging, Lewes's career is similar, in this respect, to that of Spencer, Bain, and George Eliot. His intellectual style, too, was typical: versatile, polymathic, innovative, politically dissenting, with an ear turned to Europe and the provinces rather than the traditional seats of learning, he, like Spencer and Bain, was an exhaustive constructor of an encompassing account of life and culture that would satisfy serious minds in scope as well as details.

For us today, more accustomed to an intellectual world of partiality, discontinuity, and fragmentation, this style of thinking is often characterized pejoratively—as displacement (for lost religion), as a bid for mastery and intellectual totality in an imperial age, or as merely naïve ('Positivist') faith in the clarity of the world. But, for Victorian intellectuals without ready-made institutional affiliations (guaranteeing place and forms of belief), these systems answered needs, and enabled a more generously encompassing vision of culture and the intellectual life. Lewes's career, as a novelist, playwright, actor, editor, journalist, literary critic, biographer, historian of philosophy, philosopher of science, Comtist, leading figure in London (and European) scientific circles, and eminent psycho-physiologist, is not just evidence of a flexible and omnivorous intelligence (still less of a third-rate, butterfly mind, as sometimes appears from assessments of him). Rather it is testimony to an intellectual milieu and cultural ethos that embraced science and literature, philosophy and empirical work (Lewes was a great visitor of German laboratories and cutter-up of frogs in his own basement), as well as the study of history, society, and the political life of his times. What is also distinctive about this intellectual culture is that it saw these various enterprises as essentially related.

Yet Lewes was not quite a system-builder in the manner of Bain or Spencer. Spencer's controlled (and controlling) systemization is apparent to anyone who surveys the run of his books on a library shelf with their homogeneous titles, methods, and procedure. Bain too, though not in quite this way, also offered to complete the systematic intellectual project handed to him by the tradition within which he worked, and attempted the thorough anatomy of the human mind and behaviour. Lewes's work, with the same materials and something of the same objectives, is much more piecemeal, much less sustained in its project, much better able to respond and change direction, much less tied to a single uniform vision. *Problems of Life and Mind* is an example. With its five volumes, uniform spines, and over 2,000 pages, it looks like a another swollen Spencerian performance. But in fact its nature is quite other, and what immediately strikes many readers is how confusing it is to try to get any purchase on it as a united project.

It appears—indeed is—rather sprawling and ill-organized in a way that is not merely due to the fact that it remained unfinished at his death. The whole seems to contain different elements, without a compelling sense of relationship or organization. The volumes are of different lengths and are written within different registers of address and language. Volume four, *The Study of Psychology*, for example, is a popularizing digest of contemporary ideas written in his most patient, expository manner. Other volumes are more densely technical (like volume three, which deals with advanced physiological theory, drawing on the latest European research), and an accessible introduction to the series is not best effected by an opening pair of forbidding volumes dealing with epistemological questions. Finally, the fifth and last volume is frankly speculative in a rather piecemeal fashion, which, again, is not entirely explained by the fact that it was unfinished. The whole is also irritatingly repetitive—though in this respect it is no different from comparable works by Spencer and Bain, and an early reviewer thought this a justified tactic, because of the lax habits of attention of contemporary readers.[1] Altogether, then, it is perhaps not surprising that this ungainly sequence should not have been in print since its first publication. However, it should also be said that initial sales were good, and the first volume outsold similar ventures by either Spencer or Bain. It sold 800 promptly ('a good sale', as George Eliot remarked[2]) and a second edition was requested by the publishers within a couple of months.[3]

By and large, *Problems of Life and Mind* was neglected by twentieth-century commentators. This is something to do with its bulk and unpromising form, no doubt, but it is also due to the long shadow thrown by George Eliot's reputation. Because of his varied career, and his relationship with her, certain endemic cultural prejudices have come into play, and Lewes has been seen as a

---

[1] Anon., 'Lewes's Problems of Life and Mind', *Saturday Review*, 40 (1875), 301–2.
[2] George Eliot to Mrs Bray, 22 Dec. 1873, *Letters*, v. 472.    [3] Ibid. 8.

writer who more properly belongs to the literary half of the two cultures.[4] Just as certain styles of literary criticism (like that represented by Leavis's influential *The Great Tradition*) came to terms with George Eliot's scientific interests by ignoring them, so Lewes's major work has become largely invisible. A fierce early remark by A. T. Kitchel is representative of a larger habit: praising Lewes's literary criticism, she comments that 'English criticism suffered a loss when powers like these were swamped in the scientific flood'.[5] Sister Kitchel, no doubt, had her own axe to grind, but the subsequent hostility of Leavis and the New Criticism to science created an obscurity that is only now beginning to be clarified by recent work such as that by Beer, Levine, Myers, and Shuttleworth.[6]

But, even among writers sympathetic to science and among historians of psychology, there has been a reluctance to engage fully with Lewes's work. The writer who was translated across Europe, whose psychological ideas influenced Pavlov, Rutherford, and Hughlings Jackson,[7] who was held by the major French psychologist of his day, Théodule Ribot, to have been so innovative in his theories of nervous action and consciousness that he exceeded 'all that Mr Spencer and Mr Bain have advanced on this point',[8] and who was regarded by that most laborious of historians Howard Warren to have been the culmination of nineteenth-century associationism,[9] has been surprisingly little discussed. Within the history of psychology—with its broadly synoptic purposes and assumptions and experimentalist orientation—this has been largely because of what is felt to have been his lack of influence. However, claims to influence are strange things

---

[4] A breathtakingly patronizing note to the recent edition of Arnold's letters illustrates the general problem of Lewes's reputation: 'G. H. Lewes (1817–78 *DNB*), author, editor (*Fortnightly Review*), amateur scientist, biographer of Goethe, and many other things—most notably *concubin* of George Eliot' (*The Letters of Matthew Arnold iii. 1866–70*, ed. Cecil Y. Lang (London, 1998), 192.

[5] Anna Theresa Kitchel, *George Lewes and George Eliot: A Review of the Records* (New York, 1933), 301.

[6] There is more than an incidental connection here. The general views on science and mind of many American New Critics were of a piece with those of the nineteenth-century opponents of the new psychology. John Crowe Ransom, for instance, had views on biology that were little developed from the Romantic organicism of Coleridge, and Allen Tate, as late as 1940, was willing to assert 'the belief, philosophically tenable, in a radical discontinuity between the physical and the spiritual realms' (see Allen Tate, 'The Present Function of Criticism' (originally published 1940), repr. in Ray B. West (ed.), *Essays in Modern Literary Criticism* (New York, 1952), 146). As Tate's title suggests, these arguments are a late replay of their nineteenth-century forebears. For further comment, see Rick Rylance, 'The New Criticism', in *Encyclopaedia of Literature and Criticism*, ed. Martin Coyle, Peter Garside, Malcolm Kelsall, and John Peck (London, 1990), 721–35.

[7] For general estimates of Lewes's influence and place in the history of physiological psychology, see R. E. Ockenden, 'George Henry Lewes (1817–1878)', *Isis*, 32 (1940), 70–86; R. E. Smith, 'George Henry Lewes and his "Physiology and Common Life", 1859', *Proceedings of the Royal Society of Medicine*, 53 (1960), 569–74; J. M. Forrester, 'Who Put the George in George Eliot?', *British Medical Journal*, pt. 1 (1970), 165–7. For his influence on Hughlings Jackson, see C. U. M. Smith, 'Evolution and the Problem of Mind: Part II. John Hughlings Jackson', *Journal of the History of Biology*, 15 (1982), 241–62. Jackson was a disciple of Spencer's primarily, but, significantly, accepted Lewes's version of the 'double-aspect' theory, one of Lewes's leading achievements. See esp. pp. 255–7.

[8] Ribot, *English Psychology*, 311.     [9] Warren, *History of the Association Psychology*, 138.

sometimes, and, from the standpoint of influential findings and conceptions, Lewes's claims are at least as good as those of Bain or Spencer.

The truth is, though, that other criteria are in play in such assessments. There was the profuse career, and the feeling that he properly belonged to literature. He did not attract partisans like Spencer, or seem representative of an historical transition like Bain. As a result, Lewes is regularly acknowledged as interesting, even important, and commentators plead for greater attention to his work, but in fact it receives relatively little. Recently it has been examined for supporting material for sophisticated work centred elsewhere (usually on George Eliot), but there has been little attention to the developing thought, and, quite extraordinarily, virtually nothing on *Problems of Life and Mind* as a whole entity. What commentary has been offered, largely by American scholars, is vitiated—as I shall argue more fully in the last section of this chapter—by persistently reading Lewes out of context. In many of these accounts, including the most substantial monograph on him by Hock Guan Tjoa, Lewes is reread as a Kantian Idealist, and other features of his work, career, and influence are thus pulled out of shape.

The problem, then, is twofold, for Lewes has not been read satisfactorily either in terms of his texts, or in terms of his contexts. It is only by seeing the one in terms of the other that his achievement's proper strengths and limitations can be understood. As Howard Warren recognized, Lewes has been unfortunate in that he came at the very end of a tradition of psychological enquiry. Lewes did his major work when the influential formulations (and careers) had already been made, and when the kind of totalizing project for psychology envisaged by Spencer and Bain was giving way to, on the one hand, a more cautious, and increasingly specialized kind of experimental enquiry (of a kind Lewes in fact encouraged[10]), and, on the other, the psychological modernism of Freud, which

---

[10] James Sully, a psychologist of the next generation, and one of Lewes's literary executors, noted that one problem for Lewes was that he was too general and philosophical for the scientists, and too specialized and scientific for the philosopher–psychologists (see James Sully, 'Problems of Life and Mind. Third Series. By George Henry Lewes', *Academy*, 24 Apr. 1880, 308–10). A year earlier, in his obituary tribute, Sully had stressed the value of Lewes's detailed attention to scientific fact, and his impatience with abstractions and 'logical fictions' (see James Sully, 'George Henry Lewes', *New Quarterly Review*, NS 2 (1879), 356–76). Like Spencer, Lewes, and Bain, Sully was born outside the intellectual purple, and his autobiography gives an interesting account of a relaxed, liberal-minded, and politically radical upbringing in a dissenting culture. (Sully's family were Baptists.) He pointedly contrasts his own experience with the negative account given by Samuel Butler in *The Way of All Flesh*. Butler, too, was much interested in psychological and evolutionary questions, and their careers are further illustration of the thesis advanced above concerning the intellectual culture from which mid-to-late-nineteenth-century psychology grew. Again the important points of intellectual contact are from the provinces (Bain, Spencer, Butler, George Eliot), or from autodidact or dissenting London (Lewes, Sully), and then from European sources. Sully completed his education with the physiologist Hermann Lotze at Göttingen. See Sully, *My Life and Friends*.

proposed a quite different model of analysis and different assumptions about the mind's genesis, dynamics, and relations with the world. What is true of Lewes's place in the history of psychology, is also true of his situation in relation to the history of nineteenth-century philosophy. Just as the 'experience' psychology associated with Mill, Bain, Spencer, and Lewes himself seemed to have won the major argument, there was a shift back towards the analysis of mental contents carried through by a revival in Idealist and neo-Kantian thought. This concluding chapter, therefore, will examine Lewes's work in the light of these diverse contexts, and analyse *Problems of Life and Mind* as a text of its time, which seeks to develop the tradition of enquiry in which it participated beyond itself in the light of barely grasped, developing circumstances. It is tempting (rather in the manner of Lucien Goldmann's analysis of Racine and Pascal perhaps[11]) to see the formal disorganization of the *Problems* as symptomatic of larger structural shifts in the intellectual and disciplinary culture of its day. But at the same time it is also necessary to take account of the active constituents of Lewes's project. An intellectual event is much more than a reflection of larger structural circumstances, and we need to balance a sense of Lewes's historicity—and perhaps belatedness—against an informed grasp of intentions, conscious theoretical developments, and intellectual choices and proposals.

Despite its ramshackle appearance, *Problems of Life and Mind* is coherent in its theoretical project. Indeed its apparent formal disarray is an almost necessary part of its conception. The fluidity of its structure reflects diverse elements of its purpose, contents, and arguments for powerful reasons. *Problems of Life and Mind* is about the historicality of truth, and its formal (and indeed intellectual) difficulties stem from the latent, and sometimes manifest, contradiction between its law-bound, law-discovering, scientific enterprise, grounded in Comtean Positivism, and its strong sense of the determination of intellectual and cultural life by the historical moment. The *Problems*, quite unlike texts by Spencer or Bain, is self-consciously aware of its own historicity. This is registered most commonly through a perception of the inevitable limitations of contemporary knowledge as a sufficient basis for formulating theory, and a recognition of the cultural pressures placed upon its articulation. I will come to a fuller account of this shortly, but it is worth pausing to indicate the difference in this respect from Spencer. As we have seen in the previous chapter, Spencer unrolls his truth seamlessly, converting provisional propositions into Kantlike transcendent truths, which (as Lewes recognized) conceal a dualism in an apparently materialistic, monistic realism. Spencer's conception of history in his *Psychology* appears mainly in the form of the determining structures imposed on the mind by its

---

[11] Lucien Goldmann, *The Hidden God: A Study of Tragic Vision in the 'Pensées' of Pascal and the Tragedies of Racine*, trans. Philip Thody (London, 1964).

(Lamarckian) evolutionary inheritance. But the theoretical effect of this is to freeze historical process as biology, preventing provisionality or relativism. In fact, for all the formal commitment to induction as a principle of investigation, Spencer abolishes the historicity of his own thought even at the moment of its apparent acceptance in the biology of mind. He thus pictures individuals as, simultaneously, prisoners of their own pasts, but also as free to exert choice in the long avenue of progress. As a result, his texts look—evasively—behind and before, they rarely look around, and this central, organizing conception enables Spencer's orderly, systematized account of the world. By contrast, Lewes's world is, like his texts, much messier. He is much more willing to accept provisionality, and this provisionality is the source of much of his writing's best energy and best thinking. It is also the source of some compromising contradiction.

The differences between Spencer and Lewes are not confined to the relative weight each attaches to the historicity of the present. The same structural difference is evident in their accounts of language, and the weight and nature of the attention each gives to epistemological questions. Spencer takes his view of language from the Utilitarian tradition. It is a heavily empirical account, in which language is described in ways that emphasize its indicative and nominal functions at the expense of creative usage.[12] Lewes, on the other hand, emphasizes the enabling and creative uses of language much more vigorously. This might be expected from a man with his literary interests, but it is of wider importance. For Lewes, as for Huxley, Max Müller, and other leading intellectuals in the 1860s,[13] the use of language is *the* distinctively human activity. The ability to create through language, and to manipulate the environment thereby, separates man from the animals and explains their spectacular development as a species. And, as we shall see in the next section of this chapter, this much more generous —but much more unstable—conception of language's potential is evident from Lewes's own use of it in *Problems of Life and Mind*.

A related point can be made about the epistemologies of both writers. Lewes's epistemological ideas will be the subject of more extended discussion later, but it is worth noting initially that epistemological questions are heavily foregrounded in *Problems of Life and Mind*. (They probably account for a good half of the whole text, including much of the first two volumes.) In Spencer, however, there is a progressive downgrading of their importance. He began the first edition of *The Principles of Psychology*, as Lewes does the *Problems*, with

---

[12] For Spencer's comments on language in relation to the study of the mind, see *The Principles of Psychology*, 1st edn., 475–8, and 2nd edn., ii. 123–4, 402–4. There is considerable suspicion in Spencer that language may run out of control, and needs to be reined in (see e.g. *The Principles of Psychology*, 1st edn., 49). For comment, see Burrow, *Evolution and Society*, 209–10, and, for a helpful overview, Hans Aarsleff, *The Study of Language in England, 1780–1860* (Princeton, 1967).

[13] Beer, *Darwin's Plots*, 139.

epistemological questions. But in subsequent editions they are relegated to a much less prominent role. At the same time, an ostensibly *a posteriori* account of the origin of cognitive activity gives way to a position that is effectively indistinguishable from *a priori* 'forms-of-thought' arguments, which is why his work appealed to some moderate opinion eager for compromise between the 'experience' and 'spiritualist' psychological schools. Lewes's epistemology, by contrast, refuses to let go of arguments that stress process. What is distinctive in his account is the stress on the *complexity* of the activity that constitutes human perception. What is admirable is his refusal to let it slide into a conventional descriptive or cognitive formulae. This stress on complexity is shared by George Eliot. In both writers it is backed by an ethics that stresses the way to sympathetic understanding through the recognition of the partiality of perception, and an acceptance of other ways of seeing experiences that are different from one's own.

The structural organization of Lewes's text, then, reflects some important features of the argument and content of the work. Truth claims are made complex by historical self-consciousness, a complex, process-based epistemology, and a conception and use of language that creatively challenge established models and metaphors. Despite their commitment to comprehensive accounts of the world, both Lewes's psychological work, and George Eliot's fiction in the late 1860s and 1870s, share a sense of a world of 'thick description' (to use a term from the anthropologist Clifford Geertz), which resists system at the same time as it is eager for a coherent, totalized vision. Some indication of this restlessness is given by Lewes's own account of the composition of *Problems of Life and Mind*.

Lewes thought that the *Problems* was written within the 'experience' tradition of psychological theory, but the genesis of the text was more mixed. In the 'Preface' to volume one, he writes that the project originated as far back as 1836, 'when with the rashness of ambitious youth I planned a treatise on the Philosophy of Mind in which the doctrines of Reid, Stewart, and Brown were to be physiologically interpreted'. This was abandoned because of his lack of physiological knowledge and because of his 'growing dissatisfaction with the doctrines of the Scotch school'. But it is interesting to note that he wished to integrate rival theories from the very beginning. Thereafter he looked continually for opportunities to formulate a comprehensive psychological programme. In the early 1860s he made an attempt to apply discoveries in animal psychology to the behaviour of man under the deliberately provocative title (we learn from his journal[14]) of 'The Soul and its Mechanism'. This was inspired by his growing interest in evolutionary ideas, and would have been a startlingly original—if premature—endeavour. (In the 'Preface' Lewes dismisses it as clearly erroneous.) *Problems of Life and Mind* was not, therefore, conceived, in anything like its

---

[14] Kitchel, *Lewes and Eliot*, 216.

eventual form, until the end of the 1860s—the name was chosen in January 1869[15]—and even then Lewes felt uncertain of its scope. Handicapped by what he felt was the unsatisfactory state of physiological knowledge, and the lack of a sufficiently comprehensive sense of what psychology as a science should be, the *Problems* was originally envisaged as a series of essays rather than a unified project. These essays would also look beyond psychology and encompass 'a systematic introduction to the philosophy of science'.[16]

There are several points to make about this. We might note the Victorian scale and grandeur of the enterprise, its urge for system, and desire to be comprehensive and general. But we also note the anxiety about psychology's status as a science (an anxiety typical of this period), despite the consciousness of tradition, and the worry about the sufficiency of available knowledge for the grand scheme. These worries are distinctively Lewesian—you would not find them expressed by Spencer, for example—and they follow directly from Lewes's powerful sense of the historically specific nature, and therefore provisionality, of scientific and other forms of human knowledge. Intellectual work must be understood as a product of its age and occasion. Thus, in the first volume of *Problems of Life and Mind*, he argues that science and metaphysics alike take their impetus from the questions set by the age: 'the question of originality is of quite minor importance; that of efficiency most concerns us.'[17]

Lewes was committed to this idea and it is extended in volume two. Knowledge develops, but it becomes progressively more adequate to the phenomena it describes without becoming ultimately so. 'Truths' develop from each other in this way, but from an historical point of view it is misleading to talk about 'error' in any absolute sense. Pre-Copernican theories of planetary motion, for instance, were 'right' for a long period in terms of the questions asked of them by the needs, concepts, and propositions of their age in their cultural, institutional, and intellectual relations. Thus the replacement of one theory by another is much more of an evolutionary process than an arrival at a singular, static 'truth'. A new theory develops, because it is better suited to the circumstances in which it functions. Copernican theory, for example,

---

[15]   Kitchel, *Lewes and Eliot*, 253.

[16]   George Henry Lewes, *Problems of Life and Mind*, 5 vols. (London, 1874–9), i, Preface. As noted in the Introduction, n. 27, the organization of *Problems of Life and Mind* is complex. Lewes divided it into three 'series', of which the first and third appeared as two separate volumes. *First Series*: [i] *The Foundations of a Creed* (London, 1874); [ii] *The Foundations of a Creed* (London, 1875); *Second Series*: [iii] *The Physical Basis of Mind* (London, 1877); *Third Series*: [iv] *The Study of Psychology: Its Object, Scope and Method* (London, 1879); [v] untitled (London, 1879). This division is, however, cumbersome for finding one's way around its bulk. I therefore henceforth give citations by volume number followed by page number; the reader should, however, be aware that Lewes himself did not use the volume numbers.

[17]   Lewes, *Problems*, i. 84.

was not an exhibition of the untruth of the old theory; on the contrary, that formula so far expressed real observations that, even now, in spite of Copernicus, Gallileo, Newton, and Laplace, we habitually regard the world as at rest, and only adopt the enlarged theory for astronomical purposes, when dealing with phenomena which were hardly suspected when the old theory was framed. . . . Nor have we any grounds for supposing this interpretation to be final: it embodies present knowledge, that is all.[18]

However, Lewes warns, this is not a justification for a corrosive scepticism. It implies only a continual struggle for adequacy of interpretation in specific historical circumstances.

Lewes finds an example in his own day too. He realizes that there can never be a decisive outcome to the battle between creationism and Darwinian evolutionary theory, because neither case can be established on grounds that satisfy the other. This is because 'Science is no transcript of Reality, but an ideal construction framed out of the analysis of the complex phenomena given synthetically in Feeling, and expressed in abstractions.'[19] All formulations in language, therefore, are subject to revision or challenge. But this does not mean that all propositions are equally valid. Intellectual cultures devise tests to monitor adequacy (usually through institutional pressure or testing by application). This regulates the apparent relativism, as does Lewes's emphasis on the acts of human creativity, which bring successful theories into adequate being. It is important to stress this last point, because some influential recent theories—like those associated with the 'deconstructive' arguments of Jacques Derrida and his followers —have proposed only the first, epistemologically sceptical, part of the argument and ignored the second. Thus they have failed to offer either a sufficient conception of human creativity, or a sufficient understanding of the function of knowledge propositions and language performances in human societies. As a result, the theory associated with this line of thinking has derisively dismissed writing in a 'realist' mode as mere ideological camouflage for authority structures— as, for example, in Colin MacCabe's criticism of *Middlemarch* examined in the previous chapter.

The double-edged theory offered by Lewes—that knowledge is both creatively adequate and radically provisional—is a central point in his work, and one that is shared by George Eliot. (It is, for instance, echoed by her in the opening epigraph to *Daniel Deronda* then—1875—also being written.) Testing by application is effective, but applications will themselves be historically defined. There can be no ultimately decisive tests. In volume four of the *Problems* (1879) Lewes concludes that knowledge is in fact driven by *need*: 'we only see what interests us.'[20] It is thus related not only to historical and cultural conditions, but also to the psychological conditions of the human participants in any act of knowledge

---

[18] Ibid. ii. 82–3.    [19] Ibid. 86.    [20] Ibid. iv. 42.

creation. This too is a key idea in George Eliot's thinking, where it is given a particular ethical turn. Ethical action in Eliot's fiction consists of the conscious realization of limitation, of either perception, culture, or a whole personality.[21] The important initial step—be it by Gwendolen Harleth in *Daniel Deronda*, or by that unnamed, because typical, 'observer under the softening influence of the fine arts' who is imagined looking at Dagley's run-down farm in chapter 39 of *Middlemarch*—is to become conscious of the limitations of one's own views. If we turn round Lewes's proposition, we can see its ethical bearing. If we see primarily only what interests us, perhaps our interests will become larger if we see more, and a 'growing good' (as Eliot has it) will ensue. Thus, the fact that man is a social being is morally and psychological enlarging, and man's 'higher faculties are evolved through social needs . . . Mind [is] an expression of organic and social conditions.'[22]

*Middlemarch*, however, does not only provide illustration of the ethical register of these arguments. The text is also explicitly concerned, in an informed way, with the historical and social circumstances in which biomedical research is conducted. Thus, it is frequently noted that Lydgate's interest in Bichat is a sign of his intellectual potential and seriousness, and of how up to date he is in his researches. All of which is true. What is less frequently remarked, however, is that, by the time the novel was published, serious reservations had been entered about Bichat's work that would have qualified the sense informed readers had of his achievement. His status in the history of biology, of course, was not in question, but the nature of his scientific project, and the theoretical underpinning of his research, was doubted. Thus, Huxley, for instance, could refer to him in 1874 as a 'considerable, though much overestimated anatomist'.[23] Bichat's wish—taken up by Lydgate—was to find a common substance to explain histological phenomena. Lydgate dreams of extending this to mental phenomena, to investigate the 'invisible thoroughfares which are the first lurking-places of anguish, mania and crime'.[24] But the direction of analysis taken by later biologists and psycho-physiologists was to see phenomena as non-reducible to such, essentially determinist, causes. In volume three of the *Problems* Lewes commented that Bichat was mistaken, because he attached too much importance to physiological processes at the expense of attention to the 'External Medium' with which they interacted.[25] (Lewes, of course, is using the later more sophisticated biological terminology of Claude Bernard, whose influence on his work was extensive.) Later, he also comments that Bichat was 'not sufficiently disengaged

---

[21] For illuminating discussion of these important areas, see Myers, *The Teaching of George Eliot*, esp. ch. 9.   [22] Lewes, *Problems*, iv. 6.
[23] T. H. Huxley, 'On the Hypothesis that Animals are Automata, and its History' (1874), in *Science and Culture and Other Essays*, 204.
[24] Eliot, *Middlemarch*, 194.   [25] Lewes, *Problems*, iii. 27.

from the metaphysical mode of viewing biological phenomena', and treats physiological properties as entities credited with an agency of their own.[26] In other words, Bichat worked within the biological paradigm of vitalism.[27] Instead of seeing the organism as the function of diverse, interacting influences, Bichat tends to seek reductive explanations. This way of thinking runs entirely contrary to Lewes's own physiological work, which, since the important 1859 paper given to the British Association, had stressed that the properties of nerves depended on location, and their functions depended on interaction with the environment. This is the main bias of Lewes's physiological psychology, and indeed it forms the core of his reputation. The stress he placed on 'the social factor' in psychology was what distinguished him for many of his contemporaries, and his specific point about nervous action received praise both at the time and subsequently.[28]

George Eliot, of course, was well aware of these reservations about Bichat's work. (She comments in *Middlemarch* that Lydgate's way of putting the question about 'primitive tissue' was 'not quite in the way required by the awaiting answer'.[29]) But what consequences do they have for our sense of Lydgate's hopes? Clearly, they severely qualify them. But the reservations entered are not entirely compromising, either to Bichat or to the go-ahead young doctor. What we have is a subtle account of the interaction of scientific knowledge, local culture, and a specific personality. Lydgate finds Bichat appealing, not only because he is in the van of contemporary ideas, but also because he offers reductive explanations that ignore context, just as Lydgate, both professionally and in his personal life, is unable to appreciate fully the power of social influence. In the same way, the fact that Bichat's work has been reconsidered by posterity does not diminish his achievements as a scientist, nor—following Lewes's theories of the relationship between period and intellectual need—does it diminish the success of his work for its time. Bichat both met demands set by the age and enabled further work (including that of Lewes himself). The general theory about the development of knowledge set out in *Problems of Life and Mind* is borne out in George Eliot's novel.

[26] Ibid. 64.
[27] See Elizabeth Haigh, 'The Roots of the Vitalism of Xavier Bichat', *Bulletin of the History of Medicine*, 49 (1975), 72–86, and Geoffrey Sutton, 'The Physical and Chemical Path to Vitalism: Xavier Bichat's *Physiological Researches on Life and Death*', *Bulletin of the History of Medicine*, 58 (1984), 53–71.
[28] For details of the 'social factor' in psychology, see the next section of this chapter. Several commentators praise Lewes's hypothesis about the nerves. See e.g. Ribot, *English Psychology*, 287; Sully, 'Problems of Life and Mind. Third Series', 309–10; R. R. Smith, 'George Henry Lewes and his "Physiology of Common Life"', 572. It was admired at the time by Huxley, among others, who delivered the relevant paper for Lewes.
[29] Eliot, *Middlemarch*, 178.

A historicized, evolutionary theory of knowledge thus necessarily entails limitation, for every observer's mind is 'the product of history', and all 'sentiments and opinions' are tied to the epoch and culture that produce them.[30] This, of course, will apply to *Problems of Life and Mind* itself as to any other text. To take a negative example, Lewes, like Spencer, sometimes indulged in a characteristically Victorian racial denigration of 'savage' cultures. This is a morally and ideologically unselfconscious example. Elsewhere, Lewes is more promisingly circumspect, as in his powerful awareness of the limitations placed on his work by the state of physiological knowledge. In the third volume of the *Problems*, *The Physical Basis of Mind* (1877), he enters caveats, not only about the provisionality of theoretical formulations, but also about the very foundations of physiological knowledge itself. He cites Lotze with approval to the effect that even good physiological hypotheses have an effective scientific life of only about five years, and writes that 'medical men and psychologists ought to be warned against founding theories of disease, or of medical processes, on such very insecure bases; and physiological students will do well to remember the large admixture of Hypothesis which every description of the nervous system now contains.'[31] In illustration of this general point, as we shall see, *Problems of Life and Mind* is itself unable to sort out a coherent evolutionary theory. It havers somewhat indecisively between the Lamarckian and the Darwinian hypotheses, as the various intellectual needs of the theory dictate. But it is important to recognize that this is a *historical* as much as a personal difficulty, and Lewes was, of course, by no means alone in facing it.

The recognition of the provisionality of knowledge is one reason why *Problems of Life and Mind* is so persistently concerned with epistemology and methodology. It is one source, for instance, of Lewes's reservations about Spencer's theory of knowledge. Though he is generally laudatory about his friend and ally's work, he dissents from some features of his theory. Lewes sees Spencer's 'Universal Postulate' as an unnecessary hostage to Idealism, because it seems to imply some hypothesis of '*unproved truth*' waiting to be inevitably discovered.[32] For Lewes, 'truth' can exist only in 'feeling', in sensually verifiable, and historically specific ways. It exists only in determining contexts—hence the importance of correct method. In the absence of reliable data, in a rapidly developing field, methodology becomes essential. Closing the first two volumes—*The Foundation of a Creed*—with an envoy, it is this Lewes chooses to stress. Correct method, he says, will survive the overturning of this or that result or hypothesis, and will ensure proper circumspection and verification. 'L'Envoy' is aimed, therefore, not at contemporaries whose views have hardened into 'doctrine', but at the younger generation of his readers, for it is their ideas that will 'set the conditions which determine the acceptance of new truths'.[33]

[30] Lewes, *Problems*, iii, 97.    [31] Ibid. 224.    [32] Ibid. ii. 90.    [33] Ibid. 506.

New 'truths'—or knowledge propositions—occur through the interaction of developments in empirical findings or theory with specific social and cultural situations. We have seen in Chapter 3 how Lewes had a strong—and quite accurate—sense of the way in which the post-French Revolutionary political climate had influenced the development of research in physiological psychology. This sense never left him, but the central concern of *Problems of Life and Mind* is more forward-looking. Specifically, it looks to rebuild the national culture in such a way that science will become a more integral part of British intellectual life.[34] Lewes writes that the 'absence of [science] during the last two hundred years has been a serious defect in her culture'. Contrasting Britain unfavourably with Germany, he castigates British parochialism and failure to engage with important international developments.[35] This has a strikingly modern ring to it in the context of more recent polemical jeremiads (from both left and right) on the insularity and the pro-literary, anti-scientific prejudices endemic to British culture. (The best known of these is probably that by the American Martin J. Weiner.[36])

Lewes's opportunity to redraw the map of English intellectual life was provided by the general climate of the decade or so after 1865, and it comes in the context of other, rival bids to reshape the culture during these years—most famously Matthew Arnold's anti-scientific anatomy of British spiritual debility in *Culture and Anarchy*. But within the scientific wing of opinion there was a fairly widespread sense of optimism and possibility. Major battles had been fought and not lost, and the war seemed to be being won, if only by attrition. Though neutral observers like the barrister, poet, and maverick intellectual William Smith (who had been a friend of Lewes since the 1840s, though he did not see eye to eye with him intellectually) could comment in 1870 that 'mental philosophy [was] now accustomed to the language of apology',[37] there was a firm sense among the new psychologists that the philosophical arguments of their opponents sounded increasingly weak. This is borne out by the hostile reviews that *Problems of Life and Mind* received. These were, by and large, as Lewes himself said of Richard Hutton's attack in the *Spectator*, really 'too feeble'.[38] Hutton's criticisms, and carping tone, are drawn from a different age, and are as frail in their rhetoric as their arguments. The first volume of the *Problems*, says Hutton, is difficult to

---

[34] See Hock Guan Tjoa, *George Henry Lewes: A Victorian Mind* (London, 1977), 83–104, for comment on Lewes's efforts to construct a unified and coherent world view that would embrace literature, science, history, and so on. I will discuss my reservations about Tjoa's construction of this enterprise later in this chapter.

[35] Lewes, *Problems of Life and Mind*, i. 84–6.

[36] Martin J. Weiner, *English Culture and the Decline of the Industrial Spirit 1850–1980* (Cambridge, 1981).

[37] William Henry Smith, 'Knowing and Feeling: A Contribution to Psychology', *Contemporary Review*, 14 (1870), 342.

[38] Lewes to Alexander Main, 13 Mar. 1874, in Eliot, *Letters*, vi. 30.

read, because of the 'dense mass of physiological and biological knowledge through which the reader has to push his way'. This 'desert' (what desert has a 'dense mass' of vegetation?) is inappropriate for a book about the human mind, as is Lewes's refusal to discuss the 'necessary and universal truths' of the spirit. Lewes, he concludes, is really metaphysical without admitting it, for the assertion that there are no *a priori* truths is itself an *a priori* assumption.[39] These were no longer viable arguments.

Others, however, took a similar line. An anonymous reviewer of volume one of the *Problems* in the *Westminster* in 1874 opened his commentary in the face-tious, Swiftian manner familiar from denunciations of Spencer and other evolu-tionists. He looked forward to the race of 'diviner Mammals' to come, with 'prehensile appendages' and 'high Intelligences'.[40] The aim, of course, was to denigrate the ostensibly demeaning account of man as a spiritual being in the newer psychological writing. More specific comments also followed well-trodden ground: Lewes trespasses in conventionally religious areas, his work is damag-ingly allied to Mill's (an extraordinary thing for a reviewer in the *Westminster* to say), his language is jargon, offensive to common sense, and unable to say anything about 'ourselves, our feelings, passions, sensations, thoughts, wills, and actions—nay the very fact of our existence'.[41] But what is interesting about this essay is the picture it gives of Lewes's reputation. There is early praise: Lewes is 'one of our most celebrated scientific inquirers, who, if not the greatest of philoso-phers, at least knows more about philosophy than any other living author, and whose reputation as a thinker has been founded not only on his great and var-ied knowledge, but on his supposed trustworthiness to take the common sense view on difficult problems'.[42] *Problems of Life and Mind*, therefore, he goes on to say, comes as an even greater shock.

Lewes was in fact regarded as occupying the middle ground of psycholo-gical opinion, even in the *Problems*. That text did, as Ribot noted, push some arguments—particularly over the role of society in the formation of mind, and the description of the mind–body problem—beyond the conventional limits of the period. (These were the issues also singled out by the *Westminster* reviewer for special hostility.) None the less, most observers saw that the future lay with this kind of enquiry. Another neutrally minded commentator in the *Athenaeum* in 1879, reviewing the fourth volume of the *Problems*, contrasted Lewes's work with that of Henry Calderwood, the Edinburgh Professor of Moral Philosophy whose opposition to psycho-physiology we noted in Chapter 3. Calderwood's thinking, the reviewer bluntly noted, was 'obsolete'. Though he felt reservations about Lewes's book, 'we would rather build from the foundation with Mr Lewes

---

[39] [R. H. Hutton], 'Mr Lewes's "Problems of Life and Mind"', *Spectator*, 28 Feb. 1874, 271–3.
[40] Anon., 'Mr Lewes and Metaphysics', *Westminster Review*, NS 46 (1874), 104.
[41] Ibid. 104–5.    [42] Ibid. 105.

than descend to a lower story [*sic*] from the air-built roof of Professor Calderwood'. The metaphor is a little garbled, but it would have suited Lewes's picture of his own work as methodologically reorienting psychology. The review ends recommending Lewes's book as 'decidedly the best statement in English of the problems and methods of psychology'.[43]

Certainly by the standards of, say, John Tyndall or T. H. Huxley, Lewes was moderate in tone and conclusion. Indeed, Lewes forcefully takes his distance from the extreme 'automatist' position adopted by these writers. By the mid-1870s Huxley and Tyndall were seen as putting the limit case of the new theory. Tyndall's essays were especially militant. ' "Materialism" and its Opponents' (1875) declared that the religious 'squatters' should be evicted from science's domain, and that the ultramontane intelligence was, 'through lack of exercise, virtually the underdeveloped brain of the child'. Why, protested Tyndall, should the new scientific theories always be forced onto the defensive? Why do religious writers not defend their own 'absurd cosmogony' instead of interfering in that of scientific theory? Religious writers—he has James Martineau specifically in mind —always treat assumptions as facts, whereas the new psychology claims at most that it only feels and deduces.[44] In 'Science and Man' (1877) Tyndall attempted to turn round the conservatively inclined organicist tradition in English thought. Expressing an initially surprising agreement with Carlyle, Tyndall draws out the classic organicist analogy, which compares the universe to an organism like a tree. Anti-materialists are correct, says Tyndall, the universe is not a machine. It is an energy system, like an organism. Both Carlyle's Idealist organicism and Tyndall's so-called materialism have the same basis therefore. Both imply 'the interdependence and harmonious interaction of parts, and the subordination of the individual powers of the universal organism to the working of the whole'.[45] Where the two schools part company is in the addition of an agent—like the soul or vital power—that works from outside the system, controlling or intervening in its operation. Unable to refute materialism's operational model, therefore, or explain in any plausible scientific terms how such an entity might function, the anti-materialist tactic is to resort to low abuse. Tyndall's essay was the text of an address given to the Radical Birmingham and Midland Institute, and he therefore ends attacking the political insults flung at scientific materialism, and the disgraceful blackening of individual reputations and characters (his example is Lewes's early comrade George Jacob Holyoake).

Tyndall's essays are at the rough-and-tumble end of the war of the psychological schools, but they are indicative of some of the central shifts in opinion. His polemically shrewd attempt to appropriate organicist rhetoric is of a piece

[43] Anon., 'Current Philosophy', *Athenaeum*, 27 Sept. 1879, 398.
[44] John Tyndall, ' "Materialism" and its Opponents', *Fortnightly Review*, 18 (1875), 579–99.
[45] John Tyndall, 'Science and Man', *Fortnightly Review*, NS 22 (1877), 595.

with the shift in George Eliot's conception of the functioning of the organic model. As we have observed in the previous chapter, and as has been thoroughly documented by Sally Shuttleworth, Eliot followed alterations in general biological opinion carefully. By the time she came to write *Middlemarch*, therefore, she had changed her analytic model to one that involved a much more dynamic, and indeed unstable, sense of process and energy systems.[46] Her 'natural history method' (to use Bain's term) is now a much more complicated matter. For one thing, as *Middlemarch* makes clear, organic structures can be ensnaring and predatory as well as nourishing. It depends, once more, on where you stand and how you look. A similar adjustment to, and sense of complexity in, the model is observable also in Lewes's work, as we shall see in the next section of this chapter.

The mood, then, in which *Problems of Life and Mind* was written is, from the scientific point of view, much more buoyant (and indeed intellectually rich) than that in which, say, Bain's or Spencer's early work was undertaken in the 1850s. This does not mean that opposition had fallen away, of course. Like Bain and Spencer, Lewes, too, had publication difficulties. Blackwood refused the text of the first volume of the *Problems* on religious grounds. Having, in 1873, written to Lewes that he had 'no hesitation in agreeing to publish the work [*Problems of Life and Mind*] and on the terms you propose', and having no fears that 'the cause of real religion [could be] injured by any amount of free and fair discussion such as yours is sure to be',[47] none the less Blackwood withdrew four months later. Having read only the first few sheets, he concluded that Lewes assumed 'too much a general disbelief in religion'.[48] Lewes was annoyed, but also relieved.[49] He had foreseen difficulties, even warning Blackwood that the book might give a 'metafeesical' shock to 'Scotch friends and clients'.[50] In the event Lewes had no trouble in placing the book with Trubners, a scientific publisher, to the advantage of both parties. Volume one, as we have noted, sold exceptionally well.

Lewes, of course, was alert to the difficulties of public discussion of ideas such as his. Generally, he was thought to occupy the respectable and sensible middle ground of advanced opinion, and there was no doubt that the Eliot–Lewes couple appeared impressively prestigious by, say, 1870.[51] Nevertheless, the

[46] Shuttleworth, *George Eliot and Nineteenth-Century Science*, ch. 7.
[47] Blackwood to Lewes, 17 Jan. 1873, in Eliot, *Letters*, v. 369.
[48] Blackwood to Lewes, 14 Apr. 1873, in ibid. 400.
[49] Lewes to Alexander Main, 26 May 1973, in ibid. 415.
[50] Lewes to Blackwood, 18 Jan. 1873, in ibid. 371.
[51] This was a theme in a number of Lewes's obituaries, especially in the 'scientific' press: see e.g. that in *Nature*, 19 (1878), 106–7. It was also becoming a common ploy to separate Lewes—and Eliot—from Comte, because of Comte's political associations. William Henry Smith, for example, did this in his review of Lewes's revised *History of Philosophy* for *Blackwood's* in 1868 ('Lewes's

intellectual and cultural climate remained hostile in major respects. As late as 1885, Lewes remained a man of 'negative convictions' for John Tulloch, and had 'much of a Frenchman in his ways', a damning mistake if ever there were one.[52] Thus, in two articles for the *Fortnightly* in 1876 on 'Spiritualism and Materialism', Lewes resumed some of Tyndall's themes and protested that 'the rhetoric of many spiritualists is very distasteful to serious minds' when it descends to accusations of failure in morals or conscience by individual 'materialists'.[53] As ever Lewes was conscious of the political bearing of these arguments:

The two hypotheses are not unlike Toryism and Radicalism in politics. They express one-sided views, and represent Order and Progress. Organicism claims to unite these views by showing that Progress is the development of Order. Meanwhile the Spiritualist and Tory are strong in so far as each steadfastly opposes inadequate explanations and precipitate changes; the Materialist and Radical are strong in so far as each, while protesting against prejudice and privilege, insists on actual facts and reasonable inferences. But both Spiritualist and Tory have been too apt to load their protests with threat, claiming for their own side the monopoly of moral purity. It is high time that Spiritualism should cease its exclusive pretensions to lofty aspirations and ideal aims, and cease to assume that any other hypothesis is false because desolating. The threat is held over our heads that if we do not accept the hypothesis of Spiritualism we shall be understood to deny Conscience, Justice, Love for mankind, shall regard man as no better than a brute, and banish Poetry—Morality—from the world . . . so powerful is the effect of this incessant rhetoric that few men have the courage to avow their disbelief in an extra-organic agent; and of those who do avow it, many are provoked into an equally offensive attitude, answering with defiant epigrams and noisy paradoxes.[54]

The similarities in argument between this passage and Tyndall's essays are very marked, partly because they are standard arguments from the 'materialist' camp.

History of Philosophy', *Blackwood's Edinburgh Magazine*, 104 (1868), 537–53). An anonymous reviewer of Lewes's *Aristotle: A Chapter from the History of Science* (1864) also praised Lewes's 'masterly book' before proceeding to attack the irreligious political views of Comte that were so closely associated with 'French Revolutionists' across the century. The reviewer excused Lewes from such sins, but lamented his 'combative character' and warned him not to try to be too original, and not to stress the historical and social causes of phenomena. Though Lewes took his distance from Comte in some major respects (which included the vexed matter of the status of psychology as a discipline), it was precisely the application of social and historical ideas to the analysis of the mind that *Problems of Life and Mind* proceeded to do. See Anon., 'Lewes on Aristotle's Scientific Writings', *British Quarterly Review*, 40 (1864), 51–79.

[52] Tulloch, *Movements of Religious Thought*, 250–2. In a review of various Positivist-inclined publications in 1868, Tulloch remarks that Lewes, like Mill, fails to take sufficient distance from Comte. See [Tulloch], 'The Positive Philosophy of M. Auguste Comte', *Edinburgh Review*, 127 (1868), 303–57.

[53] George Henry Lewes, 'Spiritualism and Materialism: Part 1', *Fortnightly Review*, NS 19 (1876), 482.

[54] George Henry Lewes, 'Spiritualism and Materialism: II', *Fortnightly Review*, NS 19 (1876), 717.

And Lewes is forceful and plainspoken about them. He is particularly fierce about the inhibitions placed on free enquiry, and the alignment of 'organicism' with the progressive and 'Radical' camp is again interesting. But the difference of tone is also striking. Tyndall is hectoring and provocative; Lewes is firm, but calm. The intention is different, and this in turn reveals something about the tone, intention, and structure of *Problems of Life and Mind*.

The difficult structure of the *Problems* is intimately related to the public context of its writing and reading. This is evident, not only in the theoretical emphasis given to a historicized and provisional view of human knowledge, but also at many points in the details of the text. We have seen, for example, how he wishes to look to the future, and the younger generation, but the awareness of public dispute and a public role also shapes his tone, most clearly in the splendidly clear digest of 'advanced' contemporary thinking in the fourth volume, *The Study of Psychology*, where Lewes addresses a sympathetic but only partially informed audience. Devices such as these adjustments in tone and address give *Problems of Life and Mind* a rhetorically conditional feel, which is entirely congruent with its theoretical project but is at odds with its apparently systematic, even doctrinaire, appearance in the Spencerian manner. The title of the *Problems* should, therefore, be taken to heart. Lewes is dealing with just that: a series of related problems within a complex field, whose difficulties with issues of scientific status and appropriate methodology, whose complex relationship to past enquiry, and whose fraught intellectual and social context, all make it difficult for Lewes (or anyone) to produce decisive formulations of problems, let alone answers. The result, therefore, is a text whose fragmentation and messiness are more than the result of the personal health problems that bedevilled Lewes during its production.

A possible analogy is with the Romantic long poems he so admired, for it really is quite difficult to see a coherent and satisfying way in which *Problems of Life and Mind* might have closed, even had circumstances permitted it. The *Problems* makes little effort to be systematically comprehensive, or to establish a series of logically elegant arguments that run to a conclusion. Like the long, unfinished Romantic poems of Wordsworth, Coleridge, Byron, or Keats, Lewes's text raises far too many problems for a satisfying resolution to be possible. As George Eliot realized, in late essays such as 'Notes on Form in Art' (1868), structure must be responsive to circumstances if it is to reflect the material in good faith: 'what is fiction other than an arrangement of events or feigned correspondences according to the predominant feeling?', she asks.[55] One result of this idea

---

[55] George Eliot, 'Notes on Form in Art', in *Essays of George Eliot*, ed. Thomas Pinney (London, 1963), 434.

is the increasingly 'open' endings of her last novels, and the whole line of think-ing is a late version of Coleridgean conceptions of 'organic form', given a realist twist, but continuing to be based on biological, or at least psycho-physiological, models. (The whole vocabulary of Eliot's essay is drawn from Lewes's work. 'Feeling', for instance, has here an enlarged sense beyond 'passing emotion'. It is an abstract for sensory experience across the board, and acts as a kind of epistemological guarantee in Lewes's theories.)

This kind of literary problem is one we are accustomed to considering in rela-tion to much 'modern' writing and literary theory, though in standard accounts it is rarely applied to the perennial whipping boy of post-structuralist argument, the Victorian novel. Indeed, to stretch this parallel, it could be argued that *Problems of Life and Mind* contains a kind of 'modernist' argument within a nineteenth-century 'Positivist' form (accepting the severely pejorative associations that term has acquired in many forms of recent theory). Certainly this way of thinking about the 'text' (and the multiple-volumed, open-ended form, with its emphasis on provisionality, seems to me to invite that term as coloured by this theory) is a much more promising way of thinking about it than as somehow a 'failed' or 'minor' Victorian 'system'. The tension between the two modes provides *Problems of Life and Mind* with its energy and interest. Again, the difficulty of thinking through the relationship between physiology and psychology provides an example.

Though Lewes insists quite categorically that psychology cannot proceed without physiology, he is not so polemically blasé—as, for inatance, is Tyndall —as to assume that this intellectual necessity abolishes, or indeed satisfactorily finesses, the real problems endemic to theorizing the relationship between physio-logical base and human superstructure (to use a popular nineteenth-century metaphor). Nor does he believe that the language of the one is immediately applic-able to the phenomena of the other. Two interesting and supportive reviews of volumes one and three of *Problems* by Douglas Spalding, a younger psychologist, pinpoint this very helpfully. Interestingly, the reviews are not quite coherent either in argument or tone, and veer quite sharply between courteous compliment, heavy-handed irony, and penetrating observation. They are in this respect the work of a young man, of course, but they are also, like Lewes's text, between generations. The real point of interest is Spalding's perception of the difficult-ies in *language* faced by physiological psychology. He notes that 'the popular mind' still holds, as a residue from theology, that the body is the servant of the soul. Though this is an error, it is at least intelligible, whereas the contrary pro-position, as in *Problems of Life and Mind*, that thought is governed by feeling, is, in a very real sense, unintelligible. It simply rubs common sense up the wrong way. At the same time, Spalding notes, physiological psychology is itself 'entangled in the phraseology of exploded theories' and analogies, and, in a very powerful sense, it has no adequate language of its own at its disposal. It is with the need to remake the language of psychology, on the assumption of mind–body identity, that new work should be proceeding.[56]

Spalding was clearly as radical in politics as psychology. (The *Examiner* was a radical journal, and Spalding's is to be found alongside pieces on women's rights, conditions in the Paris slums, and civil liberties in Britain.) He identifies a way in which *Problems of Life and Mind* looks backwards rather forwards. Despite pushing ahead with some of the major initiatives taken by the new psychology into areas like his radical solution to the ancient mind–body problem, and his far-reaching conception of the role of society in the formation of mind, Lewes's work none the less came as the new psychology generally was keen to seek *rapprochement* with the 'Tories and Spiritualists' (as Lewes named them). Principally, it tried to make use of some of the ideas and language hitherto monopolized by reactionary writers. One can see why, from theoretical as well as political considerations, this should be so. As the theoretical project became more sophisticated, there was a need to offer more nuanced accounts of human behaviour and of the 'higher' faculties. The sensible, indeed perhaps the only, thing to do was to make use of existing discourse, even though the language of the old might compromise the new. In Lewes's work this struggle is very evident.

The effort to make peace with spiritualism was widespread. Lewes's old positivist friend Frederic Harrison, for instance, made a bid in the *Nineteenth Century* in 1877 for the moral high ground in the 'scientific' interest.[57] Harrison's piece is not actually very successful (he ends up sounding a bit like a crusty Tory-Spiritualist himself ), but the attempt was representative. Henry Maudsley, the increasingly celebrated clinician, also argued in the *Fortnightly* that materialism, far from destroying morality, actually encouraged the moral sense. Theories of Providence destroy the moral will, and therefore abnegate moral responsibility by encouraging a self-seeking obsession with personal salvation. They can also ruin a personality: 'it is not the most elevated or the most healthy business for a person to be occupied continually with anxieties and apprehensions and cares about the salvation of his own soul.'[58] He might have been thinking of Nicholas Bulstrode in *Middlemarch*. In the second volume of *Problems* (1875), Lewes begins with the proposition that the 'Universe is mystic to man, and must ever remain so', and expresses a rather over-solicitous concern to preserve that mystery and reassure anxious readers. Science is only a re-presentation, a re-symbolization,

---

[56]  Douglas A. Spalding, 'George Henry Lewes's Problems of Life and Mind', *Examiner*, 14 Mar. 1874, 262. In 'The Physical Basis of Mind', *Nature*, 16 (1877), 261–3, Spalding extends this point to include the residue of metaphysical problems in scientific language. Very much against the grain of the usual accounts, Spalding charges Lewes with preserving *too much* metaphysical language in his work.

[57]  Frederic Harrison, 'The Soul and the Future Life', *Nineteenth Century*, 1 (1877), 623–36.

[58]  Henry Maudsley, 'Materialism and its Lessons', *Fortnightly Review*, NS 26 (1879), 260.

of still awesome phenomena. But Lewes's metaphor is then interesting and typical: '*Science is seeing with other eyes.*'[59] All is provisional, a way of seeing. We cannot search for 'scientific finality, and demand a cause of a cause, an origin of the origin. It is in this sense that mystery for ever accompanies our search, a shadow which recedes, but never lessens.'[60] With this apt, and very Eliot-like,' image for the nature of knowledge, perceptions and intellectual enquiry, it is now time to turn to the substance of Lewes's development of psychological theory.

### MIND, METAPHOR, BIOLOGY, AND MAN

*Problems of Life and Mind* is both constructive and critical. That is, it draws upon the heritage of ideas and approaches provided by the 'experience' tradition, but it also attempts to move beyond these to a different kind of model of the mind's operations. Three influences are principally at work in this. There is, first, the influence of Spencer, and, in a more general sense, Darwin, who could offer a model for the analysis of mind based on theories of general biology rather than the analysis of mental contents or speculative hypotheses about physiological processes. The second influence, a fuller account of which will be given later, comes from the need Lewes and others felt to offer a more comprehensive and humanly nuanced account of the higher human faculties. The main area of debate here concerns the challenge offered to 'materialist' psychology by neo-Kantian thought. This was represented at its best by T. H. Green, but its presence was substantial throughout the intellectual community interested in psychological questions.

The third influence was, of course, that of Comte. As we have seen, Lewes disagreed with Comte's belief that a separate discipline of psychology was unnecessary. In addition, he could not accept Comte's ill-conceived physiological ideas. None the less two of Comte's central propositions remained of abiding interest to him. The first of these was the integrational theory of knowledge implied by Comte's 'hierarchy of the sciences'. The second was the stress placed by Comte on the influence of society on the formation of mind. Comte theorized mind at the intersection of biology and sociology, which is exactly where Lewes too based his investigations. Lewes's emphasis on the social determinations of mental phenomena became, in the eyes of many of his contemporaries, his most distinctive and controversial achievement. As for the integrational model of knowledge, that is everywhere apparent in his writing, as it is in George Eliot. The theoretical bearings taken, the range of knowledge brought to bear on problems, the understanding of the functioning of society, culture, and the

[59] Lewes, *Problems*, ii, 3.      [60] Ibid. 7–8.

human personality—all these witness the acceptance of Comte's proposition that specialized knowledge is only provisionally so, and that it is necessary to look beyond speciality—and mono-causality—to understand the manifold causes of phenomena.

Yet what is also interesting is the rejection by both Lewes and Eliot of Comte's concomitant proposition that diversity of determinations can be smoothly graded into a finished hierarchy or 'system'. Lewes and Eliot may have offered nominal support to the Comteans (and in Lewes's case it went further than this in the 1850s), but their actual intellectual practice could not be comfortably assimilated into Comte's system. This is apparent in the details and shape of their most mature writing: in the messy provisionality of *Problems of Life and Mind*, in George Eliot's continually expressed anxiety about the sufficiency of her own analyses in *Middlemarch* or *Daniel Deronda*, and in Lewes's desire in the *Problems* to get psychology out of the grip of 'authorities'.

In volume four, *The Study of Psychology*, Lewes offers a critique of existing schools. There are, he writes, three kinds of psychological theory. There is the school of 'Rational Psychology', which includes the leading philosophical psychologists of whatever stamp, from Locke, through Berkeley, Hume, Hartley and the rest, to Mill. This school is non-empirical, emphasizes the operation of the conscious mind alone, and tends to focus on 'mysterious agents' or 'Psychical Principles', which analytically remove mind from determining or related phenomena.[61] The second school, the 'Empirical School' (which includes Cabanis and Gall), claims to confine itself to the data of 'Experience', but depends mainly on introspection. While often claiming to be physiological, in fact it posits a psychology that is independent of the analysis of the organism; it is only 'coquetting with Physiology'. The third or 'compromise' school uses both psychological and physiological data. Its leading practitioners are the Germans Lotze and Wundt, the Frenchman Taine, and Bain and Spencer in Britain. The stress in this work falls heavily on the 'two-fold aspect of phenomena'—that is, the desire to analyse the mind in both its physiological and psychological registers, and, if necessary (as in Bain), to keep these independent of each other. As we shall see, Lewes himself pursues the 'two-fold' analysis, but tries to develop a much more positively integrated approach.

Several points need to be made about this anatomy of the state of psychology in the mid-1870s. Lewes is, first, trying to liberate psychology from what he calls the tyranny of 'authorities in the place of reasons', and 'systems' in the place of methods. He wishes to make psychology methodologically much more responsive to its object of investigation, and to new knowledge, and less obedient to, or caught up in, scholastic or party disputes that are destructive of proper

---

[61] Lewes, *Problems*, iv. This and the following quotations are taken from pp. 3–6.

investigation. Psychology, in Lewes's view, needs to become more flexible and less speculative. This explains the relatively sparse citation or direct affiliating reference in *Problems of Life and Mind*. An analysis of the (in the Victorian manner) rather haphazard footnotes or citations in the various volumes would produce (for English readers) a rather eccentric profile, which emphasizes rather out-of-the-way European work. Though Comte and Spencer are praised, Lewes takes issue with Spencer in a number of ways, and significantly leaves Comte's work, if not some of his outline propositions, largely alone.[62] The fact is that Lewes did not want to place himself inextricably *anywhere* within present argument (except, of course, within the broadly defined 'materialist' camp). Though he was not so naïve to think that he could avoid the war of the psychological schools, his effort to adjust his tone, to make appeal to the moderate ground and European work, and above all to avoid 'system', 'doctrine', or quarrelsome 'authorities', represents a real effort to devise a way of writing for psychology that was more supple and responsive. In so doing he seeks to reconcile the old wars between the 'sensationalist' and '*a priori*' factions.[63]

Interestingly, Lewes also takes his distance from Bain and Spencer. Their 'compromise' position has advantages, and represents a significant development, but its limitations are equally striking. Despite their achievements, 'the *constitution* of the science [of psychology] has still to be effected'. Psychology lacks, first, a sufficiently clear sense of method (including a satisfactory definition of psychology's object and relationship to other fields of enquiry), and, secondly, the necessary clarity of intellectual effort to think about man *relationally*. Man is not just an individual, but a species; a part not just of nature, but of society too; not just an animal, but distinctively human; not just a body, but a mind.

To this end Lewes argues in volume one that the stony opposition between the human and the natural worlds needs supersession. Not only is the former derived from and, to an extent yet to be ascertained, determined by the latter; both can be described in such a way that they seem more fittingly related to one another. Thus Lewes turns once more to the sophisticated 'organicist' metaphor that was becoming widely deployed by writers in the materialist camp such as John Tyndall. Objecting to the truncated conception of the biological world entertained by popular prejudice, Lewes confronts the 'murder-to-dissect'

---

[62] This is not surprising; if Comte's theories were to be placed among Lewes's three groups, they would come among the other outdated lumber of the 'Empirical' school. Lewes comments that Comte was the victim of metaphor in his notion, derived from Gall, of localized faculties sited in the brain. He leagued Comte in this respect with Kant. Both extrapolated from internal observation to the hypothesis of real entities, be it phrenological anatomy or *a priori* mental forms. The metaphors of 'internal observation' and the 'internal eye' misled both. Note again Lewes's typical concern for accuracy in psychological language (see ibid. iv. 85–6).

[63] For this argument, see ibid. i. 200–47 (problem 1, ch. 2).

arguments we examined in previous chapters and accepts them: 'Theoretically taking the organism to pieces to understand its separate parts, we fall into the error of supposing that the Organism is a mere assemblage of organs, like a machine.' It is not. The

organism is not made, not put together, but evolved; its parts are not juxtaposed, but differentiated; its organs are groups of minor organisms, all sharing in a common life, i.e., all sharing in a common substance constructed through a common process of simultaneous and continuous molecular composition and decomposition; precisely as the great Social Organism is a group of societies, each of which is a group of families, all sharing a common life. . . . In a machine the parts are all different, and have mechanical significance only in relation to the whole. In an Organism the parts are all identical in fundamental characters, and diverse only in their superadded differentiations: each has its independence, although all co-operate.[64]

As a political description, the organic analogy is of ancient—and rather ruined —vintage, and had already come under scrutiny by Marx and others. But the structural conception is very important. It stresses *process* through time, a *dynamic interaction* of parts, and a *functional equality* of parts through the system. In this respect, it is theoretically homologous with Lewes's ideas about the structure and action of the nervous system proposed in his papers to the British Association in 1859 (see Chapter 3). Further, a political scenario that stresses equality and cooperation can be generated from it, which is somewhat different from the Burkean–conservative organicism that George Eliot—though not Lewes—sometimes favoured.[65]

But this is not the main point here. The major point concerns the dynamic, integrationist model with which Lewes (as indeed the later Eliot) is working.

---

[64] Lewes, *Problems*, i. 113–14.

[65] Lewes makes the point that the recent growth in cooperative societies is a healthy sign, because 'in the social organism' it is necessary to set certain specialized tasks apart 'which by their co-operation constitute society' (ibid. iii. 66). This is the leading emphasis, but Lewes is understandably cautious about making too much of analogies drawn—in Spencerian fashion—from political economy (see e.g. his strictures on the physiological 'division of labour' at iii. 218). Lewes points out that in the end such a theory can produce a conclusion that implies a class of worker fit only for certain tasks. This argument is interestingly related to his objections to Spencer's description of the nervous system in *Principles of Biology*. Lewes argues that function is dependent on structure and not the other way round (iii. 69–75). Spencer, in Lamarckian fashion, had argued that biological needs produce functions and therefore structural solutions. In political terms, Spencer's argument leads to the conclusion that an oppressed underclass, say, is the immediate result of biological necessity. In volume one of the *Problems*, Lewes gives a very George Eliot-like version of the drive to cooperation. In its ethical register it is altruistic compassion born from mutual, needful suffering: 'Enlightened by the intuition of our community of weakness, we share ideally the universal sorrows. Suffering humanises. Feeling the need for mutual help, we are prompted by it to labour for others' (i. 166). For illuminating comment on the limitations of this position, see Myers, *The Teaching of George Eliot*, pt. Two.

Drawing upon Claude Bernard,[66] and refusing the automaticist position fashionable among his psycho-physiological peers, Lewes describes an integrated structural model. On the one hand, he posits the 'Bioplasm', or 'Physiological Medium'.[67] This represents the sum of the organic conditions that determine the biological existence of the organism. By analogy, Lewes then posits a 'Psychoplasm', or psychological medium. This represents the sum of the various determining influences that bear upon psychological states. These, he claims, will be found on a spectrum from virtual 'organic' conditions (as derived, say, from hereditary factors) to the varying pressures of social life. The theoretical and descriptive homology between the two systems is essential, because the *whole* organic and mental entity is to be regarded as in immediate, continual, integrative, and enabling contact with the particular environmental medium in which it functions. These processes can be described structurally in the same way, whether this medium is (for example) human society, evolutionary stock, or general biological conditions. The use of similar language, whatever the phenomenon under consideration, is a key theoretical point, as is the second step in Lewes's formulation of these processes. Drawing now on Spencer, Lewes argues that organic processes can be examined in either their 'statical' structural conditions, or their 'dynamical' developmental conditions. 'Statical' and 'dynamical' thus describe analytical operations rather like Saussure's famous synchronic and diachronic axes in the study of language, and they serve to introduce a necessary complicating addition of time—or history—into the otherwise flat analysis.

So Lewes's model respects conditions of time, structure, and analytical parsimony. There are no essentially different analytical operations to be performed at the various levels, and the theory refuses explanations that resort to agencies that lie outside the uniform description of physical or material operations and conditions. Thus, in volume three of the *Problems*, Lewes offers a definition of physiology that embraces a descriptive and developmental perspective based on the idea of the evolution of higher forms in relation to their mediums, and the transition from passive to active existence. The study of physiology, Lewes writes, 'embraces the properties and functions of the tissues and organs—the primary conditions of Growth and Development out of which rise the higher functions

---

[66] Bernard's influence is pervasive in *Problems of Life and Mind* and is explicitly recognized at various points (see i. 116–20, iii, problem 1, ch. 3, and iv. 21). Shuttleworth's account of Bernard's influence on Lewes is first rate (*George Eliot and Nineteenth-Century Science*, esp. chs. 7 and 8). As she points out, Bernard too was influenced by Comte. Mendelsohn, 'Physical Models and Physiological Concepts', and C. U. M. Smith, *The Problem of Life: An Essay in the Origins of Biological Thought* (London, 1976), esp. 215–17, are useful accounts of Bernard's overall significance for the development of biological thought in the period.

[67] Lewes, *Problems*, i. 116–20. Lewes later substituted the less satisfactory term 'Plasmode', because another writer had begun to use 'Bioplasm' in a different way (ibid. iii. 50–9).

bringing the organism into active relation with the surrounding medium'.[68] It is significant that this volume, whose title—*The Physical Basis of Mind*—might have been thought to imply a separation of analysis akin to that of the dualistic, 'two-fold aspect' of the 'compromise' school, in fact opens by stressing the role of *society* in the formation of 'the specifically human faculties of Intellect and Conscience'.[69] In the next volume Lewes reminds us that man's 'higher faculties are evolved through social needs. By this recognition of the social factor as the complement to the biological factor, this recognition of the Mind as an expression of organic and social conditions, the first step is taken towards the constitution of our science.'[70] Lewes credits Comte with the 'general range' of this insight, but notes that he failed to see through the argument in detail. The general idea of devolving psychology to evolutionary biology *plus* the study of society also entailed a revision of traditional 'experience' school theory. In volume one of the *Problems* Lewes takes careful distance from the sensationalists: 'the doctrine of the Sensational School is wholly untenable, partly because our highest knowledge is *not* gained through the senses in any such way, but is gained through the psychological evolution of sociological material', and the senses therefore 'furnish only a small quota to the mass of human experience'.[71] How then does Lewes articulate the transition from one to the other?

One tactic is to use the same language. Alongside a sustained analogical insistence, Lewes tries to maintain descriptive homology across the various modes and registers of his psychology. Thus, describing reflex action, and wanting to force home a point about the necessity of seeing physiological processes as part of a whole functioning structure, Lewes writes that 'No organ has power of control; but the Organism will control an organ. The individual man is powerless against Society; but Society can, and does, compel the individual.'[72] (The strengths and limitations of this model for understanding society are also explored in *Middlemarch*.) Though, of course, there are crucial differences between the body and society (Lewes notes that individuals are, of course, able to exercise choice in ways bodily organs are not), none the less the analogy has a rhetorical and theoretical efficacy. This is because the retention of the same language to describe phenomena hitherto considered unlike both enables the preservation of theoretical regularity, and provides the opportunity to introduce complexity into theories that neglect either pole of the argument. But the retention of a unitary language and outlook entails a redrawing of the whole topography of the mind in such a way that a much more significant role is given to unconscious or preconscious factors. The individual's unique experiences interact with an inherited constitution that is biological and evolutionary. For example, Lewes claims that

[68] Lewes, *Problems*, iii. 7.    [69] Ibid., p. v.
[70] Ibid. iv. 6.    [71] Ibid. i. 134.    [72] Ibid. 139.

the exercise of the intelligence is a matter determined in part by instinct. In volume one of the *Problems* instinct is described, in a rather Spencerian manner, as *'lapsed* or *undiscursive Intelligence'*.[73] It thus forms the 'axiomatic' or unacknowledged basis of thought in which consciousness need play no part. This argument takes the pressure from the neo-Kantian 'forms-of-thought' objection to the 'experience' psychology and, as Lewes says, has the theoretical advantage of bringing 'the highest intellectual process . . . on a level with the process said to be its opposite'.[74] However, it does so at some cost, because it demands the acceptance of the Lamarckian theory of evolution.

We will discuss Lewes's attitudes to Lamarck in detail later, but for the time being it is enough to remark that he could see the problems entailed by Lamarck's ideas very clearly. One form this took was an increasing anxiety about Spencer's psychological theories. This is rarely expressed directly (presumably for reasons of friendship as well as intellectual politics), but the logic of Lewes's position took him away from Spencer's Lamarckian assumptions. Lewes had substantial reservations that complex questions about the exercise of the higher faculties could be answered by biological or physiological analysis alone. In volume four he writes:

Some writers who are disposed to exaggerate the action of Heredity believe that certain specific experiences of social utility in the race become organized in descendants, and are thus transmitted as instincts. With the demonstrated wonders of heredity before us, it is rash to fix limits to the specific determinations it may include; but the evidence in this direction is obscured by the indubitable transmission through language and other social institutions.[75]

Lewes is being necessarily circumspect, and in his usual manner does not name names, but there seems little doubt that he has Spencer—as the foremost theorist of this kind of Lamarckian position—in mind here. What is equally certain is the firm setting of limits to Spencer's claim.

Though, as we have seen, Lewes had adopted the argument about the hereditary derivation of instincts as a bridge to the biological description of the higher faculties, here he seriously modifies that claim. He is understandably guarded about the state of the relevant scientific findings, but is keen to ring-fence 'pure' biological explanation. This was implicit in the earlier formulations in volume one, which, very much in the manner of 'compromise school' and 'double-aspect' theory, followed a section on 'The Biological Data' with one on 'The Sociological Data'. But the connection was made only at the level of the various perspectives and emphases of a developing argument, and without explicit statement. This is a crucial point of difficulty for Lewes, as for late-nineteenth-century

---

[73] Ibid. 141.    [74] Ibid.    [75] Ibid. iv. 152.

psychology generally. Lamarckian theories of the hereditary transmission of acquired characteristics solved certain key theoretical difficulties. But leading thinkers were rightly beginning to doubt their validity, though without any strong sense of an alternative. One of the important differences between Lewes and Spencer, therefore, was Lewes's acceptance of theoretical makeshift in this crucial area, but his abandonment of a doctrinaire position on the matter. This makes his work both more unstable and potentially contradictory, but it also makes it more forward-looking, engaged, and modern.

What is also striking is Lewes's political distance from Spencer. Spencer had hitched the new biological language to Utilitarianism, and it is this—along with its old psychological baggage of self-interest and the pleasure–pain calculation—that is being rejected by Lewes in his circumscription of Spencerian psychological materialism. Lewes wants little to do with Spencer's derivation of 'certain specific experiences of social utility' from biological processes. This position is by no means surprising, because neither Lewes nor George Eliot had ever embraced Utilitarian arguments or perspectives. As William Myers rightly argues, Utilitarian theory could not provide George Eliot with any significant grip on ethical or social issues, and Eliot 'insists that suffering cannot be comfortably disposed of in a book-keeping exercise' such as the felicific calculus.[76]

Instead, both Lewes and Eliot insist on a much more complex language for describing complex human phenomena, and Lewes continued to try to marry biological to other sorts of discourse. Thus in volume four he writes of history as biology and vice versa: the 'shifting panorama of History represents a continuous evolution, a fuller and more luminous tradition, an intenser consciousness of a wider life'.[77] The phrase 'the wider life' could come from George Eliot (as indeed could the whole idea), and other aspects of Lewes's characteristic use of language overlap with that to be found in her work. Consider this proposition, also from volume four: 'We find the impersonal experiences of Tradition accumulating for each individual a fund of Knowledge, an instrument of Power which magnifies his existence.'[78] What is noticeable here is the variety of metaphor in play in a single two-clause sentence. The idea of accumulation and a 'fund of Knowledge' is drawn from economics; the idea of magnifying instruments is drawn from scientific optics (a favourite image for both Lewes and Eliot); and the idea of Power is, less happily, drawn from a nebulous area where physics, history, politics, and theology intersect. My point is not immediately concerned with the truth value of this language. Rather, I am interested in it as a language *performance* designed to elicit a complex, diffuse, and questioning response. This is quite deliberate and sustained in both writers. It is one of the significantly

[76] Myers, *The Teaching of George Eliot*, 184.
[77] Lewes, *Problems*, iv. 153.    [78] Ibid. 80.

impressive things about their work, and it mirrors an emphasis in Lewes on the importance of language for culture, and therefore for psychology. Cultural transmission, largely through language, plays a part equally significant to that of biology in the establishment of the psychological characteristics of the individual or group. This idea is especially emphasized in the last two volumes of *Problems of Life and Mind*, and the underdevelopment of it is perhaps the main regret we have that the *Problems* was ended prematurely.

Language activity such as this is a realization of theoretical proposals made by both Lewes and Eliot. It is first of all an epistemological issue, as in the extraordinarily complex idea of the 'double change of self and beholder' of which Eliot writes in *Middlemarch*. But it mainly concerns the understanding of long-term, biologically orientated processes. Virtually the closing remarks of the (unfinished) volume five of *Problems of Life and Mind* concern the relationship between biology, society, and language. At the close, Lewes writes that 'Language is to the Social Organism very much what the Nervous System is to the Body—a connecting medium which enhances all its functions.'[79] Such ideas are not peculiar to Lewes. (They are to be found early in Eliot's career in the famous 1856 essay on 'The Natural History of German Life', for instance, and she, of course, was elaborating a founding proposition of Romantic organicism.) But Lewes is keen to stress the *activity* of language, not just in terms of dynamic process, but also in terms of human agency, and this prevents his thinking sliding into metaphorical commonplace. Lewes is using a conventional notion, but he is adding to it a refreshingly new sense of the particular human possibilities in creative language use. Language is no longer only a metonym for other abstract, transindividual processes such as nation, race, or (upper-case) Culture operating with remote indifference to the activities of the individuals or groups that compose social units. Language is a matter of human use and historical opportunity. It connects individual to individual, nation to nation, epoch to epoch: 'indeed, the history of culture may serve to convince us that we have still only a rudimentary understanding of the reach and potency of symbols.'[80]

Fittingly, therefore, Lewes closes the unfinished *Problems* not with an account of biological processes, but with a salute to human empowerment and achievement. The stress had to fall on the biological substrata of human behaviour. Knowledge could not progress without this crucial realignment of thinking, but,

having shown the continuity and uniformity of sensible and ideal states as regards the neural processes which are their organic substrata, and thus excluded the hypothesis of separate organs for Thought and Feeling, we shall have to expound the operation of the Social Factor, the introduction of which is the real cause of the elevation of Animal

[79] Ibid. v. 495.    [80] Ibid.

Psychology into Human Psychology, the sensible into the ideal world, Knowledge into Science, Emotion into Sentiment, and Appetite into Morality.[81]

Lewes thought of this as his distinctive achievement, as did a number of his contemporaries, and there is no doubt that Lewes significantly reworked the methodological orientation and theoretical implications of mid-to-late-nineteenth-century psychology in this respect.[82] Lewes's consistently integrationist view of the interlocking processes of organic and social life has a number of consequences, among the most important of which is his proposal for a radical solution to the ancient dualism with which psychology struggled throughout the period covered by this study. This dualism is, of course, the ancient difficulty of the 'mind–body' problem, which, in various versions and with much political strife, has been at the centre of most of the arguments analysed in this book.

Lewes's solution to this problem is bold, and strikingly anticipates some very recent formulations of it. Simply put, he refuses to accept the problem as anything other than an analytical fiction, a product of a certain way of seeing psychological phenomena. Just as the language used to describe social and biological systems can transcend mere analogy and become adequate to each object once the whole nature of the process-based relationship between mind and medium is grasped, so Lewes believes that the habitual dualism of mind-and-body is itself merely a matter of language and convention. Like J. Z. Young, the eminent modern-day writer on brain systems, Lewes claims that the dualism inherent in our perceptions of the mind–body problem reflects a larger cultural condition. The problem stems, Lewes argues, from the habit of thinking about mind as an entity separate from the organism and society, and sovereign over each.[83] The mind–body problem is thus itself a function of a general intellectual and cultural bias. Thus Young begins his book *Philosophy and the Brain* by noting that many still claim 'that there are problems of philosophy and theology that can

---

[81] Lewes, *Problems*, v. 443.

[82] Even a hostile critic like Carveth Read thought that Lewes's emphasis on the relationship between Mind and the Social Medium was 'his signal and crowning achievement' ('G. H. Lewes's Posthumous Volumes', *Mind*, 6 (1881), 498), and George Croom Robertson, an enthusiast for Lewes's work, felt that his stress on the social context of psychological development marked his advance over both Spencer and Bain ('How we Come by our Knowledge', 113–21). Théodule Ribot, in *English Psychology*, also stressed Lewes's innovations in this respect, as did Frederic Harrison in 'The Social Factor in Psychology' (1879; repr. in Harrison, *The Philosophy of Common Sense* (London, 1907), 122–30), and W. K. Clifford, who, in his review of volume one ('*Problems of Life and Mind* by George Henry Lewes', *Academy*), saluted Lewes's conception of 'whole new science of language'. Lewes's ideas on the relations between mind, biology, and society were also prominently credited by the anonymous reviewers in the *Saturday Review* in 1873 ('Lewes's Problems of Life and Mind', *Saturday Review*, 36 (1873), 758) and the *Athenaeum* in 1879 ('Current Philosophy', *Athenaeum*, 27 Sept. 1879, 398). The conservative writer on 'Mr Lewes and Metaphysics' in the *Westminster*, however, thought it a 'somewhat strange theory' and attacked the 'excessive weight' Lewes gave to social influences (pp. 110–11).                                      [83] Lewes, *Problems*, iv. 7.

be solved without reference to the brain', but this merely displays 'the weakness produced by our intellectual and social system that separates thinkers from observers, philosophers from scientists'. The problem, Young argues, is primarily a problem of language. The philosopher and the scientist use different languages; and the difficulty with the philosopher's language is that it is imprecise and contaminated by cultural biases. The philosopher 'uses mentalistic words, often of common speech'. But it 'is very difficult to agree about the use of these, because of the privacy and variety of their subject-matter'. It is therefore necessary to reformulate the language for discussing such problems using the relatively neutral 'scientific discourse [which] almost by definition depends upon words that can be confirmed and agreed by all appropriately trained humans'.[84]

Young might overestimate the neutrality and clarity of scientific discourse, but the strength of his case does not rest there, and there is a way of extending the argument that takes account of this difficulty and preserves the advantages of Lewes's general proposition. In *Minds, Brains, and Science*, his 1984 Reith lectures, the American philosopher John Searle attacks both the conventional way of putting the mind–body problem, and the narrowly scientific solutions attached to it by recent researchers. Taking the latter problem first, Searle argues that contemporary scientific models of human behaviour—such as the various efforts to understand the brain in terms of the operations performed by computers—in fact ignore what is distinctive about human intelligence. This includes its creativity, which in turn is part of a general human ability to think 'semantically' (as Searle puts it, drawing on Chomsky's account of language usage) as well as 'formally or syntactically', which are the principles on which computers work.[85] In recent computer-based models, ostensibly neutral scientific language (in Young's terms) is in fact unhelpful, because the proposed analogy, within the framework of which the 'scientific' language operates, is not adequate to the task. (We shall return to this problem in relation to Lewes's biological model in due course.)

Despite these reservations about the adequacy of recent conceptual modelling for the mind, Searle is not proposing a return to dualistic theories—far from it. In fact, his solution to the problem is thoroughly monistic and, in its simplicity and conclusions, is remarkably similar to that offered by Lewes 100 years earlier. Searle proposes that, instead of thinking about two distinct entities (mind and body, or brain), we think about 'surface' and 'deep' features, which have a necessary, because causal, identity. This proposition, however, requires some readjustment of our sense of causation, and Searle invites us to think about cause not as a relation between two different and separate phenomena (that is,

[84] J. Z. Young, *Philosophy and the Brain* (Oxford, 1987), 1.
[85] Searle, *Minds, Brains and Science*.

involving some notion of change in the passage from 'brain' to 'mind', or cause to effect), but as an alteration in perspective and circumstances. We should understand cause as a process of *realization*, not alteration, because there is a fundamental identity between processes at a deep or infrastructural level and those at an experiential or surface level. The same phenomena, that is to say, are 'realized in' different forms. An example Searle gives is the experience of the liquidity of water at what he calls the 'macro' level of 'ordinary' experience. This experience may be different from the understanding of its chemical structure (the 'micro' level), but it does not alter the fundamental identity of the two phenomena. The same is true for brain and mind. What is more, the whole has to be understood as an interacting system whose whole nature is more than that of its components or individual properties: 'though we can say of a system of particles that it is 10°C or it is solid or it is liquid, we cannot say of any given particle that this particle is solid, this particle is liquid, this particle 10°C. I can't for example reach into this glass of water, pull out a molecule and say: "This one's wet." '[86] Searle thus concludes that 'the way, in short, to dispel the mystery is to understand the processes', and that what he ironically calls his own 'naïve mentalism' and 'naïve physicalism' are both compatible and true.[87]

I have spent some time introducing these ideas through modern writers, because it seems to me that the success, clarity, and modernity of Lewes's thought in this respect is best brought forward in this way. Lewes's science (of course) is disabled by age and error; but his methodological and philosophical grasp is startlingly similar to that of John Searle (and less completely to that of J. Z. Young), and the simplicity and elegance of his formulation of this ancient problem seem to me compelling. In *Problems of Life and Mind* Lewes conceives of the mind–body relationship in these terms: 'every mental phenomenon has its corresponding neural phenomenon (the two being as convex and concave surfaces of the same sphere, distinguishable yet identical), and . . . every neural phenomenon involves the whole Organism; by which alone the influence of the body on the mind, and the mind on the body, can be explained.'[88] Searle uses metaphors of surface and depth, or whole and structuring parts (macro and micro). These images are suggestive in that they express both integral connection and determining power. Lewes, here, uses a metaphor of two surfaces of the same shape, 'distinguishable yet identical'.

This is probably Lewes's favourite image (though it is not his only one by any means), and it probably loses something of the sense of determination offered by Searle. But it does preserve a handy sense of the analytic project on which Lewes felt himself to be embarked—that is, to give no inevitable, analytic priority to either physiological or psychological events. Like Searle, Lewes is careful to

---

[86] Searle, *Minds, Brains and Science*, 22.    [87] Ibid. 23, 27.
[88] Lewes, *Problems*, i. 112.

underline the importance of process and integral connection. The concave/convex metaphor, therefore, offers both an admirable circumspection and a methodological advantage, because it allows Lewes to try to integrate both aspects of his analysis, and to avoid the pitfalls of reductionism so graphically before him in the intellectual culture of his period. As Lewes says, the idea of 'the two-fold aspect' (another of the visual or optical images so common in Lewes's and Eliot's writing in this period[89]) enables the integration of different ways of perceiving, and organizes the various binary structures that feature so heavily in his analysis: subject and object, mind and matter, static and dynamic,[90] experience and existence, feeling and describing.[91] (The feeling/describing distinction corresponds to one Lewes makes between Perception—the consciousness of 'Reals'—and Conception—their articulation in symbols. We shall return to this later.) All this replaces 'the old Dualism' with a 'Monism, in which only one existence, under different forms, is conceived'.[92] It dissolves, Lewes claims, the Cartesian paradox of a mechanically functioning body to which is added a divine soul.[93] At the same time, though, it contests the militant materialism of 'automatists' such as Huxley and Tyndall.

*Problems of Life and Mind* is uncompromisingly opposed to automatist theories. If Lewes had begun to explore the limits of Spencer's biological paradigm, to which he was much closer, then he had no hesitation in taking his distance from Huxley. He attacks the propositions Huxley had advanced in the early 1870s (on which we have commented in Chapter 3) in the third volume of the *Problems*. Huxley's ideas are a 'legitimate expression' of 'Reflex Theory', but exaggerate the claims of that theory.[94] Specifically, Huxley's conception of reflex action is too mechanical, and he fails to offer an adequate account of consciousness. Huxley's apparent monism, in fact, is a covert dualism. By arguing that anything performed unconsciously must be automatic, and that only the brain is capable of sentience, Huxley is actually constructing a model in which consciousness is separated from the rest of the organism. Whether, with the Cartesian spiritualists, consciousness is regarded as sovereign, or, with Huxley (as we have seen in Chapter 3), it is regarded as mysterious, temporary, and circumscribed, matters little. Both models remain dualistic, because they are based upon a misleading analogy: that human beings are like machines. As a result there has been an oscillation between automatism and Idealism; the one corrects the overemphases of the other, but neither is able to get a satisfactory purchase on the problem to bypass its antagonism.[95]

---

[89] In ibid. ii. 13 Lewes uses vision as itself the key example of the interaction of the subjective and objective in mental activity.

[90] Ibid. i. 69, 76; iii. 3, 313.     [91] Ibid. ii. 16, 27; v. 229–30.     [92] Ibid. i. 122.

[93] Ibid. iv. 20–1.     [94] Ibid. iii. 403.

[95] Ibid. 309–21. This kind of argument seems to me much more powerful than the standard 'spiritualist' outcry against automatism.

By contrast, Lewes wishes to see consciousness as having a relatively auto-nomous role within its own field of activity. But this should be understood only within a general map of manifold determinations and complex, synergistic causation in which 'the *collateral product of one movement becomes a directing factor in the succeeding movement*'.[96] The word 'factor' is particularly important here, because we are dealing with not exclusive but 'overdetermined' phenomena in which acts of consciousness are causes as well as results. The important difference is, again, made by history, because it is the power to learn from experience that enables humans to become agents in their own processes. A machine has 'no *historical* factor manifest in its functions . . . no experience',[97] but the significant thing about humans is that their 'primary' tendencies can be modified or even suppressed: 'I need not dwell on the profound modifications which the human inherited mechanism undergoes in the course of experience—how social influences and moral and religious teachings redirect, or even suppress, many primary tendencies; so that "moral habits" become organized, and replace the original tendency of the organism.'[98] This is followed by a nuanced and sophist-icated account of the graduated and alterable relationship between automatic, 'secondarily automatic', and voluntary processes.

However, the overall trajectory of this analysis is clearly Lamarckian, and as a result Lewes is again returned to the theoretical impasse this tended to pro-duce. Lamarck could provide a bridge from one part of the theory to the next, but he enabled writers like Spencer, and here Lewes, only to finesse a problem, not to solve it. Lamarck was convenient, because his theories offered unitary explanations across the mental/physical divide, and seemed to do so without sacrificing significant attention to the 'higher' psychological faculties. However, this unitary theory did not make the detailed descriptive difficulties disappear. Here is Lewes's account of the will, for example. The will is 'the abstract generalized expression of the impulses which determine actions, when those impulses have an ideal origin'. General Volition is a 'still more generalized expression of all impulses which determine actions'.[99] All Lewes is doing here is passing off a taxonomic placing for a genetic description in a way familiar from the history of associationist psychology.

The difficulty concerns the adequacy of language to represent experience in both 'mental' and 'physiological' registers simultaneously. In volume five of *Problems*, when Lewes again turns to the problem of the will, he seizes gleefully on the happy double meaning of the word 'Reflection'. According to Lewes it signifies both the action of the reflex system, and an intellectual act—that is, 'the lowest and the highest psychical phenomena'.[100] In a way this represents his ideal

---

[96] Lewes, *Problems*, iii. 407.　　[97] Ibid. 326.　　[98] Ibid. 329.
[99] Ibid. 377.　　[100] Ibid. v. 399.

psychological language, in which there is a seamless movement between the physical and the mental, the convex and concave surfaces. 'The intellectual life', he writes, 'is the outcome of the affective; *it is only a mode of representation of the feelings*, which afterwards becomes their *substitute*'.[101] As for the freedom of the will, Lewes came up with a handy metaphor for a flexible statement of the determinist position. Man is like a sailing ship. He is driven by nature ultimately, but he has the power to manipulate the diverse forces in play, and therefore has an absolute freedom within sets of limiting constraints.[102] The weakness of this argument, though, is entailed in its metaphorical structure. Another way of inter-preting the metaphor could make an equally good 'spiritualist' case (the cap-tain's relationship to the vessel is as the soul's to the body), and Lewes would certainly not want that. As John Searle also recognized, the account of the will is the weakest part of this way of conceiving of the mind–body problem, because it seems to entail more than a revision of formal descriptions of behaviour.[103] It involves, in fact, the assessment of conduct, the establishment of rules for conduct, and an account of the psychological conditions under which such conduct is possible or not possible. Here, again, lies the appeal of Lamarck's theory, which can sidestep the issue rather neatly by entailing a teleologically accumulating definition of right conduct. For Spencer, the assessment of conduct can be reserved as a biological matter: the evolutionarily successful must, by definition, inherit and pass forward moral as well as physical attributes, and these attributes must, by the test of history, be right—that is, successful. For all Spencer's neo-Utilitarian opposition to the status quo, his is a deeply con-servative theory in many respects.

Lewes's critics and commentators at the time were not slow to seize on his refusal to posit an ontological distinction between physical and mental acts, nor his difficulties in giving a satisfactory account of the transition from the one to the other. For some—like Douglas Spalding—Lewes did not pursue the implica-tions of his monistic explanation far enough, nor argue sufficiently fiercely for the absolute elision of the mental and the physical.[104] Others, like the neo-Kantian philosopher Shadworth Hodgson in *Mind*, protested at what he took to be Lewes's assimilation of the philosophy of mind to material science, the mental to the physical. Hodgson argued, in a familiar way, that the two needed to be kept distinct because mental philosophy has a method and object of its own. This method and object are the analysis of the nature and quality of con-sciousness, not its origins or functions. Science was the objective analysis of mind,

---

[101] Ibid. 407; emphasis added.      [102] Ibid. iv. 103–9.
[103] Searle, *Minds, Brains and Science*, ch. 6.
[104] Spalding, 'The Physical Basis of Mind'. Spalding mentions Huxley's 'automatism' hypo-thesis approvingly.

philosophy its subjective analysis, and the two needed to be kept distinct.[105] Hodgson's piece is, therefore, a kind of last-ditch defence of introspection without the combative, critical edge that made T. H. Green's arguments for the same kind of position so much more powerful. In the event Hodgson's essays were comfortably refuted by Alexander Main—the editor of *Wise, Witty and Tender Sayings of George Eliot* (1871)—in a piece for *Mind* that pleased Lewes.[106]

Other objectors to Lewes's formulations were less easy to dismiss, however, largely because they were less willing to concede the ground that Hodgson so prematurely does in his over-respectful account of the new psychology in *Mind*, the psychologists' house journal. Among sterner critics, the burden of the argument fell upon what became known as the 'transformation problem', or the 'problem of the gap', in John Searle's terms. The gap in question is the supposition that the transition from neurological or brain activity to mental events in consciousness involves a shift in ontological status. For thinkers like Lewes or Searle there is no such problem. Searle says that 'some of the greatest intellectual efforts of the twentieth century have been attempts to fill this gap, to get a science of human behaviour which was not just commonsense grandmother psychology, but was not scientific neurophysiology either. . . . [But] all the gap-filling efforts fail because there isn't any gap to fill.'[107] Lewes says: 'all the evidence points to the . . . fact that the neural process and the feeling are one and the same process viewed under different aspects. Viewed from the physical or objective side, it is a neural process; viewed from the psychological or subjective side, it is a sentient process.'[108] None the less, throughout its history, psychology has been plagued by the problem. Even in ostensibly 'materialist' accounts, the deployment of analogies or models from other kinds of processes—such as computers or other machines—in fact produce (as Searle again says) a 'residual dualism'—as found, for example, among partisans of artificial intelligence (AI) theories: 'AI partisans believe that the mind is more than a part of the natural biological world; they believe that the mind is purely formally specifiable.' Though AI specialists themselves fulminate against 'dualism', in fact their reluctance to remain content with biological accounts of the mind inevitably introduces a transformation problem.[109] As we have seen, Lewes made exactly the same point in relation to Huxleyan automaticism.

---

[105] Shadworth H. Hodgson, 'Philosophy and Science: I—As Regards the Special Sciences', *Mind*, 1 (1876), 67–81; 'Philosophy of Mind: II—As Regards Psychology', 223–35; 'Philosophy and Mind: III—As Regards Ontology', 351–62. Hodgson's is a generalizing essay but primarily addresses itself to *Problems of Life and Mind*.

[106] Alexander Main, 'Mr. Hodgson on Mr. Lewes's View of Philosophy', *Mind*, 1 (1876), 292–4. For Lewes's comments on the piece, see Eliot, *Letters*, vi. 218. Main was more usually known to Eliot and Lewes as 'the Gusher'.

[107] Searle, *Minds, Brains and Science*, 42. See also Ramachandran, *Phantoms*, 231–2.

[108] Lewes, *Problems*, ii. 459.      [109] Searle, *Minds, Brains and Science*, 38.

However, from the standpoint of psychological theory in the 1870s, the problem was yet more acute. To common sense, it indeed seems the case that there is a clear difference between the description of neural activity, however sophisticated, and the experience of the exercise of the higher human faculties in and through consciousness. There does seem to be, at very least, the need to add something to the neurological description that can make the phenomenon recognizable and comprehensible in human terms, and, in the late nineteenth century, the perception of this problem was overdetermined by lively religious, cultural, and political contexts. Though a handful of commentators on *Problems of Life and Mind*—like the perceptive reviewer of the second volume in the *Saturday Review*[110]—applauded Lewes's efforts to think about the continuities of phenomena, most were antagonistic. Even among Lewes's supporters the issue divided opinion. James Sully was quite definite that there is a transformational problem, and that Lewes confused 'aspects' with 'conditions'. Sully argued that nerve processes do not themselves 'feel'; states of feeling are distinct and special acts of consciousness. Lewes's refusal to accept any distinction between subject and object issued in a 'scientific monism', which was to all intents and purposes itself metaphysical, because it made truth claims of a general, unverifiable, and reductionist kind.[111]

Théodule Ribot, on the other hand, recognized the strength and originality of Lewes's arguments. He saw how they advanced beyond the epistemological impasse reached by extremist physiologists (we might think of Huxley or Tyndall as examples) who could not generate a satisfactory transition from states of '*interiority*' to those of '*exteriority, or objectivity*' on the basis of which a scientist would be able to make defensibly objective claims about the world. For Ribot, Lewes solved the problem by refusing to accept the terms on which it is proposed. There is for him no transformation problem: 'the only transformation which takes place . . . is that of certain analytic factors into a synthetic fact.'[112] In other words, it is a purely formal, analytical operation. Whereas Sully wished to preserve an ontological distinction, Ribot maintains that it 'is most important to see clearly that the logical distinction between the conditions of a phenomenon, and the phenomenon itself, is simply an artifice'. This means that, when applied to psycho-physiological questions, 'we shall see that the nervous process is not the antecedent of the sensation, but that both are identical'.[113] Following Lewes (and like Searle), Ribot stresses *process*, and locates the nub of the problem in the kind of formal analytical operation one chooses to perform. The problem, therefore, is not essentially ontological; it is epistemological and descriptive. What language does one choose?

[110] Anon., 'Lewes's Problems of Life and Mind', *Saturday Review*, 4 Sept. 1875, 301–2. Lewes found the review 'very gratifying' (Eliot, *Letters*, vi. 202).
[111] Sully, 'Problems of Life and Mind. Third Series', 309.
[112] Ribot, *English Psychology*, 313.     [113] Ibid. 312.

Among the more aggressive of Lewes's critics, however, the transformation problem was a source of real difficulty. Inevitably, the anonymous *Westminster* reviewer saw the issue in religious terms. For him, certain metaphysical propositions were self-evidently true on grounds of custom and intuition. But, if Lewes's path were followed, religion and metaphysics would no longer have a language available to them, and the reviewer deplored the anti-religious aggression he detected running through *Problems*. However, like Sully and a number of other writers, he does hit upon a weak spot in Lewes's theory, which is the inadequacy of physiological knowledge to describe in detail the processes of which so much is made. He notes that, in fact, Lewes tries to bridge the gaps in available knowledge by 'throwing out dim metaphysical phrases in the hope, it would seem, that they may congeal and stiffen into some phantom bridge to span the gulf between the consciousness which consists in "neural tremors", and the real consciousness of the inner life'.[114] As we have seen, this is a real difficulty for Lewes and kindred theorists, and it is one reason why the language question is so crucial. However, in this case, the criticism is unfairly extended to support other kinds of assertion, and the writer's conclusion that the status quo is therefore valid does not necessarily follow. It should also be noted that this problem bedevilled all work—some of it much better science—in this area in the period. Darwin, for instance, also lacked a satisfactory description of the biological mechanism his general theory demanded.

Other writers focused on the same issue. Elizabeth Hamilton (Sir William's daughter), in arguments reminiscent of both her father and T. H. Green, contended that Lewes's ostensible differences with the 'automaton' or mechanistic theories of the radical materialists were in fact only nominal. There was still a huge gap between 'sentience' and 'sensibility':

We fail, therefore, to see that Mr. Lewes's theory, in replacing a mechanical by an organic view of the production of action, or rather in setting up a sensitive instead of a material mechanism, differs in any essential respect from that against which he contends; or that the word sensitive has any particular value, when sensibility is reduced to a purely vital property, and the springs of action are traced to the harmonious play of parts in a complicated organism.[115]

The argument is both strong and weak with respect to its critique of the language of physiology. It is true that an alteration in wording does not change a process, but nor does a failure in wording mean that the process does not exist. Like many such arguments in the period (as John Tyndall recognized to his fury), Hamilton's rests on the status quo. It passes the burden of proof from its own assertions to the more novel assertions of its opponents. The argument also

[114] Anon., 'Mr Lewes and Metaphysics', 130.
[115] E[lizabeth] Hamilton, 'Mr. Lewes's Doctrine of Sensibility', *Mind*, 4 (1879), 257.

suffers from a version of the problem John Searle identified with respect to models drawn from artificial intelligence. Hamilton refuses to accept biological language as sufficient to describe biological phenomena. Biology is, for her, an inert area in human terms. Like the 'automaton materialists' she opposes, Hamilton cannot see the difference between machines and bodies, and for her, therefore, by definition, it is impossible to generate human experience and acts of consciousness from machine parts.

Hamilton's argument was commonly made. 'Between the two processes, the physical and the psychical,' wrote the Congregationalist divine Thomas Herbert in 1874, 'there is a clear distinction.'[116] Indeed, each had its separate form of energy; a 'radical diversity seems to exist between all the forms of physical and psychical energy'.[117] The 'double aspect' solution, argues Herbert, 'does but vary our difficulties'.[118] Similarly, in an unfriendly review of the last two volumes of *Problems of Life and Mind*, Carveth Read, Professor of Psychology and Philosophy at the University of London (and a Millite clearly cross with Lewes for what he took to be Lewes's criticisms of Mill), chided Lewes with failing to make clear how it was that 'sentience' could be generated from 'neurility', particularly because Lewes refused to speak in terms of cause and effect. Making the whole system homologous produces an inadvertent argument for dualism, because, he claimed, Lewes's monism cannot get to grips with the problem of consciousness as formulated in the neo-Kantian critiques of the new psychology.[119]

Even moderate opinion rested its case on a dualistic ontology. William Smith's sensible, intelligent pieces for the *Contemporary Review* in 1870 on 'Knowing and Feeling' quite deliberately adopt the language of two authors close to Lewes's heart—Shelley and George Eliot—to describe the relationship between sentience and intellect. He concludes, however, that, despite the massive advances in recent knowledge, and the powerful arguments for understanding these as related phenomena, consciousness cannot be reduced to sensation. There is too massive a problem in 'tracing the threads of that delicate machinery by means of which the world of space, the world of form, and motion, transforms itself through the sensibilities of man, into a world of thought, of beauty, of intelligence'.[120]

---

[116] [Thomas Martin Herbert], 'Mind and the Science of Energy', *British Quarterly Review*, 60 (1874), 107.

[117] Ibid. 119.    [118] Ibid. 128.    [119] Read, 'Lewes's Posthumous Volumes', 483–98.

[120] William Henry Smith, 'Knowing and Feeling: A Contribution to Psychology', 342. The echo of the language of George Eliot in this quotation is very marked, and Eliot is quoted twice in the second part of the essay: 'Knowing and Feeling: Part II.—Some Further Discussion of the Will', *Contemporary Review*, 15 (1870), 424–39. Both Smith and Lewes had been champions of Shelley in the 1840s, and had remained friendly. George Eliot described Smith as 'morally and intellectually sympathetic', and speaks of Lewes's 'peculiar attachment' to him in 1872 (George Eliot to Mrs Taylor, 19 Nov. 1872, *Letters*, v. 328). Smith deploys the imagery of Shelley's well-known lyric 'When the lamp is shattered' in his argument for the integral, independent existence of a self

Liberal theological opinion, then, represented by Smith and the *Contemporary*, conceded a little ground, but insisted on maintaining a dualism. Smith is tolerant towards evolutionary theory, but he recoups the concession by taking the line also taken by several of Spencer's religious supporters—that is, to identify the evolutionary process with a sophisticated natural theology: 'To us evolution is but a name for the method of creation, and the nature of the created.'[121] Smith also makes use of the adjacent quasi-Spencerian argument concerning ultimate unknowables. The processes and forces at the bottom of things are imponderable. They can, therefore, in all significant respects, be identified with God. The chancy, regulatedly chaotic world of the Darwinian paradigm had not yet been revealed to some mainstream opinion.

### EPISTEMOLOGY AND ONTOLOGY IN *PROBLEMS OF LIFE AND MIND*

If Lewes's opponents insisted upon an ontological dualism, how did Lewes himself conceive of ontological questions? The direction of his argument goes something like this: the interaction of the world (the 'external medium') with our biological being (the 'internal medium') determines our mental structures. But, because human consciousness acts with relative independence from those determining processes, and because mental experience is in a different mode from physical experience, consciousness *appears* to be a distinctive, separate, autonomous entity. Ontologically, however, it is identical. What are usually considered ontological questions are in fact epistemological questions. They are essentially concerned with the descriptive adequacy of our chosen language to represent the real state of affairs, bearing in mind that human knowledge is circumscribed and historically determined, and therefore all language always struggles to be comprehensive.

This is a coherent and persuasive position. However, the argument suffers from difficulties. It concedes that human knowledge is relative, so one problem for Lewes (as for Eliot) is to determine the degree of that relativism and assess its significance. When does relativism become a corrosive scepticism? Another problem concerns the establishment of criteria on the basis of which knowledge is to be considered reliable and accurate (this is essentially a problem of scientific method and empirical procedure, and need not detain us long). A third, related problem concerns the instruments of knowledge: is there anything in the

---

separate from organic processes. He also uses Tennyson and Shakespeare. Smith (who was, among other things, a poet) is putting a late, liberal version of the 'literary' case against 'materialist' psychology whose harder edge we have examined in earlier chapters. Indeed some of his conclusions look forward to the Henry James–Leavis–New Critical account of Eliot, which dominated responses to her work in the early to mid-twentieth century.

[121]   Smith, 'Knowing and Feeling: A Contribution to Psychology', 351.

conditions of language or consciousness that would lead us to question their sufficiency or reliability? The fourth and last problem concerns the difficulty of generating abiding rules or principles (for example, moral rules or principles) that might guide conduct beyond the historical or personal moment of their conception. In other words, if knowledge is historical, does that not compromise truths that one might wish to recommend for their intrinsic virtues? (As we have seen, this—or a version of this—was a charge regularly levelled at the new psychology.)

Lewes's epistemology has two essential features. The first is that humans have unarguably direct, but necessarily limited, access to a reality outside consciousness and language. His epistemology is thus at bottom a direct, sensory realism. The second feature, however, concerns human modes of representation, and here Lewes is less obviously a direct realist. Indeed, he is conscious of both the provisionality and potential waywardness of knowledge propositions represented in language. These two features of the theory, which run in parallel in all of Lewes's accounts of them, are called by him the 'Logic of Feeling' and the 'Logic of Signs'. Lewes's epistemology is based on the intersection of the two, the dialogue of authority with limitation, confidence with provisionality.

The Logic of Feeling is the immediate sensory experience of the world. The Logic of Signs is the encoding or representation of that experience by language or other means. However, the one is not merely reflectively adequate to the other as in a simple correspondence theory. This is because, first, the means of representation is ultimately unreliable (that is, it is historically limited), and, secondly, human perception is itself circumscribed in both its range and efficiency. The one limitation can influence the other. The conventional means of interpreting the world that prevails in any epoch will determine what most people see and believe. What is seen may not be the real case (that the sun goes round the earth, for example). Alternatively, we may simply be unable to see enough to offer an adequate notion of what constitutes an event or phenomenon. In other words, it is inevitable that hypotheses (or, as Lewes more generally calls them, 'inferences') are formed and these may run free of their empirical or experiential basis.

There are thus two orders of phenomena, a 'Two-fold Aspect' to truth: that of Perception, and that of Conception. The former deals with the correspondence between objects and consciousness; the latter between objects in consciousness.[122] This theory is developed throughout volumes one and two of *Problems of Life and Mind*. Which of these two aspects Lewes chooses to emphasize at any given time depends upon which purpose he has in view. (For instance, is he interested in a 'scientific' or a 'historical-cultural' proposition?) Of course such

---

[122] Lewes, *Problems*, ii. 70.

a juggling of perspectives can become unstable and unsatisfying, but this is the risk Lewes runs throughout, and for interesting reasons. His weaknesses and his strengths are again related.

The separation of the two parts of Lewes's theory is essential to anchor the potential instability of the latter part. Thus a portion of Lewes's efforts in his epistemology is to keep the two separate. Once the former is invaded by the uncertainties of the latter then the materialist–realist edifice threatens to crumble, and a realist epistemology would have to fall back on a 'Symbolical or Transfigured Realism' of the kind advocated by Spencer.[123] Lewes is unhappy with this prospect, because it is but one step from the quasi-intuitionist arguments offered by the neo-Kantians. Spencer accepts that the world is ultimately unknowable, but insists that theories about it can be formed asymptotically, and that their validity is falsifiable at any point. 'Truth' is, therefore, a matter of the survival of the fittest theory, an act of intuition based on a prevailing idea and buttressed by Lamarckian-style inheritances. Lewes, however, recognizes the proximity of this to *a priori* or neo-Idealist theories, and wishes to retain a more thorough purchase on the sensory and experiential elements that form our knowledge.[124] Thus, for him, perception is more of a 'resultant' than a 'symbolical' rendering of the world.[125] Initially, these arguments may seem matters only of gradation and emphasis, but the stakes are very high. They are, for instance, related to the big contradiction in Spencer's work: that between a systemized, truth-demanding, totalized account of the world, and an epistemology that stresses provisionality and falsifiability. Lewes, as we have said, is much more committed to the 'mess' of sensory and historical experience, and the somewhat inelegant structure of his texts, and their more tortured epistemological theorizing, are at least congruent with, if not entirely caused by, this fact—as are the hesitations, slippages, revisions, and potential contradictions in some of his arguments.

Lewes needs to make a strong case for the sensory aspect of his epistemology to maintain his particular realist claims, but he also needs to acknowledge the force of the Logic of Signs, because his theory has been directed towards the historicization of knowledge. Inevitably, the latter feature engages our modern interests more closely than the former. But, though Lewes's claims about our experiential apprehension of the world are subject to knock-down arguments of a sceptical kind, and though some of his contemporary commentators (such as

---

[123] Lewes, *Problems*, i. 177.
[124] Lewes argues that Spencer's 'transcendental postulate' is akin to 'the abiding mystery which is at the root of all religion'. It opens the gates to theorizing noumena behind phenomena. Spencer, that is to say, sees the world as necessarily unknown, rather than potentially knowable (Lewes, ibid. ii. 443–52, 487).          [125] Ibid. i. 192–3.

Bain, for instance[126]) doubted that Lewes's conception of experience was exacting enough, the claims he makes about the Logic of Feeling have to be provisionally accepted before any sort of progress with the more developed theories can be made and their limits properly determined. We need to accept, therefore, that knowledge claims are anchored at some level in sensory experience; that they are verifiable by reference to it; and that the means of such verification become more exacting as history, and science, progress.

Lewes is very firm about the historicality of the Logic of Signs: 'The language we think in, and the conceptions we employ, the attitude of our minds, and the means of investigation, are social products determined by the activities of the Collective Life. The laws of intellectual process are to be read in History, not in the individual experience.'[127] Yet this passage is interesting. The ostensible opposition between individual and collective, historical experience is, from a nineteenth-century evolutionary—and especially a Lamarckian—perspective, not quite as abrupt as it at first seems. The proposition is that the individual's experience is limited by the individual's historical location. But any individual is also the inheritor of the past through culture, intellectual tradition, and, in Lamarckian or Spencerian theory, biology. In the same way that the individual inherits the past, he or she also points to the future, because our intellectual life is changing and developing. Thus the individual's historicality is both a source of limitation and a source of strength. In epistemological terms, the individual is circumscribed by the prevailing ethos and conventions, but these conventions have been questioned in the past, and are in dynamic development in the present. Lewes's sense of the positive features of historicality are evident in his language. The stress on limitation at the beginning of the passage just quoted gives way to confident talk of 'the *laws* of intellectual process' (emphasis added) at the end. And Lewes's Germanic habit of capitalizing abstract nouns gives them a rhetorical force that suggests a confident general sense of progress (or Progress) that is teleologically inflected. Thus, the passage expresses both reservation and confidence simultaneously, and it is easy to relate this to a similar bifocality in the attitude to historical locatedness to be found in *Middlemarch*, for example.

So there are the beginnings of a contradiction, or uncertainty, here. If *Problems of Life and Mind* converts ontological questions into epistemological or historical questions, then that sense of history, or of epistemological or representational uncertainty, is not functioning as a kind of radical Derridean or Nietzschean

---

[126] Alexander Bain, 'Mr. G. H. Lewes on the Postulates of Experience', *Mind*, 1 (1876), 146. Lewes replied in the same volume: see G. H. Lewes, 'The Uniformity of Nature', *Mind*, 1 (1876), 283–4. There is a succinct and intelligent discussion of the general issue by the anonymous reviewer of the second volume of *Problems of Life and Mind* in the *Saturday Review*, 40 (1875), 301.

[127] Lewes, *Problems*, i. 174.

unsettlement of order that dissolves all truth propositions into the actions of a discursive or political hegemony. Occasionally this perspective is opened up, however. Later in volume one, Lewes considers the question of point of view, or cultural relativism, in acts of perception. He imagines 'a citizen' and 'a savage' looking at each other's religious ceremonies or political assemblies. Each, of course, would have a very different sense of what was going on in each case. But this does not mean that one of them is wrong. The differences in understanding are due to the social component of their cognitive processes, and in a quite modern sense these are arbitrary. (That is, they are based on convention.) Nor does it mean that both are wrong, and that somehow there is a third perception that is right and not subject to cultural bias: there is no 'objective existence independent of all, and *unlike* each; I hold, on the contrary,' Lewes writes, 'that the objective existence *is* to each what it is felt to be'.[128] Lewes then contrasts the experience of a village labourer with that of a philosopher living in the same village, to illustrate the 'Relativity of Knowledge'. (The scenario closely resembles a theme in *Middlemarch* then being written.) Epistemological questions, therefore, have to be decided on grounds quite other than those of a supposed neutrality or independence of viewpoint. There are no ultimately satisfying accounts or causes: 'as the object is truly its *embodied history* . . . the How and the Why are essentially the same.'[129] Epistemologically, causes and conditions are identical. Cause and effect are not two different entities, and there is no point in seeking beyond history.[130]

Such a view commits Lewes to both relativism and complexity. Truths are not ultimate, they are merely, if anything, methodological. Thus Lewes has a very sophisticated sense of complex determination, and of the multiple, overdetermining factors in play in any given event. In Lewes's own words, events or phenomena are 'conjunctural', 'the coalescence of co-operant conditions'.[131] Our common conception of cause is singular, and is often hypostasized into abstract singularities like the will.[132] But in fact causation is complex and diversely interactive, just like the conditions of a phenomenon or event. These conditions we then abstract into the 'logical artifice' of theories of causation.[133] Similarly, an adequate methodology must respect the different levels of operation at which we might consider the structure of an event or phenomenon. There is no point in trying to abstract or digest complexity beyond a certain point because the regress results in unhelpful reductionism. For instance, the answer to the question 'what causes the sensation of sweetness?' can be given at different levels: psychological, physiological, or chemical, for instance. But there is no point in

---

[128] Lewes, *Problems*, i. 191.    [129] Ibid. 364.
[130] See also ibid. ii. 376–422 for further argument along these lines. Once more this view is very close to the amended account of causation offered by John Searle.
[131] Lewes, *Problems*, ii. 389.    [132] Ibid. 401.    [133] Ibid. 388.

blurring the relevant levels at which the answer might be formulated. 'It is possible for research to pursue this regress of causation to great lengths, but at each stage it *shifts the problem*; and no success in solving other problems can add one iota of causal illumination to the particular problem from which we start.'[134] This hierarchy of levels of explanation is reminiscent of the methodology recommended by modern psycho-biologists like Steven Rose, whose work we introduced in the previous chapter. But it is also reminiscent of the multiple, complex, layered account of the world to be found in Eliot's best fiction, such as *Middlemarch*. The principles involved here are just those epistemological principles at work in a passage like the 'double change of self and beholder' passage examined earlier.

Lewes confronts directly the problem of epistemological relativism that this theory presents. But his response to the problem is entailed in the historical method, and includes his refusal to accept a distinction between cause and conditions to which contemporary commentators like James Sully objected. Lewes argues that, because we cannot search for 'scientific finality, and demand a cause of the cause, an origin of the origin',[135] it is necessary to accept that knowledge is both (merely) descriptive and (necessarily) circumscribed: scientists do not 'pretend to explain Existence in itself—that is to say, apart from its relations to Consciousness—the explanation is of Things as groups of Relations'.[136] This last term is crucial to Lewes. Knowledge consists of the establishment, or description, of the connections (or 'relations') between phenomena, and cognitive activity consists of the 'correlation' of observed phenomena in (always provisional) 'groupings'. Knowledge is, therefore, indeed, 'relative' in two senses: it is both knowledge *of* relations, and it is relative in the (usually pejorative) sense that it cannot be absolute. But the fact that it is limited (a better term than relative perhaps) does not mean that it is any less secure, because even limited knowledge is referable back to experience, the Logic of Feeling, by empirical verification. Nor does the fact that knowledge is conditional (that is, it is revisable as conditions change) mean that it is any less reliable, or that things are unknowable in an absolute sense. It merely means that they are capable of other relations. The positing of an 'essence' or 'noumen' behind phenomena merely reveals an insecurity about living in the world as it is with its changes and fluctuations. Interestingly, and revealingly, Lewes's illustrating analogy is drawn from language: words are dependent for their meanings on their relationship with other language features, 'the meaning lies in the context'.[137]

The stress on complexity and relationship is the key to Lewes's epistemology and the source of his best arguments in this area. But it still remains that scientific propositions, for example, are discursive and not experiential:

---

[134] Ibid. 363.      [135] Ibid. 8.      [136] Ibid. 9.      [137] Ibid. 44.

Science deals with conceptions, not with perceptions; with ideal not real figures. Its laboratory is not the outer world of Nature, but the inner sanctuary of Mind. It draws indeed its material from Nature, but fashions this anew according to its own laws; and having thus constructed a microcosm, half objective half subjective, it is enabled to enlarge its construction by taking in more and more of the macrocosm.

Science everywhere aims at transforming isolated perceptions into connected conceptions, —facts and acts into laws. Out of the manifold irregularities presented to Sense it abstracts an ideal regularity; out of the chaos, order.[138]

It is this kind of statement that has sometimes led commentators to read Lewes's work as moving towards an Idealist position in so far as it centres its account of science upon mental constructions rather than the immediate sensory apprehension of the world. And it is certainly true that Lewes engages in a full critique of the epistemology of the 'sensational' school. For him it is reductive and misleading to claim that all our knowledge is generated from sense experience (though it is ultimately referable to it). It is the *constructive* operation of the mind that formulates knowledge propositions. In other words, hypothesis construction, or (more broadly) the ability both to make and to test *fictions*, is a central part, not just of epistemological operations, but also of the whole experience of being human, including the realms of moral and affective experience.[139]

What Lewes envisages is a self-checking system that is able to rely on the empirical basis of knowledge, but is guarded and circumspect about its extension. Inferences (signs, hypotheses, or fictions) are checked against facts (feelings or verifications). The key to all this is the idea of difference, and the dimension in which this idea operates is that of change through time. It is the differences between things, either in themselves, or as they change across time, that enables reliable cognition to occur. We can be confident in our sense of things, because they change. Science would 'tumble into chaos if this firm hold of Difference were loosened and Identity allowed to take its place'.[140] Idealism suggests that things exist independent of history, or that phenomenal history is the form in which noumenal essence reveals itself. But for Lewes 'Things exist just so long as their conditions exist.'[141] We know things because they directly impact upon our senses; we know their properties because of the variety of conditions in which we find them; and we know of conditions and laws because of change of circumstance and process. Our knowledge, therefore, as many modernists declare, is a product of a system of differences.

---

[138] Lewes, *Problems*, i. 431–2.

[139] Ibid. 288–349. For commentary, see Jack Kaminsky, 'The Empirical Metaphysics of George Henry Lewes', *Journal of the History of Ideas*, 13 (1952), 314–32; Michael York Mason, '*Middlemarch* and Science: Problems of Life and Mind', *Review of English Studies*, NS 22 (1971), 151–69; Levine, *The Realistic Imagination*, 258–66.

[140] Lewes, *Problems of Life and Mind*, ii. 435.       [141] Ibid. 435.

This is the epistemology that Lewes had been working towards since the mid-1860s (it is first set out in the lengthy 'Prolegomena' to the third edition of *A History of Philosophy from Thales to Comte* in 1867), and it is most fully explored in volume two of *Problems of Life and Mind*. It depends upon a complex, dialectical interaction of various factors. The whole depends upon difference and change; but, in order to constitute significant knowledge, the various elements of that knowledge need to be organized. This represents the significant point of disagreement between Lewes and modern theorists of 'difference' (or *différance*) such as Jacques Derrida. For the deconstructionists, the inevitable kicking-loose of representation ('writing') from reference is not matched by a concomitant wish to reorder knowledge in a more significant agreement with it. Analysis in this mode revels instead in the discursive disarray and vertigo so produced. For Lewes, however, though difference is essential for cognition, *knowledge* is produced by the reconstruction of cognitions into structured propositions, and the desire to establish the (always ultimately undiscovered) 'fluent identity throughout the manifold diversity'. The 'aim is to unify knowledge; and this can only be done by setting aside diversities'.[142] But the danger of this is that it 'converts its own distinctions into *objects*, and supplies each object with a logical subject'.[143] Lewes thus acknowledges, and makes fruitful, the structural double-bind his epistemology implies.

Lewes's epistemology is both an expression of limitation and a guarantee of progress. In psychological terms it pictures human beings as both desirous of establishing satisfactory and settled theoretical accounts of the world, and as cautious of their too exorbitant or complacent extension into propositions that become hypostasized and remote from experience. This psychological action is mirrored by the dialectic at work between difference and identity. Explanations seek to unify disparate phenomena (identity), but not at the cost of abstracting from complexity and the world's 'thick description' (difference). The key idea here is what Lewes terms the activity of 'grouping' and the 'Principle of Equivalence'. Knowledge grows by grouping and classification, as new experiences are added to earlier and substantiate or replace older hypotheses, which were themselves formed by acts of grouping whereby various data are brought into relationship.[144] The 'Principle of Equivalence' is Lewes's title for the process whereby 'logical' truth (that is, a statement in the 'Logic of Signs') is matched with a 'real' or 'material' truth.[145] Lewes contrasts this with Spencer's 'Universal Postulate': it is the 'positive statement of the negative formula advanced by Mr Herbert Spencer, as the Universal Postulate'.[146] In other words, Lewes is again keen to insist on the constructive ability of humans to obtain positive knowledge in a

---

[142] Ibid. 435.    [143] Ibid. 436.    [144] Ibid. 23, 65.
[145] Ibid. 79.    [146] Ibid. 89.

world of circumstance and provisionality. The 'positive statement' implies a desire to emphasize human agency as well as human limitation.

Once more, one of Lewes's key images for this process is drawn from language, in particular the formation of meaningful sentences. Words themselves are simply sounds until they are organized by grammar, and especially by verbs: 'The words float suspended, soulless, mere sound. No sooner are these floating sounds grasped by the copula, than in that grasp they are grouped into significance: they start into life, as a supersaturated saline solution crystallizes on being touched by a needle-point.'[147] As earlier discussed, the same image was used by George Eliot to describe the moment of realized love between Lydgate and Rosamond in chapter 31 of *Middlemarch*. But this mirrored usage is instructive, for such 'groupings into significance' can deceive as much as they can reward. The significant danger in all knowledge creation is that an abstracted assumption will betray things as they really are, just as Lydgate and Rosamond's assumptions about love and each other are products of fancy and complacent, egoistic desire, not of significant human contact.

What is true in the affective life is also true intellectually, even in modern science. Lewes, for example, protests against the popular abstraction of 'Force' by some contemporary writers on physics (including Spencer). For Lewes, this idea is a damaging abstraction, because in careless hands 'it transforms a logical into a physical distinction'. The category error (the confusion of a 'real' with a 'logical' truth in terms of the 'Principle of Equivalence') thus 'reintroduces the old Dualism in which matter is passive, destitute of qualities though capable of receiving motion, capable of housing qualities, and of becoming the temporary tenement of wandering Forces. In this scheme qualities are merely superadded', and therefore metaphysical entities entertained.[148] The problem for Lewes is similar to that presented by vitalistic theories in biology (which are regularly attacked throughout *Problems of Life and Mind*[149]), or the hypothesis of an immaterial 'spirit' or 'soul' in psychology. For Lewes, as we have seen, genuine knowledge, like the world itself, is much more complex, demanding, and contingent: 'The structure is for ever changing: the assimilation of new material and destruction of the old are incessant; and among the consequences of this incessant change there are inequalities which lead to differentiations, and these finally to Death.'[150] It is interesting that the process envisioned here is similar to that described by George Eliot in her account of the 'constantly shifting', 'double change of self and beholder' that constitutes knowledge of the town

---

[147] Lewes, *Problems of Life and Mind*, ii. 145.    [148] Ibid. i. 273–4.
[149] e.g. ibid. iii. 14, where Lewes juxtaposes the 'vitalist' to the 'organicist'—that is a scientist concerned with organic relations. See also the long discussion of the general problem at ii. 460–502, where one of the objects of Lewes's attack is Spencer's hypothesis of an 'Unknowable Force' (see esp. p. 487).    [150] Ibid. ii. 183.

of Middlemarch. But it is also interesting that, were the passage from Lewes to be quoted without a context, one would probably assume that it referred not to the formation of knowledge, but to the processes of biology. It is another example of his desire to seek a language that is operative in diverse contexts to heal the epistemological wounds of dualistic psychological theory.

## LEWES, DARWIN, AND LAMARCK

Lewes was responsive to adjustments in scientific knowledge, and we have already noted his hesitant use of Lamarckian theory. For Spencer, Lamarck's ideas provided not only a plausible account of psychological development, but also an anchor for his epistemology and ethics. If ideas and principles survive, the argument goes, they are, to all intents and purposes, 'true'. Lewes too used Lamarck's theory in this way from time to time, as here, for example: 'just as what is organized in the individual becomes transmitted to offspring, and determines the mode in which the offspring will react upon stimulus, so what is registered in the social organism determines the mode in which succeeding generations feel and think.'[151] However, Lewes's Lamarckianism was, fundamentally, of a more diffident and eventually critical kind to that of Spencer. His vacillating response to Lamarck could be considered a weak point in his work, but once again we have to contextualize such a judgement. In his attitudes to Lamarckian evolutionary theory, Lewes was both typical of his time, and a little in advance of it. For one thing, he did not, unlike Spencer, invest fully in Lamarckian ideas, and does not therefore suffer as massively as the mistake is exposed. Lewes also understood very early the import and significance of Darwin's work in a way that influenced profoundly his exploration of evolutionary paradigms and complicated already uncertain attitudes to Lamarck. Lewes, in fact, made a considerable and distinctive effort to work through the challenge represented by *The Origin of Species*, as some commentators have established.[152] Not that these scholars needed to look too far, for Lewes had the master's imprimatur: 'The articles [Lewes had written on Darwin] strike me as *quite* excellent,' Darwin wrote to him in 1868, 'I hope that they will be republished.' In the same year, Darwin proposed Lewes for membership of both the BMA and the Linnæan Society.[153]

[151] Ibid. i. 124. For similar usages see also: i. 163, 241, 416 ff.; ii. 11, 15; v. 16, 104 (where there is an explicit commendation of Spencer on the 'evolution of Life and Mind').

[152] See K. M. Newton, 'George Eliot, George Henry Lewes, and Darwinism', *Durham University Journal*, 66 (1973–4), 278–93, and, especially, Srilekha Bell, 'George Henry Lewes: A Man of his Time', *Journal of the History of Biology*, 14 (1981), 277–98.

[153] Darwin to Lewes, 7 Aug. 1868, in Eliot, *Letters*, viii. 425–6. For Darwin's recommendation of Lewes to the BMA and Linnæan Society, see Ashton, *G. H. Lewes: A Life*, 244–5; Tjoa, *George Henry Lewes*, 30.

Lewes's initial enthusiasm for Lamarckian theory is clear in his early work. In 'Hereditary Influence, Animal and Human' (1856), for example, written immediately after the publication of the first edition of Spencer's *Principles of Psychology*, and strongly under its influence, Lewes accepts the Spencerian account wholesale and casts his vision of history in its terms:

History is one magnificent corollary on the laws of transmission. Were it not for these laws, civilization would be impossible. We inherit the acquired experience of our forefathers—their tendencies, their aptitudes, their habits, their improvements. It is because what is organically acquired becomes organically transmitted that the brain of a European is twenty or thirty cubic inches greater than the brain of a Papuan, and that the European is born with aptitudes of which the Papuan has not the remotest indication.[154]

This is excitable, offensive rubbish, but Lewes does insist that it is individuals who transmit hereditary characteristics, not the species. This, while confirming his Lamarckianism, could exonerate him from the deterministic racism that Spencer favoured from time to time. The distinction between the individual and the species as the medium for biological processes remained a key issue for Lewes.

Lewes maintained similar ideas into the 1860s. In *The Physiology of Common Life* (1860)—which won much respect in the scientific community—he challenged Buckle's contention in *Civilization in England* that there is no evidence for the hereditary transmission of characteristics. Citing Spencer, he claimed there was abundant evidence:

The organization of the parent is transmitted, and with that organization all those characteristics and tendencies which the organization in activity would naturally manifest. A habit, a trick, which has been acquired, and so long established that it may be said to be *organized* in the individual—whose mechanism has *grown* in performance—will stand the same chance of being inherited, as the bulk of bone and muscle, or the sensibility of the nervous system. An idiosyncrasy which results from some organic disposition—say, for example, the repugnance to animal food—may as easily be inherited as a good constitution, or a scrofulus tendency. Explain it as we may, there is no fact more certain than that a habit once firmly fixed, once 'organized' in the individual, becomes almost as susceptible of transmission as any normal tendency.[155]

This is unequivocal. Yet by the end of the decade, having read Darwin, Lewes had begun to amend his views considerably. The turning point was a four-part account of 'Mr. Darwin's Hypotheses' Lewes wrote for the *Fortnightly* in 1868 at John Morley's request.[156] In it Lewes starts to come to terms with the challenge to Lamarckianism offered by Darwin.

---

[154] [Lewes], 'Hereditary Influence, Animal and Human', 160.
[155] Lewes, *Physiology of Common Life*, ii. 382.
[156] See Eliot, *Letters*, iv. 424.

Lewes's articles are an attack on 'metaphysical' uses of the 'development' theory; that is, the effort by many Victorian intellectuals to assimilate evolutionary thought into conventional world views. (We have seen several examples of this, principally the efforts by liberal Christian opinion—unwittingly encouraged by Spencer's work—to read evolutionary thought as a kind of natural theology.[157]) For Lewes, evolutionary theory contradicts 'metaphysical' understanding not only in its content, but also in its manner. Darwin's work, he argues, is not a finished theory, but the latest, and best, in 'an immense series of tentative gropings' whose implications are 'revolutionary'.[158] That is to say, Lewes pictures the development of evolutionary theory as a *scientific* and not a *totalizing* (Lewes would say 'metaphysical') project—rather, indeed, in the manner of his own long-meditated *Problems of Life and Mind*, which he had just begun. The difference between scientific and totalizing work lies in the former's provisionality, openness, revisability, and collective endeavour. Darwin is contributing to a developing scientific argument, even though this is itself part of a continuing battle between monism and dualism fought throughout the history of human enquiry. (Lewes, of course, is both contradictory and historically typical in his effort to combat totalizing theories by means of totalized historical schemas.)

Lewes's objections to the dualistic, 'metaphysical' reading of evolutionary thought are to be expected. Briefly, he thinks that it offers a hostage to fortune. By positing apparently agential entities ('natural selection' or 'the inheritance of characteristics'), the mechanism is separated from the process, and the terms of debate are focused there, rather than on a developing body of investigation. The construction of the argument thus favours, say, a 'religious' world view accustomed to dealing with essentially monocausal structures, rather than a contingent, messy, and provisional sense of the world's density and overdetermination. Lewes noted the fundamental equivocation in the 'natural theologizing' of evolution and offered James Martineau as an example. Such thinking, Lewes claimed, either argues for a 'separation of agencies' (biology and divinity), or elides the distinction, in which case 'the hypothesis of Creation and the hypothesis of Evolution becomes only a difference of terms'. 'Integrationist' writers, in other words, want things both ways.[159] But, in terms of the intellectual politics of the period, these were singularly unclear waters in which to sail. Lewes's articles on Darwin were attacked by J. B. Mozley, the Regius Professor of Divinity at Oxford and a leading member of the Oxford Movement.

Mozley's were mainly knock-down arguments typical of the period: evolutionary theory was 'spun out of our brain', whereas the argument from design

[157] The essays in Robert M. Young's *Darwin's Metaphor* are a fascinating discussion of this area.
[158] George Henry Lewes, 'Mr. Darwin's Hypotheses: Part I', *Fortnightly Review*, NS 3 (1868), 353.
[159] Ibid. 355, 364.

was attested by 2,000 years of conviction; man's reason demands a sense of hierarchy, which in turn reflects the hierarchical structure of the world; man's self-consciousness proves that he has an identity separate from the 'mechanisms' that form his being; his spirituality is a real presence in the world, which attests to the truth of all of these.[160] Yet Mozley was also a careful reader of Darwin and did point to an important fact about Darwin's language. He noticed that 'Natural selection figures in [evolutionary] language, indeed, as an active and creative power', undertaking tasks and carrying through processes. What is more, it is pictured as a 'designing agent'. So a cause is created that is really a result, and the argument lacks a mechanism: 'Whence does Mr. Darwin get that succession of favourable variations which is necessary for the ultimate formation of regular and highly organized species?'[161] In contemporary context, as Robert Young notes, Mozley's are worthy and important points.[162] Darwin's metaphor does indeed imply this kind of agency, and his theory does indeed lack a mechanism, and Lewes was alert to the problem in Darwin's language. He notes in volume three of *Problems of Life and Mind* that Darwin tends to see natural selection in a hypostasized way: 'the metaphorical nature of the term is not always borne in mind, so that . . . Natural Selection is said to "act on and modify organic beings", as if it were a positive condition and not the expression of the modifying process. . . . Mr. Darwin's language . . . is misleading.'[163] In other words, the 'metaphysical' terms of the argument are not merely a result of appropriation by evolutionary theory's opponents. They are a condition of its discourse in the period: hence the need for continuing linguistic vigilance.

It is quite characteristic of Lewes's thought that this subtle sense of the pressure of cultural and intellectual context should lead him to a major revision of his substantive scientific propositions. In 'Darwin's Hypotheses' Lewes quite clearly sees that Lamarck's ideas are subject to the same pressures, and will not, in their Spencerian form at least, sustain scrutiny in this spirit. Though 'we should not . . . underrate the singular importance of Lamarck's hypothesis in calling attention to the modifiability of structure through modifications of adaptation', none the less he was led into 'exaggerations by a one-sided view, which made him attribute too great an influence to one set of external conditions'.[164] In *Problems of Life and Mind* the use made of Lamarck is, therefore, balanced by certain important reservations, and the position eventually offered is, as Srilekha Bell remarks, 'a strange mixture of Lamarck and Darwin'.[165] This mixture, however,

---

[160] [J. B. Mozley], 'The Argument of Design', *Quarterly Review*, 127 (1869), 134–76. Mozley's piece was a reply to Lewes's articles and a review of Per Paul Janet's *Le Matérialisme Contemporain*.

[161] [Mozley], 'The Argument of Design', 163–6.

[162] Robert M. Young, 'Darwin's Metaphor: Does Nature Select?', in *Darwin's Metaphor*, 109–10.                    [163] Lewes, *Problems*, iii. 108.

[164] Lewes, 'Darwin's Hypotheses: I', 356.    [165] Bell, 'Lewes: A Man of his Time', 296.

is explicable as a result of the conditions of discourse on these questions in the period. What makes 'Mr. Darwin's Hypotheses' such a text of its time is the way it pits the various forms of evolutionary theory against each other. Darwin's value for Lewes is not that he offers 'the truth', but that he crystallizes certain objections Lewes also had to existing theories. His own ideas, he says, were 'very indefinite until Mr. Darwin's work came to give it shape, both by what it furnished of direct instruction, and what it suggested indirectly'.[166] But, just as Lewes is reserved about the apparent monocausality of Lamarck's proposition, so too he thinks that the '*a priori* simplicity' of radical Darwinian theory dangerously skirts metaphysical absolutes.[167] It has a 'seductive', 'speculative beauty' as a theory, which threatens to cancel variety and diversity and convert the argument into essentialist terms.[168]

The grounds of Lewes's thinking are, as might be expected, historical. 'Darwin's Hypotheses' argues for a radical historicizing of biological processes whereby biological structures are seen as a response to environmental conditions rather than the result of inner drives or processes. This was the importance of retaining some investment in Lamarck (at the risk, perhaps, from a late-twentieth-century point of view, of sounding like Lysenko), because Lamarck enabled Lewes to bring the social environment into the equation. From Lewes's perspective in the late 1860s, Darwin's theory, with its lapses of language into a voluntarist, quasi-theological register, could sound suspiciously as though mysterious agents were driving natural process. At the same time, some Lamarckian or Spencerian theories could also sound as though the cart was put before the horse, or, more technically, the structure before the function. As we have seen, Lewes consistently stressed the importance of understanding living entities as environmentally determined. Hence biological events were the result of interlocking conditions both internal and external. The theory of the inheritance of acquired characteristics seemed to offer a clear illustration of the principle that environment could determine biological structure, and this was Lamarck's appeal. But Spencer's conclusion seemed to be that function could exist independent of its structural manifestations and relationships, which was a species of error paradoxically shared by the 'materialist' psychologists' old enemies the vitalists, who posited the existence of 'Life' independent of actual living bodies. How could this paradox come about?

Lewes understood the issue very clearly. Spencer 'doesn't always bear in mind the distinction between General and Special Function'[169]—that is, he stops thinking about particular functions and, in the process of devising and articulating

---

[166] Lewes, 'Mr. Darwin's Hypotheses: Part III', *Fortnightly Review*, NS 4 (1868), 74.
[167] Lewes, 'Mr. Darwin's Hypotheses: Part IV', *Fortnightly Review*, NS 4 (1868), 492.
[168] Ibid. 494.      [169] Lewes, 'Darwin's Hypotheses: III', 70.

a hypothesis, devotes all his attention to an abstract and generalized reduction. Lewes illustrates his point with an analogy from mechanics: Spencer (as it were) thinks only about the energy properties of steam in general and not about its material manifestations in kettles or engines or anything else.[170] In time these verbal slippages towards abstraction become category conversions, and eventually a kind of intellectual about-turn is performed. What began as a theory about material forms and processes becomes one of increasing abstraction, so that material forms appear to be shadowed by abstract (and potentially immaterial) entities. This general alarm about the ways in which the forms of articulation surrender the original insight and deform knowledge is a regular theme of Lewes's work. In 'Darwin's Hypotheses', Lewes shows the same anxiety over ideas of Species or Type.[171]

Lewes is troubled by the formulation of general entities, because these threaten to become substantive and not descriptive. His reservations about the notions of Type and Species are of this kind. A Type, he says, 'is not a thing but a relation'.[172] One of his anxieties about Darwin is that Darwin's discussion of species threatens to convert a taxonomic classification into a biological entity. In so doing Darwin could lose sight of the variety of forces and factors in play. Lewes's difficulty with Darwin, that is to say, is part of his long war with reductionism. Darwin, Lewes writes, lays 'perhaps too much stress on community of blood, and not enough on community of conditions'.[173] The environmental factors that inhibit or give effect to any biological process are the important factors. The concentration on general categories like 'species', which do not take these factors into account, threatens to undo the materialist project. The fixed, taxonomic language allows entry for notions of General Plan, Type, or Mind.[174] There are also potentially grave social consequences. A notion of racial type might imply, for example, that, because Negroes have been used as slaves from the time of the Egyptian pharaohs to that of the Alabama plantation-owners (Lewes's articles were written in the wake of the American Civil War and the Governor Eyre incident), Negro slavery is inevitable, even 'natural'. In fact, all it implies is 'the concurrence of conditions which have been sufficiently uniform'.[175]

As ever, Lewes is concerned to stress environmental and historical processes as well as biological ones. This looks forward to *Problems of Life and Mind*. In volume three, Lewes's criticism of Darwin's language comes during a dramatic attempt by him to historicize *all* biological processes; even organs and histological structures owe some part of their constitution to historically operative conditions. Even when 'purely biological' factors can apparently be distinguished,

---

[170] Lewes, 'Darwin's Hypotheses: III', 69.
[171] Bell, 'Lewes: A Man of his Time', 290.    [172] Lewes, 'Darwin's Hypotheses: I', 370.
[173] Lewes, 'Mr. Darwin's Hypotheses: Part II', *Fortnightly Review*, NS 3 (1868), 628.
[174] Lewes, 'Darwin's Hypotheses: I', 361–2.    [175] Ibid. 366.

'we should only see an historical distinction, that is to say, one between effects produced by particular causes now in operation, and effects produced by very complex and obscure causes in operation during ancestral development'.[176] This, of course, is the importance of Lamarck, for Lamarck's theory expressed most fully for Lewes's generation of atheistically inclined, politically reformist, scientifically informed intellectuals the possibility of understanding life as a cumulative event involving important human dimensions as well as larger, more humanly anonymous processes.

For Spencer, Lamarck provided an essential part of his mapping of the human world. For Lewes, however, the case was more difficult. He could see pretty clearly the difficulties in Lamarck's ideas, and his work contains several substantial criticisms, but he, like most of his generation, could not see the next step through Darwinism back to the humanly centred world that is the foundation and object of all his work. In the meantime, the *Problems of Life and Mind* is an effort to grapple with complexity. It emphasizes consciousness, will, and agency, and yet continues to work with a determinist model and a knowledge of the fragility of consciousness itself. It sets out to constitute a science, and articulate the products of human reason, yet it also stresses the limitations of human understanding and the waywardness of language. It wishes to respect the individuality and distinctiveness of the human faculties and human endeavour, yet it recognizes too that big processes shape small lives, and that man is animal as well as human, and part of a species as well as a singular, particular self.

### PROBLEMS OF MIND AND CONCEPTUAL ORGANIZATION

The intriguing picture of the mind that emerges from Lewes's work is a clear product of the psychological theory of the 1860s and 1870s, but it is also strongly forward-looking. As a number of his contemporaries noted, Lewes was unusually aware of psychological dysfunction and abnormality, and *Problems of Life and Mind* recognizes the importance of hallucinations, insanity, and other clinical material for psychological investigation.[177] Lewes's work in this area was unsystematic but clearly considered, and he was similarly interested in developmental perspectives,[178] and the significance of unconscious mental processes.

Lewes was suspicious of modish ideas of 'the unconscious' by popular writers such as Eduard von Hartmann, whose *Philosophy of the Unconscious* Lewes read in both 1869 and 1872 and which sold 50,000 copies across Europe.[179] He was

---

[176] Lewes, *Problems*, iii. 107.

[177] See e.g. ibid. v. 388 ff., 394, 460. James Sully comments generally on this aspect of Lewes's work in his review of this volume in the *Academy*, 309–10.

[178] e.g. *Problems*, v. 354–5.

[179] Shuttleworth, *George Eliot and Nineteenth-Century Science*, 20.

well aware of the need to stress mental processes that occur below consciousness, but he was also concerned that 'the unconscious' might come to be seen as a separate entity independent of other psychological processes. Like Freud in his very different way, Lewes was keen to see the unconscious as a structure with a history, not as a nebulous free-standing entity like the soul or spirit.[180] In volume five of *Problems* he speaks of the 'silent growth' of character and disposition within the mind–body system, and much of this, he argues, is unconscious. These dispositions and processes form the proper 'centre' of mental life.[181] He usually preferred to term these 'sub-conscious' rather than unconscious because this implied a firmer sense of connection with (rather than an alternative to) the conscious mind.[182] It is the relays between conscious and unconscious life that hold his attention. In volume four, he attacks traditional ways of conceptualizing this problem, using Sir William Hamilton's work as an example. Traditional psychology has acknowledged phenomena outside the range of consciousness, but it then dismisses them to the limbo of unconsciousness.[183] The unconscious in this theory, therefore, is used as a kind of conceptual waste disposal for processes and phenomena it does not want to consider. Once more the effect is to separate the two strata of mental life.

Throughout *Problems of Life and Mind* Lewes is rigorously sensitive to the conceptual organization and verbal and rhetorical strategies his contemporaries used to model the mind's operations. We therefore need to examine Lewes's own practice in this respect. We have from time to time examined some of his metaphors and models, but these are only part of a larger pattern of description in *Problems of Life and Mind*, perhaps the most striking feature of which is its calculated diversity. The rhetorical organization of *Problems* is a complex mixture of clear-minded exposition, underlying which there is a studious refusal to settle into a stable set of images or models. The metaphors are jumbled up, the pattern is continually shifting, and the whole text engages in a critique or deliberate over-turning or twisting of received images. Each usage partly acts as a corrective modification of the last, and the whole is designed to encourage the reader to develop a complex, multifaceted analysis. What the individual metaphors and analogies tend to share, however, and what the overall structure is designed to enact, is a mobile, quicksilver, and (most important) energy-filled system. Lewes is not, that is to say, much interested in designing a mental topography in the way, for example, Freud and other psychoanalysts were to be. Such a model would, for him, imply a somewhat static system. Instead, he was alert, not just to the need to be cautious with metaphor and analogy lest it become substantive and

---

[180] Lewes, *Problems*, ii. 499–501.    [181] Ibid. v. 139–41.
[182] Ibid. i. 141–2.    [183] Ibid. iv. 7–8.

not illustrative,[184] but also to the heuristic desirability of incorporating change, process, and provisionality into his images to express a mental system not of 'fixed relations' (as he put it), but 'essentially a *fluctuating* [system], its elements being combined, recombined, and resolved under infinite variations of stimulation'.[185] This idea is central, and is reflected in his conception of the mechanics of the psychological system. In volume five he discusses the relationship between conscious and unconscious processes in terms of the 'groups' of neurological connections which underlie and enable them. But, he warns, 'the *group is never a fixed structure*; it is only a disposition of the elements which is easily reformed; just as in a Kaleidoscope there are certain groups of the separate pieces of glass which combine now in one way and now in another, according to impulse'.[186] Lewes may overstate the free mobility of the system, but this is a strikingly modern conception of neurological networks. It is also, I feel, an apt image for the dynamics of Victorian psychology in general, which I have borrowed in the Introduction to this book.

At this point it is worth recalling that it was Lewes (in *The Physiology of Common Life*) and not (as is often believed) William James who coined the term 'stream of consciousness'. It was an image that appealed to him, and it is elaborated in *Problems of Life and Mind*. In volume one Lewes sets out to describe consciousness not as a sovereign entity, but as a shifting and energy-based process. Consciousness is pictured as a 'mass of *stationary waves* formed out of the individual waves of neural tremors'.[187] This uses a pair of traditional metaphors—nervous action is like an energy wave, and thought processes are like the movements of water—popular with physiologically inclined associationists (and, indeed, writers such as George Eliot, or Wordsworth for that matter). But Lewes gives these an elaborate twist. He asks us to think of consciousness as a lake into which diverse currents are feeding. Stationary waves are produced when these currents inhibit and hold each other up. As new currents develop and new patterns emerge, ever-shifting configurations are produced. This 'fluctuating figure', as Lewes calls it, is a way of representing the '*psychical mood* or attitude', which takes its tone from the dominant and regular configuration.[188]

This complex image is very like those used by early twentieth-century writers and theorists (such as, for instance, both William and Henry James or the major literary modernists), which reminds us again that the break between 'the Victorian' and 'the Modern' was neither abrupt nor sharp. But it might also be noticed that, while the image has the virtue of expressing complexity and

---

[184] For example: 'Once more I warn the reader not to suppose that these physical illustrations are advanced as proofs. They are simply ways of facilitating our analogical construction of psychological processes. We do not know the real nature of these processes, but we are forced to imagine them under the forms of processes that are familiar' (ibid. v. 260).

[185] Ibid. 52.     [186] Ibid. 140–1.     [187] Ibid. i. 150.     [188] Ibid. 151.

process, and of including development in time, it is less satisfactory as a way of suggesting determining pressures and limitations, of, as Lewes puts it a little later, 'having necessarily a history at [one's] back'.[189] Lewes, therefore, turned to other kinds of metaphor. Sometimes he uses architectural metaphors of base and super-structure, or of the 'mechanical laws' that both enable and limit a building's con-struction.[190] But such 'mechanical' metaphors can also mislead. In the same volume, therefore, Lewes also attacks the use of metaphors drawn from mechanics and chemistry. 'Organic functions, we must often insist, are unlike the functions of machines.' Sensibility, or any other psycho-physiological property, 'cannot be linked to steam, or any other external motor'.[191] Nor is experience 'a mosaic', but 'a living, developing, manifold unity'.[192] Metaphors, therefore, that suggest that the parts of mental life can be decomposed or reduced to serial components are misleading. Lewes's example is the well-known—because popularized by Mill—metaphor of 'mental chemistry', which suggests that psychological processes can be combined or divided into their elements; but a feeling, says Lewes, 'cannot be taken to pieces like a salt'.[193] However, it is an interesting illustration of the rhetorical structure of *Problems* that Lewes had already used the 'mental-chemistry' metaphor positively in volume two to illustrate a better way of think-ing about the mind than that implied by traditional hierarchical models.[194] Lewes's justification for this apparent contradiction would be that metaphors are used opportunistically and heuristically, not as fixed models. Sometimes it was nec-essary to insist on integrational models, sometimes on the need to separate ana-lytically the various elements of a process. Psychology is, therefore, comparable to a spectrum (another metaphor), the colours of which shade into one another but are none the less analytically separable.[195]

Lewes had similar reservations about the language used by Bain. As we have seen, Bain used up-to-the-minute technological metaphors, but for Lewes such ideas again distort the nature of mental life. Psychological processes are not like the steam railway. Nor is the nervous system like the electric telegraph (Bain had pictured the brain as the central bureau, the ganglia as stations, and the nerves as wires), because such a metaphor implies a sender independent of an inert structure.[196] Lewes prefers a wholly organic model:

The current hypothesis, which assumes that the brain is the sole organ of the mind, the sole seat of the sensations, is a remnant of the ancient hypothesis respecting the Soul and its seat; and on the whole I think the ancient hypothesis is the more rational of the two. . . . It is the man, and not the brain, that thinks: it is the organism as a whole, and not one organ, that feels and acts. [197]

---

[189] Lewes, *Problems*, 162.    [190] Ibid. iv. 109.    [191] Ibid. 180.
[192] Ibid. 181.    [193] Ibid. 180.    [194] Ibid. ii. 146–7.
[195] Ibid. iv. 185; v. 247.    [196] Ibid. iii. 179–83.    [197] Ibid. 439, 441.

Just as consciousness is a *mode* and not a centre of the psychological life, so particular faculties and functions cannot be localized, and Lewes resisted on principle the various efforts in the period to localize brain functions in particular parts of the cerebrum.[198]

Lewes's organicism was thoroughgoing, but he was also alert to its possible misapprehension. He wanted to insist on unity, but at the same time he did not want to suggest the 'vague mysticism' and 'formless haze' of the quasi-mystical 'Panpsychism' then popular. Panpsychism, says Lewes dismissively, appeals only to minds 'eager for unity, and above all charmed by certain poetic vistas of a Cosmos no longer alienated from man'.[199] It was a throwback to older notions of the *sensorium commune*, and, he might have added, to certain versions of Romantic *Naturphilosophie* that influenced Coleridge and other vitalists. In the rhetorical structure of *Problems*, therefore, organicist ideas are counteracted by others drawn from different registers. There is a sequence that uses economics, for example, thus looking, as it were, to Bentham rather than Coleridge. Lewes compares the nervous system to the division of labour within economic production, or the growth of cooperative societies.[200] In volume four Lewes speaks, in a repeated phrase, of discovering the 'conditions of production' of psychological facts.[201] In volume five, physiology is 'the theory of the conditions of production, and Psychology, the theory of the relations of the products'.[202] Lewes, of course, is adapting both a standard metaphor and a standard discourse (that of political economy) of the period. As George Croom Robertson noted, however, this idea pulled against the main direction of Lewes's theory. It contradicted the general effort to see the mind as seamless activity, and separated the product from the means of production.[203] But its heuristic intentions are clear.

The main strand in the metaphorical organization of *Problems of Life and Mind* concerns Lewes's deployment of images that suggest energy systems rather than fixed entities. Thus the psycho-physiological system is compared to the transmission of waves in a liquid, or a trail of gunpowder that can be ignited anywhere along its length, or forces within a magnetic field, or the internal workings of a sailing ship or an engine, or the facilitation of energy discharges,

---

[198] In volume five Lewes protests against the reduction of psychology to 'Cerebral Physiology' (ibid. v. 370), just as he had resisted the phrenological theories of Gall or Comte. The localization of sensation, thought, and volition in the cerebral hemispheres, and sometimes 'particular convolutions', even 'particular cells', of them, is contested on the grounds that 'All such localizations, unless interpreted as short-hand expressions for the action of the whole organism with special reference to these organs, seem to me essentially unphysiological; and even with this very important correction they are wholly hypothetical' (p. 409). This last is a fair point, and the principle itself is clear. It stopped being a fair point, however, and the principle would need to be amended, when such localization began to be validated within a few years of Lewes writing this.

[199] Ibid. 34.     [200] Ibid. iii. 66, 73.     [201] e.g. ibid. iv. 14.     [202] Ibid. v. 41.

[203] George Croom Robertson, 'The Physical Basis of Mind', *Mind*, 3 (1878), 37.

or the movements of atoms and molecules in energy exchanges like heat loss or chemical decomposition.[204] At other points Lewes could express reservations about these same images, and insist again that they are interpretative illustrations and not representational models.[205] So the basic pattern is clear. In volume five he criticizes conventional ways of representing memory. The litter of conventional metaphors—pictures in a gallery, the photographer's plate, the specific arrangement of the nervous cells or fibres or chemical elements to facilitate certain vibrations—are all static and 'only a materialistic form of the spiritualistic hypothesis that the revival of past feelings is the unveiling of veiled images'.[206] All fail to give a sense of the mind as a complex and dynamic structure; all fail to give a sufficient sense of the *organic* processes from which mind is made; all, in seeking to stabilize organic processes in other systems, reinforce the conventional sense of the mind as a special entity transformed from and raised above its mere biology.

*Problems of Life and Mind*, then, is a performance *in* language and a performance *on* language. It is engaged in working with, and working upon, the 'shifting mass of truth and error' that is the condition of human knowledge, 'for ever becoming more and more sifted and organized into permanent structures of germinating fertility or of fossilized barrenness. Our mental furniture shows the bric-à-brac of prejudice beside the fashion of the hour; our opinions are made up of shadowy associations, imperfect memories, echoes of other men's voices, mingling with the reactions of our own sensibility'.[207] Reason jostles with custom and folly; fact with desire and prejudice. In its complexity, therefore, *Problems of Life and Mind* has a quite different verbal organization to any of the other psychological texts we have examined. Its verbal self-consciousness and rhetorical organization follow from Lewes's preferred model of mind, his epistemology, his perception of the historicality of discourse, and of the power of culture to deform and enable ideas. But it is also comparable with wider shifts in language and rhetorical organization in writing in the period, as recent critics of George Eliot have pointed out. A reading of Sally Shuttleworth's chapter on *Middlemarch* in *George Eliot and Nineteenth-Century Science* will make clear the homologies in organic modelling between that novel and the account of *Problems of Life and Mind* given here, and we have seen how the language of Eliot's fiction also records this polyvalent, multi-aspected world.

The linguistic organizations of *Middlemarch* and *Problems of Life and Mind* are related responses to a changing intellectual culture. As Gillian Beer's work has shown, similar features are shared by Hardy and Darwin too. Darwin's

---

[204] Examples of these images can be found at *Problems*, iii. 284; iv. 148; iv. 103, and v. 89, 95; v. 43; and v. 253 ff. respectively.

[205] e.g. ibid. v. 290.    [206] Ibid. 57.    [207] Ibid. iv. 167.

emphasis on 'the multiple materiality of the world' (in Beer's striking phrase) is reflected in his texts' structures. It is a profuse world organized by multiple metaphors that are mimetic of its nature. 'It is essential for Darwin's theory', comments Beer, 'that the multitudinousness and variety of the natural world should flood through his language.'[208] The same could be said for Lewes's work, and it is this that makes its so distinctive, and so modern, in the perspective of this book.

IDEAL FUTURES: LEWES'S CONVICTIONS AND APPROPRIATIONS

Of all Lewes's critics perhaps the most intellectually formidable was T. H. Green. Green's commitment to a refurbished neo-Kantianism, and his institutional base at the University of Oxford, made him an important and influential opponent who represented the strongest opposition to the new psychology in the 1870s. Like many of the figures examined in this book, Green looks both backwards and forwards in the history of psychological theory. His arguments consolidate the various objections to the new psychology made through the period, but, at the same time, they look interestingly forward to developments in our own century. Lewes died in 1878, his *Problems of Life and Mind* unfinished, but in a way this was historically apt, for the tradition of enquiry in which that work participated, and the historical moment in which it flourished, were coming to an end also. Henceforth, and for at least the next fifty years, psychological theory was to be developed within very different paradigms.

Of these at least two are visible in the specialist literature of the 1870s and 1880s. There is first an increasing desire to reformulate psychology on a more rigorously experimental basis. In a piece for *Mind* in 1886 Joseph Jacobs described 'The Need of a Society for Experimental Psychology' to combat the 'fundamental and inherent defect of subjectivity' that damages philosophically driven theories.[209] This, of course, was one more or less inevitable result of physiological work. But the range of possibilities for experimental investigation indicated in Jacobs's opening pages indicates the somewhat different sense his generation had of psychology's scope from that which became dominant in laboratory-based work as the century turned. Jacobs stresses the contributions of, not just physiologists and biologists, but 'mad-doctors', social statisticians, anthropologists, sociologists, philologists, and folklorists. He goes on to recommend the study of infant psychology—just begun in earnest by Darwin—and of fiction, especially George Eliot and Meredith. Interests of this kind are to be found casually strewn through work by Bain, Spencer, and Lewes, but here is a demand to refound

---

[208] Beer, *Darwin's Plots*, 97.
[209] Joseph Jacobs, 'The Need for a Society for Experimental Psychology', *Mind*, 11 (1886), 51.

psychology with this material at its centre and the protocols of rigorous testing as a method. (Jacobs, incidentally, remarks that advances in female education will mean a regular supply of intelligent and leisured subjects for observation.)

However, the second development remained firmly opposed to such a science. If experimental psychology became the mainstream development in the long run, the short-term victor was the more old-fashioned body of Idealist theory for which Green was the most important spokesman. Green's work was essentially critical—that is, it is more concerned with the demolition of rival 'empiricist' theories than with constructing a psychological programme. Green assumes that such a programme is already available, and it was left to others to redraw an 'Idealist' psychology for the new age. The most important development here was the analysis of modes of consciousness by James Ward in Britain and William James in America, and Ward's work represented for many (including James at one point[210]) the most interesting and coherent statements of these ideas. Some indication of Ward's work and influence will therefore be offered here. Other developments—of which the most important is undoubtedly psychoanalysis, just then being developed by Freud into a mature theory—lie beyond the scope of this study.

A confrontation between Green and Lewes might have been expected. Favourable reviewers of the early volumes of *Problems of Life and Mind* noted that the work constituted a substantial challenge to neo-Kantianism. Green himself thought that Lewes's arguments were better in this respect than those of Spencer,[211] and he was himself already engaged in a campaign against the new psychology. His long introduction to Hume's *Treatise*, published in 1874, attacked the whole Lockean tradition of which he took Hume to be the sceptical limit, and Lewes and Spencer the latest manifestations. The corrosion of ethical and spiritual values in empiricism, Green argues, follows directly from an intellectual confusion at its centre:

the physiologist, when he claims that his science should succeed metaphysic, is not dispensing with it, but rendering it in a preposterous way. He accounts for the formal conceptions in question, in other words for thought as it is common to all the sciences, as sequent upon the accidental facts which his science ascertains—the facts of animal organization. But these conceptions—the relations of cause and effect, &c—are necessary to constitute the facts. They are not an *ex post facto* interpretation of them, but an interpretation without which there would be no ascertainable facts at all.[212]

---

[210] Ward's celebrated *Encyclopaedia Britannica* essay on 'Psychology' (1886) seemed to James to be 'on the whole, the deepest and subtlest collective view of the subject which has appeared in any language' (William James, 'The Perception of Space (II)', *Mind*, 12 (1887), 183).

[211] T. H. Green, 'Mr. Lewes' Account of Experience', in *Works*, i. 446.

[212] T. H. Green, *Introduction to Hume's 'Treatise of Human Nature'*, in *Works*, i. 165.

In a characteristically opaque way, this passage gathers together Green's central psychological ideas: the defence of the primacy of human consciousness, particularly the fundamental 'forms of thought' (causation, sequence, and so on); the rejection of science as the principal mode of human enquiry in psychology; and the attack on realist epistemology. Green's essays on Spencer and Lewes are detailed elaborations of these central propositions. Their essentially polemical and critical spirit is emphasized at the close of the *Introduction to Hume*. Like Lewes, Green was bidding for the new generation. 'If . . . the attention of Englishmen "under five-and-twenty" may be diverted from the anachronistic systems hitherto prevalent among us to the study of Kant and Hegel, an irksome labour [by Green on Hume] will not have been in vain.'[213]

The stakes were not merely intellectual. Combatants and commentators alike saw wider conflicts. In a piece on 'Philosophy at Oxford' for *Mind* (increasingly the forum for such debates), Mark Pattison attacked the backwardness of Oxford philosophy, and its takeover by academics like Green who were uninspired 'by progressive knowledge'. The leading British thinkers of recent years —Mill, Spencer, Lewes, Bain, and Jevons are cited—had all emerged elsewhere, leaving Oxford intellectuals out of step with the times, Pattison claims. He therefore attacked the anti-rationalism of the Oxford Movement, and the anti-democratic, political authoritarianism of much of the work produced in the university.[214] He regretted the ingrown, 'forcing-house' atmosphere, and the attitudes of the new career intellectual—his 'mental pallor, moral indifferentism, the cynical sneer at other's efforts, the absence in himself of any high ideal'. The younger generation were infected by the institutional conservatism, and bright minds were crushed between 'ecclesiastical terror' and 'the competition machine'.[215]

Pattison's piece pleased both Lewes and Eliot.[216] It defended independent, 'provincial' intellectual culture against orthodoxy; it looked to science and 'progressive knowledge' for the future; and it concluded with a pointed and flattering comparison between Lewes and Green. Green's essay on Hume was 'elaborate and destructive', but, 'In the guise of an introduction, Mr. Green has in fact issued a declaration of war, from an idealist point of view, against the reigning empirical logic. To this challenge, Mr. Lewes's *Problems of Life and Mind* may serve as the ready-made rejoinder.'[217] It was, therefore, no surprise that Green should turn his attention to Lewes's work. The stakes were intellectual, institutional, and political.

---

[213] Ibid. 371.    [214] Mark Pattison, 'Philosophy at Oxford', *Mind*, 1 (1876), 84–6.
[215] Ibid. 94.    [216] Lewes to Pattison, 27 Dec. 1875, in Eliot, *Letters*, vi. 202.
[217] Pattison, 'Philosophy at Oxford', 96.

Green's first essay on Lewes was published in the liberal, Anglican *Contemporary Review*, which was continuing its campaign against the new psychology in a series of essays attacking leading writers or 'materialistic' arguments generally.[218] But, if the substance of the essay is familiar, its language—turgid and arcane, imitating the Germanic manner in tortuous slow motion—is less so. The tone places it in its period. The assumed audience is specialized, and his constituency is quite unlike that envisaged by, say, Lewes or Eliot who maintained admirable proportion between intellectual range and seriousness and a belief in plain communication to as wide a public as possible.

Green's essay is argumentatively shrewd, however. Its chief tactic is to seize on the transitional points in Lewes's discussion, the points of maximum difficulty and vulnerability. Thus the 'gap' between the 'physical' and the 'mental' is much emphasized. Where Lewes made use of ambiguities in language to stress a unitary process (feeling could refer to either a mental or a physical state, for example), Green found confusion and indecision. For Lewes, these ambiguities were a necessary result of 'multi-aspect' analysis, but Green demanded fast ontological distinctions. He takes the terms that Lewes uses to mediate between the various biological, personal, and socio-historical levels of his argument— experience, feeling, sense, society, history, 'medium', subjective and objective— and explores their complexities and equivocations. For example, is 'experience' an analytic construction or a series of raw physical events? If it is the former, then we can ask what mental power or faculty it is that synthesizes raw data and forms analytic abstractions. If it is the latter, we can wonder how consciousness is generated and what status it has in relation to raw experience. Lewes's arguments, Green claims, are therefore, like all those within the Lockean tradition, fundamentally equivocal. While insisting that mental life is formed from raw events, they also maintain that there is a super-added analytical power in consciousness. But on what basis can the discovery of 'relations' between events (of which Lewes makes so much) be generated? This kind of mental event— the apprehension of relationship—'would not be events but something not an event', because 'if there were nothing but events passing in time, there could be no relations'.[219] Therefore, Green argues, the consciousness of relations must be produced independently of sense experience and must be ontologically distinct from it. What is it, he asks, that synthesizes experience? The whole is an

---

[218] Green's essays on Spencer also appeared in the *Contemporary*. A second essay on Lewes was written, but withdrawn when Lewes died in 1878. It was first published in the *Works* of 1885. T. Collyns Simon's 'The Present State of Metaphysics in Great Britain' is an example of the pro-Kantian/Hegelian manner. It attacks Spencer specifically. For a non-Kantian example of the attack on the 'materialistic' psychology, see Barry, 'Battle of the Philosophies'. Barry was a theological tutor at King's College, London, who later became Deacon of Windsor and Primate of Australia.

[219] Green, 'Lewes's Account of Experience', in *Works*, i. 443.

argument for independent, Kantian 'forms of thought', and the positing of a 'self-conscious subject' ontologically distinguishable from sense experience.

Such arguments are familiar, and of a piece with the notorious difficulty in associationism highlighted by Coleridge and others. What distinguishes Green's use of them is the rigour of their application, for he extends the account to other areas of Lewes's analysis. He makes the telling point that Lewes regularly blurs the distinction between perception and conception, and coincidence and inference.[220] He also maintains that Lewes's conception of 'the real' is problematic and ambiguous, though this argument—essentially that made in the *Introduction to Hume*—is more tendentious. He argues that the 'objective' is unknowable except through the 'subjective'. To posit, therefore, a 'real' independent of the forms of human perception is to posit a fiction. There can be no 'world "outside consciousness"'. What could that be but a 'blank nothing, which we delude ourselves into supposing to be something by stocking it with abstractions from the actual content of consciousness, called "things-in-themselves"'?[221] The arguments about the ambiguities of the 'real' and the ambiguities of 'feeling' are bound together. Green asserts that hallucinatory phenomena embarrass Lewes's claims for the primacy of sense experience, and, more convincingly (the point about hallucinations might equally apply to Green's theory), that *all* feeling is a mental construction. The 'truth' of any perception therefore has little to do with externality but with the 'interpretation of feeling'.[222]

Green's own arguments might be used against him, however. He does not so much blur perception and conception as conflate them. But he does have a good point about Lewes's theory of the Logic of Feeling and the Logic of Signs. As he remarks, Lewes makes the same distinction as Green himself, only Lewes remains residually attached to the Logic of Feeling. Lewes's apparent sophistication of the sensationalist–realist epistemology is still caught in the schema of 'fact', on the one hand, and 'copy', on the other. Green manages to imply that Lewes is in fact an Idealist without the courage to admit it.[223] As we shall see, Lewes has often been misunderstood in this way.

The assumption that runs through Green's essay is that the 'biological' is incapable of generating the 'mental'. The nervous system cannot conceivably generate or operate sophisticated mental systems. There is an unbridgeable gap in both credulity and ontology: 'physiological processes are not continued into

---

[220] T. H. Green, 'Mr. Lewes's Account of the "Social Medium"', in *Works*, i. 515–16. This is the essay withdrawn from the *Contemporary* after Lewes's death.   [221] Ibid. 482.

[222] Ibid. 495. There was increasing interest in hallucinations and illusions in the period. James Sully—who was to write a book on the subject—wrote interestingly on the 'Illusions of Introspection' in *Mind*, 6 (1881), 1–18.

[223] Green, 'Lewes's Account of Experience', in *Works*, i. 447–54.

consciousness as chemical processes are into life': 'Nothing that the physiologist can detect—no irritation, or irradication, or affection of a sensitive organ—enters into it [consciousness] at all. The relations which these terms represent are all of a kind absolutely heterogeneous to and incompatible with the mutual determinations of ideas in the unity of consciousness.[224] In other words, acts of consciousness are entirely self-generating, self-regulating entities.

Underpinning this line of thought is an essentially religious faith in the benign providence of natural creation and the sovereignty of the individual subject within it. In explaining this Green reaches for the sublime cadence: 'A world which is a system of relations implies a unit, self-distinguished from all the terms related, yet determining all as the equal presence through relation to which they are related to each other; and such a unit is a conscious subject.'[225] This quotation *is* accurate incidentally, and it reveals Green struggling to create a mysticism of the sovereign, self-conscious subject. The language attempts to render the technical vocabulary and syntax of Idealist philosophy in an assertive rhythm. The effect, to my ear, is of a failed chant. It is a kind of effort at the Carlylean sublime without Carlyle's rhetorical flair or (admittedly intermittent) ironical self-consciousness.

The connection with Carlyle's generation of British intellectuals influenced by German Idealism is important. There is a real similarity between the psychological arguments of Coleridge, Carlyle, and Green, and Green's work developed the momentum of the 'Idealist revival' in Britain from the 1860s. As scholars have pointed out, this revival of interest in Idealist thought was motivated by domestic concerns, often political, and major writers often read Kant and Hegel to suit their own needs.[226] In particular, German Idealism was thought to provide a persuasive version of the 'spiritualist' case. J. H. Stirling, a Hegel-enthusiast and friend of Carlyle, claimed in *The Secret of Hegel* (1865) that: 'What we all long for is Christian simplicity, the Christian happiness of our forefathers —the simple pious soul, on the green earth, in the bright fresh air, patiently

---

[224]   Green, 'Lewes's Account of the "Social Medium" ', in *Works*, i. 476.

[225]   Ibid. 500.

[226]   Ashton, *The German Idea*; for comment on Coleridge's and Carlyle's uses—and misunderstandings—of Kant, see pp. 42–3 and 70 ff. Ashton notes that Lewes, one of her four writers, had rejected idealist philosophy by 1843 (p. 126—though I think this date is a bit early), and that he was very cool on the idealist revival (p. 211). For the political context of Coleridge's championship of idealist thought, see Butler, *Romantics, Rebels, and Reactionaries*. Hearnshaw in his *Short History of British Psychology* comments on the habit among 'anti-materialist' writers of turning to German Idealism throughout the period. His is a useful, succinct discussion of the Idealist revival and its impact on psychological thought. René Wellek also gives some detail on this history but, interestingly, ends by saluting Green in vigorous terms: 'at last in Thomas Hill Green England has borne a genius whose thought breathes the very spirit of Kant' (*Immanuel Kant in England*). It is another interesting thread of connection between New Criticism and the opponents of the new psychology in the late nineteenth century.

industrious, patiently loving . . . Hegel indeed has no object but—reconciling and neutralizing atomism—once again to restore us—and in new light and thought—immortality and freewill, Christianity and God.'[227] The jubilant, revivalist syntax is unmistakable, and these ideas were widely shared.

For Green, Stirling's book 'contrasted with everything that had been published as sense with nonsense',[228] and an essay for the *North British Review* in 1868 drew the political analogy. Green associated the Lockean tradition with scepticism and revolution and looked to the Romantic–conservative tradition in thought and literature—especially the 'mature' Wordsworth—for remedy.[229] T. Collyns Simon, another partisan, argued (again in the *Contemporary*, which was particularly encouraging to revivalists) that Hegel restored a sense of the Universal. But he did so only through the autonomous Ego. This was the key term. The individual Ego (Green's 'self-conscious subject') was directly and necessarily related to the 'Superhuman Ego', or God, though no Universal has any value other than 'such as it derives from the Individual'.[230]

The individualist bias is very pronounced, and it contrasts sharply with the emphasis Lewes places on the role of society, culture, and history in the formation of minds. Green's psychology, indeed, is almost totally without a sense of history or society at all. Though he began his second essay on Lewes with the accusation that Lewes makes too little of the 'social medium', and the achievements of human culture, it quickly emerges that Green understands something very different by these terms. Culture for him is the product of 'an active self-consciousness'.[231] The effects of culture *on* that consciousness are ignored.

The lack of any attention to history or society in Green's psychology is one objection that can be made to it, but it is part of a larger problem. Green's model of mind is deliberately static. He is not interested in what he terms 'psychogeny' (the study of the origins of mental life), only with its free-standing agency. He thus neglects change and difference in a way that is damaging for his critique of Lewes. Many of his objections stand only if the initial premisses are accepted —for instance, that consciousness cannot be understood neurologically. In a

---

[227] Quoted in Hearnshaw, *Short History of British Psychology*, 127–8.

[228] Quoted by J. H. Muirhead, 'How Hegel Came to England', *Mind*, 36 (1927), 444. Many of the accounts of first reading Hegel that Muirhead cites read like quasi- (or explicitly) religious initiations into a mystery or ritual. They often deploy—as in the very title of Stirling's *The Secret of Hegel*—the language of revelation. Given this, and the notorious complexity of Hegel himself, it is not difficult to see why the language of Green or Stirling should be as it is. The secret of Hegel in Stirling's account, by the way, is revealed by Muirhead to be Kant's old principle of the *a priori* forms (p. 443). See also Peter Robbins, *The British Hegelians 1875–1925* (London, 1982).

[229] [T. H. Green], 'Popular Philosophy in its Relation to Life', *North British Review*, NS 9 (1868), 133–62.

[230] T. Collyns Simon, 'Hegel and his Connexion with British Thought: Part 1', *Contemporary Review*, 13 (1870), 77.

[231] Green, 'Lewes's Account of the "Social Medium"', in *Works*, i. 472.

complex discussion, Green maintains that one cannot hold that consciousness is determined by physiological processes, because consciousness is not an 'event' of the same order. The laws of causality apply only to phenomena of the same ontological type: 'consciousness of an event is not itself an event,' he says.[232] But it is clear, and was clear to many of Green's contemporaries, that neurological activity does accompany conscious activity. Green's separation of the two, which follows directly from the ontological gap he assumes, leads him into some awkward corners. The 'self-conscious subject', he claims, cannot be continuous with the biological subject: 'it cannot be physically explained because it conditions the possibility of all physical explanation'.[233] This is a bit like saying that you cannot experience the taste of food because you cook it first.

It is easy to see the fundamental incompatibility of this position with that of Lewes. Lewes himself was wearily dismissive. In volume four of *Problems of Life and Mind* he comments that Green simply fails to understand what modern psychology is saying and ends up denying that the 'objective' exists at all.[234] But the central difference is not just a matter of one accepting the importance of physiology and the other not. The acceptance of physiology necessitates a different model. In it the mind is not autonomous. It is relational to the biological and social environments, determined by these environments, and subject to process and change. Indeed, the latter is in many ways the key feature of the model, for it is this dynamic structure—articulated by Lewes and twentieth-century writers like J. Z. Young alike[235]—that drives the subject to development and growth.

None the less it is worth wondering why Green's critiques of Lewes and Spencer were widely supported. At one level, of course, they articulate traditional, conservative objections in a way, and a language, that seems both briskly new and comfortably old. But there is an argumentative strength too. We have noted that Lewes in *Problems of Life and Mind* was trying hard to get away from the reductiveness that was always a difficulty for the new psychology. In his increasingly sophisticated attempts to develop the model he was, at that level, partly successful. But in his detailed analyses, and for all his expository and populist gifts, there is—as with Spencer and Bain—a feeling sometimes of remoteness from common experience, a sense that important areas of life are not being fully realized or engaged in the emphasis on determining environments.

This was certainly felt by James Ward. Ward was in many respects a figure rather similar to many of the new psychologists. He too came from a provincial nonconformist background (Birmingham Congregationalist), and was

---

[232] Green, 'Lewes's Account of the "Social Medium"', in *Works*, i. 476.
[233] Ibid. 472.    [234] Lewes, *Problems*, iv. 157.
[235] See J. Z. Young, *Philosophy and the Brain*, 79 ff.

educated in dissenting academies and in Germany, where he studied, among other things, experimental physiology. However, after the collapse of his faith, and his resignation from the ministry (he had become a Congregationalist minister in Cambridge in 1871), he became an academic, enrolling at the university in 1872 and becoming a lecturer, under the patronage of Henry Sidgwick, ten years later. The entry into Cambridge, of course, marks the significant difference between his career and those of the principal writers examined in this book. It produced an enormously influential critique of the dominant trends of thinking in the new psychology.[236]

Ward rejected the new psychology because it did not engage fully enough with actual, living consciousness and, more pressingly for a spiritually troubled man, with problems of conscience. Associationism seemed to him arid, and physiology remote from significant individual experience.[237] In *The Relation of Physiology to Psychology: An Essay* (1875) Ward attacked psychological 'materialism' (and Lewes in particular) not only for its reduction of mind to matter, but for its irrelevance. The new psychology still relied on the taxonomy of the old faculties, but did not extend knowledge of them, while, as for the physiological, technical, and other scientific detail, 'how little this means after all'.[238] He therefore looked to reformulate psychology in such a way that it became responsive to the activities of individual minds, an activity that, he held, was by definition unresponsive to the language of science.[239] His position resembles that of his mentor Henry Sidgwick on ethics. Writing in *Mind*, Sidgwick argued that evolutionary theory made no difference to the essentials of ethical debate. Unless one assumed (like Spencer) that evolutionary development inevitably produced 'the good', arguments about morals remained where they always had been.[240] Similarly, for Ward, wanting to recover a sense of psychology's responsiveness to individual living, most of the new psychological apparatus seemed irrelevant. Despite the formal rejection of his faith, he remained preoccupied by religious issues, and his intellectual work became, in a representative way, a displaced means for discussing unfinished business.[241]

Ward, then, brings together an interest in the psychology of individual consciousness (which draws upon the Idealist revival) with an informed rejection

---

[236] These and other details on Ward's career are taken from the chapter on Ward in Frank Miller Turner, *Between Science and Religion: The Reaction to Scientific Naturalism in Late Victorian England* (London, 1974). Turner's is the fullest and best account of Ward I have found.

[237] Ibid. 212–15.

[238] James Ward, *The Relation of Physiology to Psychology: An Essay* (London, 1875), 56.

[239] Ibid. 14.

[240] Henry Sidgwick, 'The Theory of Evolution in its Application to Practice', *Mind*, 1 (1876), 52–67.

[241] Turner makes an interesting comparison with Matthew Arnold in this respect: *Between Science and Religion*, 203.

of the languages of the new psychology. His work was developed by a number of contemporaries and successors—like William James, the philosopher F. H. Bradley, and (most importantly for psychological theory in Britain) G. F. Stout. Stout came under Ward's influence at Cambridge and, through his academic appointments (at Cambridge, Aberdeen, Oxford, and St Andrews), lengthy editorship of *Mind* (1891–1920), and his psychological books (especially the *Manual of Psychology* (1898), which was used as a textbook until the 1930s), did much to influence the development of psychological theory on Wardian lines.[242]

Ward partly created, partly caught, the general anti-associationist, anti-physiological mood of the moment.[243] His most famous piece, the entry on 'Psychology' for the *Encyclopaedia Britannica* in 1886, opens with a call to rethink the number of counters in the psychological game. There is, he says, another sense as important as the conventional physical senses. This is the 'internal sense', and it is in major respects the most important. Unlike the passive, ordinary senses, the 'internal sense' actively recognizes and organizes the data produced by the other senses. Consciousness and the 'internal sense' are qualitatively different *additions* to mental experience, despite the physiologists' insistence that there is no 'organ' or 'centre' in which it can be located.[244] Associationism has in its time usefully cleared out the language of psychology, but it is now time to recognize its limitations.[245]

Ward's strongest arguments, and best theoretical developments, are concerned with remodelling our picture of mental activity. Without acknowledgement, he supported Lewes's enlargement of the mental topography and free acknowledgement of subconscious processes.[246] But most persuasively he argued for an end to associationism's rigid categorization of mental life and a reconsideration of it in a modal way. The three principal modes of mental life were, he asserted, attention, feeling, and presentation (or the recognition or cognition of objects). These modes took various forms, but the advantage of thinking about psychology in this way was that the mind was pictured *at work*, as it were, rather than bound by analytical categories or taxonomic disputes.[247] Of the three modes, Ward gave most attention to attention (which may have been the principal source of his

---

[242] Turner, *Between Science and Religion*; Hearnshaw, *Short History of British Psychology*; Brett's *History of Psychology*.

[243] In 1893 Bradley actually accused Ward of not going far enough in his attacks on associationism: F. H. Bradley, 'Consciousness and Experience', *Mind*, NS 2 (1893), 211–16.

[244] James Ward, 'Psychology', *Encyclopaedia Britannica*, 9th edn., 24 vols. (Edinburgh, 1886), xx. 37–85.                                                                     [245] Ibid. 41.

[246] Ibid. 47. Ward's sketch here is almost identical to that in *Problems of Life and Mind*, which Ward had read carefully, as we shall see. Lewes, however, would not have been a helpful author to cite in terms of the intellectual politics of the period, and such arguments had been made elsewhere with different nuances.                                                             [247] Ibid. 44.

appeal to William James). This was partly because this was the most distinctive and original part of the work, but it was also because it highlighted the implications of this way of thinking for broader debates. In order to exercise the attention, one needs to posit a self or subject to do the attending, and this, following Green, was the main burden of Ward's argument.[248]

Ward partly plays a 'modernization' card, and with some justification. Associationist method had become dogmatic and obstructive. But Bain, writing in defence of a life's work against Ward's instantly successful attack, had a point too. Ward's insistence on returning to a specifically *psychological* language freed from physiological or experimentalist jargon was to be welcomed, he wrote, but it was necessary to recognize how backward-looking Ward's project actually was. Bain could see nothing but Kantianism, with some changes in nomenclature.[249] Ward's psychology did indeed carry some quite explicit traditional and conservative features. The best way of understanding these is, as ever, in context.

Ward was offered the *Encyclopaedia Britannica* essay very late, after George Croom Robertson, the original choice, became ill, and Sully, the second choice, refused the task.[250] By the time he was commissioned in 1884 Ward had already locked himself into controversy. (Though this phase of psychological controversy seems to have been particularly courteous. Both Ward and Bain, for example, are very polite, even complimentary, to each other.) Robertson had decided to use an editorial piece in *Mind* on the journal's seventh anniversary in 1883 to survey developments thus far. He expressed disappointment at the lack of progress in specifically *psychological* science, and contrasted Britain unfavourably with Germany and France in this respect. He bemoaned the lack of an institutional basis for the discipline, and its neglect by traditional institutions. He then settled to his main theme: the retrograde effect of Green's critiques of Spencer, Lewes, and the tradition of empirical psychology. As a result of these attacks, Robertson believed that it was now necessary to sever psychology from philosophy completely. The philosophical climate was so unconducive it was inhibiting scientific enquiry. Robertson wanted *psychology* not a weakly psychologized Kantianism:

There is nothing in Kant's philosophical analysis of either fact or cognition—nothing, that is to say, which from the point of view he places himself at may be unquestionably maintained—for which a positive psychological warrant cannot now be assigned;

---

[248] Ward's argument follows Green's very closely. Criticizing both Mill and Spencer, Ward argues that the only solution to the paradox identified by Mill, that 'a series of feelings, can be aware of itself as a series', is to posit a subjectivity independent of sensory processes (ibid. 39–40, 83).

[249] Alexander Bain, 'Mr. James Ward's "Psychology"', *Mind*, 11 (1886), 457–77.

[250] Turner, *Between Science and Religion*, 211.

while it is psychology that gives the clearest demonstration of the limits that should be placed upon his assertions. . . . If that be so, Psychology is amply revenged upon him for his despite.[251]

Like Lewes and Bain, Robertson was exasperated by the neo-Kantians' wish to drag psychology back fifty years.

Ward's *Encyclopaedia Britannica* article was thus an intervention in an argument, but it was a very particular intervention. The style of the piece is dictated by the occasion (it is aloof, and rather bloodless, in the *Britannica* manner), but Ward includes in it lengthy passages extracted from earlier pieces published in *Mind* in 1883, which are, as a whole, much more polemically pointed. Ward's two essays (a third was added in 1887 in reply to Bain's critique) are called 'Psychological Principles', and the first is the most directly polemical. 'Psychological Principles I: The Standpoint of Psychology' attacks the idea that psychology can be considered exclusively a science. It rejects the role of physiology, insists that introspection is a—perhaps *the*—principal psychological method, and places the self and the individual at the centre of psychology's attention. Psychology *is* philosophical, and philosophy *is* metaphysical, he asserts. The discipline can be neither a concrete science like mineralogy or botany, nor an abstract science like mathematics, because its matter consists of 'what Kant calls judgements of experience', and psychology 'never transcends the limits of the individual'.[252] Psychology 'seems in fact far more intimately related to Metaphysics, that is to theories about Being and Becoming' than it is to either epistemology or 'mechanical' science.[253] Its concerns, that is to say, are ontological, and Ward closes his essay with an explicit attack on Lewes's 'double-aspect' theory in *Problems of Life and Mind* as actually *only* physiological.

So major features of Ward's psychology looked backwards to the future. Many of the central arguments could have been taken wholesale from more or less any decade of the previous ten; and some of the rhetorical strategies too are very familiar. Literature is used as a powerful argumentative cypher for precious, sensitive, 'whole' experience threatened by meddling science. In the *Britannica* piece on 'Psychology', Keats's famous protest against science from *Lamia* is quoted: 'Do not all charms fly | At the mere touch of cold philosophy?', and a general moral is drawn about our 'repugnance' at the 'common mistake of supposing that the real is obtained by pulling to pieces rather than building up'.[254] In a later essay, an attack on Wundt's *Physiologische Psychologie*, Ward accuses Wundt of omitting that part of life Kant 'left to poetry or to speculation to contemplate the universe dramatically as a concrete unfolding', and he ended comparing

---

[251] Robertson, 'Psychology and Philosophy', 21.
[252] James Ward, 'Psychological Principles I: The Standpoint of Psychology', *Mind*, 8 (1883), 162–3.
[253] Ibid. 168.     [254] Ward, 'Psychology', 72.

modern psychology to the study of Homer as 'an arrangement of gutturals, dentals, labials and the like'. It is 'simply brain turned inside out'.[255] This might be James Martineau writing.

In the history of psychology, it is often those who are most ambitious who are most scientifically abused. Spencer is a case in point. His biological errors are scorned routinely. On the other hand, those who, like Ward or Green, make similarly comprehensive assertions in a rejection of science are rarely attacked with the same gusto. It is interesting, therefore, that Ward did commit himself to a biological speculation, and that it is identical to Spencer's. In 'Psychology' he gives some thought to racial evolution. Here was a potential problem for him, because it might invite collectivist considerations that would distract from his essentially individualist premises. Ward's solution was to resort to a kind of Lamarckian evolutionism wherein the race could be treated not as a group, but as a sort of massive individual:

it is proposed to assume that we are dealing with one individual which has continuously advanced from the beginning of psychical life, and not with a series of individuals of which all save the first have inherited certain capacities from its progenitors. The life-history of such an imaginary individual, that is to say, would correspond with all that was new, all that could be called evolution or development, in a certain series of individuals each of whom advanced a certain stage in mental differentiation.[256]

This has a clear similarity to other conservative–religious appropriations of the Lamarck–Spencer theory. It apparently accepts biology, but in fact ignores it. It preserves the individualist emphasis, but assumes all individuals are alike and disregards the messy detail of existence and circumstance. Here is the major point of disagreement with Lewes. In *Problems of Life and Mind* Lewes took issue with the neo-Lamarckian belief in the transmission of collective experience, because it was taken to support *a priori* doctrines such as the 'forms of thought'. Such a theory was, he believed, interested in products and not production, and in the hands of the neo-Kantians the argument became merely verbal and abstract.[257]

Lewes's is a provisional, fluctuating world. That of Ward and Green is smooth and confined. In the name of a sensitive response to mental detail, Ward in fact describes only a world in the head, which omits those difficulties of circumstance and complexities of determination that Lewes and Eliot's 'thick description' both relished and realized. It was no wonder that Green criticized Lewes for sticking to his 'Logic of Feeling' instead of siding wholly with the 'Logic of Signs'. And it is no accident, also, that, through F. H. Bradley, there is a direct connection with one version of twentieth-century Modernism in the agonized, solitary accidie of T. S. Eliot. Eliot wrote his doctorate on Bradley and became

[255] J. Ward, '"Modern" Psychology: A Reflexion', *Mind*, NS 2 (1893), 73, 75, 79.
[256] Ward, 'Psychology', 45.    [257] Lewes, *Problems*, iv. 171–4.

expert in portraying, first, subjectivities painfully cut off from social life, and, secondly, similar subjectivities reconciled to religious purpose through acts of solitary, trans-historical communion. Either way, one deals with processes in consciousness abstracted from the lives of others.[258]

These are large, speculative issues, well beyond the remit of this book. But the connections are real enough, though tentative. In 1887 Bain wrote a polemical essay attacking the Hamilton–Ward–Bradley development of psychological theory. He ends taking Bradley to task for picturing mental life as operating only by universals and not by details. The issue was a technical problem within associationism, but it has wider ramifications. Bradley holds (Bain maintains) 'that *particulars* can never be associated, and that what is reproduced is *universal*'. But

in common parlance we should say that our knowledge of a concrete thing is improved by repetition, and attains its very best when we have viewed it times without number, so as to detach the picture from special dates and circumstances. This is the particularity of all our familiar surroundings; it does not make the objects general in any received sense of the word; they are still looked upon by us as particulars, and when we conceive them in idea, we do so with all the more vividness for the interaction and the absence of reference to special moments of observation.[259]

Bain stresses the importance of personal, particular history. And it is hard not to think of George Eliot and Lewes in reading his discussion of the relationship between particular and general memory: so much of her fiction is couched in this vein, so much of it deals with this very issue; so much of his work rests on the uneasy but necessary dialogue of feeling and signs.

G. H. Lewes and George Eliot were both fond of the idea of the 'epoch'. It is a key word in his histories of thought and her histories of personal and social development. The nineteenth-century habit of epochal thinking—the Positivist or Marxist stages of social development, the conservative nostalgia for better epochs, even the stages of ontogenetic development in Freud—are all key features of the way men and women of the period understood time and history. But often in Lewes and Eliot there is also the recognition that process continues, change is slow, history evolves irrespective of epochal divisions. The tension provides some of the energy for their work and is a central feature of their achievement.

The history traced in this book is bounded by specific dates: 1850–1880. The bulk of the material examined in it was published in the thirty years between them, and the book has focused on the cultural circumstances of this period. Yet a discourse builds upon earlier work, and attitudes persist and are supported

---

[258] For fuller discussion, see Rylance, 'Twisting: Memory from Eliot to Eliot'.
[259] A. Bain, 'On Association Controversies', *Mind*, 12 (1887), 171.

and managed into the future. The development of psychological theory was a specialized working-out of specific intellectual and scientific problems. But it was also formed by intellectual, spiritual, and political attitudes that at first sight had little to do with the details of that theory. Looking back, many of its concerns have 'only historical' interest. The language of associationism, the ins-and-outs of Lamarckian theory or the taxonomy of the faculties, the emphasis on God at the core of the world's material management, the lack of knowledge of genetics or the constitution of the nervous system or brain structure, the limitations in understanding of race or gender—all of these require some effort by most of us to comprehend. Yet the formation of this knowledge within its own cultural circumstances is a process that continues, and many of the attitudes and problems faced by the new psychology in the period 1850–1880 are faced, some in detail, some in outline, in other periods, including our own, for we still live in the bifurcated intellectual culture that separates 'the sciences' from 'the arts'. Perhaps it is possible to see in the mid-to-late nineteenth century a culture that was not so thoroughly split. Yet no nostalgia should attach to this, for it has to be recognized that modern science is far more complicated, and much too professional and specialized for an amateur intellectual, that cultural and intellectual arrangements are different, that intellectuals have a different relationship to different institutions, the state, and each other, that the means of production and distribution of ideas is vastly different, that the world is more encompassingly international. Yet there is also a spirit of ambition and an eagerness of enquiry that is laudable in these old nineteenth-century quarrels, and an admirable effort (from my own particular position) to understand the world and people in material ways without leaving behind their humanity or their distinctive qualities as living, cultured beings. That spirit, I think, is best represented in the finest work of Eliot and Lewes, and the latter has been terribly neglected.

The reasons for that neglect have already been indicated. But it is interesting how old attitudes persist. Lewes's work was opposed by the Idealists of his day, and he made no bones about his opposition to them. Idealism, he wrote in the second volume of *Problems of Life and Mind*, 'regards things as if they had no history, and would have no future'. Whereas in reality, 'things exist just so long as their conditions exist'. Idealism was 'only theory', and Lewes sketched a critique of the purely theoretical intelligence.[260] In the same volume he dismissed Hegel in equally strong terms in arguments similar to those of Bain against Bradley. Hegel abstracts from concrete experience and emphasizes symbols and universals. In other words, Lewes says, he splits the Logic of Signs from the Logic of Feeling.[261] This is followed by a powerful passage on the ways in which 'error

---

[260] Lewes, *Problems*, ii. 435–6.     [261] Ibid. 127.

sustains itself for centuries'. We are unable to see 'perceptions' because of the power of prevailing 'conceptions', which are 'compendiously embedded in these judgements, assumptions, and superstitions.' In other words, what we would now call hegemony or ideology:

the mere enunciation of a casual connection suffices to impress the uncritical hearer with a belief of its truth; and this belief, transmitted from family to family, from generation to generation, comes to be the heritage of men who pique themselves on their rationality. Round this nucleus of fancy cluster the notions and the interests, till the fiction becomes a very serious part of life. Holy awe and abject terror guard fictions from investigation.[262]

These interests, 'philosophical no less than religious', are protected by churches, temples, mosques, and pagodas against 'the dissolving agency of Doubt, the disturbing anarchy of Investigation', and we forget the labour in thought as we forget the labour that produces the toast rack, *The Times*, and the other items of the breakfast table: 'the plantations of China, factories of Sheffield, potteries of Staffordshire, or the epitomized nation of Printing-House Square.'[263]

Clearly then, Idealism (in Oxford and Cambridge) is understood hegemonically by Lewes. It is orthodoxy, the reigning, interested fiction of the age. In an appendix to the same volume Lewes devotes further pages to 'Lagrange and Hegel: the Speculative Method'. Hegel's errors are listed and Stirling's *Secret of Hegel* attacked. Process is forgotten, science ignored, thought rules over feeling and things, the universe is reduced to the single operation of the dialectical unfolding of Spirit. To return to Hegel or Kant, he concludes, would be to give up 'all the results of research since Bichat and Lavoisier'.[264] Kant usually fares somewhat better than Hegel in *Problems of Life and Mind*, but the general tenor of the analysis remains the same: Kant was the founder of modern 'Metempirical' thinking; he was disabled by the state of biology and psychology in the late eighteenth century, but none the less had an impoverished sense of Experience.[265] Lewes pictures Kant as caught in a double-bind produced by his times:

[262] Lewes, *Problems*, ii. 131.
[263] Ibid. ii. 131, 136. This passage is very similar to one in *The Mill on the Floss*, when Eliot turns on her cultured readers and asks them, amid their graceful ironies and cushions, to remember 'the emphasis of want' in factories, mines, and fields (*The Mill on the Floss*, 385–7).
[264] Lewes, *Problems*, ii. 535. I am aware that Lewes was earlier more enthusiastic about Hegel, and had a lively interest in Hegel's aesthetics (see [Lewes], 'Hegel's Aesthetics', *British and Foreign Review*, 13 (1842), 1–49). But even at the beginning of his career Lewes was no disciple. A critique of Schlegel from the same period anticipates some of the later objections to idealism ([Lewes], 'August William Schlegel', *Foreign Quarterly Review*, 32 (1843–4), 160–81), and a review of Hamilton from 1859 indicates the settled position: Lewes wishes Hamilton's *Lectures on Metaphysics* had been published earlier; it is now too late ([Lewes], 'Philosophy as an Element of Culture', *Universal Review*, 1 (1859), 266–77).
[265] Lewes, *Problems*, i. 437–40.

The truth is that Kant tried to hold contradictory positions. The whole drift of his polemic against the ontologists was to show that knowledge was limited, relative, and could not extend beyond the sphere of possible Experience; but while thus cutting the ground from under the ontologists, he was also anxious to cut the ground from the sensationalists and sceptics, and therefore tried to prove that the mind brought with it an *a priori* fund of knowledge.[266]

Lewes, then, could find little in Kant, and nothing in the neo-Kantians. Yet the idea that Lewes was at a heart a Kantian has persisted.

Much of the commentary Lewes's work has received, particularly in America, has not fully understood the context in which that work was produced. Hock Guan Tjoa, writer of the fullest monograph on Lewes's ideas, is unnecessarily slighting of them, because due allowance is not given to context and too much is given to received images. Thus Tjoa pictures Lewes trying to ape a type of Victorian culture hero, the discoverer, by fruitlessly speculating on evolutionary or physiological themes. His real 'forte was exposition and popularization and his sallies into "original" ground served mainly to spice up an otherwise boring genre'. Lewes could not, Tjoa comments, 'refrain from adding his own embellishments' on reading Darwin's *Origin of Species*.[267] Tjoa's comments are representative. He has failed to appreciate the volatile, uncertain context in which evolutionary ideas were being developed, and projects a vision of Darwin's book that assumes it was immediately both understood and perceived to be correct. As we have seen, Lewes actually grasped the significance of the book better than most.

But there are other sources for Tjoa's false image of Lewes. Although he gives useful attention to Lewes's early political interests, he assumes, in effect, that Lewes stopped being interested in social or political issues after, say, 1850. Indeed he encourages the view that Lewes's early reading in Carlyle and Kant acted as a useful antidote to what another contemporary in the Carlyle circle, Francis Espinasse, called the 'mechanisms and Atheisms' of French materialism.[268] The effect is to draw Lewes after Carlyle, as it were, and misunderstand the larger picture. The coverage of *Problems of Life and Mind* shows similar features. *Problems*, Tjoa argues, tries to reconcile the claims of Lewes's 'seasoned empiricism' (which receives little attention) with his 'swelling need for a kind of "religious nationalism", a meaningful vision of man and things'.[269] The weight of attention falls on the latter, but this seems to me an extrapolation from certain features of George Eliot's later ideas, and not a very certain reading of Lewes's complex text. It does, however, reveal a symptomatic trait. Lewes is read, in rather clichéd terms, as seeking 'millenarian' explanations of things. He is on

---

[266] Ibid. 453–54.   [267] Tjoa, *George Henry Lewes*, 89.
[268] Ibid. 14.   [269] Ibid. 117–18.

a 'quest for certainty'. His work is 'displaced religion'.[270] The effect, in philosophical terms, is to pull it towards Idealism; the cause, one cannot help think, is the gravitational pull of American New Criticism.

It has been customary to think of Lewes in this way. For Jack Kaminsky, Lewes writes 'Empirical Metaphysics', and a similar line is taken by the British critic Michael York Mason.[271] More recently Peter Alan Dale has read him as a displaced Hegelian. Starting with Lewes's literary-critical work, Dale points to (but wildly overestimates) Lewes's 'continual fascination' with Hegel and suggests that, for Lewes, biology becomes like the Romantic Spirit or Imagination. It is a founding and structuring essence. Later, Dale argues, Lewes found support for this position in the work of the German scientist and student of Kant, Hermann Helmholtz, who stressed the constructive powers of mind in the formation of knowledge propositions. As a result *Problems of Life and Mind* posits a radically new role for symbolization *over* perception in scientific discovery (signs over feeling, that is). Lewes thus anticipates Cassirer, and overlaps with Derrida.[272]

Dale's is an Idealist recovery of Lewes that goes against Lewes's own opposition to Idealist thought, the way he was understood by his contemporaries (Idealist or materialist alike), and much of the textual evidence and contextual circumstances. *Problems of Life and Mind* has not been read very carefully; nor has Helmholtz. Helmholtz was influential on Lewes, and Helmholtz did read Kant with interest (so did Lewes). But Helmholtz also, again like Lewes, wrote in this vein (the essay was first published in *Mind* in 1878):

the assumption of knowledge of axioms from transcendental intuition is:

(1) an unproved hypothesis
(2) an unnecessary hypothesis, because it does not assert that it explains anything in our real world of concepts that could be explained without its aid, and
(3) a hypothesis completely without use in explaining our knowledge of the real world, since the propositions produced by it may be applied to the conditions of the real world only after their objective validity has been tested and established empirically.[273]

Lewes himself could not have been more forthright. In another late essay Helmholtz wrote that, though, 'in the development of concepts, inductive conclusions

---

[270] Tjoa, *George Henry Lewes*, 84, 107, 112–15.

[271] Kaminsky, 'The Empirical Metaphysics of George Henry Lewes'; Mason, '*Middlemarch* and Science: Problems of Life and Mind'. Both of these essays are, however, useful accounts of Lewes's work.

[272] Peter Alan Dale, 'George Lewes' Scientific Aesthetic: Restructuring the Ideology of the Symbol', in George Levine (ed.), *One Culture: Essays in Science and Literature* (London, 1987), 92–116.

[273] Hermann L. S. Helmholtz, 'On the Meaning of Geometrical Axioms', in *Helmholtz on Perception: Its Physiology and Development*, ed. and trans. Richard M. Warren and Roslyn P. Warren (London, 1968), 246.

acquired by the unconscious action of memory play a predominant role', it 'seems doubtful whether the ideational realm of the adult includes any forms of cognition not derived from these sources'.[274] Lewes would have been very happy with this idea. It follows coherently from his own efforts to redefine the relationship between conscious and unconscious life. But it is difficult to see how it is related to the popular Idealism of the period. Kant, Helmholtz concluded generally, had not been 'critical enough in his critique'.[275]

Lewes was working against reductive materialism and naïve sensationalist realism and, as such, his investigations are complex and subtle. Sometimes, too, they are hesitant and provisional, as we have seen, and some aspects of his thinking—such as that on the moral sense—can sometimes contradict the general tenor of his outlook and conclusions.[276] He was also interested in the complex processes involved in hypothesis formation, and was not a Millite on such subjects. But Dale's misreading of Lewes's conclusions is not really a product of his ambiguities. It is a projection of a wish that he conform to type. This construction of Lewes is also detectable in Tjoa's book and in much criticism of George Eliot until quite recently. Where Green objected to the materialism of *Problems of Life and Mind*, now Lewes is recruited to the cause. Where Lewes rejected Kant, he is now made, in important respects, to follow him. Historical perspectives are reversed. I think this is partly a product of the literary half of the two cultures' disinclination to confront scientific or materialistic beliefs. I also think, especially in America, that it is the result of the close relationship in outlook between, on the one hand, the opponents of the new psychology in the second half of the nineteenth century (particularly the neo-Kantians), and,

[274] Helmholtz, 'On the Correct Interpretation of our Sensory Impressions', in ibid. 260.

[275] Helmholtz, 'On the Meaning of Geometrical Axioms', in ibid. 246. For detailed discussion of Helmholtz's relationship to Kant in his work on visual perception that confirms this reading, see R. Steven Turner, 'Consensus and Controversy: Helmholtz on the Visual Perception of Space', in David Cahan (ed.), *Hermann von Helmholtz and the Foundations of Nineteenth-Century Science* (London, 1993), 154–204.

[276] In much the best single essay on Lewes, K. K. Collins has looked closely at some of the manuscript material pertaining to George Eliot's editing of the final volume of *Problems of Life and Mind*. Collins (also an American, incidentally) has an expert grasp of the issues, and brings out very well how Eliot's revisions nudged Lewes's text closer to Kant. She seems to have been alarmed that Lewes's theory, though strong on genetic accounts of moral belief, could not generate an independently acting moral sense, which would give 'the authority necessary to ground moral obligation' (K. K. Collins, 'G. H. Lewes Revised: George Eliot and the Moral Sense', *Victorian Studies*, 21 (1978), 475). This is in fact one of the ambiguous areas of *Problems*. Sometimes Lewes gives a solely genetic account of moral or value choices (that is, why these choices are made rather than those). But he himself seems to have been unsettled by the implications of this. He therefore writes at other points as though there were a moral sense driving through nature towards efficacious ends, 'the growing good of the world', as it were. (See e.g. *Problems*, iv. 150–1, where Lewes describes the evolution of moral ideas from primitive needs, but implies that this growth is inevitable and necessary.) This conflict is one very typical of the epoch in which Eliot and Lewes wrote.

on the other, the influential critics associated with New Critical formalism who encouraged the analysis of literary texts independently from their shaping contexts. Their views appear to have exerted a powerful gravitational pull on the subsequent development of much American criticism.

We have noted these connections in detail from time to time, but it is worth making the larger point. The formalistic orientation of New Criticism has probably been more influential in the long run than its explicit political and intellectual conservatism and it has been resumed among 'radical' avant-garde textualists associated with post-structuralism and deconstruction. The kind of textual formalism practised by both these movements is, unless in very intellectually agile hands, unlikely to encourage historically contextualizing study. As a result, the concerns and interests of the academic present are projected onto the past. While this kind of projection always occurs in historical enquiry, the recreation of context checks the conception of the past as only a hall of mirrors, as American critics of these developments like Jerome McGann have argued.[277] In psychology, as an odd replica of this process, the standard treatment of psychology's history to be found in synoptic histories of the discipline also usually leaves out the grain and texture of argument, the cultural pressures bearing upon writers, and the political and religious milieu in which ideas were formed. In these histories also, discourse is construed in the light of present interests (or purported 'scientific successes' or 'influences'). It has been the ambition of this book to place these arguments back into their proper contexts and permit the restoration of the turbulent discursive world of Victorian psychological debate.

[277] The position is well argued in Jerome J. McGann, *The Beauty of Inflections: Literary Investigations in Historical Method and Theory* (Oxford, 1985).

# Bibliography

VICTORIAN AND PRE-VICTORIAN SOURCES

Anon., 'Psychology', in *Cyclopaedia: or, an Universal Dictionary of Arts and Sciences* (London, 1788).

Anon., 'Metaphysics', in *Encyclopaedia Perthensis; or Universal Dictionary of the Arts, Sciences, Literature, &c.* (Edinburgh, 1816).

Anon., 'Psychology', in *Cyclopaedia: or, an Universal Dictionary of Arts and Sciences*, by Abraham Rees (London, 1819).

Anon., 'Metaphysics' and 'Logic', in *The Edinburgh Encyclopaedia*, conducted by David Brewster with the assistance of Gentlemen eminent in Science and Literature (Edinburgh, 1830).

Anon., 'Psychology', in *The British Cyclopaedia* (London, 1838).

Anon., 'Psychology', in *Encyclopaedia Metropolitana: or, Universal Dictionary of Knowledge* (London, 1845).

Anon., 'Notice of *The Human Body and its Connexion with Man* by James Garth Wilkinson', *Westminster Review*, NS 1 (1852), 275–9.

Anon., 'M. Comte's Religion for Atheists', *British Quarterly Review*, 28 (1858), 422–46.

Anon., 'Mr. Herbert Spencer's First Principles', *British Quarterly Review*, 37 (1863), 84–121.

Anon., 'Lewes on Aristotle's Scientific Writings', *British Quarterly Review*, 40 (1864), 51–79.

Anon., 'Mind and Brain', *British Quarterly Review*, 40 (1864), 440–63.

Anon., 'Mind', *Chambers's Encyclopaedia: A Dictionary of Universal Knowledge for the People* (Edinburgh, 1865).

Anon., 'Sir Henry Holland's *Recollections*', *British Quarterly Review*, 55 (1872), 461–78.

Anon., 'Lewes's Problems of Life and Mind', *Saturday Review*, 36 (1873), 757–8.

Anon., 'Lamarck', *Westminster Review*, NS 46 (1874), 175–99.

Anon., 'Science, Philosophy, and Religion', *British Quarterly Review*, 60 (1874), 101–26.

Anon., 'Mr Lewes and Metaphysics', *Westminster Review*, NS 46 (1874), 109–37.

Anon., 'Lewes's Problems of Life and Mind', *Saturday Review*, 40 (1875), 301–2.

Anon., 'George Henry Lewes', *Nature*, 19 (1878), 106–7.

Anon., 'Current Philosophy', *Atheneum*, 27 Sept. 1879, 398.

Arnold, Matthew, *Culture and Anarchy* (1869), ed. Ian Gregor (Indianapolis, 1971).

—— *The Letters of Matthew Arnold*, iii. *1866–70*, ed. Cecil Y. Lang (London, 1998).

Bain, Alexander, *The Senses and the Intellect* (London, 1855).

—— *The Senses and the Intellect*, 3rd edn. (London, 1868).

—— *The Emotions and the Will* (London, 1859).

—— *The Emotions and the Will*, 2nd edn. (London, 1865).

—— *The Emotions and the Will*, 3rd edn. (London, 1875).

—— *On the Study of Character Including an Estimate of Phrenology* (London, 1861).

Bain, Alexander, 'On the Correlation of Force and its Bearing on the Mind', *Macmillan's Magazine*, 16 (1867), 372–83.

—— *Mental and Moral Science: A Compendium of Psychology and Ethics*, 2nd edn. (London, 1868).

—— 'Common Errors on the Mind', *Fortnightly Review*, NS 4 (1868), 160–75.

—— 'Darwinism and Religion', *Macmillan's Magazine*, 24 (1871), 45–51.

—— *Mind and Body: The Theories of their Relation* (London, 1873).

—— 'Mr. G. H. Lewes on the Postulates of Experience', *Mind*, 1 (1876), 146.

—— *Mental and Moral Science: A Compendium of Psychology and Ethics*, 3rd edn. (London, 1879).

—— 'Mr. Spencer's Psychological "Congruities"', *Mind*, 6 (1881), 266–70, 394–406.

—— *Practical Essays* (London, 1884).

—— 'Mr. James Ward's "Psychology"', *Mind*, 11 (1886), 457–77.

—— 'On Association Controversies', *Mind*, 12 (1887), 161–82.

—— 'The Respective Spheres and Mutual Helps of Introspection and Psycho-Physical Experiment in Psychology', *Mind*, NS 2 (1893), 42–53.

—— *Autobiography* (London, 1904).

Barry, Alfred, 'The Battle of the Philosophies—Physical and Metaphysical', *Contemporary Review*, 12 (1869), 232–44.

[Barton, F. B.], 'Spencer's "Principles of Psychology"', *Reasoner*, 13 (30 Mar. 1856), 99.

[Baynes, T. S.], 'Tylor on Primitive Culture', *Edinburgh Review*, 135 (1872), 88–121.

Birks, Thomas Rawson, *Modern Physical Fatalism and the Doctrine of Evolution, Including an Examination of Mr. H. Spencer's First Principles* (London, 1876).

Borrow, George, *Lavengro: The Scholar—The Gypsy—The Priest* (1851; London, 1961).

Bradley, F. H., 'Consciousness and Experience', *Mind*, NS 2 (1893), 211–16.

[Brewster, Sir David], 'Works on Mental Philosophy, Mesmerism, Electro-Biology, &c.', *North British Review*, 22 (1854–5), 179–224.

Brontë, Charlotte, *Villette* (1853), ed. Mark Lilley (London, 1979).

[Brown, Thomas], 'Villers' *Philosophie de Kant*', *Edinburgh Review*, 1 (1803), 253–80.

—— 'Belsham's *Philosophy of the Mind*', *Edinburgh Review*, 1 (1803), 475–85.

Bulwer, Edward Lytton, *England and the English* (1833), ed. Standish Meacham (London, 1970).

Cabot, Ella Lyman, and Eyles, Edward, *Stories for Character Training: A Suggestive Series of Lessons in Ethics* (London, 1912).

Calderwood, Henry, 'The Present Relations of Physical Science to Mental Philosophy', *Contemporary Review*, 16 (1871), 225–38.

[Campbell, G. D.], 'Phrenology: Its Place and Relations', *North British Review*, 17 (1852), 41–70.

Carlyle, Thomas, *A Carlyle Reader: Selections from the Work of Thomas Carlyle*, ed. G. B. Tennyson (Cambridge, 1984).

—— *Essays: Scottish and Other Miscellanies*, 2 vols., ed. James Russell Lowell (London, 1915).

Carpenter, William B., *The Principles of Human Physiology: With their Chief Applications to Psychology, Pathology, Therapeutics, Hygiene, and Forensic Medicine*, 5th edn. (London, 1855).

—— 'The Physiology of the Will', *Contemporary Review*, 17 (1871), 192–217.

—— *The Principles of Mental Physiology with their Applications to the Training and Disciplining of the Mind and the Study of its Morbid Conditions* (London, 1874).

—— 'On the Doctrine of Human Automatism', *Contemporary Review*, 25 (1875), 397–416.

—— *Nature and Man: Essays Scientific and Philosophical* (London, 1888).

Chambers, Robert, *Vestiges of the Natural History of Creation and Other Evolutionary Writings*, ed. James A. Secord (London, 1994).

[Child, G. W.], 'Physiological Psychology', *Westminster Review*, NS 33 (1868), 37–65.

Clifford, W. K., '*Problems of Life and Mind* by George Henry Lewes. First Series. The Foundations of a Creed. Vol. 1', *Academy*, 5 (1874), 148–50.

—— *Lectures and Essays*, 2 vols., ed. Leslie Stephen and Frederick Pollock (London, 1879).

Cobbe, Frances Power, 'Unconcious Cerebration: A Psychological Study', *Macmillan's Magazine*, 23 (1870), 24–37.

—— *The Scientific Spirit of the Age: And Other Pleas and Discussions* (London, 1888).

Coleridge, S. T., *Biographia Literaria, or Biographical Sketches of my Literary Life and Opinions* (1817), ed. George Watson (London, 1975).

—— *On the Constitution of Church and State According to the Idea of Each* (1830), ed. John Barrell (London, 1972).

[Collier, James], 'The Development of Psychology', *Westminster Review*, NS 45 (1874), 377–406.

Comte, Auguste, *Auguste Comte and Positivism: The Essential Writings*, ed. Gertrude Lenzer (New York, 1975).

Courtney, William L., 'The New Psychology', *Fortnightly Review*, NS 26 (1879), 318–28.

Crowe, Catherine, *The Night-Side of Nature: or, Ghosts and Ghost Seers*, 3rd edn. (London, 1853).

Darwin, Charles, *The Origin of Species by Means of Natural Selection, or The Preservation of Favoured Races in the Struggle for Life* (1859), ed. J. W. Burrow (Harmondsworth, 1968).

—— *The Descent of Man in Relation to Sex* (1871; London, 1989).

Davidson, William L., 'Professor Bain's Philosophy', *Mind*, NS 13 (1904), 79–161.

[Dawkins, W. Boyd], 'Darwin on the Descent of Man', *Edinburgh Review*, 134 (1871), 195–235.

[de Bury, Marie Blaze], 'Victor Cousin', *North British Review*, NS 7 (1867), 162–71.

Dickens, Charles, *The Personal History of David Copperfield* (1849–50), ed. Trevor Blount (Harmondsworth, 1966).

—— *Hard Times for These Times* (1854), ed. David Craig (Harmondsworth, 1969).

—— *Great Expectations* (1860–1), ed. Angus Calder (Harmondsworth, 1965).

—— *Our Mutual Friend* (1864–5), ed. Stephen Gill (Harmondsworth, 1971).

[Duns, John], 'Professor Owen's Works', *North British Review*, 28 (1858), 313–45.

Eliot, George, *Adam Bede* (1859), ed. Stephen Gill (Harmondsworth, 1980).

—— *The Mill on the Floss* (1860), ed. A. S. Byatt (Harmondsworth, 1979).

—— *Middlemarch: A Study of Provincial Life* (1871–2), ed. W. J. Harvey (Harmondsworth, 1965).

Eliot, George, *Daniel Deronda* (1876), ed. Barbara Hardy (Harmondsworth, 1967).

—— *Essays of George Eliot*, ed. Thomas Pinney (London, 1963).

—— *The George Eliot Letters*, ed. Gordon S. Haight, 9 vols. (London, 1954–6, 1978).

—— *George Eliot's 'Middlemarch' Notebooks*, ed. John Clark Pratt and Victor A. Neufeldt (London, 1979).

[Fraser, A. Campbell]], 'Sir William Hamilton and Dr. Reid', *North British Review*, 10 (1848), 144–78.

—— 'Scottish Philosophy', *North British Review*, 18 (1853), 351–92.

[Froude, J. A.], 'Spinoza', *Westminster Review*, NS 8 (1855), 1–37.

Galton, Francis, *Herditary Genius, its Laws and Consequences* (London, 1869).

—— *Inquiry into the Human Faculty and its Development* (London, 1883).

Godwin, William, *Enquiry Concerning Political Justice and its Influence on Modern Morals and Happiness*, 3rd edn. (1789), ed. Isaac Kramnick (Harmondsworth, 1976).

[Gordon, John], 'Abernathy on Vital Principles', *Edinburgh Review*, 23 (1814), 384–98.

—— 'Functions of the Nervous System', *Edinburgh Review*, 24 (1815), 439–52.

—— 'The Doctrines of Gall and Spurzheim', *Edinburgh Review*, 25 (1815), 227–68.

Green, Joseph Henry, *Vital Dynamics: The Hunterian Oration before the Royal College of Surgeons in London 14th February 1840* (London, 1840).

—— *Spiritual Philosophy: Founded on the Teaching of the Late Samuel Taylor Coleridge*, ed. John Simon, 2 vols. (London, 1865).

[Green, T. H.], 'Popular Philosophy in its Relation to Life', *North British Review*, NS 9 (1868), 133–62.

—— *Works*, ed. R. L. Nettleship, 2 vols. (London, 1906).

Hamilton, E[lizabeth], 'Mr. Lewes's Doctrine of Sensibility', *Mind*, 4 (1879), 256–61.

Hamilton, Sir William, *Discussions of Philosophy and Literature, Education and University Reform, Chiefly from the Edinburgh Review; Corrected, Vindicated, Enlarged, in Notes and Appendices*, 2nd edn. (London, 1853).

Harrison, Frederic, 'The Soul and the Future Life', *Nineteenth Century*, 1 (1877), 623–36.

—— *The Philosophy of Common Sense* (London, 1907).

Hartley, David, *Observations on Man, his Frame, his Duty, and his Expectations* (1749; 6th edn., London, 1934).

Heath, D. D., 'Professor Bain on the Doctrine of the Correlation of Force in its Bearing on the Mind', *Contemporary Review*, 8 (1868), 57–78.

Helmholtz, Hermann L. S., *Helmholtz on Perception: Its Physiology and Development*, ed. and trans. Richard M. Warren and Roslyn P. Warren (London, 1968).

Henderson, James Scott, 'Positivism', *North British Review*, NS 10 (1868), 209–56.

[Herbert, Thomas Martin], 'Mind and the Science of Energy', *British Quarterly Review*, 60 (1874), 100–30.

Hodgson, Shadworth H., 'Philosophy and Science: I—As Regards the Special Sciences', *Mind*, 1 (1876), 67–81.

—— 'Philosophy of Mind: II—As Regards Psychology', *Mind*, 1 (1876), 223–35.

—— 'Philosophy and Mind: III—As Regards Ontology', *Mind*, 1 (1876), 351–62.

Holland, Sir Henry, *Medical Notes and Reflections* (London, 1839).

—— *Chapters in Mental Physiology* (London, 1852).

—— *Essays on Scientific and Other Subjects Contributed to the Edinburgh and Quarterly Reviews* (London, 1862).

—— *Recollections of Past Life* (London, 1872).

—— *Fragmentary Papers on Science and Other Subjects* (London, 1875).

Holyoake, G. J., 'Current Literature', *Reasoner*, 2 (2 Mar. 1856), 66.

Hume, David, *A Treatise of Human Nature*, ed. L. A. Selby-Bigge (Oxford, 1978).

[Hutton, R. H.], 'Atheism', *National Review*, 2 (1856), 97–123.

—— 'George Eliot', *National Review*, 11 (1860), 191–219.

—— 'A Questionable Parentage for Morals', *Macmillan's Magazine*, 20 (1869), 266–73.

—— 'Mr. Herbert Spencer on Moral Intuitions and Moral Sentiments', *Contemporary Review*, 17 (1871), 463–72.

—— 'Mr Lewes's "Problems of Life and Mind"', *Spectator*, 28 Feb. 1874, 271–3.

—— 'George Eliot', *Contemporary Review*, 47 (1885), 372–91.

Huxley, T. H., 'On the Physical Basis of Life', *Fortnightly Review*, NS 5 (1869), 129–45.

—— 'The Scientific Aspects of Positivism', *Fortnightly Review*, NS 5 (1869), 653–70.

—— *Hume* (London, 1879).

—— *Lessons in Elementary Physiology*, rev. edn. (London, 1886).

—— *Science and Culture and Other Essays* (London, 1892).

—— *Evolution and Ethics and Other Essays* (London, 1894).

—— 'Autobiography', in *Charles Darwin and T. H. Huxley: Autobiographies*, ed. Gavin de Beer (Oxford, 1983).

Jacobs, Joseph, 'The Need for a Society for Experimental Psychology', *Mind*, 11 (1886), 49–54.

James, William, 'On Some Omissions of Introspective Psychology', *Mind*, 9 (1884), 1–26.

—— 'The Perception of Space (I)', *Mind*, 12 (1887), 1–30.

—— 'The Perception of Space (II)', *Mind*, 12 (1887), 183–211.

—— *The Principles of Psychology* (1890), 2 vols. (New York, 1950).

—— *Selected Writings*, ed. G. H. Bird (London, 1995).

[Jeffrey, Francis], 'Stewart's *Life of Reid*', *Edinburgh Review*, 3 (1804), 269–87.

Kant, Immanuel, *The Critique of Judgement*, trans. James Creed Meredith (Oxford, 1952).

Lewes, George Henry, 'Hegel's Aesthetics', *British and Foreign Review*, 13 (1842), 1–49.

—— 'August William Schlegel', *Foreign Quarterly Review*, 32 (1843–4), 160–81.

—— *The Life of Maximilien Robespierre with Extracts from his Unpublished Correspondence* (London, 1849).

—— *Comte's Philosophy of the Sciences* (London, 1853).

—— 'Bain on The Senses and the Intellect', *Leader*, 6 (1855), 771–2.

—— 'Herbert Spencer's Psychology', *Leader*, 6 (1855), 1012–13.

—— 'History of Psychological Method', *Leader*, 6 (1855), 1036–7.

—— 'Life and Mind', *Leader*, 6 (1855), 1062–3.

—— 'Herbert Spencer's Principles of Psychology', *Saturday Review*, 1 (1856), 352–3.

—— 'Brodie's Psychological Inquiries', *Saturday Review*, 1 (1856), 422–3.

—— 'Hereditary Influence, Animal and Human', *Westminster Review*, NS 10 (1856), 135–62.

—— 'Phrenology in France', *Blackwood's Edinburgh Magazine*, 82 (1857), 665–74.

Lewes, George Henry, *A Biographical History of Philosophy from its Origin in Greece down to the Present Day*, 2nd edn. (London, 1857).

—— 'Philosophy as an Element of Culture', *Universal Review*, 1 (1859), 266–77.

—— 'Voluntary and Involuntary Actions', *Blackwood's Edinburgh Magazine*, 86 (1859), 295–306.

—— *The Physiology of Common Life*, 2 vols. (London, 1859–60).

—— *Aristotle: A Chapter from the History of Science* (London, 1864).

—— Critical Notice of *The Senses and the Intellect* and *The Emotions and the Will* by Alexander Bain, *Fortnightly Review*, 4 (1866), 767.

—— 'Mr. Darwin's Hypotheses: Part I', *Fortnightly Review*, NS 3 (1868), 353–73.

—— 'Mr. Darwin's Hypotheses: Part II', *Fortnightly Review*, NS 3 (1868), 611–28.

—— 'Mr. Darwin's Hypotheses: Part III', *Fortnightly Review*, NS 4 (1868), 61–80.

—— 'Mr. Darwin's Hypotheses: Part IV', *Fortnightly Review*, NS 4 (1868), 492–509.

—— 'Popular Lectures on Physiology', *Nature*, 1 (1870), 353.

—— *The History of Philosophy from Thales to Comte*, 2 vols., 4th edn. (London, 1871).

—— *Problems of Life and Mind*, 5 vols. (London, 1874–9).

   *First Series*: [i] *The Foundations of a Creed* (London, 1874); [ii] *The Foundations of a Creed* (London, 1875).

   *Second Series*: [iii] *The Physical Basis of Mind* (London, 1877).

   *Third Series*: [iv] *The Study of Psychology: Its Object, Scope and Method* (London, 1879); [v] untitled (London, 1879).

—— 'Spiritualism and Materialism: Part I', *Fortnightly Review*, NS 19 (1876), 479–93.

—— 'Spiritualism and Materialism: II', *Fortnightly Review*, NS 19 (1876), 707–19.

—— 'What is Sensation?', *Mind*, 1 (1876), 157–61.

—— 'The Uniformity of Nature', *Mind*, 1 (1876), 283–4.

Locke, John, *An Essay Concerning Human Understanding*, 4th edn. (1700), 2 vols., ed. John Yolton (London, 1961).

MacCall, William, *The Newest Materialism: Sundry Papers on the Books of Mill, Comte, Bain, Spencer, Atkinson and Feuerbach* (London, 1873).

McCosh, James, *The Scottish Philosophy: Biographical, Expository, Critical: From Hutcheson to Hamilton* (New York, 1875).

Main, Alexander, 'Mr. Hodgson on Mr. Lewes's View of Philosophy', *Mind*, 1 (1876), 292–4.

Mallock, W. H., *Atheism and the Value of Life: Five Studies in Contemporary Literature* (London, 1884).

—— *The New Republic: Culture, Faith, and Philosophy in an English Country House* (1877; Leicester, 1975).

Mansel, H. L., *Psychology the Test of Moral and Metaphysical Philosophy: An Inaugural Lecture Delivered at Magdalen College, Oct. 23 1855* (Oxford, 1855).

—— *A Lecture on the Philosophy of Kant* (Oxford, 1856).

—— *The Limits of Religious Thought* (Oxford, 1858).

Martineau, Harriet, *Autobiography* (1877, 2 vols.; London, 1983).

[Martineau, James], 'Cerebral Psychology: Bain', *National Review*, 10 (1860), 500–20.

—— 'The Place of Mind and Intuition in Man', *Contemporary Review*, 19 (1872), 606–23.

Masson, David, 'Bain on The Senses and the Intellect', *Fraser's Magazine*, 53 (1856), 212–30.

Maudsley, Henry, 'Materialism and its Lessons', *Fortnightly Review*, NS 26 (1879), 244–60.

Mill, James, *The History of British India*, 3rd edn., 6 vols. (London, 1826).

—— *Analysis of the Phenomena of the Human Mind* (1829), 2 vols., ed. J. S. Mill (1869; repr. New York, 1967).

Mill, John Stuart, *Auguste Comte and Positivism*, 2nd edn. (London, 1866).

—— *A System of Logic: Ratiocinative and Inductive*, 8th edn. (London, 1895).

—— *Mill on Bentham and Coleridge*, ed. F. R. Leavis (London, 1950).

—— *Autobiography*, ed. Jack Stillinger (1873; Oxford, 1971).

—— *An Examination of the Sir William Hamilton's Philosophy and of the Principal Philosophical Questions Discussed in his Writings: Collected Works of John Stuart Mill*, ix, ed. Alan Ryan (London, 1979).

—— 'Bain's Psychology', in *Essays on Philosophy and the Classics: Collected Works of John Stuart Mill*, xi, ed. J. M. Robson (London, 1978).

—— and Mill, Harriet Taylor, *Essays on Sex Equality*, ed. Alice S. Rossi (London, 1970).

Millingen, J. G., *Curiosities of Medical Experience*, 2nd edn. (London, 1839).

—— *Aphorisms of the Treatment and Management of the Insane; with Considerations on Public and Private Lunatic Asylums, Pointing out the Errors in the Present System* (London, 1840).

—— *Mind and Matter, Illustrated by Considerations on Hereditary Insanity and the Influence of Temperament in the Development of the Passions* (London, 1847).

—— *Recollections of Republican France from 1790–1801* (London, 1848).

—— *The Passions; or Mind and Matter, Illustrated by Considerations on Hereditary Insanity, etc., etc., etc.* (London, 1848).

[Mivart, St George], 'Herbert Spencer', *Quarterly Review*, 135 (1873), 509–39.

—— 'An Examination of Mr. Herbert Spencer's Psychology: Part I', *Dublin Review*, NS 23 (1874), 476–508.

—— 'An Examination of Mr. Herbert Spencer's Psychology: Part II', *Dublin Review*, NS 25 (1875), 143–72.

—— 'An Examination of Mr. Herbert Spencer's Psychology: Part III', *Dublin Review*, NS 28 (1877), 192–219.

—— 'An Examination of Mr. Herbert Spencer's Psychology: Part IV', *Dublin Review*, NS 28 (1877), 479–502.

—— 'An Examination of Mr. Herbert Spencer's Psychology: Part V', *Dublin Review*, NS 30 (1878), 157–94.

—— 'An Examination of Mr. Herbert Spencer's Psychology: Part VI', *Dublin Review*, NS 31 (1878), 412–39.

—— 'An Examination of Mr. Herbert Spencer's Psychology: Part VII', *Dublin Review*, NS 32 (1879), 141–63.

—— 'An Examination of Mr. Herbert Spencer's Psychology: Part VIII', *Dublin Review*, NS 33 (1879), 268–96.

—— 'An Examination of Mr. Herbert Spencer's Psychology: Part IX', *Dublin Review*, NS 34 (1880), 26–73.

Mivart, St George, 'Force, Energy and Will', *Nineteenth Century*, 3 (1878), 933–48.
—— 'Modern Catholics and Scientific Freedom', *Nineteenth Century*, 18 (1885), 30–47.
—— 'The New Psychology', *Nineteenth Century*, 45 (1899), 264–6.
Morrel, J. D., 'Modern English Psychology', *British and Foreign Medico-Chirurgical Review*, 17 (1856), 347–64.
Morley, John, *Nineteenth-Century Essays*, selected and introduced by Peter Stansky (London, 1970).
[Moulton, J. F.], 'Herbert Spencer', *British Quarterly Review*, 58 (1873), 472–504.
[Mozley, J. B.], 'The Argument of Design', *Quarterly Review*, 127 (1869), 134–76.
Newman, John Henry, *The Idea of a University Defined* (1873), ed. I. T. Ker (London, 1976).
Nietzsche, Friedrich, *Twilight of the Idols and The Anti-Christ*, trans. R. J. Hollingdale (Harmondsworth, 1968).
Owen, Robert, 'Essays on the Formation of Human Character' (1813–14), in *A New View of Society and Other Writings*, ed. John Butt (London, 1972).
Paley, William, *Natural Theology; or, the Evidences of the Existence and Attributes of the Deity, Collected from the Appearances of Nature* (London, 1802).
Pattison, Mark, 'Philosophy at Oxford', *Mind*, 1 (1876), 82–97.
Read, Carveth, 'G. H. Lewes's Posthumous Volumes', *Mind*, 6 (1881), 483–98.
Reid, Thomas, *The Works of Thomas Reid*, 2 vols., ed. Sir William Hamilton, 8th edn. (Edinburgh, 1895).
*Report of the Twenty-Ninth Meeting of the British Association for the Advancement of Science held at Aberdeen, Sept. 1859* (London, 1860).
Ribot, Théodule, *English Psychology*, 2nd edn. (London, 1877).
—— 'Philosophy in France', *Mind*, 2 (1877), 366–86.
Robertson, George Croom, 'Prefatory Words', *Mind*, 1 (1875), 3–6.
—— 'How we Come by our Knowledge', *Nineteenth Century*, 1 (1877), 113–21.
—— 'The Physical Basis of Mind', *Mind*, 3 (1878), 24–43.
—— 'Psychology and Philosophy', *Mind*, 8 (1883), 1–21.
Routledge, Robert, *Discoveries and Inventions of the Nineteenth Century*, 14th edn. (London, 1903).
Ryland, Frederick, *The Story of Thought and Feeling* (London, 1902).
Scripture, E. W., *The New Psychology* (London, 1897).
Seth, Andrew, *Scottish Philosophy: A Comparison of the Scottish and German Answers to Hume* (1885; repr. New York, 1971).
[Shairp, J. C.], 'Samuel Taylor Coleridge', *North British Review*, os 43, ns 4 (1865), 251–322.
—— 'Moral Theories and Christian Ethics', *North British Review*, ns 8 (1867), 1–46.
Sidgwick, Henry, 'The Theory of Evolution in its Application to Practice', *Mind*, 1 (1876), 52–67.
Simon, T. Collyns, 'The Present State of Metaphysics in Great Britain', *Contemporary Review*, 8 (1868), 246–61.
—— 'Hegel and his Connexion with British Thought: Part 1', *Contemporary Review*, 13 (1870), 47–79.
—— 'Hegel and his Connexion with British Thought: Part 2', *Contemporary Review*, 13 (1870), 398–421.

[Simpson, Richard], 'The Morals and Politics of Materialism', *Rambler*, NS 6 (1856), 445–54.

Smiles, Samuel, *Self-Help; with Illustrations of Conduct and Perseverance*, 2nd edn. (London, 1866).

—— *Character* (London, 1871).

[Smith, William Henry], 'Psychological Inquiries', *Blackwood's Edinburgh Magazine*, 77 (1855), 402–20.

—— 'Lewes's History of Philosophy', *Blackwood's Edinburgh Magazine*, 104 (1868), 537–53.

—— 'Knowing and Feeling: A Contribution to Psychology', *Contemporary Review*, 14 (1870), 342–62.

—— 'Knowing and Feeling: Part II.—Some Further Discussion of the Will', *Contemporary Review*, 15 (1870), 424–39.

Sorley, W. R., 'Psychology', in *Chambers's Encyclopaedia: A Dictionary of Universal Knowledge*, new edn. (London, 1891).

Spalding, Douglas A., 'Herbert Spencer's Psychology, Part 1', *Nature*, 7 (1873), 298–300.

—— 'Herbert Spencer's Psychology: Part 2', *Nature*, 7 (1873), 357–9.

—— 'George Henry Lewes's Problems of Life and Mind', *Examiner*, 14 Mar. 1874, 261–2.

—— 'The Physical Basis of Mind', *Nature*, 16 (1877), 261–3.

Spencer, Herbert, Notice of *Principles of Physiology, General and Comparative* by W. B. Carpenter, *Westminster Review*, NS 1 (1852), 274–5.

—— *The Principles of Psychology* (London, 1855).

—— *The Principles of Psychology*, 3rd edn., 2 vols. (London, 1881).

—— 'Morals and Moral Sentiments', *Fortnightly Review*, NS 9 (1871), 419–32.

—— 'Mr Martineau on Evolution', *Contemporary Review*, 20 (1872), 141–54.

—— *Essays: Scientific, Political, and Sperculative*, 3 vols. (London, 1891).

—— *First Principles*, 6th edn. (London, 1904).

—— *An Autobiography*, 2 vols. (London, 1904).

—— *Essays on Education and Kindred Subjects* (London, 1911).

Stephen, Leslie, *History of English Thought in the Eighteenth Century* (1876), 2 vols. (London, 1962).

Stewart, Dugald, 'An Account of the Life and Writings of Thomas Reid' (1803), in *The Works of Thomas Reid, D.D., with Notes and Supplementary Dissertations by Sir William Hamilton, Bart.*, 2 vols., 8th edn. (Edinburgh, 1895).

—— *Elements of the Philosophy of the Human Mind* (1814), ed. G. N. Wright (London, 1843).

Sully, James, 'George Henry Lewes', *New Quarterly Review*, NS 2 (1879), 356–76.

—— 'Problems of Life and Mind. Third Series. By George Henry Lewes', *Academy*, 24 Apr. 1880, 308–10.

—— 'Illusions of Introspection', *Mind*, 6 (1881), 1–18.

—— *My Life and Friends: A Psychologist's Memories* (London, 1918).

Tennyson, Alfred, *The Poems of Tennyson*, cd. Christopher Ricks (London, 1969).

Tulloch, John, 'Professor Ferrier's *Philosophical Remains*', *Edinburgh Review*, 126 (1867), 71–94.

—— 'The Positive Philosophy of M. Auguste Comte', *Edinburgh Review*, 127 (1868), 303–57.

Tulloch, John, 'Morality without Metaphysics', *Edinburgh Review*, 144 (1876), 470–500.
—— *Movements of Religious Thought in Britain during the Nineteenth Century* (1885; Leicester, 1971).
Tyndall, John, *Address Delivered before the British Association Assembled at Belfast*, with Additions (London, 1874).
—— ' "Materialism" and its Opponents', *Fortnighly Review*, 18 (1875), 579–99.
—— 'Science and Man', *Fortnightly Review*, NS 22 (1877), 593–617.
—— *Fragments of a Science: A Series of Detached Essays, Addresses, and Reviews*, 2 vols., 9th edn. (London, 1902).
Veitch, John, *Memoir of Sir William Hamilton, Bart.* (Edinburgh, 1869).
—— 'Philosophy in the Scottish Universities I', *Mind*, 2 (1877), 74–91.
—— 'Philosophy in the Scottish Universities II', *Mind*, 2 (1877), 207–34.
Ward, James, *The Relation of Physiology to Psychology: An Essay* (London, 1875).
—— 'Psychological Principles I: The Standpoint of Psychology', *Mind*, 8 (1883), 153–69.
—— 'Psychological Principles II: Fundamental Facts and Conceptions', *Mind*, 8 (1883), 465–86.
—— 'Psychological Principles III: Attention and the Field of Consciousness', *Mind*, 12 (1887), 45–67.
—— 'Psychology', *Encyclopaedia Britannica*, 9th edn., 24 vols. (Edinburgh, 1886), xx. 37–85.
—— ' "Modern" Psychology: A Reflexion', *Mind*, NS 2 (1893), 54–82.
[Wilson, H. B.], 'Theology and Philosophy', *Westminster Review*, NS 9 (1856), 221–42.
Webb, T. E., 'The Metaphysician: A Retrospect', *Fraser's Magazine*, 61 (1860), 503–17.
Wordsworth, William, *The Prelude: 1799, 1805, 1850*, ed. Jonathan Wordsworth, M. H. Abrams, and Stephen Gill (London, 1979).
—— *The Poems*, 2 vols., ed. John O. Hayden (Harmondsworth, 1977).
—— and Coleridge, Samuel, *Wordsworth and Coleridge: Lyrical Ballads*, ed. R. L. Brett and A. R. Jones (London, 1968).

MODERN COMMENTARIES

Aarsleff, Hans, *The Study of Language in England, 1780–1860* (Princeton, 1967).
Altick, Richard D., *Writers, Readers, and Occasions: Selected Essays on Victorian Literature and Life* (Columbus, 1989).
Ameriks, Karl, *Kant's Theory of Mind: An Analysis of the Paralogisms of Pure Reason* (Oxford, 1982).
Armstrong, Isobel, *Victorian Politics: Poetry, Poetics and Politics* (London, 1993).
Ashton, Rosemary, *The German Idea: Four English Writers and the Reception of German Thought 1800–1860* (Cambridge, 1980).
—— *G. H. Lewes: A Life* (Oxford, 1991).
—— *George Eliot: A Life* (London, 1997).
Baker, William, ' "A Problematical Thinker" to a "Sagacious Philosopher": Some Unpublished George Henry Lewes–Herbert Spencer Correspondence', *English Studies*, 56 (1975), 217–21.

Baldick, Chris, *The Social Mission of English Criticism, 1848–1932* (Oxford, 1983).

—— *In Frankenstein's Shadow: Myth, Monstrosity, and Nineteenth-Century Writing* (Oxford, 1987).

Barthes, Roland, *Michelet*, trans. Richard Howard (London, 1979).

Beer, Gillian, *Darwin's Plots: Evolutionary Narrative in Darwin, George Eliot and Nineteenth-Century Fiction* (London, 1983).

—— *Arguing with the Past: Essays in Narrative from Woolf to Sidney* (London, 1989).

—— *Open Fields: Science in Cultural Encounter* (Oxford, 1996).

Bell, Srilekha, 'George Henry Lewes: A Man of his Time', *Journal of the History of Biology*, 14 (1981), 277–98.

Benton, E., 'Vitalism in Nineteenth-Century Physiological Thought: A Typology and Reassessment', *Studies in the History and Philosophy of Science*, 5 (1974), 25–9.

Benson, Donald R., 'Facts and Constructs: Victorian Humanists and Scientific Theorists on Scientific Knowledge', in James Paradis and Thomas Postlewait (eds.), *Victorian Science and Victorian Values: Literary Perspectives* (New York, 1981), 299–318.

Biddiss, Michael D. (ed.), *Images of Race* (Leicester, 1979).

Block, Ed, 'T. H. Huxley's Rhetoric and the Mind–Matter Debate, 1868–1874', *Prose Studies*, 8 (1985), 21–39.

Boddy, John, *Brain Systems and Psychological Concepts* (Chichester, 1978).

Boring, Edwin G., *A History of Experimental Psychology* (London, 1929).

—— *Sensation and Perception in the History of Experimental Psychology* (New York, 1942).

Brett, G. S., *Brett's History of Psychology*, ed. and abridged by R. S. Peters, rev. edn. (London, 1962).

Briggs, Asa, *Victorian Things* (Harmondsworth, 1988).

Brown, Theodore M., 'From Mechanism to Vitalism in Eighteenth-Century English Physiology', *Journal of the History of Biology*, 7 (1974), 179–216.

Bryson, Gladys, *Man and Society: The Scottish Inquiry of the Eighteenth Century* (Princeton, 1945).

Burrow, J. W., *Evolution and Society: A Study of Victorian Social Theory* (Cambridge, 1966).

Butler, Marilyn, *Romantics, Rebels, and Reactionaries: English Literature and its Background 1760–1830* (Oxford, 1981).

—— 'The First *Frankenstein* and Radical Science', *Times Literary Supplement*, 9 Apr. 1993, 12–14.

Bynum, William F., 'The Anatomical Method, Natural Theology, and the Functions of the Brain', *Isis*, 64 (1973), 445–68.

—— Porter, Roy, and Shepherd, Michael (eds.), *The Anatomy of Madness. Essays in the History of Psychiatry*, i. *People and Ideas*; ii. *Institutions and Society*; iii. *The Asylum and its Psychiatry* (London, 1985–8).

Cahan, David, (ed.), *Hermann von Helmholtz and the Foundations of Nineteenth-Century Science* (London, 1993).

Campbell, R. H., and Skinner, Andrew S. (eds.), *The Origins and Nature of the Scottish Enlightenment* (Edinburgh, 1982).

Canguilhem, Georges, *A Vital Rationalist: Selected Writings*, ed. François Delaporte, trans. Arthur Goldhammer (New York, 1994).

Cantor, G. N., 'The Edinburgh Phrenology Debates: 1803–1828', *Annals of Science*, 32 (1975), 195–218.

Cardno, J. A., 'Bain and Physiological Psychology', *Australian Journal of Philosophy*, 7 (1955), 108–20.

Carroll, David (ed.), *George Eliot: The Critical Heritage* (London, 1971).

Chant, Colin, and Fauvel, John (eds.), *Darwin to Einstein: Historical Studies in Science and Belief* (Harlow, 1980).

Clarke, Edwin, and Jacyna, L. S., *Nineteenth-Century Origins of Neuroscientific Concepts* (London, 1987).

Coleman, William, 'Mechanical Philosophy and Hypothetical Physiology', in Robert Patter (ed.), *The Anus Mirabilis of Sir Isaac Newton 1666–1966* (Cambridge, Mass., 1970), 322–32.

Collini, Stefan, *Public Moralists: Political Thought and Intellectual Life in Britain 1850–1930* (Oxford, 1991).

Collins, K. K., 'G. H. Lewes Revised: George Eliot and the Moral Sense', *Victorian Studies*, 21 (1978), 463–92.

Cooter, R. J., 'Phrenology: The Provocation of Progress', *History of Science*, 14 (1976), 211–34.

—— *The Cultural Meaning of Popular Science: Phrenology and the Organization of Consent in Nineteenth-Century Britain* (Cambridge, 1984).

Corrigan, Timothy J., '*Biographia Literaria* and the Language of Science', *Journal of the History of Ideas*, 41 (1980), 399–419.

Cosslett, Tess (ed.), *Science and Religion in the Nineteenth Century* (Cambridge, 1984).

Daston, Lorraine J., 'British Responses to Psycho-Physiology, 1860–1900', *Isis*, 69 (1978), 192–208.

Dawkins, Richard, *The Blind Watchmaker* (Harlow, 1986).

Dennett, Daniel, *Darwin's Dangerous Idea: Evolution and the Meaning of Life* (Harmondsworth, 1995).

Denton, George Bion, 'Early Psychological Theories of Herbert Spencer', *American Journal of Psychology*, 32 (1921), 5–15.

Derrida, Jacques, *Writing and Difference*, trans. Alan Bass (London, 1978).

Desmond, Adrian, *The Politics of Evolution: Morphology, Medicine, and Reform in Radical London* (London, 1989).

—— *Huxley: The Devil's Disciple* (London, 1994).

—— *Huxley: Evolution's High Priest* (London, 1997).

Desmond, Adrian, and Moore, James, *Darwin* (London, 1991).

Donnelly, Michael, *Managing the Mind: A Study of Medical Psychology in Early Nineteenth-Century Britain* (London, 1983).

Drinker, George F., *The Birth of Neurosis: Myth, Malady and the Victorians* (New York, 1984).

Driver, C. H., 'The Development of a Psychological Approach to Politics in English Speculation before 1869', in F. J. C. Hearnshaw (ed.), *The Social and Political Ideas of Some Representative Thinkers of the Victorian Age* (London, 1933), 251–71.

Dunn, John, *Locke* (Oxford, 1984).

Dyson, George, *Darwin among the Machines* (London, 1998).

Edelman, Gerald, *Bright Air, Brilliant Fire: On the Matter of the Mind* (Harmondsworth, 1994).

Eiser, Sidney, 'Huxley and the Positivists', *Victorian Studies*, 7 (1964), 337–58.

Ender, Evelyn, *Sexing the Mind: Nineteenth-Century Fictions of Hysteria* (Ithaca, NY, 1995).

Everett, E. M., *The Party of Humanity: The Fortnightly Review and its Contributors 1865–1874* (Chapel Hill, NY, 1939).

Faas, Ekbert, *Retreat into the Mind: Victorian Poetry and the Rise of Psychiatry* (Princeton, 1988).

Figlio, Karl M., 'Theories of Perception and the Physiology of Mind in the Late Eighteenth Century', *History of Science*, 12 (1975), 177–212.

—— 'The Metaphor of Organization: An Historiographical Perspective on the Bio-Medical Sciences of the Early Nineteenth Century', *History of Science*, 14 (1976), 17–53.

Flew, Antony, *Darwinian Evolution* (London, 1984).

Forrester, J. M., 'Who Put the George in George Eliot?', *British Medical Journal*, pt. 1 (1970), 165–7.

Foucault, Michel, *Madness and Civilization: A History of Insanity in the Age of Reason*, trans. Richard Howard (London, 1967).

—— *The Order of Things: An Archaeology of the Human Sciences*, translator and editor unnamed (New York, 1973).

—— *A History of Sexuality*, i. *An Introduction*, trans. Robert Hurley (Harmondsworth, 1979).

—— *The Foucault Reader*, ed. Paul Rabinow (Harmondsworth, 1986).

Freeman, Derek, 'The Evolutionary Theories of Charles Darwin and Herbert Spencer', *Current Anthropology*, 15 (1974), 211–37.

French, Richard D., 'Some Problems and Sources in the Foundations of Modern Physiology in Great Britain', *History of Science*, 10 (1971), 28–55.

Freud, Sigmund, *Civilization and its Discontents* (1929), in *The Penguin Freud Library*, xii. *Civilization, Society and Religion: Group Psychology, Civilization and its Discontents, and Other Works*, ed. Albert Dickson (London, 1985).

Gale, Barry G., 'Darwin and the Concept of a Struggle for Existence: A Study in the Extra-Scientific Origins of Scientific Ideas', *Isis*, 63 (1972), 321–44.

Gallagher, Catherine, and Laqueur, Thomas (eds.), *The Making of the Modern Body: Sexuality and Society in the Nineteenth Century* (London, 1987).

Gay, Peter, *The Bourgeois Experience: Victoria to Freud*, i. *The Education of the Senses* (Oxford, 1984).

—— *The Bourgeois Experience: Victoria to Freud*, ii. *The Tender Passion* (Oxford, 1986).

Geertz, Clifford, *The Interpretation of Cultures: Selected Essays* (London, 1993).

Geison, Gerald L., 'Social and Institutional Factors in the Stagnancy of English Physiology, 1840–1870', *Bulletin of the History of Medicine*, 26 (1972), 30–58.

Gillespie, C. C., *The Edge of Objectivity: An Essay in the History of Scientific Ideas* (Princeton, 1960).

Goldmann, Lucien, *The Hidden God: A Study of Tragic Vision in the 'Pensées' of Pascal and the Tragedies of Racine*, trans. Philip Thody (London, 1964).

Goodfield, G. J., *The Growth of Scientific Physiology* (London, 1960).

Goodfield-Toulmin, June, 'Some Aspects of English Physiology, 1780–1840', *Journal of the History of Biology*, 2 (1969), 283–320.

Grave, S. A., *The Scottish Philosophy of Common Sense* (Oxford, 1960).

Greene, John C., *Science, Ideology and World-View: Essays in the History of Evolutionary Ideas* (London, 1981).

Greengarten, I. M., *T. H. Green and the Development of Liberal Democratic Thought* (London, 1981).

Gregory, Richard L., *Mind in Science: A History of Explanations in Psychology and Physics* (London, 1981).

Gruber, J. W., *A Conscience in Conflict: The Life of St George Jackson Mivart* (New York, 1961).

Haigh, Elizabeth, 'The Roots of the Vitalism of Xavier Bichat', *Bulletin of the History of Medicine*, 49 (1975), 72–86.

Haight, Gordon S., *George Eliot: A Biography* (Oxford, 1968).

Harrington, Anne, *Medicine, Mind and the Double Brain* (Princeton, 1987).

Haeger, J. H., 'Coleridge's "Bye Blow": The Composition and Date of *Theory of Life*', *Modern Philology*, 74 (1976), 20–41.

Harrison, J. F. C., *Robert Owen and the Owenites in Britain and America: The Quest for a New Moral World* (London, 1969).

Hatfield, Gary, 'Remaking the Science of Mind: Psychology as Natural Science', in Christopher Fox, Roy Porter, and Robert Wokler (eds.), *Inventing Human Science: Eighteenth-Century Domains* (London, 1995), 184–231.

Haven, Richard, 'Coleridge, Hartley and the Mystics', *Journal of the History of Ideas*, 20 (1959), 477–94.

Hearnshaw, L. S., *A Short History of British Psychology 1840–1940* (London, 1964).

Heimann, P. M., and McGuire, J. E., 'Newtonian Forces and Lockean Powers: Concepts of Matter in Eighteenth-Century Thought', *Historical Studies in the Physical Sciences*, 3 (1971), 233–306.

Hein, Hilde, 'The Endurance of the Mechanism–Vitalism Controversy', *Journal of the History of Biology*, 5 (1972), 159–88.

Henle, Mary, Jaynes, Julian, and Sullivan, John J. (eds.), *Historical Conceptions of Psychology* (New York, 1973).

Heyck, T. W., *The Transformation of Intellectual Life in Victorian England* (London, 1982).

Hollinger, David A., 'James, Clifford, and the Scientific Conscience', in *The Cambridge Companion to William James*, ed. Ruth Anna Putnam (Cambridge, 1997), 69–83.

Humphrey, Nicholas, *A History of the Mind* (London, 1992).

Irvine, William, *Apes, Angels and Victorians: A Joint Biography of Darwin and Huxley* (London, 1955).

—— *Thomas Henry Huxley* (London, 1973).

Jacyna, L. S., 'The Physiology of Mind, the Unity of Nature, and the Moral Order in Victorian Thought', *British Journal for the History of Science*, 14 (1981), 109–32.

—— 'Immanence or Transcendence: Theories of Life and Organization in Britain, 1790–1835', *Isis*, 74 (1983), 311–29.

—— 'The Romantic Programme and the Reception of Cell Theory in Britain', *Journal of the History of Biology*, 17 (1984), 13–48.

—— 'Principles of General Physiology: The Comparative Dimension of British Neuroscience in the 1830s and 1840s', in William Coleman and Camille Limoges (eds.), *Studies in the History of Biology 7* (London, 1984), 47–92.

Jeannerod, Marc, *The Brain Machine: The Development of Neurophysiological Thought*, trans. David Urion (London, 1985).

Jordanova, L. J., *Lamarck* (Oxford, 1984).

—— *Sexual Visions: Images of Gender in Science and Medicine between the Eighteenth and Twentieth Centuries* (London, 1989).

Kallich, Martin, *The Association of Ideas and Critical Theory in Eighteenth-Century England: A History of a Psychological Method in English Criticism* (The Hague, 1970).

Kaminsky, Jack, 'The Empirical Metaphysics of George Henry Lewes', *Journal of the History of Ideas*, 13 (1952), 314–32.

Kent, Christopher, *Brains and Numbers: Elitism, Comtism and Democracy in Mid-Victorian England* (Toronto, 1978).

Kitchel, Anna Theresa, *George Lewes and George Eliot: A Review of the Records* (New York, 1933).

Kitcher, Patricia, *Kant's Transcendental Psychology* (Oxford, 1990).

Klein, D. B., *A History of Scientific Psychology: Its Origins and Philosophical Backgrounds* (London, 1970).

Knoepflmacher, U. C., and Tennyson, G. B. (eds.), *Nature and the Victorian Imagination* (London, 1977).

Kuehn, Manfred, 'Hamilton's Reading of Kant: A Chapter in the Early Scottish Reception of Kant's Thought', in George MacDonald Ross and Tony McWalter (eds.), *Kant and his Influence* (Bristol, 1990), 315–47.

Lapointe, François H., 'Who Originated the Term "Psychology"?', *Journal of the History of the Behavioural Sciences*, 8 (1972), 328–35.

Lawrence, D. H., *Study of Thomas Hardy and Other Essays*, ed. Bruce Steele (Cambridge, 1985).

Leahey, Thomas Hardy, *A History of Psychology: Main Currents in Psychological Thought* (Englewood Cliffs, NJ, 1980).

Levere, Trevor H., *Poetry Realized in Nature: Samuel Taylor Coleridge and Early Nineteenth-Century Science* (Cambridge, 1981).

Levine, George, *The Realistic Imagination: English Fiction from Frankenstein to Lady Chatterley* (London, 1981).

—— (ed.), *One Culture: Essays in Science and Literature* (London, 1987).

Lightman, Bernard, *The Origins of Agnosticism: Victorian Unbelief and the Limits of Knowledge* (London, 1987).

Logan, Peter Melville, *Nerves and Narratives: A Cultural History of Hysteria in Nineteenth-Century British Prose* (Berkeley and Los Angeles, 1997).

Lovejoy, Arthur O., *The Great Chain of Being: A Study in the History of an Idea* (1930; repr. New York, 1960).

Lowe, E. J., *Locke on Human Understanding* (London, 1995).

MacCabe, Colin, *James Joyce and the Revolution of the Word* (London, 1978).

McFarland, Thomas, *Coleridge and the Pantheist Tradition* (Oxford, 1969).

McGann, Jerome J., *The Beauty of Inflections: Literary Investigations in Historical Method and Theory* (Oxford, 1985).

MacIntyre, Alasdair, *A Short History of Ethics* (London, 1967).

—— *After Virtue: A Study of Moral Theory* (London, 1981).

McReynolds, Paul, 'The Motivational Psychology of Jeremy Bentham', *Journal of the History of the Behavioural Sciences*, 4 (1968), 230–44.

Mandelbaum, Maurice, *History, Man, and Reason: A Study in Nineteenth-Century Thought* (London, 1971).

Mandelson, Morris, *Philosophy, Science and Perception* (Baltimore, 1964).

Marcuse, Herbert, *Eros and Civilization: A Philosophical Inquiry into Freud* (1955, London, 1969).

Marsh, Robert, 'The Second Part of Hartley's System', *Journal of the History of Ideas*, 20 (1959), 264–73.

Mason, Michael, *The Making of Victorian Sexuality* (Oxford, 1994).

—— *The Making of Victorian Sexual Attitudes* (Oxford, 1995).

Mason, Michael York, '*Middlemarch* and Science: Problems of Life and Mind', *Review of English Studies*, NS 22 (1971), 151–69.

Matus, Jill L., *Unstable Bodies: Victorian Representations of Sexuality and Maternity* (Manchester, 1995).

Medewar, P. B., *The Art of the Soluble* (London, 1967).

Mendelsohn, Everett, 'Cell Theory and the Development of General Physiology', *Archives Internationales d'Histoire des Sciences*, 16 (1963), 419–29.

—— 'Physical Models and Physiological Concepts: Explanation in Nineteenth-Century Biology', *British Journal for the History of Science*, 2 (1965), 201–19.

Micheli, Giuseppe, 'The Early Reception of Kant's Thought in England, 1785–1805', in George MacDonald Ross and Tony McWalter (eds.), *Kant and his Influence* (Bristol, 1990), 202–314.

Mischel, Theodore, '"Emotion" and "Motivation" in the Development of English Psychology: D. Hartley, James Mill, A. Bain', *Journal of the History of the Behavioural Sciences*, 2 (1966), 123–44.

Muirhead, J. H., 'How Hegel Came to England', *Mind*, 36 (1927), 423–47.

Murphy, Gardner, *Historical Introduction to Modern Psychology*, 5th edn. (London, 1949).

Murray, David J., *A History of Western Psychology* (Englewood Cliffs, NJ, 1983).

Myers, William, *The Teaching of George Eliot* (Leicester, 1984).

Newman, Charles, *The Evolution of Medical Education in the Nineteenth Century* (Oxford, 1957).

Newsome, David, *The Victorian World Picture: Perceptions and Introspections in an Age of Change* (London, 1998).

Newton, K. M., 'George Eliot, George Henry Lewes, and Darwinism', *Durham University Journal*, 66 (1973–4), 278–93.

Ockenden, R. E., 'George Henry Lewes (1817–1878)', *Isis*, 32 (1940), 70–86.

Oldfield, R. C., and Oldfield, K., 'Hartley's *Observations on Man*', *Annals of Science*, 7 (1951), 371–81.

Oldroyd, D. R., *Darwinian Impacts: An Introduction to the Darwinian Revolution* (Milton Keynes, 1980).

Olsen, Richard, *Scottish Philosophy and British Physics: A Study of the Foundations of the Victorian Scientific Style* (Princeton, 1975).

O'Neil, W. S., *The Beginnings of Modern Psychology*, 2nd edn. (Brighton, 1982).

Oppenheim, Janet, *'Shattered Nerves': Doctors, Patients and Depression in Victorian England* (Oxford, 1991).

Ospovat, Dov, *The Development of Darwin's Theory: Natural History, Natural Theology and Natural Selection, 1839–1859* (Cambridge, 1981).

Paradis, James, and Postlewait, Thomas (eds.), *Victorian Science and Victorian Values: Literary Perspectives* (New York, 1981).

Peel, J. D. Y., *Herbert Spencer: The Evolution of a Sociologist* (London, 1971).

Perkin, Harold, *The Rise of Professional Society: England since 1880* (London, 1989).

Phillipson, Nicholas, 'The Scottish Enlightenment', in Roy Porter and Mikulas Teich (eds.), *The Enlightenment in National Context* (Cambridge, 1981), 19–40.

Pratt, Carroll C., 'Faculty Psychology', *Psychological Review*, 36 (1929), 142–71.

Ramachandran, V. S., and Blakeslee, Sandra, *Phantoms in the Brain: Human Nature and the Architecture of the Mind* (London, 1998).

Read, Benjamin, 'The Early Development of Hartley's Doctrine of Association', *Psychological Review*, 30 (1923), 306–20.

Richards, Robert J., *Darwin and the Emergence of Evolutionary Theories of Mind and Behaviour* (London, 1987).

Richardson, W. Mark, and Wildman, Wesley J. (eds.), *The Relations between Religion and Science: History, Method, Dialogue* (London, 1997).

Richter, Melvin, *The Politics of Conscience: T. H. Green and his Age* (London, 1964).

Robbins, Peter, *The British Hegelians 1875–1925* (London, 1982).

Robertson, J. Charles, 'A Bacon-Facing Generation: Scottish Philosophy in the Early Nineteenth Century', *Journal of the History of Philosophy*, 14 (1976), 37–49.

Roos, David A., 'The "Aims and Intentions" of *Nature*', in James Paradis and Thomas Postlewait (eds.), *Victorian Science and Victorian Values: Literary Perspectives* (New York, 1981), 159–80.

Rose, Steven, *The Conscious Brain*, rev. edn. (London, 1976).

—— *The Making of Memory* (London, 1992).

—— *Lifelines: Biology, Freedom, Determinism* (London, 1997).

Ross, George MacDonald, and McWalter, Tony (eds.), *Kant and his Influence* (Bristol, 1990).

Rothblatt, Sheldon, *Tradition and Change in English Liberal Education: An Essay on History and Culture* (London, 1976).

Rothschuh, Karl E., *History of Physiology*, ed. and trans. Guenter B. Risse (New York, 1973).

Rousseau, G. S., 'Science and the Discovery of Imagination in Enlightened England', *Eighteenth-Century Studies*, 3 (1969), 108–35.

Rousseau, G. S., 'Nerves, Spirits, and Fibres: Towards Defining the Origins of Sensibility', in R. F. Brissington and J. C. Eade (eds.), *Studies in the Eighteenth Century III* (Toronto, 1976), 137–57.

—— and Porter, Roy (eds.), *The Ferment of Knowledge: Studies in the Historiography of Eighteenth-Century Science* (Cambridge, 1980).

Rupke, Nicolaas (ed.), *Vivisection in Historical Perspective* (London, 1987).

Ruse, Michael, *Taking Darwin Seriously: A Naturalistic Approach to Philosophy* (Oxford, 1986).

Ryan, Judith, *The Vanishing Subject: Early Psychology and Literary Modernism* (London, 1991).

Rylance, Rick, 'The New Criticism', in *Encyclopaedia of Literature and Criticism*, ed. Martin Coyle, Peter Garside, Malcolm Kersall, and John Peck (London, 1990), 721–35.

—— 'Twisting: Memory from Eliot to Eliot', in Matthew Campbell, Jaqueline Labbe, and Sally Shuttleworth (eds.), *Memory and Memorials 1789–1914* (Routledge, 2000), 98–116.

—— 'Ideas, Histories, Generations and Beliefs: Lawrence's Early Novels to *Sons and Lovers*', in Ann Fernihough (ed.), *The Cambridge Companion to D. H. Lawrence* (Cambridge, 2000).

Sacks, Oliver, *The Man who Mistook his Wife for a Hat* (London, 1986).

—— *An Anthropologist on Mars: Seven Paradoxical Tales* (London, 1995).

Sawday, Jonathan, *The Body Emblazoned: Dissection and the Human Body in Renaissance Culture* (London, 1995).

Schabas, Margaret, 'Victorian Economics and the Science of Mind', in Bernard Lightman (ed.), *Victorian Science in Context* (London, 1997).

Schiller, J., 'Physiology's Struggle for Independence in the First Half of the Nineteenth Century', *History of Science*, 7 (1968), 64–89.

Schweber, S. S., 'Scientists as Intellectuals: The Early Victorians', in James Paradis and Thomas Postlewait (eds.), *Victorian Science and Victorian Values: Literary Perspectives* (New York, 1981), 1–37.

Schofield, R. E., *Mechanism and Materialism: British Natural Philosophy in an Age of Reason* (Princeton, 1970).

Scull, Andrew, *Museums of Madness: The Social Organization of Insanity in Nineteenth-Century England* (Harmondsworth, 1979).

—— (ed.), *Madhouses, Mad-Doctors and Madmen: The Social History of Psychology in the Victorian Era* (London, 1981).

—— *The Most Solitary of Afflictions: Madness and Society in Britain 1700–1900* (New Haven, 1993).

Searle, John, *Minds, Brains and Science: The 1984 Reith Lectures* (Harmondsworth, 1984).

Semmel, Bernard, *The Governor Eyre Controversy* (London, 1962).

Severn, J. Millott, *The Life Story and Experiences of a Phrenologist* (Brighton, 1929).

Shapin, Steven, 'Homo Phrenologicus: Anthropological Perspectives on an Historical Problem', in Barry Barnes and Steven Shapin (eds.), *Natural Order: Historical Studies of Scientific Culture* (London, 1979), 41–71.

Sharlin, H. I., 'Herbert Spencer and Scientism', *Annals of Science*, 33 (1976), 457–80.

Shattock, Joanne, and Wolff, Michael (eds.), *The Victorian Periodical Press: Samplings and Soundings* (Leicester, 1982).

Sherrington, Charles S., *The Integrated Action of the Nervous System* (London, 1906).

Showalter, Elaine, *The Female Malady: Women, Madness and English Culture, 1830–1980* (London, 1987).

Shuttleworth, Sally, *George Eliot and Nineteenth-Century Science: The Make-Believe of a Beginning* (Cambridge, 1986).

—— *Charlotte Brontë and Victorian Psychology* (Cambridge, 1996).

Small, Helen, *Love's Madness: Medicine, the Novel and Female Insanity, 1800–1865* (Oxford, 1996).

Smith, C. U. M., *The Problem of Life: An Essay in the Origins of Biological Thought* (London, 1976).

—— 'Evolution and the Problem of Mind: Part I. Herbert Spencer', *Journal of the History of Biology*, 15 (1982), 55–88.

—— 'Evolution and the Problem of Mind: Part II. John Hughlings Jackson', *Journal of the History of Biology*, 15 (1982), 241–62.

Smith, R. E., 'George Henry Lewes and his "Physiology and Common Life", 1859', *Proceedings of the Royal Society of Medecine*, 53 (1960), 569–74.

Smith, Roger, 'Physiological Psychology and the Philosophy of Nature in Mid-Nineteenth-Century Britain' (D.Phil. diss., Cambridge, 1970).

—— 'The Background to Physiological Psychology in Natural Philosophy', *History of Science*, 11 (1973), 75–123.

—— 'The Human Significance of Biology: Carpenter, Darwin and the *vera causa*', in U. C. Knoepflmacher and G. B. Tennyson (ed.), *Nature and the Victorian Imagination* (London, 1977), 216–30.

Snow, C. P., *The Two Cultures*, ed. Stefan Collini (Cambridge, 1993).

Stepan, Nancy, *The Idea of Race in Science: Great Britain 1800–1960* (London, 1982).

Sutton, Geoffrey, 'The Physical and Chemical Path to Vitalism: Xavier Bichat's *Physiological Researches on Life and Death*', *Bulletin of the History of Medicine*, 58 (1984), 53–71.

Taylor, Barbara, *Eve and the New Jerusalem: Socialism and Feminism in the Nineteenth Century* (London, 1983).

Taylor, Jenny Bourne, *In the Secret Theatre of the Home: Wilkie Collins, Sensation Narrative and Nineteenth-Century Psychology* (London, 1988).

—— 'Obscure Recesses: Locating the Victorian Unconscious', in J. B. Bullen (ed.), *Writing and Victorianism* (Harlow, 1997), 137–79.

—— and Shuttleworth, Sally (eds.), *Embodied Selves: An Anthology of Psychological Texts 1830–1890* (Oxford, 1998).

Thomas, William, *The Philosophical Radicals: Nine Studies in Theory and Practice 1817–1841* (Oxford, 1979).

Thompson, E. P., *The Making of the English Working Class* (Harmondsworth, 1967).

Tjoa, Hock Guan, *George Henry Lewes: A Victorian Mind* (London, 1977).

Turner, Frank Miller, *Between Science and Religion: The Reaction to Scientific Naturalism in Late Victorian England* (London, 1974).

Turner, Frank Miller, *Contesting Cultural Authority: Essays in Victorian Intellectual Life* (Cambridge, 1993).

Turner, R. Steven, 'Consensus and Controversy: Helmholtz on the Visual Perception of Space', in David Cahan (ed.), *Hermann von Helmholtz and the Foundations of Nineteenth-Century Science* (London, 1993), 154–204.

Warren, Howard C., *A History of the Association Psychology* (New York, 1921).

Waxman, Wayne, *Kant's Model of the Mind: A New Interpretation of Transcendental Idealism* (Oxford, 1991).

Weiner, Martin J., *English Culture and the Decline of the Industrial Spirit 1850–1980* (Cambridge, 1981).

Wellek, René, *Immanuel Kant in England 1793–1838* (Princeton, 1931).

*The Wellesley Index to Victorian Periodicals 1824–1900*, ed. Walter E. Houghton *et al.*, 5 vols. (London, 1966–89).

West, Ray B. (ed.), *Essays in Modern Literary Criticism* (New York, 1952).

Wightman, W. P. D., 'Wars of Ideas in Neurological Science—from Willis to Bichat and from Locke to Condillac' in F. N. L. Poynter (ed.), *The Brain and its Functions* (Oxford, 1958), 135–45.

Williams, David, *Mr George Eliot: A Biography of George Henry Lewes* (London, 1983).

Williams, Raymond, *The Long Revolution* (London, 1961).

—— *The English Novel from Dickens to Lawrence* (London, 1970).

—— *Keywords: A Vocabulary of Culture and Society*, rev. edn. (London, 1983).

—— *Problems in Materialism and Culture: Selected Essays* (London, 1980).

Winch, Donald, 'The System of the North: Dugald Stewart and his Pupils', in Stefan Collini, Donald Winch, and John Burrow (eds.), *That Noble Science of Politics: A Study in Nineteenth-Century Intellectual History* (Cambridge, 1983), 23–61.

Wylie, Ian, *Young Coleridge and the Philosophers of Nature* (Oxford, 1989).

Yeo, Richard, *Defining Science: William Whewell, Natural Knowledge, and Public Debate in Early Victorian Britain* (Cambridge, 1993).

Yolton, John (ed.), *John Locke: Problems and Perspectives* (Cambridge, 1969).

—— *Thinking Matter: Materialism in Eighteenth-Century Britain* (Minneapolis, 1983).

Young, J. Z., *Philosophy and the Brain* (Oxford, 1987).

Young, Robert M., *Mind, Brain and Adaptation in the Nineteenth Century: Cerebral Localization and its Biological Context from Gall to Ferrier* (Oxford, 1970).

—— *Darwin's Metaphor: Nature's Place in Victorian Culture* (Cambridge, 1985).

Zohar, Danah, *The Quantum Self* (London, 1990).

# Index